Historical Fiction

Genreflecting Advisory Series

Diana T. Herald, Series Editor

Junior Genreflecting: A Guide to Good Reads and Series Fiction for Children
Bridget Dealy Volz, Cheryl Perkins Scheer, and Lynda Blackburn Welborn

Genreflecting: A Guide to Reading Interests in Genre Fiction, 5th Edition
Diana Tixier Herald

Now Read This II: A Guide to Mainstream Fiction, 1990–2001
Nancy Pearl

Christian Fiction: A Guide to the Genre
John Mort

Strictly Science Fiction: A Guide to Reading Interests
Diana Tixier Herald and Bonnie Kunzel

Hooked on Horror: A Guide to Reading Interests in Horror Fiction, 2d Edition
Anthony J. Fonseca and June Michele Pulliam

Make Mine a Mystery: A Reader's Guide to Mystery and Detective Fiction
Gary Warren Niebuhr

Teen Genreflecting: A Guide to Reading Interests, Second Edition
Diana Tixier Herald

Blood, Bedlam, Bullets, and Badguys: A Reader's Guide to Adventure/Suspense Fiction
Michael B. Gannon

Rocked by Romance: A Guide to Teen Romance Fiction
Carolyn Carpan

Jewish American Literature: A Guide to Reading Interests
Rosalind Reisner

African American Literature: A Guide to Reading Interests
Edited by Alma Dawson and Connie Van Fleet

Historical Fiction

A Guide to the Genre

Sarah L. Johnson

Genreflecting Advisory Series
Diana T. Herald, Series Editor

LIBRARIES UNLIMITED
A Member of the Greenwood Publishing Group
Westport, Connecticut • London

British Library Cataloguing in Publication Data is available.

ISBN: 1-59158-129-X

First published in 2005

Libraries Unlimited, 88 Post Road West, Westport, CT 06881
A Member of the Greenwood Publishing Group, Inc.
www.lu.com

Printed in the United States of America

The paper used in this book complies with the
Permanent Paper Standard issued by the National
Information Standards Organization (Z39.48–1984).

10   9   8   7   6   5   4   3   2   1

Contents

Acknowledgments

This is the place where I finally get the chance to formally thank everyone who supported me during the writing of this book. I have been reading and collecting historical novels for over twenty years, and there's little I enjoy more than discussing worthwhile reads with fellow enthusiasts. This book gives me the welcome opportunity to share my thoughts and recommendations with the greater reading community, and for this I'm very thankful.

Richard Lee of the Historical Novel Society and Duncan Smith of NoveList first encouraged my interest in historical fiction by putting me to work and agreeing to publish articles and book reviews that I wrote. My colleagues at Booth Library, Eastern Illinois University, encouraged me in the writing process and tactfully asked me how things were progressing with the book. I especially appreciated their support, and that of Dean Allen Lanham, during the month of August 2003, when I was awarded a Booth Library Summer Research Grant that gave me time to work on the manuscript.

Teresa Basinski Eckford, Sue Feder, Rachel Singer Gordon, and John Vallely all sent me comments on chapters relating to their fields of expertise. My father Steve Lewis, editor/publisher of Mystery*File, read the mystery, Western, and thriller chapters and recommended more titles to include. I am particularly grateful to Trudi Jacobson of the University at Albany Libraries, one of my fellow editors at the *Historical Novels Review*, for reading each chapter as it was completed and providing detailed notes on suggested changes. Trisha Ashley of the Romantic Novelists Association answered my questions on RNA's awards. Barbara Ittner and Diana Tixier Herald kept me on the right track throughout. Last but certainly not least, I couldn't have completed this book without the encouragement of my husband, Mark, who never blinks an eye when I mention that we're out of bookshelf space again.

A small number of the annotations in this book appeared previously, in longer versions, in either the *Historical Novels Review* or *Murder: Past Tense*.

All errors and omissions are, of course, my own. If you discover titles you believe were inadvertently omitted, or if you have books that you'd like to recommend, please drop me a line via e-mail (cfsln@eiu.edu). I will be happy to consider them for future editions.

Finally, I am grateful to the hard-working historical novelists whose works are listed within these pages. Without them, this book would not exist. I have been privileged to have corresponded with many of them during my lengthy exploration of their world, and some have become friends in the process. Please keep on writing!

Sarah L. Johnson
Booth Library, Eastern Illinois University
January 2005

Introduction

What is history but a fable agreed upon?—Napoleon Bonaparte

If I had one prediction for the millennium it would be that all of us, including novelists, shall be spending a lot of time—more than ever before—looking backward.—Thomas Mallon[1]

Purpose and Scope

In the early twenty-first century, historical fiction has finally come into its own. Always popular on library and bookstore shelves, historical novels frequently appear on bestseller lists; examples from 2004 include Neal Stephenson's *The Confusion*, Anne Tyler's *The Amateur Marriage*, and Jimmy Carter's *The Hornet's Nest*. In addition, they are often recommended as choices for book discussion groups (Anita Diamant's *The Red Tent*, Donna Woolfolk Cross's *Pope Joan*, and many more). Reader and publisher interest shows no signs of diminishing. Between 2000 and 2003, over one-third of *Booklist* Editors' Choice titles in adult fiction were historical novels. Now more than ever, librarians and other professionals who work with readers need to develop a greater familiarity with the genre. This includes knowledge of general characteristics, its appeal to readers, benchmark and representative titles, and publishing trends.

Historical Fiction: A Guide to the Genre aims to provide guidance in all of these areas. Its primary audience is librarians, both readers' advisors and collection development specialists, curious to learn more about historical fiction and reader interests. Readers and fans of the genre can use it to locate interesting titles and discover more about their own reading tastes. Aspiring historical novelists can read the chapter introductions and annotations to see what's being published by whom, and where their own work might fit into the canon.

Historical fiction overlaps several other genres. For instance, historical romance is a subset both of historical fiction and of romance. Most general readers' advisory tools address historical fiction, but place novels in overlapping subgenres, like historical romance or historical mystery, within the other category. While this may suit readers of other genres just fine, it doesn't work as well for readers who specifically seek out historical settings. This book presents historical fiction, in all its variety, in a single volume to make it easier for librarians and readers to locate worthwhile books.

Most readers' advisors know historical fiction when they see it, though exact definitions are tricky. As in the latest *Genreflecting* volume (2000), here "historical fiction" includes novels set prior to the middle of the last century in which the historical backdrop plays a strong role in the story. This guide makes no claims to comprehensiveness, for all-inclusive coverage would mean filling several more volumes. This book focuses on English-language novels for adults that have been published between 1995 and mid-2004, in particular those commonly found in American public library collections (as indicated in OCLC's WorldCat). Many classic titles and other genre favorites are also included.

With these guidelines in mind, selection was done regardless of format, recognizing that many worthy titles are published only in paperback. Series titles are listed in full, in their appropriate reading order—which may or may not reflect publication order. In all, over 3,800 titles are categorized, described, and in most cases annotated.

This guide considers historical fiction in its broadest sense, recognizing today's tendency toward "genre-blending." To satisfy as many tastes as possible, subgenres like time-slip novels, alternate history, and historical fantasy each have their own chapters. While purists may not consider them appropriate, many reader favorites, like Connie Willis's *Doomsday Book* and Judith Tarr's <u>Hound and Falcon Trilogy</u>, fall within these categories.

Organization of This Book

As a genre, historical fiction is incredibly diverse, ranging from the delightful Regency romances of Georgette Heyer to Ken Follett's action-packed World War II adventures. This diversity presents challenges for readers' advisors. Most genre tools arrange historical novels by time period and place, with indexes by subject or theme. This book takes a different approach. Like other volumes in the *Genreflecting Advisory Series*, this guide is organized by subgenre, which more closely reflects reader interests. For example, while Margaret Mitchell's *Gone with the Wind*, Jeff Shaara's *Gods and Generals*, and Charles Frazier's *Cold Mountain* all take place during the American Civil War, their styles are very different, and readers who enjoy one might not automatically enjoy the others. This guide places each title in its appropriate category: Mitchell with romantic epics, Shaara with other traditional historical novels on the Civil War, and Frazier with literary historical novels set during that time period. The subject index will help omnivorous readers who can't get enough of a particular time period or place, or who wish to access titles that fall into different subgenres.

Each chapter, covering one subgenre within historical fiction, begins by explaining its appeal to readers. Chapters are divided into subcategories or themes, which are based mostly around eras/locales, but not always. (In the latter case, keywords after each annotation will provide the historical context.) The introduction for each theme analyzes common characteristics, which can include historical background that will be useful for readers. Annotations for individual novels include author, title, publisher, original publication date, and number of pages, followed by a concise plot summary. When novels appear as part of a series, annotations may be provided for the series as a whole rather than for each title.

For the most part, only novels published in the United States, or widely available to American readers, are included. If a book was previously published in another country (usually Great Britain) significantly before the American publication date, this information is given in parentheses. Sometimes an American publisher will discontinue a series even though new volumes continue to appear in Britain. Because readers of a series will want to know what happens next, this book provides information on later titles regardless of where they were published.

The following icons designate special features of novels or series:

🏮 = Winner of one or more literary awards, specifics of which are mentioned in the annotation.

✍ = Biographical novels, that is, novels in which a historical personage is one of the main characters. These people are listed in the historical character index.

★ = Classic or benchmark novels within the subgenre, works to which newly published titles are frequently compared. These may or may not be older novels.

📖 = Novels especially appropriate for reading groups for book discussion. For more information on selecting novels for reading groups, see the section labeled "Choices for Book Discussions" in Chapter 1.

YA = Although this book concentrates on novels for adults, some of them may be suitable for young adults, either because they feature young people or because the subject matter may interest them. This icon denotes these titles.

Although most titles clearly fit within a single subgenre, a selected number will fit into more than one. Full annotations for these titles are placed where, in the author's opinion, they fit most appropriately. "See" and "see also" references appear throughout the book, in both the chapter introductions and the annotations. For example, many thrillers appeal to mystery readers, and fans of Arthurian historical fiction may also enjoy Arthurian fantasy.

Literary historical novels (Chapter 10) deserve special mention here, because some novels in this category can easily fit more than one subgenre. For example, Cormac McCarthy's *Blood Meridian* and Ivan Doig's *Dancing at the Rascal Fair* can be considered literary Westerns, while Anne-Marie MacDonald's *Fall on Your Knees* appeals to readers of both literary fiction and sagas. When works of literary fiction appear in other chapters, they are given the designation **Literary** in bold type at the end of the annotation.

Cross-genre titles are the hardest to classify, for obvious reasons. For a small number of novels listed in the literary chapter (e.g., Anita Diamant's *The Red Tent*, Stephanie Cowell's *Nicholas Cooke* and others, Tracy Chevalier's *Girl with a Pearl Earring*), deciding whether they fit better as literary or traditional historical novels is a judgment call for the readers' advisor and the reader. Though annotated in Chapter 10, they have strong appeal for readers who enjoy traditional historicals. Likewise, Dorothy Dunnett's beloved *Lymond Chronicles*, listed in Chapter 8 alongside other swashbuckling tales, straddles the adventure, literary, and traditional subgenres. For many readers, these remarkable novels seem to "have it all"—compelling plots, brilliantly described historical settings, fascinating characters, and clever or lyrical language. They can be appreciated on many levels, which can explain why they are popular with so many different types of readers. While consulting this book, readers' advisors should keep in mind the cross-genre appeal of these perennial favorites, most of which are denoted as classic or benchmark titles (★). For more information on these types of works, see Chapter 1, under the section "Genre-Blending."

Suggestions for Use

Although the organization of this book will be intuitive to most readers, not everyone will be consulting it for the same purpose. Readers' advisors, both in libraries and bookstores, may wish to discover titles of interest to themselves and their patrons. Collection development librarians may use it to fill in gaps or build new collections in areas they haven't covered. Readers looking for what books to read next, or read-alike titles for their favorite novels, can use this book to discover new material. Following are some general guidelines for usage:

1. The main table of contents lists subgenres, themes, and subcategories within themes. Readers searching for a particular type of novel should begin here.

2. To learn about novels similar to ones you or other readers have enjoyed, consult the author/title index to see in what chapter the book is located. Read-alike titles are grouped together within a chapter's subsections, which are based on time period/place or other themes.

3. To discover worthwhile books by a certain author, use the author/title index to see where they are located. Some authors write in more than one subgenre, so their novels may be scattered throughout the book. For example, Karen Harper now writes the Elizabeth I series of historical mysteries, among other things, but during the 1990s, she also wrote many well-researched historical romances. Be aware that many authors also have extensive backlists, and this book may not include every novel they have ever written.

4. To find books set during a particular time period and place regardless of subgenre—Victorian England, for instance—use the time/place index to cut across the chapters and locate worthwhile titles.

5. To learn more about overall publishing trends, consult Chapter 1, specifically the section labeled "Recent Trends in Historical Fiction." For explanations about the appeal of more specific types of novels, like historical mysteries or adventures set during the Age of Sail, see the introductions to chapters and themes. Use the main table of contents to locate the section you want. To find more specific subjects or themes (e.g., pirates, artists, epistolary novels), the subject index can help.

If this book helps you learn more about the vibrant historical fiction genre, or suggests worthwhile titles for you or other readers to consider, it will have served its purpose. Happy reading!

Notes

1. Thomas Mallon, "History, Fiction, and the Burden of Truth," in *Writing Historical Fiction: A Virtual Conference Session* (Albany, NY: Department of History, University at Albany, SUNY, 1998). Available: http://www.albany.edu/history/hist_fict/Mallon/Mallons.htm (Accessed August 4, 2004).

Chapter 1

The Appeal of the Past

Defining Historical Fiction

At first glance, historical fiction seems a relatively easy genre to define. While it's true that it basically means "fiction set in the past," this definition brings up a number of questions. For instance, how far back must a novel be set to make it historical—a hundred years, fifty years, ten years? To readers born in the 1960s, novels set during World War II may be considered suitably historical, but older readers who vividly remember the 1940s may not agree.

Even if librarians can agree on a definition that historical fiction includes any works that are set, for example, more than fifty years in the past, whose past are we talking about, the reader's or the author's? Take, for example, F. Scott Fitzgerald's *The Great Gatsby*, both written and set in the 1920s. How about Jane Austen's novels, written during England's Regency period and set slightly beforehand? These works are obviously set in the historical past, and they provide considerable information on customs of the times. By this definition, though, any contemporary novel will become "historical fiction" at some point in the future. When readers ask for historical fiction, this usually isn't what they mean.

In this book, "historical fiction" is defined as fictional works (mainly novels) set before the middle of the last century, and ones in which the author is writing from research rather than personal experience. This usually means that the novels will take place before the author's life and times. Most autobiographical novels wouldn't fit these criteria, but they are included here on occasion if they are newly written works set in the 1940s or earlier.

Some novels written in past centuries or decades (e.g., works by Austen, Fitzgerald, Edith Wharton, and others) may appeal to historical fiction fans, but they must contain enough historical detail to evoke times past. In addition, some novels set in the 1950s, 1960s, and even later may fit some readers' definitions of historical fiction, especially readers who weren't yet born at the time and who wish to experience what life was like then. These novels are beyond the scope of this book, but readers' advisors should be aware that readers may not have the same definition of historical fiction that they do, and should adjust their readers' advisory interview accordingly.

A Brief History

Historical fiction is one of the oldest forms of storytelling. Members of long-ago cultures, from Babylonia to ancient Greece and Rome, proudly recounted tales of their forebears' heroism and defeats. Many of these stories have passed down to us over the years. Early works we consider to be classics—Shakespeare's *Hamlet*, Goethe's *Faust*, even Homer's *Odyssey*—are fictionalized retellings of events that occurred long before the author's time. Today's novelists continue to revisit the same characters and themes, proving that the legacy of these ancient tales has endured.

In literary circles, Sir Walter Scott's *Waverley* is generally considered to be the first historical novel. Published anonymously in 1814, *Waverley* was the first novel in Scott's popular series about eighteenth-century Scottish history. What made it unique among its predecessors was Scott's attempt to accurately portray the background and qualities of ordinary people involved in the 1745 Jacobite rebellion against the British crown. With its subtitle " 'Tis Sixty Years Since," *Waverley* established the original cutoff date for historical fiction. To modern readers, its prose seems old-fashioned and cumbersome, but its popularity inspired many devoted followers and imitators. Among other successful historical novels of the nineteenth century are Nathaniel Hawthorne's *The Scarlet Letter* (1850, about Puritan New England), Charles Dickens's *A Tale of Two Cities* (1856, about the French Revolution), and Tolstoy's *War and Peace* (1869, about early nineteenth-century Russia). Considered classics today, they were the bestsellers of their era—critically acclaimed yet popular reading.

During the twentieth century, historical fiction saw both its highest and lowest points. Some of the most highly praised and enduring historical novels were written and published during this time. To name a few: the novels of Sigrid Undset's Kristin Lavransdatter trilogy, which helped win her the Nobel Prize for Literature in 1928, and Anya Seton's *Katherine* (1954), which even historians of the Middle Ages took seriously and recommended as an accurate portrayal of Chaucer's England. The genre also got wide recognition in the form of Westerns, the most prolific subgenre from the early twentieth century through the 1950s. Then historical romances exploded onto the market in the 1970s, with their lavish tales of wild passion and star-crossed lovers set against vividly rendered historical backdrops.

The extreme popularity of historical fiction, in its many guises, contributed to its overall perception as a lowbrow form of literature. All genre fiction has suffered critical disdain to some degree, and continues to do so. This should surprise no one. As usually happens when the market is flooded with novels in a certain genre, as was the case with historical fiction in the mid-twentieth century, the quality declines. In a 1950 article for *Masses and Mainstream* ("Reply to Critics") , author Howard Fast, a historical novelist himself, wrote: "This is an era of many historical novels, few of them good, and very few indeed which have more than a nodding acquaintance with fact."

His comments weren't unique by any stretch. Over and over again, comments from authors and the media implied that historical fiction was a genre very rarely done well. Either these novels were bad history—costume dramas, in which modern-day characters were dressed up and paraded around in period garb—or bad fiction, where the author crammed in so much research that it overwhelmed the plot. Many well-known historical novelists first made their mark in the 1950s through the 1980s, such as Maurice Druon, Zoé Oldenbourg, John Jakes, Rosemary Sutcliff, and even Howard Fast himself. However, their works were admired as exceptions to the rule.

Things picked up in the mid- to late 1990s, when literary authors started looking back to the past for inspiration. All of a sudden, their historical novels began winning major literary prizes. Margaret Atwood's novel *Alias Grace*, about a housemaid tried for her employer's murder in 1843, garnered the Pulitzer Prize for Literature in 1996. Appendix A in this guide lists many other examples. However, many works of literary fiction, no matter the time period in which they were set, were typically not considered historical novels by the press, by their publishers, and even by the authors who wrote them, even though they seemed to follow all the rules.

There are many examples. "I rely on the work of great historians, but I'm not a historical novelist," declared Charles Johnson in an interview (1998) with the *Sacramento Bee*, referring to *Dreamer*, his novel about the life of Martin Luther King Jr. Anita Diamant's *The Red Tent* (1997), in which a well-known biblical story is seen through the eyes of the character Dinah, was labeled by its publisher as contemporary women's fiction. *Cold Mountain* (also 1997), which beautifully evokes the pointless loss caused by the Civil War, was more frequently termed literary fiction. If another possible label fit, the book wore it. Historical fiction was everywhere, but nowhere: It had become the genre that dared not speak its name.

This has changed to some degree in the early twenty-first century (though some labeling problems persist; see "Of Publishers and Labels," below). It has finally become fashionable again to talk about the historical novel in public. Publishers are actively promoting their books as "upmarket historical fiction"—novels, in other words, that one wouldn't be embarrassed to be caught reading on the subway. The success of films like *Gladiator*, *Elizabeth*, *Girl with a Pearl Earring*, and even *Cold Mountain*, the latter two of which were based on novels, demonstrates people's huge and growing interest in historical topics. *Booklist* has devoted several recent issues to historical fiction, and *The Historical Novels Review*, a book review magazine co-edited by the author of this guide, publishes 800 reviews of new historical novels each year. The genre is prolific, healthy, and going strong. Long may it continue.

Recent Trends in Historical Fiction

It has been said that historical novels, since they attempt to re-create the past, have a certain timeless quality that novels in other genres don't have. This isn't exactly true. While some classic titles—like those by Georgette Heyer, Mary Renault, and James Michener—have remained in print almost continuously since their original publication, they are the exceptions that prove the rule. Writing styles change over time, and novels that seemed unique and affecting in years past may seem drab or overly formal today. Even historical novels written as little as thirty years ago may seem dated, due to changing tastes in subject matter, overly flowery language, or the use of words or phrases that seem politically incorrect. Instead, one might say that because of its reliance on the past, which is fixed and unchanging, historical fiction must keep reinventing itself to remain interesting.

New Angles on Old Topics

While biographical and wartime novels remain popular, readers and authors continue to look for new angles on the same historical characters and events. There have been many novels published about Anne Boleyn, but Philippa Gregory's award-winning *The Other Boleyn Girl* was the first major novel to observe her from the viewpoint of her sister Mary—one of Henry VIII's mistresses. Robin Maxwell's *The Secret Diary of Anne Boleyn*, which is much more sympathetic to Anne, tells her life story in the form of a diary written for her daughter, the future Queen Elizabeth I. Both Gregory's and Maxwell's works are historical novels in the traditional sense, but they look at the historical record, and historical characters, in unique ways.

Social History

Topics chosen for historical novels often reflect trends in history. Beginning in the 1970s, social history came to the forefront in academic circles. A new crop of scholars started to take interest in women's and minorities' roles in history, and relevant programs —women's studies, African-American studies—were formed at universities. Historical novels written before then often concerned themselves with the movers and shakers of times past—great men and the countries they ran or conquered. Since that time, there has been more emphasis, both in history and historical fiction, placed on people and themes that previously remained in the background.

This shift from political to social history uncovered much fertile ground for historical novelists. While retellings of well-known events and famous people continue to be popular, today's historical novels are just as apt to emphasize more neglected topics, such as common people's daily lives and how they were affected (or not) by major events. An example is Geraldine Brooks's *Year of Wonders*, about how a young widow helps her village survive the plague in seventeenth-century England. In the last decade, there has also been considerably more importance placed on women's roles, those of racial minorities, members of the serving class, gays and lesbians, and members of non-Western cultures. This is especially true in literary historical fiction, where viewpoints seem to have shifted from that of the colonizers—Great Britain in particular—to that of the colonized. One occasionally gets the feeling that writers go out of their way to discover minor historical tidbits worthy of writing a novel about, the more obscure the better. Regardless, the shift to social history, and less familiar subjects, seems to have worked in their favor. As shown in Appendix A, many historical novels of this type have been on the radar of literary prize committees within the last ten years.

Genre-Blending

The historical fiction genre easily combines with many other genres: mystery, romance, fantasy, thrillers and suspense, even Christian fiction. Although traditional historical novels (Chapter 2) have a devoted audience, it's in the other subgenres that historical fiction has been the most abundant and popular lately. Historical mysteries are being published at an astonishing rate, so far with no noticeable decline in quality. Literary historical fiction, which always existed to some degree, got a significant boost with Charles Frazier's 1997 novel *Cold Mountain* and continues to flourish.

Titles that incorporate elements of more than one subgenre are among the most popular of all, for they appeal to the widest possible audience. Take, for example, Diana Gabaldon's <u>Outlander Saga</u>, a bestselling combination of romance, time-travel, and adventure set against a well-researched backdrop of both World War II-era England and eighteenth-century Scotland and America. Literary thrillers like David Liss's *A Conspiracy of Paper* mix mystery, action/adventure, suspense, and the intellectual writing style of literary fiction. Even traditional historical novels have been known to add elements of other genres. Cecelia Holland's novel *The Angel and the Sword* adds some minor fantasy elements to what is otherwise a traditional retelling, though an exciting one, of a medieval European legend.

What Do Readers Look For?

Although trends come and go, the overall appeal of historical fiction remains unchanged. Readers seek out authors who evoke or re-create the past by providing detail on all aspects of life in earlier times: customs, food, clothing, religious beliefs, architecture, and much more. This historical frame must be presented as authentically as possible so as not to shatter the illusion, but accuracy in historical facts isn't nearly enough to satisfy readers. If that were the case, they would be content with nonfiction history books. Many avid fiction readers find straight history texts to be dry and lifeless, with their reliance on facts and dates rather than people's personal experiences. The "fiction" part of historical fiction adds emotional intensity, something that straight history can't easily provide. The best historical novelists make the history an integral part of the story but weave it in gradually so that readers aren't overwhelmed.

In reading historical novels, readers enjoy immersing themselves in the day-to-day lives and mindsets of people who lived in earlier eras. Readers want to learn firsthand about the hopes and dreams of people who lived long ago, marveling at how different their experiences are from those of people today. At the same time, historical fiction makes the unfamiliar seem familiar. Many novels express the same overarching theme: Despite changes in politics, culture, and religion over the years, human nature doesn't change.

Most important of all, historical novel readers want to be entertained. They want to be seduced into believing that the historical world an author creates is real. At their best, historical novels bring the past to life, through emotionally involving stories and well-developed, sympathetic characters that reflect their time.

Appeal Factors in Historical Novels

Readers choose and enjoy historical novels based on a variety of factors. In *Readers' Advisory Service in the Public Library* (ALA, 1997), Joyce Saricks and Nancy Brown discuss "appeal factors"—qualities that may cause readers to like or dislike a particular novel. Experienced readers' advisors use these features to make recommendations on what patrons might want to read next. Traditionally, bibliographies of historical fiction have been organized by time period and country, but this isn't the only way to match historical novels with readers. In discussing with library patrons what they enjoyed about a particular historical novel, readers' advisors should make note of elements other than era and locale. Appeal factors for individual novels are detailed in the annotations in this guide and are explained further here.

Time Period

Some readers are omnivorous in terms of the eras they want to read about. For example, Civil War buffs may choose to read as many novels as they can about the period, to get as many different perspectives as possible. I personally know several historical novel buffs who refuse to read anything set after the end of the Tudors' reign in England. For these readers, the index to this book will prove fruitful. These readers will also appreciate comprehensive book-length bibliographies such as Lynda G. Adamson's *American Historical Fiction* and *World Historical Fiction*, which are organized primarily by locale and era.

Geographic Setting

With historical fiction, geographic setting often goes hand in hand with time period in terms of reader preference. For example, some American readers will avoid American settings in favor of British or European ones, preferring to read about a place that isn't quite so familiar to them. Others will use historical novels about the United States during the antebellum period, the Great Depression, the World Wars, etc., to place themselves inside the mindsets of people—often their own ancestors—who lived during those times.

Amount and Type of Historical Content

How much historical detail do authors include in their novels, and what type of history do they focus on—political, social, economic? While historical readers often prefer novels in which descriptions of customs, fashion, décor, politics, food, etc., are provided in great detail, others may prefer works in which the background is more lightly sketched. (This book concentrates on the former.) In addition, while some historical novels—such as those by Jeff Shaara, Colleen McCullough, and even Jean Plaidy—focus on major political events and the people who shaped them, others concentrate on an era's social history. Specific historical events rarely figure in the plotlines of Catherine Cookson's British regional sagas or Janette Oke's prairie romances. Instead, these novels focus on female characters' daily lives and how they and their families survived the times. The lack of reference to exact dates and outside events doesn't diminish their value as historical fiction.

Level of Realism

Some historical novel readers prefer a romanticized version of history, one that emphasizes the glory and heroism of past eras. These readers may appreciate traditional stories of knights riding victoriously into battle, the glitz and glamour of royalty, and long, sprawling epics of historical women and men who overcome many obstacles and emerge triumphant. These novels may mention the adverse sides to life in past eras, but they aren't dwelt upon.

Other readers will prefer a gritty, more realistic portrayal of history. These readers will appreciate novels that don't gloss over subjects like poverty, fear of religious persecution, serious portrayals of battle, and the struggle to survive during periods of poverty, hunger, and war. Much literary fiction falls into this category, as do many mysteries (Anne Perry's two series) and even traditional historical novels (Charmaine Craig's *The Good Men*). This is not to say that stories in the latter category are grim and depressing, simply that they present life in historical times with a more authentic flavor. Of course, it's possible for novels to be glorious, romantic, and realistic all at the same time—historical military adventure fiction, for example. (For a related topic, see also the section dealing with violence and sexual content, below.)

Author

Historical fiction read-alikes are often chosen with the assumption that authors will stick with the same style from book to book. Strictly within the historical fiction genre, this is often the case, especially with novels in series—but not always. Some authors focus on the period and era in which they have the most expertise: Pauline Gedge writes primarily about ancient Egypt, for example. Some prolific historical novelists like Cecclia Holland are able to master many different historical settings but use a similar style throughout. Within literary historical fiction, authors will likely change themes from novel to novel (e.g., Tracy Chevalier, Beryl Bainbridge, Thomas Mallon), yet they will remain within that particular subgenre. One must be careful with author read-alike suggestions, though, as they may not always work. For example, recommending Colleen McCullough's hefty Roman political novels to readers who enjoyed her Australian family saga *The Thorn Birds* may not be appropriate.

Pacing

The pacing of historical novels—leisurely, action-packed, or somewhere in between—is often reflected in their subgenre category. This is analyzed in greater detail in the chapter introductions. For example, literary historical novels, many of which are character-centered, unfold their action slowly, and characters' motivations may not be apparent from the outset. Military adventure novels, such as those by Bernard Cornwell, seem to move a mile a minute, with the pace rarely flagging during major battle scenes.

Type of Character

Both historical and fictional characters feature in historical novels, and readers may prefer one over the other. Even when the plot revolves around an actual historical event, one in which royalty or other statesmen may figure, the story may be shown from the point of view of a well-known historical character (Margaret George's *Autobiography of Henry VIII*) or a secondary character, real or fictional, who observes the action from a close distance (Beryl Bainbridge's *According to Queeney*). In recent years, well-known historical stories have been fictionally retold by fully fleshed out characters that few had written about before (India Edghill's *Queenmaker*, about Michal, King David's wife and queen). Readers may also want to read about particular types of characters in earlier societies: royalty, nobility, clergy, merchants, sailors, soldiers.

Characterization

Different from character type, characterization refers to how well the author has developed his or her characters, and how well the reader gets to know them. Do readers get to know characters' personalities early on, or are they developed throughout the novel? Are they easily recognizable "types," or are they multifaceted? Are the characters easy to sympathize with and understand, or are they presented at a distance?

Subject and Theme

Certain subjects and themes resonate across historical periods and subgenres—race relations, colonialism, political revolutions, art and music, and many more. These are noted within the annotations, and readers can discover read–alikes of this type within the subject index. Other themes are less tangible, such as male-female relationships, women's roles, and the role of religion in historical times. Readers' advisors can develop greater familiarity with these themes by reading relevant novels in the genre.

Dialogue

Considerable debate has raged among authors and readers about how authentic characters' dialogue should be. After all, if novelists were to observe historical accuracy in its purest form, many of their characters would be speaking something other than modern English. To convey authentic atmosphere, authors frequently use slightly more formal dialogue than one would speak in casual conversation today. In her romances *For My Lady's Heart* and its sequel *Shadowheart*, Laura Kinsale has her characters use authentic Middle English phrasings to convince readers of her medieval settings. Regency romances wouldn't be the same without their witty, sparkling dialogue, which reflects the flirtatiousness and propriety of the era. Others (Lindsey Davis, Simon Scarrow) go the opposite route, placing modern idiom in their protagonists' mouths. For some readers, this emphasizes the similarities between the authors' ancient Rome and now, since people used slang and raunchy language in all eras. Other readers find that modern use of language in historical fiction throws them out of the period completely.

Language

Language used in a narrative may be lyrical and poetic, as is the case with much literary historical fiction, or it may be more straightforward. It may be descriptive or spare. And as with characters' dialogue, the language of a narrative may or may not reflect the historical era. A novel may be told in a slightly formal voice, as if to evoke the language used in earlier times, or it may be modern.

Violence and Sexual Content

Readers often have strong preferences about how much violence or sexual content they want to read about. Nearly all historical novelists deal with these issues to some degree. Battle scenes can be related both on-screen and off, as can bedroom scenes. While some readers find that gritty descriptions of blood and violence give them an authentic feel for the period, they may offend others. The "cozy" versus "hard-boiled" distinction in historical mysteries, mentioned within Chapter 7, reflects the level of violence. Likewise, explicit sexuality in a novel—mainly in romantic fiction, but in other subgenres as well—may be acceptable to some readers. Others will prefer that characters' private lives be kept private.

Determining Historical Accuracy

Historical accuracy is important, if not critical, to readers of historical fiction. Although minor slip-ups may not pass their notice, significant blunders will draw readers out of the story, making them suspicious of the novel's overall quality. Mistakes on individual word usage may not matter, but incorrect dates, or placing historical characters in times or places when they weren't really there, aren't nearly as forgivable. The more familiar readers are with the period, the less tolerant they will be of anachronisms or other errors. While most historical fiction buffs have certain novelists whose research they trust, they read unfamiliar authors with a more critical eye.

What does this mean for readers' advisors who want to assure patrons that a historical novel truthfully reflects its era? In short, there's no easy way to positively determine historical accuracy without personal expertise on the period and people in question—at least as much as the authors know themselves! Readers can develop this familiarity through study of primary or secondary sources, such as historical biographies and narrative histories, or through formal coursework. Many historical novel fans also read biographies and historical nonfiction. But few librarians—and even most readers—have the time to do extensive research on any single book. While any and all background knowledge is helpful, a Ph.D. in history isn't necessary for readers' advisory work.

A more realistic question to answer is how well librarians and readers can judge the amount of research that went into a historical novel. Developing a familiarity with benchmark authors and novels is highly recommended. Librarians can also keep up with well-researched novels, and the authors who write them, through discussions with people who read frequently in the genre. Reading published reviews can be helpful, though reviewers may not address historical accuracy. Even if they do, the reviewers—especially those from the popular press—may or may not be history experts.

Historical novelists often provide reader aids that serve as clues to their own research techniques. Because some of them—especially authors' notes, epilogues, and genealogical tables—involve spoilers, readers should be judicious in consulting them before reading. Examples are as follows:

- *Bibliographies*, which list sources consulted by the author in the writing process, can convince readers of an author's thoroughness. They also provide suggestions for additional reading.

- *Authors' notes*, provided at the end, can provide sources as well as details on where and how the novel diverged from the historical record. It isn't unusual for authors to change minor facts and dates for the story's sake. Readers can forgive this to some degree, provided the authors don't change history too drastically—and provided they come clean about it.

- *Epilogues* tell readers what happened after the story ends, wrapping up any necessary details on historical characters or events.

- *Genealogical tables*, especially in the case of historical characters, provide names of people, the relationships between them, and dates of birth and death.

- *Glossaries* of unfamiliar or foreign words or phrases used in a novel lend authenticity to the authors' dialogue, language, and depth of research.

- *Photographs* of places and people are usually included in novels based on authors' own family history, like Lalita Tademy's *Cane River* or Janice Woods Windle's Western family sagas. They may also appear in other biographical novels.

- *Diagrams and maps* of geographic regions accurate to the period in question ("England in the mid-twelfth century") , battlefields, traveling routes, and so forth, provide historical background and help readers follow characters through the story. They are often provided on novels' endpapers.

- *Footnotes* may be used within the novel itself to give historical background on certain people or places. Since they interrupt the story's flow, they aren't very common. Authors are more apt to provide a bibliography instead.

The absence of any of these features doesn't necessarily signify anything. Literary historical novels rarely use them, for example. However, their presence can aid readers and librarians in determining depth of research. Of course, the best way of determining how trustworthy an author's research might be is to *read*—especially works by benchmark authors. Even if authors write in more than one subgenre or historical period, their research techniques tend to stay consistent throughout.

Of Publishers and Labels: Locating Historical Fiction

Although librarians actively select historical fiction for their collections, and current titles are nearly always found in bookstores, historical novels are almost never shelved separately. Rather, they are shelved with other genres—historical mysteries in Mystery, historical romance and romantic historicals in Romance. Traditional and literary historical novels will likely be found mixed in with the general fiction collection.

Historical fiction is occasionally given useful subject headings in an online catalog, such as "Elizabeth I, Queen of England, 1533-1603—Fiction" for novels about Elizabeth Tudor. While librarians may be used to searching OPACs in this way, Library of Congress subject headings, especially for anything history-related, are not exactly intuitive. Who would think to look under "United States—History—Revolution, 1775-1783—Fiction" for

novels about the American Revolution? It's hard enough to type, let alone to remember the exact dates. Patrons can't be expected to know these tricks of the library trade.

It doesn't help that relevant novels in publishers' catalogs will rarely be labeled "historical fiction" even though they are set in the past and seem to fulfill the necessary criteria. Some publishing imprints that actively acquire historical fiction, such as Forge and Crown, will label their novels correctly on the spine. Most won't, however, instead substituting a nonspecific genre label such as plain old "Fiction." The problem is not that historical fiction is too narrow to deserve its own section in libraries and bookstores, but that it's too broad, and that it overlaps with other genres. Regardless of the category label, blurbs in publishers' catalogs and on the dust jackets will offer a good sense of when and where a novel is set. (For names and addresses of relevant publishers, see Chapter 15.) To get around the shelving issue, some libraries use spine labels that designate fiction with historical settings.

Promoting Historical Fiction Collections

Even though historical fiction rarely has a section of its own, many librarians cater to genre readers by hosting book discussions on relevant titles, developing annotated bibliographies, and creating book displays.

Choices for Book Discussions

Many historical novels make good choices for book discussion groups. Specific titles are noted in this guide. The books chosen should not be unduly lengthy, in order to keep the group's attention. They should also be in print. Literary historical novels tend to be good choices, as do literary historical mysteries (annotated as such in Chapter 7). They speak not only to the time period but also to the human experience, which can raise a lot of discussion points. Because literary novels usually aren't as lengthy as others, this can work to librarians' advantage. Examples include Charles Frazier's *Cold Mountain* (assuming it hasn't been overdone by this point), Tracy Chevalier's *Girl with a Pearl Earring*, Geraldine Brooks's *Year of Wonders*, and just about any historical novel by Kathryn Harrison.

Other good choices are novels that either feature characters ahead of their time or that present social issues resonating with readers today. Examples of these issues include gender roles (Donna Woolfolk Cross's *Pope Joan*; Rebecca Kohn's *The Gilded Chamber*), race (Barbara Chase-Riboud's *Sally Hemings*; Lalita Tademy's African-American family saga *Cane River*), or religion (Charmaine Craig's *The Good Men*). Novelist Donna Woolfolk Cross in particular has gone out of her way to market her novel to book discussion groups, and librarians can arrange for her to talk one-on-one with their book groups via her Web site (www.popejoan.com). A good selection of discussion titles may be found at ReadingGroupGuides.com, under Find a Guide, then Historical Fiction. NoveList also provides discussion questions for many historical novels.

Bibliographies and Displays

With locally created bibliographies, it is important to provide annotations. This is due to the different subgenres a novel may fall into, as well as the appeal factors, as noted above. The best annotations will include at least the title, author, original publication date, and number of pages. A brief summary (including when and where the novel takes place) and descriptive commentary should follow. The summary should touch on the book's contents without giving away major plot points ("spoilers") , since these can ruin a book for potential readers. Exceptions can be made in cases where the historical outcome is generally known: that the Union won the Civil War, for instance. Librarians should comment on any appeal factors—apparent depth of research, characterization, language, etc.—that distinguish one book from another.

Although it's common to base historical fiction bibliographies around a particular time period and locale, theme-related lists and book displays also make good sense. They may include titles that:

- Serve as read-alikes for a currently popular historical novel, or an older novel that has recently been turned into a film: military novels of ancient Greece for the movie *Troy*, historical naval adventure for Patrick O'Brian's *Master and Commander.*

- Revolve around an interesting or timely subject or theme: Islam through the ages, novels on historical women for Women's History Month in March, biographical novels on American presidents for Presidents' Day.

- Describe an interest or cultural heritage shared by many library patrons: African-American historical novels, sagas with family trees for genealogically minded readers.

Because historical fiction is such a diverse genre, the possibilities for displays and annotated lists are almost endless.

Final Recommendations

To cater to readers, librarians should recognize that historical fiction is as valid a genre as romance, mystery, science fiction, or any of the other major fiction genres. Because it's rarely shelved separately, and because publishers may not label historical novels as such, librarians may need to expend extra effort on developing and promoting their historical fiction collections. This book can help in that regard. For example, does your library have a readers' advisory Web site that lists other genres but omits historical fiction? This is common, but it's a fault easily remedied. Because historical fiction includes novels of so many different styles, those who enjoy the genre should be able to find something appropriate to both their mood and their reading tastes. Librarians who remain well-informed about historical fiction, in all its great diversity, can only serve their patrons better.

References

Barton, David. 1998. "Facts of Fiction." *Sacramento Bee*, May 5. Available: http://www.sacbee.com/static/live/lifestyle/bookclub/archives/johnson2.html (Accessed October 13, 2004).

Fast, Howard. 1950. "Reply to Critics." *Masses and Mainstream*, 53–64. Available: http://www.trussel.com/hf/reply.htm (Accessed October 13, 2004).

Chapter 2

Traditional Historical Novels

Traditional historical novels are the type of books that readers usually picture when they think of historical fiction. They transport readers to a far-off time and place and allow them to vicariously experience the past through the eyes of another. Their authors are story-tellers first and foremost, and their goal is twofold: to portray a historical period as realisti-cally as possible and to entertain. The novels have protagonists that readers can root for and strong plotlines that keep readers glued to the pages to find out what happens next. Their appeal lies in the authors' ability to make historical figures and events come alive.

There is no standard pattern to traditional historicals, but for the most part, plots unfold in a straightforward, linear fashion. They tend to be long books, with 300-plus pages as the norm. Although they aren't as action-packed as are adventure novels, the authors keep the plots moving at a nice pace. Most storylines end optimistically, with the protagonist over-coming considerable adversity to reach his or her goals. Even though most traditional historicals don't make use of literary stylistics and multi-layered storylines, the overall quality of the writing is high.

The characters may be real-life historical figures whose lives are imagined against an accurately presented background, or they may be fictional creations placed by the author in a historical period to show how they react to their time. Alternatively, there may be a mix of historical and fictional characters present in the novel, with interaction between them. Tra-ditional historical novels are more likely than those in other subgenres to be biographical, since novels of this type have a predetermined, linear plot: They follow one character through the major events of his or her life. Jean Plaidy's many novels about British and Eu-ropean royalty are good examples of this. Whether the characters are real or fictional, the history influences the course of events, playing a strong role in the story rather than simply serving as a backdrop.

Readers typically look for traditional historicals set in particular places or during specific time periods. The most common settings include prehistoric Europe and America, ancient Greece and Rome, Egypt, England/Great Britain, and the United States. In the latter two cases, medieval times and the U.S. Civil War are among the most popular time periods. (Those set in the historical American West, also a highly popular locale, form a separate subgenre and are covered in Chapter 6.) Novels set elsewhere in the world—such as Canada, Asia, Africa, Australia, or Central and South America—aren't found nearly as frequently, for many publishers today feel that traditional historicals with unusual locales are unmarketable. These settings flourish in works of literary fiction and adventure novels, however, and readers in search of current historical fiction set in more distant lands may wish to consult Chapters 8 and 10.

Prehistoric Europe and Asia

Many authors set their novels in Europe or Asia before the time of recorded history. They attempt to re-create life in prehistoric times as accurately as possible, combining archaeological research with a good dose of imagination. Works with pre-contact Native Americans are frequently called "Prehistoric" as well. These are annotated later on in this chapter, at the beginning of the United States section.

Auel, Jean.

Earth's Children Series. ★

With her Earth's Children series, Jean Auel set the standard for prehistoric fiction. Her heroine Ayla, a young Cro-Magnon woman living in Europe some 30,000 years ago, searches for acceptance and companionship after she is left alone in the world. Auel's novels, all incredibly detailed with plentiful descriptions of flora and fauna, are based on years of anthropological research into prehistoric society. They also have a strong romantic element (including some explicit sex).

The Clan of the Cave Bear. Crown, 1980. 468pp.

Ayla, left alone after a disaster kills the members of her tribe, is taken in by the Clan of the Cave Bear, a group of Neanderthals. They distrust her because of her unusual appearance—blue eyes, blond hair, and lack of a flat forehead. Cast out by her adoptive clan, Ayla searches far and wide for others like herself.

The Valley of Horses. Crown, 1982. 502pp.

When Ayla comes upon a fertile valley, she forms a kinship with the horses of the steppe. It is only when a young hunter named Jondalar discovers her cave that she finds human acceptance.

The Mammoth Hunters. Crown, 1985. 645pp.

Ayla and her lover Jondalar meet up with people who look like Ayla, the Mamutoi (Mammoth Hunters). Because she was raised by "Flatheads," Ayla doesn't immediately trust them, and they feel the same about her. Ayla and Ranec, master carver of the Mamutoi, are mutually attracted to one another, which arouses Jondalar's jealousy.

The Plains of Passage. Crown, 1990. 760pp.

Jondalar and Ayla journey across the grasslands of Ice Age Europe to his homeland, where Jondalar plans to introduce her to his family.

The Shelters of Stone. Crown, 2002. 749pp.

At last, the pair reach their destination—Jondalar's tribe, the Zelandonii. Ayla fears they won't accept her, even though she's pregnant with Jondalar's child. Some of the Zelandonii are prejudiced against Flatheads and any who associate with them. They don't entirely approve of Ayla and Jondalar's relationship, either.

Cornwell, Bernard.

Stonehenge: A Novel of 2000 BC. **HarperCollins, 1999. 448pp.**

Three brothers of the Ratharryn tribe—Lengar the warrior, Camaban the sorcerer, and Saban, an early engineer and builder—vie with one another for control. Camaban first has the idea to build a great monument to the sun god, and Saban, the protagonist, makes his idea real. Like his <u>Warlord Chronicles</u> set in Arthurian Britain, Cornwell's Bronze Age saga doesn't stint on gritty detail or gore.

Dann, John R.

Song of the Axe. **Forge, 2001. 479pp.**

Around the time of the ice age that occurred 30,000 years ago, Agon (Axe Man) rescues blond-haired Eena (Spear-Woman) from rape by brutal Neanderthal shaman Ka. Rather than kill her to appease her family's ghosts, the two run off together, fall in love, and raise a family. Ka's descendants continue to pursue them over the years. The writing is a bit choppy, and there are violence and gore aplenty, but the romance and mystical atmosphere are conveyed well.

Holland, Cecelia.

Pillar of the Sky. **Knopf, 1985. 534pp.**

At the dawn of the Bronze Age in what is now southern Britain, Ladon defies tradition by naming his own son as his heir rather than his sister's child Moloquin. Outcast from the tribe, Moloquin is taken in by the clan's storyteller. After considerable struggle, he eventually becomes the tribe's leader and oversees the construction of Stonehenge.

Mackey, Mary.

<u>Earthsong Trilogy.</u>

In Europe of 4300 BC, Marrah is the young priestess of the Xori people, a matriarchal society. Their life is transformed by the arrival of Stavan, a warrior whose people pose a threat to their peace-loving ways. Her world on the brink of extinction, Marrah journeys with Stavan across the steppe to form a new society where the Mother Goddess reigns supreme.

The Year the Horses Came. HarperSanFrancisco, 1993. 377pp.

The Horses at the Gate. HarperSanFrancisco, 1995. 321pp.

The Fires of Spring. Onyx, 1998. 378pp.

Tarr, Judith.

Prehistoric Series.

Tarr's prehistoric novels focus on the matriarchal tribes of Europe and Asia, their mystical beliefs in a Mother Goddess, and how women's power was connected to their bond with horses. All can be read alone.

White Mare's Daughter. Forge, 1998. 496pp.

In Eastern Europe circa 4500 BC, priestess Sarama is led by the goddess of the White Mare away from her patriarchal tribe, in search of a new land where women rule. It is then up to Sarama to teach her new society about the training of horses and about possible invasion by her own original tribesmen. The invading force happens to be led by her twin brother.

Lady of Horses. Forge, 2000. 415pp.

In this prequel to *White Mare's Daughter*, the progenitors of the Celts are nomadic tribes that live on the Asian steppe. Among these savage people lives Sparrow, daughter of a tribal shaman, who is chosen by the Horse Goddess to serve her.

Daughter of Lir. Forge, 2001. 415pp.

Rhian was born to be the heir of the Mother of the City of Lir. Due to evil omens about her birth, she is hidden and raised as a potter's daughter instead. Rhian experiences terrifying visions of war that predict the demise of their matriarchal culture. Along with her blood brother Emry, she hopes to capture a chariot and use it against the people who challenge her world's existence.

The Shepherd Kings. Forge, 1999. 512pp.

This work continues the themes of both Tarr's prehistoric and Egyptian novels. Lower Egypt has been overrun by barbarian tribes known as the Hyksos, or Shepherd Kings, whose mastery of horses and chariots enables them to overtake Pharaoh's armies. An Egyptian slave named Iry is chosen by the Horse Goddess to be her servant, to the surprise and horror of the Hyksos.

Thomas, Elizabeth Marshall.

Reindeer Moon Series. `YA`

Thomas, an anthropologist, sets her novels in Siberia of 20,000 years ago.

Reindeer Moon. Houghton Mifflin, 1987. 338pp.

From the spirit world, Yanan details the existence of her brief life as a young woman growing up in a reindeer-oriented society in prehistoric Siberia.

The Animal Wife. Houghton Mifflin, 1990. 289pp.

Kobi, a man of Yanan's tribe, abducts a woman from a rival tribe whom he names Muskrat. Their relationship is passionate yet stormy, and she conceals a secret from him that changes his view of the world.

Biblical

Men and women from the Bible are placed in historical contexts. While religion plays a role in these novels, it is not the focal point; the emphasis is on historical authenticity and the portrayal of societies during biblical times. Biblical settings are also very common in Christian fiction (covered in Chapter 11).

Card, Orson Scott.

Women of Genesis series.

Card dramatizes the lives of well-known biblical matriarchs. Though published by a Mormon press, these novels (republished by Forge in paperback) are fairly mainstream. The next book will be called *The Wives of Israel*, about all of Jacob's wives and concubines.

Sarah. Shadow Mountain, 2000. 390pp.

Princess Sarai fully expects to become a priestess of Asherah when grown, but her destiny lies instead with the man called Abram. When they fall in love, she forsakes her heritage to follow him into the desert and join him in worship of his God (who changes her name to Sarah). Throughout her life's trials and tribulations, not the least of which is her barrenness, Sarah is a strong woman, fully worthy to be the wife of Abram (who later calls himself Abraham). She uses her strength to her advantage in her rivalry with her selfish older sister Qira, Lot's wife. Card's characters are not wooden archetypes but human characters who frequently speak in modern dialogue.

Rebekah. Shadow Mountain, 2001. 413pp.

When an accident results in the deafness of Rebekah's father, she and brother Laban communicate with him in writing. This love of learning stays with her all her life. Though unaware of her own beauty, Rebekah knows she is destined for a greater role than that of a farmer's wife. When she's approached by the steward of Abraham's household, who wants a wife for his master's son Isaac, she is eager to follow her destiny.

Rachel and Leah. Shadow Mountain, 2004. 418pp.

Due to her "tender eyes," Laban's oldest daughter Leah is excused from helping her nomadic family with their animals. Though not exactly jealous of her younger sister Rachel, Leah knows that Rachel is the beauty of the family. When Jacob, a handsome relative, appears in their camp, both Leah and Rachel fall in love with him—as do two of the family's servants, Zilpah and Bilhah.

Chamberlin, Ann.

Leaving Eden. Forge, 1999. 240pp.

Na'amah, the daughter of Adam and his first wife, the goddess Lilith, tells the story of her father's loneliness; the attraction he feels for Eve, a woman from another tribe; and his punishment (banishment from Eden) for taking a mate while a child of his first wife still lives. This novel gently pokes fun at the true power held by men in prehistoric/biblical times, for here God is a woman.

Tamar. **Forge, 1994. 463pp.** ✍

Tamar arrives at King David's court when her mother, the high priestess Maacah, joins his harem and becomes one of his wives. Forbidden to worship her own faith, Tamar struggles against the power that the masculine God of Jerusalem holds over David and his people. Tamar also has prophetic abilities. Though she realizes what lies in store for her half-brother Absalom, she is powerless to stop it.

Edghill, India.

Queenmaker. **St. Martin's Press, 2002. 376pp.** ✍📖

King Saul's daughter Michal, hardly given mention in the Bible apart from her great love for David, emerges as the power behind the throne in Edghill's debut novel. Married off to another when David loses her father's favor, Michal overcomes her girlish infatuation for him when she sees how he murders his way to power and prestige. Little by little, she learns to beat him at his own game, befriending Bathsheba and helping to raise the future King Solomon in a nurturing, feminine environment.

Wisdom's Daughter. **St. Martin's Press, 2004. 408pp.** ✍📖

Bilqis, Queen of Sheba, comes to King Solomon's court in Israel to find a female heir to rule her lands after her death. She finds the perfect candidate in Baalit, Solomon's beloved daughter. Baalit has a brilliant mind and a willingness to lead, but in her father's court, she takes second place to her brothers. Bilqis's choice provokes controversy in the royal court.

George, Margaret.

Mary, Called Magdalene. **Viking, 2002. 630pp.** ✍

Mary of Magdala's life resembles that of any young Jewish girl in the first-century Near East, though she makes one big mistake: concealing an idol of the pagan deity Ashara from her family. Mary agrees to an arranged marriage in an attempt to escape possession by the evil goddess, but relief only comes through the commands of Jesus, the Messiah, whom she has no choice but to follow after her own family abandons her. The remainder of the novel follows the Bible story closely, so there are few surprises. Though the novel is slow in spots, George does a credible job of re-creating the historical atmosphere in which Mary Magdalene must have lived.

Halter, Marek.

Canaan Trilogy. ✍📖

Future volumes of what Harek calls "the feminine Bible" will include novels about Moses's wife Zipporah and Ezra's sister Lilah.

Sarah. Crown, 2004. 310pp.

Sarai, daughter of a wealthy Sumerian man in the city-state of Ur, flees an arranged marriage by drinking a potion that makes her barren. For six years, she lives as a priestess of Ishtar. When she meets her childhood love Abram again, she escapes and joins his nomadic tribe. God changes her name to Sarah. Then the familiar biblical story begins to unfold.

Hunt, Angela Elwell.

The Shadow Women. **Warner, 2002. 390pp.** ✍

The "shadow women" in the life of Moses—his sister Miryam, his adoptive mother Merytamon, and his Bedouin wife Zipporah—tell their own versions of Moses's story. Christian novelist Hunt succeeds somewhat in her first work of mainstream fiction, but it is still fairly lightweight in comparison to Anita Diamant's *The Red Tent* (Chapter 10) and India Edghill's *Queenmaker.*

Kohn, Rebecca.

The Gilded Chamber. **Rugged Land, 2004. 336pp.** ✍ 📖

A new retelling of the story of Esther, the Persian queen who saved the Jews from extinction. King Xerxes of Persia has banished his wife Vashti for disobedience. Now, members of the king's household roam the kingdom in search of a new wife. Hadassah, a Jewish orphan betrothed to her cousin Mordechai, is chosen to be Xerxes's bride. Hadassah, instructed by Mordechai never to reveal her Jewish heritage, takes the new name Esther and joins Xerxes's royal harem. What makes Kohn's novel unique is the detail she presents about women's lives in ancient times.

Lotan, Yael.

Avishag. **Toby Press, 2002. 226pp.** ✍

King David lies dying, and the job of Avishag the Shunammite is to warm his bed. They never become lovers, but David's sons Solomon and Adoniyah both fall in love with Avishag. This causes problems with the royal succession.

Ray, Brenda.

The Midwife's Song. **Karmichael, 2000. 243pp.**

Puah, a young Hebrew midwife, dares to defy orders given by Pharaoh to kill all male Hebrew infants. With the help of her husband Hattush, she saves the infant Moses from certain death. In doing so, Puah becomes a heroine for her people.

Other Ancient Civilizations

Egypt

Egypt at the time of the Pharaohs is a popular setting for traditional historicals. They give readers the opportunity to learn about life along the Nile in ancient times, the polytheistic Egyptian religion, and the politics of the time.

Essex, Karen.

Kleopatra Series. ✍📖 **YA**

In her two-book series, Essex re-establishes Kleopatra's reputation as an intelligent political leader rather than the promiscuous femme fatale of legend. In keeping with the author's historically authentic interpretation, Essex uses the Greek spelling of Kleopatra's name. Most other novels about Kleopatra focus almost exclusively on her reign, but this series spends a good deal of time on her childhood.

Kleopatra. Warner, 2001. 382pp.

Kleopatra grows up with a talent for both language and politics; as such, she proves very unlike her lazy father King Ptolemy XII. Exiled to Rome as a young girl, Kleopatra gathers information that will lead her to rule Egypt one day.

Pharaoh. Warner, 2002. 482pp.

Kleopatra, aged twenty-two, determines that the best hope for Egypt is for her to form an alliance with the Roman Empire. She puts Egypt above all, joining herself politically and romantically with Caesar, and after his death, Antony.

Falconer, Colin.

When We Were Gods. **Crown, 2000. 462pp.** ✍

Falconer's Cleopatra VII, just eighteen years old when she comes to power, is a politically astute woman who always has the future of her country in mind. She keeps this goal to the forefront when she conducts affairs with both Julius Caesar and Mark Antony.

Gedge, Pauline.

Gedge, a native New Zealander now living in Canada, has written a number of novels of ancient Egypt, including her earlier novels *Child of the Morning* (about the female pharaoh Hatshepsut), *The Twelfth Transforming*, and *Scroll of Saqqara*.

Thu Series.

This duology tells the story of Thu, an ambitious Egyptian peasant girl who is not content with her station in life.

Lady of the Reeds. Soho, 1994. 513pp. (Original title: *House of Dreams.*) ✍

Thu follows Hui, Pharaoh's physician and seer, from her home in Aswat to the royal court, where she rises to become the concubine of Ramses III.

House of Illusions. Moyer Bell, 1997. 448pp. ✍

Thu, who has been living in her home village of Aswat for the past seventeen years, reveals the story of murder and conspiracy that forced the Pharaoh to exile her from court. When she is back in a position to take revenge on those who sought her ruin, she doesn't know whether the end would justify the means.

Lords of the Two Lands. ✍ **YA**

Circa 1550 BC, the Setiu (better known as the Hyksos) people, nomad invaders originating from Asia Minor, have overrun Egypt for the past 200 years. Gedge's trilogy dramatizes rebellions launched by descendants of the original Egyptian rulers in an effort to regain control of their country. Ultimately successful, the princely Tao family ushers in Egypt's Eighteenth Dynasty.

The Hippopotamus Marsh. Soho, 2000. 371pp.

The Oasis. Soho, 2001. 536pp.

The Horus Road. Soho, 2002. 504pp.

George, Margaret.

The Memoirs of Cleopatra. **St. Martin's Press, 1997. 976pp.** ✍

Cleopatra narrates the story of her rich and passionate life as Queen of one of the wealthiest kingdoms in the world. One of George's strengths is her ability to weave the personal aspects of a ruler's life with her political role and actions.

Holland, Cecelia.

Valley of the Kings. **Forge, 1997. 240pp.** ✍

In the 1920s, Howard Carter narrates his tale of the discovery of King Tutankhamun's tomb. The scene then switches to 3,500 years earlier, when Tutankhamun fights with his beautiful mother, Nefertiti, for control of the kingdom. Tutankhamun died mysteriously as a youth, and this novel suggests the reason why. Originally published in 1977 under the pseudonym Elizabeth Eliot Carter.

Jacq, Christian.

Ramses Series. ✍

The books in Jacq's Egyptian series, all bestsellers in his native France, tell the story of the pharaoh Ramses II, starting from his childhood circa 1300 BC as the chosen heir of the pharaoh Seti through his survival of numerous palace intrigues. Ramses rules Egypt for more than sixty years with the help of advisors and his beautiful wife Nefertari. Though Jacq's narrative style tends to be fairly simplistic, there is action, adventure, and romance galore.

The Son of Light. Warner, 1997. 384pp.

The Eternal Temple. Warner, 1998. 368pp.

The Battle of Kadesh. Warner, 1998. 377pp.

The Lady of Abu Simbel. Warner, 1998. 384pp.

Under the Western Acacia. Warner, 1999. 368pp.

The Stone of Light.

It is the tail end of the reign of Ramses II. The scene switches to the Place of Truth, a secret village where talented artisans craft beautiful objects of art exclusively for the Valley of the Kings.

Nefer the Silent. Atria, 2000. 400pp.

The Wise Woman. Atria, 2000. 432pp.

Paneb the Ardent. Atria, 2001. 400pp.

The Place of Truth. Atria, 2001. 384pp.

Queen of Freedom Trilogy. &

In the seventeenth century BC, when Egypt was overtaken by the barbarian Hyksos tribes, the country's survival lies in the hands of one strong woman, Queen Ahotep.

The Empire of Darkness. Atria, 2003. 384pp.

The War of the Crowns. Atria, 2004. 384pp.

The Flaming Sword. Atria, 2004. 384pp.

Tarr, Judith.

King and Goddess. Forge, 1996. 384pp. &

Hatshepsut, Egypt's famous female Pharaoh, was maligned after her death by the nephew whose throne she usurped. Her name was eradicated, her monuments destroyed. Tarr's novel reestablishes Hatshepsut's reputation by detailing her rise to power and her accomplishments. Forced to marry her odious half-brother and serve as his chief wife, Hatshepsut knows she has the wisdom and power within her to rule. Her love for the scribe Senenmut helps her survive to become "king and goddess."

Lord of the Two Lands. Forge, 2003. 315pp. &

In 336 BC, a time when Egypt was ruled by Persia, Alexander, King of Macedonia, is ready to extend his empire by defeating King Darius of Persia. Meriamnon, daughter of the last Egyptian pharaoh, tries to convince Alexander to liberate her country before the Persians despoil it.

Pillar of Fire. Forge, 1995. 448pp. &

Akhenaten was the pharaoh notorious for abandoning the ancient gods of Egypt in favor of a monotheistic religion in which the sun god Aten was worhipped. In Tarr's interpretation of historical events, Akhenaten and the biblical Moses are one and the same. Her version of Akhenaten's life, as told in the third person by a Hittite slave girl who serves his daughter, is a retelling of Exodus.

Throne of Isis. Forge, 1994. 349pp. &

Cleopatra's cousin Dione, by Cleopatra's side at all major events in her life, provides a unique perspective on the well-known warrior queen, focusing on her relationships with Caesar and Antony. Tarr keeps us at a slight distance from her characters, so the reader never gets into Cleopatra's head. In this, Tarr portrays her heroine as those closest to her may have seen her.

Greece

Many historical novels set in ancient Greece are based on epic poems, like the *Iliad* and *Odyssey*, or on figures of the era (Sappho, Alexander the Great). Even if the stories are invented, they have the ring of legend.

Bradshaw, Gillian.

The Sand-Reckoner. **Forge, 2000. 351pp.** ✍

> Archimedes (ca. 287–212 BC), one of the greatest mathematicians and engineers of the ancient world, forsakes his happy life studying philosophy at Ptolemy's Museum in Alexandria when his ailing father calls him home to Syracuse. There he takes up a post building catapults as an engineer for King Hieron, who is battling the Roman army during the Second Punic War. Archimedes also falls in love with Hieron's sister.

Fast, Howard.

Spartacus. **1950. 351pp.** ✍ ★

> Fast's classic novel about the doomed Roman slave leader Spartacus (ca. 109–71 BC), written in response to the author's imprisonment for Communist sympathies, was originally self-published. It went on to become a bestseller. The story of Spartacus's revolt against the cruel injustices of the Roman Empire is framed by people's recollections of him after the rebellion is put down.

Franklin, Sarah B.

Daughter of Troy. **Avon, 1998. 402pp.**

> Briseis, the rightful queen of Lyrnessos, narrates her version of the Trojan War, from the time she is carried off by Prince Achilles as a spoil of war, through their love affair, her abduction by King Agamemnon of Mycenae, and her foreknowledge of Achilles's death. (Franklin is the pseudonym of fantasy author Dave Duncan.)

Freedman, Nancy.

Sappho: The Tenth Muse. **St. Martin's Press, 1998. 336pp.** ✍

> Ruled by her passions, the great lesbian poet Sappho is lustful and temperamental, a strong woman who stands up for herself in business dealings and marries a man as aristocratic as she. Hardly the feminist retelling one might expect about the famous Greek poet, Freedman's novel shows Sappho's poetry as only one of many aspects of her personality, and her love for a man to have been the greatest love of her life.

Hand, Judith.

The Amazon and the Warrior. **Forge, 2004. 368pp.**

> During the Trojan War, Penthesilea, Queen of the Amazons, raises up an army to take revenge on Achilles. Years earlier, Achilles had killed her mother. Penthesilea wants revenge, even though it may mean abandoning her lover, Damonides.

Voice of the Goddess. **Pacific Rim, 2001. 381pp.**

Leesandra of Keftiu, a goddess-worshipper living on the island of Crete circa 1600 BC, dedicates herself to preserving their peaceful way of life, which is being threatened by Indo-Europeans arriving from mainland Greece. Joining her is her star-crossed lover Alektrion of Kalliste. When the nearby island of Santorini is destroyed by a volcanic eruption, the society's continued survival becomes even more precarious.

Jong, Erica.

Sappho's Leap. **Norton, 2003. 320pp.** ✍ 📖

Sappho, famous for the erotic love poetry she wrote over 2,600 years ago, is a woman ahead of her time. Her adventures start early: At fourteen she is seduced by an older man, a poet, but married off to another when their liaison is discovered. When her marriage ends and her daughter is kidnapped, she begins a journey of a lifetime that ranges from her home of Delphi to Egypt and the land of the Amazons. This is sharp, visionary fiction from an author well known for her portrayals of exuberant feminine sexuality.

McCullough, Colleen.

The Song of Troy. **London: Orion, 1998. 404pp.**

The classic saga of the Trojan War is narrated by its major players: the beautiful Helen, who precipitated the war; soldier and wayfarer Odysseus; Priam, Troy's king; Achilles, warrior prince; and Agamemnon, King of Mycenae, whose launch of a thousand ships meant the sacrifice of his daughter. This is McCullough's least-known historical novel. Published in Australia and Britain, it is widely available in the United States.

Mitchison, Naomi.

The Corn King and the Spring Queen. **Harcourt Brace, 1931. 721pp. (Alternate title: *The Barbarian*.)** ★

Along the shores of the Black Sea in 228 BC, a witch-girl named Erif Der marries Tarrik, the Corn King, a pagan ruler who is her family's deadly rival. Though compelled by her father to put an end to his power, Erif and Tarrik fall in love. However, her father's curse causes her to flee Scythia, first to Sparta and later to the dissolute country of Egypt. Earthy, heroic, and magical, this is Mitchison's masterwork.

Pressfield, Steven.

Pressfield writes stirring tales of personal and military glory set in ancient Greece. With their powerful action scenes, they will also appeal to readers of adventure fiction.

Gates of Fire. **Doubleday, 1998. 386pp.** ★

In 480 BC, at the Battle of Thermopylae, a brave force of 300 Spartans fought a hopeless battle against the invading armies of Persia's King Xerxes. Though the Spartans all lost their lives, they managed to hold off Persia for seven days, giving the Greeks enough time to rally their forces and repulse a Persian invasion later on. The story is told in flashback by Xeones, a Spartan squire captured by King Xerxes, who recounts his story from boyhood until that fateful day.

The Last of the Amazons. **Doubleday, 2002. 400pp.** ✍

Around 1250 BC, Theseus, King of Athens, happens upon a land populated by female warriors who call themselves "tal Kyrte." The Greeks call them Amazons. When Antiope, their Queen, falls in love with Theseus and betrays them for his sake, she calls down the wrath of her entire tribe. Their story is framed by the tale of Selene, an Amazon captured by the Greeks who fights to return to her former way of life.

Tides of War. **Doubleday, 2000. 426pp.** ✍

Fifty years after Thermopylae, Alcibiades (ca. 450–404 BC), an Athenian soldier raised in Sparta, brings Greece to glory during the Peloponnesian War. Valiant, ambitious, handsome, and well spoken, Alcibiades embodies the best of Athens. When his arrogance gets the best of him and popular opinion turns against him, Alcibiades turns against the Athenians as well, fighting for Sparta against his former city.

The Virtues of War. **Doubleday, 2004. 301pp.** ✍

Alexander the Great narrates the tale of his own life (356–323 BC) in all its complexity. A brilliant student, fearless military commander, and passionate lover of women and men, Pressfield's Alexander is a soldier at heart. He illuminates a glorious era when war was the only true way of life, and victory was men's greatest accomplishment.

Renault, Mary.

The late classicist and novelist Mary Renault (a pseudonym for Eileen Mary Challans) set the standard for historical fiction set in ancient Greece. Renault expects a lot from her readers. She doesn't hand-hold them through history; instead she simply presents events as they happen, in stark, descriptive language.

<u>Alexander the Great trilogy.</u> ✍ ★

Renault's trilogy is primarily a heroic character study of Alexander. She relates his life through a succession of dramatic episodes, illustrating the major events and people that shaped his personality from childhood on.

Fire from Heaven. Pantheon, 1969. 375pp.

In the first novel, Renault details the young Alexander's troubled relationships with his father, King Philip of Macedon, and his overprotective mother, Queen Olympias; his first kill, which brought him into manhood; the taming of the unruly horse Bucephalus; and his tutoring by the Greek philosopher Aristotle.

The Persian Boy. Pantheon, 1972. 419pp.

A promising youth and an even stronger man and leader, Alexander forges a strong relationship with a eunuch slave-boy, Bagoas, who becomes his lover. Bagoas is present for all of the major events in Alexander's life: military victories, assassination attempts, his marriage to two women, and also Alexander's love for another man.

Funeral Games. Pantheon, 1981. 335pp.

The darkest of the three novels, *Funeral Games* deals with Alexander's heirs and their impossible task of holding the realm together after his death.

The Last of the Wine. **Pantheon, 1956. 389pp.** ★

During the Peloponnesian War in the fifth century BC, when the rivalry between Athens and Sparta comes to a head, Alexias—a young Athenian of noble birth—studies philosophy with Sokrates. He also develops a close bond with one of Sokrates's followers, a youth named Lysis. The story of their love affair is tied in with the fall of Athens after the Spartan victory.

The Mask of Apollo. **Pantheon, 1966. 371pp.** ★

In the fourth century BC, Nikeratos, a tragic actor from Athens, travels from there to Sicily and back, acting in a variety of productions. A golden mask of Apollo, symbolic of the golden age of the Greek theater, accompanies him wherever he goes. He meditates upon its meaning before forming any opinions about events in his life, such as his relationship with Dion of Syracuse (a historical figure) and the potentially harmful influence of Plato's philosophies.

The Praise Singer. **Pantheon, 1978. 288pp.** ★ ✍

Simonides of Keos, the great lyric poet of the fifth century BC, becomes the apprentice of Kleobis the bard, an Ionian singer. After the death of Kleobis, Simonides joins the court of the Pisistratids in Athens, where he is a witness to their rise and fall.

Theseus series. ✍ ★

Renault humanizes the legend of Theseus, King of Athens, a historical figure.

The King Must Die. Pantheon, 1958. 338pp.

Theseus grows up as the unacknowledged son of an Athenian king in a land that is still partly matriarchal. *The King Must Die* follows his life through the time he is sent to Crete as a tribute to King Minos.

The Bull from the Sea. Pantheon, 1962. 343pp.

Successfully escaping from the labyrinth, Theseus returns to Athens in glory, forming relationships with two women: Hippolyta, the woman he loves, and Phaedra, the Cretan woman he marries.

Sundell, Thomas.

A Bloodline of Kings. **Crow Woods, 2002. 484pp.** ✍

In this lengthy novel about Philip of Macedon, the story begins with one birth, that of Philip himself, and ends with another, that of his son Alexander, later "the Great." In the intervening pages, Sundell takes us through the life of an extraordinary man, Philippos of the Makedones, whose brilliant military career during the fourth century BC was overshadowed by that of his more famous son. Philippos earns Macedon a place on the political playing field of the ancient Hellenes and makes it the equal of powerful city-states such as Athens and Thebes.

The Roman Empire

Novels set throughout the Roman Empire focus not only on political developments within the city of Rome itself but also on its rulers' conquests of lands throughout Europe. As the soldiers of Rome seek to bring yet more lands under the Empire's umbrella, they clash with the Celtic tribes of Europe and the British Isles, who fight fiercely in defense of their territory.

Bradshaw, Gillian.

The Beacon at Alexandria. **Houghton Mifflin, 1986. 376pp.**

In Alexandria in AD 293, a young woman named Charis disguises herself as a man in order to study medicine. She becomes the physician to the city's leading archbishop. When he dies, the city is thrown into chaos as religious factions vie for power.

Island of Ghosts. **Forge, 1998. 319pp.**

In the second century AD, Roman Emperor Marcus Aurelius orders 8,000 horsemen from the barbarian Sarmatian tribe to serve him in Britain. The warrior-prince Ariantes is one of these Sarmatians. He struggles to stay true to his heritage while helping the Romans put down uprisings among renegade Druids.

Render Unto Caesar. **Forge, 2003. 464pp.**

Hermogenes, an Alexandrian Greek in Rome of 16 BC, attempts to collect on a debt owed to him by Tarius Rufus, a Roman consul. In doing so, he encounters considerable prejudice against himself and his people, who are considered "Greek trash" by the supposedly noble Romans. Cantabra, a female former gladiator, rescues Hermogenes and protects him against the consul's minions. When Hermogenes overhears Tarius Rufus plotting against a high-ranking member of Roman society, he needs all the help he can get.

Breem, Wallace.

Eagle in the Snow. **Putnam, 1970. 320pp.** ★

In the early fifth century AD, General Paulinus Maximus, commended for his bravery in fighting off Celtic barbarians along Hadrian's Wall in Britain, gets called to perform a second duty. The powers that be in Rome ask him to take a single legion to defend Gaul against attack by thousands of native German tribesmen. Reissued by Rugged Land in 2003, with an introduction by Steven Pressfield.

Dietrich, William.

Hadrian's Wall. **HarperCollins, 2004. 356pp.**

It is AD 367, and the wall built to separate Roman Britain from the land's northern barbarians still stands. Valeria, daughter of a Roman senator, heads north to Hadrian's Wall for an arranged marriage. Her escort, a veteran soldier named Galba, can't hide his jealousy of Valeria's proposed husband Marcus, who will be replacing him as commander. When Valeria arrives, she gets caught up in a web of passion, revenge, and war.

Gillespie, Donna.

The Light Bearer. Berkley, 1994. 788pp.

The clash between the might of the Roman Empire and the valiant tribes of Germania circa AD 50 to AD 90 come alive in this tale of Auriane, daughter of a Chattian chieftain. She becomes a warrior after Roman invaders murder her people. Word of her exploits reaches as far as Rome, where the Emperor Domitian swears to capture and defeat her. Marcus Julianus, a Roman senator and imperial advisor, grows intrigued by reports of Auriane; he knows that he is destined to meet this remarkable woman.

Graves, Robert.

Claudius Series. ✍ ★

The Emperor Claudius wryly observes a number of events leading up to his reign. Behind his outward infirmities and unfortunate stutter lies a sharp and ever-inquiring mind.

I, Claudius. H. Smith and R. Haas, 1934. 494pp.

As a young man, Claudius finds himself ignored by the other Julio-Claudian rulers because they believe he is too dim-witted and sickly to bother eliminating. Claudius has the dubious benefit of watching all of the political machinations, debauchery, and bloodshed of the rulers who preceded him, such as Augustus, Tiberius, and Caligula.

Claudius the God and His Wife Messalina. H. Smith and R. Haas, 1935. 583pp.

Against all odds, the intellectual Claudius has become emperor after Caligula's death. He reigns for thirteen years before he, too, is murdered (this is a natural end for Roman emperors). He isn't completely immune to tyranny himself, though he justifies his actions in his usual witty manner. The most blatant examples of vice are left to his beautiful wife, Messalina, who plots his downfall.

Grundy, Stephan.

Attila's Treasure. Bantam, 1996. 549pp.

Hagan, a Burgundian warrior prince, is sent to abide with Attila and his Huns as a foster son/hostage around AD 415. It is a bloody, tumultuous era, and Grundy's battle scenes are appropriately realistic and rousing. His novel, despite the title, is not about the historical Attila (Gothic for "little father") but a fictional one of Attila's predecessors. There are some minor fantasy elements, particularly in Grundy's evocation of the Otherworld, but the majority of the book is straightforward historical fiction.

Harris, Robert.

Pompeii. Random House, 2003. 278pp. **YA**

Well-to-do Romans flock to seaside resorts during the summer of AD 79. Marcus Attilius Primus, a young engineer, is responsible for the aqueduct bringing water to townspeople living on the Bay of Naples. When drought threatens the region, Attilius rushes to Pompeii to remedy the fault. There he discovers corruption and imminent danger. Rich with suspense, despite the foregone conclusion—the eruption of Mount Vesuvius.

Leckie, Ross.

Punic War trilogy.

Leckie is best when re-creating the battles of Rome's Punic Wars, but his characterizations of great men like Hannibal and Scipio are just as intriguing, for both are portrayed almost negatively—something unusual in biographical novels.

Hannibal. Regnery, 1996. 245pp. ✍

Hannibal, born and bred in North Africa in the second century BC and brought up to hate all Romans, relates in the first person how he made his legendary march across the Alps, with armies and elephants, to conquer Rome. His is a bloodthirsty story, but he finds romance, too, with a beautiful Spanish woman named Similce.

Scipio: The Man Who Defeated Hannibal. Regnery, 1998. 304pp. ✍

Publius Cornelius Scipio Africanus, the man who established Rome's dominance in the ancient world by conquering Carthage and defeating its leader, dedicates his memoirs before his death to his secretary, Bostar. But Bostar, Hannibal's former geographer, also has his own story to relate. The differences between their two versions make this an intriguing novel.

Carthage. Canongate, 2001. 240pp.

The (fictional) bastard sons of Hannibal and Scipio take up where their fathers left off, battling it out to the death as Rome and Carthage vie for supremacy in the ancient world.

McCullough, Colleen.

The Masters of Rome. ✍ ★

In her six novels about the decline of the Roman Republic and the birth of the Roman Empire, McCullough demonstrates her mastery of the politics, culture, and personalities of the era. Erudite and impressively detailed, the novels come complete with maps, glossaries, and black-and-white drawings done by the author. The length of the series as a whole may daunt new readers; they are best read in order. McCullough's obvious hero is Gaius Julius Caesar, though many of the other historical personages she depicts are equally fascinating.

The First Man in Rome. Morrow, 1990. 896pp.

The year 110 BC is the beginning of the end for the Roman Republic, as foreshadowed by the rise to prominence of two unlikely statesmen. Gaius Marius is a New Man from the Italian provinces who rises above his humble origins to become consul for an unprecedented six terms. His right-hand man and political competitor is Lucius Cornelius Sulla, a man of noble birth who comes from the slums of the Subura to challenge Marius for the title of First Man in Rome.

The Grass Crown. Morrow, 1991. 894pp.

When the aging Gaius Marius decides to seek an unprecedented seventh term as consul, his one-time student and friend Sulla becomes his rival. As the two vie for dominance, they must also fight to save Rome from rebellions elsewhere in Italy and from the schemes of a barbarian leader, Mithridates, King of Pontus.

Fortune's Favorites. Morrow, 1993. 878pp.

Fortune's favorites—the three men who dominated Roman politics circa 80 BC—are Lucius Cornelius Sulla, returning from exile to become a power-crazed dictator; Pompey the Great, member of a wealthy provincial family; and Gaius Julius Caesar, a young politician with a promising future. Amid their rivalry for power in Rome, the city's leaders must subdue rebellions in places as far away as Spain. They also put down the dangerous slave revolt led by Spartacus.

Caesar's Women. Morrow, 1996. 695pp.

Despite the title, this is more about Caesar the man and his rise to prominence in Rome beginning in 68 BC than about the noblewomen who surrounded him, but McCullough's female characters are equally as impressive. These include Caesar's shrewd and intelligent mother, Aurelia; his flighty young second wife, Pompeia; his scheming mistress Servilia; and his adored daughter, Julia.

Caesar: Let the Dice Fly. Morrow, 1997. 664pp.

In 54 BC, Caesar's ambitions know no bounds. Having conquered Gaul, he turns his attention to Rome itself, though the members of the Senate are growing nervous about how far Caesar will go in his quest for power. His one-time ally—the general Pompey, who is also his son-in-law—becomes his adversary, though even he cannot turn the tide away from Caesar.

The October Horse. Simon & Schuster, 2002. 792pp.

In 48 BC, Caesar—at the height of his power—is in Egypt, helping to determine the outcome of a civil war between King Ptolemy and his sister-wife, Queen Cleopatra. Though Cleopatra becomes the mother of Caesar's only son, Caesarion, the son can never inherit his father's responsibilities. In the meantime, Caesar's enemies—Marc Antony, Marcus Brutus, and others—pretend to be his friends. Their jealousy of his position, and their desire to return Rome to its republican ways, lead to both Caesar's assassination and the rise of his great-nephew, Octavian.

Park, Paul.

The Gospel of Corax. **Soho, 1996. 297pp.** ✍

Corax, a Roman slave and healer wanted for the murder of his master, escapes his master and makes a pilgrimage to the source of the Ganges River, the land of his father's birth. Along the way he meets a rebel named Jeshua with a similar mission. The two make their way to the spiritual center of the Himalayas. Park's down-to-earth version of Jesus may offend some Christian readers, as will

Corax's homosexuality, but Park includes plenty of authentic historical detail as the pair make their way east.

Ripley, Alexandra.

A Love Divine. **Warner, 1996. 712pp.**

Little is known of Joseph of Arimathea, save the traditional story that he gave up his own tomb for Jesus. In this fictional biography, Ripley follows the legend of Joseph, a Jewish seaman in Roman-occupied Palestine who learns of Jesus's miracles firsthand and spreads the word of his teachings throughout the Roman Empire. The majority of the novel takes place in Palestine, showing Joseph as a young man who falls in love with his childhood friend. He befriends Emperor Augustus and King Herod and becomes father to a crippled daughter whose infirmities lead him to Jesus. At journey's end, he arrives at last in the British Isles, where he founds Glastonbury Abbey.

Schweighardt, Joan.

Gudrun's Tapestry. **Beagle Bay, 2003. 268pp.**

In the fifth century, Attila the Hun is the scourge of the western Roman Empire. A young Burgundian woman named Gudrun takes it upon herself to rid the world of this terror in revenge for his destruction of her home and livelihood. Based on the *Poetic Edda*.

Scott, Manda.

Boudica Series.

A projected four-book series about the Celtic warrior queen Boudica. Her true name is Breaca, while "Boudica" is a title meaning "bringer of victory." Not just a war story, Scott's series has strong elements of Celtic spirituality. The next book will be *Dreaming the Hound.*

Dreaming the Eagle. Delacorte, 2003. 465pp.

Breaca, daughter of an Eceni warrior in first-century Britain, wants to become a spiritual leader for her people. Fate has something else in mind. When her mother Graine is killed, Breaca takes vengeance, becoming a warrior herself at a young age. She becomes her people's greatest hope, since the Romans are set on eliminating the Celtic tribes during their invasion of the British Isles.

Dreaming the Bull. Delacorte, 2004. 344pp.

The Romans, under Emperor Claudius, have overtaken Britain. Breaca's half-brother Bán, believing that his sister and her family were killed, joins the Roman cavalry. He continues to deny his past, but his heart never really abandons his Celtic roots. When Breaca's lover Caradoc is captured, only Bán can save him.

Spinrad, Norman.

The Druid King. **Knopf, 2003. 412pp.** ✒

Spinrad, best known for his science fiction, switches genres in this page-turner about Vercingetorix, the legendary Druid king of Gaul who is a French national hero today. Trained as a youth by the Romans themselves, Vercingetorix uses this knowledge against them. He unites the warring Gallic tribes against the incursion of Roman forces under Julius Caesar.

The British Isles

Early Middle Ages

These novels take place between the fall of Rome in the fifth century AD and the Battle of Hastings in 1066, a period commonly known as the Dark Ages. However, historians now reject that term because it implies lack of development and activity—which certainly wasn't true.

General

These powerfully felt, serious novels tell of conflicts between Celtic and Roman Christianity, as well as the incursion of Angles, Saxons, and Jutes into the British Isles.

Bragg, Melvyn.

The Sword and the Miracle. **Random House, 1996. 541pp. (Original title: *Credo*.)** ✒

Beginning in AD 657, Bega, an Irish princess fated to become a saint, and Padric, a British prince and warrior, sacrifice their romance for Bega's belief in a greater calling. She believes her destiny is to spread the word of God to the pagan peoples of the British Isles. Padric, her teacher and mentor, has an all-encompassing desire to fight the invading Northumbrians and re-create the kingdom of Rheged, which was torn apart after the Romans came. The novel, unfortunately given a pseudo-Arthurian title in the United States, depicts the struggles between Celtic mysticism and Celtic Christianity—and between the Celtic and Roman versions of Christianity—that took place in the British Isles during the seventh century. This culminated in the Synod of Whitby.

Dunnett, Dorothy.

King Hereafter. **Knopf, 1982. 721pp.** ✒

Renowned historical novelist Dunnett's novel of the historical Macbeth is both enlightening and controversial: the former because it deftly illuminates eleventh-century Scotland and Scandinavia, a land still wild and pagan; the latter because it presumes that Scotland's King Macbeth and the Norse nobleman Thorfinn, Earl of Orkney, were one and the same. Her Macbeth, unlike Shakespeare's, is a brilliant strategist, an unrecognized hero who has his country's best interests at heart. Groa, his consort and queen, is his perfect ally and mate. Challenging and lengthy, the novel will nonetheless reward those readers who make it through.

Godwin, Parke.

The Last Rainbow. **Bantam, 1985. 358pp.**

The last volume of Godwin's Arthurian trilogy (see below) can stand alone equally well. It is a spiritual, fantastical depiction of the life of St. Patrick in fifth-century Ireland, and his relationship with a woman of the Prydn (the same Pictish tribe to which Morgana, Arthur's lover, belongs in Godwin's novel *Firelord*).

Holland, Cecelia.

The Kings in Winter. **Atheneum, 1968. 208pp.**

Early eleventh-century Ireland, supposedly united under the reign of High King Brian Boru, is a land rife with blood-feuds, rebellions, and continual raids by Danish Vikings. Muirtagh, the fictional chief of the Clan ó Cullinane, decides against his better judgment to side with Maelmordha, the King of Leinster, against Brian Boru. Brian had destroyed Maelmordha's army years earlier in his attempt to claim the crown. In their bid to rid Ireland of its High King, the rebels enlist the help of the Danes. Their actions culminate in the Battle of Clontarf.

Horsley, Kate.

Confessions of a Pagan Nun. **Shambhala, 2001. 181pp.** 📖 **YA**

Though the title implies a juicy tell-all, here "confessions" is meant in another sense: a spiritual disclosure of sins at the end of one's life. The story is written as the memoir of a nun, Gwynneve, living in fifth-century Ireland during its transition from paganism to Christianity. Gwynneve is brought up to follow Druid ways, but when monks come to convert her people, she retreats into St. Brigid's Convent in Kildare. Here she passes the time copying manuscripts, but her unorthodox opinions attract unwanted attention.

Lawhead, Stephen.

Patrick. **Morrow, 2003. 464pp.** ✐

Lawhead's story of St. Patrick's "missing years" begins as the protagonist, not yet a legendary figure, is born to a Welsh family in the late fourth century and given the name Succat. At sixteen, he is captured by raiders and forced to serve as a slave in Ireland for seven years, which hardens both his body and his character. After escaping, Succat experiences adventures in Gaul and Rome. There, he makes the monumental decision to return to Ireland and spread the word of the new Christian faith.

Llywelyn, Morgan.

Lion of Ireland. **Houghton Mifflin, 1980. 522pp.** ✐ **YA**

In the tenth century, Brian Boru emerges as the High King of a united Ireland—the greatest leader the country has ever known. As a young boy, Brian sees the devastation that Norse raiders can wreak and swears that he will drive them from the country once and for all. He keeps his promise. His opponents include not only the Vikings but also some of his fellow countrymen and members of his own family.

Pride of Lions. **Forge, 1996. 351pp.** ✍ **YA**

After Brian Boru's death in 1014, his fifteen-year-old son Donough decides to take up the reins of kingship. His path is blocked by his brother Teigue and his scheming mother, Gormlaith, who wants to use her son to regain power for herself. When past alliances crumble, Donough travels to Scotland, arranging a marriage for himself despite his affection for a pagan woman back in Ireland.

Osborne-McKnight, Juilene.

The author's historical novels of early Ireland blur the lines between historical fiction and fantasy. Her later novels are annotated in Chapter 14.

I Am of Irelaunde. **Forge, 2000. 301pp.** ✍

The author, an accomplished storyteller, gives her gifts full rein in her novels of Ireland's distant past. Magonus Succatus Patricius, not yet the renowned saint we call Patrick, has been sent to Ireland as a missionary, though the ways of the Irish people baffle him. Via visitations from Osian, a warrior-poet who has been dead for 200 years, Patrick learns of the heroic deeds of the Fianna, the great Irish warriors, and learns to love and accept his own Irishness.

Rathbone, Julian.

The Last English King. **St. Martin's Press, 1999. 381pp.**

Rathbone's depiction of events leading up to the Battle of Hastings in 1066 is irreverent and unabashedly anachronistic, but also entertaining and—despite this seeming contradiction—well researched. Three years after the battle, Harold's last surviving bodyguard expiates his survivor's guilt by recounting his story of King Edward, Harold, and the tyrant King William to a monk who is wandering with him toward the Holy Land.

Rice, Sile.

The Saxon Tapestry. **Arcade, 1991. 395pp.** ✍

In eleventh-century England, a Christian land still rife with pagan customs, Edward the Confessor is king. Vikings and Normans surround him like hungry beasts, waiting to claim his throne. After the Normans kill Edward's successor, King Harold, at Hastings in 1066, the Saxons' last hope lies in the romantic outlaw Hereward the Wake. Hereward has just returned from Ireland with fighting on his mind. While Rice's novel isn't as gritty and authentic as other accounts of England before the Conquest, in its imagery and language it evokes the ancient Anglo-Saxon sagas.

Tranter, Nigel.

High Kings and Vikings. **Trafalgar Square, 1998. 344pp.** ✍

In the midst of Scotland's Dark Ages, when its people were in constant danger from Viking raids, Cormac mac Farquhar, Thane of Glamis, becomes one of his country's defenders. He finds personal happiness with a Scottish noblewoman.

Arthurian Historical Novels

Here, authors place the legendary King Arthur and his coterie in a well-researched historical context, omitting any fantastical or magical aspects of the legend. Arthurian fantasy novels, which include paranormal elements, are annotated in the historical fantasy chapter.

Cornwell, Bernard.

The Warlord Chronicles.

In his trilogy, Cornwell portrays sixth-century Britain as a place of bloody clashes between the Celts, led by a powerful warlord named Arthur, and the Saxons. He also contrasts Christianity with the old Druidic religions.

The Winter King. St. Martin's Press, 1996. 431pp.

After the Romans depart, Britain erupts in chaos. Arthur emerges as a great leader, but he makes enemies by eloping with the feisty Guinevere instead of marrying his rightful bride.

Enemy of God. St. Martin's Press, 1997. 417pp.

Though Arthur has established order in the form of the round table, it becomes increasingly clear that his son Mordred will never be a suitable king. Arthur's ideals are also shattered by the betrayal of Guinevere and Lancelot.

Excalibur. St. Martin's Press, 1998. 436pp.

Arthur, deserted by his queen, sees peace slipping out of his grasp. Mordred believes he can seize power by bringing the old gods back to Britain, but his plan will be foiled if Arthur agrees to Christian baptism.

Godwin, Parke.

Arthurian Trilogy.

Legendary figures Arthur and Guinevere appear both larger than life and fully human in this dramatic series.

Firelord. Doubleday, 1980. 396pp.

Godwin's Arthur is a Romanized Celt who becomes King of the Britons and holds off the Saxon invasion as long as he can. The Faerie folk here are not magical creatures but a Pictish tribe living in primitive conditions.

Beloved Exile. Bantam, 1984. 422pp.

Few novels speak about the fate of Arthur's queen after the fall of Camelot. In what is perhaps the most powerful portrayal of Guenevere yet in fiction, Godwin presents her as a middle-aged widow, undone by Arthur's death but strong enough to try to unite the people of her realm. Betrayed into captivity, Guenevere emerges triumphant, even as a slave to a Saxon warlord.

The Last Rainbow. Bantam, 1985. 358pp.

Novel about St. Patrick; annotated in the previous section.

Hollick, Helen.

Pendragon's Banner Trilogy.

Hollick's version of the Arthurian legend begins in AD 450, as Uthr Pendragon joins forces with Cunedda of Gwynedd to oust the tyrant Vortigern from power. Uthr's secret son Arthur and Cunedda's daughter Gwenhwyfar become star-crossed lovers; Lancelot doesn't play a role here. The author adds other new touches to the well-worn tale, including Arthur's nasty ex-wife Winifred, who schemes to save the kingdom for her own son.

The Kingmaking. St. Martin's Press, 1995. 604pp.

Pendragon's Banner. St. Martin's Press, 1996. 547pp.

Shadow of the King. St. Martin's Press, 1997. 560pp.

Sutcliff, Rosemary.

Sword at Sunset. **Coward-McCann, 1963. 495pp.** ★

Sutcliff's Arthur is the great Romano-Celtic leader who successfully routs the Saxons until his final defeat at Camlann. Her battle scenes are particularly well done. During her lifetime, Sutcliff wrote a number of highly regarded historical novels of Roman Britain for young people. In this, her first adult novel, she reuses characters from an earlier work for young adults, *The Lantern Bearers*.

Whyte, Jack.

The Camulod Chronicles. (Original series title: A Dream of Eagles.)

Whyte's series is placed firmly in the fourth and fifth centuries as Roman armies are withdrawing from Britain. It can most accurately be called a pre-Arthurian series, as the story begins long before Arthur's birth and foreshadows the coming of the great Briton leader.

The Skystone. Forge, 1996. 352pp.

In AD 367, Roman soldiers Publius Varrus and Caius Britannicus, destined to become Arthur's great-grandfathers, decide to remain in the land they have always known rather than return to Rome with their comrades. They found a colony named Camulod that is designed to preserve the civility of Roman culture against invasion. Using stone from a meteorite, Publius forges a sword called Excalibur.

The Singing Sword. Forge, 1996. 352pp.

It is AD 395, and the Roman legions have departed. Now the residents of Camulod are truly on their own, forced to fend for themselves against Saxons and other invaders. To this end they ally themselves with the Celtic people under one king, Ullic Pendragon. They also develop their own cavalry.

The Eagles' Brood. Forge, 1997. 412pp.

Caius Merlyn Britannicus, known in other novels as the wizard Merlin, is the new commander of the fortress of Camulod. He was born on the same day as his cousin Uther Pendragon. The two are the best of friends and allies until a woman named Cassandra comes between them.

The Saxon Shore. Forge, 1998. 496pp.

Merlyn, preserver of his ancestors' dreams, is the keeper of Excalibur and the protector of his young cousin Arthur after the death of his father, Uther. In order that Arthur might grow up to unite the peoples of Britain—the Romans, Hibernians, and Celts—Merlyn leads his cavalry far and wide. He consolidates the boy's claims until he reaches the Saxon Shore, where Vortigern, self-proclaimed High King of Britain, still rules.

The Fort at River's Bend. Forge, 1999. 351pp.

After an assassination attempt on the eight-year-old Arthur, Merlyn brings him to the port of Ravenglass, where they take refuge in an abandoned Roman fort—a good place for Arthur to grow to manhood. Merlyn's old enemy Peter Ironhair of Cornwall threatens their safety.

The Sorcerer: Metamorphosis. Forge, 1999. 352pp.

In the second half of the story begun in *Fort at River's Bend*, Merlyn is co-ruler at Camulod with his brother Ambrose, and his ward Arthur is nearly ready to take up the reins of kingship. Peter Ironhair and other enemies still encroach on Camulod. While Arthur is off visiting his father's people to learn about their culture, Merlyn decides to rid the colony of its foes once and for all.

Uther. Forge, 2001. 623pp.

Though marketed as the seventh volume of the <u>Camulod Chronicles</u>, in reality *Uther* is the beginning of a trilogy that retells events from *The Eagle*'s Brood from Uther's point of view. Part Celt, part Roman, Uther is most loyal to the Celtic peoples, which costs him his friendship with Merlyn. He also falls in love with Ygraine of Ireland, wife of his bitter enemy.

Woolley, Persia.

<u>Guinevere Trilogy.</u>

Woolley's trilogy of novels about Guinevere concentrates on the human characters behind the Arthurian legend. Over the course of the novels, Gwen grows from a tomboy living in Northern England to a mature queen known for her honesty and courage. While there are no fantasy elements here, the tales contain all of the other elements that make Arthurian fiction so popular: brave men and women, noble quests, drama, treason, betrayal, and a little romance.

Child of the Northern Spring. Poseidon, 1987. 428pp.

Queen of the Summer Stars. Poseidon, 1990. 415pp.

Guinevere: The Legend in Autumn. Poseidon, 1991. 432pp.

High Middle Ages

This era covers the period between 1066, the year of the Norman Conquest, and 1485, when Richard III's fall at the Battle of Bosworth signaled the ascent of the Tudor monarchs. Novels set during this time cover the lives of England's Plantagenet kings (and their counterparts in Scotland and Wales), feudal societies, and people's relationship with the church.

Baer, Ann.

Down the Common: A Year in the Life of a Medieval Woman. **M. Evans, 1996. 234pp.**

> As the title suggests, this is the fictional re-creation of the life of a medieval woman, Marion, wife of Peter the carpenter. Neither character nor plot development is paramount, but readers will come away with a better idea of the day-to-day concerns, both secular and spiritual, of women living in a feudal society.

Chadwick, Elizabeth.

Lords of the White Castle. **St. Martin's Press, 2002. 614pp.** ✍

> In the late twelfth century, from the time he was accused of cheating at a game of chess, courtier Fulke FitzWarin has had a rivalry with Prince John. This impedes Fulke's family's quest to regain their estate. When John becomes king, his vindictiveness is far-reaching, and Fulke is forced to turn outlaw to regain his family's lands. This doesn't help the romance he aspires to, for Maude le Vavasour, his true love, is promised by her father to another man. Based on the true story of a man who may be the original Robin Hood.

The Winter Mantle. **St. Martin's Press, 2003. 506pp.** ✍

> One year after the Norman Conquest, Judith, the strong-willed niece of William the Conqueror, falls in lust and love with Waltheof, Earl of Huntington, and he with her. They're determined to wed, and do, but Waltheof, a Saxon earl, soon regrets having pledged his fealty to William. This has immense consequences for their marriage and daughter, as well as for all of England. All of the main characters are historical figures. The sequel, *The Falcons of Montabard*, appears in this chapter under "The Middle East."

Falconieri, David.

The Beggar's Throne. **MacAdam/Cage, 2000. 391pp.** ✍

> During the Wars of the Roses, the future Edward IV seeks to consolidate power for the House of York despite changing loyalties even among his own followers. In an intertwining tale, the fictional Miller brothers find themselves on opposite sides of the York–Lancaster conflict. The author brings a human touch to this well-known time in history, and there is hardly a character given short shrift.

Follett, Ken.

The Pillars of the Earth. **Morrow, 1989. 973pp.** ★

> While the Empress Maud and King Stephen fight a civil war for England's throne, Philip, a monk who becomes prior of the fictional town of Kingsbridge,

and Tom, a master builder, join forces to achieve their dream. Divisions in the community mimic the intrigues dividing all of England. Surprisingly, this epic novel of the building of a Gothic cathedral in twelfth-century England was thriller writer Follett's most successful book. Though criticized for the modern outlook of its characters, it has also been praised for the strength of its storytelling.

Horsley, Kate.

The Changeling of Finnistuath. **Shambhala, 2003. 339pp.** 📖 **YA**

In fourteenth-century Ireland, a peasant girl named Grey (short for Gregory) is raised as a boy, for her father had vowed to kill any more daughters he had. When she discovers that she's really a woman, Grey travels far and wide, taking on new roles during her life—monk's helper, mother, whore, warrior—to pin down her true identity. The repression of the Church overshadows her life, as does the Black Death.

Kaufman, Pamela.

The Book of Eleanor. **Crown, 2002. 510pp.** ✍

Eleanor of Aquitaine, queen of both England and France, tells her story in the first person from prison, where she has been sent by her tyrannical husband, Henry II, for inciting her sons to rebel against him. She speaks of her unhappy marriage to Louis VII of France, its eventual annulment, her romance with her childhood sweetheart Baron Rancon, and her fury at being forced to marry Henry II for political reasons. Eleanor's relationship with Rancon, as portrayed here, is completely fictional.

Pargeter, Edith.

Pargeter also wrote the Brother Cadfael series of medieval mysteries (Chapter 7) under the pseudonym Ellis Peters.

The Bloody Field. **Viking, 1972. 313pp. (Original title:** *A Bloody Field by Shrewsbury.***)** ✍

Harry "Hotspur" Percy's rebellion against Henry IV was a precursor to the Wars of the Roses. Pargeter gives psychological insight into the lives of three men involved in the conflict, beginning in the year 1399: the new king Henry IV, reclaiming his rights after the death of Richard II; Hotspur, the Northumbrian knight initially loyal to Henry; and Prince Hal, caught between the two because of his previous admiration for King Richard.

Heaven Tree Trilogy. **Warner, 1993. 899pp.** ★

Harry Talvace, a master stone carver, is apprenticed to Ralf Isambard, a villainous nobleman who has a passion to build a great cathedral. Madonna Benedetta, Isambard's mistress, loves Harry, but he chooses to marry his childhood sweetheart. Their stories continue in the subsequent books. The series is most often found in American libraries as an omnibus volume. The three novels, the latter two of which were never published separately in the United States, are *The Heaven Tree, The Green*

Branch, and *The Scarlet Seed*. Pargeter herself believed that this trilogy of feudal life in early thirteenth-century England was her greatest work.

Penman, Sharon Kay.

Penman's lengthy, sweeping novels of medieval England make the lives of long-ago royalty and nobility accessible. While most incorporate a romantic sub-plot, they also include an incredible, though not overwhelming, amount of detail on the politics of the time. All are considered classics of the genre, works against which all other novels of the Middle Ages are measured.

Plantagenet Trilogy. ✍

Intricately detailed novels about the early Plantagenets, their lives and loves. The trilogy is expected to continue with *The Devil's Brood*, about the rebellious children of Henry II and Queen Eleanor.

When Christ and His Saints Slept. Holt, 1995. 746pp.

After the only legitimate son of King Henry I drowns with the White Ship in 1120, the English succession falls into confusion. Maude, King Henry's proud daughter and the widow of the German emperor, is forced by her father to marry Geoffrey of Anjou, a younger man whom she detests and whom England doesn't want as a ruler. Stephen, Henry's nephew, believes that the people will accept him as ruler more readily than Maude and Geoffrey. He quickly has himself crowned King of England after Henry's death. Thus begins twenty years of bloody civil war, a time when people said that Christ and his saints slept. Penman's is one of the few novels to portray the Maude–Stephen relationship as the bitter rivalry it most likely was, rather than as a forbidden romance.

Time and Chance. Putnam, 2002. 528pp.

Maud's son Henry II, the vigorous young Plantagenet king, finds that his political and religious differences with Thomas Becket cause insurmountable problems. Eleanor of Aquitaine, a beautiful, strong-willed heiress, progresses believably from Henry's beloved queen to his bitter former confidante. And Becket, the king's chancellor and boon companion, suddenly develops a loyalty to the church that sets him against many, Henry most of all.

The Sunne in Splendour. Holt, Rinehart & Winston, 1982. 936pp. ✍ ★

Richard III, best known from Shakespeare as the hunchbacked traitor who killed his nephews to steal England's throne, is restored to his proper place in Penman's novel. Here, Richard is both a loyal brother to Edward IV and an intelligent leader himself. Passionately in love with his queen, Anne Neville, with whom he would prefer to have a quiet life, Richard becomes caught up in forces beyond his control as the Wars of the Roses divide families and friends. Penman also tells the story of Richard's elder brother Edward IV, the charming monarch whose ambitious wife costs him some supporters, and whose early secret marriage to a noble-woman throws the succession into confusion.

Welsh Trilogy. ✍

Three epic biographical novels set in thirteenth-century England and Wales.

Here Be Dragons. Holt, Rinehart & Winston, 1985. 704pp.

In the early thirteenth century, Joanna, the illegitimate daughter of King John, marries Llewelyn, Prince of North Wales, in an uneasy truce between their realms. After she grows to love her husband, Joanna finds it difficult to take sides.

Falls the Shadow. Holt, 1988. 580pp.

In his crusade for the rights of the common man, Simon de Montfort, the French-born Earl of Leicester, becomes more English than the English themselves. His romance and marriage to Nell Plantagenet, sister of Henry III, is one of legend, for she had been sworn to chastity after the death of her first husband. Simon's bitter rival is his brother-in-law the king, whose incompetent rule leads England's nobles to rise up in rebellion, with Simon as their leader.

The Reckoning. Holt, 1991. 592pp.

It is now 1271, and Simon de Montfort has been dead for five years. Llewelyn of Wales (grandson of Llewelyn the Great from *Here Be Dragons*), once betrothed to Simon's daughter Ellen, decides to go ahead with their marriage after all. Unfortunately, their romance isn't destined to last. The daughter of a traitor now married to one of England's greatest enemies, Ellen becomes a pawn in the game of England's king, Edward I, to take control of Wales once and for all.

Plaidy, Jean.

The Norman Trilogy. ★ ✍

Biographical novels about the Norman kings of England. Plaidy traces their lives from the childhood of William the Conqueror through the civil wars of Stephen and Matilda (two of William's grandchildren). Note: Matilda is called Maude in other novels, such as those by Sharon Kay Penman.

The Bastard King. Putnam, 1979. 319pp.

William the Conqueror, the illegitimate son of the Duke of Normandy and a tanner's daughter, grows up knowing he will be his father's successor. His stormy relationship with the feisty Matilda of Flanders, who believes herself too proud to wed a bastard, develops into love. She supports his bid to become King of England after Edward the Confessor's death.

The Lion of Justice. Putnam, 1979. 385pp.

King William and Queen Matilda's son Henry, nicknamed "Beauclerc," never expected to be king, but the death of his brother William Rufus works to his advantage. Henry seals his ambition with his marriage to Edith of Scotland (renamed as yet another Matilda), who is a descendant of the Anglo-Saxon kings of England.

The Passionate Enemies. Putnam, 1979. 318pp.

After Henry's queen Matilda dies, he marries the much younger Adelicia of Louvain to beget more legitimate children, for his son William had been killed in a shipwreck in 1120. When this plan fails, Henry's only hope lies in his daughter Matilda, whom his nobles will never accept as their monarch. Matilda's chief rival for the throne is her cousin, Stephen of Blois, with whom she has a passionate affair.

The Plantagenet Saga. ★ ✍

Many readers have learned about English history from Jean Plaidy's novels, and those in her Plantagenet Saga are among the best known. In fifteen volumes, they trace the history of the Plantagenet monarchs from Henry II and Eleanor of Aquitaine in the twelfth century to Henry VII and his Plantagenet wife Elizabeth of York in the fifteenth. Plaidy' writes straightforwardly and sticks close to historical fact. These novels, which include family trees, follow directly upon her Norman Trilogy, above. They are listed in historical order.

The Plantagenet Prelude. Putnam, 1980. 333pp.

Eleanor of Aquitaine, Queen of France, is not content with her dull marriage to Louis VII. She convinces him to divorce her, whereupon she marries Henry Plantagenet, heir to England's throne.

The Revolt of the Eaglets. Putnam, 1980. 330pp.

Henry II, the first Plantagenet king, is growing older, but there is nobody he can turn to. Because of his infidelity, his queen, Eleanor of Aquitaine, turns his sons against him.

The Heart of the Lion. Putnam, 1980. 331pp.

Though Richard I is king, he spends most of his time on Crusade against the Saracens rather than at home. In the meanwhile, his mother rules England in his stead, his wife Queen Berengaria languishes for want of attention, and his brother John plots to seize the throne.

The Prince of Darkness. Putnam, 1978. 317pp.

What the unscrupulous King John wants, he must have. When he casts eyes upon the very young Isabella of Angoulême, he decides that she will be his queen even though she is betrothed to another.

The Battle of the Queens. Putnam, 1981. 366pp.

Not long after King John's death in 1216, his widow Isabella of Angoulême marries her original betrothed, Hugh de Lusignan, a vassal of the King of France. However, she never gives the French crown the honor it is due. This prompts the intelligent Dowager Queen of France, Blanche of Castile, to watch Isabella's behavior closely.

The Queen from Provence. Putnam, 1979. 286pp.

Eleanor of Provence, the beautiful wife of Henry III, turns him into a devoted husband but a very weak king. Her greed and extravagance give her a bad reputation among England's people, and Henry's emptying of the royal treasury leads to the revolt of England's barons under Simon de Montfort.

The Hammer of the Scots. Putnam, 1981. 318pp. (Original title: *Edward Longshanks.*)

Though the marriage between Edward I and Eleanor of Castile is a happy one, his reign is one of constant war: with Scotland, Wales, and his eldest son, the future Edward II, whose weak morals predict that he will be an equally weak king.

The Follies of the King. Putnam, 1982. 331pp.

While Edward II lavishes too much attention on his favorites, particularly Piers Gaveston, his wife Isabella of France plots to topple him from power with the help of her lover, Roger Mortimer.

The Vow on the Heron. Putnam, 1982. 350pp.

The young Edward III decides to start his reign on a positive note, punishing his mother and her lover for their part in the murder of his father, Edward II. Edward marries a good woman, Philippa of Hainault, who gives him many children, but his conviction that he can inherit France's crown through his mother begins the Hundred Years' War.

Passage to Pontefract. Putnam, 1982. 366pp.

Edward III''s grandson Richard II, one of England's weakest kings, must contend with the Peasants' Revolt of 1381 as well as with the schemes of his uncle, John of Gaunt, and those of John's son Henry Bolingbroke.

The Star of Lancaster. Putnam, 1981. 320pp.

Though as a youth he was foolhardy and reckless, Henry IV's son Prince Hal shows his true and valiant colors in his victory against France at Agincourt during the Hundred Years' War.

The Sun in Splendour. Putnam, 1983. 365pp.

During the Wars of the Roses, Edward IV is a man who lets his passions run away with him, as shown by his marriage to beautiful widow Elizabeth Woodville. Though she bears him numerous children, the succession is threatened after Edward's death because of a secret from his past.

Epitaph for Three Women. Putnam, 1983. 333pp.

Henry VI becomes King of England at the age of only nine months, leaving the realm in chaos. This novel deals with three women who have great influence on his life: Katherine of Valois, his mother, whose romance with Welshman Owen Tudor causes a scandal; Jeannette d'Arc, the girl from Domrémy whose sacrifice haunts Henry all his life; and his aunt-by-marriage, Eleanor of Gloucester, who turns to witchcraft to help her husband Duke Humphrey gain the throne.

Red Rose of Anjou. Putnam, 1983. 348pp.

During the Wars of the Roses, Margaret of Anjou, of a long line of strong-minded French women, fiercely guards the rights of her husband, Henry VI, throughout his madness. She is equally protective of their son, England's heir.

Uneasy Lies the Head. Putnam, 1984. 345pp.

At the death of his brother, Prince Arthur, young Henry becomes the heir to the Tudors. It is up to his father, Henry VII, to deal with the realm's current problems, which include pretenders such as Perkin Warbeck and the beautiful, homesick Spanish princess, Catherine of Aragon, who will eventually become Henry's bride.

The Queen's Secret. **Putnam, 1990. 311pp.** ✍

Katherine of Valois, daughter of an insane father and a promiscuous mother, becomes the prize won by England's Henry V after his victory at Agincourt during the Hundred Years' War. After a short but happy marriage, her husband dies, leaving her and her baby son at the mercy of England's power-hungry nobles. It is no wonder that she falls in love with a handsome Welshman named Owen Tudor, though their relationship must be kept secret. Part of the <u>Queens of England</u> series.

The Reluctant Queen. **Putnam, 1991. 299pp.** ✍

During the Wars of the Roses, Lady Anne Neville has no desire to be Queen of England; all she wants is to marry her childhood love, King Edward IV's younger brother Richard. Instead, her father, Warwick the Kingmaker, marries her off to the Prince of Wales, the king's greatest enemy. Part of the <u>Queens of England</u> series.

Reisert, Rebecca.

The Third Witch. **Washington Square Press, 2001. 400pp.**

The "Scottish play" (*Macbeth*) is retold in the first person by Gilly, the youngest of the three witches from *Macbeth*, and the one who correctly prophesies that he will become King of Scotland. Growing up, she's raised by two weird and elderly herb-women who live in a forest hut. The driving force of her existence is revenge against the man—Macbeth—who destroyed her childhood. To this end, she disguises herself as a kitchen slave and infiltrates the king's castle and household, weapons in hand. Reisert admits she was more faithful to Shakespearean times than to eleventh-century Scotland, and the ending is a bit pat, but it's fascinating to see the familiar play from a new point of view.

Riley, Judith Merkle.

<u>Margaret of Ashbury Series.</u> ★ `YA`

Fourteenth-century England is the setting for Riley's novels of early feminism, religion, and romance. These are reader favorites. Margaret's story continues in a sequel, *The Water-Devil*, regretfully available only in the German language.

A Vision of Light. Delacorte, 1989. 442pp.

In 1355, twice-married Margaret of Ashbury hears a mysterious voice advising her to do something unusual and possibly heretical: write a book about her life. Since she is unlettered herself, Margaret enlists Brother Gregory, a Carthusian friar, to take on the task, something he would not have done were he not afraid of starving. Still, he cannot help but become engrossed in Margaret's fascinating life story, which includes midwifery, witchcraft, and the Black Death.

In Pursuit of the Green Lion. Delacorte, 1990. 440pp.

In this sequel to *A Vision of Light*, twenty-three-year-old Margaret has been kidnapped by her late husband's relatives. She is rescued by Gregory de Vilers, formerly her chronicler Brother Gregory, whose money-grubbing family is equally as odious. Though Margaret and Gregory decide to marry for her protection, there is little affection between them at first. Their love intensifies as she travels to France to rescue him from capture during the Hundred Years' War.

Tranter, Nigel.

Tranter died in 2000 at the age of ninety, and throughout his long life he produced a wide output of historical novels, mainly about the history of his native Scotland. His dialogue can be abrupt, but his research was meticulous. Through his novels, many readers have discovered a painless way of learning more about Scottish history.

Courting Favour. Trafalgar Square, 2000. 330pp. ✍

Beginning during the last years of David II's reign in the mid-fourteenth century, this novel sees John, the young Earl of Dunbar and March, through the numerous errands he makes on behalf of King David and his successors: the wise yet aging Robert II, whose daughter John marries, and Robert's son, the weak and ineffectual Robert III. Most notably, John must negotiate on Scotland's behalf with England's John of Gaunt to stop Scots/English border warfare.

The End of the Line. Trafalgar Square, 2001. 378pp. ✍

George the Cospatrick, tenth Earl of Dunbar and March, is asked by his queen to request England's help in quelling a possible civil war in Scotland. But Scotland and England have traditionally been enemies, and George's son faces distrust over his father's supposed treachery.

Envoy Extraordinary. Trafalgar Square, 1999. 328pp. ✍

In 1249, after his father is killed on Crusade and King Alexander II of Scotland dies of a fever, Patrick, Earl of Dunbar, becomes an advisor to the child king, Alexander III. He helps Scotland overcome threats to its trade by Norse and Viking raiders.

The Islesman. Trafalgar Square, 2003. 390pp. ✍

In the late thirteenth century, Angus Og MacDonald, Lord of the Isles, serves as leader and protector of his people, scattered on remote islands throughout the Hebrides and on the Scottish mainland. Joining forces with Robert the Bruce, Angus does all he can to save his land from English occupation.

The Lion's Whelp. **Trafalgar Square, 1998. 320pp.** ✍

> After James I of Scotland is murdered in 1437, his seven-year-old son James II comes to the throne. Fortunately for the realm, Alexander Lyon, Thane of Glamis, becomes one of young James's greatest protectors.

Robert Bruce Trilogy. ✍ ★

> In 1296, a time when King Edward I of England wants to subdue the Scots and bring them into England's fold, Scotland desperately needs a leader. Their hero is Robert the Bruce, who makes it his mission to unite the Scots against their English enemies, whatever the price.

> ***The Steps to the Empty Throne.*** St. Martin's Press, 1971. 351pp.

> ***The Path of the Hero King.*** St. Martin's Press, 1972. 349pp.

> ***The Price of the King's Peace.*** St. Martin's Press, 1972. 348pp.

Sword of State. **Trafalgar Square, 1999. 394pp.** ✍

> Patrick, Earl of Dunbar, of the ancient Cospatrick line, befriends Alexander II of Scotland in the early thirteenth century. Dunbar serves as the king's "sword of state" through court rivalries and threats from the English and Norsemen.

Waldo, Anna Lee.

Madoc Series. ✍

> In legend, Madoc, a twelfth-century Welsh prince, was one of the early discoverers of America.

> ***Circle of Stones.*** St. Martin's Press, 1999. 428pp.

> Brenda, the mistress of Prince Owain of Wales, flees to her native Ireland when a prophecy insists that Owain put their son Madoc to death. Brought back to Owain's court, Brenda sees her political power grow as she uses her diplomatic skills and her druidic healing abilities to good effect. In the meantime, druids train young Madoc to lead them from Wales to the New World.

> ***Circle of Stars.*** St. Martin's Press, 2001. 499pp.

> It is 1151, and as prophesied, Madoc leads his people to America, a difficult voyage involving ten ships. After arriving in this untamed land, he meets a beautiful girl named Cougar, who, like him, was chosen by the gods to lead her people.

The Tudor Era

The year 1485 marked the ascent of Henry VII, the first Tudor king, to England's throne; the year 1603 saw the death of his granddaughter, Elizabeth I. Most novels set during the Tudor era focus on the royal court, with all its pomp and splendor. Other common subjects include religious dissension, as Henry VIII declares himself head of the Church of England in order to marry Anne Boleyn, as well as the political rivalry between Henry's daughter Elizabeth and her Catholic cousin, Mary Queen of Scots.

Dunn, Suzannah.

The Queen of Subtleties. Morrow, 2004. 288pp. ✍

Anne Boleyn writes a long letter to her daughter, Elizabeth, explaining some of the decisions she made in her life. Lucy Cornwallis, confectioner to Henry VIII, dreams of romance with Mark Smeaton, a handsome court musician involved in Anne's downfall. Lucy relates her own story as she watches the king fall in love with Anne. Dunn's frank, conversational prose feels more appropriate to the twenty-first century than Tudor England.

George, Margaret.

The Autobiography of Henry VIII. St. Martin's Press, 1986. 932pp. ✍ ★

Henry himself narrates the story of his life, omitting nothing: the relationships with his six wives, in bed and out; his struggles with the church; the pageantry of the court; and much more. His fool, Will Somers, plays straight man to Henry, interjecting words about the real story behind Henry's narrative. "A whale of a book, about a whale of a king," wrote novelist Mary Stewart about this work, George's first major biographical novel.

Mary Queen of Scotland and the Isles. St. Martin's Press, 1992. 870pp. ✍

George's second epic novel shows the personal history behind the tragic figure who was Mary, Queen of Scots. Mary's life opposes that of her cousin Elizabeth in nearly every respect. Adored as a child, Mary grows up in splendor first in Scotland and then at the French court, where she becomes queen at age sixteen. As an eighteen-year-old widow, she returns to Scotland a relative stranger, a Catholic in a newly Protestant land. Extremely intelligent, but of poor judgment where men and politics are concerned (and in Scotland, these are one and the same), Mary knows great passion in her life, but betrayals first by her people and then by Elizabeth lead to her downfall.

Gregory, Philippa.

🎗 *The Other Boleyn Girl.* Touchstone, 2002. 672pp. ✍ 📖

This intricate tapestry of a novel traces the rise and fall of Mary Boleyn, who becomes Henry VIII's mistress at the age of fourteen, and the subsequent rise and fall of her sister Anne. Gregory's portrait of the Boleyn family is not a sympathetic one, for the sisters' parents are more than willing to sacrifice the pair's happiness for their own ambitions. Anne, ruthless in her pursuit of the crown, shares their sentiments. Mary yearns for a way to escape, eventually finding it in the arms of a man who loves her. Parker Romantic Novel of the Year Award.

The Queen's Fool. Touchstone, 2004. 494pp. ✍ 📖

In 1553, nobleman Robert Dudley chooses Hannah Green, a Jewish girl living with her bookseller father in London, to be his personal fool. Hannah goes to court as a member of young King Edward's entourage, though in reality she serves as Lord Robert's spy. Later, as the fool and confidant of Edward's successor Queen Mary, a surprisingly sympathetic woman, Hannah witnesses the religious and political intrigues pervading the country—ironically so because she must feign belief in Catholicism to avoid the Inquisition. With her gift of second sight, Hannah's abilities are much in demand, since both Lord Robert and Princess Elizabeth want to know what the future holds for them and the realm. Like Mary Boleyn in *The Other Boleyn Girl*, Hannah must choose between the wondrous, dangerous life at court and the joys of living as a commoner's wife.

The Virgin's Lover. Touchstone, 2004. 441pp. ✍ 📖

It is 1558. Bloody Mary has died, and Queen Elizabeth I has finally come to the throne. All of England rejoices—everyone, that is, except Amy, neglected wife of Elizabeth's favorite companion, Robert Dudley. As Lord Robert's fortunes rise and rumors spread about his intimacy with the queen, Amy grows sad with jealousy. Meanwhile, Elizabeth faces challenges to her position from supporters of Mary, Queen of Scots, and Elizabeth's own courtiers suggest she forget about Robert and marry for the good of the realm. Just as romantic matters come to a head between Elizabeth and Robert, someone solves their problem for them.

Holt, Victoria.

My Enemy the Queen. Doubleday, 1978. 348pp. ✍

Elizabeth I is a beloved and strong queen, but she never forgets the people who once betrayed her. Lettice Knollys, daughter of Elizabeth's cousin Catherine, comes to court at a young age. The queen holds her in affection because of their blood relationship. However, Lettice finds it hard to regain Elizabeth's favor after her marriage to the queen's favorite, Robert Dudley. The author also wrote biographical novels as Jean Plaidy.

Irwin, Margaret.

Elizabeth Trilogy. ✍ ★ YA

Irwin's charming re-creation of the youth of Queen Elizabeth follows her from childhood, to imprisonment at her sister Queen Mary's behest, and finally to her arrival at court. There, Elizabeth tries desperately to avoid Mary's jealousy when her husband Philip develops an interest in her. The novels' titles explain their basic storyline.

Young Bess. Harcourt, Brace, 1945. 274pp.

Elizabeth, Captive Princess. Harcourt, Brace, 1948. 246pp.

Elizabeth and the Prince of Spain. Harcourt, Brace, 1953. 251pp.

Llywelyn, Morgan.

Grania. Crown, 1986. 437pp. ✍

The "she-king of the Irish seas" is Grace O'Malley, called Grania in the Irish tongue. The equal of any man in strength and ferocity, Grace fights with gusto aboard ship and serves as the unofficial leader of her clan—and the symbol of

Irish freedom. Her foil and alter ego is Queen Elizabeth of England, who is determined to break Grace's control of the Irish waters.

Maxwell, Robin.

The Queen's Bastard. **Arcade, 1999. 436pp.** ✍

Maxwell has taken gaps in the historical record and historians' reference to an "Arthur Dudley" to surmise that Elizabeth I had an illegitimate son by her lover Robert Dudley, Earl of Leicester. Born in 1588 and replaced with a stillborn child by the queen's lady in waiting, Arthur is placed with an adoptive family, not knowing his identity until his father's death. Meanwhile, Elizabeth and Robert console each other over the presumed loss of their baby.

The Secret Diary of Anne Boleyn. **Arcade, 1997. 281pp.** ✍ **YA**

In her secret diary, Anne Boleyn leaves a record of her life for her daughter Elizabeth to find and read one day. Here Anne records her innermost thoughts: the life she lived as a strong woman surrounded by powerful men who professed loyalty and then betrayed her; her love/hate relationship with Henry VIII; and her love for her daughter. In reading her mother's diary, Elizabeth can't help but see parallels to her own life.

Virgin: Prelude to the Throne. **Arcade, 2001. 243pp.** ✍

A nubile adolescent in 1547, Princess Elizabeth can't help but be intrigued by the attentions paid to her by handsome nobleman Thomas Seymour, even though he is married to her stepmother and guardian, Catherine Parr. The pregnant Catherine watches, heartbroken, as her callous husband attempts to seduce Elizabeth, secretly planning to marry her himself and become king.

The Wild Irish. **Morrow, 2003. 393pp.** ✍

The Irish Rebellion against the English in the sixteenth century is largely unknown today, making it prime material for historical novelists. Maxwell has based her novel on the rebellion, fictionalizing the events leading up to a historic meeting between Grace O'Malley, pirate queen and rebel leader, and Queen Elizabeth herself at London's Greenwich Castle in 1593.

Miles, Rosalind.

I, Elizabeth. **Doubleday, 1994. 595pp.** ✍

In her own voice, Queen Elizabeth I narrates her story as a memoir she sets down at the end of her life. In it, she reveals the inner woman behind her outer public persona, someone who struggles to balance her own needs with that of her country.

Plaidy, Jean.

In the Shadow of the Crown. **Putnam, 1989. 379pp.** ✍

Mary Tudor recounts her own version of her self-described sad and bitter life. Though Mary is the firstborn child of Henry VIII, she finds herself declared illegitimate after her father has his marriage to her mother, Katherine of Aragon, annulled. This reinforces Mary's own Catholicism, for she is her mother's loyal daughter. Her adherence to the True Faith gains her many enemies and the notorious nickname of Bloody Mary. Part of the <u>Queens of England</u> series.

The Lady in the Tower. **Putnam, 1986. 405pp.** ✍

From her prison in the Tower of London, Anne Boleyn narrates her story, from her happy childhood in England and France, to her separation from the man she loved, to her unhappy relationships with the Church and with Henry VIII—a man she regrets ever becoming involved with. Part of the <u>Queens of England</u> series.

Mary Queen of Scots series. ✍

An understanding portrait of Scotland's tragic queen, told in two novels.

Royal Road to Fotheringay. Putnam, 1968. 349pp.

Mary, the beautiful and tragic Queen of Scots, lives for passion, from her youth growing up at the French court through her marriage to France's young king, her return to Scotland, and her marriage to the unpopular Lord Darnley.

The Captive Queen of Scots. Putnam, 1970. 410pp.

Queen Mary's third marriage, to the ambitious Lord Bothwell, angers her enemies further. This results in her flight to England and her eventual capture by Queen Elizabeth.

Queen of This Realm. **Putnam, 1985. 570pp.** ✍

Realizing how unlikely it was for her ever to have become queen, Elizabeth I surrounds herself with loyal supporters, though she knows she must remain master of them all. Elizabeth narrates her own life story in typical Plaidy style: straightforward and dramatic. Part of the <u>Queens of England</u> series (see this chapter and Index).

The Rose Without a Thorn. **Putnam, 1994. 255pp.** ✍

Katherine Howard is forced to abandon her true love, Thomas Culpepper, when she attracts the attention of Henry VIII. Her promiscuous past catches up to her after she becomes the king's fifth wife. Part of the <u>Queens of England</u> series.

The Tudor Novels. ✍

Plaidy's biographical novels of royalty in Tudor England are listed in historical order, but they can all stand alone.

The Thistle and the Rose. Putnam, 1973. 318pp. (Originally published in Britain in 1963.)

In early sixteenth-century England, Henry VIII's sister Margaret is sent north to Scotland to marry its monarch, James IV, but she finds his attention occupied by mistresses. When James and the Scots army are defeated at Flodden Field in 1513, Margaret struggles to hold onto the kingdom and her son.

Mary, Queen of France. Three Rivers, 2003. 287pp. (Originally published in Britain in 1964.)

Princess Mary, Henry VIII's younger and favorite sister, had extracted a promise from her brother to let her marry a man of her choosing after the death of her first husband, Louis XII of France. Still, Henry is known to be temperamental, and Mary knows she risks his wrath in marrying her secret love, Charles Brandon.

Katharine of Aragon. Three Rivers, 2005. 672pp.

A biographical novel of Katharine of Aragon, Henry VIII's first wife, whom he divorced to marry Anne Boleyn. This is an omnibus volume of the author's previously published <u>Katharine of Aragon</u> trilogy, comprising *Katharine, The Virgin Widow*; *The Shadow of the Pomegranate*, and *The King's Secret Matter.*

The King's Pleasure. Doubleday, 1969. 372pp. (Originally published in Britain in 1949.)

Everyone in England is subject to the king's pleasure, as Anne Boleyn discovers when she sets her sights on marrying Henry VIII.

St. Thomas's Eve. Putnam, 1970. 284pp. (Originally published in Britain in 1954.)

When Henry VIII makes plain his intent to break away from Catholicism to divorce his wife and marry Anne Boleyn, Sir Thomas More defies him, but it costs him his life.

Murder Most Royal. Putnam, 1972. 542pp.

Anne Boleyn and Catherine Howard, first cousins, become Henry VIII's second and fifth wives respectively, and both of their lives end on the executioner's block.

The Sixth Wife. Putnam, 1969. 252pp. (Originally published in Britain in 1953.)

Katherine Parr, a twice-widowed noblewoman, would have preferred to marry her chosen love, Thomas Seymour, but Henry VIII's wish that she become his sixth wife cannot be denied.

The Spanish Bridegroom. Putnam, 1971. 338pp. (Originally published in Britain in 1954.)

Philip II of Spain, the Catholic monarch who married England's Mary Tudor, has a happy first marriage, which results in a son. After his first wife's death he feels resigned to duty, taking the pathetic, older Mary Tudor as his second wife. In the meanwhile, his son Carlos gives him nothing but trouble, particularly when Philip later marries Carlos's betrothed, Elisabeth of France.

Gay Lord Robert. Putnam, 1971. 317pp. (Originally published in Britain in 1955.)

Robert Dudley, Earl of Leicester, is Queen Elizabeth's favorite, which is why a scandal erupts when his wife Amy is mysteriously found dead.

Prescott, H. F. M.
The Man on a Donkey. Macmillan, 1952. 631pp. ★

Henry VIII, in his eagerness to marry Anne Boleyn, destroys England's monasteries in his plan to take over the Church. When he takes their wealth for himself and his courtiers, rebellion begins to brew in the North. This classic historical novel, republished by Phoenix Press in 2002, has stood the test of time well.

Tannahill, Reay.
Fatal Majesty. St. Martin's Press, 1999. 466pp. ✍

This biographical novel focuses not so much on the personalities of Mary, Queen of Scots, and her cousin Queen Elizabeth, as on the political intrigues that followed Mary upon her return to Scotland from France. As such, it is not as personally involving as it could have been, but the historical facts are accurately presented. A strong sense of drama pervades the novel, even though the outcome (Mary's execution) is never in doubt.

Tiffany, Grace.
My Father Had a Daughter. Berkley, 2003. 291pp. ✍ **YA**

Judith Shakespeare grows up in the countryside around Stratford, while her father's life revolves around the London stage. When her twin brother Hamnet drowns, Judith blames herself. She is horror-stricken after reading a draft of her father's latest play, *Twelfth Night*, which seems to make light of the event. She travels to London in male garb, hoping to sabotage the play, but instead finds herself falling in love with the theatrical world.

Will. Berkley, 2004. ✍ **YA**

William Shakespeare leaves his wife Anne at home in Stratford with their three children, though not without some guilt. He heads to London to make his fortune at the theater. Will grows in confidence and fame, transforming from starving actor to witty playwright. As his star rises, he attracts the attention of Queen Elizabeth and the enmity of handsome player Christopher Marlowe.

Tranter, Nigel.
The Admiral. Trafalgar Square, 2001. 247pp. ✍

Andrew Wood gains the admiration of his king, Scotland's James III, with his exploits as a pirate-slayer, so much so that he is named Lord High Admiral. His efforts in defense of his country incur the wrath of England's Henry VII.

The Stuart Era

With the death of Elizabeth I in 1603 came the end of the Tudor era. At this time her cousin James VI of Scotland, the son of Mary Stuart, Queen of Scots, moved south to London and became King James I of both England and Scotland. Thus were the two warring kingdoms united under a single monarch. The end of the Stuart era was marked by the death of Queen Anne in 1714. Historical novels set during this time include depictions of Cromwell's Protectorate, the restoration of Charles II to the throne in 1660, and the continuing rivalry between Protestants and Catholics.

Gregory, Philippa.

Tradescant Series.

> Biographical novels about the two John Tradescants, the elder and the younger, both gardeners for the Stuart monarchs.

> *Earthly Joys.* St. Martin's Press, 1998. 440pp.

> At the beginning of the reign of James I in 1603, humble gardener John Tradescant becomes the unlikely confidant of his employer, royal advisor Sir Robert Cecil. When Cecil dies, Tradescant comes into the service of the Duke of Buckingham, a dissolute courtier who is hated by the people for his spendthrift ways. After Charles I's accession, Tradescant's wife and son are suspicious of the growing Catholic influence at court, although Tradescant owes his livelihood to rich nobles' desires for beautiful gardens—and the secret missions he conducts for the queen.

> *Virgin Earth.* St. Martin's Press, 1999. 576pp.

> In this stand-alone sequel to *Earthly Joys*, John Tradescant the Younger inherits his father's passion for gardening as well as his penchant for involvement in royal affairs. Fleeing to the Virginia colony to avoid fighting for Charles I in England's Civil War, he finds a home with members of the Powhatan tribe, and love with one of their women.

Plaidy, Jean.

Myself My Enemy. Putnam, 1989. 382pp.

> On her deathbed, Henrietta Maria of France, Dowager Queen of England, wonders how much she herself was to blame for the problems of the realm. Loyal to her husband Charles I, she stands by him and his belief in the divine right of kings, even as it leads them and England inexorably toward civil war. Part of the Queens of England series (see this chapter and Index).

The Pleasures of Love. Putnam, 1992. 329pp.

> Catherine of Braganza, England's only Portuguese queen, is married to Charles II solely for political reasons, but she hopes that a loving relationship will come from the union. Instead, what she finds is a ribald court in which the king and his many mistresses rule the day. However,

when she attracts the people's enmity because of her barrenness, her husband becomes her strongest defender. Part of the <u>Queens of England</u> series.

The Stuart Saga. ★ ✍

Seven biographical novels about the Stuart kings of England and their entourage, all told in Plaidy's usual straightforward style. *The Wandering Prince*, *A Health Unto His Majesty*, and *Here Lies Our Sovereign Lord* form a trilogy about Charles II. The rest can easily stand alone. These are listed in historical order.

The Murder in the Tower. Putnam, 1974. 286pp.

Though married to the Earl of Essex, Frances Howard will do anything to have Henry, the Prince of Wales, as her lover. When he proves unattainable, she turns to Robert Carr, one of the favorites of King James I, but his friend Thomas Overbury stands in their way.

The Wandering Prince. Putnam, 1971. 318pp.

Prince Charles, in exile after his father's execution, is seen from the point of view of two important women in his life: his sister Henriette, Duchess of Orleans, and his mistress Lucy Water.

A Health Unto His Majesty. Putnam, 1972. 284pp.

During the glory of the Restoration, Charles II occupies England's throne. His wife Catherine of Braganza and his favorite mistress, Barbara Villiers, tell their stories of his glorious reign.

Here Lies Our Sovereign Lord. Putnam, 1973. 317pp.

Nell Gwyn, the orange seller and actress who captured the heart of Charles II, tells her version of the Merry Monarch's life.

The Three Crowns. Putnam, 1965. 363pp.

William of Orange, the Dutch nephew of Charles II, doesn't approve of the vice rampant at the English court, but is willing to marry his young cousin, fifteen-year-old Mary, for a chance at England's throne.

The Haunted Sisters. Putnam, 1977. 317pp.

For Mary and Anne Stuart, daughters of the exiled Catholic monarch James II, thoughts of their father bring them nothing but regret. Both believe that England is better off with a Protestant ruler, but the knowledge that they betrayed their father haunts them to the end of their days.

The Queen's Favourites. Putnam, 1978. 427pp.

Sarah Churchill, Duchess of Marlborough, and her poor relation Abigail Hill are the true power behind Queen Anne's reign. They manipulate her for their own political ends.

William's Wife. Putnam, 1993. 276pp. ✍

Daughter of the Duke of York and niece of Charles II, Lady Mary of York, the future Mary II, narrates her life story. Forced into a loveless marriage with her Dutch cousin, she sacrifices personal happiness for royal duty. Part of the <u>Queens of England</u> series.

Tranter, Nigel.

Honours Even. **Trafalgar Square, 1996. 358pp.**

The future Charles II leaves exile in the Netherlands in 1649 to get to know his Scottish subjects, but the Lord Protector, Oliver Cromwell, covets the Honours of Scotland, symbols of the nation. Scotland, naturally, isn't willing to give them up.

Triple Alliance. **Trafalgar Square, 2001. 228pp.**

Colonel James Stansfield, a Roundhead left behind in Scotland during Cromwell's protectorate, allies himself with two Haddington lairds. The three men establish a great textile enterprise, an alliance that has political ramifications for them all.

The Georgian Era

England's Georgian era began in 1714 with the death of Queen Anne and the ascension of her distant cousin, George of Hanover, to the throne; it ended over a hundred years later in 1837 with the ascension of his descendant, Queen Victoria. Many traditional historicals deal with Georgian royalty and the consequences of their personal and political decisions. This includes the American Revolution, a war that George III is blamed for losing.

Chase-Riboud, Barbara.

Hottentot Venus. **Doubleday, 2003. 336pp.** ✍ 📖

Born in a Dutch colony in South Africa in 1789, Sarah Baartman accompanies her English husband to London at age twenty. He convinces her that traveling abroad will bring her fame and fortune. Instead, she is dubbed the "Hottentot Venus" and paraded around naked in freak shows in both London and Paris. A tragic story of racism, exploitation, and the effects of colonialism.

Cline, Edward.

Sparrowhawk Series.

In this series, Cline fictionalizes the philosophical and political origins of the American Revolution, explaining how it began as a revolution of ideas long before any actual battles took place. It is only natural that the story begins in Britain, with the protagonists meeting up and traveling across the Atlantic later on. Cline acknowledges the influence of Ayn Rand's novels in his work. Elements of Rand's Objectivist philosophy —of man as a heroic being who values reason above all—are well evident.

Sparrowhawk: Book One, Jack Frake. MacAdam/Cage, 2001. 360pp.

Jack Frake, a commoner, grows up in a village in 1740s Cornwall. Falling in with a group of smugglers with ideas far above their station, Jack assists their cause. For his pains he is sentenced to eight years' servitude in the American colonies.

Sparrowhawk: Book Two, Hugh Kenrick. MacAdam/Cage, 2002. 425pp.

Hugh Kenrick, born into the nobility, angers his father and uncle when he joins a secret society of free-thinkers who question the right of kings to rule. When his involvement with them becomes public, and Hugh gets in trouble with the law, his family sends him to Philadelphia for his own good.

Sparrowhawk: Book Three, Caxton. MacAdam/Cage, 2003. 233pp.

Jack Frake and Hugh Kenrick meet up in the American colonies in 1759 and discover they have many beliefs in common.

Sparrowhawk: Book Four, Empire. MacAdam/Cage, 2004. 290pp.

In 1764 Hugh Kenrick, a member of the Virginia House of Burgesses, tries to muster enough support among his fellow legislators to protest the Stamp Act.

Gregory, Philippa.

A Respectable Trade. HarperCollins, 1995. 480pp. 📖

Frances Scott, a former aristocrat living in genteel poverty in 1787 Bristol, thinks she is making a worthy sacrifice—her marriage to a dockside shipping merchant in exchange for his protection and name. A respectable trade, in other words. She doesn't realize that his fortune lies in African slavery, another so-called respectable trade. When Frances falls in love with Mehuru, a Yoruba priest trained to be a house servant, she begins to question her country's endless greed.

Norman, Diana.

Makepeace Burke Series.

Norman, a well-regarded English historical novelist, delivers a tale of politics and romance with her trademark wit.

A Catch of Consequence. Berkley, 2003. 386pp.

When Boston tavern keeper Makepeace Burke rescues an English aristocrat from drowning in Boston harbor, she and her brother are branded as traitors. The Englishman, Sir Philip Dapifer, offers to marry her and bring her back to England. Makepeace accepts. A female tavern keeper with colonialist sympathies is hardly welcome in upper-crust society, and Sir Philip's former wife proves a formidable enemy. But Makepeace is a fighter, determined to keep her home and her husband whether anyone else likes it or not.

Taking Liberties. Berkley, 2004. 464pp.

Diana Stacpole, a former countess, gained her freedom when her repressive husband died. She travels to Plymouth to find the son of a friend who disappeared in the fight with the American colonies. There, Diana meets nouveau riche Makepeace Hedley, who is in Plymouth looking for her missing daughter. The two women band together in their quest, forging a friendship that endures despite class differences.

Plaidy, Jean.

The Georgian Saga. ✍

Plaidy's Georgian saga encompasses the entire reign of the House of Hanover, from the birth of Sophia Dorothea, George I's wife, in Celle in 1666 through the accession of Queen Victoria in 1837. Like all of Plaidy's novels, they stick fairly close to historical fact.

The Princess of Celle. Putnam, 1985. 335pp. (First published in Britain in 1967.)

Sophia Dorothea, the beautiful, spoiled Princess of Celle, is forced into an unhappy marriage with her loutish first cousin, George Lewis of Hanover.

Queen in Waiting. Putnam, 1985. 399pp. (First published in Britain in 1967.)

Wilhelmina Caroline, Princess of Ansbach, never expects to be Queen of England. Much more intelligent than her boorish husband, George Augustus of Hanover, she serves as intermediary between him and her stubborn father-in-law. Caroline waits patiently for years before England's throne becomes vacant.

Caroline, the Queen. Putnam, 1986. 413pp. (First published in Britain in 1968.)

Queen Caroline and her prime minister, Robert Walpole, are the true rulers of England, but she hides, even from those closest to her, an illness that threatens her life.

The Prince and the Quakeress. Putnam, 1986. 318pp. (First published in Britain in 1968.)

Before he becomes King George III, the young Prince of Wales makes a secret marriage with a beautiful Quaker woman, Hannah Lightfoot, who bears him several children. This is Jean Plaidy's most controversial novel, as the evidence for Hannah's marriage has not been accepted as fact.

The Third George. Putnam, 1987. 352pp. (First published in Britain in 1969.)

Officially wedded to Charlotte of Mecklenburg-Strelitz, hardly a great beauty, George III finds contentment in his marriage but has to contend with his unruly brood of fifteen children and those pesky American colonies.

Perdita's Prince. Putnam, 1987. 346pp. (First published in Britain in 1969.)

While he is still Prince of Wales, the future George IV becomes enraptured by Mary Robinson, an actress whom he calls Perdita for one of the roles she plays on the stage.

Sweet Lass of Richmond Hill. Putnam, 1988. 381pp. (First published in Britain in 1970.)

Because he cannot officially wed Maria Fitzherbert, a twice-widowed devout Catholic, the Prince of Wales marries her secretly, though he knows their union will never be recognized. Diane Haeger's romantic novel *The Secret Wife of King George IV*, annotated in Chapter 4, deals with the same subject.

Indiscretions of the Queen. Putnam, 1988. 352pp. (First published in Britain in 1970.)

In order to beget a legitimate heir, the future George IV marries his first cousin Caroline of Brunswick, an uncouth and unconventional woman—though he is hardly any great prize himself.

The Regent's Daughter. Putnam, 1989. 381pp. (First published in Britain in 1971.)

Princess Charlotte of Wales, caught between an overbearing mother and a cold father, continually searches for love and acceptance.

Goddess of the Green Room. Putnam, 1989. 351pp. (First published in Britain in 1971.)

Dorothy Jordan, a talented actress in the theaters of Drury Lane, becomes the mistress of George III's son William, Duke of Clarence, and bears him ten illegitimate children.

Victoria in the Wings. Putnam, 1990. 349pp. (First published in Britain in 1972.)

With the death of Princess Charlotte, King George III has no legitimate heirs, so there is a race among his sons to be the first to marry and have a child. The Duke of Kent's daughter Victoria will become the next in line to the throne, assuming she survives childhood.

Warner, Janet.

Other Sorrows, Other Joys. **St. Martin's Press, 2003. 368pp.** ✍

Catherine Sophia Boucher, called Kate, can't help but fall in love with visionary poet William Blake. Kate struggles to balance her conventional attitudes against William's avant-garde ideas about religion, politics, and even love. She endures his dalliances with other women (including Mary Wollstonecraft) and sees his psychic abilities first-hand. Their marriage survives it all.

The Victorian Era

Queen Victoria gave her name to the years of her reign, the period between 1837 and 1901. These novels either evoke the propriety of the era or contrast it with the plight of the less fortunate.

Ceely, Jonatha.

Mina. **Delacorte, 2004. 324pp.** `YA`

In 1848, after losing her family to the Irish famine, a fifteen-year-old Irish Catholic girl named Mina disguises herself as a boy and joins the household of an English estate. As a servant, "Paddy" gets to know the ins and outs of the kitchen and gradually befriends Mr. Serle, the estate chef. Mina reveals her true identity to him, telling Mr. Serle about her personal losses and her difficult flight from Ireland to Liverpool.

Harrod-Eagles, Cynthia.

I, Victoria. St. Martin's Press, 1996. 415pp. ✍

In this novel, described as "the autobiography Queen Victoria might have written," Victoria recollects her long, eventful life in a series of diary entries. Her voice feels authentic, similar to the tone used in the real-life queen's letters to family, and her words reveal the thoughts of the private woman who existed behind the crown.

Hunt, Caroline Rose.

Primrose Past: The 1848 Journal of Young Lady Primrose. ReganBooks, 2001. 251pp.

Packaged to look like a Victorian journal, this charming novel, written by a famed hotelier, purports to be exactly that: the re-created diary of a fifteen-year-old girl known only as Cygnet. She reports in a fairly leisurely fashion on the events of the day and happenings in her family. When her parents go on a journey, suspense picks up as Cygnet finds in their belongings a letter that causes her to question her parentage.

Plaidy, Jean.

The Queen Victoria Series. ✍

Plaidy's four-volume series covers the entire life of Queen Victoria (1818–1901): her overprotected childhood, her relationship with Lord Melbourne as a young queen, the love she finds with her consort Prince Albert, and the last years of her reign.

The Captive of Kensington Palace. Putnam, 1976. 288pp.

The Queen and Lord M. Putnam, 1977. 268pp.

The Queen's Husband. Putnam, 1978. 382pp.

The Widow of Windsor. Putnam, 1978. 351pp.

Victoria Victorious. Putnam, 1986. 569pp. ✍

Queen Victoria, reigning over England for sixty-four years, tells the story of her life in uncomplicated fashion. While Plaidy delves somewhat into politics, the emphasis here is on Victoria's domestic life: her husband Albert, her family, and her devoted servant John Brown. This covers the same ground as Plaidy's Queen Victoria series, above, but is told in the first person. Part of the Queens of England series (see this chapter and Index).

Tennant, Emma.

Adèle: Jane Eyre's Hidden Story. William Morrow, 2002. 240pp.

The center of this Victorian-style gothic is Adèle Varens, the young ward of Edward Rochester and Jane Eyre's pupil. She grows up in vibrant

Paris, the daughter of an actress, and misses it constantly. Still, the gloomy aspects of Thornfield Hall intrigue her, and while she watches the blossoming romance between her guardian and her governess, she can't resist paying secret visits to the attic, where Mr. Rochester's great secret resides. A sequel to Charlotte Bronte's *Jane Eyre*.

Twentieth Century

In comparison to literary historicals (Chapter 10) and sagas (Chapter 5) set in the British Isles during the twentieth century, the number of traditional historicals is fairly limited.

Beauman, Sally.

Rebecca's Tale. **Morrow, 2001. 448pp.**

Du Maurier's heroine, the beautiful first wife of Maxim de Winter, narrates her own story here, by way of a letter received by Colonel Julyan, the magistrate in charge of the case, twenty years after her death in the 1930s. Did her husband murder her, and what was Rebecca really like? Her story is retold from four different perspectives, all the while paying homage to the original text.

Llywelyn, Morgan.

The Irish Century.

These novels are a set of interlinked, politically astute stories about Irish citizens' experiences in the Easter Rising, the Irish War of Independence, and Ireland's Civil War. Llywelyn, an Irish citizen, is a well-known chronicler of Irish myth and history. *1972* will be the next volume.

1916: A Novel of the Irish Rebellion. Forge, 1998. 441pp. `YA`

Ned Halloran, a teenager orphaned after the *Titanic* disaster of 1912, returns to Ireland to enroll at Saint Enda's School in Dublin. There he meets scholar and patriot Patrick Pearse, who introduces him to Ireland's bloody history and the need for its freedom from the tyrannical British Empire. By the time of the Easter Rising in 1916, Ned is a believer and an active participant in the fight for Irish independence.

1921: A Book of the Irish Century. Forge, 2001. 427pp.

Beginning in 1917, Henry Mooney is a newspaper reporter whose political beliefs are less radical than his friend Ned Halloran's, but he still supports the Republican cause. Rather than fight, he uses his journalistic skills to rail against the British, but his romance with a Protestant Anglo-Irish woman confuses his loyalties.

1949: A Novel of the Irish Free State. Forge, 2003. 416pp.

In *1921*, Ireland was painfully divided into two states: the Catholic Free State and the Protestant Northern Ireland. Ursula Halloran, Ned Halloran's adopted daughter, has inherited her father's drive and passion for political change. Because unwed motherhood is unacceptable in her Catholic homeland, she is forced to leave Ireland when she becomes pregnant.

Europe

The Middle Ages

This period roughly covers the years AD 476–1492, between the fall of the Western Roman Empire through Columbus's "discovery" of the New World. Topics include religious wars of medieval Europe, the origins of the Crusades, and, less commonly, the personal lives of European monarchs.

Anderson, Poul.

Mother of Kings. Tor, 2001. 444pp. ✍

In the tenth century, Gunnhild, the witch daughter of a Norse chieftain, marries Eirik Blood-Axe, the favored son of Norway's king, and bears him nine children. The pair briefly become King and Queen of England, but in this cruel and dangerous era, no one who seizes power can ever hope to hold it for long. Anderson, a well-known chronicler of Norse fantasies, writes Gunnhild's story in a poetic, stark fashion. This was marketed as a fantasy novel but reads more like the historical re-creation of an ancient Viking saga.

Burnham, Sophy.

The Treasure of Montségur. HarperSanFrancisco, 2002. 276pp. ▣

Jeanne Béziers, on the run from the Inquisition after her people were exterminated in the siege of Montségur, relates her story. In the early thirteenth century in southern France, a baby girl is found in a meadow. Adopted by a Cathar noblewoman, Jeanne is taught the peaceful ways of her people. She finds love and acceptance with the Cathars, but when danger approaches, Jeanne is forced to sacrifice her beliefs for a chance to escape with the secret of the Cathar treasure.

Craig, Charmaine.

The Good Men. Riverhead, 2002. 389pp. ✍ ▣

In 1320, the Inquisition asks Grazida Lizier, a young widow from Montaillou, France, to speak about her heretical Cathar beliefs as well as her adulterous, incestuous relationship with the village priest, Pierre Clergue—a man who has Cathar sympathies himself. When the Inquisition learns about Clergue's beliefs and his sexual proclivities, they come to Montaillou to investigate. Craig, a half-Burmese actress who was the model for Pocahontas in the Disney movie, has crafted a thoughtful story out of Grazida's historical testimony.

Cross, Donna Woolfolk.

Pope Joan. Crown, 1996. 422pp. ▣ ✍ **YA**

In the ninth century, as legend has it, a young woman disguised as a man claimed St. Peter's throne and served as Pope for two years. Cross's well-researched interpretation of the life of Pope Joan features a young woman, Joan of Ingelheim, who is taught Latin by her brother and takes his place after he is killed in a Viking raid. Disguised as the Christian scholar Brother John Anglicus, Joan heads to Rome, where she becomes a part of the papal inner circle. Her secret is revealed at a most inopportune moment.

Druon, Maurice.

The Accursed Kings. ✍ ★

Druon's classic series of the brutal fourteenth century in France begins with the legendary words uttered by Jacques DeMolay, Grand Master of the Templars, while being burned at the stake: that King Philippe IV "The Fair" (1268–1314) and his descendants would be cursed for eternity. Within one generation, the Capetian Kings of France had died out, to be replaced by their cousins, the Valois. The seventh and last volume, *Quand un Roi Perd la France* (*When a King Loses France*), the story of Queen Clémence's young son Jean, has never been translated into English; publishers felt it didn't live up to the standards of the rest of the series.

The Iron King. Scribner, 1956. 269pp.

In 1313, Philippe the Fair, a strong, powerful king in the prime of his life, has three grown sons and a beautiful daughter, Isabelle. Within a year after disbanding the Templars by burning their leader for witchcraft, he too is dead.

The Strangled Queen. Scribner, 1957. 213pp.

Marguerite of Burgundy, a sensual, intelligent woman married to the boorish and cruel Louis X, decides to take a lover. She pays for it with her life, for without a Pope on the Vatican throne, her husband cannot obtain an annulment.

The Poisoned Crown. Scribner, 1957. 224pp.

His first wife Marguerite now dead, Louis X takes the young princess Clémence of Hungary as his second wife.

The Royal Succession. Scribner, 1958. 254pp.

Louis X has died, but his wife Clémence is pregnant. For the time being France is without a king, and the western world still without a Pope.

The She-Wolf of France. Scribner, 1960. 335pp.

English nobleman Roger Mortimer escapes from the Tower of London, heads to exile in France, and begins an affair with England's Queen Isabella—Philippe IV's daughter, who visits France to drum up support against her husband, Edward II.

The Lily and the Lion. Scribner, 1961. 294pp.

Edward III, Isabella's son, is now England's king. In France, the first Valois monarch, Philippe VI, gets involved in a feud with two of the throne's previous claimants.

Gordon, Noah.

The Last Jew. Thomas Dunne, 2000. 348pp.

During the Inquisition of 1492, Queen Isabelle and King Ferdinand issue an edict that expels all Jews from Spain, despite the fact that the Jews have lived there all their lives. Some convert to Catholicism and remain, others flee, and yet more retain the outward appearance of Christianity while practicing their Judaism in secret. Yonah Toledano of Toledo is one of the latter. He wanders for years, taking on various occupations, holding on to his religion and finding his true purpose later in life.

Holland, Cecelia.

The Angel and the Sword. Forge, 2000. 304pp.

After the death of her mother the Queen, Ragny, a Princess of Spain in the ninth century, flees the kingdom disguised as a man when her disreputable father tries to rape her and steal her throne. Accompanied by her manservant and a guardian angel, Ragny cuts off her hair, travels to the Kingdom of Francia, and becomes Roderick, who wields his sword on behalf of his adopted land. Based on the French legend of Roderick the Beardless.

Corban Loosestrife Series.

The adventures of Corban Loosestrife in tenth-century Jorvik (modern York, England), Scandinavia, and across the Atlantic and back. Holland's latest effort is a projected five-volume series, all told in stark language.

The Soul Thief. Forge, 2002. 300pp.

Young Corban searches for his twin sister Mav, captured during a brutal Viking raid on their family's Irish settlement. In his travels he encounters a number of memorable characters, including Eric Bloodaxe, his witch-wife Queen Gunnhild, and the mysterious, powerful Lady of Hedeby.

The Witches' Kitchen. Forge, 2004. 384pp.

Fifteen years after the events in *Soul Thief*, Corban Loosestrife and his wife Benna live in Vinland with their son Conn, Corban's sister Mav, and her son Raef. When Corban is summoned back to Denmark, he heeds the call. Conn and Raef accompany him, leaving the women behind. Back in Scandinavia, Corban once again gets involved with the brutal politics of the age.

Great Maria. Knopf, 1974. 519pp. ★

Maria, the daughter of a Norman robber baron in southern Italy, marries not Roger d'Alene, the knight she adores, but his older brother Richard. As Richard's territory increases with each of his conquests, their station gradually rises. Richard and Maria's relationship is stormy, passionate, and occasionally violent, but it feels real, as does the world they inhabit. Holland's novel, one of her best, is based on the Norman conquest of Sicily in the eleventh century.

Kalogridis, Jeanne.

The Burning Times. **Simon & Schuster, 2001. 390pp.** 📖

Michel, a Dominican novice in fourteenth-century France, is charged with determining whether the Franciscan nun named Mother Françoise is a witch or a saint. She decides to relate her story to no one but him. Born Sybille de Cavasculle, she becomes a midwife and a worshipper of the Goddess Diana under her grandmother's tutelage. Gifted with the power to heal, Sybille takes refuge with the Franciscans to escape the Inquisition. Throughout her life, Sybille continues to search for the elusive man destined to be her soul mate.

Mackin, Jeanne.

The Queen's War. **St. Martin's Press, 1991. 452pp.** ✍

In 1173, Eleanor of Aquitaine, Queen of England, has created a court of her own in the French city of Poitiers while her husband King Henry amuses himself in England with his mistress. While Eleanor enlists the support of her sons against their father, a young peasant girl named Lucie, rescued by Eleanor from punishment, becomes the object of desire among the chivalrous men in Eleanor's court of love.

Marcantel, Pamela.

An Army of Angels. **St. Martin's Press, 1997. 578pp.** ✍

Thirteen years old in 1425, Jehanne the Maid begins hearing saints' voices that tell her she must leave her village to follow her destiny as France's military leader and savior. In her novel about Joan of Arc, Marcantel makes her heroine a devout, flawed, very human figure, one dedicated to her mission even unto death.

Morrison, Blake.

The Justification of Johann Gutenberg. **Morrow, 2002. 256pp.** ✍

In the year 1464, in the city of Mainz, the man known as Johann Gutenberg sits down to write a justification for his life's work—the printing press—and dedicates it to a scribe whom his new invention has left unemployed. His story (narrated by Gutenberg in a rather lofty tone) is one of desperate schemes, romantic entanglements, and finally financial ruin, for in the end he never thought that his work would amount to anything.

Oldenbourg, Zoé.

The realism of Oldenbourg's novels may make readers uncomfortable, for they are full of the cruelty, suffering, and intense piety felt by the people of medieval France. Few of her novels end optimistically, for her thesis is that society's requirements were so strict that personal happiness could only be found outside its bounds, and then only fleetingly.

The Cornerstone. **Pantheon, 1955. 482pp.**

In this sequel to *The World Is Not Enough*, it is now the thirteenth century, and Ansiau of Linnières has gone on pilgrimage. Two of his descendants, one stout and brutish, the other thoughtful and philosophical, take care of his estate in his absence.

Destiny of Fire. **Pantheon, 1961. 378pp.**

In 1209, Ricord de Montgeil and his family, proud vassals of the Count of Toulouse, are considered heretics by the Church because of their Cathar beliefs. Though they are destined to become victims of the Fourth Crusade, they carry on as best they can, their faith undiminished.

The Heirs of the Kingdom. **Pantheon, 1971. 563pp.**

In the eleventh century, Jacques and Marie, two teenagers whose families are artisans, are happy and in love. When they decide to join a group of pilgrims on the First Crusade to Jerusalem, they have no idea how eye-opening and arduous a journey it will be.

The World Is Not Enough. **Pantheon, 1948. 509pp.** ★

In the Champagne region of France in the late twelfth century, a girl named Alis is married to Ansiau of Linnières, though both are barely out of childhood. When her husband leaves to go on Crusade, it is left to Alis to manage her family and their fief.

Tarr, Judith.

The Eagle's Daughter. **Forge, 1995. 352pp.** ✍

Aspasia, a fictional Byzantine princess in the tenth century, relates the story of her niece Theophano (a historical figure), who married Holy Roman Emperor Otto II, son of Otto the Great. After her husband's death in battle, Theophano becomes Regent for her young son, which leads to a war for succession amongst her husband's cousins. Aspasia, no shrinking violet herself, finds love with King Otto's Moorish physician.

Undset, Sigrid.

Kristin Lavransdatter trilogy. ★

First published in 1920–1922 in Norwegian, and translated several years later into English, Undset's trilogy spanning the life of one woman in fourteenth-century Norway helped garner the author the Nobel Prize for Literature in 1928. Her heroine, Kristin Lavransdatter, defies her family to marry Erlend Nikulausson, the man she loves beyond reason. She gives him seven sons and manages their estate of Husaby while he is off on political business, but their marriage is not always happy. Besides a love story, Undset's novels provide a detailed picture of life in medieval Norway. Tiina Nunnally's recent translation, less stiff and formal than the original translation, makes the novels accessible to a modern audience. Information on this edition is given below, though there are many others. Undset also completed a four-volume series, The Master of Hestviken, set in medieval Norway.

The Wreath. Penguin, 1997. 288pp. (Alternate title: *The Bridal Wreath.*)

The Wife. Penguin, 1999. 352pp. (Alternate title: *The Mistress of Husaby.*)

The Cross. Penguin, 2000. 430pp.

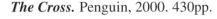

Weinstein, Lewis.

The Heretic. University of Wisconsin Press, 2003. 392pp. 📖

Previously self-published, this novel of the Inquisition in fifteenth-century Europe features a family of secret Jews whose forebears were forced to convert to Christianity. Through a meeting with Johann Gutenberg, Seville natives Gabriel and Tomas Catalan become early printers of Hebrew books. Their friendship with Princess Isabel gains them recognition, but when Tomas falls in love with a Jewess, their pretense of Christianity is jeopardized.

The Renaissance and Reformation

The Renaissance in Europe saw many exciting developments in art, literature, and science. During the same time, the Protestant Reformation swept over Europe. These novels cover the period between Columbus's arrival in North America (1492) and the Treaty of Westphalia, which put an end to the political and religious rivalries of many European nations after the Thirty Years War (1618–1648).

Elegant, Robert.

Bianca. St. Martin's Press, 2000. 348pp. (First published in Britain in 1992.) ✍

Lady Bianca Capello, a Venetian noblewoman, defies the expectations for her sex by running off with a handsome Florentine rather than submit to marriage with the old man her father chooses for her. Unhappy in her marriage, Bianca attracts the attention of Francesco de'Medici, prince regent of Tuscany. While her presence is tolerated by his wife, Bianca's cousin Mario tries to use her as a diplomatic weapon, and Francesco's brother stops at nothing to bring her down.

Ennis, Michael.

Duchess of Milan. Viking, 1992. 580pp. ✍

In Italy in the 1490s, two young women, first cousins, vie with one another for the greatest title of all: Duchess of Milan. Isabella d'Aragona is the twenty-year-old wife of Gian Galeazzo Sforza, the Duke of Milan, but her husband's uncle Lodovico Sforza, called "Il Moro," rules in his stead. Beatrice d'Este, married to Il Moro, quickly learns that her cousin and childhood friend is also her most bitter rival. Amid a court replete with Machiavellian intrigue, the two women's schemes change the fate of the nation.

Grunwald, Henry.

A Saint, More or Less. Random House, 2003. 234pp. ✍

Nicole Tavernier, a peasant newly arrived in Paris in 1594, wanders the streets of Paris claiming to work miracles with her healing. She joins the household of Barbe Acarie, a devout Catholic woman. They band together to cure the sick and bring hope back to a country torn by religious wars. When word of Nicole's accomplishments reaches King Henry of Navarre, Barbe starts doubting her charge's talents and begins to discredit her.

LaFond, Carolyn Street.

The Painter's Daughter. **Frederic C. Beil, 2002. 320pp.** ✍

LaFond's retelling of the life of Alessandra Lippi, daughter of the renowned Italian painter Fra Lippo Lippi, is best seen as a fictional portrait of fifteenth-century Florence. The beautiful Alessandra loves Sandro Botticelli, her godfather, for whom she models, but he has eyes only for his art.

Park, Jacqueline.

The Secret Book of Grazia dei Rossi. **Simon & Schuster, 1997. 572pp.** 📖

Grazia dei Rossi, the Jewish wife of the Pope's physician and herself the secretary of Isabella d'Este, writes her memoirs as a legacy for her son. In them, she reveals her continual struggle being a Jewish woman in a Christian man's world, someone who has been torn continually between love and responsibility.

Plaidy, Jean.

Evergreen Gallant. **Putnam, 1973. 384pp. (First published in Britain in 1963.)** ✍

In the late sixteenth century, there was little hope that Huguenot Prince Henri of Navarre would come to the French throne, despite his royal blood and his marriage to Catherine de Medici's beautiful and passionate daughter Margot. Best known for his succession of mistresses and his conversion to Catholicism upon gaining the throne, Henri IV becomes one of France's best-loved monarchs.

The Medici Trilogy. ✍

At the age of fourteen, Catherine de Medici, Queen Consort to Henry II of France in the sixteenth century, is removed from her Italian merchant family and married to France's heir. The series portrays her life up to the St. Bartholomew's Day Massacre in 1572, after which she is distrusted and feared by all, including her own family.

Madame Serpent. Putnam, 1975. 332pp.

The Italian Woman. Putnam, 1975. 299pp.

Queen Jezebel. Putnam, 1976. 380pp.

Puzo, Mario, and Carol Gino.

The Family. **Regan, 2001. 373pp.** ✍

With *The Godfather*, Mario Puzo made a name for himself as a chronicler of blood loyalty in a large Italian-American family. In his final novel, set amid the splendor and decadence of fifteenth-century Rome, he chronicles the story of the Borgias, the ultimate crime family. Its members include father Rodrigo (aka Pope Alexander VI) and his children Lucrezia, Cesare, Juan, and Jofre. Alexander, as head of the operation, takes control by engineering marriages between his children and Italian nobility, and even pushing them toward incest with each other. *The Family* was completed by Puzo's companion Carol Gino after his death.

Riley, Judith Merkle.

The Master of All Desires. **Viking, 1999. 386pp.** ✍

Riley's historical novel, set in sixteenth-century Paris, mixes fiction with a touch of romance and the fantastic. Queen Catherine de Medici, determined to discover the secret of her husband's attraction to his mistress Diane de Poitiers, seeks out the Master of All Desires, the disembodied head of a magus who grants all wishes asked of him. Nostradamus, the court astrologer, knows that these wishes can backfire on the giver and wants to warn his queen of the danger. However, the head is now in the possession of a young bluestocking poet, Sibille de la Roque, who wishes for nothing more than true love.

The Serpent Garden. **Viking, 1996. 467pp.**

If a marriage between Henry VIII's younger sister Mary and the elderly king of France takes place, it is due primarily to the efforts of miniature painter Susanna Dallet, even though women aren't eligible for membership in the painters' guild. Arriving in France as part of Princess Mary's entourage, Susanna doesn't realize she brings with her a manuscript that conceals secrets of the French court.

Rucker, Rudy.

As Above, So Below. **Forge, 2002. 320pp.** ✍

In sixteen chapters, each of which is preceded by one of his subject's masterworks, science fiction author Rucker illustrates key episodes in the life of Peter Bruegel, the Flemish painter who flourished in sixteenth-century Brussels and Antwerp (in modern-day Belgium). Through Bruegel's encounters with colorful characters and his observations on matters both artistic and earthy, Rucker brings the enigmatic artist to life.

Stone, Irving.

The Agony and the Ecstasy. **Doubleday, 1961. 664pp.** ✍ ★

In the mid- to late twentieth century, Irving Stone wrote a number of successful biographical novels, predominantly featuring artists and the struggles they encountered during the creative process. His work about Italian Renaissance painter/sculptor Michelangelo is one of his best. Not only is the story intensely personal, but in its realistic portrait of society in Renaissance-era Florence and Rome, it reaches near-epic status.

Early Modern and Twentieth-Century Europe

The years between the Treaty of Westphalia in 1648 and the early twentieth century saw a number of political and social changes sweep through Europe, including the French Revolution, the Napoleonic Wars, and the Russian Revolution.

Alexander, Robert.

The Kitchen Boy. Viking, 2003. 229pp. ✐

On the night of July 16, 1918, Empress Aleksandra recorded in her journal that the Romanovs' kitchen boy, Leonka Sednyov, was sent away. In the early hours of the following morning, she, her family, and all other members of the Romanov household were brutally murdered. In this believable page-turner, Alexander imagines that Leonka had returned to witness that fateful event, later escaping to America. His granddaughter discovers his story after his death.

Alleyn, Susanne.

A Far Better Rest. Soho, 2000. 360pp.

At the end of *A Tale of Two Cities*, Sydney Carton gives his life at the guillotine so that his look-alike friend Charles Darnay can live out a full life with his wife Lucie, the woman they both love. Here Carton's actions are explained in more detail, as Alleyn imagines his personal history from his youth, through his missing years in London, until his final sacrifice.

Davenport, Will.

The Painter. Bantam, 2003. 323pp. ✐

Rembrandt van Rijn, the famous Dutch painter, made a mysterious trip to Hull, England, in 1662. His imagined story, which includes a challenge he made to poet Andrew Marvell over ship captain's wife Amelia Dahl, intertwines with a modern-day tale. In the twenty-first century, Amelia's descendant Amy Dale, restoring her ancestor's old house, finds Amelia's diary and gets caught up in her own game of seduction with two different men. Davenport is best known for the time-slips he wrote as James Long.

Gulland, Sandra.

<u>Josephine Bonaparte Trilogy.</u> ✐ 📖

Gulland retells the life of Josephine Bonaparte, a grand lady if ever there was one, in first person through her diary entries.

The Many Lives and Secret Sorrows of Josephine B. Scribner, 1999. 448pp.

As a fourteen-year-old on Martinique in 1777, Marie-Josephe-Rose Tascher hears a prediction from a voodoo priestess that one day she will be queen, unlikely though that seems. By 1779, Rose is on her way to France, by way of an arranged marriage to nobleman Alexandre de Beauharnais. Left widowed and penniless after the French Revolution, she meets a short, gauche, ambitious soldier named Napoleon, who renames her Josephine.

Tales of Passion, Tales of Woe. Scribner, 1999. 384pp.

Josephine and Napoleon are newly married in 1796, but she spends most of her time waiting in Paris while he's off on his military adventures in

Europe and Egypt. His star continues to rise, while she relies on her innate charm to ward off her unpleasant, scheming in-laws.

The Last Great Dance on Earth. Scribner, 2000. 373pp.

In 1800, Josephine and Napoleon have been married for four years and love each other passionately, but many factors serve to tear them apart: her barrenness, his Corsican relatives' disapproval of her, and England's war against France.

Lee, Tanith.

The Gods Are Thirsty. **Overlook, 1996. 514pp.** ✍

Camille Desmoulins, journalist and patriot, exposes the sensual excesses of the privileged class despite great personal danger to himself. Lee is best known for her vivid novels of fantasy and horror, and given her style, the French Revolution is an appropriate subject. Though overlong and occasionally dry, it is an educational read.

Mackin, Jeanne.

The Frenchwoman. **St. Martin's Press, 1989. 378pp.**

Julienne rises from poverty in Paris to become Marie Antoinette's favorite dressmaker. When revolution threatens, and it appears the queen's life is in danger, Marie Antoinette entrusts Julienne with a royal diamond that she hopes will ensure the Dauphin's future. The atmosphere in France proves too volatile, however, and Julienne is forced to flee to the Pennsylvania colony called Azilum, which had been created as a refuge for the queen—one she tragically never got to use.

Mantel, Hilary.

A Place of Greater Safety. **Atheneum, 1993. 748pp.** ✍ ★

Three men—George-Jacques Danton, Maximilien Robespierre, and Camille Desmoulins—make their way from the French provinces to Paris in 1787, where they join forces against the repressions and tyrannies of the monarchy. However, they soon become caught up in events beyond their control, with Robespierre in particular becoming more fanatical than those he is trying to overthrow. Mantel gets inside all three men's heads, explaining their motivations as well as their fears when they realize they may have gone too far.

Piercy, Marge.

City of Darkness, City of Light. **Fawcett, 1996. 477pp.** ✍

Piercy's novel of events leading up to and during the French Revolution focuses on six characters: actress Claire Lacombe, Madame (Manon) Roland, merchant Pauline Leon, and revolutionaries Robespierre, Danton, and Condorcet—all historical personages. The lives of all six don't converge until later in the story. The multiple viewpoints can be confusing, but the characters are all appropriately brave, and the author's political arguments are apt.

Sienkiewicz, Henryk.

Fire and Sword Trilogy.

First published in Polish in 1883–1889, this epic trilogy of war, love, and adventure set around the attempted Turkish invasion of seventeenth-century Poland, a classic tale of Polish heroism, has recently been translated for modern readers by W. S. Kuniczak. These editions are listed below:

With Fire and Sword. Hippocrene, 1991. 1135pp. ★

The Deluge. Hippocrene, 1991. 2 vol. 1808pp.

Fire in the Steppe. Hippocrene, 1992. 716pp.

Spicci, Joan.

Beyond the Limit. **Forge, 2002. 490pp.** ✍

The inspirational story of Sofya Kovalevskaya, the first woman to earn a doctorate in mathematics, begins in Russia in 1865. Sofya dreams of studying math at the university level, but this is unheard of for a woman. To achieve her goal, she arranges her marriage with a Russian publisher. Though Sofya unexpectedly falls in love with her husband, her sister's revolutionary activities prove troublesome, and European universities initially deny her entrance on account of her gender.

Stephenson, Neal.

Baroque Cycle.

An ambitious, sprawling three-book series set in England, Europe, and colonial America during the Baroque era, covering 1600 through 1750. It was a great time of scientific and cultural discovery. Stephenson explores the age to its fullest, with frequent digressions about politics, science, finance, and the arts. This creates a richly detailed atmosphere, but it bogs down the story. The final book will be *The System of the World.*

Quicksilver. Morrow, 2003. 927pp.

Quicksilver is divided into three books. In the first, Enoch Root (an ageless character from Stephenson's previous science fiction novel, *Cryptonomicon*) journeys to Massachusetts in 1713 to find Daniel Waterhouse. Waterhouse, scientist extraordinaire, is needed back in England to settle the rivalry between Isaac Newton and Gottfried Wilhelm Leibniz about the true origin of calculus. The second book starts in the 1660s. Jack Shaftoe—called "King of the Vagabonds"—rescues an Englishwoman named Eliza from a Turkish harem, where she had been captive for years. They travel across continental Europe. Jack trains Eliza as a spy, while she plots revenge against her former captors. The paths of all of these characters cross in the novel's third part.

The Confusion. Morrow, 2004. 816pp.

It is now 1689. Crafty Jack Shaftoe escapes from his stint as a galley slave and goes after a Spanish pirate ship supposedly loaded with treasure. This leads to some dramatic shipboard adventures. Eliza, Countess de la Zeur, has become a notorious spy and the confidant of European monarchs. While trying to escape to England with her newborn baby, she is captured by a French privateer.

Zimler, Richard.
Hunting Midnight. **Delacorte, 2003. 512pp.**

Zimler's second historical novel (after *The Last Kabbalist of Lisbon*, see Chapter 9) has the same threads of Jewish mysticism that pervaded his first, but this time the setting is the Iberian Peninsula and the American South in the nineteenth century. In Porto, Portugal, circa 1800, young John Zarco Stewart discovers that his family descends from converted Jews who had practiced in secret since the Inquisition. After his best friend dies, a mystical bushman named Midnight, a freed slave whom his father brings back from his African travels, becomes his mentor. Napoleon's invasion of Portugal brings an abrupt end to John's childhood, and his discovery of secrets from his father's past propels him first to England and then to the American South.

The United States

Pre-Contact Native Americans

These novels re-create the lives of Native Americans before the arrival of European settlers. Most are tales of survival that recount early societies' relations with each other and with the natural world. Even though some take place around AD 1000 or later, they are often called "prehistoric" because they are set prior to recorded history. Novels set in prehistoric Europe and Asia are annotated at the beginning of this chapter.

Gear, W. Michael, and Kathleen O'Neal Gear.
The First North Americans. ★ YA

This lengthy series takes readers on visits to various locations throughout prehistoric North America. The Gears, a husband–wife writing team, are archaeologists by profession, and their novels are based on thorough anthropological and ethnographic research. Besides their fascinating storylines, which include a cast of characters appropriate to their time, books in this series include elements of romance and mystery. They can be read in any order.

People of the Wolf. Tor, 1990. 435pp.

At the end of the last Ice Age thousands of years ago, a dreamer who follows the Wolf leads his people across the ice bridge leading from Asia to North America.

People of the Fire. Tor, 1991. 467pp.

When the central Rockies and Great Plains regions of North America are stricken by drought thousands of years ago, a group of settlers struggle to keep their dreams alive.

People of the Earth. Tor, 1992. 587pp.

Along America's Northern Plains, White Ash, a dreamer who was cast out by the Earth People as a child and taken in by the Sun People, finds her prophetic visions of famine and death returning.

People of the River. Tor, 1992. 400pp.

The Mound Builders, living around the Cahokia settlement in the Mississippi River Valley, deal with the failure of the corn crop.

People of the Sea. Forge, 1993. 425pp.

In California 11,000 years ago, when the mammoths are disappearing from the earth, a young woman flees from her murderous husband west toward the sea.

People of the Lakes. Forge, 1994. 608pp.

Star Shell, daughter of a Hopewell chief living in the Great Lakes region 2,000 years ago, saves her people from the harmful influence of a totemic mask.

People of the Lightning. Tor, 1995. 414pp.

In prehistoric Florida, a young albino seer named White Lightning Boy carries a prophecy of destruction to his fishing village.

People of the Silence. Forge, 1996. 493pp.

At the height of the Anasazi empire, located in New Mexico circa AD 1150, a young woman named Cornsilk may be the person whom the cruel Great Sun Chief has been seeking, the secret result of an illicit relationship between his wife and another man.

People of the Mist. Forge, 1997. 432pp.

Along the Chesapeake Bay 600 years ago, Red Knot is murdered before her marriage can take place. This precipitates a war among the people of the entire Algonquin Nation.

People of the Masks. Forge, 1998. 416pp.

A dwarf boy named Rumbler, living among the Iroquois of upstate New York and Ontario circa AD 1000, holds the power of the spirit world. When he is captured, he and a young woman he has befriended escape and try to find his father.

People of the Owl. Forge, 2003. 563pp.

The Poverty Point settlement in northeastern Louisiana was America's largest city 4,000 years ago, and fifteen-year-old Salamander is its new leader. Salamander's people think he is really too young for the role, and each of his wives is ordered to kill him.

People of the Raven. Forge, 2004. 494pp.

Over 9,000 years ago in the Pacific Northwest, two rival tribes struggle to stay alive at a time of great environmental change. Based on the recent discovery of Kennewick Man.

Harrison, Sue.

Ivory Carver Trilogy.

Prehistoric Alaska circa 7000 BC.

Mother Earth Father Sky. Doubleday, 1990. 313pp.

After young Chagak's family and tribe are killed by the Short Ones, she grows up very quickly. Chagak escapes her family's enemies by heading out across the Bering Sea in search of shelter, but trouble arises when she is asked to marry one of the men who massacred her family.

My Sister the Moon. Doubleday, 1992. 449pp.

Kiin, promised to one of the sons of Chagak and her mate Kayugh, is raped, kidnapped, and sold away from her people by her own younger brother.

Brother Wind. Morrow, 1994. 490pp.

On the Aleutian Islands, Kiin must leave the tribe of the First Men to journey back to the Walrus People after their leader kills her husband. In a parallel story, Kukutux of the Whale Hunters faces starvation after her husband is killed and her tribe abandons her.

Storyteller trilogy.

Harrison's second trilogy is set in the icy Aleutian Islands beginning in 6480 BC.

Song of the River. Avon, 1997. 484pp.

A healer named K'os adopts a clubfooted male baby after the Near River people rape her and abandon him. She names him Chakliux. Twenty years later, Chakliux, now grown to manhood, becomes a revered storyteller for the Cousin River tribe. He is unknowingly sent back to his birth people as part of K'os's revenge against them.

Cry of the Wind. Avon, 1998. 448pp.

The Near River and Cousin River tribes, once friendly, are now bitter rivals. Chakliux, the leader of Cousin River, loves Aqamdax, though both are married to others. They both try to evade K'os's scheming, for in her revenge she will lash out at anyone, including her adopted son.

Call Down the Stars. Morrow, 2001. 446pp.

Many years later, two storytellers, Yikaas and Qumalix, relate to each other the stories of their ancestors, including the continuing saga of K'os, Chakliux, and Aqamdax, for their own tribespeople.

Sarabande, William.

The First Americans.

This series about the first Americans who crossed the land bridge that stretched across the Bering Strait in prehistoric times was published in mass market paperback. "William Sarabande" is a pseudonym for author Joan Lesley Hamilton Cline.

Beyond the Sea of Ice. Bantam, 1987. 373pp.

Corridor of Storms. Bantam, 1988. 423pp.

Forbidden Land. Bantam, 1989. 434pp.

Walkers of the Wind. Bantam, 1990. 420pp.

Sacred Stones. Bantam, 1987. 373pp.

Thunder in the Sky. Bantam, 1992. 455pp.

Edge of the World. Bantam, 1993. 465pp.

Shadow of the Watching Star. Bantam, 1995. 495pp.

Face of the Rising Sun. Bantam, 1996. 486pp.

Time Beyond Beginning. Bantam, 1998. 486pp.

Spirit Moon. Bantam, 2000. 640pp.

Shuler, Linda Lay.

Time Circle Quartet.

Shuler's heroine is Kwani, the spiritual leader of the Anasazi people who lived in New Mexico 200 years before Columbus. Because of her blue eyes, her tribe initially calls her a witch and casts her out. A mystical Toltec Indian named Kokopelli rescues her and shows her where her powers lie. Eventually she comes to be revered as She Who Remembers, though people continue to be jealous of her powers. The series continues with the story of Kwani's daughter Antelope, who has inherited her mother's abilities. Though called a "quartet," the fourth volume was never published.

She Who Remembers. Arbor House, 1988. 400pp.

Voice of the Eagle. Morrow, 1992. 654pp.

Let the Drum Speak. Morrow, 1996. 446pp.

Spinka, Penina Keen.

Picture Maker series.

In her first novels for adults, young adult novelist Spinka introduces Gahrahstah, a Native American girl living along North America's east coast in the fourteenth century.

Picture Maker. Dutton, 2002. 463pp.

Called Picture Maker for her capacity to foretell events through her drawings, Gahrahstah uses her prophetic abilities to save the Ganeogaono people. Picture Maker is captured by the Algonquins, who treat her brutally, but her journey doesn't end there. Her travels take her from Canada to Greenland, where the Norse have settled.

Dream Weaver. Dutton, 2003. 464pp.

Ingrid, born to Gahrahstah and a Norse settler of Greenland, does not fit in as one of her father's people. Christian missionaries pity her family for their heathen beliefs. In search of belonging, she retraces the steps of her mother's original journey, finally returning to her birthplace on North America's east coast.

Colonial America

Before the United States became a country, it was home to a variety of European settlements. These novels recount early settlers' experiences in the American colonies and their encounters with America's Native American inhabitants.

Burgess, Dean.

An Unclean Act. Permanent Press, 2002. 288pp. ✍

> Despite Puritans' plans to establish a community of religious freedom in America, they were, ironically, rather intolerant of others' beliefs. In 1661, when Massachusetts settler Thomas Burge makes a fateful decision to leave his unhappy marriage and establish a household with the Quaker woman he loves, it is considered an "unclean act." His action brings about the first recorded divorce in the American colonies.

Chance, Megan.

Susannah Morrow. Warner, 2002. 416pp.

> In this realistic, dark novel of the Salem witch trials of 1692, fifteen-year-old Charity Fowler has just lost her mother in childbirth on the very night her mother's sister, Susannah Morrow, arrives on her family's doorstep. Charity's father Lucas, a strict Puritan, looks askance at the worldly Susannah, though he's attracted to her against his will. In search of acceptance, Charity falls in with a group of manipulative girls who condemn Susannah as a witch, while Lucas finds himself caught in between.

Cline, Edward.

Sparrowhawk Series.

> Annotated in full under "British Isles, Georgian Era." The later volumes take place in colonial America.

Coyle, Harold.

Savage Wilderness. Simon & Schuster, 1997. 519pp.

> The French and Indian War in the 1750s was a bloody conflict when the French and English battled ferociously for control of the American colonies. Coyle, the author of Civil War novels and modern thrillers, makes this history personal through the stories of three men: a Scottish national exiled from his homeland in the Great Clearances and forced to fight for England, a country he despises; a British army captain whose military knowledge fails him in the American wilderness; and the bastard son of a French nobleman who learns how to fight from his American Indian allies.

Hudson, Joyce Rockwood.

Apalachee. **University of Georgia Press, 2000. 400pp.**

The South in the early eighteenth century was an amalgam of Native and Spanish cultures, but with the arrival of the English in the Carolinas, the dynamics of colonial society changed. In 1704, the Native American wise woman Hinachuba Lucia lives with her people, the Apalachee, in what is now the panhandle of eastern Florida. Driven from her homeland when English soldiers arrive, Lucia is sold into slavery on a Carolina plantation, separated from her husband, and forced to follow Christianity.

Kilian, Michael.

Major Washington. **St. Martin's Press, 1998. 353pp.** ✍ **YA**

Before George Washington was the first American president, he was an untried major who gained experience fighting in the French and Indian War on the side of the English. Kilian focuses on the years 1753 to 1755, as seen through the eyes of Washington's fictional colleague Thomas "Tick" Morley. During this time, Washington makes three forays into the Allegheny wilderness; conducts an affair with Sally Fairfax, his best friend's wife; and develops into the man who became a great leader, bad teeth and all.

Lamb, Cynthia.

Brigid's Charge. **Bay Island Books, 1997. 296pp.** ✍

This novel of the origin of the Jersey Devil legend begins in New Jersey's Pine Barrens in 1704, when an English woman named Deborah Smith arrives from England to marry Japhet Leeds. Deborah, a healer, adapts well to her husband's Quaker beliefs, though she keeps her own faith closely guarded. Her closest friend is her former servant Erin, who shares her belief in the goddess Brigid. When Deborah becomes pregnant with her thirteenth child at age fifty, it arouses suspicions of witchcraft. Based on the author's family history.

Moss, Robert.

Firekeeper Series. ✍

An interconnected set of biographical novels set on America's early frontier.

The Firekeeper. **Forge, 1995. 512pp.**

Moss alternates between the white and the Iroquois point of view in his novel of Sir William (Billy) Johnson, a leader of both peoples who convinces the Iroquois to fight against the French. This assures an English victory in the French and Indian War of the eighteenth century. Two women become involved with Billy and his escapades: Cat Weissenberg, a refugee from Germany, and an Iroquois shamaness named Island Woman.

The Interpreter. Forge, 1997. 346pp.

In 1710, Conrad Weiser, a native of the German Palatinate who fought for England against France, leaves England for the American colonies. The colonists, astonished to find themselves indentured servants, rebel against England, with Conrad as their leader. He grows ever closer to the Mohawks, learning their language and serving as interpreter between them and the settlers.

Robson, Lucia St. Clair.

Mary's Land. **Ballantine, 1995. 465pp.** ✍

In 1638, two women leave England for Lord Baltimore's new colony of Maryland. Margaret Brent, an upper-class Catholic, arrives with her sister and brother in search of religious freedom. Anicah Sparrow, a young pickpocket, becomes an indentured servant.

Seton, Anya.

The Winthrop Woman. **Houghton Mifflin, 1958. 586pp.** ✍ ★

In early seventeenth-century America, Elizabeth Fones finds the strength within herself to survive the repressive nature of the Massachusetts Bay Colony, of which her uncle John is the governor. Married twice to others, at last she finds some semblance of personal freedom and love with her third husband, William Hallet.

Swerling, Beverly.

Shadowbrook. **Simon & Schuster, 2004. 490pp.**

During the French and Indian War in the 1750s, Quent Hale, younger son of a landowning family in upstate New York, joins forces with his half-Indian stepbrother Cormac Shea. Their hopes: to keep their family plantation, Shadowbrook, safe from takeover by the French, and to provide a homeland for the Indians to occupy after the war ends. As both Quent and Corm were adopted into the Potawatomi tribe as children, they feel the continual pull between both cultures. Nicole Crane, a half-English, half-French young woman, undergoes a similar struggle. Having vowed to join a convent in Quebec, Nicole finds her loyalties divided when she falls in love with Quent.

Thom, James Alexander.

Follow the River. **Ballantine, 1981. 399pp.** ✍

In 1755 Virginia, Shawnee Indians abduct Mary Ingles, a twenty-three-year-old pregnant wife and mother, along with her children. Determined to find a way back to her people, Mary escapes many months later with the help of an old Dutch woman. Even her rescuer ends up becoming her enemy. Based on a true story.

The American Revolution

Novels set between 1775 and 1783, when Americans fought for independence from Great Britain, are action-oriented tales of war and patriotism.

Cameron, Christian.

Washington and Caesar. **Delacorte, 2004. 578pp.** ✍

In 1773, a new slave named Caesar arrives to work on Mount Vernon, George Washington's Virginia estate. Caesar escapes the plantation, and after war is declared, he joins the British Army to fight for his own freedom. He and other Loyalists form a fighting unit made up of former slaves. At the end, both master and former slave fight for freedom on opposite sides. Cameron portrays both Washington and Caesar fairly, showing their heroic characteristics as well as their failings.

Carter, Jimmy.

The Hornet's Nest. **Simon & Schuster, 2003. 465pp.**

Ethan and Epsie Pratt, backwoods homesteaders in Georgia in the 1770s, befriend two neighbors, Kindred and Mavis Morris, and learn about the plight of the American Indians. As war breaks out, the Pratts and the Morrises are reluctantly forced to take sides. One doesn't often think of the American Revolution taking place in the Deep South, yet this is the setting for Carter's first novel—the first ever to be written by a former president of the United States.

Fast, Howard.

Citizen Tom Paine. **Duell, Sloan & Pearce, 1943. 341pp.** ✍ ★

Paine, an Englishman who becomes a devotee of the idea of a free republic, writes the treatise "Common Sense" in defense of his beliefs. In this way Paine has a tremendous impact on the American Revolution and the formation of a new nation. Among Fast's many novels about the American Revolution (including *April Morning*, *Freedom Road*, and *The Last Frontier*), this is perhaps his best.

Harr, John Ensor.

Dark Eagle. **Viking, 1999. 512pp.** ✍

Dark Eagle is an epic defense of Benedict Arnold's treasonous behavior in the Revolutionary War, during which he plotted to turn West Point and the U.S. Commander in Chief, George Washington, over to the British army. Though one of the Americans' strongest leaders, Arnold is not treated well by either his fellow generals or the Congress. He is the classic tragic hero, switching sides only when it becomes clear that his country has turned against him.

Lussier, Paul.

Last Refuge of Scoundrels. **Warner, 2000. 313pp.**

In his revisionist novel of the American Revolution, Lussier shifts his focus from the Founding Fathers to the people who, in his view, were really behind the making of the United States. Among them are John Lawrence, a merchant's son, and his lover Deborah Simpson, a patriotic prostitute who dresses as a man and serves in the Continental Army (and whose story is based on the real-life exploits of soldier Deborah Sampson). They interact with people both fictional and real, including career aristocrat George Washington, the bumbling John Hancock, and Ben Franklin, closet Lothario.

Martin, William.

Citizen Washington. **Warner, 1999. 583pp.** ✍

After Washington's death, a young man is sent to interview the people who knew him best before the truth becomes lost to history. Through the accounts of a slave at Mount Vernon, Alexander Hamilton and other political associates, and wife Martha, Washington emerges as an imperfect yet heroic individual.

Shaara, Jeff.

Revolutionary War Series. ✍

Shaara based many of his famous characters' conversations on their actual words, as recorded in historical documents.

Rise to Rebellion. Ballantine, 2001. 491pp.

The time between the Boston Massacre in 1770 and the signing of the Declaration of Independence in 1776 saw the beginnings of a new nation, and Shaara tells the story of its major players with aplomb. All of his characters—idealistic lawyer John Adams, overseas diplomat Benjamin Franklin, British General Thomas Gage, and colonial army commander George Washington—are well known to history.

The Glorious Cause. Ballantine, 2002. 638pp.

In the conclusion to *Rise to Rebellion*, the story changes from talk to action, as George Washington takes the offensive by crossing the Delaware River and attacking the enemy. Also well portrayed are Nathaniel Greene, Washington's greatest and most reliable commander; Lord Cornwallis, the capable British general; and Benjamin Franklin, now a great statesman.

Thom, James Alexander.

The Red Heart. Ballantine, 1997. 448pp. ✍

During the Revolutionary War, Miami Indians abduct five-year-old Frances Slocum from her Quaker family in northeastern Pennsylvania. Over time, Frances adapts to her new culture, taking the Miami name Maconakwa. Sixty years later, after the Indians are beaten, her family finally locates her, but Maconakwa has to decide whether or not to return to them. Based on a true story.

Thom, James Alexander, and Dark Rain Thom.

Warrior Woman. Ballantine, 2003. 480pp. ✍

On the eve of the Revolutionary War, the army of Virginia prepares to attack the Shawnee tribe. Nonhelema, female peace chief of the Shawnee and a Christian convert, preaches a message of peace to her people. When they ignore her words, she reluctantly rides into battle. Her story is a tragic one, for despite her consistent message of peace, both the Shawnee and the white men ultimately betray her. Co-written by Thom and his wife Dark Rain, a member of the Shawnee Nation.

The Early United States

Novels set between the end of the Revolution (1783) and the beginning of the Civil War (1861) tell of the political growth and expansion of the United States. Common themes include fictional biographies of America's presidents, relationships with Native American tribes, and the growth of slavery in the South.

Byrd, Max.

Jackson. **Bantam, 1997. 421pp.** ✍

In 1828, journalist David Chase is assigned to write a tell-all biography of Andrew Jackson, who is running for president against incumbent John Quincy Adams. Adams's supporters want Chase's book to reveal scandals from Jackson's life, such as his treasonous collusion with Aaron Burr and his notoriously bad temper. As Chase grows to admire Jackson's sharp political acumen, a long-held secret about Jackson's wife emerges, and Chase must decide whether to reveal it.

Jefferson. **Bantam, 1993. 424pp.** ✍

Jefferson's personal secretary William Short narrates this tale of the great man and future president during his tenure in Paris, circa 1784–1789, when he served as ambassador to France. There, Short encounters luminaries such as Ben Franklin and John Adams and watches his master succumb to the charms of beautiful Maria Cosway.

Card, Orson Scott.

Saints. **Forge, 2001. 624pp. (Originally published in 1984 as *A Woman of Destiny*.)** ✍

Card's mainstream novel of Dinah Kirkham, one of Mormon leader Joseph Smith's many wives, details the Mormon experience in America yet remains accessible to non-believers. Growing up in poverty in industrial England in the 1830s, Dinah trusts no one fully after her father abandons the family. She discovers her own strength after traveling to America in search of a better life.

Chase-Riboud, Barbara.

Sally Hemings Series. ✍ ★ 📖

The author tells of race relations in early nineteenth-century America through the story of Thomas Jefferson's slave mistress.

Sally Hemings. Viking, 1979. 384pp.

This controversial novel fueled the fire of the debate about whether President Thomas Jefferson had an affair with a slave, his wife's half-sister, after Martha Jefferson's death. Here Sally Hemings, proud and respectable despite her lack of choice in the matter, is given back her dignity.

The President's Daughter. Crown, 1994. 467pp.

In 1822, on her twenty-first birthday, Harriet Hemings, the red-haired slave daughter of Sally Hemings and Thomas Jefferson, is allowed to leave Monticello and pass into white society. After she marries, she receives a package in the mail indicating that someone knows her secret. Little is known of the real Harriet Hemings; this is her fictional biography.

Griesemer, John.

Signal & Noise. **Picador, 2003. 593pp.**

Griesemer's mammoth novel of the laying of the first transatlantic cable in the 1850s and 1860s encompasses two continents and many more personalities. While this may seem an odd subject for a work of fiction, it is considerably more lively than it sounds, touching on issues such as the arrival of "modern" technology, spiritualism, the horrors and the aftermath of the Civil War, and the eccentrics who were Victorian England's greatest engineers.

Mackin, Jeanne.

The Sweet By and By. **St. Martin's Press, 2001. 293pp.** ✍

When modern-day magazine writer Helen West conducts research for an essay on Maggie Fox, the nineteenth-century founder of American Spiritualism, she begins to feel a kinship with her subject. Their stories, told in parallel, have striking similarities. Both Maggie and Helen mourn for the love of their life and earnestly wish that they could communicate with their loved ones after death.

Marcus, Martin.

Freedom Land. **Forge, 2003. 352pp.** ✍

In 1835, when half-British, half-Creek Billy Powell is accused of a murder he didn't commit, he heads south to Freedom Land, a village in the Florida Everglades that serves as a sanctuary for a motley group of Seminole Indians and escaped slaves. When the U.S. government organizes efforts to recapture the slaves and remove the Seminoles to Oklahoma, it is up to Freedom Land's residents to protect themselves and their territory. Now called Chief Osceola, Powell and his American Indian, black, and white followers do just that. Their successful defense is known today as the Second Seminole War, the only Indian war that the United States ever lost.

Nevin, David.

The American Story.

The books in Nevin's series, all of which work as stand-alone novels, dramatize the political history and growth of the United States between 1800 and 1860 through the intermingled stories of historical and fictional characters. Two more novels in the series, *Dream West* and *Meriwether*, are annotated in Chapter 6.

1812. Forge, 1996. 414pp. ✍

Nevin details the events leading up to America's "other" war with Britain, the War of 1812, through the eyes of the great personalities that shaped this early country: Andrew and Rachel Jackson, President James and Dolley Madison, and military genius Winfield Scott.

Eagle's Cry. Forge, 2000. 447pp. ✍

After George Washington dies in 1799, the newly formed government of the United States is threatened from within and without. While Thomas Jefferson and James Madison try to live by their democratic principles, Aaron Burr attempts to create a Federalist empire in the northeast, and Napoleon Bonaparte's gain of New Orleans and the Louisiana Territory may mean the end of American expansion.

Treason. Forge, 2001. 431pp. ✍

In 1803, Jefferson is president and Aaron Burr his vice president, but Burr's own Democratic Party shuns him for his failed attempt to steal the 1800 election from Jefferson. After mortally wounding Alexander Hamilton in a duel, Burr is completely discredited politically. He joins with General James Wilkinson in a scheme to persuade the New Orleans territories, newly purchased from France, to revolt against an American takeover. Secretary of State James Madison tries to stop them.

Robson, Lucia St. Clair.

Light a Distant Fire. **Ballantine, 1988. 415pp.** ✍

As a child in what is now Florida, young Osceola is saved by his grandmother when Andrew Jackson and his men attack their Seminole village. He survives to become the leader of his people, defending them against the governmental forces that unjustly invade their lands.

Shaara, Jeff.

Gone for Soldiers. **Ballantine, 2000. 424pp.** ✍

Before the Civil War, many of the major players from the earlier Shaara trilogy fought on America's behalf in another cause, the Mexican War of 1846–1848. General Winfield Scott, a veteran of the War of 1812, fights with the U.S. Army against arrogant Mexican General Santa Anna. Robert E. Lee, an untried engineer, is at Scott's side, developing the skills of command that will serve him well in the Civil War.

Slotkin, Richard.

🎗 *Abe: A Novel of the Young Lincoln.* **Holt, 2000. 478pp.** ✍ 📖

Tracing young Abe Lincoln's personal growth from a two-year-old toddler to a strapping twenty-three-year old, Slotkin takes us step by step through the stages that turned him into a man of greatness: the tragedy of his mother's early death, a flatboat journey down the Mississippi to New Orleans, and his arrival in New Salem, Illinois. His Abe is a folksy, adventurous frontiersman whose story is told with authenticity and humor. Michael Shaara Award.

Zaroulis, Nancy.

Call the Darkness Light. **New American Library, 1979. 659pp.**

In the 1840s, orphaned Sabra Palfrey goes to work in the mills of Lowell, Massachusetts. Despite the harsh working conditions, she learns a sense of independence, which is to change her life in unforeseen ways. This lengthy novel encompasses the broad spectrum of life in nineteenth-century New England, including utopianism, anti-Irish prejudice, the plight of women, and more.

The Civil War

Between 1861 and 1865, friends and families were torn apart as people were forced to take sides between the Union and the Confederacy. While many novels cover the actual battles, others deal with political decisions, social issues such as race and slavery, and the difficulty of conducting daily life during wartime.

Ballard, Allen B.

Where I'm Bound. **Simon & Schuster, 2000. 316pp.** **YA**

In this novel of African Americans' contributions to the Civil War, Joe Duckett, a part-black, part-American Indian former slave, flees harsh treatment on a Louisiana plantation to join the Union army. He serves with distinction in the Third United States Colored Cavalry. What drives him is his dream of reuniting his entire family, including a wife and daughter left behind on the plantation and two children who were sold away.

Bean, Fred.

Lorena. **Forge, 1996. 284pp.**

In late 1864, Lorena Blaire is one of four female nurses recruited by the Union to infiltrate the forces of Confederate General John Bell Hood and report back to General Grant on their activities. She does her job well, but her opinion of the Confederacy changes when she meets Dr. Jonathan Cross, an honorable doctor from Texas who has never owned slaves.

Burke, James Lee.

White Doves at Morning. **Simon & Schuster, 2002. 320pp.**

New Iberia, Louisiana, during the Civil War and Reconstruction is the setting for this traditional historical by a well-known mystery writer. As in all his novels, universal themes—the desire for freedom, the responsibilities of loyalty—are made very personal. Willie Burke, the author's ancestor, loyally defends his homeland by fighting for the Confederacy, reluctantly so. Interacting with him are Abigail Dowling, a Massachusetts native and abolitionist; Flower, a slave whom Willie teaches to read; and Ira Jamison, a southern plantation owner who is also Flower's father.

Carter, Alden R.

Bright Starry Banner. **Soho, 2004. 452pp.**

Over a very short time—December 31, 1862, through January 2, 1863—Union and Confederate soldiers clashed in what was one of the bloodiest Civil War battles ever fought. Despite this, the Battle of Stones River in Murfreesboro, Tennessee, is nearly forgotten today. Carter revives the action through a series of vignettes, which he re-created by reading journal entries of actual participants like writer Ambrose Bierce.

Croker, Richard.

To Make Men Free. **Morrow, 2004. 427pp.**

This is another vigorous fictional portrait of a Civil War battle, this time Antietam (September 17, 1862). Known as the bloodiest day in American history, when over 22,000 men died, Antietam brought the Union the victory it so desperately needed. The Union success also tied in directly to Lincoln's famous Emancipation Proclamation. Many historic figures (Robert E. Lee, the Lincolns, George McClellan, Stonewall Jackson) appear here.

Ehrlich, Ev.

Grant Speaks. **Warner, 2000. 401pp.** ✍

In 1885, Civil War general and former President Ulysses Grant passed away after completing his famous memoirs, which revealed his personal experiences during the war and in the White House. Ehrlich, the Undersecretary of Commerce under President Clinton, has penned a sly rebuttal to Grant's tome, imagining that Grant as the country knew him was an impostor. This very different Grant retells his life story in an outrageous, satirical fashion.

Foote, Shelby.

Shiloh. **Random House, 1952. 226pp.** ★

Foote's novel takes us into the minds of both Union and Confederate soldiers participating in the Battle of Shiloh, fought over two days in April 1862 in the Tennessee woods. After the success of this novel, Foote went on to publish his famous history of the Civil War.

Fortschen, William R.

We Look Like Men of War. **Forge, 2001. 192pp.**

Sam Washburn, born a slave in 1850, had escaped his bonds and headed north to freedom. Now he returns south to defend his liberty by fighting for the Union. He joins a "colored regiment" as a drummer boy, and his experience—based on the author's research for his doctoral dissertation—vividly demonstrates African Americans' real experiences during the Civil War.

Fowler, Robert H.

The Battle of Milroy Station. **Forge, 2003. 320pp.**

The Battle of Milroy Station never happened, but in Fowler's version, it very well might have. At the beginning of the war in an unnamed Confederate state, Andrew Jackson Mundy, aide-de-camp of General Evan Martin, discovers the length to which his superior officer will go to obtain battlefield fame. These events haunt him many years later, when Mundy is asked to become the running mate of William McKinley in the 1896 presidential election. The reason he turns down this honor has to do with General Martin's past actions, which are gradually revealed.

Jakober, Marie.

🏵 *Only Call Us Faithful.* **Forge, 2002. 381pp.** ✍

As Miss Elizabeth ("Liza") Van Lew discovers, it isn't easy being a Union sympathizer in Richmond, Virginia, the heart of the Confederacy, in 1861. After her death, Liza's ghost reveals the important role she played during the Civil War. Ever loyal to her country, Liza organizes a Union spy ring that manages to run successfully until the war's end. Although her anti-slavery feelings are well known to the general populace, it proves impossible for the rebels to catch her. Michael Shaara Award.

Kantor, MacKinlay.

🏵 *Andersonville.* **World Publishing, 1955. 733pp.** ★

The Andersonville prison camp in southwestern Georgia, infamous for the horrific, inhumane treatment of over 50,000 Union prisoners, is the setting for this gritty novel. The realism of this novel is unremitting, making it at times almost too painful to read. There are some hopeful images, particularly in seeing how war can also bring out the best in basically good people. Pulitzer Prize.

Long Remember. **Coward-McCann, 1934. 411pp.** ★

Kantor's first novel, set in the peaceful town of Gettysburg, Pennsylvania, in summer 1863, features Daniel Bale, a soldier with pacifist tendencies. He reluctantly comes to accept the necessity of war as the Battle of Gettysburg rages around him.

McCaig, Donald.

🏵 *Jacob's Ladder.* **W. W. Norton, 1998. 525pp.**

In 1857 Virginia, Duncan Gatewood falls in love with Maggie, a light-skinned, thirteen-year-old female slave, but when his father finds out, he sells Maggie south along with her baby son Jacob. While Duncan is sent off to the Virginia Military Institute and ends up fighting for Lee, Maggie is rescued by the slave-master who sold her off, Silas Omohundru, who rescues her from a southern brothel and marries her. In the meantime, a Gatewood slave who also loved Maggie runs away and joins the Northern army to take revenge against his former masters. Michael Shaara Award.

McColley, Kevin.

The Other Side. **Simon & Schuster, 2000. 382pp.**

Living on a small Ohio farm, seventeen-year-old Jacob Wilson wants to avoid involvement in the Civil War. This changes when he falls in love with a runaway slave his father hides on their land. When militiamen discover her and destroy their property, he kills one of them, runs away from home, and falls in with Quantrill's Raiders, a nasty group of thugs who thrive on violence.

McCrumb, Sharyn.

Ghost Riders. **Dutton, 2003. 333pp.** ✍ 📖

When her husband signs up with the Confederates, Malinda Blalock disguises herself as his brother and joins him. After they scheme to get discharged, they turn into outlaws on the opposite side. Their story intertwines with that of Zebulon Vance, a mountain boy who becomes North Carolina's governor, and a present-day tale about ghosts appearing on the battlefield of a Civil War re-enactment. McCrumb's theme is a strong one: During the Civil War it was impossible to tell what side people were on, and it was even harder to stop fighting once peace was made. Like *The Songcatcher* (Chapter 5), this is part of McCrumb's <u>Ballad Novel</u> series featuring the folk living in the Appalachian Mountains of North Carolina and Virginia.

Moreau, C. X.

Promise of Glory. **Forge, 2000. 302pp.**

The Battle of Antietam on September 17, 1862, when Robert E. Lee undertook his first attempted invasion of the North, was the bloodiest day of the whole Civil War. Moreau tells the story of that fateful day in Maryland from the point of view of its major players.

Nagle, P. G.

<u>Far Western Civil War Series.</u>

Nagle's novels explore a part of the North–South conflict that is rarely discussed, let alone explored in fiction: the Civil War in the Far West. Books in her series, which follow the same set of characters, are best read in order. They will appeal to readers of traditional historicals as well as Westerns.

Glorieta Pass. Forge, 1999. 441pp.

The Battle of Glorieta Pass, largely unknown today, was called the "Gettysburg of the West." In 1861, when federal troops in the West are called back East to fight for the Union, the Confederacy sees its opportunity to move in. The side that wins New Mexico Territory will gain unhindered access to Colorado and the California coast. Among the characters caught up in the conflict are Alastar O'Brien, an Irish immigrant miner fighting for the Union with the Colorado Volunteers; Jamie Russell, a Texas boy fighting for the Confederates; Lt. Charles Franklin, a wealthy man's son turned Union soldier; and Laura Howland, a young woman from Boston who has just lost her father and now stands to lose even more.

The Guns of Valverde. Forge, 2000. 412pp.

The Confederates of Texas, crushed by their defeat at Glorieta Pass, see a way to regain some ground by stealing Union artillery at the Battle of Valverde. Jamie Russell, a Confederate quartermaster taken prisoner by Alastar O'Brien, plans a way to get the artillery back to Texas. Wounded, Jamie is nursed back to health by Laura Howland, who is in love with his captor.

Galveston. Forge, 2002. 378pp.

In 1863, when war hero Jamie Russell accompanies his sister Emma to their aunt's home in Galveston, Texas, he expects to spend some quality time helping Emma recover from the loss of her true love at Valverde. What he finds is a city vulnerable to naval attack from the Union.

Red River. Forge, 2003. 396pp.

The Mississippi and Red Rivers are the South's primary corridors for moving supplies for trade. If the North can cut off this route, it may hasten the end of the war. Many of the characters from Nagle's previous books reunite in this tale of Union–Confederate encounters along the Red River and in Louisiana's plantation country.

O'Brien, Patricia.

The Glory Cloak. **Touchstone, 2004. 348pp.** ✍ 📖

At the outbreak of the Civil War, Susan Gray and her distant cousin Louisa May Alcott travel to Washington, D.C., to serve as nurses for the Union Army. There they meet Clara Barton, the Civil War heroine who becomes their mentor. John Sulie, an injured soldier, intrigues both of the women, but he may not be who he seems. A novel of women's friendship during the turmoil of war.

Parry, Richard.

That Fateful Lightning. **Ballantine, 2000. 355pp.** ✍

Ulysses S. Grant, fighting a losing battle against throat cancer in 1884, looks back on everything he has accomplished. He determines that he was a failure in everything but war. In writing his memoirs, encouraged to do so by both his wife Julia and author Mark Twain, Grant relives his most heroic moments, hoping that the proceeds from his writings will help keep Julia and his children from poverty after his death.

Shaara, Michael, and Jeff Shaara.

Civil War Trilogy. ✍ ★ YA

Like few before them, these novels succeed in bringing readers into the minds of the leaders who fought on both sides of the Civil War. Nearly all of the characters are historical, but the principal players are Confederate General Robert E. Lee, Union commander Ulysses S. Grant, Confederate General Thomas "Stonewall" Jackson, Winfield Scott Hancock (the Union commander at Gettysburg), and Joshua Chamberlain, the Union leader who accepted Lee's surrender at Appomattox. When *The Killer Angels* was first published in 1973, it hardly made waves in the literary world, despite winning the 1975 Pulitzer Prize. Five years after Shaara's death, after the release of the associated film *Gettysburg,* it finally reached bestseller status. At that point Jeff Shaara, Michael's son, took on the project of writing the prequel and sequel to his father's classic novel. A rare coin dealer, Jeff Shaara had no previous writing experience, but all of his novels have become bestsellers.

Shaara, Jeff.

Gods and Generals. Ballantine, 1996. 498pp.

Shaara's four protagonists—Generals Lee and Jackson in the South, Chamberlain and Hancock in the North—prepare strategies that lead them through the Battles of Fredericksburg and Chancellorsville. This novel takes place between 1858 and 1863, ending just before Gettysburg.

Shaara, Michael.

The Killer Angels. McKay, 1974. 374pp.

A dramatic portrait of the Battle of Gettysburg, which killed more men than any other battle on American soil. The entire novel occurs over a very short time period, June 29 through July 3, 1863. More literary than Jeff Shaara's two novels, this masterpiece sees the action mostly from the viewpoints of Confederate Generals Robert E. Lee and James Longstreet. Pulitzer Prize.

Shaara, Jeff.

The Last Full Measure. Ballantine, 1998. 560pp.

The trilogy concludes as Lee, Grant, and Chamberlain lead their armies during the last two years of the Civil War. It begins as Lee retreats from Gettysburg and follows them and their men through 1865. Later chapters reveal each man's fate after the war.

Trotter, William R.

Sands of Pride Series.

These lengthy novels take place along the North Carolina seacoast during the Civil War.

The Sands of Pride. Carroll & Graf, 2002. 754pp.

The action takes place from just before North Carolina's secession in 1861 through July 1863. Fort Fisher, a fortress just south of Wilmington that is literally built of sand, is the lifeline for the Confederacy. Over two dozen characters, both fictional and real, populate the novel. These include North Carolina governor Zebulon Vance, Confederate President Jefferson Davis, Confederate spy Belle O'Neal, plantation owners, bushwhackers, merchants, British diplomats, and more. Trotter's nonfiction series about the Civil War in North Carolina served as background material for Charles Frazier's *Cold Mountain* (Chapter 10).

The Fires of Pride. Carroll & Graf, 2003. 560pp.

After the South's defeat at Gettysburg in 1863, the South rallies to defend Fort Fisher, called the Alamo of the Confederacy. Like the previous book, this sequel centers on Wilmington, North Carolina, and its residents.

Wheeler, Richard S.

The Exile. Forge, 2003. 336pp. ✍

A biographical novel of Thomas Francis Meagher, an Irish patriot and American Civil War hero. Banished to Van Diemen's Land (Tasmania) for his role in inciting the Irish to rebel against the English in 1848, Meagher escapes and makes his way to New York. There he gets caught up in corrupt Tammany Hall politics and joins with other Irish to fight in the Union Army. Meagher is ruined and disillusioned by the war, and Andrew Johnson appoints him to be acting governor of the Montana Territory. There he faces even harsher conditions.

Reconstruction and the Gilded Age

The years right after the Civil War were hard on everyone. Both the North and South recuperated from their losses and struggled to rebuild their cities and towns. As the later years of the nineteenth century approached, prosperity was just around the corner. Novels set in 1880s and 1890s America tend to focus on Gilded Age society and its excesses.

Byrd, Max.

Grant. **Bantam, 2000. 362pp.** ✍

In 1880, when Ulysses Grant is being considered for a third term as president, journalist and Civil War veteran Nicholas Trist is sent to interview him and write about the campaign. As Trist pursues romantic encounters with a senator's wife, he reveals his portrait of a man who achieved great success in war but suffered later from alcoholism, poverty, and the throat cancer that eventually ended his life.

Chance, Megan.

An Inconvenient Wife. **Warner, 2004. 404pp.** 📖

Lucy Carelton, unable to meet the demands of society in 1884 New York City, is diagnosed officially with "hysteria." Her wealthy husband William, desperate for a cure, brings her to see Dr. Victor Seth, a hypnotist with newfangled techniques. Under Victor's guidance, Lucy blossoms. She begins to understand that her problems were caused by an unhappy childhood and loveless marriage. At that point Lucy becomes more inconvenient than ever, as William feels threatened by her newfound passion and independence.

Cohen, Paula.

Gramercy Park. **St. Martin's Press, 2002. 357pp.**

In 1894, Italian tenor Mario Alfieri arrives in Manhattan with hopes of making his debut at the Metropolitan Opera. While looking for a house in Gramercy Park to rent, he encounters 19-year-old Clara Adler, recently bereft of a rich guardian who left her nothing in his will. Clara's pitiful state and mysterious background attract the womanizing Mario, who falls in love and marries her. Her enemies—including the lawyer controlling her guardian's estate—stop at nothing to ruin their happiness.

Due, Tananarive.

The Black Rose. **One World/Ballantine, 2000. 375pp.** ✍

Madam C. J. Walker was America's first black female millionaire, the owner of a vast empire of hair care products designed to prevent black women's hair from breaking and splitting. This may seem a minor accomplishment, but when the former Sarah Breedlove developed her product in the late nineteenth century, it gave African-American women a sense of beauty and worth. Sarah's rise from poverty in the Louisiana Delta to fame and fortune is an inspirational story. Due, a noted science fiction author, based her novel on research conducted by Alex Haley.

Reid, Van.

Moosepath League series. **YA**

Van Reid just may be New England's answer to Garrison Keillor. This series is a funny and entertaining collection of quirky Yankee tall tales, replete with eccentric, colorful characters, all set in Maine at the very end of the nineteenth century. In these charming re-creations of the serial adventures from Victorian newspapers, there are digressions aplenty, but that's all part of the fun.

Cordelia Underwood, or, the Marvelous Beginnings of the Moosepath League. Viking, 1998. 400pp.

Mollie Peer, or, The Underground Adventure of the Moosepath League. Viking, 1999. 336pp.

Daniel Plainway, or, The Holiday Haunting of the Moosepath League. Viking, 2000. 385pp.

Mrs. Roberto, or, The Widowy Worries of the Moosepath League. Viking, 2003. 336pp.

Fiddler's Green. Viking, 2004. 320pp.

Uris, Leon.

O'Hara's Choice. HarperCollins, 2003. 416pp.

Veteran historical novelist Uris's final novel (he died in 2003) glorifies the career of an imaginary U.S. Marine, Zachary O'Hara. After the Civil War, first-generation Irish-American Zach gets the chance to convince the Secretary of the Navy of the Corps' importance. Along the way he falls in love with Amanda Blanton Kerr, an independent and headstrong woman. Both Zach's superiors and Amanda's father disapprove of their relationship.

Twentieth Century

The early twentieth century was a time of cultural and technological discovery, and inventions created during that time were used both in daily life and in war. Most of these novels take place during World War I, the Great Depression, and World War II. Race relations are another popular topic.

Baldacci, David.
Wish You Well. **Warner, 2000. 401pp.** 📖 **YA**

The author, best known for his modern legal thrillers, has crafted an old-fashioned coming-of-age novel set in 1940s New York City and Virginia that makes use of his courtroom expertise. When Louisa Mae (Lou) Cardinal's father is killed, she and her younger brother move from the city to rural Virginia to live on a farm with her great-grandmother, also called Louisa. In the hard environment of the Appalachian Mountains, they learn about life, love, and growing up. There are also lessons to be learned in the elder Louisa's battle against a coal company that exploits the poorer classes.

Boyne, Walter.

Dawn over Kitty Hawk. **Forge, 2003. 400pp.** ✍

In this novel about Orville and Wilbur Wright, Boyne, a former director of the National Air and Space Museum, not only illustrates how they achieved their dream of building the first powered aircraft but also tells about the people who both helped and hindered their goals. This includes their sister Katherine, their controlling father Milton, and numerous competitors.

Callanan, Liam.

The Cloud Atlas. **Delacorte, 2004. 368pp.**

At the end of World War II, Japan launched thousands of balloon bombs and set them northeast to Alaska. In Callanan's novel, Louis Belk, eighteen years old in 1944, is a young sergeant set to defuse them before the public discovers they exist. While in Alaska, Belk becomes romantically involved with Lily, a Yup'ik woman who insists she can foresee where the bombs will drop next. Belk, Lily, and Belk's superior officer form an unlikely love triangle. With its emphasis on the mysterious Alaskan landscape in wartime, the novel is suspenseful and occasionally harrowing.

Dalton, David.

Been Here and Gone: A Memoir of the Blues. **Morrow, 2000. 432pp.**

Aged 102 in 1998, former bluesman Coley Williams reminisces about his life as a backup singer to some of the greatest blues legends in America. His story also recounts the black experience in the United States in the twentieth century. Growing up a black tenant farmer in Mississippi in the 1920s, Coley survives the Great Depression and lives through the early Civil Rights Movement. His voice is homespun, raunchy, and real.

DeJohn, Jacqueline.

Antonio's Wife. **HarperCollins, 2004. 431pp.**

In 1908, Italian opera singer Francesca Frascatti leaves Naples for America to find her daughter, Maria Grazia, whom she gave up to pursue a music career. During the day, she and detective Dante Romano roam the streets of Manhattan to find Maria Grazia before the Black Hand does. Mina DiGianni, a Neapolitan seamstress, becomes Francesca's dresser and confidante. While taking refuge at the theater from her abusive husband Antonio, Mina falls in love with Dante.

Fleming, Thomas.

Conquerors of the Sky. **Forge, 2003. 544pp.**

A reminiscence of the first hundred years of flight, Fleming's novel sees the development of the aviation industry from the point of view of Buchanan Aircraft, a (fictional) fledgling California company in the 1930s that became one of the greatest airplane manufacturers of the twentieth century.

Hoopes, Roy.

Our Man in Washington. **Forge, 2000. 380pp.** ✍

In 1920s Baltimore and Washington D.C., reporters H. L. Mencken and James M. Cain take on fictional roles as amateur investigators, checking out the truth behind sex scandals and other corruption in the Harding administration.

Kemper, Marjorie.

Until That Good Day. **Thomas Dunne, 2003. 320pp.** 📖

In 1930s Louisiana, traveling salesman John Washington has a secret that he keeps from everyone: He has African ancestry, and his family has successfully passed as white since Reconstruction. Almost everyone, that is, for John reveals his past only to his black mistress, Odessa. His daughter Vivien relates his story. The novel is loosely based on the author's own family history.

Reasoner, James.

The Last Good War series.

The continuing adventures of the Parker family on all fronts during World War II. Readers of family sagas may enjoy these novels, but they have more action and adventure than is typical for that subgenre.

Battle Lines. Forge, 2001. 379pp.

Brothers Joe and Dale Parker, Joe's friend Adam, and Adam's girlfriend Catherine all end up enlisting in the military for a fairly contrived reason. Dale has been having an affair with a banker's wife, and the banker threatens to ruin him unless the Parkers enlist. What happens to the four friends is fairly predictable as well, as they all learn very quickly that war is not nearly as clear-cut or romantic as they imagined. It's a fairly light read, as war novels go, but the history is accurate, and the author's message comes through loud and clear.

Trial by Fire. Forge, 2002. 445pp.

Joe and Dale Parker see action while assisting the British in North Africa. Catherine and Adam, now married, are stationed in the Pacific, with Catherine as a navy nurse during the Battle of the Coral Sea and Adam as a Marine at Wake Island.

The Zero Hour. Forge, 2003. 496pp.

In 1942, as the action in both Africa and in the Pacific grows more heated, the Parker brothers fight with the British against Rommel, while Adam fights in the Solomon Islands with the Marines.

Wouk, Herman.

<u>Captain Victor Henry Series.</u> ★

Wouk's large-scale series, a combination of traditional historical novel and family saga, takes us behind the scenes to explore the historical background of America's involvement in World War II. The action is seen through the eyes of the fictional Henry family, most notably Navy Captain Victor "Pug" Henry, who serves as one of Roosevelt's advisors. Captain Henry's sons and daughter likewise become caught up in the fray. The books read as one very long novel.

🎗 *The Winds of War.* Little, Brown, 1971. 885pp.

Pulitzer Prize.

War and Remembrance. Little, Brown, 1978. 1042pp.

Canada

Very few recent novels in this subgenre take place in Canada, though they proliferate in both literary historicals (Chapter 10) and sagas (Chapter 5).

Fleming, Thomas.

A Passionate Girl. **Forge, 2004. 416pp.**

Part of Fleming's Stapleton saga; annotated in Chapter 5.

Roberts, Kenneth.

Arundel. **Doubleday, 1933. 486pp.** ★

During the harsh winter of 1775, Steven Nason, a soldier from Maine fighting in the Continental Army, joins Benedict Arnold on his march to take the fort of Quebec from the British. Not only is this a moving coming-of-age story, but it is also a vivid portrait both of the doomed march on Quebec and of the great Arnold before he turned traitor.

Latin America, the Hispanic Southwest, and the Caribbean

Most of these novels are set in early Mexico and other Spanish territories in North America (including modern New Mexico and Arizona), from the Spanish conquest in the sixteenth century through the Hapsburg Empire in the nineteenth. The difference between them and Western historical novels featuring Native Americans (Chapter 6) can be slight.

Falconer, Colin.

Feathered Serpent. **Crown, 2002. 374pp.** ✍

As a child, the young Aztec girl Malinali realizes that the legendary god Quetzalcoatl, or Feathered Serpent, will soon be returning to earth. Sold into slavery with the Maya, Malinali encounters Hernán Cortés, whom the Aztecs believe is Feathered Serpent in the flesh. She becomes his translator and lover, and in doing so helps him conquer Montezuma's empire in the name of Spain. She realizes only later in life that she and all of Mexico were deceived by the invader. There is plenty of sex and violence, and Falconer does well in presenting the Spanish conquest of Mexico in the sixteenth century from a feminine viewpoint.

Farcau, Bruce.

A Little Empire of Their Own. **Vandemere, 2000. 344pp.** ✍

In 1914, Charlotte, the former Habsburg Empress of Mexico, lives as a mad recluse in a shabby Belgian palace. She is still canny enough, though, to conceive a plot of revenge against the European dynasties that abandoned her husband Emperor Maximilian to his tragic fate in the 1860s. The story of their betrayal is told in flashback through the diary of Ricardo Gallardo, a Mexican war officer.

Harrigan, Lana M.

Ácoma: A Novel of Conquest. **Forge, 1997. 383pp.**

In 1598, Spanish conquistadors arrive in the land north of Mexico City, name it Nuevo México, and claim all of it for Spain. The Ácoma of the Áco pueblo along the Rio Grande are subjugated, turned into slaves, and mutilated for their attempted rebellion. One of their men, Rohona, wakes up from a fever to find himself a slave in the de Vizcarra household. The husband is a gold-mad maniac, but Rohona finds forbidden love with his gentle wife, María Angélica.

K'atsina: A Novel of Rebellion. **Forge, 1998. 350pp.**

In the mid-seventeenth century, the Inquisition, a formidable institution in Europe, has reached New Spain as well. Because of their continued "heretical" beliefs in ancient religions, the natives are in danger. They pray to their ancestors' spirits, the k'atsinas, to rescue them. When Augustín, a native of the Áco pueblo in training for the Jesuit priesthood, falls in love with a young Spanish woman, he finds his loyalties torn.

Hartmann, William K.

Cities of Gold. **Forge, 2002. 541pp.**

Two parallel stories unfold, both set in Arizona but 450 years apart. In 1989, Kevin Scott, a city planner hired by a corporation, surveys the area surrounding Tucson for possible development. In 1539, a Spanish explorer named Fray Marcos de Niza reports that he has found Coronado's seven cities of gold, which is the catalyst for Spanish colonization of the Southwest. In his research, Kevin discovers the truth about de Niza's claims, and this results in a legal battle over the appropriate use of land.

McCafferty, Kate.

Testimony of an Irish Slave Girl. **Viking, 2002. 206pp.** 📖

Cot Daley, an Irish girl kidnapped from her homeland and forcibly brought to Barbados, narrates a harrowing tale of white slavery in the seventeenth-century Caribbean. The treatment of the Irish is no better than that of the Africans, and the two groups join together in a slave revolt. Because Cot's story is told in flashback, it loses some immediacy, but the author successfully illuminates a time and event not widely known today.

The Middle East

Exotic drama set in long-ago times and in distant lands: Byzantium at its zenith (fifth through ninth centuries), the time of the Crusades to the Holy Land, and the inner lives of harem women in the later Ottoman Empire.

Bradshaw, Gillian.

The Bearkeeper's Daughter. **Houghton Mifflin, 1987. 310pp.** ✍

Sixth-century Constantinople, ruled by Justinian I and Theodora, is a city in its prime. Rumor has it that the empress was once a courtesan, the daughter of a bearkeeper. When a man claiming to be her illegitimate son turns up, she finds a place for him as a scribe, keeping his true identity secret from her husband.

Imperial Purple. **Houghton Mifflin, 1988. 324pp.**

Demetrias, a silk weaver in fifth-century Tyre, gets caught up in political conspiracies when she receives an order to weave a cloak of imperial purple, something that only those of the emperor's bloodline are permitted to wear.

Chadwick, Elizabeth.

The Falcons of Montabard. **St. Martin's Press, 2004. 480pp.**

It is 1120. Atoning for a crime he inadvertently committed, Sabin FitzSimon, bastard son of an English earl, makes a pilgrimage to the Holy Land. Along the way he joins the entourage of nobleman Edmund Strongfist. Edmund warns Sabin away from his daughter Annais, though they are immediately attracted to one another. This is a sequel to *The Winter Mantle*, annotated in "High Middle Ages," although the characters here are fictional. Both novels can be read independently.

Chamberlin, Ann.

Reign of the Favored Women Series. ✍

Chamberlin's trilogy of the royal women of the sixteenth-century Ottoman Empire explores gender roles and power both in and out of the harem.

Sofia. Forge, 1996. 364pp.

In 1562, Sofia Baffo, daughter of the governor of Corfu, is sold into slavery with orphaned sailor Giorgio Veneiro when their ship is overtaken by Turks. Brought to Constantinople, the proud and haughty Sofia rises high in the royal seraglio, while Giorgio, now a eunuch called Abdullah, must deal with the loss of his manhood.

The Sultan's Daughter. Forge, 1997. 348pp.

The eunuch Abdullah watches over the woman he loves, the Sultan's daughter Esmikhan, and sorrows with her over her failure to bear a child to her husband, the Grand Vizier. In the meantime Sofia, now called Safiye, secures her role as consort to Murad, the Sultan's heir.

Reign of the Favored Women. Forge, 1998. 384pp.

Safiye, the mother of Sultan Murad's heir, schemes with Machiavellian adroitness so that her son Muhammad will rule the Ottoman Empire one day. Plotting against her is Murad's mother, Nur Banu, who continues to rule the harem.

Duggan, Alfred.

In the 1950s and 1960s, Duggan (1903–1964) wrote many historical novels set in ancient Greece, the Roman Empire, and the Middle Ages. Though his writing style seems a bit stiff today, his novels are highly regarded for their accurate portrayal of the times. His best-known novels about the Crusades, below, were reprinted by Cassell in 2003.

Count Bohemond. **Pantheon, 1965. 281pp.** ✍ ★

This is another novel of the First Crusade, this time told from the viewpoint of one of its leaders. Bohemond, son of Robert Guiscard, rises from his position as a minor Norman overlord in Sicily to become a convincing diplomat and strong military commander.

Knight with Armour. **Coward-McCann, 1950. 306pp.**

Sir Roger, a Norman knight, heads south on the First Crusade in the late eleventh century. His adventure lasts three years and culminates in the taking of Jerusalem in 1099. Roger's revulsion toward the supposed "infidel" Turks is hardly politically accurate today, but it's appropriate to the era.

Falconer, Colin.

The Sultan's Harem. **Crown, 2004. 464pp.** ✍

Sultan Suleyman, called the Magnificent, has one main weakness: the Tartar concubine called Hürrem. Hürrem, constrained by her sex to remain in the harem, stops at nothing—gossip, poison, even murder—to achieve her goals of ruling the empire herself. Set in the sixteenth-century Ottoman Empire.

Goodman, Anthony.

The Shadow of God. **Sourcebooks, 2002. 444pp.** ✍

For 145 days in the year 1522, the Greek island of Rhodes, the last remaining Christian outpost in the Near East, was under siege by the Ottoman Turks under their young leader Suleiman the Magnificent and 200,000 Muslim warriors. Philippe de L'Isle Adam leads the Greek defense, and with 500 European knights tries to protect the fortressed city. Scenes showing the clash of cultures and the splendor of the Ottoman Empire are handled equally as well as the brutal battle and torture scenes.

Holland, Cecelia.

The Belt of Gold. **Knopf, 1984. 305pp.** ✍

In ninth-century Constantinople, Empress Irene is the sole ruler of Byzantium, but her throne is hardly secure. Into this hotbed of political intrigue comes a Frank named Hagen, on pilgrimage to the Holy Sepulcher, who becomes involved with one of Irene's handmaidens.

Jerusalem. **Forge, 1996. 318pp.** ✍

In 1187, Ranulph Fitzwilliam, a member of the Knights Templar, fights to save Jerusalem from the Islamic forces of Saladin. He must also reconcile his vow of chastity with his love for the Princess Sibylla, who struggles to hold her kingdom together after the death of her brother, the leper king Baudouin.

Rivele, Stephen J.

A Booke of Days. **Carroll & Graf, 1996. 436pp.**

To expiate his past sins, Roger, Duke of Lunel, leaves his wife home in Provence while he goes on Crusade to Jerusalem in 1096. In his journal, he recounts his adventures and his changing thoughts about the Turks, whose civilized behavior contrasts with the barbarism he observes among his Christian compatriots. He also falls in love with Yasmin, a Turkish poetess, provoking yet another crisis of faith and guilt.

Tarr, Judith.

Queen of Swords. **Forge, 1997. 464pp.** ✍

In the twelfth century, Lady Richildis, a Frankish noblewoman, journeys to Jerusalem in search of her brother Bertrand and ends up at the court of Melisende, Queen of the Crusader state of Jerusalem. Both are strong women, necessarily so; after chafing under the rule of her husband, Fulk of Anjou, Melisende claims the kingdom for herself when he dies in battle.

Taylor, Debbie.

The Fourth Queen. **Crown, 2003. 345pp.** ✍ 📖

In the eighteenth century, Helen Gloag leaves her Scottish homeland on a ship bound for Boston, where she heads in search of a better life. Kidnapped by Barbary pirates, she is sent to a Moroccan slave market, where she is purchased and brought to the imperial palace. Navigating the politics of the harem, she becomes the emperor's favorite and is selected to become his fourth and last official wife. This means that her life is in danger from the many other jealous women who would like to usurp her place.

Turteltaub, H. N.

Justinian. **Forge, 1998. 511pp.** ✍

In the late seventh century, Justinian II, Emperor of Byzantium, is an arrogant ruler, determined to expand the holdings of the Eastern Roman Empire at all costs. His self-centeredness causes the nobility to turn against him. Mutilated and exiled with his bodyguard to the faraway lands across the Black Sea, Justinian spends his time plotting his return to the throne. How he successfully regains his power ten years later is the story of the novel. The author is Byzantine scholar and alternate history novelist Harry Turtledove writing under a pseudonym.

Wallach, Janet.

Seraglio. **Doubleday, 2003. 316pp.** ✍ 📖

The author, a historian of the Middle East, gives credence to the tale that Empress Josephine's young cousin Aimée du Buc de Rivery was kidnapped by Algerian pirates while en route from France to her home in Martinique. Aimée is brought to the seraglio of the Ottoman ruler. Renamed Nakshidil, she becomes the ruler of the harem and the mother of the future sultan. Her tale is told in retrospect by her companion, a eunuch named Tulip, who is conveniently present at nearly every event of her life.

Asia, Africa, and the Antipodes

These novels make the exotic seem familiar—either via Western protagonists who discover new lands and peoples, or by telling the stories of sympathetic characters from faraway countries. There are still comparatively few traditional historical novels set in Asia or the South Pacific, and even fewer in Africa. Because of this, some older titles are listed below. For additional titles with non-Western settings, readers should investigate literary historical novels (Chapter 10) and the Romance chapter (Chapter 4) under romantic epics.

Ali, Thalassa.

<u>Singular Hostage Series.</u> `YA`

An involving saga of court intrigue, romance, and adventure in India during the British Raj. The last volume, *The Companions of Paradise*, will appear in 2005.

A Singular Hostage. Bantam, 2002. 349pp.

In 1838, young Englishwoman Mariana Givens travels to visit relatives in India to find a husband. She falls in love with the country instead. Mariana's affinity for translation leads her to join the entourage of India's Governor General on a mission to the Maharajah of Punjab, who holds babies hostage in hopes of ensuring their fathers' loyalty. She takes on new responsibility when she grows protective toward Saboor, a little boy whose life is threatened.

A Beggar at the Gate. Bantam, 2004. 301pp.

It is 1840. Mariana has married Hassan Sahib, Saboor's father, which alienates her from the British community in India. Mariana's relatives strongly disapprove of the relationship and pressure her to get a divorce. She hesitates, as she has grown close to Saboor, and wants to explore her husband's religious beliefs further.

Brennert, Alan.

Moloka'i. St. Martin's Press, 2003. 389pp. 📖

At the age of seven, Rachel Kalama's family discovers that she has leprosy. They send her from the tropical paradise of Honolulu to the isolated leper colony on the island of Moloka'i. There, she makes friends and forms a new family with other lepers, including her uncle Pono, whose relatives have abandoned them. Rachel grows to adulthood on Moloka'i and marries. Despite the tragic subject, this is an uplifting story.

Buck, Pearl S.

Best known for her masterwork *The Good Earth*, Pulitzer and Nobel Prize winner Pearl Buck, daughter of American missionaries in China, also wrote historical novels set in her adopted homeland.

Imperial Woman. J. Day, 1956. 376pp. ★ ✍

A biographical novel of Tzu-Hsi, the last Empress of China in the late nineteenth century, this begins not with her reign but with her younger years, when she was known as Yehonala—before she was hand-picked by the emperor to be his concubine. In the imperial court, Yehonala loses her innocence and learns how to navigate her way through personal and political intrigues.

Peony. J. Day, 1948. 312pp. ★

In nineteenth-century Kaifeng, a prominent Chinese city with a significant Jewish population, a Chinese girl named Peony becomes a bondmaid to a wealthy Jewish family. The entire cast of characters struggles with the problems of religion and assimilation.

Cooney, Eleanor, and Daniel Altieri.

The Court of the Lion. Morrow, 1989. 920pp. ✍

This lengthy, incredibly detailed novel of the T'ang dynasty brings eighth-century China to life. When Emperor Minghuang's favorite son dies unexpectedly, rumors of murder flood the court, and the emperor retreats into his grief. His empress banished under charges of witchcraft, his favored consort gone mad, there is nothing to prevent Mongol invader An Lu-shan from taking over the empire—nothing, that is, except the sagacity of Kao Li-sheh, the loyal chief eunuch.

Dion, Frederic.

The Blue Wolf. St. Martin's Press, 2003. 384pp. ✍

First published in France and England under the pseudonym "Homeric," Dion's novel is a large-scale biographical novel of Temudjin, better known as Genghis

Khan, the Mongol warrior who consolidated power for himself in the late twelfth and early thirteenth centuries. His power proves his downfall. His former friends grow jealous, and his enemies begin to gather.

Elegant, Simon.

A Floating Life: The Adventures of Li Po. **Ecco, 1997. 312pp.** ✍

T'ang Dynasty (eighth-century) poet Li Po is the subject of this biographical novel, in which the great writer narrates his life story—with all its adventures—to a young boy named Wang.

Holland, Cecelia.

Until the Sun Falls. **Atheneum, 1969. 491pp.**

It is 1237, and Genghis Khan has been dead for ten years. The Mongol armies, under their greatest general Sabotai, storm across Russia and Eastern Europe, conquering cities one by one. The action is seen from the point of view of Psin, Khan of the Merkits, but in her portrait of a complex man fully of his time, Holland also shows his relationships with his wives and children.

McCullough, Colleen.

Morgan's Run. **Simon & Schuster, 2000. 604pp.** ✍

In 1787, Richard Morgan is a gunsmith and tavern keeper who makes the mistake of reporting on his boss's illegal activities. In revenge, he is falsely accused of a crime and transported as a felon to Australia's Botany Bay colony. The voyage is difficult, but Morgan stands out for his bravery, and on Norfolk Island he discovers love and a new life. McCullough took a break from her <u>Masters of Rome</u> series (annotated in the beginning of this chapter) to write this novel based on the life of her husband's ancestor.

Shaw, Patricia.

Shaw writes exciting historical novels set in Australia, most of which are fictional portraits of the early settlers of Queensland. While her novels have waned in popularity in the States, she continues to publish frequently in her native Australia, and in Britain and Canada.

Cry of the Rain Bird. **St. Martin's Press, 1995. 346pp.**

Corby Morgan and his wife Jessie leave England with dreams of buying a sugar plantation in Australia, but once they've arrived, trouble sets in. Not only do they have to weather harsh storms, they have difficulty managing their aboriginal workers, and both are tempted by extramarital affairs.

Fires of Fortune. **St. Martin's Press, 1996. 407pp.**

In nineteenth-century Brisbane, Ben Buckman is appalled that a wealthy doctor won't treat his Aborigine mother simply because of her race.

When she dies for lack of treatment, Ben lashes out at this injustice and pays the price. He is redeemed by the love of Phoebe, the doctor's daughter.

Where the Willows Weep. **St. Martin's Press, 1995. 376pp.**

In late 1850s Australia, Laura Maskey is nothing but trouble to her parents, particularly when she runs away from an arranged marriage. Her preferred suitor is cattle station owner Paul MacNamara, but he gets drawn into the violence that springs up between ranchers and the Aborigines.

Chapter 3

Multi-Period Epics

Novels in this chapter can be called epic in every sense of the word. Through them, readers can view a culture from its beginnings in the distant past until today. Most take the form of a series of chronological snapshots, which demonstrate how characters in a number of different time periods react to the eras in which they live. Other novels focus on an object, legacy, or faith that is passed down through the centuries, affecting a number of people over the years. Taken in their entirety, multi-period epics give us a comprehensive picture of a civilization or geographic area, showing how the land and its people have changed over time. While character development of these novels' human inhabitants is not always their strong point, the setting itself may be the most important character of all.

Multi-period epics may not only be hard to put down, they can also be hard to pick up. Literally, that is, because these hefty tomes can easily number well over 500 pages, typically of miniscule type. Meticulously researched, they are packed to the brim with words, characters, and history. Though this is not a large subgenre, it is an important one, for the process of historical change as told through fiction is what historical novels are all about.

Since some multi-period epics focus on the generations of one particular family over a thousand years or more, they can be thought of as the ultimate family saga, though their scope is broader than most that fall into this category. Readers who enjoy these novels may also want to investigate sagas (Chapter 5), in particular those that belong to a multi-part series. Christian fiction (Chapter 11) also boasts several multi-period epics.

Worldwide Scope

Nothing less than the entire history of the world, retold as an epic novel; Barbara Wood's novel stands apart.

Wood, Barbara.

Wood's epic novels (see also *Sacred Ground*, later in this chapter) aren't written with the same level of detail as those of James Michener or Edward Rutherfurd, but her writing has a spiritual flavor the others lack.

The Blessing Stone. St. Martin's Press, 2003. 464pp.

Wood retells world history in her own distinct fashion, through eight historical episodes linked via a mysterious blue stone. The stone becomes a talisman for a young woman in prehistoric Africa, who alone of her tribe has the ability to rely on reason over instinct. The subsequent stories tell of matriarchal tribes of the ancient Near East, goddess-worshippers in the Jordan River Valley, early Christian martyrs in first-century Rome, abbey life in late Anglo-Saxon England, a young woman's adventures in sixteenth-century Germany and Asia, passion and revenge in 1720 Martinique, and wagons west on the nineteenth-century American frontier. To Wood's credit, the stories are all unique: some light, some dark, some more realistic than others.

The British Isles

Long novels exploring the fascinating history of the British Isles from their pagan, prehistoric past through today, concentrating mainly on cities in England and Ireland.

Rutherfurd, Edward.

With his lengthy, epic sagas of the history of England, Rutherfurd can be called the British heir to James Michener's legacy, but without the strong social agenda of his predecessor.

The Dublin Saga.

When complete, this two-volume series will encompass the entire known history of Dublin, Ireland, from its prehistoric past through the twentieth century. Family trees included.

The Princes of Ireland. Crown, 2004. 776pp.

Beginning in pre-Christian Ireland and continuing through the sixteenth century, Rutherfurd introduces a wide cast of characters who interact with one another and the land. Historical periods include the times of the great High Kings of Tara, the coming of St. Patrick, Viking raids and the founding of Dublin in the tenth century, the glory of Brian Boru's leadership, the Norman invasion in the twelfth century, and Henry VIII's desecration of Dublin's churches and monasteries. Throughout it all, Ireland's political and religious struggles with England loom large.

The Forest. **Crown, 2000. 598pp.**

The New Forest, which encompasses a hundred thousand acres in southern England, is best known as the place where King William Rufus, the Conqueror's son, was mysteriously killed by an arrow. This novel begins in 1099, a year before Rufus's death, and continues to the present. Rutherfurd enlivens this mystical place with lively characters, from noblemen and ladies to humble woodcutters and peasants.

London. **Crown, 1997. 829pp.**

From its Roman origins through the signing of the Magna Carta and up to the modern day, Rutherfurd recounts the history of London through a series of interconnected stories that detail the lives of its inhabitants. Some of the families from *Sarum* who left the countryside for the big city make an appearance here.

Sarum. **Crown, 1987. 897pp.** ★

Sarum is the old Roman name for Salisbury, England, the home of Stonehenge. In a series of interconnected vignettes, this area's history over 10,000 years is seen through the eyes of five families living on the Salisbury Plain from the last Ice Age until the 1980s.

Welch, Robert.
Groundwork. **Dufour, 1997. 202pp.**

Welch's novel of the past 400 years of Irish history manages to achieve something of the scope of Michener without the length: More than just a family saga, it's a novel of Ireland in microcosm. Through vignettes detailing the lives of the Condon and O'Dwyer families of County Munster, the author illuminates Anglo–Irish relations from Elizabethan times up to the twentieth century. **Literary.**

Wright, Patricia.
♠ *I Am England*. **St. Martin's Press, 1987. 398pp.**

The story of Furnace Green, a small village in the countryside of Sussex, England, is rendered in five separate installments: from the worshippers of the pagan god Tiw in AD 70, past the years just following the Norman Conquest, up through the forging of the cannon that helped defeat the Spanish Armada in the sixteenth century. Georgette Heyer Historical Novel Prize.

That Near and Distant Place. **St. Martin's Press, 1988. 431pp.**

The lives of the residents of Furnace Green continue in this sequel to *I Am England*, which takes up the story of this Sussex village beginning with Cromwell's rebellion and continuing until the modern day.

Europe

Religious and social conflicts, prevalent throughout European history, are the themes here. The Jews, persecuted for their beliefs for the past 2,000 years, take center stage in Gross's and Halter's epic novels.

Gross, Joel.

The Books of Rachel. Seaview, 1979. 440pp.

Over 500 years, beginning in Spain in the fifteenth century, the first daughter born to each successive generation of the Cuheno family is given the name Rachel, along with the heirloom of a family diamond. These women, all proud of their Jewish heritage, rely on their faith to survive difficult and painful times, from the Spanish Inquisition through the horrors of the Second World War.

The Lives of Rachel. New American Library, 1984. 424pp.

In this continuation of the story begun in *The Books of Rachel*, New Yorker Rachel Kane is visiting Jerusalem's Western Wall, a major symbol of her Jewish faith, with her husband, in the present day. Here, she begins to imagine the lives of her distant ancestors. Via this introduction, Gross takes us even farther back in time to link together the lives of five strong, courageous women bearing the name of Rachel—in ancient Judea, Rome of 63 BC, fifth-century London, eighth-century Byzantium, and eleventh-century Mainz.

Halter, Marek.

The Book of Abraham. Holt, 1986. 722pp.

Abraham the Scribe is the ancestor both of the author and of this novel, which recounts the struggles that European Jews have encountered over the past 2,000 years. Its sweep takes us from their origins in first-century Jerusalem to early medieval Toledo to 1940s Warsaw—where the author's grandfather, another Abraham, encounters the Gestapo.

The Children of Abraham. Arcade, 1990. 377pp.

Though not an epic in itself, Marek's second novel continues where *The Book of Abraham* left off, detailing the lives of the Halter family throughout the twentieth century, dispersed throughout the world after the horrors of the Holocaust. Standing alone, this is also an adventure story, as Halter and his cousins scour the globe to solve a relative's murder.

Michener, James A.

James Michener's panoramic historical novels are meticulously researched presentations of the history of a place as seen through the eyes of its inhabitants. Many include family trees on the endpapers, detailing the genealogy of the families involved in the story from beginning to end. Though entertaining, Michener's epics don't shrink from exploring serious themes, such as the repression of one race or people by another. Michener is so well associated with this subgenre that the term "Micheneresque" is frequently used to describe all other novels written in this style. *Poland* is Michener's only European epic; the remainder are listed according to their setting.

Poland. **Random House, 1983. 556pp. ★**

> Part fiction, part fact, *Poland* retells the story of the country's many struggles for freedom from 1204 until the present, from the points of view of three families living in a small village. More than anything else, it conveys the spirit of Polish national pride, which somehow manages to survive unscathed through the centuries even though the land and its people do not.

Rutherfurd, Edward.

Russka. **Crown, 1991. 760pp.**

> The author's only epic with a non-British setting, in *Russka* he continues to write on a broad canvas, this time telling the story of Russia and its people from the first century AD until the present. Three rival families —the noble Babrovs, the merchant Suvorins, and the peasant Romanovs (later, revolutionaries and rulers)—vie for supremacy as their descendants rise and fall in power with the times.

Williams, Jeanne.

The Cave Dreamers. **Avon, 1983. 573pp.**

> In this feminine version of the Michener-style epic, Ezda, a woman living in Basque country in prehistoric times, is the guardian of the "cave of always summer," a secret haven for women that is beautifully painted with images of birds. In six separate historical episodes, we see the history of the Basque people from then until today, as the secret of the cave is passed from mother to daughter over many generations.

The Heaven Sword. **Avon, 1985. 448pp.**

> The heaven sword of the title was forged at a pagan altar on an island in ancient Scandinavia and passed from woman to woman down through the ages. It follows the female descendants of one family from Lapland to Byzantium to Mexico, strengthening the bonds between women and their chosen men over time.

The United States

Written by Americans, these epics demonstrate pride in the authors' national heritage. Most are about the history of the original thirteen colonies, though Michener and Barbara Wood both add some cultural diversity to the mix.

Hamill, Pete.

Forever. **Little, Brown, 2003. 613pp.**

> Hamill, a well-known journalist, pays homage to his hometown in this unusual literary epic. While most epic historical novels show stages of a locale's development through their contemporary inhabitants, this work sees over 250 years of the Big Apple, New York City, from 1740 until

September 11, 2001, through the eyes of a single man. Cormac O'Connor is an Irishman who has been given a remarkable gift. In exchange for having saved the life of a former African slave, Cormac is rewarded with immortality as long as he never leaves the city's bounds.

Jakes, John.

Charleston. Dutton, 2002. 464pp.

This Southern city's story is told through members of the Bell family, beginning with Sydney Greech, its progenitor, who in 1720 is convinced by his fiancée to change his surname to the more aristocratic-sounding Bell. Jakes recounts the history of Charles Town (later Charleston), South Carolina, over several generations from the years just prior to the Revolution up through Reconstruction.

Martin, William.

Annapolis. Warner, 1996. 685pp.

In this patriotic military epic, the Staffords and the Parishes, two seafaring families in Annapolis, Maryland, in the mid-eighteenth century, observe their city change through eight generations—from their arrival in the New World through the Civil War and continuing on to the modern day.

Back Bay. Crown, 1979. 437pp.

The history of Boston is seen through six generations of the powerful Pratt family, each of whose members—from colonial America until the present—must deal with a family curse until one descendant finally figures out the solution.

Cape Cod. Warner, 1991. 652pp.

The author jumps back and forth in time in this epic homage to Cape Cod, as seen through the eyes of several prominent families from the time of the Pilgrims until the early 1990s.

Harvard Yard. Warner, 2003. 580pp.

Martin's most recent novel is as much the history of New England and America as it is the history of Harvard University in Cambridge, Massachusetts. Peter Fallon, a historian introduced in *Back Bay*, learns about the hidden existence of a long-lost Shakespearean play, one possibly given by the Bard himself to Harvard's founder. To discover its current whereabouts, Fallon sorts through documentation belonging to the Wedge family, the play's original guardians, down through the generations. His searches reveal 300 years of Harvard's history, from the time of the witch hunts through the 1960s. A combination epic and bibliomystery.

Michener, James A.

Alaska. Random House, 1988. 868pp. ★

From prehistory to the Klondike Gold Rush to its successful bid for statehood in 1959, Michener retells the history of America's forty-ninth state in epic form. In essence, *Alaska* is a saga of exploitation and neglect, both of the land's native peoples and of its natural resources.

🎗 *Centennial*. Random House, 1974. 909pp.

> Written partly to celebrate the bicentennial of the United States, *Centennial*'s story is that of Colorado, which was granted statehood in 1876. Set in the fictional town of Centennial, Colorado, Michener takes us from the dinosaur era up to 1974, with chapters detailing relations among the land, its animals, Native Americans, and the state's white settlers. Western Heritage Award.

Chesapeake. Random House, 1978. 865pp.

> In 1583, a Susquehannock Indian named Pentaquod is led downstream to the Chesapeake Bay, and here he settles in with the native peoples and raises a family. From then to the arrival of John Smith to the Watergate scandal of the 1970s, Michener writes of the lives of the people who lived along the eastern shores of Maryland and Virginia.

Hawaii. Random House, 1959. 937pp.

> The great Pacific melting pot that is America's fiftieth state is shown in incredible detail in this novel, which takes us from prehistory until the middle of the twentieth century. Hawaii's growth from a volcanic island paradise until statehood in 1959 is shown through the eyes of the ethnic groups who contributed to its development and exploitation, including the English, Americans, Japanese, Chinese, and native Hawaiians.

Texas. Random House, 1985. 1,096pp. ★

> Among Michener's "big books," at over 1,000 pages this is the grandfather of them all. A Governor's Task Force composed of Texans from a variety of ethnic backgrounds comes together to decide on an appropriate curriculum for a required seventh-grade history class. Each chapter retells a story describing a different period in Texas history, from its beginnings as a Spanish colony in the sixteenth century until the middle of the 1980s. The state of Texas is presented as colorful, vivid, and larger than life.

Sandburg, Carl.
Remembrance Rock. Harcourt, Brace, 1948. 1067pp.

> Best known for his poetry and biographical studies, Carl Sandburg was also a successful novelist. He tells of the United States' beginnings from 1608 England through the bombing of Pearl Harbor.

Wood, Barbara.
Sacred Ground. St. Martin's Press, 2001. 340pp.

> The 2,000-year history of the fictional Topaa tribe on the California coast is introduced by way of Erica Tyler, a present-day anthropologist who fights to rescue artifacts from a mysterious cave revealed after a recent earthquake. In a parallel storyline, Marimi, a Topaa Indian from long ago, and her descendants struggle for freedom both for the land and for themselves.

Zaroulis, Nancy.

Massachusetts. Fawcett, 1991. 709pp.

Bartholomew Revell arrives in Plymouth aboard the Mayflower in 1620. As his station rises from apprentice to merchant to shipping magnate, so do his family's prospects. Over the next 350 years, Zaroulis takes us through the growth of her home state through dramatizations of major historical episodes: the Salem witch trials, encounters with the Indians, the Boston Tea Party, industrialization and anti-Irish prejudice in the state's mill towns, and the Sacco and Vanzetti trials. Naturally, there's at least one Revell family member present at all of these events.

Canada

Members of the First Nations and white settlers both appear in these two volumes about Canadian history.

Assiniwi, Bernard.

The Beothuk Saga. St. Martin's Press, 2000. 341pp.

The Beothuk were the native people of Newfoundland, the first inhabitants of the North American continent to meet European explorers a thousand years ago. In this somber epic, through Adin (the first Beothuk) and his descendants, we see European history through the eyes of a tribe whose members, the victims of white men's diseases and cruel bounty hunting raids, were completely annihilated by the early nineteenth century. **Literary.**

Cruise, David, and Allison Griffiths.

Vancouver. HarperCollins, 2003. 752pp.

Cruise and Griffiths, a Canadian husband-and-wife team best known for their nonfiction exposés, were asked by HarperCollins to write the ultimate epic about Vancouver, British Columbia—the most cosmopolitan of cities. It begins in 13,000 BC in what is now Alaska, when young Manto of the Yupick tribe settles there with his wife, and ends twelve episodes later, in 2003, with another woman of native descent. In between, the authors take us through sixteen centuries of the city's exciting history, with focus on immigrants' experiences and the role of the family.

Latin America and the Caribbean

Four novels about the culturally diverse and occasionally violent history of countries located south of the American border.

Michener, James A.

Caribbean. Random House, 1989. 672pp. ★

In the first sentence, Michener describes the chief character of his novel as the alluring Caribbean Sea, and in doing so begins a tale of the islands and people who inhabit them from the year 1310 to the 1980s. Sixteen vignettes illustrate the history of the Caribbean and its invasion by a variety of European cultures, including the Spanish, English, and French.

Mexico. **Random House, 1992. 625pp.** ★

Norman Clay is an American journalist, born in Mexico, who returns to his homeland after twenty years' absence to report on a showdown between two famous bullfighters. One of them is of Indian ancestry, the other Spanish. In the process, Norman gets caught up in the story of his own Mexican ancestors, who come from three different ethnic groups: Mexican Indian, Spanish, and English. The stories, taking place over a 1,500-year period, range from the gory sacrifices of the native Mexican tribes to the coming of the Spaniards to the war with the United States in the mid-nineteenth century.

Uys, Errol Lincoln.

Brazil. **Simon & Schuster, 1986. 1000pp.**

The Cavalcantis and da Silva families are the protagonists of this sprawling epic saga that sees the country of Brazil from its beginnings as a Portuguese colony in the fifteenth century to its growth into a modern nation in the twentieth century. Through it all, readers will view clashes with the native tribes, prospecting expeditions in the Brazilian wilderness, and the growth of the land's coffee empires. Uys, a native South African, was James Michener's research assistant during the writing of *The Covenant*, and this is evident in his style.

Williams, Jeanne.

So Many Kingdoms. **Avon, 1986. 379pp.**

This epic history of Brazil is shown through the eyes of six of its women, beginning with Rachel, a Portuguese orphan who arrives in the nineteenth century to marry a wealthy plantation owner.

The Middle East

Michener, James A.

The Source. **Random House, 1965. 989pp.**

During a present-day archaeological dig at the fictional site of Makor ("the source") in modern-day Israel, anthropologists recover layer upon layer of artifacts, each of which belongs to a different period of the region's history. The dig is a framework around which the author builds his tale, which recounts fifteen separate episodes over 12,000 years of the history of the Middle East. Not all the stories end happily, which is in keeping with the violent history of the region.

Africa

Michener, James A.
The Covenant. Random House, 1980. 877pp.

South Africa over the last 15,000 years gets the Michener treatment in *The Covenant*. The focus here is on three families—the African Nxumalos, the Afrikaner Van Doorns, and the English Saltwoods—who interact with each other as well as with the native peoples.

Chapter 4

Romancing the Past

Romantic historical novels involve readers emotionally with engaging stories that celebrate the love between two people—most typically a woman and a man. Readers enjoy romances because they provide a means of escaping from their day-to-day lives into a world where love takes center stage. Romances set in the past let readers live vicariously through the experiences of lovers from earlier periods of history, which makes the sense of escapism even more paramount. While being entertained, readers can see how the political atmosphere, social factors, and everyday life of the times influence the actions of the heroes and heroines.

While traditional romance novels conclude with happily-ever-after endings, the novels in this chapter don't always follow this formula. Historical romantic fiction can be divided into three categories, depending on the scope of the novel and also on whether the history or the romance is more prominent in the storyline. The eras, geographical settings, and pace used by the authors of historical romantic fiction will also differ for each subcategory.

Romantic epics feature sweeping drama, vividly described, colorful settings, and star-crossed romances. They play out on a wide canvas, and their heroes and heroines often get caught up in major political events from history. A classic example is Margaret Mitchell's *Gone with the Wind. Romantic historicals*, set on a smaller scale than romantic epics, strike a balance between the romance and the historical content: Both are equally important to the storyline. Both romantic epics and romantic historicals tend to be long books, and the couples in these novels may or may not have a happy ending.

Historical romances, on the other hand, follow the formula of the romance genre in that the romance ends happily. The romantic story also forms the major plotline of the book; although historical details are important, major political events occur in the background. These novels tend to be shorter than romantic epics or romantic historicals, though there are exceptions. (People who enjoy reading family sagas with a romantic aspect should also investigate romantic sagas in Chapter 5.)

Romantic Epics

Romantic epics are novels in which a protagonist, usually female, searches for love in a vibrantly described historical setting. These lengthy novels contain sweeping drama, lush historical imagery, and larger-than-life characters who waltz in and out of history, typically interacting with many real-life characters and events. Romantic epics feature star-crossed lovers who take on the world to stay together, though they are continually forced apart—by duty, circumstance, or choice. The heroines are bright, beautiful, and courageous, while the heroes are attractive, dashing, and intriguing. The pair may or may not be perfect for each other, though they find themselves passionately drawn together, often against their better judgment.

Exotic settings are common to these novels, and many romantic epics are set in more than one location, as the heroine and hero undertake dangerous voyages or are forced to live their own lives when they are separated from one another. The brilliantly described locale, painted on a broad canvas yet illustrated down to the last detail, plays into the dramatic impact of these novels, as if to emphasize that these are extraordinary people living in extraordinary times.

Many of these novels take place against a wartime setting or a period of political upheaval, which adds to the drama and tension. The historical events in these novels usually play a strong role both in keeping the hero and heroine apart and in bringing them back together. Social factors, such as class barriers between the pair, can also serve as a challenge to the protagonists.

There is no standard pattern to the plot of romantic epics. Both the hero and heroine may find love with more than one partner, although only one of them is typically his or her true soul mate. Although these novels usually end optimistically, the hopeful conclusion may or may not refer to the romance. In most romantic epics, the heroine emerges triumphant, confident that the decisions she's had to make were the best ones for her, given the tumultuous times she was forced to live in.

Readers who appreciate the broad sweep of history in romantic epics may also appreciate multi-period epics (Chapter 3). Also, some historical fantasy novels (Chapter 14), like Marion Zimmer Bradley's *The Mists of Avalon* and Diana Paxson's *The White Raven*, may also appeal to fans of romantic epics, as they follow a strong-willed heroine on a romantic, magical journey.

Donati, Sara.

Wilderness Series.

Sequels to James Fenimore Cooper's *The Last of the Mohicans*, Sara Donati's novels are set on the New York frontier in the late eighteenth century. Donati has also written a literary historical novel (*Homestead*, Chapter 10) under her real name, Rosina Lippi.

Keywords: New York—Early United States

Into the Wilderness. Bantam, 1998. 691pp.

In 1792, Englishwoman Elizabeth Middleton, a spinster at age twenty-nine, comes to her father's lands in New York State ostensibly to become a schoolteacher. Soon she discovers that her father has plans to marry her off to wealthy doctor Richard Todd. However, the man she loves is Nathaniel Bonner, a rough outdoorsman who is the son of "Hawkeye" Bonner, the hero of Cooper's classic novel. Elizabeth's future inheritance—her father's lands—is the source of the rivalry among Nathaniel, Todd, and the Mahican tribespeople, who believe the land to be their own.

Dawn on a Distant Shore. Bantam, 2000. 463pp.

Elizabeth and Nathaniel are happily married with twins, but fate keeps them apart. To rescue his father, Nathaniel travels to Montreal, but when his own life is in jeopardy, Elizabeth bundles up her children and takes them on a frozen journey north.

Lake in the Clouds. Bantam, 2002. 613pp.

In 1802, Hannah Bonner, Nathaniel's daughter by his Mahican first wife, struggles with her mixed-race identity and her decision to pursue a career in medicine. While nursing a runaway slave back to health, she puts her family in danger, but the bounty hunter assigned to recapture the slave turns out to be Hannah's childhood sweetheart, Liam Kirby.

Fire Along the Sky. Bantam, 2004. 624pp.

This latest volume picks up the Bonners' story ten years after *Lake in the Clouds* ends. Hannah Bonner comes home to Paradise a changed person, and war with Britain is on the horizon. Elizabeth and Nathaniel's son Daniel itches to head to war, while his sister Lily lives her own life in Montreal.

Donnelly, Jennifer.
The Tea Rose. **Thomas Dunne, 2002. 544pp.**

Fiona Finnegan is an Irish working-class girl in East London of 1888. After her father's murder, she is torn from her lover Joe Bristow and flees to America with her younger brother to avoid being hunted down by the tea baron responsible for her father's death. It takes ten years of hard work, but Fiona builds a tea empire of her own from the ground up—always dreaming of the day when she can return home and take revenge on the man who destroyed her family.

> **Keywords:** England—Victorian Era; New York—Reconstruction and Gilded Age

Fitzgerald, Valerie.
Zemindar. **Bantam, 1981. 763pp.**

Laura Hewitt, a twenty-four-year-old spinster, accompanies her wealthy cousin Emily to colonial India in 1857. There she falls in love both with India and with Oliver Erskine, the half-brother of Emily's new husband. Unlike many of the British, Oliver is sympathetic to the plight of India's people, and, though English, is accepted by them. Though Oliver can predict the coming of the Sepoy Rebellion, he is powerless to stop it, and he and Laura are soon caught up in one of the bloodiest revolts in modern history. Georgette Heyer Historical Novel Prize.

> **Keywords:** India—19th Century

Gabaldon, Diana.

Outlander Series. ★

A combination of time travel, epic romance, and plentiful historical detail make Gabaldon's novels hard to pigeonhole. They are enjoyed by numerous romance fans but are meatier than most works in the genre. The story begins as Claire Randall, a former combat nurse during World War II, goes back in time to eighteenth-century Scotland, where she falls in love with Scotsman Jamie Fraser. But Claire is married, and she remains torn between her present-day husband and the romantic Scotsman who lived two centuries earlier. The series sees Claire and Jamie trying to prevent the loss of Scottish lives at the Battle of Culloden in 1745, and, much later, riding out the trouble that the American Revolution will bring to the colonies and to England. Claire's certain knowledge of what the future holds, though, is only of so much help when the pair are forced to live through it all. A nonfiction work by Gabaldon, *The Outlandish Companion* (Delacorte, 1999), provides background to the series.

Keywords: Scotland—18th Century; North Carolina—American Revolution

Outlander. Delacorte, 1991. 627pp.

Claire Randall, back from her stint in World War II and on her second honeymoon with her husband in Scotland, touches a boulder within an ancient stone circle. This brings her back in time to 1743 Scotland, where she becomes caught up in a world filled with spies, rebellions, and a handsome red-haired Scotsman named Jamie Fraser. RITA Award.

Dragonfly in Amber. Delacorte, 1992. 743pp.

In 1968, twenty years after her adventures in *Outlander*, Claire's husband Frank has died. Claire and her adult daughter Brianna journey to Scotland, hoping to learn what happened to Claire's eighteenth-century husband, Jamie, after she left him to return to the present. Claire revisits her past adventures with Jamie, in which the pair do all they can to prevent Bonnie Prince Charlie from returning to Scotland in 1745. In a contemporary story, Claire puzzles over the best way to tell Brianna about her true paternity.

Voyager. Delacorte, 1994. 870pp.

After discovering that Jamie survived the 1745 Battle of Culloden, Claire travels back into the past to find her lost love. After reuniting passionately with him, the pair escape the wrath of the English by fleeing to the West Indies, where Jamie's nephew has been taken prisoner aboard a pirate ship.

Drums of Autumn. Delacorte, 1997. 880pp.

Claire and Jamie turn up in 1760s Charleston, South Carolina, where they live among unhappy expatriate Scots and try to prevent the American Revolution. Their daughter Brianna, romantically involved with a man from the present day, travels back into the past herself to try to prevent Claire and Jamie's deaths.

The Fiery Cross. Delacorte, 2001. 979pp.

In the Carolinas in 1771, the American Revolution will soon be under way, and Claire knows that war is unavoidable. Brianna and her husband Roger are happily married with a son, but all of their lives will be threatened if Jamie fights against England in the upcoming war.

Goudge, Elizabeth.

The Child from the Sea. **Coward-McCann, 1970. 736pp.** ✍

The romantic and tragically short life of Lucy Walter, the Welsh mistress and possibly secret wife of England's Charles II in the mid-seventeenth century, is portrayed here with great sympathy. According to most historians, Lucy was a woman of loose morals who took advantage of her relationship with the future king. In Goudge's eyes she becomes his loving but wronged first wife, initially accepted by his family but abandoned for political reasons when it came time for Charles to claim his throne.

> **Keywords:** England—Stuart Era

Hague, Nora.

Letters from an Age of Reason. **Morrow, 2001. 648pp.**

This epistolary novel—told entirely in the form of letters and diaries—recounts the love story of Arabella Leeds, born and bred in New York's high society in the 1860s, and Aubrey "Bree" Paxton, a "high yellow" Southern house servant who can easily pass for white. They tell their own stories separately, recounting their meeting one day when both are visiting Europe. Arabella has no idea that in their own country, Bree would be considered black, and therefore completely inappropriate as a love interest. By that point, of course, it's too late.

> **Keywords:** Louisiana—Early United States; England—Victorian Era

Kaye, M. M.

The Far Pavilions. **St. Martin's Press, 1978. 957pp.** ★

In her most famous novel, Kaye weaves a tapestry of romance, war, and adventure set between the Sepoy Mutiny of 1857 and the second Afghan War. Ashton Pelham-Martyn, known as Ash, is a British subject raised in India who returns to England for a military education. Due to his upbringing, he discovers he really doesn't belong in either world, something that attracts him to Anjuli, an Indian princess of mixed race. The story is not only theirs, however, but also that of the Indian subcontinent in the last half of the nineteenth century, with its complicated class restrictions and shaky political situations.

> **Keywords:** India—19th Century

Shadow of the Moon. **Messner, 1957. 351pp.**

Against the backdrop of the Great Sepoy Mutiny in 1857 India, Winter de Ballesteros, of English-Spanish noble heritage, falls in love with the dashing Alex Randall, her husband's aide.

> **Keywords:** India—19th Century

Trade Wind. **Coward-McCann, 1963. 492pp.**

In 1859 Zanzibar, Boston blueblood Hero Athena Hollis falls under the spell of Rory Frost, a slave trader and overall scoundrel.

Keywords: Zanzibar—19th Century

Kellerman, Faye.

The Quality of Mercy. **Morrow, 1989. 607pp.** ✍

Shakespeare's Dark Lady and the daughter of Queen Elizabeth's Jewish physician —one and the same? Rebecca Lopez is the beautiful daughter of a family of Spanish Jews who disguise themselves as Anglicans to avoid the Inquisition. Will Shakespeare is still an up-and-coming playwright, not yet the brilliant actor or wordsmith that history knows him to be. The two fall in love while investigating the death of Will's mentor and friend, though their closeness promises danger for them both. It is a bawdy tale appropriate to its era, though Kellerman's portrayal of Queen Elizabeth as a closet lesbian goes a bit too far.

Keywords: England—Tudor Era

Koen, Karleen.

Through a Glass Darkly Series.

Adventure in romance in the wildly decadent London and Paris of the early eighteenth century, and later, in pre-Revolutionary America.

Through a Glass Darkly. **Random House, 1986. 738pp.**

As fifteen-year-old Barbara Alderley grows to womanhood, her grandmother, the Duchess of Tamworth, plans for her to marry her late husband's friend, Roger Montgeoffry. While Barbara falls in love easily with the much older Roger, and he's intrigued by the husky-voiced Barbara, he loves her mainly for the lands he acquires through their marriage. This isn't the only secret that Roger's keeping from her, either.

Keywords: England—Georgian Era

Now Face to Face. **Random House, 1995. 733pp.**

In the sequel to *Through a Glass Darkly*, Barbara Montgeoffry, Countess Devane, is a twenty-year-old widow in 1721. She sails to Virginia to make something out of her family's tobacco plantation. She steadily grows stronger and more mature, not hesitating to take action against the evils of slavery. Barbara returns home only when the timing is right, and becomes romantically involved with a Jacobite spy.

Keywords: Virginia—Colonial Period

Liu, Aimee E.

Cloud Mountain. **Warner, 1997. 574pp.** ✍

In 1906 San Francisco, Hope Newfield meets Liang Po-yu, a Chinese scholar and revolutionary, while she is teaching his students how to speak English. They fall in love, marry, and raise a family, ignoring the prejudice that comes with mixed-race unions. After 1911, the entire family moves to Shanghai in the pursuit of freedom in the new Republic, but the land proves dangerous for them all. Liu wrote this novel based on the lives of her own grandparents.

Keywords: California—20th Century; China—20th Century

Martin, James Conroyd.

Push Not the River. Thomas Dunne, 2003. 432pp. ✍

Countess Anna Maria Berezowska, a noblewoman in late eighteenth-century Poland, fights for herself and her country during a time of great upheaval in Polish history: the rise and fall of the Third of May Constitution, a document that promised democratic reform for the Polish people. Sent away to live with her Aunt Stella after her parents' deaths, Anna falls in love with Jan Stelnicki, a patriot who fights for his country's independence, but their romance is stalled by war and the romantic manipulations of Anna's beautiful, selfish cousin Zofia. Through it all, Anna emerges as an indomitable heroine. Martin's novel is based on the actual diary of Anna Maria, which for a time was sealed in wax to hide its scandalous contents from the eyes of later generations. A sequel is expected.

Keywords: Poland—Early Modern Era

McLeay, Alison.

Oliver Trilogy.

Scottish novelist McLeay's trilogy sweeps from early nineteenth-century North America to Victorian England to the twentieth-century Orient.

Passage Home. Simon & Schuster, 1990. 606pp. (Original title: *The Wayward Tide.*)

Naïve Rachel Dean, the daughter of a Newfoundland family in 1827, learns the hard way that men cannot be held against their will. As a child she develops an immediate bond with a restless wanderer named Adam Gaunt. Years later, in Liverpool, she encounters Adam again and seduces him, convincing him to marry her and take her to America. When Adam is reported dead, she is left to make her own way on the American frontier. But Rachel is a survivor, supporting herself and her son out West as a singer in a classic Wild West saloon. She eventually makes her way back to Liverpool, where she marries an older man in the shipping business. Just when she thinks her dreary life is set in stone, things take an unexpected turn.

Keywords: The West—Early United States; England—Victorian Era

Sea Change. Simon & Schuster, 1992. 444pp. (Original title: *Sweet Exile.*)

Kate Summerbee, the "river brat" daughter of a Mississippi riverboat captain, has lived her entire life aboard ship. In the summer of 1862, after one crazy night of passion with British shipping magnate Matthew Oliver in New Orleans, Kate's stubborn father insists that they marry. When Matthew doesn't return for her as expected, Kate makes her own way to his home of Hawk's Dyke in Liverpool. There, she is caught between two equally attractive and compelling men: Matthew and his father, Adam Gaunt. McLeay does a great job writing from the point of view of an outspoken Southern girl who never loses her brashness or pluck.

Keywords: Louisiana—Civil War; England—Victorian Era

After Shanghai. St. Martin's Press, 1996. 418pp.

Clio Oliver, born in Shanghai in 1910, is called back to England after her grandfather Matthew's funeral. There she meets members of other branches of her squabbling family, including the mysterious Catherine and her illegitimate son, Stephen Morgan. Circumstances return her to Shanghai, where she arrives with her husband to live, though she is torn between the two cultures and two very different men.

Keywords: China—20th Century

Mitchell, Margaret.

Gone with the Wind. Macmillan, 1936. 1037pp. ★

Margaret Mitchell's epic of the Old South during the Civil War years—later made into a popular epic film—features raven-haired heroine Scarlett O'Hara, a Southern belle on a Georgia plantation who can't figure out which man is truly best for her until it's too late. Though debonair Rhett Butler is her soul mate, she only discovers this after mooning for years over Ashley Wilkes, who never returns her affection. Some sections, particularly the portrayal of blacks, are seen today as racially offensive, though the historical context of the time in which Mitchell was writing should be taken into account. Pulitzer Prize.

Keywords: Georgia—Civil War

Moore, Ann.

Gracelin O'Malley Trilogy. 📖

Moore's trilogy, the first two novels of which have been published, follows a young Irishwoman's romantic yet tear-filled journey from 1840s Ireland to the Pacific Northwest. The trilogy will conclude with *'Til Morning Light.*

Gracelin O'Malley. New American Library, 2001. 398pp.

In Ireland at the time of the potato famine, young Protestant Gracelin O'Malley is married off to Bram Donnelly, the lord of the manor, to save her family from starvation. He turns out to be an abusive drunk, though his wealth helps her provide for the starving poor of the local countryside. She finds her true love in her brother's Catholic friend Morgan, who believes as passionately in social change as she does.

Keywords: Ireland—19th Century

Leaving Ireland. New American Library, 2002. 378pp.

More somber than *Gracelin O'Malley*, this sequel sees Gracelin on a journey to America via Liverpool with her daughter, for she is wanted for murder back in

Ireland. After surviving a difficult sea voyage, Gracelin arrives in New York City in 1849 only to confront anti-Irish sentiment and unsanitary living conditions.

> **Keywords:** New York—Early United States

Ripley, Alexandra.

Scarlett. Warner, 1991. 823pp.

The Civil War is over, and Scarlett O'Hara—after gallivanting about to a variety of Southern cities—takes a trip to Ireland to visit her relatives before returning home to live happily ever after with her adored Rhett. Ripley shows a more mature Scarlett, and she also injects some new history into the narrative, depicting how the luckless Irish were treated by their rude English overlords. Ripley, author of a number of Southern romantic historical novels, was hand-picked by the Mitchell estate to write an authorized sequel to *Gone with the Wind*.

> **Keywords:** Georgia—Reconstruction and the Gilded Age; Ireland —19th Century

Robson, Lucia St. Clair.

Walk in My Soul. Ballantine, 1985. 644pp. ✍

Tiana Rogers, a young Cherokee woman from Tennessee, becomes the first love of the great Sam Houston. Their romance is overlaid with tragedy, however, as Tiana's people are destined to be banished to Oklahoma in the 1830s in what is now called the Trail of Tears.

> **Keywords:** Tennessee—Early United States

Ryman, Rebecca.

<u>Olivia and Jai Series.</u>

Romance combines with fierce caste conflict in nineteenth-century British India.

> **Keywords:** India—19th Century

Olivia and Jai. St. Martin's Press, 1990. 644pp.

In the 1840s, Olivia O'Rourke, a spirited, freethinking American, arrives at the Calcutta mansion of her aunt and uncle, Sir Joshua and Lady Bridget Templewood, to live with them and perhaps find a husband. At one of their house parties, she runs into a mysterious man known as Jai Raventhorne, an attractive half-caste man who is Joshua's fiercest rival in business. The tormented Jai has a score to settle with the Templewoods, and Olivia is in his way. Despite Jai's continual warnings that she is caught up in business she can't understand, Olivia pursues him relentlessly until he is forced into an act of betrayal so devastating it tears her family apart.

The Veil of Illusion. St. Martin's Press, 1995. 632pp.

In this sequel to *Olivia and Jai*, Maya Raventhorne has never believed that her father had anything to do with the Bibighar Massacre of 1857, in which hundreds of European women and children were killed by Indian revolutionaries. While she sees society-conscious Christian Pendlebury as her ideal suitor, his family has doubts, particularly because Maya herself is of mixed race and tainted by her father's supposed treason. A better match for her may be fiery newspaper reporter Kyle Hawkesworth, but they clash on nearly every issue.

Shalimar. **St. Martin's Press, 1999. 456pp.**

This novel takes place during the years of the Great Game, when Britain fought with Russia and China for control of trade and territory along the Silk Road of Central Asia. To solve her brother's gambling debts, Emma Wyncliffe, a young Englishwoman living in Delhi in 1890, is forced to marry Damien Grenville. He is handsome, enigmatic, and dangerous, and spends most of his time trying to root out the location of the secret Yasmina Pass through the Himalayas before the Russians do.

> **Keywords:** India—19th Century

Scott, Joanna Catherine.

Cassandra, Lost. **St. Martin's Press, 2004. 321pp.** ✎

When Baltimore heiress Cassandra Owings's father denies her permission to marry Lieutenant Benedict van Pradelles, they run off together. In Paris during the Reign of Terror, Cassandra cares for Benedict's dying mother while his father shelters her from the rabble outside their doors. While there, she forms an unbreakable bond of friendship with Jean Lafitte, a French teenager. Fifteen years later Cassandra and Benedict are raising a large family in Spanish New Orleans. When Jean reenters their lives, Cassandra finds she can't resist the pull of adventure again. **Literary.**

> **Keywords:** France—Early Modern Era, Louisiana—Early United States

Scrupski, Barbara.

Ruslan. **Crown, 2003. 447pp.**

In Czarist Russia in the nineteenth century, Countess Alexandra Korvin, seeing no easy solution to her life of poverty, disguises herself as a man and joins the military. She serves under an army captain named Ulyanov. Though he had fallen in love with Alexandra long before, she fights against her attraction to him.

> **Keywords:** Russia—Early Modern Era

Selinko, Annemarie.

Désirée. **Morrow, 1953. 594pp.** ✎ ★ **YA**

Bernardine Eugénie Désirée Clary, daughter of a prosperous silk merchant from Marseilles, becomes the first love of Napoleon Bonaparte. He breaks off their engagement after meeting Josephine. On the rebound, she meets and quickly marries another man, Count Bernadotte, who later becomes King of Sweden. The heroine's search for love and acceptance pervades the novel, though the romantic aspects are more lighthearted than deeply felt.

Keywords: France—Early Modern Era; Sweden—Early Modern Era

Seton, Anya.

Avalon. **Houghton Mifflin, 1965. 440pp.** YA

In this poignant love story, Merewyn, a Cornish peasant girl, and Rumon de Provence, a French prince, begin an adventure that takes them from the coast of Cornwall to Iceland, Greenland, the North American coast, and finally to the royal court of tenth-century England.

Keywords: England—Early Middle Ages

Katherine. **Houghton Mifflin, 1954. 588pp.** ✍ ★ YA

Katherine de Roet, a poor commoner, grows up in a convent and marries knight Hugh Swynford, by whom she has two children. Her sister Philippa weds the poet Geoffrey Chaucer. When Katherine's path brings her into the royal circle, she meets John of Gaunt, Duke of Lancaster and King Edward III's third son, with whom she falls passionately in love. Their romance must wait until the deaths of both their spouses, but by then John is forced to marry for political reasons. For the rest of their lives, Katherine and the duke remain devoted to each other, and their illicit union (and four illegitimate children) causes scandals to ripple through fourteenth-century England. Meticulously researched, and based on historical figures, Seton's classic romance has served as the inspiration for many of today's romance novelists.

Keywords: England—High Middle Ages

Simons, Paullina.

The Bronze Horseman. **Morrow, 2001. 637pp.**

In 1941 Leningrad, as the Germans approach the city's borders, sixteen-year-old Tatiana Metanova becomes romantically involved with Alexander Belov, a Red Army officer, not knowing that he's the man that her sister loves. To save her lover's life, Tatiana feigns affection for another soldier who has the potential to destroy Alexander. While Tatiana and Alexander's love struggles to survive, so do the members of Tatiana's family, slowly starving to death in their small apartment as the Germans lay siege to their city. A sequel, *Tatiana and Alexander/The Bridge to Holy Cross* (alternate title), has been published overseas.

Keywords: Russia—World War II

Small, Bertrice.

Bertrice Small writes sensual, fast-paced romantic novels complete with beautiful heroines and irresistible heroes who live and love with great passion. They also have the wealth and intelligence to vie for power with the greatest monarchs of their day. Her books are hard to categorize.

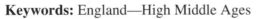

While all of Small's novels (others of which are historical romances) are typically found in the romance section of bookstores, they don't always follow the conventions of the genre. The happily-ever-after ending is there, but Small's heroines become romantically and sexually involved with more than one partner, and her settings are as exotic as those of the best romantic epics. Her earliest heroines are based on historical individuals. Explicit sexual content.

Adora. **Ballantine, 1980. 440pp.** ✍

Theodora Cantacuzene, daughter of the Emperor of Byzantium in the fourteenth century, falls in love with Prince Murad, though she is married off for political reasons to his father, the Sultan of the Ottoman Empire.

Keywords: Ottoman Empire—14th Century

Beloved. **Ballantine, 1983. 465pp.** ✍

In the third century AD, Zenobia, Queen of Palmyra, falls in love with Marcus Alexander Britainus, a Roman soldier, despite the Roman Empire's desire to conquer her world.

Keywords: Syria—Roman Period

The Kadin. **Avon, 1978. 441pp.** ✍

Lady Janet Leslie is kidnapped from her home in late fifteenth-century Scotland and sold into slavery in Turkey, where she finds passionate love and political intrigue in the Sultan's harem.

Keywords: Ottoman Empire—15th Century

Ware, Ciji.

Island of the Swans. **Bantam/Fawcett, 1989. 533pp.** ✍

The true story of Jane Maxwell and her lifelong love, Thomas Fraser, and how their romance is interrupted by war with the American colonies. By the time Thomas returns home, Jane—believing him dead—has arranged for marriage with Alexander, Duke of Gordon, who refuses to give her up. Beginning in 1760s Scotland, the action sweeps to the London court and to early nineteenth-century America. Revised edition issued by Fawcett in 1998.

Keywords: England—Georgian Era, Scotland—18th Century

Winsor, Kathleen.

Forever Amber. **Macmillan, 1944. 972pp.** ★

In seventeenth-century England at the time of the Restoration, young Amber St. Clare rises from poverty on the streets of London to become the favorite mistress of Charles II. She is the quintessential heroine: beautiful, ruthless, and lusty. She is also somewhat naïve, for despite all of her great fortune and her many affairs (which she enjoys with great gusto), she constantly longs for the one man that she can never have. Historical detail is one of the book's strong points, and Amber emerges triumphant from events such as the Plague and the Great Fire of London in 1666. A bestseller in the 1940s, the novel was banned in Boston for its overly racy content.

Keywords: England—Stuart Era

Romantic Historical Novels

Romantic historicals are historical novels with a strong romantic element. Historical events and characters are integral to the plot of romantic historicals, so much so that these novels could not realistically take place in any other location or time. While they take place on a smaller scale than romantic epics, their background is nonetheless realistically drawn.

Although the romance has a strong role in the development of the storyline and characters, it is not always the most important. The protagonist may have other problems to contend with, such as saving the family name or fortune, protecting herself and her land against invaders, or avoiding political controversy or capture. These elements may play as much of a part in the story as does the romance.

Many authors of romantic historicals (e.g., Diane Haeger, Parke Godwin) were inspired by the real-life romantic tales of historical figures, such as British or European royals and nobles. Others create believable fictional characters that interact with one another against a well-realized historical background. With approximately equal weight given to the historical setting and the romance, romantic historicals give readers a realistic feel for the courtship practices of past eras. Medieval settings are common, as are novels set in the American West, Victorian England, and Europe during wartime. While some authors (Elizabeth Chadwick, Caroline Stickland) write exclusively in one historical period, others (Diane Haeger, Rosalind Laker, Virginia Ellis) write novels set in a variety of locations and eras.

Unlike historical romances, romantic historicals may or may not end on an optimistic note. Historical fiction readers find this unpredictability to be appealing, for it keeps them turning the pages to discover whether the heroine and hero will end up together. The protagonist may also have more than one love interest within the novel, as might his or her partner. Many older romantic historicals, written before the happily-ever-after ending and single-partner elements became the norm in romances, are considered classics of the romance genre today.

Fans of romantic historicals may also enjoy traditional historical novels (Chapter 2) with a strong romantic element, such as those written by Megan Chance, Jean Auel, and Jean Plaidy. Romantic Westerns, novels of the American West with a romance storyline, are found in Chapter 6.

Prehistoric

Readers who enjoy these romantic tales of prehistoric Europe should also investigate traditional historical novels (Chapter 2) set during the same time period.

Wolf, Joan.

Prehistoric Trilogy. YA

Wolf's prehistoric trilogy is set in the French Pyrenees, home to the cave paintings at Lascaux, beginning about 14,000 years ago.

Daughter of the Red Deer. Dutton, 1991. 420pp.

Alin, priestess of the matriarchal Red Deer tribe, is one of sixteen young women captured by men of the Tribe of the Horse, a male-centered group who need to replace the women that they've lost. There she falls in love with Mar, their leader.

The Horsemasters. Dutton, 1993. 401pp.

The Kindred are a group of tribes who live peacefully in the valleys of the Pyrenees in southern France. Arika, the chief priestess of the Tribe of the Red Deer, is too busy worrying about her squabbling family to pay attention to the warnings about conquering tribes from the north. When her son Ronan is cast out of the tribe, he learns from the northerners the power of horsemanship, but he must ally himself with Nel, the Kindred girl he loves, for their people to survive.

The Reindeer Hunters. Dutton, 1994. 368pp.

Matriarchal and patriarchal tribes once again find themselves in conflict. When the reindeer leave the fertile lands of the valleys of the Pyrenees, Alane of the Kindred agrees to marry Nardo of the Norakamo to seal an agreement between their people on the rights to hunting grounds.

The Roman Empire

Davis, Lindsey.

The Course of Honor. **Mysterious Press, 1998. 327pp.** ✍

In the first century AD, Caenis serves as a slave in the household of Antonia, a Roman matron, the daughter of Mark Antony. She later becomes the grandmother to both Caligula and Claudius. In her household, Caenis meets a soldier named Vespasian, and the two fall in love. Their romance continues for years, through Vespasian's unlikely elevation to the imperial throne, but tradition forbids an emperor to marry a slave, even a former one. Davis is best known for her Roman mysteries (Chapter 7), but this historically-based love story was the first novel she wrote.

Europe and the British Isles

The Middle Ages

Here, romances develop between members of opposing political and cultural groups in medieval times (circa the fifth to fifteenth centuries AD): the Normans and the Saxons, the English Plantagenets and the French Angevins, and the lower and upper classes of medieval England.

Baltuck, Naomi, and Deborah Baltuck.

Keeper of the Crystal Spring. **Viking, 1998. 437pp.**

In 1086, Aldyth is a young Saxon woman who's the foster daughter of Sirona, a seer and wisewoman. Though Aldyth has dedicated herself to the Goddess of the Crystal Spring and vows never to marry, she's pursued by two different men: the attractive Bedwyn, an outlaw and childhood friend, and Gandulf, son of a Norman lord.

Borchardt, Alice.

Devoted Series.

Much has been made of Borchardt's relationship to vampire novelist Anne Rice, her younger sister. Borchardt's first novels show Rice's fantasy influence to some degree, but not as much as her later titles (Chapter 14). These novels are set in tenth-century France.

Devoted. Dutton, 1995. 467pp.

Elin is a young woman of the Forest People who's gifted with second sight. Herself a prisoner of the Vikings and victim of their cruelty, Elin warns Owen, Bishop of Chantalon, of his imminent capture. They manage to escape together, and in gratitude, Owen decides to marry her.

Beguiled. Dutton, 1997. 482pp.

Elin and Owen's marriage had held strong against the Viking invaders, but Elin sees more danger ahead, for their child and for the people of Chantalon. When Owen goes to obtain help to fight the enemy, Elin is left to defend Chantalon as best she can.

Chadwick, Elizabeth.

There are two romance novelists who write as Elizabeth Chadwick. The author of the books named below is the British Chadwick, who writes romances, romantic historicals, and traditional historical novels set in medieval times.

The Champion. **St. Martin's Press, 1998. 499pp.**

In 1193, Alexander de Montroi decides to leave the monastery to join his brother Hervi on the European tournament circuit. He's too busy to pay attention to Monday de Cerizay, a friend's daughter who becomes his brother's ward. One night of passion has serious consequences for them both.

The Conquest. **St. Martin's Press, 1997. 458pp.**

In 1066, after the Norman Conquest takes from her all that she holds dear, a Saxon widow named Ailith is forced to take refuge with her Norman neighbors. Eventually she becomes chatelaine at the English estate of Rolf de Brize, one of the Norman invaders, becoming his mistress even though he has a wife and family of his own back in Normandy.

Daughters of the Grail. **Ballantine, 1995. 409pp.**

In the mountains of southern France in 1207, young Bridget is not a Cathar, but members of her family belong to this so-called heretical sect at a time when the Catholic Church has made a commitment to rid itself of them. A descendant of Mary Magdalene, Bridget must find a way to continue a bloodline that has lasted well over a thousand years. Raoul de Montvallant, a Catholic, is sympathetic to the Cathars. Although Bridget loves him, she knows that he's devoted to his wife. Raoul's conscience forces him to turn against the Church's ruthless policies of intolerance, even if it means his own destruction. It is left to the next generation to right these wrongs.

The Love Knot. **St. Martin's Press, 1999. 474pp.**

During the civil war between King Stephen and Empress Matilda that rocked England in the twelfth century, knight Oliver Pascal honors the deathbed wish of a friend to take her son and her widowed maid Catrin, the boy's nurse, into his household. Oliver and Catrin fall in love, but in a land ravaged by civil war, no outcome is ever certain.

The Marsh King's Daughter. **St. Martin's Press, 2000. 408pp.**

Miriel Weaver, given to a nunnery by her stepfather against her will, sees a chance at freedom in Nicholas de Caen, a soldier of fortune who is the only survivor of King John's drowned supply train. She persuades him to take her with him when he's recovered, but they part on bad terms. When they meet again years later, she has become a prosperous wool merchant, and he is a successful trader.

Godwin, Parke.

Lord of Sunset. **Avon, 1998. 466pp.** ✍

Harold Godwinesson, Earl of Wessex, lives for twenty years with his handfasted wife, Edith of Nazeing, whom he cannot marry in the Church. When politics call him to England's throne, he's forced to marry another woman, despite his love for Edith and the many children they have together. Edith and Harold tell their stories in alternating chapters, she beginning on that fateful day in 1066 when she was asked to identify her husband's body at Hastings.

Gower, Iris.

Best known for her British regional sagas (Chapter 5), Gower also wrote two romantic novels based on medieval British royalty.

Destiny's Child. **Severn House, 1999. 224pp. (Originally published in Britain in 1975 as *Bride of the Thirteenth Summer*, under the name Iris Davies.)** ✍

During the Wars of the Roses in the fifteenth century, Lady Margaret Beaufort, heiress of the Lancastrian line, is married in her thirteenth year to Edmund Tudor, son of Catherine of France and Owen Tudor. He dies just before his son, the future Henry VII, is born.

A Royal Ambition. **Severn House, 1999. 222pp. (Originally published in Britain in 1974 as *Tudor Tapestry*, under the name Iris Davies.)** ✍

Catherine of France, Henry V's widow, would prefer to marry Welsh gentleman Owen Tudor, but men of the royal court have their own plans for her. Not quite as detailed as Rosemary Hawley-Jarman's *Crown in Candlelight*, below, Gower's tale is nonetheless well researched.

Graeme-Evans, Posie.

The Innocent. **Atria, 2004. 406pp.** ✍

Anne, a beautiful young peasant girl, is raised in secrecy in the forests of fifteenth-century England after political foes kill her mother. In 1465, Anne arrives at the London court of King Edward IV. With her knowledge of herbs, she saves the life of Edward IV's queen and quickly becomes the royal healer. Before Anne knows it, she and the king are caught up in a passionate affair. First of a forthcoming trilogy.

Hawks, Kate.
The Lovers. Avon, 1999. 324pp.

Hawks (a pseudonym for Parke Godwin) links the traditional legend of Trystan and Yseult to a historical context. When King Arthur banishes Trystan to Gaul after his affair with his uncle's wife, Arthur's Irish servant Gareth joins him and helps him fight off the invading Franks. It's here that Gareth falls in love with Isolt, Trystan's neglected and unloved wife.

Headlee, Kim.
Dawnflight. Sonnet, 1999. 500pp.

Lancelot plays no part in Headlee's version of the Arthurian legend, in which Guinevere (Gyanhumara), warrior chieftainess of a Celtic tribe, betrays an alliance with a Brytoni nobleman when she falls in love with Arthur, the Pendragon of Britain.

Herbert, Kathleen.
Dark Age Trilogy.

This is the correct chronological order for Herbert's trilogy of strong-willed women during England's early medieval period, though the publication dates suggest otherwise.

Bride of the Spear. St. Martin's Press, 1988. 297pp.

Fifty years after the death of King Arthur, Taniu, neglected daughter of the cruel King Loth of Lothien, is betrothed against her will to Owain of Cumbria—but she has other ideas. A retelling of the Welsh legend of the Lady of the Fountain.

❦ *Queen of the Lightning.* St. Martin's Press, 1984. 255pp. ✍

Riemmelth of Cumbria is forced into a political alliance with Oswy of Northumbria, though her heart is promised to another. Georgette Heyer Historical Novel Prize.

Ghost in the Sunlight. St. Martin's Press, 1986. 335pp. ✍

In the seventh century, Alchflaed, daughter of King Oswy, makes a political marriage to keep the peace. In doing so she stirs up ghosts from the past, such as the memory of her late mother's first love.

Jarman, Rosemary Hawley.
Crown in Candlelight. Little, Brown, 1978. 477pp. ✍

Katherine of Valois, youngest daughter of the mad King Charles of France in 1405, makes a political marriage with Henry V—the victor of Agincourt who is her country's greatest enemy. They grow to love one another, but after his death, humble Welsh knight Owen Tudor captures

Katherine's heart. Their liaison, given his nationality and her position as mother of the next king, is completely unacceptable.

Jones, Ellen.

Beloved Enemy. Simon & Schuster, 1994. 565pp. ✍

Eleanor of Aquitaine, a duchess in her own right at fifteen, yearns for both love and power, neither of which she finds in her marriage to the monkish Louis VII of France. After giving birth to only girls, she convinces him to divorce her, where-upon she marries Henry, Prince of Anjou, a lusty creature who can satisfy her two desires.

The Fatal Crown. Simon & Schuster, 1991. 556pp. ✍

Jones imagines the stormy relationship between Maud, Empress of Germany, and her royal cousin, Stephen of Blois, as a passionate, adulterous affair. The two fall in love in England before Maud, daughter of Henry I, is married off to the much older German emperor. When she returns, Stephen lays claim to the throne that Maud's father promised her. Entertaining and romantic, though there's no histor-ical evidence that their real-life relationship was like this.

Llywelyn, Morgan.

Strongbow: The Story of Richard and Aoife. O'Brien, 1993. 155pp. ✍ **YA**

This short novel, reissued in 1996 for the adult market, tells in alternating chap-ters the story of Strongbow, aka Norman knight Richard de Clare, and Aoife (Eva), an Irish princess who marries Richard and fights alongside him for her homeland.

Meade, Marion.

Stealing Heaven. Morrow, 1979. 415pp. ★ ✍

The love story of Heloise and her tutor, Peter Abelard, scandalized twelfth-cen-tury France. Heloise's own letters from that time testify to her endless devotion to the husband she lost to the contemplative life and to her uncle's devastating re-venge on him. Meade retells their timeless story from Heloise's point of view.

Pargeter, Edith.

The Marriage of Meggotta. Viking, 1979. 283pp. ✍ **YA**

Beginning in 1230, Meggotta de Burgh had been brought up with the expectation of marrying her father's ward, Richard de Clare. Though the pair, barely out of childhood, are in love, they risk Henry III's wrath if they marry—for the king has a different political match in mind for Richard.

Roberson, Jennifer.

Marian Series.

A retelling of the Robin Hood legend set in late twelfth-century Nottingham.

Lady of the Forest. Kensington, 1992. 593pp.

In 1194, Sir Robert of Locksley turns his back on his noble heritage to pursue his own sort of justice. Marian of Ravenskeep thinks she wants no more from him than to know how her Crusader father died, but the pair fall in love at first sight.

Lady of Sherwood. Kensington, 1999. 372pp.

The sequel to *Lady of the Forest* begins in 1199. The heroic King Richard of England has died, only to be succeeded by the treacherous Prince John—Robert of Locksley's archenemy. Lady Marian herself joins the band of merry men by heading into Sherwood Forest herself and training to be a warrior.

Watson, Elsa.

Maid Marian. **Crown, 2004. 307pp.**

After her much older husband dies, Marian Fitzwater becomes the ward of Richard the Lionheart. Because she doesn't want Eleanor of Aquitaine to sell her into another marriage, Marian throws herself on the mercy of Saxon outlaw Robin Hood. In Sherwood Forest, Marian learns that arrangements were made for her to marry her late husband's brother, and many members of his family have died suspiciously.

The Renaissance and Reformation

Romances set amid political and courtly intrigue in France, Italy, Scotland, and England during the sixteenth century.

Haeger, Diane.

Courtesan. **Pocket Star, 1993. 568pp.** ✍

In sixteenth-century France, Diane de Poitiers, a beautiful noble widow, captures the heart of the much younger Henri de Valois, future king of France. The affair scandalizes the country, for she had also been his father's mistress. Their love remains true for many years, through Henri's elevation to the throne and his marriage to Catherine de'Medici.

Kay, Susan.

❦ *Legacy.* **Crown, 1986. 648pp.** ✍

In this colorful and entertaining biographical novel, Elizabeth I's great love is Robert Dudley, Earl of Leicester, though part of her hates her need for and dependence on men. Georgette Heyer Historical Novel Prize.

Lennox, Judith.

The Italian Garden. **St. Martin's Press, 1993. 471pp.**

In Renaissance-era Italy and France, Joanna Zulian's uncle exploits her talent by denying her credit for her own artistic creations. Her star-crossed lover is mercenary soldier Toby Dubreton, but despite their strong connection, they're continually torn apart.

Westcott, Jan.

The Border Lord. **Crown, 1946. 464pp.** ✍

This adventurous love story between Francis Hepburn, Earl of Bothwell, and Anne Galbraith, set along the Scottish border in the late sixteenth century, is based on historical characters.

Seventeenth Century

The English Civil War and the Restoration (mid-seventeenth century) are common settings for romantic historicals, while European settings are much less frequent.

Armitage, Aileen.

A Passionate Cause. **Severn House, 2000. 204pp. (First published in the UK in 1971, as *King's Pawn* by Aileen Quigley.)** ✍

In the mid-seventeenth century, young Topaz Birke gives shelter to an attractive Englishman, Charles Barlow, during his travels in Germany. Soon she has given her heart to the mysterious stranger. After he departs for England, she finds herself pregnant and travels far to be with him, only to discover that he isn't who she thought he was.

Barnes, Margaret Campbell.

With All My Heart. **Macrae Smith, 1951. 284pp.** ✍ **YA**

Catherine of Braganza, a Portuguese princess, doesn't have the easiest time being married to Charles II, a monarch whose dalliances with other women seem limitless. Though at first she believes he cares only for her dowry, she's continually touched by his genuine affection for her.

Laker, Rosalind.

Circle of Pearls. **Doubleday, 1990. 519pp.**

Julia Pallister is daughter of a Royalist household in Puritan-era Sussex who's torn between two men: architect Christopher Wren and Puritan Adam Warrender. Most of Laker's historicals illustrate a particular trade taken up by her heroines, and here the chosen industry is ribbon embroidery.

The Golden Tulip. **Doubleday, 1991. 585pp.** **YA**

In Netherlands in the seventeenth century, Francesca Visser, an artist's daughter, is determined to make a name for herself as a painter, but her father's financial straits might force her to marry instead. Together with Pieter Van Doorne, a tulip grower who loves her, they devise a plan for Francesca to avoid this fate.

Lord, Elizabeth.

Frances Cromwell Series. ✍

Frances Cromwell, Oliver Cromwell's youngest daughter, chooses to follow her heart.

Shadow of the Protector. Severn House, 2002. 215pp.

In 1649, after the execution of King Charles I, Frances rebels against her Puritan upbringing. Though she strongly desires to marry one of her father's chaplains, Cromwell is against the match.

Fortune's Daughter. Severn House, 2002. 183pp.

Six years later, determined to escape the influence of her overbearing father, the Lord Protector, Frances Cromwell dreams of marrying Lord Robert Rich. She gains what she desires, for a change, and finds her political sympathies changing at the same time.

Roberson, Jennifer.
Lady of the Glen. **Kensington, 1996. 416pp.**

In 1692, countless members of the MacDonald clan of the Scottish Highlands were massacred at Glencoe by order of England's William III. That much is known at the outset. The Campbells were a rival clan whose laird aided the English monarch. This sets the stage for a tale of two star-crossed lovers, Catriona Campbell and Alasdair Og MacDonald, born to be enemies but destined to live and love passionately.

Eighteenth Century

Unlike those of earlier time periods, most romantic historical novels set in eighteenth-century Britain and Europe are set in the countryside or in small villages rather than at royal courts.

Fleming, James.
The Temple of Optimism. **Miramax, 2000. 316pp.**

In a country village in Derbyshire in 1788, Edward Horne returns home from London to sell his estate. His neighbor, Sir Anthony Apreece, wants Edward's land for himself, while Edward falls more and more deeply in love with Daisy, Sir Anthony's beautiful wife. The novel, written in a formal, witty style, shows the emotions that seethe behind the respectability of England's landed gentry in the eighteenth century. **Literary.**

Hawks, Kate.
Watch By Moonlight. **Morrow, 2001. 223pp.**

In this novel based on Alfred Noyes's poem "The Highwayman," innkeeper's daughter Bess Whateley throws in her lot with handsome gentleman Jason Quick even though she knows he's on the run from the law. Readers unfamiliar with the poem should hold off reading it until the end, as it gives away the plot. Set in 1763 Dorset.

Hucker, Hazel.
Cousin Susannah. **St. Martin's Press, 1995. 371pp.**

In 1794, when farmer's daughter Susannah Trotter becomes pregnant after an affair with wealthy James Manningford, she seduces a local curate and convinces him that the child is his. James tries to do his best by the couple, but doesn't realize until after they're married that he wants Susannah for himself.

Jacobs, Anna.
Replenish the Earth. **Severn House, 2001. 284pp.**

In 1735 Dorset, Sarah Mortonby is surprised to learn that she has inherited her late mother's family home. She falls in love with it, despite its neglected condition, and refuses to sell it to her unscrupulous new neighbor, Mr. Sewell. When her maid urges her to marry, her first choice is her handsome bailiff, who can help her restore the estate. But Sewell will not be ignored, either by Sarah or the local village.

Laker, Rosalind.
The Sugar Pavilion. **Doubleday, 1994. 370pp.**

In late eighteenth-century Paris, Sophie Delcourt has dreams of becoming a confectioner, but when she flees the Revolution for safety in Brighton, England, she's forced to start all over again. Fortunately, she has determination and wit, not to mention two suitors from which to choose.

Nineteenth Century

The political and economic changes sweeping Britain and Europe in the nineteenth century once more take center stage in these novels of lovers kept apart by political and religious differences or by social circumstance.

Byatt, A. S.
🏵 *Possession: A Romance*. **Doubleday, 1990. 555pp.**

Annotated in Chapter 10.

Eden, Dorothy.
Never Call It Loving. **Coward-McCann, 1966. 319pp.** ✍

Katharine O'Shea, called Kitty by those who taunted her about her affair, has an extramarital relationship with Charles Stewart Parnell, a politician who had worked long and hard for Home Rule for his native Ireland. When Katharine's husband finally sues for divorce, it's the beginning of the end for Parnell's political career.

Haeger, Diane.
The Secret Wife of King George IV. **St. Martin's Press, 2000. 373pp.** ✍

Though Prince George is forced to marry his cousin, the unclean and uncouth Caroline of Brunswick, his heart remains with his first wife, Maria Fitzherbert, whose Catholic religion made their union illegal by the laws of England. Their story begins in 1784, thirty-six years before George became king.

Hardy, Charlotte.

Far from Home. St. Martin's Press, 1997. 420pp.

Brid Flynn, a poor Irish Catholic girl, convinces herself that Lord Harry Leighton will marry her, so she follows him to London. Predictably, she's soon proven wrong, but her sorry circumstances inspire the spunky Brid to create a new life for herself.

Hart, Mallory Dorn.

A Glass Full of Stars. John James, 1999. 544pp.

During the Napoleonic Wars in Reims, France, Caroline Jeunot plans on continuing a prosperous winery after her husband dies. Then she discovers that Thierry de St.-Mazur, an artillery major, is now its partial owner. While struggling for control of the winery, the two fall in love. Thierry goes off to fight and is reported missing, leaving Caroline to journey alone to Russia to promote her sparkling champagne.

Hodge, Jane Aiken.

Caterina Series.

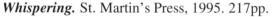

Political and romantic happenings in nineteenth-century Portugal, an unusual setting for romance novels.

Whispering. St. Martin's Press, 1995. 217pp.

When teenager Caterina Gomez's Portuguese father asks her to travel to Oporto, Portugal, in the early nineteenth century, she agrees only reluctantly. While there, she and her two traveling companions get caught up in political and romantic intrigue.

Caterina. St. Martin's Press, 1999. 256pp.

The sequel to *Whispering* begins in 1832 in Portugal. Caterina Fonsa, née Gomez, has established her own household. In this era of turmoil, her freethinking ways and satirical political cartoons, which she draws under a pseudonym, may spell danger for herself and her son.

Laker, Rosalind.

Banners of Silk. Doubleday, 1981. 469pp.

Louise Vernet is an impoverished dress designer in Second Empire Paris who's helped by a *grisette* (working-class girl), Catherine Allard, who takes her in and teaches her more about the trade. Their search for love is set against a well-realized backdrop of the French clothing industry, in particular the early beginnings of Charles Worth, whose stylish creations were soon sweeping the continent.

Tree of Gold. Doubleday, 1986. 350pp.

Gabrielle Roche, daughter of one of the most prominent families in Lyons's silk industry during Napoleonic times, is attracted against her will to Nicholas Devaux, her rival in business, though she's promised to another.

McLeay, Alison.

The Dream Maker. St. Martin's Press, 1999. 320pp.

The Napoleonic Wars are over, and they have brought the St. Serf family in England nothing but poverty and disgrace. Sixteen-year-old Flora finds friends among a group of social outcasts, but when she runs into the handsome Darius Elder, the son of the banker who called in her family's loans, she conceives an unexpected passion for him.

Roberts, Ann Victoria.

Louisa Elliott Series.

A multi-generational story of forbidden love, set in England and Ireland in the late nineteenth and early twentieth centuries.

Louisa Elliott. Contemporary, 1989. 650pp.

In Victorian-era York and Dublin, Louisa Elliott tries to overcome the shame of her illegitimate birth by working as a governess and living an upright, scandal-free life. Though her cousin Edward loves her unreservedly, passion leads Louisa into the arms of handsome Robert Duncannon, an officer with the Royal Dragoons. She becomes his mistress, even knowing that he can never marry her.

Morning's Gate. Morrow, 1991. 639pp. (Original title: *Liam's Story.*)

This sequel to *Louisa Elliott* begins in the present day. Zoe Clifford comes to York in search of her family history. Her research leads her to Stephen Elliott, a distant cousin, and the pair discover long-hidden secrets about the family of her great-grandmother, Letitia Duncannon Elliott. They find parallels to their own lives in the story of Letitia's brother Liam, who in the early twentieth century grows up with a crush on Georgina Duncannon, Robert Duncannon's daughter, not realizing that she's his half-sister. Distraught, he flees England for Australia, later returning to fight for his country on the battlefields of World War I.

Moon Rising. St. Martin's Press, 2001. 360pp. ✍

In the seaside town of Whitby in the 1880s, Damaris Sterne, a fishergirl, poses for atmospheric photographs taken for the tourist trade. She begins a passionately erotic affair with the much-older (and married) Bram Stoker, recounting to him local legends of Whitby, many of which he later incorporates into his masterwork. Their encounter is remembered in the first person by Damaris twenty years later, who has since become a respectable widow and matron. The eerie gothic atmosphere of *Dracula* carries over into Roberts's work, which fictionalizes the novel's origins.

Stickland, Caroline.

Stickland, a British author, writes novels set in Thomas Hardy country—Wessex, England, in the mid-nineteenth century. Her first novel, *The Standing Hills* (1986), was shortlisted for the Betty Trask Award and the Georgette Heyer Historical Novel Prize.

***An Ancient Hope.* St. Martin's Press, 1994. 252pp.**

In this retelling of the story of the prodigal son set in nineteenth-century Dorset, Theodosia Farnaby and her dowry—the family ropeworks— come between her two cousins, rivals both in business and in love.

***The Darkening Leaf.* St. Martin's Press, 1996. 286pp.**

When lovers Philobeth Alleyn and Frederick North rescue a woman from a shipwreck on a Dorset beach in 1847, they don't expect that it will change their relationship for good, as the captivating Ellen Farebrother intrigues Frederick more day by day.

Twentieth Century

Love blossoms during wartime throughout twentieth-century Europe. Just like in real life, not all of the stories end happily. See also wartime sagas in Chapter 5.

Barnett, Jill.

***Sentimental Journey.* Pocket, 2001. 436pp.**

Kitty Kincaid, the courageous daughter of a famed research scientist, is captured by the Nazis in North Africa—and only ingenious U.S. Army officer J. R. Cassidy can save her. And in London, Royal Air Force pilot Charlotte "Charley" Morrison is torn between two different men. As the title suggests, this is a sentimental, heartfelt tale, a look at the men and women of the Greatest Generation.

Gavin, Catherine.

***The Snow Mountain.* Pantheon, 1974. 509pp.** ✍ **YA**

Olga Nikolaevna, the twenty-three-year-old daughter of Czar Nicholas II, manages to escape her family's clutches long enough to conduct a brief but heartfelt romance with a Russian soldier who serves her family. Their love story (fictional) is made more poignant because of the tragedy that will inevitably follow.

Gilbert, Anna.

🎗 ***The Treachery of Time.* St. Martin's Press, 1996. 445pp.**

In the years just before World War I in a small English village, two child-hood friends, Daniel and Esther, rescue an abandoned girl. Years later, after they fall in love and plan to marry, the girl returns and threatens to come between them. Catherine Cookson Award (a short-lived British award).

Grayson, Emily.

***Night Train to Lisbon.* Morrow, 2004. 224pp.**

In 1936, Carson Weatherell, daughter of well-to-do Yankees, goes on a European tour with her aunt and uncle. On a train heading to Lisbon, she meets Alec Breve, a dashing physics graduate student, and they fall in love. Carson's uncle informs her that Alec may be a German spy, which changes her attitude about him . . . at first.

Waterloo Station. **Morrow, 2003. 208pp.**

Eighteen-year-old Carrie Benedict learns about life and love from her grandmother, who tells her a story of her youth during the war years. Maude Latham, eighteen in the year 1938, travels to Oxford to study, where she falls in love with her literature tutor, Stephen Kendall. But Stephen is already married, and his position in the Royal Navy means that the lovers will soon be separated. Maude signs up as a trauma nurse, even knowing that she will be unable to communicate with Stephen.

Greig, Andrew.

The Clouds Above. **Simon & Schuster, 2000. 254pp.**

In the summer of 1940, during the Battle of Britain, a RAF pilot named Len Westbourne falls in love with Stella Gardam, a radar trainee with the WAAF. Both know that the survival of their romance is unlikely in these dangerous times. Len and Stella tell their stories in alternating chapters.

Haig, Kathryn.

Apple Blossom Time. **St. Martin's Press, 1998. 459pp.**

Laura Ansty has always been told that her father died a hero during World War I, but given the reluctance of the villagers to discuss his exploits, she is not so sure. When World War II approaches, she has to put her questions aside to do her part. After she finds love while at her assigned post in Egypt, she discovers that true romance and answers to her past must be found closer to home.

Harvey, Caroline.

The Brass Dolphin. **Doubleday, 1997. 313pp.**

In 1938, Englishwoman Lila Cunningham and her father become caretakers for Villa Zonda, a house on Malta, to improve their financial situation. There Lila discovers danger, as the German bombing of the island makes her fear for her life. She also finds love with the titled nephew of a British expatriate, ignoring the affection that a Maltese schoolmaster has for her. British novelist Joanna Trollope writes romantic historicals under this pseudonym, Caroline Harvey, though few have been published in the United States.

Hull, Jonathan.

Losing Julia. **Delacorte, 2000. 358pp.**

Patrick Delaney, a World War I veteran, now resides in a California nursing home. He recalls his stint during the war, when he lost his best friend Daniel. Patrick also fondly remembers the passionate affair he had ten years later in Paris with Julia, the beautiful woman who had been Daniel's lover.

Laker, Rosalind.

Orchids and Diamonds. **Doubleday, 1995. 293pp.**

Juliette Cladel joins her sister in the dressmaking business in early twentieth-century Paris. When her lover Count Nikolai Karasvin returns to Russia to marry his fiancée, the pregnant Juliette decides to get on with her life. She marries a Venetian designer and moves with him to Venice, continuing her line of work there, but she never forgets her first love.

MacDonald, Malcolm.

Rose of Nancemellin. **St. Martin's Press, 2001. 411pp.**

In 1910, Irish lady's maid Rose Tremayne rescues a handsome man from drowning off the shores of Cornwall, and her talent for mimicry convinces him that she's not a servant but a privileged daughter of the house. Her behavior gets her canned. She relocates to the London theater district with no money but considerable acting ability.

Oldfield, Pamela.

Riding the Storm. **Severn House, 2000. 256pp.**

In this novel of historical romantic suspense set in the 1930s, gentle widow Kate Harper arrives at the English country estate of Highstead to marry the master, crime writer Robert Dengaul. But she soon finds that evil lurks behind his mansion's calm façade.

Purcell, Deirdre.

Ashes of Roses. **Signet, 1994. 523pp. (Original title: *Falling for a Dancer*.)**

In post-World War II Ireland, after Catholic schoolgirl Elizabeth Sullivan becomes pregnant after a brief affair with a traveling actor, her parents give her two choices: join a home for unwed mothers or marry a man they choose. She decides to marry Neeley Scollard, who lives in remote Beara on the Irish coast. At seventeen, she becomes mother to Neeley's four children as well as her own son, a boy called Francey, and does her best by them all despite Neeley's neglectful treatment. Beth, her sensuality awakened by her earlier affair, finds little to rekindle her passions until a younger, more attractive man comes along. The sequel to this book is *Roses After Rain* (British title *Francey*), not annotated due to its modern setting.

The United States

Colonial America

Love stories set in the wild and as-yet-untamed American colonies in the seventeenth century.

Riefe, Barbara.

Iroquois Series. **YA**

Riefe's trilogy features members of the Mohawk tribe living in what is now New York State.

The Woman Who Fell from the Sky. Forge, 1994. 332pp.

At the end of the seventeenth century, spoiled Englishwoman Margaret Addison Lacroix is traveling north to Quebec to meet her husband-by-proxy when her ship is attacked by Mohawks. The Oneidas who rescue her see her as an Iroquois spirit, but she's forced to endure a number of other violent encounters before she finds love with a kindly Oneida, Two Eagles.

For Love of Two Eagles. Forge, 1995. 378pp.

In 1700, Margaret Addison has married her Oneida warrior, but when he's reported dead while on a mission of vengeance, she attempts to take her baby son back with her to her family in England. To do so, she must brave the wilderness and the danger of Mohawk warriors on her way to the port of Boston.

Mohawk Woman. Forge, 1996. 378pp.

In 1710 in what is today New York, Singing Brook and Sky Toucher of the Mohawk tribe defy their families to be together, but the world intervenes when the British ask Sky Toucher for his help against the French.

The American Revolution

Romantic historical novels set at the time of America's founding (the 1770s, and just before and after).

Bittner, Rosanne.

Westward America Trilogy.

An extended romantic series/family saga set in the late eighteenth and early nineteenth centuries, as settlers populated the Ohio River Valley and moved westward.

Into the Wilderness: The Long Hunters. Forge, 2002. 288pp.

In the Allegheny Mountains of Pennsylvania in 1752, Noah Wilde, frontiersman and British spy, saves sixteen-year-old Jessica Matthews from an attack by the Ottawa Indians. They fall in love, but Noah must leave her behind when he's called back to work for the British. Fortunately, Jess is a survivor.

Into the Valley: The Settlers. Forge, 2003. 272pp.

Bittner's series continues with the sons of Noah and Jessica. Luke Wilde, a farmer in the Ohio River Valley in 1780, figures he would have the same life whether the colonists or the British were in charge. His fiancée Annie Barnes feels differently. Annie can't deny her attraction to Luke's brother Jeremiah, a fervent patriot, though she doesn't think he's right for her.

Into the Prairie: The Pioneers. Forge, 2004. 288pp.

In the early nineteenth century, Noah's grandson Jonah Wilde moves his wife Sadie and son Paul to the Indiana prairie to settle on a farm. Along the way, they get caught up in trouble with the land's native inhabitants, the Shawnee.

Clark, Mary Higgins.

Mount Vernon Love Story. **Simon & Schuster, 2002. 224pp.** ✍ **YA**

George Washington, post-presidency in 1797, relives the successes and failures in his life, particularly the luck that caused him to choose widowed Martha "Patsy" Custis as his wife. Though sketchy on historical details, it will still likely peak readers' interest in the real life of America's founding father. Clark's debut novel, first published in 1969 as *Aspire to the Heavens*, was re-released for her fans after her name became synonymous with contemporary suspense.

Rae, Catherine M.

Marike's World. **Thomas Dunne, 2000. 186pp.**

In New York in the year 1776, a young Dutch woman named Marike Dykeman is forced to separate from Philip Bogardus when he's called away to fight the British. After she discovers that she's pregnant, Marike must devise a way to save her reputation and the child she carries until her lover returns home.

Nineteenth Century

Romantic novels set during America's early growth as a nation—just before, and during, the U.S. Civil War (1861–1865). Romantic Western novels, those which are set on the American Western frontier in the nineteenth century, are featured in Chapter 6.

Charbonneau, Eileen.

The Randolph Legacy. **Forge, 1997. 416pp.** **YA**

In the early nineteenth century, Judith Mercer, a young Quaker woman, sails home to America on an English ship. There she encounters a crippled, amnesiac man known as Washington. His existence has been kept a secret from the captain, who was the cause of his injuries at a young age. When Judith discovers the young man's true identity as the heir to the Southern Randolph plantation, she is pleased to see him restored to his proper place. However, she fears their burgeoning romance will not survive social barriers (his family are slaveholders) and their difference of religion.

Ellis, Virginia.

The Wedding Dress. **Ballantine, 2002. 292pp.** **YA**

Julia and Victoria, two Virginia sisters widowed in the Civil War, realize that the days of romance have likely passed them by. They decide to sew a wedding dress for their younger sister, Claire, in the hopes of finding her a husband when it's completed. Though the war has claimed the lives of most eligible Southern men, they force themselves to remain optimistic. When Sergeant Monroe Tacy arrives with a final message to Julia from her late husband, he seems to be the answer to their prayers.

Haeger, Diane.

My Dearest Cecelia. St. Martin's Press, 2003. 288pp. ✍

At a ball at West Point Academy in 1837, Southern belle Cecelia Stovall meets the man who will become the love of her life: Northern military man William Tecumseh Sherman. Their love survives for years despite misunderstandings, marriages to others, and the opposing sides they take when the Civil War breaks out. General Sherman avoided Cecelia's hometown of Augusta during his infamous march through Georgia, and his longtime affection for her may have been the reason why. Loosely based on history.

Stone, Irving.

The President's Lady. Doubleday, 1951. 338pp. ✍ **YA**

Stone gives life to the love story between Andrew Jackson, military hero and American president, and Rachel Donelson, a girl of the Tennessee frontier, and the uphill battle they fought to clear her name, after they and the American public discovered that her abusive first husband had not officially gone through with their divorce.

Twentieth Century

Like novels of the same time period in Europe, most works in this section feature stories of wartime romances.

Ellis, Virginia.

The Photograph. Ballantine, 2003. 321pp. **YA**

Just after the Japanese attack Pearl Harbor, seventeen-year-old Maddy Marshall joins her sister-in-law Ruth in Miami. A photograph taken the night of her brother Davey's departure for the war, when Maddy met the man she came to love, gradually changes to reflect the reality of the group's situation. Only Ruth can view the changes in the photo.

Florence, Ronald.

The Last Season. Forge, 2000. 348pp.

In Newport, Rhode Island, in 1941, a Portuguese fisherman's daughter named Sera falls in love with a Navy lieutenant and gets caught up in the romance and glitter of the Newport social set. But reality soon sets in, with their vast differences in social class and world war on the horizon.

Rae, Catherine M.

Flight from Fifth Avenue. St. Martin's Press, 1995. 186pp.

Maida Jardine flees from her family's Fifth Avenue apartment in 1911 to avoid an arranged marriage with a rich and cruel English nobleman. She heads west on an orphan train and works for a time in the Triangle Shirtwaist Factory, and manages to find both adventure and romance before returning home. The late Catherine Rae wrote many light romantic historical novels of upper-class New Yorkers.

Wilson, Susan.

Hawke's Cove. **Pocket, 2000. 282pp.**

> Evangeline "Vangie" Worth is left behind on her New England island home in 1944 when her husband John goes off to fight in World War II. She strikes up a friendship with Joe Green, a jack-of-all-trades who shows up at her door looking for work. Their relationship turns into love when John is reported missing in action. John, however, is still alive, and when he returns home to Massachusetts, the lovers can hardly bear to part.

Canada

In these romantic novels set in Canada, the beauty of America's northern neighbor comes alive in all its splendor.

Davis, Kathryn Lynn.

Sing to Me of Dreams. **Pocket, 1990. 549pp.**

> In 1861 on Vancouver Island in British Columbia, a baby girl named Tanu, born to a Salish woman and a white trader, is destined to be the tribe's shaman. Later renamed Saylah, she leaves her people for the white world after an outbreak of scarlet fever forces her to face her limitations. Saylah joins the household of Julian Ivy, who's drawn to her healing power, but she finds herself torn between his love and her heritage.

Johnson, Janice.

Winter of the Raven. **Forge, 1995. 381pp.**

> In the 1880s, Kate Hewitt grows up with her missionary father among the Haida of the Queen Charlotte Islands, where she pursues photography as a hobby. After her father is murdered, she gets stranded in Victoria until Luke Brennan comes along. Kate believes him to be one of the many artifact-hunters who want to exploit the Haida for their beautiful carved statues, but she can't resist when he offers her the opportunity to accompany him as a photographer on his mission. Some mystery elements.

MacNeil, Robert.

Burden of Desire. **Doubleday, 1992. 466pp.**

> After a freighter explodes in Halifax harbor on December 6, 1917, a clergyman and a psychiatrist sorting through the wreckage locate the passionate diary of a young woman—who then becomes an object of desire for them both.

Asia, Africa, and the Antipodes

The unusual settings imbue these romantic novels, and their heroes and heroines, with a larger-than-life quality.

Bradshaw, Gillian.

Horses of Heaven. **Doubleday, 1991. 448pp.**

> The ancient Hellenic kingdom of Bactria (modern-day Afghanistan) in 140 BC, several generations after the death of Alexander the Great, is the unusual setting for a tale of star-crossed lovers. Mauakes, the ruler of neighboring Ferghana, takes Heliokleia, a princess of Bactria, as his bride in his alliance with her country. She's not as attracted to her boorish, older husband as she is to Itaz, the son of his first marriage.

Cheng, François.

Green Mountain, White Cloud: A Novel of Love in the Ming Dynasty. **St. Martin's Press, 2004. 224pp.**

> This short, delicately written novel of forbidden love is set at the very end of the Ming Dynasty in seventeenth-century China. Dao-sheng, a former musician, dares to cast a glance at Lady Lan-ying, who is betrothed to another. He pays for his crime with decades of hard labor. Thirty years later, when Lan-ying is ailing, they are reunited, and their love is rekindled.

Johnson, Janice Kay.

The Island Snatchers. **Forge, 1997. 383pp.**

> After Anne Cartwright's missionary husband dies soon after reaching Hawaii in the 1850s, she takes on a role as nurse to the islanders. It's here she falls in love with Dr. Matthew McCabe. Together they fight the evils of smallpox and search for the truth behind Matthew's father's supposed suicide.

Oxnam, Robert B.

Ming. **St. Martin's Press, 1995. 270pp.**

> At the end of the Ming Dynasty in seventeenth-century China, two lovers are caught on opposite sides of the conflict between protecting the old ways and fighting the invading Manchus. While Meihua yearns to embrace the learning that's forbidden to a woman, Longyan, a second son, has the opposite problem. He turns to the military after a learning disability prevents him from fulfilling his destiny as a scholar.

Soueif, Ahdaf.

The Map of Love. **Anchor, 1999. 529pp.**

> Annotated in Chapter 10.

Sundaresan, Indu.

Nur Jahan Series. ✍ 📖

> The real-life romance between Emperor Jahangir and his Empress, Nur Jahan, in sixteenth-century India.

The Twentieth Wife. Pocket, 2002. 384pp.

> In Mughal India in 1577, an eight-year-old named Mehrunnisa, born into poverty, watches Prince Salim (later Jahangir) at his first wedding. She falls in love

with him instantly and decides that he will be her husband one day. Over time, the pair grow closer, but their romance must survive her first marriage, her husband's murder, and other machinations both political and within the harem before they find their way back to each other. Her dream comes true twenty-six years later, when she becomes his twentieth wife, known as Nur Jahan, Light of the World.

The Feast of Roses. Atria, 2003. 400pp.

In this sequel to *The Twentieth Wife*, Mehrunnisa, the first woman that Jahangir has married for love, becomes the power behind the throne. Her husband helps her cope with unscrupulous court ministers and powerful harem women.

Historical Romances

In novels of historical romance, the love story takes center stage. While historical events, customs, and values are present in the story and may serve to advance the plot, they function primarily as a background to the romance. If any battles or political developments occur within the novel, for the most part they take place off-stage. This keeps the focus on the main characters and their growing relationship. As a rule, historical romances have an optimistic, happily-ever-after ending.

Historical romances vary considerably in terms of how much period detail the author weaves into the story, and reader preferences will vary as well. People who simply want to read a well-written love story in a non-modern setting may not want to be overwhelmed with historical details. Other readers will want exactly the opposite. There are a number of readers and even authors in the genre who lament the lack of history-intensive romances being published today. Some authors of historical romance classics, such as Roberta Gellis and Karen Harper, now write primarily in other genres, such as historical mystery, women's fiction, or contemporary suspense.

While the market for history-intensive romance may not be as strong now as it was twenty years ago, many historical romance authors today do considerable background research for their novels. They take care to ensure that their facts are correct and that their characters behave in ways appropriate to their era. There is some controversy about whether romances featuring feisty, freethinking heroines should automatically be considered anachronistic. Those who disagree mention that historical novels in general are written about characters who stand apart from the norm (Eleanor of Aquitaine is frequently used as an example), and they have a point. The debate will no doubt continue.

Some settings in historical romance are more common than others. In novels set in the British Isles, medieval settings are popular, as are novels set in the Regency period, the Georgian period, and in Victorian times. Among American settings, the frontier West is perhaps the most popular. Historical romance novels set in other times or locations—such as ancient times, the American Revolution and Civil War, and Asia and Australia—are harder to come by. Bloody battle scenes, after all, have little appeal for the romance reader, and publishers seem to feel that unusual settings deflect attention from the love story. (Librarians interested in learning why some settings are more popular than others should read Kristin Ramsdell's "Getting Behind Reader Taboos: What's Wrong with France?," published in the July 2002 issue of *Romance Writers Report.*) Other unpleasant aspects of life in times past, while they certainly existed, are not dwelt upon in most historical romances.

Authors listed in this section do their best to create characters and plotlines that faithfully reflect their time period. In all of these novels, the historical background features strongly in the story. With so many historical romances published each month, comprehensiveness is next to impossible; the following list provides a selected bibliography. Only authors' most significant or newest titles are provided here, but many writers have a lengthy backlist of titles that would be equally appropriate for readers who enjoy a good dose of history with their romance. (Not all of these authors limit themselves to historical romance titles, however.) Also, publishers frequently bring older paperback titles by popular authors back into print so that they can reach a new audience—and so that readers and librarians can purchase fresh copies for their collections.

Novels in this section are categorized chronologically. Sensuality levels are indicated as either **Sweet** (kisses and little beyond that; no sex), or **Sensual** (descriptions of sexual intimacy between the couple). Novels described as **Very sensual** include very explicit descriptions of sex.

Ancient Civilizations

Very few romance novels are set during ancient times, though they do exist. With their long-ago historical setting, larger-than-life heroes and heroines, and compelling plots, these romances read like ancient legends.

French, Judith E.

Roxanne Series. ✍

The romantic adventures of Roxanne of Persia, best known to history as the wife of Alexander the Great. French's romances are unique not only for their ancient world setting (fourth century BC) but because her heroine loves more than one man during her life. **Sensual.**

The Conqueror. LoveSpell, 2003. 355pp.

Roxanne, the most beautiful woman in all of ancient Persia, finds love in a political match with Alexander the Great. His attraction to other women—and his need to conquer the world—occasionally takes a backseat to their romance.

The Barbarian. LoveSpell, 2004. 368pp.

Alexander the Great is dead, and Roxanne awakens in Alexandria with no memory of her past save a few recollections of having borne a child. When a barbarian named Kayan enters her tent and tells her that they once loved one another long ago, she puts her trust in him. The two of them escape from Egypt and make their way home to Persia.

Lovelace, Merline.

Lady of the Upper Kingdom. **Harlequin Historicals, 1996. 296pp.**

In ancient Egypt, Captain Philip Tauron, friend of Alexander the Great, falls in love with Lady Farah, an unapproachable priestess. **Sensual.**

Robinson, Suzanne.

Heart of the Falcon. **Avon, 1990. 272pp.**

Ancient Egypt: After the death of her father, Anqet flees to Thebes to escape from her uncle's unwelcome suit—and finds safety and danger in the arms of the mysterious Count Seth. Reissued in 1997. **Sensual.**

Verrette, Joyce.

Regretfully out of print, Joyce Verrette's excellent Egyptian romances, written before ancient settings became unfashionable, bring the period to life. **Sensual.**

Dawn of Desire. **Avon, 1976. 475pp.**

Love between heirs of rival nations, Princess Nefrytatanen and Prince Amenhemet "Ameni," blossoms along the River Nile.

Desert Fires. **Avon, 1978. 410pp.**

The continued romance of Nefrytataten and Ameni, now king.

Sunrise of Splendor. **Fawcett Gold Medal, 1978. 557pp.**

Princess Sharula, not content to be a harem woman, wants Ramessa to make her his Queen.

Winged Priestess. **Fawcett Gold Medal, 1980. 318pp.**

Nefrytatanen defies the gods themselves for the love of her husband, King Amenhemet.

Medieval Romances

Most medieval romances are chivalrous love stories featuring knights and their ladies. They are set between the fifth and fifteenth centuries in the British Isles or elsewhere in Europe. While most medieval noblewomen had a fair amount of independence, arranged marriages were the norm. In these stories the arranged marriage often serves as the catalyst for the romance.

Beverley, Jo.

With their vivid descriptions of England in the Middle Ages, Jo Beverley's well-written medieval romances are among the most popular of the genre. Dark and realistic at times, they feature independent-minded heroines caught up in political intrigue who must work through emotional barriers to find happiness. **Sensual.**

Dark Champion. **Signet, 1993. 376pp.**

In twelfth-century England, Imogen of Carrisford turns to FitzRoger of Cleeve when enemies besiege her castle.

Lord of Midnight. **Topaz, 1998. 378pp.**

Early twelfth century: When she marries a man to save her family home, Claire of Summerbourne doesn't realize that the handsome stranger may have killed her father.

Lord of My Heart. **Signet, 1992. 376pp.**

In 1068, just after the Norman Conquest, Madeleine de la Haute Vironge marries Aimery de Gaillard to get her uncle off her estate, but Aimery may be a traitor to the crown.

The Shattered Rose. **Zebra Books, 1995. 415pp.**

After two years away, Galeran of Heywood returns from the Crusades in the early 1100s only to find his wife Jehanne with a newborn baby, an illegitimate daughter the Church wants to take away from her.

Canham, Marsha.

Robin Hood Trilogy.

A trilogy of romantic adventure set during the time of England's King John in the late twelfth and early thirteenth centuries. **Sensual.**

Through a Dark Mist. **Dell, 1991. 472pp.**

Lady Servanne de Briscourt is en route to her marriage when her party is attacked by the Black Wolf and his men.

In the Shadow of Midnight. **Dell, 1994. 407pp.**

Lady Ariel de Clare, niece of the Marshal of England, flees an arranged marriage with the help of Eduard, the bastard son of the Black Wolf, who sees her safely to Wales. Eduard, though, has his own plans—to rescue Eleanor, Princess of Brittany, from King John's clutches.

The Last Arrow. **Dell, 1997. 454pp.**

Brenna Wardieu, the Black Wolf's daughter, an archer of great skill, falls in love with a mercenary sent to challenge her brother in a tournament. What Griffyn Renaud de Verdelay doesn't know, however, is that Brenna and her brother are sworn to protect the lost Princess of Brittany against King John, while she fears that he has been assigned to kill her.

Chadwick, Elizabeth.

Chadwick's earliest novels are well-researched historical romances set in the dark, occasionally grim setting of twelfth-century England and Wales. **Sensual.**

Ravenstow Series.

Historical romances that double as an extended family saga, set around the earl-dom of Ravenstow in the twelfth century.

The Wild Hunt. St. Martin's Press, 1991. 370pp.

During the Welsh border wars, Guyon of Ledworth weds the much younger Lady Judith of Ravenstow to protect her lands. Betty Trask Award.

The Running Vixen. St. Martin's Press, 1992. 330pp.

A sequel to *The Wild Hunt*, featuring a romance between Guyon's gentle daughter Heulwen and his foster son Adam de Lacey.

The Leopard Unleashed. St. Martin's Press, 1993. 328pp.

Renard, heir to the earldom of Ravenstow, returns from the Crusades with his mistress Olwen, a half-Welsh tavern dancer, and must choose between her and Eleanor de Mortimer, his betrothed.

Shields of Pride. **Ballantine, 1994. 325pp.**

In 1173, when Henry II of England tries to bring his rebellious sons into line, Linnet de Montsorrel and her young son come under the protection of the king's mercenary, Joscelin de Gael.

Cody, Denée.

The Conquered Heart. **Kensington, 1995. 353pp.** ✍

In the twelfth century, Eve MacMurrough, Princess of Leinster, expects to despise Richard de Clare, the Norman knight whom her father orders her to marry. Their relationship soon grows into respect and love. **Sensual.**

The Court of Love. **Kensington, 1996. 410pp.**

Julianna, Countess of Rosmar, one of Eleanor of Aquitaine's companions, must get the permission of both Eleanor and her son, King Richard, before marrying commoner Stephan de Mandeville. Without this consent, their love and lives are in danger. **Sensual.**

Queen of the May. **Kensington, 1997. 346pp.**

Giselle, living as an outlaw in Sherwood Forest in King Richard's England, wounds Alexander de Mandeville, the new lord of Wolfhurst, with one of her own arrows—but soon regrets it. **Sensual.**

Crenshaw, Nadine.

Viking Gold. **Zebra, 1995. 382pp.** ✍

In this intelligent Viking-era romance set in the ninth century, Princess Aasa captures the heart of Olaf, Prince of Norway, though she's promised to his widowed father, the king. **Sensual.**

Gellis, Roberta.

The Roselynde Chronicles. ★

A panoramic series of romantic novels set between the reigns of Richard the Lion-Heart and his nephew Henry III (late twelfth to early thirteenth centuries), featuring one beautiful, strong-willed woman—Alinor of Roselynde—and her children and grandchildren. The political history of England, Wales, and indeed all of Europe plays a major role in the plotline of the series. All of Gellis's historical romances, most of which are set in medieval England, are recommended for their impeccable research and skillful storytelling. This six-book series will be reprinted in 2005 by Harlequin, along with a new volume, *Desiree*. **Sensual.**

Roselynde. Playboy Press, 1978. 495pp.

Lady Alinor Devaux, mistress of Roselynde at the beginning of King Richard's reign, defies her namesake and queen by marrying Sir Simon Lemagne, the warden of her estates, for he is thirty years older and not of her station.

Alinor. Playboy Press, 1978. 558pp.

Following the death of her great love Simon, Lady Alinor Lemagne surprises herself with her attraction to her late husband's handsome former squire, Ian de Vipont.

Joanna. Playboy Press, 1978. 560pp.

Beautiful red-haired Joanna, daughter of Alinor and Simon, lets her passions rule her except when it comes to love. She turns down suitor after suitor until she meets a knight named Geoffrey.

Gilliane. Playboy Press, 1979. 494pp.

At the time of King John's death in 1204, Gilliane, forced for political reasons to marry a man she hates, becomes the prisoner—and the star-crossed lover—of Adam Lemagne, Alinor and Simon's son.

Rhiannon. Playboy Press, 1982. 381pp.

Simon de Vipont, one of medieval England's most eligible bachelors, fights for the hand of Rhiannon, daughter of a Welsh prince.

Sybelle. Jove, 1983. 404pp.

Sybelle, daughter of Joanna and Geoffrey and the heiress to Roselynde, vows to wed no man—that is, until she meets Walter de Clare.

Haycraft, Molly Costain.

The daughter of classic historian/historical novelist Thomas Costain, Haycraft wrote a series of historical romances based on the lives of royal women. **Sweet.**

The King's Daughters. **Lippincott, 1971. 247pp.** ✍ **YA**

Elizabeth, the youngest daughter of Edward the First, sees her sisters married off one by one, mostly for political reasons, but yearns for a romance of her own.

The Lady Royal. **Lippincott, 1964. 253pp.** ✍ **YA**

Isabella, daughter of Edward III, has already turned down more suitors than she can count, to her parents' dismay. She doesn't count on the persistence of French nobleman Enguerrand de Coucy. History fans take note: De Coucy is the focus of Barbara Tuchman's award-winning nonfiction history of the fourteenth century, *The Distant Mirror*.

My Lord Brother the Lion Heart. **Lippincott, 1968. 320pp.** ✍ **YA**

Princess Joan, sister of Richard the Lion Heart and the widowed Queen of Sicily, must find a way to avoid being married off to a Saracen for political gain.

Hunter, Madeline.

Hunter's medieval novels stand out in the romance field for their well-researched backdrop of fourteenth-century England, Scotland, and Wales and her frequent choice of men and women of the merchant class as her protagonists. The love stories between these strong-willed and intelligent men and women are intimately entwined with the political intrigue of the day. **Sensual.**

By Arrangement. **Bantam, 2000. 389pp.**

When a mere merchant named David de Abyndon succeeds in obtaining the hand in marriage of Lady Christiana Fitzwaryn, he must do all he can to win her heart as well.

By Design. **Bantam, 2000. 373pp.**

Joan, a talented sculptress who had once known a better life, can't hide her fury when a Freemason named Rhys tries to rescue her from punishment—and ends up purchasing her instead.

By Possession. **Bantam, 2000. 371pp.**

Addis de Valence, finally home from the Baltic Crusades, can't hide his growing attraction to Moira Falkner, a serf from his late wife's household. She refuses to compromise herself by becoming his mistress.

Lord of a Thousand Nights. **Bantam, 2002. 384pp.**

Lady Reyna Graham, widow of a Scottish lord, disguises herself as a courtesan to seduce the man who is holding siege to her keep.

The Protector. **Bantam, 2001. 368pp.**

As France and England fight over the lands of Brittany, Morvan Fitzwaryn, brother of Christiana from *By Arrangement*, takes refuge on the Breton lands of Anna de Leon when the Black Plague strikes.

🎗 *Stealing Heaven.* **Bantam, 2002. 320pp.**

Marcus de Anglesmore makes the mistake of falling in love with an enticing Welsh witch named Nesta, the sister of the woman he had agreed to marry. RITA Award.

Ingram, Grace.

Red Adam's Lady. **Stein and Day, 1973. 320pp.** ★

In this bawdy and adventurous medieval romance, the night after Red Adam of Brentborough ruins Lady Julitta's honor by abducting her, he does the unthinkable and marries her. She insists on keeping him at arm's length. **Sweet.**

Kinsale, Laura.

For My Lady's Heart Series.

Kinsale evokes the harsh medieval world through the dark portrayal of her protagonists and her authentic Middle English dialogue. **Sensual.**

For My Lady's Heart. Berkley, 1983. 423pp.

In fourteenth-century England, Melanthe del Monteverde, an Italian princess with a seeming heart of stone, chooses a knight, Ruck of Wolfscar, to be her champion in regaining her father's English lands. Inspired by the courtly poem *Sir Gawain and the Green Knight.*

Shadowheart. Berkley, 2004. 502pp.

Allegreto, the mysterious Italian who protected Princess Melanthe in Kinsale's earlier book, is given a novel of his own. A young assassin, Allegreto heads to Italy to assert his birthright in the principality of Monteverde. He kidnaps Elena, the long-lost Monteverde heir, who journeys home to claim her lands.

Lide, Mary.

Sedgemont Series.

Ann of Cambray, daughter of a Celtic woman and a Norman warrior in the twelfth century, falls in love with Raoul of Sedgmont, the man whose ward she becomes. Together they play the political game of standing up for their own rights while avoiding the potential wrath of Eleanor of Aquitaine. The three children of Ann and Raoul are just as proud and passionate as their parents, and like them, their fates revolve around the whims of the royal family. **Sensual.**

Ann of Cambray. Warner, 1984. 432pp.

Gifts of the Queen. Warner, 1985. 368pp.

A Royal Quest. Warner, 1987. 374pp. (Original title: *Hawks of Sedgemont.*)

Martyn, Isolde.

The Knight and the Rose. **Berkley, 2002. 452pp.**

In the year 1322, to escape her brutal husband, Lady Johanna Fitzhenry must find a willing man to swear that the two of them were married first. Hope arrives in the form of Gervase de Laval, who claims to be a scholar, but while she grows steadily closer to him, he is concealing his true identity from her. Martyn's novel is based on a medieval court case. **Sensual.**

🎗 *The Maiden and the Unicorn.* **Bantam, 1999. 429pp. (Original title: *The Lady and the Unicorn.*)** ✍

It is 1470, the height of the Wars of the Roses. Margery Huddleston, the ward of Warwick the Kingmaker, is sent to France on a mission for the Yorkist King Edward IV. There, she attracts the attention of Sir Richard Huddleston, who may or may not be working for the Lancastrians. RITA Award. **Sensual.**

Moonlight and Shadow. **Berkley, 2002. 460pp. (Original title: *The Silver Bride*.)**

At the end of the Wars of the Roses, silver-haired Heloise Ballaster, a maid of honor to Anne of Warwick, is forced by her merchant father to marry Sir Miles Rushden at swordpoint. **Sensual.**

Ryan, Patricia.

Best known for her medieval romances, below, the author recently began a nineteenth-century mystery series under the name P. B. Ryan (Chapter 7).

🎗 *Silken Threads.* **Topaz, 1999. 340pp.**

In this twelfth-century romance inspired by Hitchcock's *Rear Window*, a mercenary must rescue his lord's illegitimate daughter from her abusive husband. After breaking his leg in the attempt, he recovers at the nearby home of Joanna Chapman, a silk merchant's beautiful widow. From her storeroom, he can observe all the goings-on across the way. RITA Award. **Sensual.**

The Sun and the Moon. **Signet, 2000. 338pp.**

Phillipa de Paris, an Oxford intellectual, joins forces with one of King Henry's spies to help save England from another civil war. Sequel to *Silken Threads*. **Sensual.**

Samuel, Barbara.

A Bed of Spices. **Harper, 1993. 343pp.**

In 1348 Strassburg, Prussia, Frederica der Esslingen falls in love with Solomon, a Jewish merchant's son. Samuel also writes romances under the name Ruth Wind. **Sensual.**

Squires, Susan.

Danegeld. **LoveSpell, 2001. 358pp.**

In England's Dark Ages, Britta, a Saxon wicce with a wounded heart, feels compelled to heal Karn, a Viking warrior, despite the fact that he was captured while raiding her village. It is considerably more grim than most romances, but in this sense perhaps more realistic for its time period. **Sensual.**

Danelaw. **LoveSpell, 2003. 374pp.**

To keep the Goddess alive in the early Middle Ages, Epona, a priestess who serves the power of the horse, must find the man who can help her give birth to a girl-child. **Sensual.**

Wolf, Joan.

Born of the Sun. **New American Library, 1989. 407pp.** YA

In sixth-century Britain, eighty years after the death of Arthur, Celtic princess Niniane falls in love with Ceawlin, illegitimate son of the Saxon king. **Sensual.**

The Edge of Light. **New American Library, 1990. 371pp.** ✍ YA

Alfred the Great fights off the Danish invasion in ninth-century Britain with the help of his beautiful wife, the Mercian princess Elswyth. **Sensual.**

The Road to Avalon. **New American Library, 1988. 358pp.** YA

It is post-Roman Britain, and most of the standard elements of the traditional Arthurian tale are here, with some exceptions that set Wolf's tale apart. Magic doesn't exist, giving it a historically authentic flavor. Morgan rather than Gwenhwyfar is Arthur's soul mate, though because she is the half-sister of his mother, Igraine, they are forbidden to marry. **Sensual.**

Tudor and Renaissance Era

Most romances set during England's Tudor period, or during the Renaissance in Europe (a less frequent setting), are love stories set against the political intrigue of royalty. The ribald court of Henry VIII, a larger-than-life figure known for his romantic exploits, serves as a backdrop to many romances between beautiful noblewomen and their chosen men.

Barnes, Margaret Campbell.

The Tudor Rose. **Macrae Smith, 1953. 313pp.** ✍ ★ YA

Henry VII is rarely seen as a hero these days, but in this classic romance he is the savior of Elizabeth of York, who turns to him rather than marry her brothers' likely murderer, her uncle Richard III. **Sweet.**

Cody, Denée.

The Golden Rose. **Kensington, 1998. 343pp.**

Catherine, Lady of Rosmar, returns home to find her castle occupied by Andrew Mandeville, desperate to reclaim his family's ancient seat. Political intrigue abounds in 1499 England, and soon it engulfs Catherine and Andrew, who find they must work together if they are to survive. **Sensual.**

Domning, Denise.

Lady in Waiting. **Topaz, 1998. 380pp.**

In the court of Elizabeth I, Kit Hollier's plans to deflower one of the queen's ladies come undone when he falls in love with her. **Sensual.**

Feather, Jane.

Kiss Trilogy.

A trilogy set amid political intrigue in Tudor England, featuring Lady Guinevere Mallory and her two daughters, Penelope and Philippa. **Sensual.**

The Widow's Kiss. **Bantam, 2001. 464pp.**

The wealth of Lady Guinevere Mallory, four times a widow, attracts Henry VIII's attention when soldier Hugh of Beaucaire questions her ownership of a plot of land.

To Kiss a Spy. **Bantam, 2002. 314pp.**

Lady Penelope (Pen) Bryanston, convinced that her baby didn't die at birth, agrees to accept the investigative services of French spy Owen d'Arcy if she'll report back to him on Princess Mary's activities.

Kissed by Shadows. Bantam, 2003. 469pp.

Lady Philippa (Pippa) Nielson doesn't realize that she's being used as a pawn of Queen Mary's to secure the Spanish succession to the English throne—or that her friend Lionel Ashton may be on their side. Some elements of the plot, while not surprising given the ruthless time period, may disturb romance readers.

Feyrer, Gayle.

The Prince of Cups. **Dell, 1995. 471pp.**

In fifteenth-century Italy, it's foretold by her great-grandmother in the Tarot cards that Veronica Danti will have a Prince of Cups in her future. **Very sensual.**

Gellis, Roberta.

The Dragon and the Rose. **Playboy, 1977. 363pp.** ✍

As in Margaret Campbell Barnes's *The Tudor Rose*, mentioned above, Elizabeth of York and Henry Tudor are the romantic protagonists, but Gellis doesn't flinch from either court politics or battle scenes. **Sensual.**

Henley, Virginia.

A Woman of Passion. **Delacorte, 1999. 450pp.** ✍

Elizabeth "Bess" Hardwick is a real-life Elizabethan heroine who married four times, becoming more powerful with each successive husband. Her story is overly romanticized to conform to the genre, and Henley's tendency to give sexy modern nicknames to her Elizabethan characters requires some suspension of disbelief. Hers is a sympathetic, exciting portrait of the Countess of Shrewsbury, who hasn't received much positive press because of her role as jailer to Mary, Queen of Scots. **Very sensual.**

Holling, Jen.

Bride of the Bloodstone Trilogy.

Set in 1542, Holling's trilogy of romances features members of two warring families along the English–Scots border: the Grahams and the Maxwells. They also have a touch of the paranormal, as the family feud began over possession of a magical stone. **Sensual.**

Tempted by Your Touch. Sonnet, 2002. 374pp.

Robert Maxwell hopes to make peace with the Grahams by wedding the beautiful Caroline Graham, but Caroline's brother may be using her as a tool for his revenge.

Tamed by Your Desire. Sonnet, 2002. 331pp.

Escaping from an unwanted arranged marriage, Fayth Graham falls right into the hands of her family's enemy, Alex Maxwell—who must choose between keeping her and regaining the Bloodstone.

Captured by Your Kiss. Sonnet, 2003. 331pp.

Mona Graham and Patrick Maxwell resolve their families' differences by finding the lost treasure—and falling in love.

Osborne, Maggie.
Chase the Heart. Morrow, 1987. 324pp.

In Elizabethan England just after the Armada's defeat, Lady Nellanor Amesley, the ward of the late Robert Dudley, Earl of Leicester, finds that her benefactor left her a casket of letters containing secret information—information that could alter the royal succession. Dudley's widow, realizing their contents, has sold them off to Philip of Spain, so Queen Elizabeth sends Nell and Lord William Steele off on a mission to retrieve them—or face death if they fail. Osborne also writes Western romances. **Sweet.**

Small, Bertrice.
Friarsgate Inheritance Series.

A series set both in Scotland and around the Tudor court of Henry VIII. The next volume will be *Philippa*, about Rosamund's daughter. **Very sensual.**

Rosamund. New American Library, 2002. 375pp.

Twice-widowed Rosamund Bolton, mistress of Friarsgate on the English–Scots border, fights for her inheritance with the help of the king, Henry VIII, who draws her into his circle.

Until You. New American Library, 2003. 371pp.

Having secured her inheritance, Rosamund travels north to visit her friend, Queen Margaret of Scotland, Henry VIII's sister. While there, she has a passionate romance with Patrick Leslie, Earl of Glenkirk (father of Janet Leslie, heroine of Small's romantic epic *The Kadin*). They undertake a mission for Margaret's husband James IV against England.

O'Malley Saga. ★

Skye O'Malley, a rival to Queen Elizabeth herself, finds love and adventure in the Elizabethan court and in the exotic lands of the Middle East. The later volumes in this series deal with the romantic intrigues of the members of Skye's family, who voyage to Ireland, Turkey, and remote India. There's not as much historical detail here as in Small's romantic epics, and her character names are more romantic than realistic, but they have the same sweep and passion. The saga continues in the Skye's Legacy series (see under "Seventeenth Century," below). **Very sensual.**

Skye O'Malley. Ballantine, 1980. 461pp.

Skye, the most beautiful woman in Ireland, gets involved with many men on her travels from Ireland to Algiers to London—and finds love with Niall Burke.

All the Sweet Tomorrows. Ballantine, 1984. 610pp.

Believing that her beloved Niall is dead, Skye marries a cruel nobleman, only to discover that Niall is being held captive in Algiers.

A Love for All Time. New American Library, 1986. 534pp.

Queen Elizabeth herself arranges a marriage between Conn O'Malley, Skye's baby brother, and plain heiress Aiden St. Michael. They fall in love, but Aiden's relatives betray her and sell her into slavery in the Ottoman Empire.

This Heart of Mine. Ballantine, 1985. 690pp.

Velvet de Marisco, daughter of Skye and her husband Adam de Marisco, is presented as a prize to the Grand Mughal of India, who marries her and gives her a daughter.

Lost Love Found. Ballantine, 1989. 483pp.

Valentina St. Michael, daughter of Conn and Aiden, searches for the truth about her parentage in the seventeenth-century Ottoman Empire.

Wild Jasmine. Ballantine, 1992. 658pp.

Velvet's daughter, Yasaman Kama Begum, flees India in search of her mother's family when her half-brother makes unwanted advances toward her.

Seventeenth Century

The English Civil War in the seventeenth century was a time of intense political and religious rivalry, as Royalists fought against Roundheads (Puritans) for control of England. Romances set during the Civil War and Restoration vividly contrast the plain Puritan lifestyle with that of the more glamorous Royalists. Not surprisingly, most of this era's romantic heroes fall into the latter group. Pamela Belle's novels, under "Romantic Sagas" in Chapter 5, are also set during this era. Seventeenth-century Europe is a less frequent setting for these novels.

Feather, Jane.

Bride Trilogy.

Three female friends living during the English Civil War distrust all men and vow never to marry. Of course, they all end up breaking their promise. **Sensual.**

The Hostage Bride. Bantam, 1998. 346pp.

Royalist nobleman Rufus Decatur accidentally abducts Portia Worth, the bastard relative of the Marquis of Granville, a Roundhead sympathizer.

The Accidental Bride. Bantam, 1999. 328pp.

Cato, Marquis of Granville, enters into an arranged marriage with seventeen-year-old Phoebe, who is both the awkward sister of his late wife and a good friend of his daughter.

The Least Likely Bride. Bantam, 2000. 322pp.

In 1640, scholarly Olivia Granville, her head buried in a book, falls down a cliff and awakens aboard a pirate ship captained by a handsome Royalist.

Small, Bertrice.

Skye's Legacy.

The Skye's Legacy novels continue the story of Skye O'Malley's descendants (earlier volumes in the series listed earlier), up through the time of the Restoration. The escapades get steadily more outlandish—how many members of Skye's family have been kidnapped into slavery in the Middle East by now?– but Small's fans will enjoy watching how the stories unfold. **Very sensual.**

Darling Jasmine. Kensington, 1997. 378pp.

James Leslie vows to win back the love of his life, Jasmine de Marisco, though she has fled to France to escape an arranged marriage to him. As the mother of King James's only grandson, her search for freedom isn't destined to last.

Bedazzled. Kensington, 1999. 374pp.

In 1625, Barbary pirates capture a ship carrying Lady India Lindley, Jasmine's daughter, just after her elopement with an English nobleman.

Besieged. Kensington, 2000. 340pp.

Lady Fortune Lindley, Jasmine's second daughter, agrees to marry an Irish Protestant aristocrat to claim her family's Ulster inheritance.

Intrigued. Kensington, 2001. 409pp.

Lady Autumn Rose Leslie, Jasmine's youngest daughter, finds adventure and romance in seventeenth-century England and France.

Just Beyond Tomorrow. Kensington, 2002. 329pp.

Jasmine's son Patrick Leslie, the new Duke of Glenkirk, finds a wife in heiress Flanna Brodie, but she doesn't understand his unwillingness to help Prince Charles (the future Charles II) regain his father's throne.

Vixens. Kensington, 2003. 439pp.

First cousins Fancy Devers, Diana Leslie, and Cynara Stuart, the next generation of O'Malley descendants, set Charles II's Restoration court ablaze with their beauty.

Smith, Haywood.

Secrets in Satin. **St. Martin's Press, 1997. 352pp.**

During the English Civil War, the Catholic Elizabeth, Countess of Ravenwold, is only too glad when her abusive husband dies, but nobody else understands her newfound sense of freedom. Certainly not Edward, Viscount Creighton, a Protestant aristocrat who is matched with her against his will by King Charles I himself. **Sensual.**

Shadows in Velvet. **St. Martin's Press, 1996.**

Philippe Corday must quickly end his *affaire* with La Grande Mademoiselle, Louis XIV's first cousin, before he's married to a young convent-raised aristocrat named Anne-Marie. The pair soon get caught up in political machinations on the princess's behalf. **Sensual.**

Georgian Romances

The majority of these romances are set in England during the reign of George III in the 1760s, before his madness made him unable to rule. Others are set in the 1830s, when his son George IV was on the throne in his own right. Like romances set in the Regency period, Georgian romances tend to feature members of the upper classes. Some of them fit into the Regency romance style (below), with light, witty dialogue and banter. Others reflect the treacherous and often erotic undercurrent hidden beneath the propriety of English society.

Abrams, Nita.

Couriers Series.

> Abrams's well-researched romantic novels of adventure, intrigue, and espionage in England and Europe during the Napoleonic Wars (early nineteenth century) feature members of a Jewish family. **Sensual.**

A Question of Honor. Zebra, 2002. 382pp.

> Captain Richard Drayton, a British spy in Napoleonic Spain, believes that Rachel, his niece's young (and Jewish) governess, may be hiding something.

The Exiles. Zebra, 2002. 384pp.

> In Vienna, a city swarming with intelligence activity, a mysterious swordsman rescues Elizabeth de Quincy from thieves.

The Spy's Bride. Zebra, 2003. 380pp.

> Eloise Bernal agrees to an arranged marriage with James Roth Meyer, not knowing his true identity as master British spy James Nathanson.

Beverley, Jo.

Malloren Series.

> Beverley's Malloren novels, about an aristocratic family of four brothers and two sisters, are set in 1760s Georgian England—when highwaymen roamed the roads in search of adventure. **Sensual.**

My Lady Notorious. Avon, 1993. 380pp.

> Lady Chastity Ware disguises herself as a highwayman to save her family and captures a coach occupied by Cyn Malloren.

Tempting Fortune. Zebra, 1995. 444pp.

> Poor, plain spinster Portia St. Claire believes that notorious gambler Lord Arcenbryght (Bryght) Malloren may have been her family's downfall.

Something Wicked. Topaz, 1997. 374pp.

> Lady Elfled Malloren, unmarried and bored, attends the Vauxhall Gardens Masquerade in disguise—and experiences a night of passion with her family's archenemy, Fort, the Earl of Walgrave.

Secrets of the Night. Topaz, 1999. 338pp.

Because Rosamunde Overton's husband can't provide the needed heir, she looks for a lover to do the job, and finds him in Lord Brand Malloren.

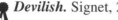 *Devilish.* Signet, 2000. 372pp.

When Bey Malloren, the Marquess of Rothgar, and Diana, Countess of Arradale, are thrown together, sparks fly, though both have sworn never to marry. RITA Award.

Winter Fire. Signet, 2003. 311pp.

Having been caught in a passionate embrace with the Marquess of Ashart, Lord Rothgar's cousin, Genova Smith must pretend to love him to protect her reputation.

Canham, Marsha.

Scotland Trilogy.

A trilogy of romances set in Jacobite-era (1745) England and Scotland, when Catholics made a vain attempt to help Scotland's Bonnie Prince Charlie gain England's throne. The first two have been reissued. **Sensual.**

Pride of Lions. Paperjacks, 1988. 407pp.

After Alex Cameron wins her in a duel, proud Catherine Ashbrooke discovers that her new husband is a Jacobite spy.

Blood of Roses. Knightsbridge, 1989. 599pp.

When the Jacobite Rebellion threatens to tear married lovers Catherine and Alex Cameron apart, she runs away from their Highland home and joins him in fighting the English.

Midnight Honor. Dell, 2001. 388pp. ✍

Lady Anne MacKintosh, loyal to Scotland and Bonnie Prince Charlie, can't understand why her devoted husband Angus Moy, chief of Clan Chattan, insists on taking sides with the hated English. Based on the life of a historical Scottish heroine.

Grant, Tracy.

Shores of Desire. Dell, 1997. 400pp.

Robert Lescaut, a Napoleonic army officer, falls in love with Emma Blair, a lookalike for his late wife, on a mission to Scotland. Grant's romantic tale shows her proficiency in writing tales of romantic espionage (Chapter 9). **Sensual.**

Putney, Mary Jo.

Bride Trilogy.

Putney's trilogy of romantic adventure in late Georgian-era England also incorporates exotic settings—India, China, and Australia. The books take on the difficult theme of intercultural relations in the early nineteenth century. **Sensual.**

The Wild Child. Ballantine, 1999. 310pp.

Kyle Renbourne makes a deal with his younger twin brother. If Dominic agrees to woo his promised wife, Lady Meriel Grahame, on his behalf, Kyle will give him a share of his inheritance. Meriel has not spoken since the night her parents were murdered in colonial India, and it's up to Dominic to break down her defenses.

The Child Bride. Ballantine, 2000. 310pp.

Troth Mei-Lian Montgomery, the mixed-race daughter of a Scottish trader and his Chinese concubine, disguises herself as a male interpreter and spy in 1830s China. Kyle Renbourne, oddly attracted to the translator he's hired, discovers her true identity and asks her to accompany him on a dangerous mission.

The Bartered Bride. Ballantine, 2002. 336pp.

On the fictional tropical island of Maduri in 1834, widow Alexandra Warren is rescued by sea captain Gavin Elliott after being trapped into slavery while traveling from Australia home to London. The rough slave trade of the East Indies contrasts nicely with the proper atmosphere of late Georgian England.

Ross, Julia.

Ross is the pseudonym for Jean Ross Ewing.

The Seduction. **Berkley, 2002. 368pp.**

When Alden Granville-Strachen, the Viscount Gracechurch, loses everything in a card game, he is given one chance to redeem himself: seduce a young widow living in the English countryside. **Sensual.**

The Wicked Lover. **Berkley, 2004. 400pp.**

Robert Sinclair Dovenby, better known as "Dove," inexplicably finds a young man hiding in his bedroom. He knows that the intruder is really a woman but doesn't discern her true identity: Sylvie Georgiana, Countess of Montevrain, who was sent to investigate his covert activities. **Sensual.**

Ware, Ciji.
Wicked Company. **Bantam, 1982. 695pp.**

Sophie McGann, a Scottish lass in 1761 London, wants to be a playwright, but certain men want to take credit for her talent. **Sensual.**

Regency-Era Romances

Romances set during England's Regency period (1811–1820), when the Prince of Wales (later George IV) ruled in his mad father's stead, are typically novels of manners. Most of these lighthearted love stories are set among the upper crust in London, though the scene can shift to the nearby countryside during the summer as members of the aristocracy flock to the seashore. Regency authors are meticulous about their research, thoroughly checking all of their facts from their characters' titles down to their garments, jewelry, and mannerisms. Fans revel in the characters' sparkling dialogue, reminiscent of that of the great Jane Austen, and also in the obligatory happy ending.

Regency novels can be divided into two categories, depending on the level of physical intimacy between the couple. In the first category, **Regency romances,** the stories tend to be fairly "sweet," with little more than kisses exchanged by the pair, and the focus is on the romantic pair and their acceptance by society. In the second category, **Regency historicals,** stories are considerably more sensual and take place not just in Society, but in the world at large.

There are exceptions to these rules, however. The late Georgette Heyer, though she wrote in other historical periods as well, is the *grande dame* of the Regency romance, and her work continues to be popular in libraries. Most Regency authors are prolific; here is a selected bibliography of their novels.

Balogh, Mary.

The Bedwyns.

Balogh's latest series tells the story of the Bedwyns, six brothers and sisters who find romance and adventure in Regency England. **Regency historicals.**

A Summer to Remember. Delacorte, 2002. 320pp.

Rakish Kit Butler, Viscount Ravensburgh, fakes his engagement to Miss Lauren Edgeworth to rid himself of his unwanted fiancée, Freyja Bedwyn. A lead-in to the Bedwyn series.

Slightly Married. Dell, 2003. 342pp.

Colonel Aidan Bedwyn fears commitment until he encounters Eve, an independent woman who needs his protection.

Slightly Wicked. Dell, 2003. 342pp.

Judith Law shares one night of reckless passion with a handsome stranger, not knowing he was one of England's most eligible bachelors, Rannulf Bedwyn.

Slightly Scandalous. Dell, 2003. 374pp.

Lady Freyja Bedwyn, a proud and handsome spinster at twenty-five, fights her attraction to Joshua Moore, Marquess of Hallmere.

Slightly Tempted. Dell, 2004. 356pp.

Beautiful Lady Morgan Bedwyn, the youngest sister, becomes more than an instrument of revenge for the rakish Gervase Ashford, Earl of Rosthorn.

Slightly Sinful. Dell, 2004. 368pp.

Alleyne Bedwyn, presumed dead at the Battle of Waterloo, is rescued by Rachel York, who has taken refuge in a Belgian brothel. The two hatch a scheme to preserve Rachel's inheritance.

Slightly Dangerous. Delacorte, 2004. 344pp.

Wulfric Bedwyn, the aloof Duke of Bewcastle, is the head of the Bedwyn family. Even he is not immune to love, as he discovers when an unlikely woman catches his eye: Christine Derrick, a dazzling widow.

Beverley, Jo.

Deirdre and Don Juan. **Avon, 1993. 217pp.**

Upon hearing that his long-estranged wife has died, Mark Juan Carlos Renfrew, Earl of Everdon (aka Don Juan), becomes engaged against his will to the plain wallflower Lady Deirdre Stowe. One of her best-known novels; Beverley also writes romances set in the Georgian and medieval periods. **Regency historical.**

Chesney, Marion.

Daughters of Mannerling.

Chesney (who also writes police procedural mysteries as M. C. Beaton, and historical mysteries under her own name) writes short, lighthearted romances. This series focuses on the six privileged daughters of one aristocratic couple, Sir William and Lady Beverley of Mannerling: Isabella, Jessica, Abigail, Abigail's twin Rachel, Belinda, and Lizzie. After their father gambles away their opulent estate, the girls devise their own ways of regaining their home and finding love. **Regency romances.**

The Banishment. St. Martin's Press, 1995. 151pp.

The Intrigue. St. Martin's Press, 1995. 150pp.

The Deception. St. Martin's Press, 1996. 168pp.

The Folly. St. Martin's Press, 1996. 165pp.

The Romance. St. Martin's Press, 1997. 164pp.

The Homecoming. St. Martin's Press, 1997. 153pp.

Heath, Sandra.

With several novels appearing each year, Heath is a prolific British author. **Regency romances.**

False Steps. **Signet, 2003. 300pp.**

Cassian Stratford, Marquess of Lansdale, believes that Winifred "Freddie" Smith is a lady of fashion, but she's really the daughter of a lodging house owner.

Lavender Blue. **Signet, 2003. 240pp.**

Jovian Cathness, Duke of Chavanage, has taken to the bottle, much to the dismay of his longtime love Lady Anthea Wintour.

Hern, Candice.

Ladies' Fashionable Cabinet Trilogy.

These novels revolve around the *Ladies' Fashionable Cabinet*, a magazine that dispensed well-meaning advice to fashion- and socially conscious English women during the Regency period. **Regency historicals;** Hern also writes Regency romances.

Once a Dreamer. Avon, 2003. 376pp.

Mrs. Eleanor Tennant, a respectable widow, is surprised to discover that the advice columnist called The Busybody—the interfering woman who told her impetuous niece to elope—is really a romantic man named Simon Westover.

Once a Scoundrel. Avon, 2003. 374pp.

Anthony Morehouse, upon discovering that he has won not a piece of furniture but a ladies' magazine in a card game, loses his heart to the editor of the *Ladies' Fashionable Cabinet*, Edwina Parrish.

Once a Gentleman. Avon, 2004. 384pp.

Nicholas Parrish has to marry Pru Armitage, one of his bluestocking employees at the *Cabinet*, after she falls asleep at her desk and mistakenly spends the night at his townhouse.

Heyer, Georgette.

With her well-researched and witty portrayals of all classes of life in Regency England, Heyer set the standard by which other Regency romances are measured. Some of her most popular works are listed. For a complete list of titles, see the Georgette Heyer Web site (www.georgette-heyer.com). **Regency romances.**

Arabella. **Putnam, 1949. 284pp.**

Delightful misunderstandings between Arabella Tallant, daughter of a poor country parson embarking on her first London season, and nobleman Robert Beaumaris.

Bath Tangle. **Putnam, 1955. 312pp.**

Fiery redhead Lady Serena Carlow ends up as the ward of Ivo Barrasford, marquis of Rotherham, a man whom she jilted.

A Civil Contract. **Putnam, 1962. 393pp.**

A gentle story of the growing relationship between mismatched partners Captain Adam Deveril and Jenny Chawley, a plain and slightly plump merchant's daughter.

Frederica. **Dutton, 1965. 384pp.**

The romantic escapades of the Merrivale siblings in Regency-era London, particularly those of Frederica, the most outgoing of the bunch.

The Grand Sophy. **Putnam, 1950. 307pp.**

Sophia Stanton-Lacy takes on more than she bargained for when she goes to stay with her cousins, the Ombersleys.

The Toll-Gate. **Putnam, 1954. 310pp.**

Mystery and romance, as Captain John Staple discovers a connection between an unattended toll-gate and beautiful orphan Miss Nell Stornaway.

Hunter, Madeline.

Seducer Series.

The dark and dangerous heroes of Hunter's early nineteenth-century romances, set in the aftermath of the Napoleonic Wars, are all members of the Hampstead Dueling Society, a group of men proficient in the art of the duel, political intrigue, and seduction. **Regency historicals.**

The Seducer. Bantam, 2003. 419pp.

1818: Diane Albret, kept secluded in a French school for twenty years, doesn't understand why her guardian, Daniel St. John, risks scandal by bringing her back to England with him.

The Saint. Bantam, 2003. 432pp.

Bianca Kenwood has no intention of giving up a promising career as a singer, not even for her darkly handsome guardian, Vergil Duclairc.

The Charmer. Bantam, 2003. 400pp.

Against her better judgment, Sophia Raughley follows nobleman's son Adrian Burchard from Paris to England in 1831 because her political power is needed in Parliament.

The Sinner. Bantam, 2004. 372pp.

Dante Duclairc and Fleur Monley agree to a marriage in name only to solve their money issues: he owes his creditors too much, and she wants to prevent her stepfather from stealing her fortune.

Kelly, Carla.

Kelly writes about ordinary (non-aristocratic) heroes and heroines who find themselves in extraordinary situations. Kelly is a North Dakota-based author who writes exceptional Regencies as well as gritty Western stories (Chapter 6). **Regency romances.**

The Lady's Companion. Signet, 1996. 223pp.

After her father gambles away their fortune, Susan Hampton becomes a lady's companion and falls in love with her employer's bailiff. RITA Award.

Miss Milton Speaks Her Mind. Signet, 1998. 224pp.

Jane Milton has cared for her cousin's orphaned son for years, but the boy may be illegitimate.

Mrs. Drew Plays Her Hand. Signet, 1994. 223pp.

Roxanna Drew, a vicar's widow with two daughters, restores a dower house owned by an attractive nobleman. RITA Award.

The Wedding Journey. Signet, 2002. 231pp.

Captain Jesse Randall marries Nell Mason to save her from being mistreated by her father.

Manning, Jo.

Reluctant Guardian Series.

Manning based her first novel on a real-life story. **Regency romances.**

The Reluctant Guardian. Regency Press, 1999. 224pp.

Sir Isaac Rebow, an experienced military man, is less than thrilled to play nurse-maid to his pretty London cousins until he discovers how charming young Mary truly is.

Seducing Mr. Heywood. Five Star, 2002. 248pp.

Lady Sophia Rowley, the socialite spurned by Isaac Rebow in *The Reluctant Guardian*, has recently lost her third husband. She discovers an unexpected attraction to the vicar who's been made guardian of her two stepsons.

Paquet, Laura.

Denham Series.

Paquet's books feature unconventional heroes and heroines with unusual careers for the period: architect, businesswoman, playwright. **Regency romances.**

Lord Langdon's Tutor. Zebra, 2000. 224pp.

Though determined not to marry him by arrangement, Miss Clarissa Denham agrees to tutor Lord Langdon in the art of mixing in society.

Miss Scott Meets Her Match. Zebra, 2002. 224pp.

Elizabeth Scott, owner of an import business, flees her unscrupulous cousin and lands in the arms of nobleman Spencer Willoughby (a secondary character in the previous book).

Mr. McAllister Sets His Cap. Zebra, 2003. 224pp.

After Emily, Lady Tuncliffe, the married elder sister of Clarissa Denham, loses her disreputable husband in a riding accident, she grows attracted to the architect hired to renovate her London town house.

On Bended Knee. Zebra, 2003. 284pp.

Regency novellas by Alice Holden, Kate Huntington, and Laura Paquet, the last of which completes the Denham series with the story of the youngest Denham sister, Lucinda, who loves a playwright.

Quinn, Julia.

Bridgerton Family Series.

Novels starring members of the large Bridgerton family; filled with the author's delightfully witty dialogue and smart characterization. **Regency historicals.**

The Duke and I. Avon, 2000. 371pp.

To avoid being set up by matchmakers, Daphne Bridgerton fakes her engagement to Simon Basset, Duke of Hastings.

The Viscount Who Loved Me. Avon, 2000. 376pp.

Kate Sheffield falls in love with reformed rake Viscount Anthony Bridgerton while trying to protect her half-sister Edwina from his suit.

An Offer from a Gentleman. Avon, 2001. 377pp.

Sophie Beckett, a Regency-era Cinderella who's forced into servitude by her wicked stepmother, falls in love at first sight with Benedict Bridgerton at a ball but runs away at the stroke of midnight.

Romancing Mr. Bridgerton. Avon, 2002. 370pp.

Penelope Featherington, on the shelf at age twenty-eight, has loved Colin Bridgerton for years. When he returns from his travels, he starts to see her in a different light.

To Sir Phillip, With Love. Avon, 2003. 372pp.

Eloise Bridgerton strikes up a pen-pal relationship with Sir Phillip, not realizing he's not really the charming noble gentleman of her dreams.

When He Was Wicked. Avon, 2004. 384pp.

Michael Stirling, Regency rake, becomes an earl on his cousin's death. He feels especially distraught because of the attraction he feels for his cousin's wife, Francesca Bridgerton Stirling.

South, Sheri Cobb.

South writes refreshingly unconventional Regencies: many of her characters come from the lower or working classes but don't aspire to change their social station. **Regency romances.**

Miss Darby's Duenna. **PrinnyWorld, 1999. 217pp.**

To keep an eye on his fiancée, with whom he's unfashionably fallen in love, Harry Hawthorne disguises himself as his own grandmother and chaperones her around London—at least until his grandmother shows up in person.

Brundy Trilogy.

A trilogy about the delightful Brundy couple, their friends, and their acquaintances.

The Weaver Takes a Wife. PrinnyWorld, 1999. 234pp.

To settle her father's debts, Lady Helen agrees to marry Ethan Brundy, a nouveau riche mill owner with a heart of gold and a horrendous Lancashire accent. Nobody expects the marriage to succeed—certainly not the haughty bride herself.

Brighton Honeymoon. PrinnyWorld, 2000. 240pp.

Orphaned Polly Hampton pretends to be Ethan Brundy's long-lost sister. He knows she's lying and asks his friend to help unmask her, but the pretty Polly's charms soon have him enthralled.

French Leave. PrinnyWorld, 2001. 229pp.

Lord Waverly, the experienced rake who was once Lady Helen Brundy's suitor, finds his match in Lisette Colling, a naïve young woman whom he finds escaping from a French convent.

Victorian and Edwardian Romances

Life in Victorian England (1837–1901) is normally thought of as prim and proper, and many Victorian romances include heroines or heroes who rebel against the strict rules of conduct imposed by society. Rather than focusing primarily on the upper classes, as do most Georgian and Regency romances, these works feature the rich, the working class, and the poor—and the differences among them. Romances set during the brief Edwardian period (1901–1910), when Victoria's son Edward was on the throne, are similar in tone.

Ashworth, Adele.

♠ *My Darling Caroline.* **Jove, 1998. 352pp.**

Lady Caroline Grayson would rather be a botanist than settle down and marry. She certainly doesn't expect a husband to support her choice of career—until her father forces her to marry the Earl of Weymerth. RITA Award. **Sensual.**

Someone Irresistible. **Avon, 2001. 384pp.**

Amid the world of scientific discovery in 1851 London, a paleontologist finds love with an upper-class woman who has long admired him. **Sensual.**

When It's Perfect. **Avon, 2002. 384pp.**

In 1855, an Egyptologist, returning from abroad after his sister's death, uncovers secrets his sister may have told to the working-class woman who was designing her wedding clothes. Sequel to *Someone Irresistible.* **Sensual.**

Winter Garden. **Jove, 2000. 340pp.**

A French spy in southern England in 1849, Madeleine DuMais's abilities are put to the test when she meets her partner in crime. **Sensual.**

Feather, Jane.

Matchmaker Trilogy.

In this Edwardian trilogy, three well-bred sisters who run a matchmaking service (and secretly write a scandal sheet) discover the men who are the best matches for them. **Sensual.**

The Bachelor List. Bantam, 2004. 343pp.

Constance Duncan battles wits with Max Ensor, Member of Parliament, who doesn't believe in women's suffrage.

The Bride Hunt. Bantam, 2004. 370pp.

When an earl threatens to sue their newspaper, and the sisters can't afford a barrister, Prudence Duncan bargains with Sir Gideon Malvern: If he will defend them, they will find him a bride.

The Wedding Game. Bantam, 2004. 384pp.

Dr. Douglas Farrell approaches the sisters' matchmaking service with the hope of finding a rich wife he can marry for convenience. He soon discovers that Charity Duncan suits him better.

Harper, Karen.
The Wings of Morning. **Dutton, 1993. 373pp.**

On the island of St. Kilda in the Outer Hebrides in the 1850s, Abigail MacQueen is determined to help cure the disease that took the lives of her family members. Her quest takes her to Victorian London and to America, where she finds love again with a handsome sea captain. **Sensual.**

Tarr, Hope.
Tempting. **Jove, 2002. 308pp.**

Simon Belleville, a Member of Parliament who's head of Her Majesty's Morality and Vice Commission, is intrigued by an innocent woman he finds in a Covent Garden brothel. **Sensual.**

Americana Romances

While historical romances set in the United States are less common than those set in England, a number of prominent authors use American history as a backdrop. Most use small-town or rural settings and reflect day-to-day life in early America. Romances set in the American West in the nineteenth century are listed in a separate section, later this chapter.

Garlock, Dorothy.

Dorothy Garlock's Americana romances are full of homespun period detail of the Midwest during Prohibition and the Depression years. **Sweet.**

1920s Missouri Series.

Realistic romances set in rural Missouri during Prohibition.

The Edge of Town. Warner, 2001. 370pp.

Julie Jones is the caretaker for her large family of five siblings, but her responsible nature can't prevent her from falling for Evan Johnson. Luckily for Julie, Evan is nothing like his father, the town drunkard.

High on a Hill. Warner, 2002. 385pp.

The region swarms with homemade whiskey operations and countless bootleggers. Annabel Lee Donovan's father is one of these, picking up and moving every few months to evade the law. When they move to a house high on the hill above Henderson, Missouri, Annabel quickly adapts to the ways of their new town, though she doesn't realize at first that handsome ex-lawman Corbin Appleby is on her father's trail.

A Place Called Rainwater. Warner, 2003. 400pp.

Jill Jones, younger sister of Julie from *The Edge of Town*, moves from Missouri to Rainwater, Oklahoma, to help her Aunt Justine run her hotel.

Her childhood friend Thad Taylor, who sees himself as Jill's protector, follows her there.

Great Depression Series.

Love flourishes on the Kansas and Oklahoma plains during the Great Depression.

With Hope. Warner, 1998. 464pp.

In 1932 Oklahoma, Miss Henry Ann Henry, named for her father, has trouble hanging on to her family farm. Neighbor Tom Dolan brings hope and trouble into her life.

With Song. Warner, 1999. 440pp.

Seward County, Kansas, 1935. When gangsters' bullets take the lives of her parents, Molly McKenzie plots with lawman Hod Dolan to catch the killers.

With Heart. Warner, 1999. 433pp.

Newspaper woman Kathleen Dolan, part-owner of the Rawlings, Oklahoma, *Gazette* in 1938, comes up against men who want to see her fail, but rancher Johnny Henry comes to her rescue.

After the Parade. Warner, 2000. 397pp.

Returning home as a hero from World War II, Johnny Henry struggles to rebuild his life with wife Kathleen. An immediate sequel to *With Heart.*

Route 66 Series.

More down-to-earth romances from Garlock. All take place along Route 66, the fabled road heading west during the Great Depression.

Mother Road. Warner, 2003. 416pp.

In Sayre, Oklahoma, circa 1932, garage owner Andy Connors is bitten by a snake. While recovering in a hospital in Oklahoma City, he asks his old friend Yates to watch over his children as well as the woman, Leona Dawson, who cares for them.

Hope's Highway. Warner, 2004. 386pp.

After his brother's suicide, Brady Hoyt and his niece hitch a ride in Elmer Kinnard's caravan heading west to California. He and Margie Kinnard, Elmer's daughter, eye one another, though Margie fully intends on pursuing a career in Hollywood.

Song of the Road. Warner, 2004. 416pp.

Mary Lee Clawson, a poor pregnant widow, comes home to the motor court she owns in Cross Roads, New Mexico. She faces all sorts of family problems. Ex-con Jake Romero, one of her renters, has recently returned to town to clear his name.

Grayson, Elizabeth.

Moon in the Water. **Avon, 2004. 480pp.**

In mid-nineteenth-century America, Chase Hardesty, a riverboat pilot, marries pregnant Ann Rossiter to give her child a name. They gradually fall in love on a trip north along the Missouri River. **Sensual.**

Guhrke, Laura Lee.

Breathless. **Sonnet, 1999. 389pp.**

In Shivaree, Georgia, in 1905, sparks fly when librarian Lily Morgan meets up with her ex's lawyer, who made her a social outcast during her scandal-ridden divorce five years earlier. **Sensual.**

The Charade. **Sonnet, 2000. 448pp.**

In 1775 Boston, runaway indentured servant Katie Armstrong becomes an unlikely double agent, but she falls in love with the man whose identity she's compelled to unmask. **Sensual.**

Harper, Karen.

Circle of Gold. **Dutton, 1992. 393pp.**

In early nineteenth-century Kentucky, Rebecca Blake is left with a Shaker sect after her father's death, but she earns their scorn after falling in love with a visiting British aristocrat. The pair return to his English estate, but she never forgets her country origins. **Sensual.**

River of Sky. **Dutton, 1994. 407pp.**

In 1835 St. Louis, when Kate Craig's riverboat captain husband dies unexpectedly, she takes it upon herself to pay off his debts. Kate also discovers that her husband had kept an Indian wife, Blue Wing of the Mandan tribe. The two women become friends and take Kate's riverboat up to trade with the Mandans, but Kate can't decide which of their two male passengers intrigues her more. **Sensual.**

Landis, Jill Marie.

Magnolia Creek. **Ballantine, 2002. 367pp.**

A year after the Civil War, Dru Talbot returns to his home in rural Kentucky only to find that his wife Sara believed herself a widow—who in his absence had gotten romantically involved with a Yankee and borne him an illegitimate daughter. **Sensual.**

Lindstrom, Wendy.

🎗 *Shades of Honor.* **St. Martin's Press, 2002. 320pp.**

Just after the Civil War, Union soldier Radford Grayson returns to his hometown of Fredonia, New York. Soon he has his brother's fiancée Evelyn thinking that she chose the wrong brother to marry. RITA Award. **Sweet.**

The Longing. **St. Martin's Press, 2003. 320pp.**

Just after the events in *Shades of Honor*, Amelia Drake marries her late father's business rival, Kyle Grayson, to save her reputation. What begins as a marriage of convenience slowly turns into something more, but secrets from the past prevent their growing closer. **Sensual.**

Maderich, Robin.

Faith and Honor. **Warner, 1986. 345pp.**

> Reissued by a new publisher in 2003, Maderich's history-intensive romance features Faith Ashley, a widow in colonial Boston who is rescued from British harassment by a man with plenty of secrets. **Sensual.**

Sparks, Kerrelyn.

For Love or Country. **Forge, 2002. 292pp.**

> In pre-Revolutionary Boston, Quincy Stanton—Royalist by day, patriot spy by night—becomes intrigued by Virginia Munro, a patriot he initially believes to be an indentured servant. **Sensual.**

Wiggs, Susan.

Great Chicago Fire trilogy.

> A trilogy of historical romances set around the Great Chicago Fire in 1871. **Sensual.**

The Hostage. Mira, 2000. 402pp.

> On the night of the Chicago Fire, Deborah Sinclair, a Chicago debutante, is kidnapped and held for ransom by a handsome rogue, who takes her to his cabin on remote Isle Royale in Lake Superior.

The Mistress. Mira, 2000. 400pp.

> Thinking they're about to die, Kathleen O'Leary, an Irish Catholic maid, makes an impulsive marriage with a rich bachelor, though they're both pretending to be something they're not.

The Firebrand. Mira, 2001. 400pp.

> Five years after the Chicago Fire, a suffragette bookstore owner clashes with a big-city banker, not realizing at first that the baby she saved that night is his long-lost daughter.

Williamson, Penelope.

The Passions of Emma. **Warner, 1997. 432pp.**

> Emma Tremayne moves in high society in late-nineteenth century Bristol, Rhode Island, completely unaware of the plight of the lower social classes until pregnant millworker Bria McKenna enters her life. One of the Irish despised by the privileged rich, Bria is dying of consumption, and loves her husband Shay so devotedly that she's anxious to see him settled before she goes. She and Emma become the best of friends, and Emma can't help but feel guilty about falling in love with Bria's husband. **Sensual.**

Frontier and Western Romances

Romances set in the western United States during the nineteenth century include freethinking female heroines and men as wild and untamed as the Western frontier. Below is a selection of these titles. "Prairie romances," a phrase more often used to describe Christian-centered romances set on the Western frontier, are annotated in Chapter 11.

Bittner, Rosanne.

Savage Destiny Series.

Bittner, who has moved from traditional Western romances to Western romantic historicals to inspirational Western romances, populates her romances with true-to-life characters and historically authentic locales. Her novels also show a profound respect for the Native American way of life. The seven novels feature the romantic adventures of Abigail Trent, a frontier girl, her lover/husband Zeke Monroe, a half-Cherokee scout, and members of their family. Readers of romantic sagas (Chapter 5) may also enjoy these tales. The first six were reprinted in 1996 to coincide with the release of *Eagle's Song*. **Sensual.**

Sweet Prairie Passion. Zebra, 1983. 463pp.

Ride the Free Wind. Zebra, 1984. 445pp.

River of Love. Zebra, 1984. 413pp.

Embrace the Wild Land. Zebra, 1984. 446pp.

Climb the Highest Mountain. Zebra, 1985. 441pp.

Meet the New Dawn. Zebra, 1986. 477pp.

Eagle's Song. Zebra, 1996. 445pp.

Grayson, Elizabeth.

Color of the Wind. **Bantam, 1999. 432pp.**

Wyoming, 1882: Boston illustrator Ardith Merritt fulfills a deathbed promise to deliver her stepsister's children to their father—the man who once broke her heart. **Sensual.**

Painted by the Sun. **Bantam, 2000. 448pp.**

Shea Waterston, a traveling photographer, has been trying to find her son once again, after having had to send him on an orphan train west ten years earlier. When she stops in Colorado Territory to photograph a hanging, she doesn't expect her unintentional stay in Judge Cameron Gallimore's jail to change her life. **Sensual.**

Heath, Lorraine.

Rogues of Texas.

A group of friends, all dashing Englishmen, find romance in late nineteenth-century Fortune, Texas. Heath, the daughter of an Englishwoman and a Texan, includes elements of her dual heritage in these novels. **Sensual.**

A Rogue in Texas. Avon, 1999. 374pp.

Grayson Rhodes, an English nobleman, comes to Texas to make his own way in the world. He falls in love with Abbie Westland, the strong-minded widow on whose land he works.

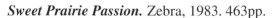

Never Love a Cowboy. Avon, 2000. 376pp.

Jessye Kane, a saloonkeeper's daughter, will partner with English blueblood Harrison Bainbridge in business—but not in love.

Never Marry a Cowboy. Avon, 2001. 374pp.

Though still mourning the death of his first love back in England, Kit Montgomery agrees to grant Ashton Robertson's dying wish by marrying her.

The Outlaw and the Lady. Avon, 2002. 375pp.

Lee Raven, a notorious outlaw, abducts Angela Bainbridge after seeing her when he robbed a bank. He doesn't realize that she's blind.

Landis, Jill Marie.

Summer Moon. Ballantine, 2001. 404pp.

In 1869, Kate Whittington heads from Maine to Texas in response to a newspaper ad from a widower seeking a wife, only to find out that he's not the one who penned their delightful correspondence. **Sensual.**

Lovelace, Merline.

The Garretts of Wyoming.

Sensual Western romances set on the northern Great Plains (Dakota Territory) in the mid- to late nineteenth century. Some family saga elements; the series follows the stories of three generations of the Garrett family. The plot and characters incorporate the author's background in the U.S. military. **Sensual.**

The Horse Soldier. Mira, 2001. 384pp.

Not realizing that her husband, Major Andrew Garrett, was alive and in a Union prison camp during the Civil War, Julia Robichard married again. Eight years later, after her second husband has disappeared, Julia reunites with Andrew at an army fort in Montana Territory.

The Colonel's Daughter. Mira, 2002. 384pp.

An outlaw named Black Jack Sloan rescues Suzanne Bonneaux, daughter of Julia and stepdaughter of now-Colonel Andrew Garrett, after her coach is waylaid by thieves.

The Captain's Woman. Mira, 2003.

In 1898, on the eve of the Spanish–American War, journalist Victoria Parker impulsively gets engaged to Captain Sam Garrett, though he's in love with another. After they marry, she follows him to Florida and then to Cuba, where he sees action with Teddy Roosevelt's Rough Riders.

The Oklahomans.

A romantic series (planned as a trilogy) tracing the early history of Oklahoma, which in 1805 was part of the Louisiana Purchase. The next volume will be *Untamed*, about Daniel Morgan's son. **Sensual.**

A Savage Beauty. Mira, 2003. 374pp.

Sergeant Daniel Morgan, a married man, tries to ignore his attraction to Louise Therese Chartier, a half-Osage frontier widow who accompanies his military expedition west.

Osborne, Maggie.

Osborne writes realistic, Western historical romances set in the nineteenth century both before and after the Civil War. **Sensual.**

The Best Man. **Warner, 1998. 424pp.**

Freddy, Alex, and Les—the three daughters of a man who wanted only sons—have to drive a herd of cattle from Texas to Dodge City, Kansas, to get their inheritance. Along the way, each of them falls in love.

The Bride of Willow Creek. **Ivy, 2001. 358pp.**

Angelina "Angie" Bartoli Holland heads to the small town of Willow Creek, Colorado, intending to ask her long-estranged husband for a divorce.

Prairie Moon. **Ivy, 2002. 358pp.**

In post-Civil War Texas, lawman James Cameron brings Della Ward the last letter written by her late husband.

♣ *The Promise of Jenny Jones.* **Warner, 1997. 384pp.**

Jenny Jones, condemned to die in a Mexican jail, gets a second chance at life by bringing a dying woman's young daughter to California. RITA Award.

The Seduction of Samantha Kincade. **Warner, 1995. 384pp.**

In nineteenth-century Colorado, the love of a good man transforms Samantha Kincade from a seventeen-year-old bounty hunter with a lust for vengeance into a woman with a great capacity for love.

Shotgun Wedding. **Ivy, 2003. 360pp.**

Annie Malloy agrees to marry sheriff Jesse Harden to have a father for her unborn baby.

A Stranger's Wife. **Warner, 1999. 362pp.**

To get out of an Arizona jail and see her six-year-old daughter again, Lily Dale agrees to impersonate the long-lost wife of a Colorado gubernatorial candidate.

Williamson, Penelope.

Williamson, who began her writing career as a romance novelist, has most recently written historical mysteries (see Chapter 7) set in Jazz Age New Orleans. **Sensual.**

Heart of the West. **Simon & Schuster, 1995. 591pp.**

In 1879 New England, proper Bostonian Clementine Kennicutt jumps at the chance to escape her pious father, elope with cowboy Gus McQueen, and live with him on his Montana ranch. Her dreams of life out west don't prepare her for the reality of frontier life—the harsh weather, the stark living conditions, and definitely not the attraction she feels for her husband's ne'er-do-well brother.

The Outsider. Simon & Schuster, 1999. 464pp.

Rachel Yoder, a woman of the Plain People, struggles to raise her son alone on a remote Montana sheep farm in 1886. Her late husband was unjustly hanged for cattle rustling, so Rachel does her best to conform to the law. But she can't resist helping Johnny Cain, a wounded outlaw who turns up on her doorstep. Williamson offers more than just a satisfying romantic tale in her realistic portrait of the Amish and the wild Western frontier.

Chapter 5

Sagas

Historical novels that focus on characters' domestic lives and family relationships over time comprise the subgenre of sagas. Most sagas follow several generations of one family or of multiple families, revolving around a matriarchal or, less frequently, a patriarchal figure who serves as a dominant and guiding force in the lives of family members. Alternately, sagas may follow groups of friends from their younger days until middle or old age.

Because they tell involved stories, or series of stories, sagas tend to be long books. They often appear in multiple volumes, which gives readers a sense of continuity and a feeling that life continues to unfold throughout the march of history. Some sagas include family trees to aid readers in sorting out the names and relationships of the numerous characters and their descendants. The plots of sagas commonly include a good deal of romance and adventure; readers of romantic historicals and romantic epics (Chapter 4) may enjoy these books as well.

Sagas allow their readers to feel emotionally invested in the characters, and to see how the changing times affect the characters' lives. The emphasis is usually on social and economic rather than political history. The protagonists don't necessarily serve as instruments of change for large-scale historical events, but they find their lives greatly affected by sweeping changes around them. While historical events may not always be at the forefront, the background of sagas is nonetheless accurately presented.

Lengthy single-volume novels are often labeled as "sagas" in publishers' blurbs, though most of these don't fit the saga definition. The popularity of sagas peaked in the 1970s and 1980s, with benchmark series such as R. F. Delderfield's Swann Family Saga and John Jakes's North and South trilogy appearing during this time. Therefore, many of the novels in this chapter are older. Although the majority appearing today are reprints from British publishers, this subgenre still commands a devoted readership, predominantly among women. Family sagas are also frequently published for the Christian market, and these are annotated in Chapter 11.

Beginning in the late 1990s, a number of literary novelists (Ann-Marie MacDonald, Alistair MacLeod, Amitav Ghosh) jumped onto the saga bandwagon, giving these novels even greater visibility—and a wider readership. (Sagas written in a literary style are tagged with the word **Literary** in bold at the end of the annotation.) Traditional settings such as Britain, America, and Australia still appear regularly, but the subgenre continues to evolve in ethnic diversity, with a number of authors (Lalita Tademy, Nomi Eve, Bernice Morgan) basing their novels on their own unique cultural heritage.

Classic Sagas

These sagas are classic stories of family life through history, complete with strong men, courageous women, domestic squabbles, and class conflict. Illicit romance and black sheep are often thrown in as well. The appeal of these stories often hinges on character as well as setting, and these novels usually also contain minor elements of adventure.

The British Isles

Classic British sagas, very popular in the 1970s and 1980s, portray the domestic side of life in the British Isles.

Delderfield, R. F.

<u>Swann Family Saga.</u> ★

In 1858, British army officer Adam Swann returns from service in India with a determination to succeed in commerce. He marries Henrietta, a mill owner's daughter, and together they raise a brood of children, all of whom have their own romantic adventures. The final novel sees the Swann clan at the beginning of World War I, as they and England itself are gradually moving into the modern age.

God Is an Englishman. Simon & Schuster, 1970. 687pp.

Theirs Was the Kingdom. Simon & Schuster, 1971. 798pp.

Give Us This Day. Simon & Schuster, 1973. 767pp.

Graham, Winston.

<u>Poldark Saga.</u> ★

The twelve-volume Poldark Saga, complete in 2002, is an extended family saga set in Graham's trademark location, the bleak Cornwall coast in the late eighteenth and early nineteenth centuries. The initial volume, first published in 1945 in Britain, begins as Captain Ross Poldark, returning home from fighting in the American Revolution, finds his sweetheart engaged to his cousin and his crumbling estate in need of repair. He takes as his wife Demelza, daughter of a brutal local miner, and transforms her into a woman suited to his station. The two have a stormy relationship, complicated by class differences and their passing affections for others. Poldark's archenemy is neighbor George Warleggan, and their two families continue to vie for power throughout most of the series. Readers who are looking for scenes of drama, romance, class conflict, family troubles, and, of course, illegal smuggling along the rocky Cornish coast, will find plenty of it here. The Poldark Saga was later dramatized in several installments by the BBC. Graham died shortly after publication of the last volume, at age ninety.

The Renegade. Doubleday, 1951. 344pp. (Original title: *Ross Poldark.*)

Demelza. Doubleday, 1953. 320pp.

Venture Once More. Doubleday, 1954. 283pp. (Original title: *Jeremy Poldark.*)

The Last Gamble. Doubleday, 1955. 347pp. (Original title: *Warleggan.*)

The Black Moon. Doubleday, 1974. 424pp.

The Four Swans. Doubleday, 1977. 479pp.

The Angry Tide. Doubleday, 1978. 476pp.

Stranger from the Sea. Doubleday, 1982. 445pp.

The Miller's Dance. Doubleday, 1983. 372pp.

The Loving Cup. Doubleday, 1985. 440pp.

The Twisted Sword. Carroll & Graf, 1991. 510pp.

Bella Poldark. London: Macmillan, 2002. 530pp.

Lofts, Norah.

Suffolk House Trilogy. ★

The story of a house in Suffolk is told in the first person by its many inhabitants from 1381, when peasant Martin Reed escapes from serfdom and makes his fortune, until its declining years in the mid-1950s. Unusually for a saga written decades ago, Lofts's tone is never sentimental, and along the way she makes history come alive.

The Town House. Doubleday, 1959. 403pp.

The House at Old Vine. Doubleday, 1961. 408pp.

The House at Sunset. Doubleday, 1972. 370pp.

Tallboys Trilogy. ★

Sir Godfrey Tallboys, a knight in fifteenth-century England, is captured by Moors while en route to Spain to participate in a tournament. He's rescued by a young Moorish girl, Tana. Six years later, he and Tana, who is pregnant with his child, return to England. Godfrey's loyal wife Sybilla welcomes them both, not realizing who the father of the girl's baby is. These romantic complications carry over to the next generation.

Knight's Acre. Doubleday, 1975. 253pp.

The Homecoming. Doubleday, 1975. 282pp.

The Lonely Furrow. Doubleday, 1976. 308pp.

MacDonald, Malcolm.

Stevenson Family Saga.

This series of four novels centers on the railroad boom of the 1840s through 1870s, as residents of Victorian England found their lives economically affected by this revolutionary new form of transportation. Nora and John Stevenson are deeply involved in the railroad business, which lifts them up from poverty, while their friends the Thorntons are of a more genteel background. More than once Nora's financial genius saves the Stevensons from financial ruin. She emerges as a strong matriarch, holding the family together while their fortunes continue to improve. The fourth book features their troublesome daughter, Abigail, a liberated woman who becomes a writer.

The World from Rough Stones. Knopf, 1975. 535pp.

The Rich Are With You Always. Knopf, 1976. 483pp.

The Sons of Fortune. Knopf, 1978. 466pp.

Abigail. Knopf, 1979. 389pp.

The United States

These novels depict the widespread political and social changes sweeping through U.S. history, as seen from the point of view of a single family.

Fast, Howard.

The Immigrants.

Twenty years in the making, this saga by the late historical novelist Howard Fast focuses on the Lavette family of California, beginning with Italian immigrant Dan Lavette, who survives the San Francisco earthquake of 1906 and becomes a businessman to be reckoned with. The heroine of the following five books is his daughter Barbara, a noted foreign correspondent whose journeys abroad give her an education in life and love. *An Independent Woman*, which ends in the modern day, shows Barbara as her family's beloved matriarch, still fighting for what she believes in.

The Immigrants. Houghton Mifflin, 1977. 389pp.

Second Generation. Houghton Mifflin, 1978. 441pp.

The Establishment. Houghton Mifflin, 1979. 365pp.

The Legacy. Houghton Mifflin, 1981. 359pp.

The Immigrant's Daughter. Houghton Mifflin, 1985. 321pp.

An Independent Woman. Harcourt Brace, 1997. 252pp.

Jaffe, Rona.

The Road Taken. **Dutton, 2000. 388pp.**

The story of Rose Smith, born January 1, 1900, is a chronicle of the entire twentieth century in America. After Rose and her husband relocate from Bristol, Rhode Island, to a New York City brownstone, they and their growing family participate in many of the changes transforming the country. Stepmother Celia can't resist the call of the city, and younger brother Hugh becomes a gay activist despite himself. In the latter half of the book, Rose's daughters take center stage: Peggy is content as a suburban housewife, while Joan gets caught up in the freedom of the 1960s and Ginger is determined to study medicine. While the novel can serve as a useful history lesson, Jaffe's skill is most apparent in her accurate picture of family relationships.

Jakes, John.

Crown Family Saga.

A rags-to-riches immigrant saga set in early nineteenth- and twentieth-century Chicago.

Homeland. Doubleday, 1993. 785pp.

In the 1890s, Berlin native Pauli Kroner leaves Germany for America to join his uncle, Joseph Crown, who has made a fortune in the Chicago brewing industry. A typical immigrant in many ways, Pauli believes that America is a land where fortunes are waiting to be won. The Crowns are high society, and they mingle with the likes of Theodore Roosevelt and Thomas Edison. After Pauli (renamed Paul) clashes with his uncle, he goes out on his own, surviving Chicago's slums, and using his newfound skills as a cinematographer in the Spanish–American War.

American Dreams. Dutton, 1998. 495pp.

Paul's cousins Fritzi and Carl, Joe Crown's children, are the protagonists in this second installment, which picks up circa 1906. After Fritzi gives up on having a successful stage career in New York, she lands in Hollywood, becoming a silent film actress. Her brother Carl lives life dangerously, first as a race car driver and then as a World War I flying ace. As in *Homeland*, Jakes introduces a number of historical personalities into the story, such as Mary Pickford, Henry Ford, and D. W. Griffith.

Plain, Belva.

The Sight of the Stars. Delacorte, 2004. 311pp.

In 1907 New Jersey, nineteen-year-old Adam Arnring, not content with running the family business, hops a train out west. He lands in Chattahoochee, Texas, where he happens upon a job in a family-owned department store. Over time, his expertise stands him in good stead. He takes over the business and marries the founder's niece, Emma Rothirsch, and they raise a family. The novel continues throughout the rest of the twentieth century, detailing how the Arnrings cope with tragedies, betrayals, and family secrets.

Canada

These novels of Canadian family life in the late nineteenth to early twentieth centuries are beloved by Canadians and Americans alike.

Bacon, Charlotte.

Lost Geography. **Farrar, Straus & Giroux, 2000. 259pp.**

> This lyrical saga of four generations of women begins with Margaret Evans, a nurse in 1930s Saskatchewan, then follows her daughter Hilda in Toronto, Hilda's daughter Danielle in Paris, and finally Margaret's great-granddaughter Sophie, in Paris and Manhattan in the 1990s. Migration is the novel's central theme; despite being uprooted either by choice or by need, each woman is thoughtful, independent, and determined to pursue love on her own terms. **Literary.**

De la Roche, Mazo.

The Whiteoaks of Jalna. ★

> De la Roche's classic saga of 100 years and five generations of the Whiteoak family of southern Ontario still circulates in some libraries. The story begins in the 1850s, as the Whiteoak matriarch and patriarch decide to settle in a small town on Lake Ontario and raise their family there. The author returned to earlier periods in the Whiteoak family's history in her later volumes, which means that to follow the entire Jalna story from its beginning, the books must be read in a different order than they were published. With her death in 1961 came the end of the series.

The Building of Jalna. Little, Brown, 1945. 366pp.

Morning at Jalna. Little, Brown, 1960. 263pp.

Mary Wakefield. Little, Brown, 1949. 337pp.

Young Renny. Little, Brown, 1935. 324pp.

Whiteoak Heritage. Little, Brown, 1940. 325pp.

The Whiteoak Brothers. Little, Brown, 1953. 307pp.

Jalna. Little, Brown, 1927. 347pp.

Whiteoaks of Jalna. Little, Brown, 1929. 384pp.

Finch's Fortune. Little, Brown, 1931. 443pp.

The Master of Jalna. Little, Brown, 1933. 379pp.

Whiteoak Harvest. Little, Brown, 1936. 378pp.

Wakefield's Course. Little, Brown, 1942. 406pp.

Return to Jalna. Little, Brown, 1948. 462pp.

Renny's Daughter. Little, Brown, 1951. 376pp.

Variable Winds at Jalna. Little, Brown, 1955. 359pp.

Centenary at Jalna. Little, Brown, 1958. 342pp.

MacDonald, Ann-Marie.

Fall On Your Knees. **Simon & Schuster, 1996. 508pp.** 📖

> New Waterford, Cape Breton, Nova Scotia, in the first years of the twentieth century is the setting for this multigenerational saga. When piano tuner James Piper marries teenager Materia Mahmoud against the wishes of her Lebanese family, it sets in motion a chain of events that frequently lead to misery. James loves his

daughters, particularly Kathleen, the eldest, but he behaves less than honorably toward them. This makes for some disturbing scenes. Oprah's Book Club. **Literary.**

Multi-Volume Sagas

These multi-volume sagas allow readers to live through an extended sweep of history through many generations of a single family. In doing so, they can trace the history of an entire country. In this way these sagas are similar to multi-period epics (Chapter 3), though these novels emphasize characterization more than a single geographic location. Several classic sagas, listed in the previous section, can fit this category as well (e.g., Mazo de la Roche's Whiteoaks of Jalna series). See also Philippa Carr's Daughters of England series, under Romantic Sagas.

The British Isles

Anand, Valerie.

Bridges Over Time.

Anand takes us through 900 years (1040–1969) of one family's journey to regain their lost social standing. Its progenitors are Sir Ivor de Clairpont, a Norman knight captured and enslaved in Northumbria just before the Conquest, and his wife, the indomitable bondswoman Gunnor. Anand's characters are sympathetic and genuine, and her unsanitized portrait of England's social history will appeal to readers who appreciate gritty realism in their historical fiction. Although these novels are connected, they can also be read independently. The final volume, *The Dowerless Sisters* (published only in Britain), takes the story of the Whitmeads through 1969. (Anand also writes historical mysteries under the pseudonym Fiona Buckley.)

The Proud Villeins. St. Martin's Press, 1992. 310pp.

Ivon de Clairpont, a Norman knight, is among a group taken hostage by Danish forces in 1040. After unsuccessfully chafing against his bonds of slavery, he eventually settles down with Gunnor, a fellow thrall. He never ceases to remind his family, particularly grandson Ivon Oddeyes, of their noble heritage.

The Ruthless Yeomen. St. Martin's Press, 1993. 342pp.

In the thirteenth century, Ivon's descendants are now villeins on the holdings of Sir Henry Rushley of Oxfen. Owning nothing themselves, they are subject to the orders of their overlord, as Isabel of Northfield discovers when she tries to escape her family's legacy of serfdom. Her ambitions for the family are eventually achieved through her descendants, yeomen who become involved with peasant leader Wat Tyler's rebellion in 1381.

Women of Ashdon. St. Martin's Press, 1993. 373pp.

Susannah Whitmead, born in 1460, becomes the lady of Ashton Manor through marriage. Her granddaughter Christina, in an attempt to hold on to her grandmother's beloved house, becomes involved in the anti-Catholic conspiracies of Tudor times.

The Faithful Lovers. St. Martin's Press, 1994. 373pp.

When bachelor and secret Royalist Ninian Whitmead rescues a young Indian girl from a shipwreck off the Cornwall coast and makes her his wife, acceptance is not forthcoming from the Puritan community. This leads to tragedy for Ninian during England's Civil War. In later generations, their descendants fight among themselves in an attempt to prevent Henrietta Whitmead's marriage to the cousin she loves.

The Cherished Wives. St. Martin's Press, 1996. 341pp.

Two branches of the family join with the marriage of gentle Lucy-Anne Browne to her second cousin George Whitmead in the late eighteenth century, but wedded bliss eludes the couple. When the obnoxious and overbearing George disappears on long voyages with the East India Company, Lucy-Anne quietly takes a lover.

Harrod-Eagles, Cynthia.

The Morland Dynasty.

The Morland Dynasty traces the history of the Morland family from their origins during the fifteenth-century Wars of the Roses through the twentieth century. The series currently numbers twenty-six volumes, and the author plans to write three more, which will take the Morlands through the Second World War. Her characters, though fictional, interact with well-known historical figures, such as Richard, Duke of York in the fifteenth century, and there is usually at least one Morland family member present at every major event in England's history. Though all but the first six volumes were published only in Britain and the Commonwealth, the entire series has been published in paperback by Time Warner UK. These editions are available in the United States through Trafalgar Square, a distributor of British books.

The Founding. Dell, 1980. 496pp.

The Dark Rose. Dell, 1981. 528pp.

The Distant Wood. Dell, 1981. 383pp. (Original title: *The Princeling.*)

The Crystal Crown. Dell, 1981. 445pp. (Original title: *The Oak Apple.*)

The Black Pearl. Dell, 1983. 429pp.

The Long Shadow. Dell, 1983. 383pp.

The Chevalier. London: Macdonald, 1984. 414pp.

The Maiden. London: Macdonald, 1985. 413pp.

The Flood-Tide. London: Macdonald, 1986. 416pp.

The Tangled Thread. London: Macdonald, 1987. 416pp.

The Emperor. London: Macdonald, 1988. 416pp.

The Victory. London: Macdonald, 1989. 400pp.

The Regency. London: Macdonald, 1990. 624pp.

The Campaigners. London: Macdonald, 1991. 624pp.

The Reckoning. London: Macdonald, 1992. 486pp.

The Devil's Horse. London: Little, Brown, 1993. 482pp.

The Poison Tree. London: Little, Brown, 1994. 438pp.

The Abyss. London: Little, Brown, 1995. 480pp.

The Hidden Shore. London: Little, Brown, 1996. 471pp.

The Winter Journey. London: Little, Brown, 1997. 494pp.

The Outcast. London: Little, Brown, 1998. 463pp.

The Mirage. London: Little, Brown, 1999. 448pp.

The Cause. London: Little, Brown, 2000. 504pp.

The Homecoming. London: Little, Brown, 2001. 518pp.

The Question. London: Little, Brown, 2002. 515pp.

The Dream Kingdom. London: Little, Brown, 2003. 640pp.

The United States

Fleming, Thomas.

Stapleton Family Saga.

Master historical novelist and historian Fleming has written a multi-part, loosely connected saga of the Stapleton family, members of which take part in many notable events in American history. The fictional Stapletons are loosely based on the Stevenses and Stocktons, two prominent New Jersey families. They are listed in historical order but can easily be read independently.

Rulers of the City and *Promises to Keep*, two more works in the saga, are modern novels about local New Jersey politics.

Remember the Morning. Forge, 1997. 379pp.

On the shores of Lake Ontario in 1721, five-year-olds Catalyntie Van Vorst, of Dutch lineage, and Clara Flowers, a former slave, are captured by the Seneca Indians. Released at age seventeen, they have difficulty re-adjusting to their former lives. Catalyntie, thought ugly by the Seneca, now finds that she's the sought-after one, while Clara is expected to abandon her independence to serve her friend as a slave. Both love the same man, Malcolm Stapleton, an aspiring soldier who is searching for his own identity.

Liberty Tavern. Doubleday, 1976. 502pp.

Before the Civil War divided families and friends, there was the American Revolution, which did the same but across continents. Jonathan Gifford, owner of the Liberty Tavern in Monmouth County, New Jersey, is torn between his loyalty to England and his family's desire to support the Patriots.

Dreams of Glory. Warner, 1983. 492pp.

During the harsh winter of 1780, Washington's rebel army is close to starving at their winter quarters in Morristown, New Jersey. The British plan to end the war once and for all by capturing the brave American leader. Helping to foil these plans is Hugh Stapleton, a congressman and spy, and Caleb Chandler, a clergyman who is coerced into working—or feigning to work—as a double agent. In this maze of espionage, George Washington himself comes across as the ultimate spymaster, ironically so for a man who supposedly could not tell a lie.

The Wages of Fame. Forge, 1998. 461pp.

Beginning in 1827 and ending just before the Civil War, in this novel Hugh Stapleton's heir and grandson George is a force to be reckoned with in politics. His rival for Caroline Kemble's affections is John Sladen, no dummy himself. Both become senators from different states and reunite in Washington for the final showdown as the country heads toward war with Mexico. Caroline, George's wife and John's former lover, comes through as the true force behind her husband's political clout.

When This Cruel War Is Over. Forge, 2001. 301pp.

In 1864, the Civil War has raged for three years. Southern belle Janet Todd goes secretly recruiting for the Sons of Liberty, an organization that seeks to stop the war by uniting the Midwest into another Confederacy. Paul Stapleton, a Union officer, has grown weary of the lengthy war, and his patriotic loyalties are torn when he falls in love with Janet.

A Passionate Girl. Forge, 2004. 416pp. (Originally published in 1979 in paperback.)

The Fenians were a group of Irish nationalists who revolted against British tyranny in the mid-nineteenth century. Many Irish-Americans with Fenian sympathies became involved in the American Civil War to gain military experience. In 1865, Irish citizens Bess Fitzmaurice and her brother emigrate to the United States, becoming involved in the Fenian invasion of Canada's English colony. When the U.S. government withdraws its support for the Irish rebels, Bess returns to the States and becomes romantically involved with former Union General Jonathan Stapleton.

The Spoils of War. Putnam, 1985. 524pp.

This novel of how the people of the North helped their country survive after the Civil War begins in 1866 and lasts through 1900. It begins as Jonathan Stapleton, a New York banker, decides to marry his brother's beautiful widow Cynthia, a Southern woman of genteel poverty who longs for love and acceptance.

Jakes, John.

The Kent Family Chronicles. ★

Jakes's epic saga of the American experience as seen through the eyes of the Kent family begins at the time of the American Revolution and continues through America's westward expansion and frontier settlements of the 1880s. It begins as

Philip Kent, the bastard son of a French noble, leaves Europe for America at the time of the Revolution. He becomes a soldier, fighting on the side of his newly adopted country. Later installments see members of the Kent family through the nation's early years, the Civil War, Reconstruction, and the arrival of large groups of immigrants in the 1880s—all the while demonstrating the strength of the American spirit. This well-regarded series has inspired several TV miniseries and has never gone out of print since its initial publication.

The Bastard. Pyramid, 1974. 635pp.

The Rebels. Pyramid, 1975. 539pp.

The Seekers. Pyramid, 1975. 639pp.

The Furies. Pyramid, 1976. 537pp.

The Titans. Pyramid, 1976. 633pp.

The Warriors. Pyramid, 1977. 688pp.

The Lawless. Jove, 1978. 800pp.

The Americans. Jove, 1980. 800pp.

Settle, Mary Lee.

Beulah Quintet. ★

The five books in Settle's <u>Beulah Quintet</u> cover the settling of West Virginia, beginning in the mid-eighteenth century and continuing through the 1980s. The action centers on the fictional town of Canona: its people, their society, and their personal and political freedoms. *Prisons*, though written after *O Beulah Land* and *Know Nothing*, reaches back to seventeenth-century England to show how one man fought against Cromwell's conservative Puritan regime. Other subjects touched on within the series include the eighteenth-century settling of West Virginia, slavery in the years before the Civil War, and miners' strikes in the early twentieth century. The last novel, *The Killing Ground*, features Hannah McKarkle, a modern-day writer who comes back to Canona to research her heritage, bringing the story full circle.

Prisons. Putnam, 1973. 256pp.

O Beulah Land. Viking, 1956. 368pp.

Know Nothing. Viking, 1960. 334pp.

The Scapegoat. Random House, 1980. 278pp.

The Killing Ground. Farrar, Straus & Giroux, 1982. 385pp.

Thane, Elswyth.

Williamsburg Chronicles. ★

In the 1940s and 1950s, the late Elswyth Thane (1900–1981) wrote a series of interconnected novels about the Sprague and Day families of Williamsburg, Virginia, from the American Revolution until World War II.

The later books are set partially in England and, accurately reflecting the time period when they were written, speak to anti-German sentiment during the war. Popular with romance readers.

Dawn's Early Light. Hawthorn, 1943. 317pp.

Yankee Stranger. Hawthorn, 1944. 306pp.

Ever After. Hawthorn, 1945. 334pp.

The Light Heart. Aeonian Press, 1947. 341pp.

Kissing Kin. Meredith, 1948. 374pp.

This Was Tomorrow. Hawthorn, 1951. 319pp.

Homing. Hawthorn, 1957. 489pp.

Sagas with a Sense of Place

In these family sagas, the sense of place feels so strong that it becomes almost a character of its own. The lives of the novels' characters are intimately tied to the region where they live.

British Regional Sagas

British regional sagas are heartwarming tales that deal with the realities of working-class life in England, Scotland, and Wales, mostly in the nineteenth and early twentieth centuries. Their protagonists, nearly all female, struggle to create better lives for themselves and their families through hard work, education, and marriage with people of higher social standing. However, for those women who decide to "marry up," class differences often cause as many problems as they solve, to their frequent disappointment. The benchmark novelist in this category is Catherine Cookson, whose "clog and shawl" sagas (nicknamed for the outfits worn by the women on her novels' covers) remain immensely popular in Britain today.

Cookson, Catherine.

The late Catherine Cookson (1906–1998), the originator of the British regional saga, wrote over a hundred novels of family, romance, hard work, and triumph, mostly set against a well-researched backdrop of industrial northeast England and the surrounding countryside in the nineteenth century. Her compelling stories frequently begin with one woman's journey from poverty to happiness and continue to focus on her family, friends, and descendants. Cookson based many of her novels on her own background, growing up as the illegitimate daughter of a poverty-stricken woman in Tyne Dock, Northumberland. Many British authors have followed Cookson's immensely popular style. Although few of these works are available in the United States, read-alike authors commonly found in American libraries include Iris Gower, Anna Jacobs, Claire Rayner, and Jessica Stirling.

The Black Candle. **Summit, 1989. 488pp.**

In 1883, young Bridget Mordaunt makes good on the running of the candle and blacking factories she inherited from her father, but her relationship with two aristocratic brothers leaves a legacy of love and heartache that lasts three generations.

The Desert Crop. **Simon & Schuster, 1999. 318pp.**

When schoolboy Daniel Stewart's abusive father Hector marries Irishwoman Moira Conelly, some of his children object. But Daniel befriends the kindly Moira, whose youth is lost in continual pregnancy. He helps keep the family farm afloat, despite his drunken father's neglect and his refusal to pay for the medical education Daniel longs for.

The Fifteen Streets. **Simon & Schuster, 2002. 331pp. (First published in Britain in 1952.)**

The Fifteen Streets is the slum district of Tyneside, Northumberland, where Irish Catholic dockworker John O'Brien and his siblings grow up in poverty. His involvement with his younger sister's teacher, Mary Llewellyn, ignites resentment in her wealthy, snobbish family.

The Golden Straw. **Simon & Schuster, 1995. 494pp.**

In Victorian times, milliner Mabel Arkwright gives her assistant Emily Pearson a broad-brimmed, golden straw hat. Emily later inherits Mrs. Arkwright's business, but the straw hat proves her undoing, as well as that of her children and grandchildren. It all begins when the hat attracts the attention of unscrupulous womanizer Paul Steerman.

A House Divided. **Simon & Schuster, 1999. 365pp.**

Matthew Wallingham, blinded in action during World War II, falls in love with his nurse, Liz Ducksworth, though both of them have family problems and secrets to contend with. His wealthy family does not' accept working-class Liz, and Liz's abusive former fiancé takes revenge on her for leaving him.

Kate Hannigan Series. 📖

These two books, Cookson's first published novel and her last, are partly autobiographical, loosely following the life stories of Cookson's mother Kate and Cookson herself. Both take place in the slums of Tyneside's "fifteen streets" in the Edwardian period.

Kate Hannigan. Simon & Schuster, 2004. 305pp. (Originally published in Britain in 1950.)

Lovely Kate Hannigan falls in love with Dr. Rodney Prince, the well-to-do doctor who delivers her illegitimate daughter, Annie. Their long-term affection causes her neighbors (and Rodney's mean-spirited wife) to gossip spitefully about her.

Kate Hannigan's Girl. Simon & Schuster, 2000. 287pp.

This sequel to *Kate Hannigan* picks up with Kate's daughter Annie in the 1920s. Despite her mother's happy and prosperous marriage, Annie is humiliated by her own illegitimate birth. She faces the same religious prejudice that her mother faced. Even worse, she must compete for everything, including mathematician Terence Macbane, with the scheming Cathleen Davidson. Originally written much earlier than 2000, *Kate Hannigan's Girl* was rejected by Cookson's publisher for its controversial content, but was later accepted and released as her 100th published novel.

The Mallen Trilogy. ★

The Mallens are a family accursed, as shown by the white streak of hair borne by the sons of the ruthless Thomas Mallen, Squire of High Banks Hall, who loses his fortune amid scandal in the 1850s. Not even his illegitimate, deaf daughter Barbara is immune from his tyrannical legacy, as demonstrated by the effect the Mallen curse has on her three sons.

The Mallen Streak. Dutton, 1973. 282pp.

The Mallen Girl. Dutton, 1973. 282pp.

The Mallen Lot. Dutton, 1974. 309pp. (Original title: *The Mallen Litter.*)

My Beloved Son. Simon & Schuster, 1991. 380pp.

Strong-willed Ellen Jebeau, a poor widow taken in by her rich brother-in-law's family in 1926, won't let anything get in the way of creating a better life for herself and her son.

The Obsession. Simon & Schuster, 1997. 317pp.

In England's North Country in Victorian times, twenty-one-year-old Beatrice Steel goes to any length to keep her family home, Pine Hurst, for herself after the unexpected death of her debt-ridden father. This includes alienating her family and forcing her sister's suitor to marry her instead.

The Silent Lady. Simon & Schuster, 2002. 351pp.

The long-lost Irene Baindor, reappearing at her solicitor's offices in 1955, is nearly mistaken for a street woman and dismissed. Irene is hardly recognizable as the beautiful, musically talented woman who was mysteriously thrown out of her husband's house twenty-six years earlier. Now she returns to tell her remarkable tale.

Tilly Trotter Trilogy.

Beginning in 1836, Matilda Trotter, called Tilly, learns the hard way that beauty can be both a gift and a curse. Growing up with her grandparents in Tyneside in County Durham (as Cookson did herself), Tilly falls on hard times. Accused of witchcraft and barely escaping with her life, she goes to work at the local mill. Mistress to a rich, married man for years, after he dies she is forced out of their home by his jealous daughter. At this point the ever-resourceful Tilly heads to America, where she becomes a frontier wife. Her frontier adventures over at the ripe old age of thirty-five, Tilly heads back to her homeland.

Tilly. Morrow, 1980. 372pp. (Original title: *Tilly Trotter.*)

Tilly Wed. Morrow, 1981. 310pp. (Original title: *Tilly Trotter Wed.*)

Tilly Alone. Morrow, 1982. 1982. (Original title: *Tilly Trotter Widowed.*)

The Upstart. **Simon & Schuster, 1996. 348pp.**

> In nineteenth-century England, would-be gentleman Samuel Fairbrother, a tradesman who has made his fortune in boot manufacturing, gets advice from butler Roger Maitland on how to succeed in a rich man's world. What he doesn't count on is his daughter Janet's growing love for the well-meaning, intelligent Roger.

Drummond, Emma.
Knightshill Saga.

> Many of Emma Drummond's historical novels (including those she wrote as Elizabeth Darrell or under her real name, Edna Dawes) deal with romance and conflict in exotic lands, and these are no exception. In 1896, the elderly Sir Gilliard Ashleigh, a formerly military man, treats his grandchildren the way he would his subordinates. Obsessed with making sure his family line continues, he browbeats his surviving grandchildren into heeding him, inflaming passions and destroying marriages. The action sees family members through the Boer War and adventure in the Australian outback.

> *A Question of Honor.* St. Martin's Press, 1992. 346pp.

> *A Distant Hero.* St. Martin's Press, 1997. 424pp.

> *Act of Valour.* St. Martin's Press, 1998. 457pp.

Doughty, Anne.
The Woman from Kerry. **Severn House, 2003. 320pp.**

> Rose McGinley, whose family was evicted from their home in Donegal, Ireland, during the 1861 Clearances, finds that her childhood poverty gives her the strength to carry on as she grows into adulthood.

Gower, Iris.
Sweyn's Eye Series.

> Set amid the copper works of industrial Swansea, South Wales, in the years up to and following World War I, the six novels in this series focus on three women of the city, their families and friends, and their romantic entanglements. Mali Llewelyn, a copper worker's daughter, struggles to escape from the poverty of Copperman's Row through marriage to the heir to the business. Fisherman's daughter Katie Murphy is less lucky in love, and the tragedy she encounters makes her strong. Mary Jenkins, Mali's and Katie's employer at the local laundry, grows as a business-woman in tough times, but takes a while to settle down with the right man. Gower's novels are being reissued by Severn House.

> *Copper Kingdom.* St. Martin's Press, 1983. 320pp.

> *Proud Mary.* St. Martin's Press, 1985. 372pp.

> *Spinner's Wharf.* St. Martin's Press, 1985. 383pp.

> *Morgan's Woman.* St. Martin's Press, 1987. 384pp.

Fiddler's Ferry. St. Martin's Press, 1987. 377pp.

Black Gold. St. Martin's Press, 1988. 384pp.

Jacobs, Anna.

Jacobs, an Australian author with English roots, is best known for her romantic family sagas and historical novels set in eighteenth- and nineteenth-century England.

Gibson Family Saga.

Annie Gibson, born in 1820 in a mill town in industrial Lancashire, England, is the appealing heroine. After her mother's death, Annie is forced to raise her younger siblings. She falls on hard times, discovers and loses love, and gradually rises up from poverty, always vowing that one day she'll leave Salem Street behind forever. The final three volumes, centered on Annie and her growing family, have not been published in the United States; these include *Ridge Hill*, *Hallam Square*, and *Spinners Lake*.

Salem Street. St. Martin's Press, 1995. 486pp.

High Street. St. Martin's Press, 1996. 359pp.

The Kershaw Sisters.

A new series set in pre-World War I Lancashire. Jacobs has written three more novels (*Our Polly*, *Our Eva*, and *Our Mary Ann*) about the Kershaw family, though these have not yet been published in America.

Our Lizzie. Thomas Dunne, 2003. 320pp.

Lizzie Kershaw survives both parental and marital abuse. The war brings freedom for Lizzie, as she flourishes on the home front, working in a munitions factory while her husband is away fighting on the continent.

Kirkwood, Gwen.

Lochandee Saga.

Family troubles in 1930s and 1940s Scotland.

The Laird of Lochandee. Severn House, 2002. 314pp.

In 1930s Scotland, Connor Maxwell takes in young Rachel O'Brien after her father dies, but his wife treats her worse than a servant. When she falls in love with Ross, the son of the house, and becomes pregnant, the pair must face his parents' wrath if they are to stay together.

A Tangled Web. Severn House, 2003. 288pp.

At the end of World War II, Ross and Rachel are married, but secrets from the past threaten their happiness.

Sole, Linda.

Bridget O'Rourke Series.

Sole's latest saga takes place on the London docklands between the late nineteenth century and World War II.

Bridget. Severn House, 2002. 252pp.

Bridget O'Rourke is the only responsible member of her impoverished family. Her possible savior is Joe Robinson, though his ties to the criminal underworld threaten their livelihood.

Kathy. Severn House, 2004. 248pp.

Kathy Cole trains as a nurse during World War I and falls in love with Bridget's younger brother Tom.

Amy. Severn House, 2004. 251pp.

Bridget's daughter Amy Robinson works in her aunt's dress shop in London and befriends the daughter of one of her mother's old rivals.

Emma Robinson Saga.

British shopgirl Emma Robinson marries Dick Gillows to save her reputation and have a father for her illegitimate child, but he turns out to be unscrupulous, violent, and abusive. She discovers that Dick married her only to take over her family's shop, so she fights to stop him and to make her own life for herself and her son James. After Emma is widowed, she marries a good friend, Jon Reece, who goes off to fight in France during World War II. When she falls in love with a handsome American, she regrets her hasty marriage.

The Ties that Bind. Severn House, 1999. 248pp.

The Bonds that Break. Severn House, 2000. 250pp.

The Hearts that Hold. Severn House, 2001. 256pp.

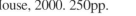

Stirling, Jessica.

Jessica Stirling, the pseudonym of Scottish novelist Hugh C. Rae, has written over twenty historical sagas set in nineteenth- and twentieth-century Scotland. His earlier novels (pre-1984) were co-written with Peggie Coughlan, also under the Stirling name.

The Burnsides.

Urban family saga set in mid-twentieth-century Glasgow.

The Penny Wedding. St. Martin's Press, 1995. 394pp.

After her mother dies during the Great Depression, seventeen-year-old Alison Burnside feels obligated to give up her dreams of a medical career. Hope arrives in the form of her four older brothers, who agree to help her out, and Jim Abbott, who becomes her tutor and a romantic interest.

The Marrying Kind. St. Martin's Press, 1996. 359pp.

Alison Burnside, now a third-year medical student in pre-World War II Glasgow, must choose between her attachment to Jim Abbott, her ailing fiancé, and the freedom offered to her by new career opportunities and a romance with a handsome, disreputable Irishman.

The Conways Trilogy.

An urban family saga set in early twentieth-century Glasgow, similar in tone to the Burnsides series. *Wives at War* will be the next volume.

Prized Possessions. St. Martin's Press, 2001. 412pp.

In Depression-era Glasgow, Lizzie Conway fights to keep her three teenage daughters out of poverty, hoping that one day they'll be able to move out of the slums. It doesn't help that she has to keep paying off the money her deceased husband stole from the Mafia. Babs and Polly, strong-willed girls both, get involved with the wrong men and end up learning about their mother's mistakes the hard way.

Sisters Three. St. Martin's Press, 2002.

Still in the Gorbals slums of Glasgow on the eve of World War II, Polly and Babs raise their own families and try to keep their gangster husbands out of trouble. Trouble brews when Rosie, the deaf youngest sister, becomes romantically involved with a policeman.

Isle of Mull Trilogy.

Series set on the Isle of Mull off the Scottish coast, late nineteenth century.

The Island Wife. St. Martin's Press, 1998. 410pp.

In 1878, the lives of the Campbells, tenant farmers on the Scottish island of Mull, are forever changed with the arrival of the Baverstock brothers and Michael Tarrant. While Austin Baverstock attracts red-haired Biddy's attention, she's also intrigued by Michael, and competes with plain sister Innis for his affections.

The Wind from the Hills. St. Martin's Press, 1998. 449pp.

Beginning in 1891, the Campbell sisters discover that marriage to their chosen suitors has come at a price, yet they still cannot forget their bitter rivalry.

The Strawberry Season. St. Martin's Press, 2000. 468pp.

At the end of the nineteenth-century, sixteen years after the events in *The Island Wife*, pregnant Fay Ludlow arrives on the quiet Isle of Mull, disrupting the lives of its residents.

The Piper's Tune. St. Martin's Press, 2002. 486pp.

In late Victorian and early Edwardian Glasgow, Lindsay Franklin has the chance to take part in the family's shipbuilding business. In doing so, she attracts the attention of a number of notable men, not the least of whom is her handsome Irish cousin, Forbes McCullough.

Shamrock Green. St. Martin's Press, 2003. 480pp.

Sylvie McCulloch, proprietor of the Shamrock Hotel in World War I-era Dublin, falls in love with Francis Hagarty, a wounded soldier who is brought to the Shamrock to recuperate. Her husband Gowry becomes furious when he discovers that Francis is using the hotel to store arms that he has smuggled in. Due to circumstances beyond his control, Gowry leaves Ireland to fight in the war. Sylvie and daughter Maeve remain behind. The Easter Uprising of 1916 looms just around the corner.

The Workhouse Girl. **St. Martin's Press, 1997. 472pp.**

In Victorian Scotland, Nancy Winfield, servant and former workhouse girl, is the only ally of Cassie Armitage during her unhappy marriage to the nasty Reverend Robert Montague—and both Nancy and the deceitful reverend have secrets that they're not revealing.

Thorne, Nicola.

Broken Bough Saga.

One family's journey from poverty to respectability in Dorset, England, in the early twentieth century.

The Broken Bough. Severn House, 2001. 217pp.

Cathy Read, widowed after her husband's accidental death, must find a way to care for her three growing daughters: Verity, Addie, and Peg. She marries Lord Ryland's head gardener and has more children, but money is still tight.

The Blackbird's Song. Severn House, 2001. 219pp.

In 1924, Peg Hallam leaves Dorset for London to become a Fleet Street journalist. Her sister Verity, already living in the city as a nurse, tries to steer her clear from trouble, but Peg determines to break out on her own.

The Water's Edge. Severn House, 2002. 216pp.

Peg Hallam, engaged to another, comes in close contact with a previous crush, Hubert Ryland, while participating in the General Strike in 1926.

Oh, Happy Day! Severn House, 2002. 218pp.

Now Lady Ryland, the former Peg Hallam has found stability and love, but her half-brother Ed's marriage to Maisie, a former nightclub dancer, threatens the family's respectability.

American Regional Sagas

These sagas give readers a good feel for family life in different regions of the United States: New England, the Midwest, the South, and the West.

New England

Gautreau, Norman G.

Sea Room. **MacAdam/Cage, 2002. 311pp.** 📖

This saga of a French-Canadian family of lobster trappers living in the small town of Buck Harbor, Maine, takes place during World War II. Ten-year-old Jordi is devastated when his father, Gil, signs up with the army and becomes a medic overseas, as the two had always been close, and Jordi had hoped that they would build a boat together. While the family tries to cope with Gil's absence, his mother and grandmother do their own part for the war effort by cultivating their land. After Gil is killed toward the end of the fighting, Jordi's grandfather Pip and other relatives and friends help Jordi hold on to his dream. **Literary.**

Graver, Elizabeth.
  Unravelling. **Hyperion, 1997. 298pp.** 📖

Set in early nineteenth-century New England, this literary saga focuses on the troubled relationship between Aimee Slater, a New Hampshire farm girl, and her mother. The story jumps back and forth between the major events in Aimee's life: her childhood; her flight from her family home to the textile mills of Lowell, Massachusetts, at age fifteen; and the pain she experiences when her mother forces her to give up her newborn twins, the result of Aimee's never-ending search for love. Later life finds Aimee living alone at the edge of her parents' property; having found independence at last, she can at last reconcile herself to her and her mother's past actions. **Literary.**

The Midwest

Flagg, Fannie.
  Standing in the Rainbow. **Random House, 2002. 493pp.** 📖

The amusingly quirky characters of Flagg's latest novel are fully human and completely entertaining. Dot Smith, better known as "Neighbor Dorothy," re-counts the trials and tribulations of small-town life in Elmwood Springs, Missouri, from 1946 up until the present day. It's a fond look back to the halcyon days of childhood, and even if things really weren't that way in reality, they are remembered as such anyway.

Ryan, Arliss.
  The Kingsley House. **St. Martin's Press, 2000. 420pp.** ✍

Using the occupants of a longtime family residence in Livonia, Michigan, as her focal point, Ryan recounts 150 years in the life of small town Midwestern America. In 1843, Nathan Kingsley, the author's third great-grandfather, lovingly builds a home for his future wife Mary. More a pioneer settlement than a town, Livonia slowly grows over the years to become a burgeoning suburb of Detroit and eventually a small city. Nathan and Mary survive their first venture as unsuspecting abolitionists along the Underground Railroad, their granddaughter Gertrude overcomes early tragedy to live on as the family matriarch, and in 1977 her granddaughter Laura saves the house from demolition by having it physically moved to a historic preservation site, where it can be visited today.

The South

Donald, Elsie Burch.
  Nashborough. **HarperCollins, 2001. 416pp.**

Nashborough is a fictional town in the Deep South presided over by the wealthy Nash and Douglas families, joined by the marriage of the Douglas heir to Dartania Nash. As the twentieth century progresses, their traditional society ways lose out to financial hardships, intermarriage with families previously considered unequal, and racial tensions. Though some of the prose has a soap opera-ish quality, and many characters are not very likeable, the author captures the atmosphere of the Southern way of life. **Literary.**

Fletcher, Inglis.

Carolina Series. ★

Fletcher's seven-volume series about the people of Albemarle County, North Carolina, will appeal to readers in search of a meticulously researched fictional history of the South. The novels have stood the test of time well, and they are a painless way to learn about the early history of the state. Fletcher has also written five more novels set in North Carolina, though these don't form part of the same story.

Raleigh's Eden. Bobbs Merrill, 1940. 662pp.

Men of Albemarle. Bobbs Merrill, 1942. 566pp.

Lusty Wind for Carolina. Bobbs Merrill, 1944. 509pp.

Toil of the Brave. Bobbs Merrill, 1946. 547pp.

Roanoke Hundred. Bobbs Merrill, 1949. 492pp.

Bennett's Welcome. Bobbs Merrill, 1950. 451pp.

Queen's Gift. Bobbs Merrill, 1952. 448pp.

Jekel, Pamela.

Pamela Jekel has spent much of her literary career writing multigenerational family sagas set in the Southern United States. Her work is frequently compared to James Michener's, though she focuses on individual personalities and their relationships to one another as much as the land. Refreshingly, she doesn't neglect to include the perspectives of the country's Native American inhabitants. Her earlier sagas include *Bayou*, set in Louisiana's Delta country and in New Orleans, and *Columbia*, set in the Pacific Northwest.

Deepwater. **Kensington, 1994. 495pp.**

Between the early eighteenth century and the Civil War, four generations of women raise families along the Carolina coastline. While the introductory material tells of their precursors on Roanoke just before Virginia Dare's birth, the real meat of the novel begins with Leah Hancock, a strong woman on a tobacco settlement who manages to escape to Cape Fear with her daughters when Indians attack her family.

Natchez. **Kensington, 1995. 482pp.**

Covering 150 years of life in Natchez, Louisiana, the novel begins with newly arrived settler Josiah Fleming, who takes another bride when his wife and children die on the voyage south from Connecticut. The pair gives rise to five generations of strong-minded women who deal with hardships such as war, death, and plantation disasters. The family melodrama can seem soap opera-like at times, but the author's research is accurate, and the plot is entertaining.

River Without End. **Kensington, 1997. 436pp.**

A novel of the Old South, told with broader sweep than her earlier novels. Here Jekel writes a saga of the people living alongside Florida's Suwannee River between 1790 and 1976, though most of the action takes place in the nineteenth century. It begins with a group of runaway slaves heading toward freedom who find refuge among the Seminole tribes of Florida. They stick together throughout numerous incursions onto their land, from the Spanish to Andrew Jackson's troops in 1818 to Union soldiers in the Civil War. Their leader is Osceola, champion against the white invaders, and his descendants carry on his legacy.

McCrumb, Sharyn.

The Songcatcher. **Dutton, 2001. 368pp.** 📖 ✍

Part of McCrumb's <u>Ballad</u> series of novels set in modern Appalachia, this installment also incorporates a strong saga component in the form of a ballad originating in eighteenth-century Scotland and passed down over generations in America. Its journey begins in 1751, as Malcolm McCourry, a character based on one of McCrumb's own ancestors, is kidnapped from his home in Islay and taken aboard ship. He makes his way to the mountains of North Carolina, where he raises two families. His reminiscences alternate with the story of John Walker and his relationship with estranged daughter Linda, a folksinger calling herself Lark McCourry, who tries to make it home before he dies. Lark remembers a song from her childhood and tracks it down, with the help of wisewoman Nora Bonesteel, in the hopes that it will revive her flagging career.

Miller, Charlotte.

Behold, This Dreamer Trilogy.

The difficulties of life on a family farm in early twentieth-century Alabama. **Literary.**

Behold, This Dreamer. NewSouth, 2000. 510pp.

In the 1920s, Janson Sanders, son of a poor white tenant farmer and his Cherokee wife, makes his own way in the world after his parents' deaths. Although he dreams of eventually regaining his parents' land, he finds work at a plantation house in Georgia. He falls in love with the owner's daughter, Elise Whitley, though her cruel father and brothers make their lives difficult.

Through a Glass Darkly. NewSouth, 2001. 341pp.

Janson and Elise, now married, return to his relatives in Alabama after her father disowns them. During the Great Depression, they struggle to hold on to their dreams and raise a family despite the poverty that envelops them.

There Is a River. NewSouth, 2002. 301pp.

During the war years, Janson is called up to fight while Elise and her family learn how to provide for themselves. Their independence comes in handy after Janson returns home wounded. This saga extends over three generations until the 1980s, when family farms are once again in crisis.

Price, Eugenia.

Over her lifetime, the late Eugenia Price wrote a number of bestselling historical novels set in the Deep South before, during, and after the Civil War. Her meticulously researched novels are family sagas and sentimental love stories, all based on the lives of real people—so-called average citizens who manage to triumph over heartbreak, war, and other adverse circumstances. Price took inspiration from names she saw on gravestones and took it upon herself to discover the stories of these people who had passed on. Her portrayals of charming characters and her heartwarming evocations of days gone by appeal to all age groups. Many of her historical novels, gentle reads originally published by the mainstream press, have been reissued for the Christian market.

Florida Trilogy. ✍

In her second series Price found inspiration in the strength of the people of St. Augustine, Florida, between 1791 and the Civil War. John McQueen, Mary Evans, and Margaret Fleming, three historical personages, are the hope and inspiration of their spouses and families.

Don Juan McQueen. Lippincott, 1974. 384pp.

Maria. Lippincott, 1977. 352pp.

Margaret's Story. Lippincott & Crowell, 1980. 394pp.

Georgia Trilogy. ✍

Anne Couper Fraser of St. Simons Island, Georgia, and her Scottish soldier-husband, John, are the protagonists of this extended romantic saga beginning during the War of 1812 and ending during the Civil War.

Bright Captivity. Doubleday, 1991. 631pp.

Where Shadows Go. Doubleday, 1993. 646pp.

Beauty from Ashes. Doubleday, 1995. 627pp.

St. Simons Island Trilogy. ✍ ★

Begins in post-Revolutionary Maine and ends on St. Simons Island, Georgia, just after the Civil War. James Gould, James's son Horace, and northerner Anson Dodge make the South their home, renew their faith, and discover love. Price wrote the volumes of this trilogy in the opposite order of their chronology.

Lighthouse. Lippincott, 1971. 342pp.

New Moon Rising. Lippincott, 1969. 281pp.

The Beloved Invader. Lippincott, 1965. 284pp.

Savannah Quartet. ★ ✍

Beginning with Philadelphian Mark Browning, who arrives in Savannah as a young man, the Browning, Mackay, and Stiles families of antebellum Georgia interact with one another, find romance, and find themselves divided on the issue of slavery.

Savannah. Doubleday, 1983. 595pp.

To See Your Face Again. Doubleday, 1985. 546pp.

Before the Darkness Falls. Doubleday, 1987. 455pp.

Stranger in Savannah. Doubleday, 1989. 755pp.

The Waiting Time. Doubleday, 1997. 373pp. ✍

Just before the Civil War, transplanted Bostonian Abby Allyn Barnes finds her-self the unexpected owner of a rice plantation and a hundred slaves after her hus-band's death and does the right thing by setting them free. She finds a new love interest in Thad Greene, her late husband's overseer. Price's last novel, *The Wait-ing Time,* was completed just weeks before her death in 1996.

The West

Western sagas are annotated in Chapter 6.

African Sagas

Families of European descent learn to survive in the wilds of Africa.

Smith, Wilbur.
<u>Ballantyne Novels</u> and <u>Courtney Family Saga.</u>
These adventure-filled series are annotated in Chapter 8.

Wood, Barbara.
Green City in the Sun. **Random House, 1988. 699pp.**
Nairobi, Kenya, is the green city in the sun, and Sir Valentine Treverton ar-rives here in 1919 with his fragile wife Rose and determined sister Grace. Val-entine dreams of transforming the Kenyan wilderness into profitable coffee plantations, while Grace, a medical doctor, wants to bring modern medicine to the poverty-ridden land. Their plans are derailed by the Mathenge family, the land's original inhabitants, who place a curse on the Trevertons that lasts over several generations.

Australian Sagas

Family tales of the strong men, women, and children who settled in Australia, from its days as a British penal colony through the early twentieth century.

Fletcher, Aaron.
<u>Outback Saga.</u>
The entries in this five-volume saga of the colonists and convicts who settled the untamed Australian outback were published as paperback originals. They have since been reissued.

Outback. Leisure, 1978. 447pp.

Outback Station. Leisure, 1991. 470pp.

Walkabout. Leisure, 1992. 476pp. Later reissued as *Walk About.*

Wallaby Track. Leisure, 1994. 479pp.

Outback Legacy. Leisure, 1996. 442pp.

Long, William Stuart.

The Australians.

One of the extended family sagas charting the development of a nation that were issued by Book Creations in the 1980s, this installment takes on the settling of Australia from its earliest years as a prison colony, to later years of British rule, to its growth as its own nation. The later volumes include a genealogical table. The earlier volumes in the series were issued simultaneously in hardcover by Gregg and in paperback by Dell, and the later ones only in paperback.

The Exiles. Gregg, 1979. 677pp.

The Settlers. Gregg, 1980. 541pp.

The Traitors. Gregg, 1981. 615pp.

The Explorers. Gregg, 1982. 505pp.

The Adventurers. Gregg, 1983. 447pp.

The Colonists. Gregg, 1984. 404pp.

The Gold Seekers. Gregg, 1985. 349pp.

The Gallant. Dell, 1986. 431pp.

The Empire Builders. Dell, 1987. 440pp.

The Seafarers. Dell, 1988. 402pp.

The Nationalists. Dell, 1989. 449pp.

The Imperialists. Dell, 1990. 486pp.

McCullough, Colleen.

The Thorn Birds. **Harper & Row, 1977. 533pp.** ★

Paddy Cleary and his wife Fiona arrive from New Zealand with their family in the 1940s to run Drogheda, a large sheep station in the Australian outback owned by Paddy's rich sister Mary Carson. Despite their responsibilities, Mary continually treats her brother's family like poor relations, suitable for hard work but not much else. Paddy and Fiona's only daughter, Meggie, grows up admiring the family's itinerant priest, Father Ralph de Bricassart. Despite Ralph's avowed celibacy, Mary wants him for herself. Meggie's growing love for Ralph causes them nothing but pain over the years, as he's continually torn between Meggie and the Church. His choice has immense repercussions for the next generation of Clearys. This passionate multigenerational saga was made into a popular yet controversial television miniseries.

The Touch. **Simon & Schuster, 2003. 454pp.**

In 1872, Elizabeth Drummond voyages from Scotland to Sydney to marry her cousin Alexander Kinross, a former ne'er-do-well who struck it rich in Australia's gold mines. Realizing that he would rather have married her beautiful sister, Elizabeth knows she has a difficult life ahead. Her problems multiply when she meets Alexander, whom she dislikes instantly, as well as his beautiful mistress, Ruby. Their unhappiness carries over to the next generation.

McKinley, Tamara.

The Jacaranda Vines. **St. Martin's Press, 2001. 406pp.**

Jacaranda Vines is a vineyard in modern Australia, a billion-dollar corporation that may be divided up. The death of its owner, wine tycoon Jock Witney, has left his family burdened with debt. His elderly, long-suffering widow, Cordelia, has her own reasons for wanting to keep the family business together. She takes her granddaughter Sophie on a tour of the outback, telling her stories of the vineyard's history, which begins in the 1830s in Sussex and continues through present-day Australia.

Matilda's Last Waltz. **St. Martin's Press, 1999. 440pp.**

After the death of her husband and young son, Jenny Sanders learns that she has inherited Churinga, a sheep station in the Australian outback. The city-bred Jenny travels to Churinga and finds herself increasingly attracted by the wide-open landscape and intrigued by diaries left by the station's former owner, Matilda Thomas, beginning in the 1920s. As Matilda struggles to keep the neighboring squires from taking over the ranch, she encounters more and more danger.

Windflowers. **St. Martin's Press, 2002. 368pp.**

Claire Pearson, a veterinarian in modern Sydney, returns to her family's cattle ranch in Queensland after her great-aunt Aurelia calls her home. She dreads the reconciliation, as she and her mother Ellie have long been estranged. Ellie decides that it's time to lay bare the family secrets once and for all, and she and Aurelia gradually reveal a story that begins in 1936 and contains revelations about Claire's own parentage. McKinley's characterizations are occasionally thin; her strength is in her descriptions of the barren, beautiful Australian landscape.

Romantic Sagas

Romantic sagas are family stories that also incorporate a strong romantic element. Readers who enjoy novels of this type should also investigate romantic epics and romantic historicals (Chapter 4).

Aitken, Rosemary.

Cornish Sagas.

A series of novels set in the Cornish mining town of Penvarris circa 1910.

Stormy Waters. Severn House, 2001. 216pp.

Wilhelmina Nicholls, called Sprat, becomes romantically involved with Denzil Vargo, but his drunken father and family secrets threaten to tear them apart.

The Silent Shore. Severn House, 2002. 208pp.

In this sequel to *Stormy Waters*, Sprat Nicholls, unable to deal with what she's learned back in the mining town of Penvarris, has fled to London, but she yearns continually for the peaceful life she once led at home.

The Granite Cliffs. Severn House, 2003. 250pp.

The mining life in Penvarris in Edwardian times can be treacherous, as Daniel Olds learns to his disappointment. Though he grows closer to Victoria Flower, the vicar's daughter, their differing social circumstances present a challenge in their close-knit community. This novel stands on its own.

Bacon, Margaret.

Northrop Hall Series.

After the horrors of World War I, life at the magnificent family residence of Northrop Hall won't ever be the same.

Northrop Hall. Severn House, 2003. 256pp.

When war breaks out in Europe in 1914, and Lady Arndale of Northrop Hall dies in an accident, her son Charles takes over management of the estate. Daughters Diana and Laura take on more grown-up roles. The social fabric of their world is changing, as the roles of master and servant are occasionally swapped; and the women of the family find themselves taking on greater responsibilities—and gaining respect for it.

The Years Between. Severn House, 2003. 256pp.

After the war, Diana and her husband James work tirelessly to transform Northrop Hall into a home for wounded soldiers, but their marriage feels the strain.

Belle, Pamela.

The Herons of Goldhayes. ★

A series of romantic family sagas set during England's Civil War in the seventeenth century. Critics' comments likening Belle's series to M. M. Kaye's romantic epic *The Far Pavilions* (Chapter 4) are well deserved.

The Moon in the Water. Berkley, 1984. 528pp.

Thomazine Heron, orphaned at a young age, goes to live with her distant Heron cousins at their Suffolk manor, Goldhayes. There she finds friendship with cousin Lucy and true love with her cousin Francis. However, she was betrothed as a child to another cousin, the cold Dominic Drakelon, and Thomazine's guardian refuses to let her wed Francis instead.

The Chains of Fate. Berkley, 1984. 511pp.

Discovering that her beloved Francis is indeed alive, in contrast to what she and her family had been told, Thomazine heads north to Scotland to find him. Their romance is thwarted by politics and their scheming cousin Meraud.

Alethea. Berkley, 1985. 578pp.

After the Restoration of Charles II to England's throne, Alethea Heron, daughter of Francis and Thomazine, flees to London to become an artist when her older half-brother's attentions make her uncomfortable. Though determined never to marry, she becomes romantically involved with the debonair Earl of Rochester and succeeds in her artistic endeavors in a man's world.

Wintercombe Series.

Belle's second series set during England's Civil War, like the first, interweaves real and fictional characters to create a historically accurate portrait. Unlike the Royalist Heron family, the St. Barbes are Puritans living at Wintercombe, a large house in Somerset.

Wintercombe. St. Martin's Press, 1988.

Silence St. Barbe, the young second wife of a Puritan soldier and mother of a growing family, continues to run her household despite its being garrisoned by the King's Men. Though offended by the rough manners of the commanding officer, Lieutenant-Colonel Ridgeley, Silence feels attracted to his second-in-command, kindly Captain Nick Hellier.

Herald of Joy. St. Martin's Press, 1989. 501pp.

After George St. Barbe dies in 1651, his wife Silence holds the family together. Her problems are compounded by her eldest stepdaughter, Rachael, whose jealousy of Silence makes her bitter and vengeful. Cavalier Nick Hellier, the father of Silence's daughter Kate, comes into her life once again, and her children shelter him at the risk of their own lives.

A Falling Star. St. Martin's Press, 1990. 500pp.

In 1685, Silence and Nick Hellier have been married for many years, and Silence becomes a great-grandmother. Monmouth's Rebellion divides the residents of Philip's Norton, their peaceful village in Somerset. When Silence's grandson and heir Alexander St. Barbe comes home to Wintercombe, it throws the family into turmoil. Most affected are his cousin Charles, who has guarded the estate in Alex's absence, and his French cousin Louise, attracted to Alex against her better judgment.

Treason's Gift. St. Martin's Press, 1993. 546pp.

Though Alex and Louise are married, their relationship is frequently stormy. In 1686, while Louise St. Barbe deals with a tragic miscarriage, her unfaithful husband Alex heads to the Netherlands to help restore Protestantism, in the form of William and Mary, to England's throne.

Carr, Philippa.

Daughters of England.

Philippa Carr, one of the many pseudonyms of the prolific Eleanor Burford Hibbert (also known as Victoria Holt and Jean Plaidy), wrote a series of historical romantic suspense novels that form an extended family saga, reaching back to Tudor England and ending just before World War II. Journals passed from mother to daughter tie the earlier books together, as does the lengthy family tree on the novels' endpapers. Although Carr's later works abandoned the "secret diary" theme and didn't rely as much on historical events for plot development, they continued to focus on the female descendants of the same extended family. Each of Carr's heroines goes through a trial by fire of sorts, either facing near-certain death or discovering the passionate nature that lies beneath her seemingly placid demeanor. Carr's final novel, *Daughters of England,* despite its title, is a stand-alone romantic historical novel set in seventeenth-century England.

The Miracle at St. Bruno's. Putnam, 1972. 384pp.

The Lion Triumphant. Putnam, 1973. 380pp.

The Witch from the Sea. Putnam, 1975. 341pp.

Saraband for Two Sisters. Putnam, 1976. 384pp.

Lament for a Lost Lover. Putnam, 1977. 381pp.

The Love Child. Putnam, 1978. 371pp.

The Song of the Siren. Putnam, 1979. 336pp.

Will You Love Me in September. Putnam, 1981. 324pp. (Original title: *The Drop of the Dice.*)

The Adulteress. Putnam, 1982. 334pp.

Knave of Hearts. Putnam, 1983. 288pp. (Original title: *Zipporah's Daughter.*)

Voices in a Haunted Room. Putnam, 1984. 335pp.

The Return of the Gypsy. Putnam, 1985. 348pp.

Midsummer's Eve. Putnam, 1986. 334pp.

The Pool of St. Branok. Putnam, 1987. 339pp.

The Changeling. Putnam, 1989. 368pp.

The Black Swan. Putnam, 1990. 350pp.

A Time for Silence. Putnam, 1991. 349pp.

The Gossamer Cord. Putnam, 1992. 367pp.

We'll Meet Again. Putnam, 1993. 304pp.

Davis, Kathryn Lynn.

The Rose Clan.

A heartfelt romantic saga set in nineteenth- and twentieth-century Scotland, featuring the three very different daughters of world traveler Charles Kittridge.

Too Deep for Tears. Pocket, 1989. 550pp.

Charles Kittridge, an English diplomat, returns to Glen Affric in the Scottish Highlands to see his wife, Mairi Rose, before he dies, and to bring together the three daughters he has' never met. Mairi's daughter Ailsa was conceived the night before Charles left Scotland for London in 1840. Although she loves her homeland, she has married an Englishman, whose life she finds stifling. Wan Li-an, Charles's half-Chinese daughter, hates him for giving her the blue eyes that made her an outcast. Genevra Townsend, the youngest, is the result of Charles's liaison with a gentlewoman stationed with her husband in India. Genevra resents him for ruining her mother's life and for her own illegitimacy. Their reunion brings both joy and pain, not only for themselves but also for Mairi, who can't help but think of his other relationships when she looks at her long-lost husband.

All We Hold Dear. Pocket, 1995. 501pp.

In 1988, when she turns eighteen, Eva Crawford's parents gently inform her that she was adopted, a fact she has a hard time dealing with. Her attempt to understand herself through her past leads her to her mother's friend in Glasgow, who gives her a chest full of journals telling the story of her ancestors, Ailsa Rose Sinclair and her daughter Alanna.

Somewhere Lies the Moon. Pocket, 1999. 530pp.

Eva Crawford, a student in Edinburgh, can't commit to marriage with her lover, Rory, until she gains a greater understanding of her past. The author takes us back to the three half-sisters, Ailsa, Li-An, and Genevra. They reunite once again in Scotland to help Ailsa's daughter, Ena, adjust to becoming a woman.

Gellis, Roberta.

The Roselynde Chronicles.

Annotated in Chapter 4.

Gregory, Philippa.

Wideacre Trilogy.

Like an eighteenth-century version of the television show *Dynasty*, this saga overflows with greed, drama, and desperate scheming, but the historical research behind it is well done, and it has more substance than most works of this type. Gregory's trilogy features three strong-willed women who strive to succeed in a world that mistreats members of the female sex. As they find to their detriment, excessive greed comes at a great price.

Wideacre. Simon & Schuster, 1987. 556pp.

Beatrice Lacey is obsessed with her ancestral home, Wideacre Hall, but as an eighteenth-century woman, her rights are ignored in favor of her brother, Harry, though, is no match for the determined Beatrice, who will resort to any-thing—incest, blackmail, and other corrupt acts—to ensure that she'll never have to leave Wideacre Hall.

The Favored Child. Pocket, 1989. 472pp.

Beatrice Lacey's greed has ruined Wideacre, her former Sussex estate. Her two heirs, cousins Julia and Richard, grow up in innocence in the nearby dower house, not knowing that they're more closely related than they've been told.

Meridon. Pocket, 1990. 439pp.

The lost Lacey heir, a young gypsy called Meridon, joins a traveling cir-cus, but mysterious dreams keep calling her home.

Harrod-Eagles, Cynthia.

The Kirov Saga.

This trilogy set in Russia between 1803 and 1917 features three English-women who fall in love with men of the Russian nobility and with the coun-try itself. All deal with issues of life in a foreign country, the pageantry of Russian history, and the attraction of a possible romance with dark, brooding Russian noblemen—even though they are already married.

Anna. St. Martin's Press, 1991. 631pp.

Fleur. St. Martin's Press, 1993. 406pp.

Emily. St. Martin's Press, 1993. 514pp.

Harvey, Caroline.

Legacy of Love. **Viking, 2000. 385pp.**

British novelist Joanna Trollope, best known for her modern women's fiction, also writes historical romantic fiction under the pseudonym Caroline Harvey. Her second novel to be published in the United States begins in the 1840s, as young Englishwoman Charlotte Brent marries an Army officer to escape from her boring life at home. Her husband's ca-reer takes them to Kabul, where she falls in love with a dashing ne'er-do-well. In late Victorian times, Charlotte's granddaughter Alexandra similarly struggles with maturity and passion, as does Alexandra's daughter Cara, who comes of age during World War II. Harvey's *A Second Legacy* (2001), set in the 1960s, features Cara's daughter Alexia.

Howatch, Susan.

Susan Howatch's romantic family sagas can be enjoyed on their own and as reinterpretations of well-known stories from British history.

Cashelmara. **Simon & Schuster, 1974. 702pp.** ★

This is a romantic multi-generational saga centered on a large ancestral home in Victorian times, this time the Galway estate called Cashelmara, owned by a noble English family. Readers who think they see parallels between Howatch's characters and the royal families of fourteenth- and fifteenth-century England (Edward I, his sons, and his grandchildren) would not be wrong.

Penmarric. **Simon & Schuster, 1971. 735pp.** ★

Howatch recasts the now-timeless saga of Henry II, his high-spirited queen Eleanor of Aquitaine, and their warring sons Richard the Lion Heart and King John on a Cornish landscape between 1890 and World War II. When grim Cornish landowner Mark Castallack brings his slightly older bride Janna home to Penmarric, they begin a love-hate relationship that extends to the next two generations of their descendants. The author tells the story in the first person from the points of view of multiple narrators. Their individual personalities stand out when scenes are revisited from different perspectives.

The Wheel of Fortune. **Simon & Schuster, 1984. 973pp.**

Beginning in 1913, the large Welsh estate of Oxmoon is the setting for a glitter-filled tale of the Godwins, their rivalries and doomed romances, and a family curse that leads to madness. Readers familiar with Anya Seton's *Katherine* will find some of the same characters here, but in more modern guises.

Laker, Rosalind.

To Dance with Kings. **Doubleday, 1988. 564pp.**

Four generations of women of Versailles feature in this romantic family saga. It begins in 1664 as peasant Jeanne Dremont, a fan maker, makes a promise to her newborn daughter Marguerite that she will not grow up in poverty. Marguerite, her daughter Jasmin, Jasmin's daughter Violette and Violette's daughter Rose grow up alongside the palace, where the Bourbon kings (Louis XIV, the Sun King, through Louis XVI) reign in splendor—at least until the Revolution, which affects Rose, companion to Marie Antoinette, most of all. Laker also writes romantic historical novels (Chapter 4).

MacDonald, Malcolm.

Cornish novelist Malcolm MacDonald also writes classic British sagas. His novels appear in Britain under the pseudonym Malcolm Ross.

The Carringtons of Helston. **St. Martin's Press, 1998. 409pp.**

Just before World War I, the Carrington siblings, Will and Leah, accompany their father to their grandfather's Cornwall home. Their purchase of a farm antagonizes their neighbors, the Liddicoats. All won't be lost for them, however, if Clifford Liddicoat succeeds in playing matchmaker between the wealthy Leah and one of his own sons.

For I Have Sinned. **St. Martin's Press, 1995. 391pp.**

In World War I-era England, young Salome McKenna decides to play hide-and-seek just before her parents leave for a lengthy cruise. When she emerges, they have left her behind. She is rescued by a well-meaning bystander, Marion Culham-Browne, who thinks Salome looks just like the daughter she lost seven years earlier. When Marion takes Salome back to Ireland, it causes problems in her marriage.

Kernow & Daughter. **St. Martin's Press, 1996. 391pp.**

At the beginning of the twentieth century, Cornishman Barney Kernow refuses to believe that his daughter Jessica may be a better choice to run the family business after him than any of her three brothers. Jessica, an independent sort, caves into pressure to get married, but nothing upsets her plans more than when she falls in love with her fiancé.

Tamsin Harte. **St. Martin's Press, 2000. 345pp.**

After her father dies, life in early twentieth-century Cornwall is no longer so comfortable for Tamsin and her mother. They open a boardinghouse to make ends meet, an action that reveals who their true friends really are. In deciding which man to marry, Tamsin must decide whether to follow her heart, her head, or her desire to regain her social standing.

Tomorrow's Tide. **St. Martin's Press, 1997. 327pp.**

Years after fourteen-year-old Jennifer Owens rescues an abandoned baby and takes him to an orphanage, she becomes a nurse, stars in a film, and falls for Barry Moore, who leaves to fight in World War I. When Barry comes home wounded, Jennifer must choose between love and her career—and discovers the fate of the child she found long ago.

The Trevarton Inheritance. **St. Martin's Press, 1996. 395pp. (Original title: *Crissy's Family*.)**

When her parents are killed, Crissy Moore has no choice but to approach her grandmother, a snobby rich woman who had disowned her mother for marrying the family's coachman. While her vindictive grandmother tries to tear the family apart, Crissy does her best to keep her five siblings together, though her determination causes trouble with her beau. Set in nineteenth-century Cornwall.

Oldfield, Pamela.

Chloe Blake Saga.

Saga set in 1890s Sussex, England.

Changing Fortunes. **Severn House, 2002. 256pp.**

Chloe Blake serves as a companion to an invalid, Jessica Matthews, to pay her own way to America, where her father lives. Her lively manner affects all of the Matthews family, even Jessica's bitter spinster daughter, in a positive way.

New Beginnings. **Severn House, 2003. 256pp.**

In this sequel to *Changing Fortunes*, Chloe Tyler, now a widow returning from America, becomes a housekeeper to sheep farmer Jack Bourne, but his family doesn't accept her presence.

Early One Morning. **Severn House, 2002. 256pp.**

Nancy Franklin, daughter of a horse trainer in 1903 England, must care for her younger brother and guard his inheritance after her stepmother runs off and her father commits suicide. She finds help and solace from a kindly widower, one of the horses' owners.

Purcell, Deirdre.

Ashes of Roses. **Signet, 1994. 523pp. (Original title:** *Falling for a Dancer.***)**

Annotated in Chapter 4.

Saxton, Judith.

Harvest Moon. **St. Martin's Press, 1997. 536pp.**

Laurie and John, two boys born in 1912, become great friends despite their different upbringing: Laurie is the heir to a great estate, whereas John's family owns the local hop farm. They also befriend tomboy Foxy Lockett, a working-class girl who is in love with John. She is left behind when the two leave for the Spanish Civil War. When they return, their financial situations have changed, and Foxy must decide whether her relationship with John has survived.

Someone Special. **St. Martin's Press, 1995. 536pp.**

April 21, 1926, is the birthday of Princess Elizabeth, who later becomes Queen Elizabeth II. Sharing the same birthday are Anna, daughter of a society woman, and Nell, who with her mother escapes their impoverished circumstances to join a traveling fair. The three grow up during the Depression and the 1940s, with the two other girls keeping track of the path that Elizabeth takes to adulthood.

Sole, Linda.

Rose Saga.

In France in the late nineteenth century, Jenny Heron is sent off to a convent school in Paris to curb her precocious ways. She makes friends there, but their romantic attitudes rub off on her. She later finds romance with her guardian's son in the Loire Valley, but tragedy brings her to her grandmother's home in Cornwall, where she uncovers some secrets about her heritage. In the final volume, Jenny's daughter Julia falls in love with and marries a military captain who has secrets of his own.

The Rose Arch. Severn House, 2001. 219pp.

A Cornish Rose. Severn House, 2001. 248pp.

A Rose in Winter. Severn House, 2002. 256pp.

This Land, This Love. **St. Martin's Press, 1998. 319pp.**

In this romantic saga set in turn-of-the-century England, farmer Aden Sawle loves Rebecca Cottrel, a publican's daughter. She considers him not of her station and dreams of marrying Sir Victor Roth, her best friend's fiancé. When Rebecca's father is murdered, she consoles herself by marrying Aden. Though he becomes a wealthy landowner, their mutual trust grows more tenuous, as both have regrets over previous lost loves. Secrets that they have kept from each other are eventually revealed.

Steel, Danielle.

Granny Dan. Delacorte, 1999. 223pp.

After her grandmother dies, aged ninety, the unnamed narrator discovers that the woman she knew as Granny Dan had a life before she was old. Danina Petroskova is a prima ballerina who dances for Czar Nicholas II in the early twentieth century and who, her promising career over after an accident, falls in love with the married physician who treats her. Steel's portrait of Czarist Russia is stereotypically glittery, but it is a smooth read by an author who knows how to tug at the heartstrings.

Tannahill, Reay.

A Dark and Distant Shore. St. Martin's Press, 1983. 592pp.

In 1803, when she is seven years old, Vilia Cameron's father sells off the family residence, the romantic Scottish castle of Kinveil, to pay his debts. Vilia determines to reclaim her ancestral home at any cost. Her quest forms a romantic saga that covers the entire nineteenth century and the length and breadth of the far-flung Victorian empire.

In Still and Stormy Waters. St. Martin's Press, 1994. 520pp.

In this romantic saga loosely based on the rivalry between Elizabeth I and Mary, Queen of Scots, the dual protagonists are cousins Sophie and Rachel Macmillan. In Victorian London, Rachel is the illegitimate daughter of wealthy Scotsman Daniel Macmillan. Though she is later legitimized, her newfound family never fully accepts her. Sophie grows up in Hong Kong as the privileged daughter of another Macmillan branch, not knowing, as Rachel does, what it's like to have to fight for what she wants. Both vie for possession of the family estate, the Scottish castle of Juran, and the love of the same man, Rainer Blake.

🎗 *Passing Glory.* Crown, 1989. 598pp.

The author tells the story of the Brittons, in peace and in war, from the day of Queen Victoria's funeral in 1901 until the coronation of Elizabeth II in 1953. Returning to his family's aristocratic country home as a war hero in 1918, Matt Britton refuses to fall back into his usual role of son of the house. This causes a rift between him and his less-than-loving father, who thinks he's crazy to take up flying instead of joining the family shipbuilding business. To explain this warring family's complicated history, the author jumps back to 1901, when four-year-old Matt horribly embarrasses his mother during Queen Victoria's funeral procession. The romantic elements of this saga develop gradually. Parker Romantic Novel of the Year.

Return of the Stranger. St. Martin's Press, 1996. 376pp.

Upon Josiah Smith's death in 1894 Scotland, his house passes not into the hands of Grace, his widow, but to a complete stranger named Max McKenzie—or so his children think. As Grace soon reveals to daughters Tassie and Selina, Max was the product of an illicit relationship between their mother and father while Grace was still married to her first husband.

Though Max appears kind, the Smiths find themselves forced to move from the only home they've ever known. As Tassie grows closer to an investigative journalist who doesn't believe Max's version of events, the story that Max has told the Smiths begins to unravel.

Glitz, Glamour, and Riches

Sagas featuring families involved in the glamorous worlds of show business and high finance.

Adler, Elizabeth.
Fortune Is a Woman. **Delacorte, 1992. 433pp.** ★

In this glitzy saga, Francie Harrison, an American heiress, loses everything in the San Francisco earthquake of 1906 but manages to rise again, emerging triumphant at last. Together with Lai Tsin, a mysterious Mandarin immigrant, and Annie Aysgarth, a young lass from Yorkshire, she manages to build up a multibillion-dollar hotel and trading empire, but finds that money alone won't make her happy.

Collins, Joan.
Star Quality. **Hyperion, 2002. 354pp.**

Four generations of women, beginning with Irish maid Millie McClancey during World War I, become involved with the wrong men and with the burgeoning entertainment industry, deriving more success from the latter. The action moves from the music halls of early twentieth-century London, to the early years of Broadway, to the silver screen in mid-century Hollywood, to life working on a soap opera in the 1980s. It's not meant to be serious literature and shouldn't be taken as such, but Collins's novel is an entertaining, appropriately glitter-filled romp.

Howatch, Susan.
The Rich Are Different. **Simon & Schuster, 1977. 658pp.**

These two Howatch sagas (she has since written a number of well-regarded sagas surrounding the Anglican Church in the 1960s) are not as popular as her romantic sagas (*Penmarric* and *Cashelmara*) but include the same elements of romance, revenge, and family secrets. Here Howatch creatively revisits the historical story of Caesar, Cleopatra, and Mark Antony, who have taken the form here of 1920s American banker Paul Van Zale; Englishwoman Dinah Slade, who petitions Paul to save her family home; and Steve Sullivan, Paul's right-hand man and Dinah's lover.

Sins of the Fathers. **Simon & Schuster, 1980. 608pp.**

The sequel to *The Rich Are Different* continues with the story of Paul's nephew, millionaire Cornelius Van Zale (aka Octavius Caesar), and his life in the world of New York high finance.

Rayner, Claire.

The Performers Family Saga.

Trained as a nurse and midwife, Claire Rayner has incorporated her medical background into her twelve-part <u>Performers</u> family saga set in Victorian England. The novels focus on the Lucas and Lackland families, both involved in medicine and the Victorian theater. Anglophiles will recognize the titles as names of London landmarks. The last four novels in the series were never published in hardcover in America, though the entire series was brought back into print in 2002 by House of Stratus (London and New York) in matching trade paperback editions.

Gower Street. Simon & Schuster, 1973. 351pp.

The Haymarket. Simon & Schuster, 1974. 320pp.

Paddington Green. Simon & Schuster, 1975. 348pp.

Soho Square. Putnam, 1976. 311pp.

Bedford Row. Putnam, 1977. 278pp.

Covent Garden. Putnam, 1978. 276pp. (Original title: *Long Acre.*)

Charing Cross. Putnam, 1979. 306pp.

The Strand. Putnam, 1981.

Chelsea Reach. London: Weidenfeld and Nicolson, 1982.

Shaftsbury Avenue. London: Weidenfeld and Nicolson, 1983.

Piccadilly. London: Weidenfeld and Nicolson, 1985.

Seven Dials. London: Weidenfeld and Nicolson, 1987.

Stewart, Fred Mustard.

The Savages.

The prolific Stewart's latest family saga, which centers on commerce whiz Justin Savage and his descendants, features the usual family rivalry but also swashbuckling adventure at sea. There is name dropping aplenty as members of the Savage clan hobnob with the rich and famous, from Winston Churchill to Teddy Roosevelt to William Randolph Hearst. Character development isn't a strong point, as Stewart's cardboard characters tend to speak in cliché-ridden dialogue, particularly in the later volumes of the series. Readers who enjoy glittery, fast-paced adventures will find the series entertaining.

The Magnificent Savages. Forge, 1996. 383pp.

Justin Savage, the illegitimate son of an American shipping magnate, signs up as a cabin boy on a ship bound for China. Though he escapes his half-brother's murderous intentions, the ship is waylaid by pirates. Justin must abandon his dream of marrying Samantha, a missionary's daughter, as he is forced to marry Madame Ching, the pirate queen, instead.

The Young Savages. Forge, 1998. 304pp.

In the 1880s, Justin Savage is now the leader of one of New York City's most prominent banking families. His son Johnny, disillusioned with finance, heads out west with his Harvard buddy Teddy Roosevelt, while his half-sister, the half-Chinese Julie Savage, aims to head back to China but falls in love with a rogue in San Francisco.

The Naked Savages. Forge, 1999. 304pp.

Johnny Savage has finally come into his own as family patriarch and head of the banking empire, and he and his growing brood continue to amass wealth and take on globetrotting adventures. Johnny joins Teddy Roosevelt's Rough Riders in Cuba, injuring himself in the process, but this brings him closer to his family. In the meanwhile, his children and stepchildren have their usual array of dalliances in love, money, and booze.

The Savages in Love and War. Forge, 2001. 304pp.

In the late 1930s, Nick Savage, Johnny's son, has taken over as leader of the wealthy Savage clan. His greatest concern is keeping their worldwide assets—in New York, Hong Kong, and Paris—safe during the war years. The adventures of Nick and family grow steadily more unrealistic.

Vincenzi, Penny.

Spoils of Time Trilogy.

Vincenzi, a bestselling author in Britain, makes her American debut with this family saga set in England during the *belle époque* of the Edwardian era, the First World War, and the twenties. The remaining volumes, in print overseas, are *Something Dangerous* and *Into Temptation.*

No Angel. Overlook, 2003. 640pp.

Celia Lytton, a woman of aristocratic birth and bearing, is used to getting her way. This shows in her dealings with her husband Oliver, a publishing magnate; her own children; Sylvia Miller, whose daughter comes to live with the Lyttons; and a children's book author who falls under Celia's influence.

Sagas of Ethnic and Cultural Heritage

These sagas focus on the cultural heritage of a family or families that has been passed down through the generations. They are about cultural identity as much as they are about family ties. These novels can deal with stories of immigrant life and the adjustments made by older members of a family after their arrival in the United States long ago, or they can use the form of a saga to illustrate how ethnic groups' experiences have changed over the years. Many authors of these family sagas belong to the ethnic group they write about and use their works to celebrate the cultural legacy left them by their forebears.

African-American

These novels depict the struggles and triumphs of African-American families in American history, from the early days of slavery through the Civil Rights era, and their complicated relationships with members of white families.

Briscoe, Connie.

A Long Way from Home. HarperCollins, 1999. 348pp. ✍

Montpelier, the Virginia home of former president James Madison, is also home to a family of slaves. After Madison dies in 1836, the lives of Susie and her daughter Clara become hellish, as both are continually harassed both verbally and sexually. Clara's daughter Susan, sold to a wealthy Richmond banker who may be her own father, could pass for white if she so chooses. Susan (Briscoe's own ancestor) eventually marries a free black man and obtains freedom after the Civil War, attaining her mother's and grandmother's dream. **Literary.**

Gurley-Highgate, Hilda.

Sapphire's Grave. Doubleday, 2003. 248pp.

In 1749, at the beginning of this family saga spanning over 200 years of African-American women's history, a proud woman from Sierra Leone is captured and brought aboard a slave ship. After she reaches America's shores, she gives birth to a daughter called Sapphire, so called for her blue-black complexion. Like her mother, Sapphire is strong in spirit but has a beauty that brings unwelcome attention from men—a problem experienced by her descendants as well. Over the years, on the North Carolina plantation where many of them reside, they strive for dignity, respect, and the right to choose their own way of life.

Haley, Alex.

🎗 *Roots.* Doubleday, 1976. 688pp. ✍ ★

Haley's classic saga of African Americans' journey from their African homeland through years of slavery and discrimination in America and finally to freedom is considered a masterpiece of social history. It was also the subject of one of the most watched TV miniseries of all time. The story begins with Kunta Kinte, Haley's distant ancestor in 1750s Africa, who is captured by slavers and brought to America; it concludes six generations later with Haley's father. Haley's novel influenced thousands if not millions of people, both black and white, to pursue genealogy as a hobby. *Roots*, a fictionalized biographical saga, was originally marketed as nonfiction but is now considered—after considerable controversy over whether certain scenes in the book were real or fictionalized—more along the lines of a historical novel. Pulitzer Prize.

Haley, Alex, and David Stevens.

Alex Haley's Queen: The Story of an American Family. **Morrow, 1993. 670pp.** ✍

Queen, the story of Alex Haley's father's family, was completed by fellow researcher David Stevens after Haley's death in 1992. It begins with Haley's Irish great-great-grandfather, James Jackson, who comes to America and settles on an Alabama plantation. His son Jass's illicit relationship with the beautiful slave, Easter, results in the birth of Queen, who becomes Haley's grandmother. Like *Roots*, this is a very personal story that encapsulates the African-American experience.

Mama Flora's Family. **Scribner, 1998. 393pp.**

Haley's second posthumous novel, which Stevens completed from his writings, stars Mama Flora, a sharecropper's daughter in 1920s Tennessee who passes on her dream of power, independence, and freedom to the next two generations of her family. Her strength and belief in education propel her, son Willie, and niece Ruthana through landmark events of the twentieth century such as World War II, the Civil Rights Movement, and organization of the Black Muslims.

Hill, Donna.

Rhythms. **St. Martin's Press, 2001. 352pp.**

Cora Harvey, a Baptist preacher's daughter who is the pride and joy of 1920s Rudell, Mississippi, must abandon her dream of becoming a singer when she is raped by a white man. Her daughter and granddaughter, both with white blood, escape Rudell's repressive rural atmosphere for the lights of the big city, but their family's past continues to disturb their happiness. **Literary.**

LeBlanc, Whitney J.

Blues in the Wind. **River City, 2002. 333pp.**

The culture of Louisiana Creoles between the 1930s and the start of the Civil Rights Movement is brought to life in this family saga of the Fergersons. Philip Fergerson marries Martha, a beautiful woman of lighter complexion than he, and settles down to life as a school principal. But the blues come into his life in the form of Martha's brother, LightFoot Broussard. The music's passion turns his family life upside down. Blues legends B. B. King and Robert Johnson make appearances.

Mills, Elizabeth Shown.

Isle of Canes. **Ancestry, 2004. 583pp.** ✍

François, an Ewe carpenter, arrived in Louisiana on a slaver's ship in 1735. His daughter Marie-Thérèse, known as Coincoin, lives in slavery for decades before becoming the mistress of Pierre Metoyer, a Frenchman who first buys her, then frees her. She proceeds to do the same for her own children. Augustin, Coincoin's son, becomes patriarch to a large family and achieves the Southern antebellum version of the American dream. Augustin's daughter-in-law Perine, a strong woman built in Coincoin's image, keeps his memory alive during the Civil War and Jim Crow era. Mills's saga of the Metoyers, a historical family both black and white and yet neither, challenges all perceptions of racial boundaries. Mills is an eminent genealogist.

Peacock, Nancy.

Home Across the Road. **Longstreet, 1999. 249pp.**

As slaves on the Roseberry plantation in Civil War-era North Carolina, the black Redd family had always served the white Redds. In 1971, the housekeeper, China Redd, is on her deathbed and ready to tell the true story of her ancestors, which will be utterly unlike the one told by white matron Lydia Redd in her published memoirs. Their story begins when plantation owner Jennis Redd impregnates Cally, his slave. From that point on, the families' lives run in parallel, but the black Redds' station continues to improve while that of the white Redds declines. **Literary.**

Tademy, Lalita.

Cane River. **Warner, 2001. 418pp.** ✍ 📖

This saga of four successive generations of African-American women living on a Creole plantation along Louisiana's Cane River is similar to *Roots* in its initial concept (based on the author's own ancestors), scope, and emotional impact. It begins with Elisabeth, a slave on a Virginia plantation who is sold south to someone in Louisiana, and ends four generations later with Tademy's great-grandmother Emily, a light-skinned, beautiful former slave. The women live side by side with white men of French ancestry, bearing their children—sometimes willingly, sometimes not. All must fight for their and their children's rights in a society where mixed-race relationships are never formalized, and illegitimate black children of white men are ignored in favor of their legitimate white half-siblings. Oprah's Book Club.

Walker, Margaret.

Jubilee. **Houghton Mifflin, 1966. 497pp.** ★

A character based on the author's great-grandmother, Vyry is born to a white plantation owner and his black slave just before the Civil War. Walker's meticulously researched novel takes the reader through Vyry's day-to-day life, from the years of slavery on a Southern plantation through Reconstruction. A powerful woman, she endures years of physical and verbal abuse at the hands of her master's wife and others. She emerges angry, yet stronger. This was one of the first novels to vividly depict the experience of slavery from a black woman's point of view.

Asian

Chinese

The stories of Chinese and Chinese-American families, both in Asia and in the United States. Many of these families struggle to find a balance between traditional Chinese values and more modern ways of life.

Lord, Bette Bao.

The Middle Heart. **Knopf, 1996. 370pp.** `YA`

In 1932 China, three children—young master Steel Hope, his servant Mountain Pine, and gravedigger's daughter Firecrackers (disguised as a boy)—make a vow to remain "blood brothers of the Middle Heart." Their journey takes them through love and loss during the major events of twentieth-century China, such as the Japanese occupation and the Communist revolution.

Spring Moon. **Harper & Row, 1981. 464pp.** `YA`

Spring Moon, a daughter of the Chang family in late nineteenth-century China, has her feet bound "for her own good," but she breaks with tradition by becoming educated. Her story and that of her family continue over five generations, as China enters the modern age.

Rui, Li.

Silver City. **Metropolitan, 1997. 276pp.**

Between the 1920s and the Cultural Revolution, four generations of the Li and Bai clans live in the salt-mining town of Silver City in northwestern China. The two families vie for power as their lives are greatly affected by the changing times—the influence of the West and the arrival of Communism. Their story is told in retrospect, after most of the Li family are executed by Communists in the 1950s.

Tan, Amy.

Tan's literary family sagas are annotated in Chapter 10.

Tsukiyama, Gail.

Night of Many Dreams. **St. Martin's Press, 1998. 275pp.** 📖

Joan and Emma Lew, sisters, grow up in Hong Kong in the years before World War II. When the Japanese invasion begins, they and their family—which includes their traditionally minded mother, independent Auntie Go, and a devoted servant named Foon—pick up and move to Macao. They later return, but Emma wants more out of life, relocating to San Francisco to attend school. Their businessman father seems to travel effortlessly between their home and Japan, which may not be very realistic, but for readers looking for a gentle, easy read that's strong in family spirit, this one will suit. **Literary.**

Japanese

In Japan and in America, the ties between generations of Japanese women remain strong.

Houston, Jeanne Wakatsuki.

The Legend of Wild Horse Woman. **Kensington, 2003. 329pp.** 📖

In an internment camp in 1942 in Manzanar, California, a Japanese woman named Sayo reveals her past history to her daughter, Hana, and her granddaughter, Terri. Born in 1902 under the Fire Horse sign, Sayo grows up being told that her fiery temperament will prevent her from marrying. Her birth date disguised, Sayo marries into the powerful Matsubara family by proxy and moves to America to join her husband. As Sayo adapts to a new culture and a difficult married life, she develops an inner strength, which she communicates to her descendants. **Literary.**

Minatoya, Lydia.

The Strangeness of Beauty. **Simon & Schuster, 1999. 224pp.** 📖

This is the autobiographical novel (or I-Story, as the narrator calls it) of Etsuko, a young Japanese woman living in Seattle in 1922, who returns to Japan with her sister Naomi's daughter after Naomi dies in childbirth. Back in Japan, between 1922 and 1939, Etsuko and Hanae try to rediscover their heritage while, in some very funny scenes, they try not to upset the delicate balance of Etsuko's mother's samurai household. In the meantime, world events are encroaching on Japan, which brings all three women closer together. **Literary.**

South Asian

Sagas reflecting the author's homelands of India, Burma, Malaysia, and Sri Lanka (formerly Ceylon). They offer a close glimpse of family traditions not often seen by Western readers.

Davidar, David.

The House of Blue Mangoes. **HarperCollins, 2001. 418pp.**

Solomon Dorai is the headman of the village of Chevathar, India, in this literary multigenerational saga. His family's tale begins in 1899, as Solomon is forced to mete out justice after a local girl is raped in an act of caste rivalry. His decision in this no-win situation has tragic consequences. His children and grandchildren carry on the family legacy. The author uses lush prose and minimal dialogue to convey the social changes pervading India in the first half of the twentieth century. **Literary.**

Ghosh, Amitav.

The Glass Palace. **Random House, 2001. 474pp.**

In 1885, as the British invade Burma and lead the royal family away from the Glass Palace into exile in Mandalay, eleven-year-old Rajkumar spies an even younger girl, Dolly, a beautiful maid in the retinue of one of the country's princesses. Twenty years later, their paths cross again, when both have gained both stature and wealth. Over the next hundred years, their lives and those of their descendants, spouses, and friends mirror the allegiances and conflicts of their countries of Burma, India, and Malaysia. **Literary.**

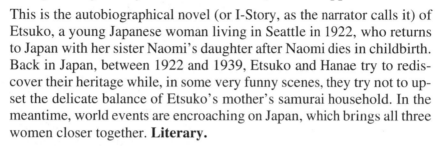

Manicka, Rani.

The Rice Mother. **Viking, 2003. 480pp.**

Lakshmi, a Ceylonese girl, is sold into marriage to a Malaysian man at the age of fourteen. By nineteen, she has had six children. The Japanese invasion disrupts their household, but she remains determined to improve their state in life. In this exotic land over the next fifty years, her children, grandchildren, and great-grand-children tell their own stories of war, love, ghosts, and superstition. This lyrical novel of family ties among women should appeal to fans of Isabel Allende and Amy Tan. **Literary.**

Selvadurai, Shyam.

Cinnamon Gardens. **Hyperion, 1999. 354pp.**

This novel of family values and romantic entanglements by a Canadian writer of Sri Lankan heritage opens in Ceylon in 1927, then a British colony. Annulakshmi is a young woman who worries about being trapped into an arranged marriage; her uncle Balendran is a closet homosexual who worries about his secret life being revealed. The family's upper-crust lifestyle does not insulate them from the problems of the time, such as racial conflict and societal expectations. **Literary.**

Canadian

Canada's history, like that of the United States, encompasses the stories of many immigrant families.

MacLeod, Alistair.

No Great Mischief. **W. W. Norton, 2000. 283pp.** 📖

In 1779, Calum MacDonald leaves the Scottish Highlands with his family, bound for a better life in Nova Scotia. In modern times, his descendant Alexander Mac-Donald works as an orthodontist in Ontario, though his heart has never left his home island of Cape Breton. While on a visit to his eldest brother in Toronto, Alexander's thoughts return to the earlier part of the century, spent growing up with his grandparents and twin sister on the island. His memory goes back even further to encompass earlier generations' stories of loyalty and loss. **Literary.**

Morgan, Bernice.

Cape Random Series.

These two novels, relating one family's struggles and triumphs in Newfoundland from the early nineteenth century until the present, were originally written as one book. Only the first half has been published in the United States, but because it ends with a cliffhanger, many readers of *Cape Random* will be compelled to find and read the sequel.

Cape Random. Shambhala, 2002. 369pp. (Original title: *Random Passage.*)

In the early 1800s, members of the extended Andrews family make their way from Weymouth, England, to unknown prospects in the remote, uncivilized, God-forsaken place known as Newfound Land. On the island of Cape Random, the Vincent family introduces them to a new way of life. Lavinia Andrews, the pensive seventeen-year-old daughter, records their experiences in her journal. The story of the family's settlement is gritty and utterly unromanticized. All characters have unique personalities, from the dreamy Lavinia and her fun-loving brother Ned to the lusty, determined newcomer Mary Bundle, to mysterious storekeeper Thomas Hutchings, whose story is told at the end of the book.

Waiting for Time. St. Johns, Newfoundland: Breakwater Books, 1995. 232pp.

This sequel to *Cape Random* is the story of Mary Bundle, who at seventeen has barely escaped a life of thievery by finding passage on a ship to Newfoundland. Her life spans nearly a hundred years. Events formerly seen through others' eyes in *Cape Random* are retold from Mary's point of view, meaning that many events only hinted at in the earlier book are finally revealed. Mary's tale is introduced through the discoveries of a modern-day Andrews descendant, but these modern bits are less compelling than those set in earlier times.

European

German

Hegi, Ursula.

The Vision of Emma Blau. **Simon & Schuster, 2000. 432pp.**

Stefan Blau emigrates from Burgdorf, Germany (the setting for Hegi's earlier *Stones from the River,* Chapter 10) in the early twentieth century in search of the American dream. He settles in a small New Hampshire town on Lake Winnipesaukee, voyaging to Burgdorf once to marry and bring back his bride, Helene Montag. Over the next ninety years and two generations, their apartment house, called the Wasserburg, is the center of a story of sibling rivalry and anti-German prejudice. **Literary.**

Irish

Family sagas of the Irish-American immigrant experience.

Dorris, Michael.

Cloud Chamber. **Scribner, 1997. 316pp.** 📖

In this continuation of sorts of *A Yellow Raft in Blue Water*, his 1987 family saga of Native American women, Dorris picks up the tale with the paternal ancestors of his previous heroine, Rayona. It begins with her great-great-grandmother, Rose Mannion, who flees English-dominated Ireland in the nineteenth century for Kentucky. The members of her family, including their present-day descendants on the plains of Montana, are a mixed-race and warring bunch who love and hate with equal intensity. **Literary.**

Moore, Ann.

<u>**Gracelin O'Malley Trilogy.**</u>

Annotated in Chapter 4, under "Romantic Epics."

Shea, Christine.

Moira's Crossing. **St. Martin's Press, 2000. 248pp.**

Moira and Julia O'Leary emigrate from Ireland to Boston after their mother's death in childbirth and the later death of their young sister, Ann. Over the next three generations, their differing personalities clash, but they remain dependent on each other as they grow older and raise families. **Literary.**

Williams, Niall.

The Fall of Light. **Warner, 2002. 305pp.**

After his wife leaves him, gardener Francis Foley takes his four sons and high-tails it out of the country, taking with him the telescope belonging to his employer. His four sons and he are soon separated, each having his own individual adventure, roaming through Hungary, Africa, and America. In the end, Francis finds that all he really wants is to be back together with his family. An adventuresome family saga set during Ireland's potato famine (1840s). **Literary.**

Italian

The lives of close-knit Italian and Italian-American families in the early twentieth century.

Ardizzone, Tony.

In the Garden of Papa Santuzzu. **Picador USA, 1999. 339pp.**

In the early twentieth century, poor Sicilian farmer Papa Santuzzu directs his seven children to make a better life for themselves in "La Merica," which they do, a few at a time. As a result, the members of the close-knit clan end up scattered throughout the country—not really the end result that their father and mother had envisioned for them. Their individual stories, told as a series of vignettes, are sprinkled with magic realism and Sicilian folklore. **Literary.**

Ermelino, Louisa.

The Black Madonna. **Simon & Schuster, 2001. 252pp.** 📖 **YA**

In New York City's Little Italy between the 1940s and 1960s, three Italian-American women depend on each other and their prayers to the Virgin Mary (the Black Madonna) to help themselves and their families survive their blue-collar tenement life. **Literary.**

The Sisters Mallone. **Simon & Schuster, 2002. 292pp.** 📖

Helen, Mary, and Gracie Mallone (formerly Malloni) are raised by their grandmother, Anona, not in Little Italy but in Hell's Kitchen, a region heavily populated by the Irish. All three look out for each other, particularly with regard to their love lives, as adultery and abuse are all too common. In this black comedy, the sisters are too smart to let little things like philandering husbands and the Mafia get them down. Set in 1920s through 1950s New York City. **Literary.**

Marciano, Francesca.

Casa Rossa. **Pantheon, 2002. 340pp.** 📖

When Casa Rossa, a farmhouse in Puglia (southern Italy), is being sold, its owner Alina Strada takes the opportunity to reflect on its previous occupants—her grandmother Renee, who served as the inspiration for her painter grandfather, but left him for another woman during the era of Nazi Germany; Alina's mother Alba; and finally Alina and her sister Isabella. They all survive Italy's turbulent political life in the twentieth century. **Literary.**

Trigiani, Adriana.

The Queen of the Big Time. **Random House, 2004. 261pp.** 📖

Nella Castelluca, middle daughter of an Italian-American farming family living outside Roseto, Pennsylvania, in the 1920s, wants to become a teacher and leave small-town life behind. Circumstances force her into factory work, but her romance with local heartthrob Renato Lanzara keeps her dreams alive. Alas, he leaves town just as things heat up, and Nella becomes engaged to another man. Renato returns on the eve of their wedding. Though generations pass, Nella never forgets her first love. A novel about making the most of what you have. **Literary.**

Polish

Pietrzyk, Leslie.

Pears on a Willow Tree. **Bard/Avon, 1998. 272pp.**

In sixteen self-contained chapters, four generations of women of the Polish-American Marchewka family learn to survive and gradually assimilate into the wider American culture. Beginning with Rose, who adopts her new name upon coming to America from Poland in 1919, and ending with her great-granddaughter Amy, who receives old family photographs from her mother while teaching school in Thailand, the Marchewka women hold family gatherings, prepare traditional meals, and both fight and embrace their culture. **Literary.**

Hawaiian

Davenport, Kiana.

Shark Dialogues. **Atheneum, 1994. 492pp.** 📖

Pono, the matriarch of a Hawaiian family, calls her four granddaughters home to tell them stories of their own rich heritage, which in many cases parallels that of Hawaii itself. Her story begins in 1834, as her great-grandmother, a Tahitian princess named Kelonikoa, meets a one-eyed white man who came ashore at Lahaina, Maui. Over the next 150 years, Hawaii deals with continual invasions by foreigners, outbreaks of leprosy, and many political changes. Davenport presents the tale of her native land as a melting pot of cultures, intermingling episodes of folklore and history. **Literary.**

Jewish

These novels express the strong ties among Jewish families, whose members pass on religious and cultural traditions from the Middle East, Eastern Europe, and America to subsequent generations.

Eve, Nomi.

The Family Orchard. Knopf, 2000. 316pp. 📖 ✍

Eve based her lyrical saga on 200 years of her own family's history, from her third great-grandparents, who emigrated from Eastern Europe to Jerusalem in 1837, to herself and her new husband, living in Boston in the 1990s. The stories of each successive generation are earthy, quirky, and imbued with history, legend, and love. The orchard of the title represents the family's actual livelihood—a citrus grove in Israel—as well as the figurative trees that hold the family together as each new generation and spouse is grafted on in turn. **Literary.**

Freud, Esther.

Summer at Gaglow. Ecco, 1998. 242pp.

Gaglow is a country estate in East Germany where, in the year 1914, the Jewish Belgard family resides. The three Belgard sisters have a simmering conflict with their mother, Marianna, while their father, grain merchant Wolf, deals with pressing financial matters. The focus here is on young Eva, who comes of age during a time when her comfortable world is falling apart. The novel flashes back and forth to Eva's granddaughter Sarah, an actress in modern-day London, who grows intrigued with Gaglow when she hears that the estate may soon revert to her family. **Literary.**

López-Medina, Sylvia.

Sigiuriya. HarperCollins, 1997. 320pp. ✍

Bianca de Lucena, daughter of a Jewish merchant, encounters Amahl Cozar, a Moslem general, who assists her in her efforts to help Jews escape from cities where the Inquisition is rampant. Their children, raised as Jews, face the same sort of persecution and are forced to marry outside the faith to save themselves. López-Medina based her novel on her mixed-faith ancestors' experiences surviving the Spanish Inquisition in fifteenth-century Andalusia.

Ragen, Naomi.

The Ghost of Hannah Mendes. Simon & Schuster, 1998. 384pp. ✍

Catherine da Costa, realizing that she is dying, calls her adult granddaughters to her side with one last request: that they travel to Europe to collect the lost pieces of a sixteenth-century manuscript written by their ancestor, Hannah Mendes. Suzanne and Francesca Abraham, modern women who don't like each other very much, comply reluctantly with their grandmother's request. Their quest soon turns up fascinating tidbits —and men—that soon get them hooked. The manuscript fragments they turn up re-create the life of Doña Gracia Mendes (whose birth name was Hannah), a Sephardic Jew from Portugal who lived through the Spanish Inquisition.

Singer, Katie.

The Wholeness of a Broken Heart. **Riverhead, 1999. 369pp.**

Hannah Felber, a young Jewish woman, has always enjoyed a close relationship with her mother, Celia. All comes crashing to a halt when Hannah asserts her independence. Stunned by her mother's abandonment of her, Hannah looks to her Eastern European ancestors for clues to her unusual behavior. Hannah's two great-grandmothers, Channa (Hannah's namesake) and Leah, are both strong-minded, straight-talking women. Through them, Singer speaks about the American immigrant experience both from the point of view of those newly arrived in a strange land (Channa) and those left behind in the old country (Leah). **Literary.**

Latin American

These family sagas celebrate Latin American culture and society, both in the United States and in the authors' native countries (Chile, El Salvador, Mexico, Puerto Rico, Cuba, and the Dominican Republic).

Allende, Isabel.

Daughter of Fortune Series.

Annotated in Chapter 10.

The House of the Spirits. **Knopf, 1985. 368pp.** ★

The Truebas, a close Chilean family with supernatural interests and talents, is at the heart of Allende's best-known novel. Their matriarch is the spiritual Clara del Valle, who became mute at a young age, who breaks her silence to announce that she'll soon be marrying her late sister's former fiancé, Esteban Trueba. Together they raise two sons, Jaime and Nicolas, and daughter Blanca, who enrages her father by falling in love with his foreman. The story continues into the next generation, as the entire family, including Blanca's daughter Alba, becomes more politically involved while Chile moves toward Pinochet's military coup of 1973. The author is a relative of the assassinated former president of Chile, Salvador Allende. **Literary.**

Benitez, Sandra.

❦ *Bitter Grounds.* **Hyperion, 1997. 444pp.**

El Salvador's turbulent political history is chronicled over three generations beginning in 1932, when Mercedes Prietas and her daughter Jacinta begin work on the Contreras' coffee plantations. Jacinta grows to rely more and more on Elena Contreras's family as her own life falls apart, and the reverse is true as well. American Book Award. **Literary.**

Cisneros, Sandra.

❦ *Caramelo.* **Knopf, 2002. 442pp.** **YA**

Celaya Reyes, or Lala, is the youngest child and only daughter of a proud Mexican-American family. Admitting she can be an unreliable narrator, she tells the story of her heritage through portraits of three generations of her family, taking them from Mexico City in the early twentieth century to Chicago and San Antonio, traveling back and forth across the border as they visit their relatives in Mexico. Her relatives are identified by their memorable qualities, as a child would: the Awful Grandmother, Little Grandfather, Uncle Fat-Face, etc. Their stories are as unique as their monikers. ALA Notable Book. **Literary.**

Ferré, Rosario.

Eccentric Neighborhoods. **Farrar, Straus & Giroux, 1998. 336pp.**

In this colorful, literary family saga written in the tradition of Gabriel García Márquez, two Puerto Rican families—the Rivas de Santilannas and the Vernets —are seen through the eyes of Elvira Vernet, their mutual descendant. While her mother's family included wealthy sugar plantation owners, her father's forebears were nouveau riche Cuban immigrants who made their fortune in the cement industry. **Literary.**

Garcia, Cristina.

Monkey Hunting. **Knopf, 2003. 251pp.**

This literary saga begins with Chen Pan, a farm boy who leaves China for Cuba in search of fortune. He doesn't expect to end up an indentured servant, forced into backbreaking labor on a sugar plantation. Eventually he escapes and marries mulatto former slave Lucrecia, and in Havana's Chinatown, the two raise a family who are just as Cuban as they are Chinese. The story continues into the 1970s, when their descendants become embroiled in China's Cultural Revolution and America's involvement in Vietnam. **Literary.**

Rosario, Nelly.

Song of the Water Saints. **Pantheon, 2002. 246pp.**

Three generations of Dominican women are the focus of this literary novel of strong family ties and female power in a land where women are not often valued. In the early twentieth century, Graciela yearns to make more of herself than rural life can offer. Her daughter Mercedes, of a strong religious bent, is left alone to raise herself after her stepfather's death. She marries and moves to New York City, where she brings up her granddaughter Leila, whose restlessness calls to mind the free spirit of her forebear Graciela. **Literary.**

Middle Eastern

Croutier, Alev Lytle.

Seven Houses. **Atria, 2002. 306pp.**

Beginning in Smyrna, Turkey, in 1910, Esma is a young widow living alone with her two sons. Though her sons' tutor Süleyman wishes to court her, his intentions are foiled by Esma's brother, who later brings Esma's children to live with him on his silk plantation. Her descendants grow up under Western influences. Granddaughter Amber emigrates to America, but she later returns home. In this literary saga from the Turkish-born author of *The Palace of Tears* (Chapter 10), the residences owned by the Ipekci family partially narrate the story. **Literary.**

Wartime Sagas

During wartime, when separation and loss become a way of life, families and communities band together for comfort and strength. Wartime sagas express both the stresses and the joys of these difficult times.

The British Isles

The war disrupts family life in Britain during World Wars I and II, yet it also brings people closer together. Romances blossom, but when couples are forced to separate, the women left behind rely on support from their parents, siblings, and friends. Because these novels are told from a woman's perspective, they will appeal most to female readers.

Bingham, Charlotte.

Chestnut Tree Series.

This series is the American debut of bestselling British saga writer Charlotte Bingham. Here she tells how World War II changes the lives of women in the Sussex fishing village of Bexham. The last volume (available overseas) is *The Moon at Midnight*, set in the 1960s.

The Chestnut Tree. St. Martin's Press, 2003. 322pp.

In 1939, the women of Bexham decide to work for the war effort however they can. Beautiful Judy Melton gets engaged to the soldier she loves but must find a way to go on after they lose touch; socialite Meggie Gore-Stewart uses her fluency in French to serve as a spy overseas; shy Mattie Eastcott and her neglected mother suddenly find strengths they didn't know they had; and Rusty Todd outgrows her tomboyish ways and finds love on her own terms. A sentimental tearjerker in places, the novel accurately presents how the women of England gave their all in this trying time.

The Wind off the Sea. St. Martin's Press, 2004. 368pp.

When well-to-do American traveler Waldo Astley decides to settle in Bexham in 1947, he encounters a village in turmoil. The women are happy to have their men home, but they feel stifled at having to give up their wartime careers. Waldo himself is the catalyst for a number of changes in village life.

Harrison, Sarah.

Flowers Series.

Coming-of-age sagas set during World War I and World War II.

The Flowers of the Field. Coward, McCann & Geoghegan, 1980. 490pp.

Thea, Dulcie, and Primmy, three young women growing up during World War I, find their lives irrevocably changed by love and the coming of war. Harrison depicts in great detail the action both on the front in Europe and back at home in London and Kent.

A Flower That's Free. Simon & Schuster, 1984. 766pp.

This sequel to *The Flowers of the Field* is the story of Kate Kingsley, born in Kenya but of English origins, who travels back to England in 1936 to visit relations. Life in London proves trying, as she finds British society overly rigid, and it's not until World War II is over that Kate finally obtains some personal freedom.

Hely, Sara.

War Story. Thomas Dunne, 2003. 448pp.

At Dulcimer Hall in 1939, Scottish nursemaid Maggie Dunlop's station in life has changed for the better, as she is loved by all of her charges. When the family is evacuated to America as war breaks out, she makes the mistake of falling in love with David Voist, an American pilot and her employer's very married relative. When they encounter one another in London later on during the war, they have some tough decisions to make.

Howard, Elizabeth Jane.

Cazalet Chronicles.

Between 1938 and 1947, three generations of the well-to-do Cazalet family live and thrive on their Sussex estate. The plot moves fairly slowly and tends to focus on the day-to-day lives of the characters, their servants, and pets. Howard's series is just as much about the values important to the British upper class in the pre- and post-war years as it is about the wider world they live in. Particularly poignant are the views of the grandchildren, cousins Polly, Clary, and Louise, who yearn for love and excitement. They find both to some degree.

The Light Years. Pocket Books, 1990. 434pp.

Marking Time. Pocket Books, 1991. 405pp.

Confusion. Pocket, 1994. 341pp.

Casting Off. Pocket, 1996. 482pp.

Mayhew, Margaret.

Our Yanks. St. Martin's Press, 2002. 339pp.

The author's homage to the brave Americans who fought for her homeland during World War II, *Our Yanks* is an old-fashioned tale set in the English village of King's Thorpe, which is overrun by members of the American 8th Army Air Force in August 1943. The men—boisterous, glamorous, and exciting—gradually charm the residents, and many wartime romances bloom.

Palmer, Elizabeth.

The Dark Side of the Sun. St. Martin's Press, 2000. 312pp.

Mary Fox grows up in rural England alongside the Harding family on the estate where Mary's mother works as a governess. Mary becomes best friends with Nettie, the Harding daughter who is of her own age, and falls in love with Godfrey, the eldest son, not realizing that he is homosexual. When Britain enters the war, Mary and the Harding siblings do their best to participate, Mary working for the War Office. Glamorous Nettie, now calling herself Venetia, throws parties for American soldiers and trades sexual favors for war-related confidences. Though Mary and the Hardings are separated for a time, everything comes full circle when the death of Mary's mother lets loose some family secrets.

Pilcher, Rosamunde.

Coming Home. **St. Martin's Press, 1995. 728pp.** ★

Rosamunde Pilcher is known for her comfortably overstuffed sagas, but *Coming Home*, her gift to all women and men who grew up during the war years, is her only historical novel. Sent to boarding school at the Porthkerris Council School in Cornwall in 1935, while her parents are in Singapore, thirteen-year-old Judith Dunbar meets Loveday Carey-Lewis. As Judith comes of age during World War II, she finds love and loss. Her friendship with Loveday and the warm, welcoming Carey-Lewis family keeps her centered. Parker Romantic Novel of the Year.

Saxton, Judith.

Still Waters. **St. Martin's Press, 1998. 503pp.**

Growing up in the Norfolk countryside between World War I and World War II, Tess Delamere has a happy childhood, but she is haunted by memories she believes are associated with her mother's death. She gets some answers with Ashley Knox, a sweetheart she meets at boarding school. Mal Chandler, an RAF pilot from Australia, has some unanswered questions of his own. When Mal meets Tess at a dance, sparks fly, but the war has a way of ending many relationships abruptly, and there is no guarantee who will be alive at the end.

You Are My Sunshine. **St. Martin's Press, 2000. 433pp.**

Four teenage women become friends and take on new wartime roles. Kay Duffield marries hastily before sending her man off to war and joining up for service herself. While training as a barrage balloon operative ("bop"), she meets shy Emily Bevan, of a Welsh sheepfarming family; Jo Stewart, a bit of a tomboy and troublemaker; and Biddy Bachelor, who barely survived the bombing that killed her family in Liverpool. The four survive the war together, becoming closer than sisters.

Summers, Rowena.

Caldwell Family Saga.

Beginning in 1939 in Bristol, England, the lives of the three Caldwell sisters—Imogen, Elsie, and Daisy—change in ways they could not have imagined when their father's business is bought out by the Preston family, their mother dies in an accident, and the war begins.

Taking Heart. **Severn House, 2000. 252pp.**

When the family haberdashery business goes under, Imogen Caldwell decides that they must take in lodgers to make ends meet. Though she loses her fiancé when their way of life changes, she becomes romantically involved with Robert Preston, the man responsible for her family's situation.

Daisy's War. Severn House, 2001. 288pp.

In 1940, Daisy Caldwell trains as a nurse, and sister Imogen helps out with the war effort by becoming a driver. Elsie stays on the sidelines, though she is dragged into current events when her husband is injured in the war.

The Caldwell Girls. Severn House, 2002. 256pp.

Elsie Caldwell struggles to take care of both her new baby and her wounded husband, relocating to Yorkshire to live with her in-laws, while Daisy has regrets not following in her mother's footsteps on the stage.

Dreams of Peace. Severn House, 2002. 246pp.

Daisy and Imogen find their romantic plans thwarted because of the war, and Vanessa Brown, a young evacuee living with their Aunt Rose in London, finally grows up.

The United States

Portrayals of family life on the American home front; the Civil War (1861– 1865) is a common setting.

Coleman, Lonnie.

Beulah Land. ★

The Beulah Land series, which spans most of the nineteenth century, is a plantation saga set in Highboro, Georgia, a small farming town fifty-three miles northwest of Savannah. Its owners, Arnold and Deborah Kendrick, are a slave-owning family, so the story's realism may make modern readers uncomfortable. The Kendricks and their neighbors, the Davises, live their lives in the antebellum South amid family dramas, including occasional affairs with slaves, until the Civil War comes and forces them to readjust.

Beulah Land. Doubleday, 1973. 495pp.

Look Away, Beulah Land. Doubleday, 1977. 492pp.

The Legacy of Beulah Land. Doubleday, 1980. 430pp.

Jakes, John.

North and South Trilogy. ★

Jakes's epic family saga of life in America before, during, and after the Civil War tells the story of two families—the Mains and the Hazards— over three generations, beginning in 1842 and lasting through Reconstruction. The prologue introduces both families' progenitors by showing their individual arrivals in America from England and France in the 1680s, and sows the seeds for their future leadership in the iron and rice industries. At West Point, the Hazards from Pennsylvania meet and befriend the Mains of South Carolina. When the Civil War begins, members of the two families find themselves on opposite sides. During Reconstruction, the families struggle to rebuild themselves as well as their country.

Jakes's characters interact with historical figures such as John Brown and George Custer and play major roles in well-known historical events. Perhaps best of all, Jakes never romanticizes the war or its aftermath. The first book of this saga was made into one of the most successful TV miniseries of all time.

North and South. Harcourt Brace Jovanovich, 1982. 740pp.

Love and War. Harcourt Brace Jovanovich, 1984. 1019pp.

Heaven and Hell. Harcourt Brace Jovanovich, 1987. 700pp.

Lent, Jeffrey.

In the Fall. **Atlantic Monthly, 2000. 542pp.**

Annotated in Chapter 10.

Price, Charles F.

Price's grim but sensitively written series of one Southern family's Civil War experience is based on his own family history.

Hiwassee. Academy Chicago, 1996. 188pp.

In 1863, Judge Madison Curtis, owner of a decent-sized plantation in the Hiwassee River Valley of western North Carolina, has two sons off fighting for the Confederacy at Chickamauga while his oldest son, Andy, wounded in a previous encounter, recuperates at home. When a band of murdering thugs loyal to the Union comes calling, Andy goes into hiding while the judge finds an ingenious method to prevent his home from being torched.

Freedom's Altar. John F. Blair, 1999. 291pp.

The Civil War is over, and Judge Curtis, his family decimated, tries to find a way to expiate his guilt over the way he saved his home. He also comes to terms with his involvement in slavery. When Daniel McFee, the judge's former slave, comes back to the only home he's ever known, he signs on as a sharecropper on the Curtis plantation. McFee's plans to bring peace to the ravaged and lawless land are thwarted by Nahum Bellamy, a warped abolitionist who wants to destroy the white Southern way of life.

The Cock's Spur. John F. Blair, 2000. 311pp.

Ves Price, a moonshiner in 1880 North Carolina, is a would-be suitor of Becky Curtis, the judge's last surviving daughter. The Curtis farm, now in shambles, is taken care of by Hamby McFee, a former slave. Hamby also trains winning birds for cockfighting rings. In his odd means of livelihood, he finds a way to save Ves from danger.

Where the Water-Dogs Laughed. High Country, 2003. 298pp.

This fourth of Price's realistic historical novels set in late nineteenth-century Appalachia picks up with mixed-race Hamby McFee and his encounter with a large black bear, in fulfillment of a Cherokee myth about the balance of light and dark. Intertwined with this is the story of the courtship of the author's grandparents.

Reasoner, James.

Civil War Battle Series.

The Brannons are a farming family from Culpeper County, Virginia, in the 1860s. This extended family saga finds widowed mother Abigail running the farm after her husband's death while her sons do their best to serve the Confederacy well. Although each book is centered on a particular battle, the fighting takes place mostly offstage, with the focus remaining on the growing Brannon clan, their marriages, and their struggle to remain united while romantic intrigues and the Civil War keep them apart.

Manassas. Cumberland House, 1999. 336pp.

Shiloh. Cumberland House, 1999. 360pp.

Antietam. Cumberland House, 2000. 383pp.

Chancellorsville. Cumberland House, 2000. 408pp.

Vicksburg. Cumberland House, 2001. 399pp.

Gettysburg. Cumberland House, 2001. 403pp.

Chickamauga. Cumberland House, 2002. 394pp.

Shenandoah. Cumberland House, 2002. 416pp.

Savannah. Cumberland House, 2003. 432pp.

Appomattox. Cumberland House, 2003. 432pp.

Chapter 6

Western Historical Novels

Western historical novels are defined not only by a time period and place but also by several overarching themes: freedom, opportunity, and strength of character, all of which symbolize the American Western experience. They are novels of adventure, discovery, and survival. On the other hand, they are also novels of civilization and its effects, for they demonstrate the impact that settlement and exploration has had on the lands of the Western frontier and their native peoples.

Novels of the historical American West can be divided into two categories: *historical Westerns* and *traditional Westerns* (also known simply as "Westerns") . It's important for readers' advisors to know the difference between the two, but the dividing line between them isn't always clear. This chapter deals primarily with historical Westerns, though a select number of traditional Westerns with significant historical detail and a strong sense of place are included.

A typical plot for a traditional Western goes something like this. A tough but morally upright man rides alone into a Western scene, fights off Indians or outlaws, and proceeds to save the day—after which he mysteriously rides off into the sunset, literally or figuratively. These novels, usually fairly short, are set somewhere west of the Mississippi River, although the exact locale is not always given. They take place sometime between the end of the Civil War (1865) and the Massacre at Wounded Knee (1890), the horrific event that finally ended the U.S. government's Indian wars and signaled the end of the American frontier. Traditional Westerns evoke a strong sense of time and place with their brilliant descriptions of the unspoiled Western landscape. Setting is extremely important to traditional Westerns, as "the West" is seen as the place where freedom can be found, where simple moral goodness triumphs, and where characters find their destinies. However, specific historical events and locales tend not to figure in the story, although there are exceptions.

While traditional Westerns still command a devoted audience, the genre as a whole has evolved into something new. Today's Western novels have been relabeled as historical Westerns, historical fiction, frontier fiction, or simply "novels of the West." These descriptions reflect their wide-ranging content. Historical Westerns tend to be longer than traditional Westerns, with a meatier, more detailed plot. While many are still adventure stories at heart, they may or may not be fast-paced. Character development is important, and the protagonists' moral dilemmas aren't nearly as black and white as traditional Westerns made them out to be.

Historical Westerns require an accurate historical setting, for historical fiction fans won't be satisfied without it. The timeframe is also broader, covering the entire experience of Western exploration and settlement. This ranges from the mid-sixteenth century, when Spanish explorers first encountered the Plains Indian tribes of the Southwest, all the way through the first few decades of the twentieth century. In between, historical events commonly portrayed include the settlement of the Western frontier (as told from both male and female points of view); the U.S. government's Indian wars; the westward expeditions of Lewis, Clark, and their contemporaries; the California Gold Rush; and the fight to win Texas from Spain.

In comparison to traditional Westerns, historical Westerns offer more diverse subjects. They don't hesitate to take on complex social issues, such as race relations, white settlers' poor treatment of the Indians, and the hard lives of women eking out a living on the Western frontier. The most recent examples are less stereotypical in their portrayals of white settlers and Native Americans than those written decades earlier. While traditional Westerns rarely had female, Native American, or African-American protagonists, these characters are common to historical Westerns. Because they try to be true to the era in which their works are set, novelists in this genre strive to be historically accurate, which is why terms like "Indian" appear within their pages. On the other hand, Western historical novelists often take a balanced point of view, showing native–white relations from both sides.

Historical Westerns are holding steady in the marketplace, with a few publishers (most notably Forge and Five Star, but some other trade and university presses as well) actively publishing new works from both familiar and debut authors. Leisure, the Western imprint of Dorchester, publishes mainly traditional Westerns but also some historical Westerns. While some of the novels mentioned in this chapter are apt to be found within "Western" collections in libraries or bookstores, others will be found mixed in with the rest of the fiction, as is the case with most historical novels. Two major organizations for Western writers, Western Writers of America (WWA, founded 1953) and Women Writing the West (WWW, founded 1994), actively promote the field and their authors' works to readers and the media. Both groups sponsor awards for excellence in Western writing, the Spur and the Willa Cather Award (or WILLA), respectively.

This chapter subdivides historical Westerns by theme, rather than by specific era or locale. Because many include elements of adventure, readers who enjoy that aspect of Western historicals may wish to investigate Chapter 8 for additional historical adventure titles. In addition, readers interested in other novels of Native American history, such as those set in prehistoric North America and in colonial times, will find them primarily in Chapters 2 and 10.

Traditional Westerns

These action-packed, mostly male-centered novels tell of independence and survival in the historical American West. They may feature outlaws and lawmen fighting each other and the Indians; other common topics include cattle drives, ranching, shootouts, treasure hunts, and male camaraderie. While most are told from the viewpoint of white settlers, the novels listed here are more culturally sensitive than most traditional Westerns. They also have better character development and use an accurate historical backdrop. Most take place during the usual timeframe for Westerns, the late 1860s through the 1890s. A sampling is presented.

Blakely, Mike.

Moon Medicine. **Forge, 2001. 416pp.**

In the 1840s, intellectual Honore Greenwood flees Paris, France, after dueling over a woman. His escapades have only begun. He traipses through the Wild West on a variety of adventures—fighting Indians, falling dangerously in love with a beautiful New Mexican *señorita*, and rescuing children from raids. Called Plenty Man by the Comanche, Honore recalls everything from the viewpoint of old age.

Spanish Blood. **Forge, 1996. 312pp.**

In 1870, Bart Young comes to New Mexico Territory with dreams of fortune. He finds it in the form of an old, forgotten Spanish land grant hidden in the mountains near Sacramento.

Vendetta Gold. **Forge, 1998. 256pp.**

Roy Huckaby, newly released from a Texas prison, swears to live an exemplary life from then on. But then a dying man hands him a treasure map, which leads Huckaby into romance, war, and more danger.

Bowman, Doug.

The Guns of Billy Free. **Forge, 1998. 287pp.**

In the 1870s, Billy Free flees Mississippi after being accused of a murder he didn't commit. Always one to shoot first and think later, Billy doesn't take any chances. He knows that if the posse catches him, he'll be a dead man.

The H&R Cattle Company. **Forge, 1997. 231pp.**

Brett Rollins and Zack Hunter make their fortune on the Texas plains with a deck of cards and a six-shooter.

Houston. **Forge, 1998. 286pp.**

Joe Plenty, left for dead in a Kansas gully after five ranch hands shoot the ranch's owners, survives to tell notorious gunfighter Camp Houston what he saw. But Camp is no ordinary cowboy; he takes time to befriend the locals rather than rushing through a job. His thoroughness helps him nab the killers.

Pilgrim. **Forge, 2001. 284pp.**

Eli Pilgrim, formerly a pig farmer from Ohio, starts his life over as a Texas ranch hand just after the Civil War. He kills a would-be robber in self defense, but when the dead man's brothers kill the ranch owner, Eli vows revenge on them.

The Quest of Jubal Kane. **Forge, 1999. 315pp.**

Jubal Kane, a fifteen-year-old Texas farm boy, was the lone witness to his parents' cold-blooded murder in 1866. Taking the law into his own hands seven years later, Jubal tracks down the killers himself.

West to Comanche County. **Forge, 2000. 303pp.**

In lawless Comanche County, Texas, in 1870, after rancher Kirb Renfro finds that his wife Ellie has been raped and murdered, he takes off after the perpetrators.

Brandvold, Peter.

Dakota Kill. **Forge, 2000. 288pp.**

Mark Talbot, back in Dakota Territory after seven years of adventure in Mexico and the West, discovers that a bunch of things had happened while he was gone: His brother was murdered five years earlier, rich land baron King Magnusssen wants control of his land, and Magnussen's daughter Suzanne wants Talbot for herself.

The Romantics. **Forge, 2001. 350pp.**

Jock Cameron, hired to guide Adrian Clark and his beautiful Mexican wife Marina to a secret hoard of Spanish gold in the Arizona desert in 1879, knows that what they're searching for probably doesn't exist. It doesn't stop them from trying, not even with a crazy ex-Confederate officer and bloodthirsty Apaches on their trail.

Estleman, Loren.

Black Powder, White Smoke. **Forge, 2002. 318pp.**

Honey Boutrille, an ex-slave and bordello owner in 1880s Louisiana, kills a man for mutilating one of his prostitutes, so he flees west to escape the noose. Out in San Francisco, Twice Emerson kills a Chinese immigrant for the hell of it and decides to relocate to the Rockies rather than get caught. As both Boutrille and Emerson evade the law, two men follow them, one who hopes to write Boutrille's biography and another man who wants to put Emerson in a Wild West show. The paths of all four men collide dramatically in Denver.

Page Murdock Series.

In this ongoing series, frontier lawman Page Murdock, a U.S. deputy, brings order to the lawless Wild West, taking on corruption, rebellious Indians, and evil gangs from Mexico to the Canadian North. The earliest volumes have recently been reissued.

The High Rocks. Doubleday, 1979. 182pp.

Stamping Ground. Doubleday, 1980. 178pp.

Murdock's Law. Doubleday, 1982. 184pp.

The Stranglers. Doubleday, 1984. 179pp.

City of Widows. Forge, 1994. 254pp,

White Desert. Forge, 2000. 236pp.

Port Hazard. Forge, 2004. 301pp.

Johnston, Terry C.

Plainsmen Series.

A historically sensitive sixteen-book series, mostly featuring scout and lawman Seamus Donegan. Over a decade and more, Donegan fights in numerous real-life battles against Indian tribes of the Western plains, such as the Fetterman Massacre (1866), the Battle of Beecher Island (1868), the Modoc War (1872–1873), the Battle of Palo Duro (1875), the Nez Perce War (1877), and more in between. Maps and photos are provided. The last three volumes, though still considered part of the series, leave Seamus Donegan behind to form a stand-alone trilogy based on the Nez Perce War, when the U.S. Army forced the Nez Perce tribe to leave Idaho. Chief Joseph valiantly defends his people, inching them ever closer to Canada, though American soldiers pursue them even there. The final volume retells the last days of Crazy Horse. The bloody violence is not for the squeamish.

Sioux Dawn. St. Martin's Paperbacks, 1990. 427pp.

Red Cloud's Revenge. St. Martin's Paperbacks, 1990. 384pp.

The Stalkers. St. Martin's Paperbacks, 1990. 278pp.

Black Sun. St. Martin's Paperbacks, 1991. 386pp.

Devil's Backbone. St. Martin's Paperbacks, 1991. 426pp.

Shadow Riders. St. Martin's Paperbacks, 1991. 374pp.

Dying Thunder. St. Martin's Paperbacks, 1992. 402pp.

Blood Song. St. Martin's Paperbacks, 1992. 359pp.

Reap the Whirlwind. Bantam, 1994. 493pp.

Trumpet on the Land. Bantam, 1995. 639pp.

A Cold Day in Hell. Bantam, 1996. 480pp.

Wolf Mountain Moon. Bantam, 1997. 424pp.

Ashes of Heaven. St. Martin's Paperbacks, 1998. 398pp.

Cries from the Earth. St. Martin's Paperbacks, 1999. 458pp.

Lay the Mountains Low. St. Martin's Press, 2000. 495pp.

Turn the Stars Upside Down. St. Martin's Press, 2001. 329pp. ✍

Kelton, Elmer.

Slaughter Series.

A two-volume series about the extermination of the wild buffalo, which marks the end of the Plains Indians' way of life. Prolific Western author Kelton tells this action-packed story from both white and Native American perspectives. Set in 1870s Texas.

🎗 *Slaughter.* Doubleday, 1992.

After the Civil War, Confederate soldier Jeff Layne saves the life of Englishman Nigel Swithwick and helps him adapt to life out West. As buffalo hunters, the two men clash with the natives, who fiercely defend their homeland. Spur Award.

The Far Canyon. Doubleday, 1994. 323pp.

Sick of all the killing, Jeff Layne leaves buffalo hunting and returns to his ranch in south Texas, only to find that his old nemesis Vesper Freed has staked a claim there. Meanwhile Crow Feather, his old enemy from *Slaughter*, hates the idea of reservation life and puts down new roots in a canyon bottom with his family.

Swarthout, Miles Hood.

🎗 *The Sergeant's Lady.* Forge, 2003. 302pp.

In southern Arizona Territory in the 1880s, Miss Martha Cox is a rancher's sister who can shoot and fight as well as a man. She and her brother Jacob get caught up in the U.S. Cavalry's wars against the Apache when she falls in love with Sergeant Ammon Swing. Swarthout, son of *The Homesman* author Glendon Swarthout, based this novel on a short story his father wrote in the 1950s. Spur Award.

Wister, Owen.

The Virginian: A Horseman of the Plains. Macmillan, 1902. 504pp. ★

In the rangeland surrounding Medicine Bow, Wyoming, a rancher known only as "the Virginian" takes justice into his own hands. Over time, the enigmatic young Southerner goes from ranch tenderfoot to ranch foreman. New England schoolmarm Molly Stark loves the morally upright cowboy, but given his violent past, she knows he'd never fit in with her family back home. This classic is said to have established the literary "code of the West," a path of honor that all cowboys should follow. Widely reprinted.

Celebrity Characters

These biographical novels fictionalize the lives of famous characters from the Old West, both male and female. Among historical happenings featuring legendary outlaws and lawmen, two events loom large. One is the 1881 showdown at the O.K. Corral in Tombstone, Arizona, where the Earp brothers and Doc Holliday fought the Clanton gang. The other is the bloody Lincoln County War of the late 1870s, when two rival factions—one of which included William Bonney, aka Billy the Kid—fought over control of military contracts in Lincoln County, New Mexico.

Barry, Desmond.

 The Chivalry of Crime. **Little, Brown, 2000. 473pp.** ✍

In 1892, fifteen-year-old Joshua Benyon wants nothing more than to be a great "shootist" like the famed gunslinger Jesse James. Robert Ford, the man who eventually put an end to James's murderous sprees, tells Joshua the story of James's life. Joshua discovers the consequences of violent crime the hard way. Spur Award.

Braun, Matt.

Doc Holliday: The Gunfighter. **St. Martin's Paperbacks, 1997. 312pp.** ✍

Dr. John H. Holliday, a gentleman and dentist from the South, flees his rough past, takes up gambling, and gains a reputation as the fiercest gunfighter in the West.

Brooks, Bill.

Bonnie and Clyde: A Love Story. **Forge, 2004.** ✍

In 1932, former Texas waitress Bonnie Parker abandons her poverty-stricken existence and heads out on a murderous shooting spree with her partner, Clyde Barrow. Robbing banks throughout the Southwest, Bonnie and Clyde—presented as "Romeo and Juliet with guns"—vow to live and die together, letting nobody get in their way. A tale of passionate love and tragedy, neither of which could exist without the other.

Pretty Boy. **Forge, 2003. 316pp.** ✍

Depression-era bank robber Charley "Pretty Boy" Floyd, dying in an Oklahoma cornfield, looks back on his frenetic life, framing it in his own voice as well as those of family and beloved friends. Floyd lives his life to the fullest, in constant search for thrills, fast cars, and loose women—to the dismay of his loyal wife, Ruby.

The Stone Garden: The Epic Life of Billy the Kid. **Forge, 2001. 284pp.** ✍

In this revisionist Western, William H. Bonney—Billy the Kid—and his lover Manuella reveal what really happened after the 1881 ambush in which Sheriff Pat Garrett supposedly killed Billy. In this version of the legend, Garrett knowingly kills the wrong man and keeps his secret hidden from the public, who are all too ready to rejoice at Billy's death. Twenty-seven years later, the tide of public opinion turns against Garrett, while Billy dreams of the old days and observes how his legend has survived.

Coleman, Jane Candia.

Doc Holliday's Woman. **Warner, 1995. 325pp.** ✍

"Big Nose" Kate Elder, born Mary Katharine Harony in Hungary in 1850, loses her immigrant parents at a young age and makes her own way in America, a single woman in a man's world. She falls in love with gambler Dr. John "Doc" Holliday against her better judgment, pursues him throughout the Old West, and witnesses the final showdown at the O.K. Corral in Tombstone, Arizona.

I, Pearl Hart. **Five Star, 1998. 222pp.** ✍

The first mistake Pearl Taylor makes is falling in love with gambler Frank Hart, for whom she leaves her well-to-do Ontario home. She follows him to various Wild West shows across America as well as to the Chicago World's Fair. Behind the legend of the "Bandit Queen" lies a life of desperation, for Pearl—abused and neglected by her husband Frank—only turns to stagecoach robbery to earn money to feed her three children. In 1899, she becomes the first woman to be sentenced to the Yuma Penitentiary.

Eickhoff, Randy Lee.

And Not to Yield. **Forge, 2004. 432pp.** ✍

Famed gunslinger Wild Bill Hickok was born with the name James Butler Hickok to an abolitionist farming family. Educated and determined, he travels throughout the country, succeeding in nearly all his endeavors—spying for the Union in the Civil War, Indian fighting, shooting, gambling, the law, and loving women.

The Fourth Horseman. **Forge, 1998. 416pp.** ✍

John Henry "Doc" Holliday's life ends in tragedy at the O.K. Corral shootout in Tombstone, Arizona, in 1881, and his earlier life serves as a prelude to his last self-destructive act. As a young man in 1860s Georgia, Holliday kills a man who brags of raping his mother. Sent out West to escape from the law, Holliday becomes a frontier dentist but loses himself in gambling and drink.

Eickhoff, Randy Lee, and Leonard C. Lewis.

Bowie. **Forge, 1998. 304pp.** ✍

The larger-than-life story of Jim Bowie, who gave his name to the Bowie knife and died in glory with his comrades at the Alamo, is revealed via a multitude of interviews. Over thirty men and women bear witness to his extraordinary life on the frontier, from his early partnership with pirate Jean Lafitte through the many duels he fought and the card games he won and lost.

Estleman, Loren.

Billy Gashade. **Forge, 1997. 351pp.** `YA`

A teenager gets mixed up with the wrong people during the draft riots in New York City in 1863. His wealthy judge father gives him a new name, Billy Gashade, and sends him out West to hide. Billy becomes an itinerant piano player in a series of Western saloons and encounters many famous people—Billy the Kid, George Custer, Calamity Jane, Wild Bill Hickok, and more.

🏵 *Journey of the Dead.* **Forge, 1998. 251pp.** ✍

In the 1880s, Francisco de la Zaragoza, a 129-year-old Mexican alchemist searching for the philosopher's stone in the New Mexican desert, comes upon Sheriff Pat Garrett, still in mourning for having killed Billy the Kid. Garrett hopes that Zaragoza can ease his pain, for he's being haunted by Billy's ghost. The two ponder life's questions together. Spur Award; Western Heritage Award.

Fackler, Elizabeth.

Billy the Kid. **Forge, 1995. 512pp.**

> Throughout his life, drifter Billy the Kid knows how to look out for himself, justifying each act as one of self-preservation. He's also loyal to a fault, and he proves it by going after the men who killed his friend, Englishman John Tunstall, in the bloody Lincoln County War. Set in New Mexico Territory in the 1870s and 1880s.

Lyon, Suzanne.

<u>Butch Cassidy Series.</u>

> The fictionalized life story of Butch Cassidy, starting before he formed the Hole-in-the-Wall Gang.

Bandit Invincible: Butch Cassidy. **Five Star, 1999. 351pp.**

> Born Robert Leroy Parker to a Mormon family from Utah, Cassidy adopts the name of an older acquaintance he meets while ranching. Rather than settle down into humdrum poverty, Cassidy leaves the family farm, finds romance with Mary Boyd Rhodes, and becomes an honorable outlaw.

El Desconocido: Butch Cassidy. **Five Star, 2002. 263pp.**

> The continued adventures of Butch Cassidy, nicknamed El Desconocido —"the Stranger"—because few people can easily recognize him.

McMurtry, Larry, and Diana Ossana.

Pretty Boy Floyd. **Simon & Schuster, 1994. 444pp.**

> In 1920s Oklahoma, farmer Charles Floyd's life starts out with the best intentions, but it derails fast after he's arrested for armed robbery. He leaves his wife and child behind and heads out on a series of bank robberies and shooting sprees across the West. In its reliance on dialogue and action, the novel reveals its film script roots.

Olds, Bruce.

🎗 *Bucking the Tiger.* **Farrar, Straus, and Giroux, 2001. 371pp.**

> Olds takes a multifaceted, literary approach to the life of Doc Holliday, whose story has been retold many times. A much more admirable character than the Holliday from Paul West's retake on the legend (below), here Doc forms a true love relationship with Kate Haroney and meditates on how he's managed to cheat death. ALA Notable Book. **Literary.**

Parker, Robert B.

Gunman's Rhapsody. **Putnam, 2001. 289pp.**

> Wyatt Earp loads up his wagon and gets out of Dodge City, taking along two of his brothers, their women, and Mattie, the woman he calls his wife. In the silver mining town of Tombstone, Arizona, Earp becomes deputy sheriff and meets other recognizable characters like Bat Masterston and Doc Holliday. Earp also falls in love with Josie Marcus,

the sheriff's girlfriend, which is a catalyst for the famous 1881 shootout at the O.K. Corral. A spare, minimalist take on the legend.

West, Paul.

O.K.: The Corral, the Earps, and Doc Holliday. **Scribner, 2000. 302pp.** ✍

Consumptive dentist John Henry "Doc" Holliday stars in this gritty, character-centered retelling of the prelude to the shootout at the O.K. Corral. In his thoughtful letters to his cousin Mattie, a nun, Holliday reveals his innermost thoughts on the Earps, his prostitute girlfriend Big Nose Kate, and his own self-destructive behavior. **Literary.**

Wheeler, Richard S.

♣ *Masterson.* **Forge, 1999. 253pp.** ✍

In 1919, New York City journalist William Barclay "Bat" Masterson wields a pen rather than a six-shooter, but he's bothered by the legends that still surround him. With his wife Emma, a former showgirl, Bat takes one last trip out West. In Western cities he once knew well—Cheyenne, Dodge City, Leadville, and Los Angeles—Bat makes peace with his past. Spur Award.

Zollinger, Norman.

Meridian: A Novel of Kit Carson's West. **Forge, 1997. 416pp.** ✍

Brad Stone, a mapmaker on John C. Frémont's Third Expedition in 1845, is thrilled to meet his childhood hero, legendary mountain man Kit Carson. Carson and Brad become friends, and Carson brings him home to Taos, where Brad meets and falls in love with Ana Barragán. The lovers are forced to part, and Brad accompanies Frémont and Carson on their journey. They participate in many well-known events: California's Bear Flag revolt, the conquest of California, and the Taos Rebellion of 1847.

Frontier and Pioneer Life

These novels portray the day-to-day lives of both men and women during the Westward Expansion.

Wagons West

Men, women, and families make their way westward from the United States to the Western frontier in search of open land and new opportunities. They travel in wagon trains across the prairie, making do with minimal comfort. Their journeys are fraught with hardship, in the form of the harsh landscape, conflicts with their fellow settlers, and Indian raids. For frontier novels told from a feminine viewpoint, see "Women on the Frontier," later in this chapter.

Brown, Dee.

The Way to Bright Star. **Forge, 1998. 352pp.** `YA`

In 1902, former circus performer Ben Butterfield tells about the high point of his life. Back in 1862 he and two friends are asked to transport a Yankee officer's contraband—two camels—from Texas to his home in Bright Star, Indiana. While en route, the trio meet a number of colorful characters, and Ben finds love with a girl with the unlikely name of Queen Elizabeth Jones.

McMurtry, Larry.

Boone's Lick. **Simon & Schuster, 2000. 287pp.** `YA`

Shay Cecil, aged fifteen, narrates the tale of his large family's difficult journey from Boone's Lick, Missouri, to Wyoming Territory in the 1860s. His mother Mary Margaret, tired of caring for four children by herself, wants to track down Shay's errant father, who had left them over a year before. Mary Margaret, as wily a heroine as any in Western fiction, stops at nothing to keep her family safe and fed along the way.

Reynolds, Clay.

Franklin's Crossing. **Dutton, 1992. 536pp.**

In 1873, Moses Franklin, a former Virginia slave, is hired to take a wagon train of settlers across North Texas to Santa Fe. The settlers, a mixed group of Northerners and Southerners, don't trust a black man to lead them, and wagonmaster Cleve Graham uses Franklin as a scapegoat when things don't go their way. When they accidentally stumble into Comanche territory, many settlers pay the price with their lives. Franklin's only real ally is Aggie Sterling, a horse trader's daughter. Some violent scenes.

Wheeler, Richard S.

The Fields of Eden. **Forge, 2001. 383pp.** ✍

In the 1840s, settlers from all walks of life—missionaries, immigrant Irish, and fortune-hunters—converge on the Oregon Trail. But the British Hudson Bay Company still controls Oregon Territory and is reluctant to see Americans encroaching on its border. Dr. John McLoughlin, chief factor of Hudson's Bay at Fort Vancouver, feels sorry for the hungry pioneers but is torn by his loyalty to the British Crown. Told from multiple viewpoints.

Life in Pioneer Towns

After the difficult journey westward ends, pioneers have the chance to settle down and begin their lives anew. They band together to form communities, setting up businesses, saloons, and newspapers, hoping the railroad will come to town and connect them with the wider world.

Dillard, Annie.

The Living. **HarperCollins, 1992. 397pp.** ★ 📖

In the late nineteenth century, families originally from the Midwest settle near Puget Sound and find that pioneer life is both more difficult and more rewarding than they imagined. Ada and Rooney Fishburn's youth works in their favor, as they prove more resilient than most. With the help of Lummi Indians and other families, the Fishburns survive to see the small Whatcom Settlement grow into a prosperous community, complete with shops, railroad, and prospectors in search of gold. Dillard describes the pioneers' back-breaking labor with the same intensity as she does the beautiful landscape of the Northwest coast. **Literary.**

Phillips, Scott.

Cottonwood. **Ballantine, 2004. 304pp.**

Bill Ogden is the resident photographer, saloon-owner, and all-around Lothario in the pioneer town of Cottonwood, Texas, in the 1870s. All of Cottonwood's residents wait patiently for prosperity to come to town via the railroad. When Chicago developer Marc Leval announces his plans for Cottonwood, it seems their dreams may come true. But Leval's wife Maggie proves to be too much for Bill to handle, as do the evil schemes of one farm family. A wry parable on one town's unwitting descent into sin.

Reynolds, Clay.

The Tentmaker. **Berkley, 2002. 389pp.**

After an unremarkable stint in the Civil War, Gil Hooley heads out West to set up shop as a tentmaker in some frontier town—he doesn't care which one. Fate steps in when his wagon breaks down in the middle of nowhere, Texas. One by one, other folks happen by, and with Hooley's handmade tents as their shelter, many even stay. It's soon apparent to all but Hooley that he's got a full-fledged town on his hands, but a violent gang of thugs stops at nothing to put an end to it all. A powerful tale of belonging, loyalty, and even love, served up in realistic, gritty Western style.

Wheeler, Richard S.

🎗 *Drum's Ring.* **New American Library, 2001. 296pp.**

Bad news for Angie Drum, publisher of the local newspaper in Opportunity, Kansas, in the 1870s: She has uncovered a ring of corrupt town officials, and at the center of them is her own son, Opportunity's mayor. Spur Award.

Restitution. **Signet, 2001. 298pp.**

Long before he became a pillar of the community in Cottonwood, Utah, Truman Jackson had a disreputable past as a bank robber, though he never got violent. When Truman and his wife Gracie decide to come clean, the townspeople condemn rather than forgive them.

Sam Flint Series.

A trilogy of novels about itinerant frontier newspaperman Sam Flint, who starts up weekly newspapers in a series of Old West towns. His curiosity and journalistic integrity get him in trouble with the local townsfolk. Set in the 1870s.

Flint's Gift. Forge, 1997. 352pp.

Sam Flint proves such a good publicist for the quiet town of Payday, Arizona, that it starts to attract undesirable characters.

Flint's Truth. Forge, 1998. 348pp.

Flint sets up shop in Oro Blanco, New Mexico, a town where men have made their fortunes in gold. When Flint gets wind of a conspiracy involving the mine owners, everyone in Oro Blanco wants him to keep quiet about it.

Flint's Honor. Forge, 1999. 320pp.

In Silver City, Colorado, Flint threatens to expose his competitor, corrupt newspaper editor Digby Westminster. The problem is that Flint has few people on his side except the town whore and a quirky typesetter.

The Witness. Forge, 2000. 298pp.

Daniel Knott works as a bookkeeper for Amos Burch, a rich philanthropist in Paradise, Colorado, in the 1890s. When Daniel spies Burch in flagrante delicto with a woman who isn't his wife, and Burch's wife sues for divorce, Daniel has to decide whether to accept a bribe and compromise his principles. A Western morality tale.

African Americans on the Frontier

The important roles African Americans had in the development of the West were for years overlooked or downplayed in fiction, but these novels make up for it. Nicknamed "buffalo soldiers" by Native Americans, brave black soldiers defend their country with honor, despite overt racism, inadequate supplies, and the presence of the Ku Klux Klan. See also Margaret Blair Young and Darius Aidan Gray's black Mormon trilogy in the next section.

Carlile, Clancy.
Children of the Dust. Random House, 1995. 428pp.

Gypsy Smith, a half-African American, half-Cherokee gunfighter and scout, meets his future wife while escorting black sharecroppers north in 1889 to participate in the Oklahoma Land Rush. On the night before his wedding, the Klan attacks him and leaves him for dead. Gypsy vows retribution on the Klan and local lawmen, who do nothing to protect him.

Durham, David Anthony.
Gabriel's Story. Doubleday, 2001. 291pp. 📖

In the 1870s, fifteen-year old Gabriel Lynch reluctantly accompanies his mother and younger brother from Baltimore to dusty Kansas, where his

widowed mother hopes to start a homestead and reconnect with her first love. Distrusting his new stepfather and hating their rough living conditions, Gabriel sulks and pines for adventure. He finds it after running away to Texas with a group of cowboys, but their flight degenerates into a wild spree of burglary, rape, and murder. A literary tale of lost innocence. **Literary.**

Lewis, J. P. Sinclair.

Buffalo Gordon Series.

The Western adventures of Nate Gordon, a runaway slave from Louisiana. Well-researched but clumsily written in places, and Nate's constant heroism is almost too good to be true.

Buffalo Gordon. Forge, 2001. 480pp.

During the Civil War, Nate joins the Union Army, returns to Louisiana, and recruits other African-American men for the all-black 9th Cavalry. Despite many incidents of racism and violent encounters with Cheyenne and Comanche warriors, he and his regiment keep the West safe for settlers.

Buffalo Gordon on the Plains. Forge, 2003. 444pp.

Assigned to the plains of Kansas, Nate and company fight the deadly Dog Soldiers, fierce warriors of the Cheyenne. He must also get his pregnant lover Cara back after her former master captures her.

Willard, Tom.

Buffalo Soldiers. **Forge, 1996. 331pp.**

Former slave Augustus Sharps, member of the all-black 10th Cavalry in 1869, serves his regiment with distinction. Over the next thirty years, he and his wife Selona raise a family on the plains, protect settlers from Indian attacks, and endure the prejudice of his fellow townspeople. The first volume in the author's Black Sabre Chronicles, which traces African-American contributions to the U.S. military.

Mormons on the Frontier

These novels show Mormons' roles in the development of the West—and not just Utah.

Card, Orson Scott.

Saints. **Forge, 2001. 624pp.**

Annotated in Chapter 2.

Freeman, Judith.

Red Water. **Pantheon, 2002. 324pp.** ✍ 📖

The Mountain Meadows Massacre—September 11, 1857—was the dark day when 120 settlers on their way to California were slaughtered by a group of Mormons and Indians. John D. Lee, a Mormon who was one of the perpetrators, was the only person ever tried for the crime. Freeman tells the story from the point of view of three of Lee's nineteen wives, each of whom has a different perspective on the man they all loved. **Literary.**

Grey, Zane.

Riders of the Purple Sage. Harper & Brothers, 1912. 334pp. ★

In the town of Cottonwoods, Utah, in the late nineteenth century, Jane Withersteen, a young Mormon woman, defends her ranch against other Mormons, who try to get control of her property by marrying her off. She's alone in her efforts until a stranger named Lassiter comes riding into town. Lassiter seeks out Jane, since she's the only one who knows the story behind his secret. This was the first, best known, and probably the most popular of Zane Grey's eighty-odd novels. Though a bit clichéd today, it has been widely reprinted.

Young, Margaret Blair, and Darius Aidan Gray.

<u>Standing on the Promises Trilogy.</u> ✍

A trilogy about black Mormon pioneers, based on historical characters. Detailed historical notes lend authenticity. The novels will also interest readers of inspirational (Mormon) historical fiction.

One More River to Cross. Bookcraft, 2000. 337pp.

The pioneer journeys of two historical characters close to LDS leader Joseph Smith. In the 1830s, Elijah Abel carries the message of the Mormon Church on a series of missions throughout the West. Jane Manning James and her husband Isaac settle in Nauvoo, Illinois, and make their home with the Smith family.

Bound for Canaan. Bookcraft, 2002. 432pp.

Among the Mormons making the trek from Nauvoo to Salt Lake City are Elijah Abel and his family, and Jane Manning James and hers. Despite their personal connections to Joseph Smith, and the ending of the Civil War, Elijah and Jane are still denied equal status in the Church. Set between 1839 and 1891.

The Last Mile of the Way. Bookcraft, 2003. 448pp.

The story of the Abel and James families continues into the mid-twentieth century.

Western Explorers and Adventurers

The daring exploits of the men and women who were among the first to explore the Western frontier. The novels in this section tend to be fast-paced, action-packed adventures.

Mountain Men

White men in search of adventure head West as fur trappers, living on their own in the Rocky Mountains and trading with Indians for supplies. The ultimate survival stories, these novels feature independent souls who live off the land, becoming as free and untamed as the wilderness that surrounds them. Most are set in the 1820s through 1850s, before the arrival of settlers.

Blevins, Win.

🏵 *So Wild a Dream.* **Forge, 2003. 398pp.**

Sam Morgan yearns for a more adventurous life than what Morgantown, Pennsylvania, can offer. In 1822 he takes off down the Ohio River, learns the fur trade, and befriends Indian guides and legendary mountain men—whose dream of freedom he follows. Projected to be the first in a new series. Spur Award.

Fisher, Vardis.

🏵 *Mountain Man.* **Morrow, 1965. 372pp.** ★

After his wife is murdered, fur trapper Sam Minard goes after her killers. In Kate Bowden, a strong-minded widow who took her own revenge on the perpetrators who killed her husband and children, Sam finds a kindred spirit. Beautiful descriptions of the Yellowstone National Park region combine with a fast-paced story of survival and retribution. It isn't politically correct in the least, and the hatred some mountain men felt for the Indians comes through loud and clear. This novel inspired the Robert Redford movie *Jeremiah Johnson.* Western Heritage Award.

Gear, W. Michael.

Richard Hamilton Series.

Gear, who co-wrote the prehistoric First Americans series (Chapter 2) with his wife, also wrote several solo novels set in the 1820s. He uses intellectual Richard Hamilton as a vehicle to dispel "politically correct" myths about the Plains Indians, a violent people who tried to exterminate every other culture they encountered, including other native tribes.

The Morning River. Forge, 1996. 382pp.

In 1835, Richard Hamilton, a snobby philosophy student from Boston, finds himself alone in the Missouri wilderness while on business for his father. Robbed and beaten, Richard is sold as an indentured servant on a keelboat and sent on a voyage of a lifetime up the Missouri River. He grows up fast when he saves the life of Heals like a Willow, a Shoshoni medicine woman.

Coyote Summer. Forge, 1997. 427pp.

As Richard's romantic feelings toward Willow grow stronger, Willow leaves him in the Rocky Mountains to minister to the Shoshoni's spiritual needs. Richard's journey to get her back leads him into more danger and a new understanding of what it means to be "civilized."

Johnston, Terry C.

The late Terry C. Johnston (1947–2001) is best known for two series, Titus Bass and The Plainsmen (earlier this chapter). His novels of the early Western frontier are enhanced by thorough historical research and his personal experience roaming the Western mountains and plains. Johnston died of cancer just after completing *Wind Walker.*

Titus Bass Series. (Also called Mountain Man Series.) ★

Johnston's Western adventures about Titus "Scratch" Bass—fur trapper, fearless mountain man, and all-around survivor—are hardly politically correct, but they reflect an important part of American history. Titus's story goes from the early 1800s, as he grows up as a Kentucky farm boy, through the 1850s, when he settles down with his Crow family in the Rocky Mountains. In between, Titus hunts buffalo, fights off Indians, endures numerous hardships, and tries to prevent white settlers from taking over the West. The books, written as a set of three trilogies, are listed in historical order.

Dance on the Wind. Bantam, 1995. 517pp.

Buffalo Palace. Bantam, 1996. 405pp.

Crack in the Sky. Bantam, 1997. 481pp.

Carry the Wind. Green Hill, 1982. 571pp.

BorderLords. Jameson, 1985. 455pp.

One-Eyed Dream. Jameson, 1988. 432pp.

Ride the Moon Down. Bantam, 1998. 427pp.

Death Rattle. Bantam, 1999. 429pp.

Wind Walker. Bantam, 2001. 461pp.

Wheeler, Richard S.

Skye's West Series.

Barnaby Skye, legendary mountain man and guide in the 1820s through the 1860s, has an unlikely past. A reluctant seaman pressed into service with Britain's Royal Navy, Skye saw his chance at freedom at Fort Vancouver and jumped ship. His penchant for getting into trouble continues to follow him. "Mister Skye," as he prefers to be called, makes his living fur trapping and escorting missionaries and settlers to various locations out West. Over time, he acquires two wives—Many Quill Woman of the Crow tribe, whom he calls Victoria, and a younger Shoshone woman named Mary—as well as an ugly, bad-tempered horse named Jawbone. The cultural differences between Skye and his wives, as well as their odd domestic arrangement, are both touching and funny. The novels, numbered as given in the order below, can be read in almost any order, though *Rendezvous* takes Skye back to his early days—his military past.

Sun River. Tor, 1989. 314pp.

Bannack. Tor, 1989. 314pp.

The Far Tribes. Tor, 1990. 313pp.

Yellowstone. Tor, 1990. 312pp.

Bitterroot. Tor, 1991. 356pp.

Sundance. Tor, 1992. 346pp.

Wind River. Tor, 1993. 342pp.

Santa Fe. Forge, 1994. 345pp.

Rendezvous. Forge, 1997. 349pp.

Dark Passage. Forge, 1998. 318pp.

Going Home. Forge, 2000. 315pp.

Downriver. Forge, 2001. 304pp.

The Deliverance. Forge, 2003. 318pp.

Early Explorers

In the early nineteenth century, early explorers like John Charles Frémont, Meriwether Lewis, William Clark, and John Wesley Powell mapped the Western frontier and opened it up for further settlement. Some of these biographical novels take a revisionist stance, portraying these American legends in less than a heroic light. Others take their familiar stories and retell them from the point of view of others in their parties.

Cleary, Rita.

River Walk. **Five Star, 2000. 278pp.** ✍

John Collins, a member of Lewis and Clark's expedition across the North American continent in 1804–1806, has had little to say in the historical record. Cleary (one of Collins's descendants) re-creates what his journey with the famous pair must have been like, struggling to fit in with a mixed company of Americans, French Canadians, and natives. Collins reaches a turning point when he falls in love with Laughing Water, a widow of the Mandan tribe, since desertion of the group for any reason is forbidden.

Hall, Brian.

I Shall Be Extremely Happy in Your Company. **Viking, 2003. 419pp.** ✍ 📖

Timed to mark the bicentennial of the Lewis and Clark expedition, Hall's novel takes a revisionist approach by looking beyond its characters' near-mythic status. It is told by four different protagonists—Lewis, Clark, Sacagawea, and her husband Toussaint Charbonneau—whose viewpoints rarely agree. Not only do we see the damage inflicted on the land and on Native Americans by the journey and its aftermath, but Hall also develops the inner life of Sacagawea, whom he clearly admires, and of Meriwether Lewis, who succumbs to depression after his return to civilization. **Literary.**

Nevin, David.

Dream West. **Putnam, 1983. 639pp.** ✍

In 1844, John Charles Frémont and his wife, a U.S. senator's daughter, Jessie Benton Frémont, set out to map the lands of the Western frontier. Their accurate surveys of the region serve to open up Western lands for settlement and further exploration. Jessie frequently isn't given credit for her efforts in America's westward expansion, but in Nevin's book they are romantic and professional partners who support each other through thick and thin. An old-fashioned historical novel of America's "manifest destiny" movement, and the first entry in Nevin's <u>American Story</u> series (continued in Chapter 2, and below).

Meriwether. **Forge, 2004. 348pp.** ✍

Meriwether Lewis, tired of being relegated to a desk job as part of President Jefferson's staff, finally gets his chance to let his adventurous spirit free. He teams up with a friend, William Clark, to make the legendary Corps of Discovery trip west to the Pacific. Though burdened with occasional depression, Lewis doesn't let his moodiness get the best of him until the expedition is over. Part of Nevin's <u>American Story</u> series.

Tenney, Jeffrey W.

🏵 *Corps of Discovery.* **IUniverse, 2001. 452pp.** ✍

The epic American adventure of Lewis and Clark has been retold in fiction many times. Where Tenney's version differs is in the characterization. Rather than see it through the eyes of Lewis or Clark, Tenney pieces the journey together through the viewpoints of York, Clark's black servant; John Colter and John Collins, two other explorers; Sacajawea; and George Drouillard, their interpreter. This self-published novel came out of nowhere to win a Spur Award in 2002.

Thom, James Alexander.

Thom has chronicled American history from both the native and the European points of view; see Chapter 2 for his other historical novels.

From Sea to Shining Sea. **Ballantine, 1984. 931pp.** ✍ ★

At once a family saga, military adventure, and fictional history of America's westward expansion, Thom's novel gives life to the brilliant sons and daughters of John and Ann Rogers Clark of Virginia. In particular their son George Rogers Clark, an American Revolutionary war hero, succeeds in defending America's Western lands against British incursion. Another son, George's younger brother William, gains fame and fortune through his journey, with Meriwether Lewis, to reach the Pacific Ocean in 1803—1805. The authentic dialogue evokes the early American period nicely, as do the realistic descriptions of the wilderness and plains. Some violence.

Sign-Talker. **Ballantine, 2000. 466pp.** ✍

Lewis and Clark need a hunter and interpreter for their Corps of Discovery and find their man in George Drouillard. Son of a Frenchman and a Shawnee woman, Drouillard both admires and fears what the white explorers will mean for America's native peoples. For the most part, Drouillard remains a passive observer of the beautiful landscape and the human failings he sees in the group's leaders. But as the expedition continues on to the Pacific and back, his tolerance grows thin.

Vernon, John.

The Last Canyon. **Houghton Mifflin, 2001. 336pp.** ✍

> In 1869, explorer John Wesley Powell, accompanied by nine companions, makes the first recorded effort to travel the length of the Grand Canyon. Navigating the mighty Colorado proves difficult, with its treacherous rapids and the presence of the Paiute Indians—a surprise to Powell's party, since they had expected the region to be completely barren and uninhabitable. In alternating chapters, each group (white and Paiute) tells its version of events. **Literary.**

Wheeler, Richard S.

Eclipse. **Forge, 2002. 380pp.** ✍

> Most novels about Meriwether Lewis and William Clark focus on their Western expedition; Wheeler's version begins in 1806, right after they return home and are forced to adjust to their newfound fame. Clark marries a younger cousin and settles down to married life in St. Louis, where he supervises America's Indian affairs. Lewis, on the other hand, returns from his trip ill in both mind and body. Consumed by syphilis, Lewis flounders in his new job as commissioner of the Louisiana Territory.

Native Americans

In contrast to traditional Western novels, in which Indians are portrayed as hostile, violent, or unintelligent, these novels depict Native Americans sympathetically and/or relate the story from their point of view. Additional novels of Native American life can be found in Chapter 2.

General

These novels introduce readers to the customs and history of different Native American tribes, presenting America's westward movement from a very different viewpoint than traditional Westerns. The authors write with sensitivity, relating the degradation and extreme hardship that Indians suffered at the hands of white men. Some novels are told from the point of view of white men "adopted" into Indian tribes rather than from that of Native Americans themselves. The two series by Robert Conley and Don Coldsmith begin several centuries earlier than most, telling of Indians' day-to-day lives in the sixteenth and seventeenth centuries, and how their lives changed upon their first encounters with Spanish settlers.

Blake, Michael.

<u>**Dances with Wolves Series.**</u>

> More readers will be familiar with the Kevin Costner film *Dances with Wolves* than with Blake's original book version, but since Blake also wrote the screenplay, there are many similarities. In both, images of the beautiful Western landscape form a backdrop to a dramatic story of the clash between white and native cultures. However, in Blake's novels it is the Comanche, not the Lakota Sioux, whom Dunbar encounters.

Dances with Wolves. Newmarket, 1991. 324pp. ★

After a heroic stint in the Civil War, Lieutenant John Dunbar chooses a frontier post out West for his next assignment. But the outpost is deserted, which forces him to turn to the Comanche for survival. Though his initial encounters with them are violent, Dunbar eventually joins the Comanche tribe and gets to appreciate their way of life. He grows romantically attracted to Stands with a Fist, a white woman living with the Comanche, and becomes a Comanche warrior himself, adopting the name Dances with Wolves. When the U.S. Army comes looking for him, Dunbar has to decide whether to stay with the Comanche.

The Holy Road. Villard, 2001. 339pp.

Eleven years after *Dances with Wolves*, Dunbar has married Stands with a Fist, and they have three children. He hasn't left the white world behind, though. Texas Rangers, intent on subjugating the Indians, kill half his village and kidnap Dunbar's wife and baby daughter. Because of his white skin, Dunbar realizes that he's the only warrior who can rescue them.

Blakely, Mike.

Comanche Dawn. Forge, 1998. 413pp.

Called a Comanche version of Ruth Beebe Hill's *Hanta Yo*. Blakely charts the rise of the Comanche Nation from their point of view. In 1687, the Comanche are introduced to the horse, and their future leader, a young man called Horseback, is born. With his beautiful wife Teal by his side, Horseback becomes an expert warrior and rider. Thanks to his efforts, the Comanche split from the Shoshone to form their own tribe, the most powerful force on the southern plains. Blakely includes a Shoshone/Comanche glossary.

Blevins, Win.

🎗 *Stone Song.* Forge, 1995. 400pp. ✍

His Crazy Horse (better known as just Crazy Horse), the greatest warrior of the Lakota Sioux, leads his people to victory against Custer and his troops at the Battle of the Little Big Horn. His Crazy Horse is an enigma even to his people, but he fights with all he has to prevent the Sioux way of life from being destroyed. Spur Award.

Chiaventone, Frederick.

🎗 *Moon of Bitter Cold.* Forge, 2002. 398pp. ✍

Relieved to see the end of the Civil War, many Americans head westward in 1866. When too many white men encroach on Native Americans' lands, Lakota chief Red Cloud forges an alliance among the four major tribes—the Sioux, Cheyenne, Arapaho, and Crow—that leads them to victory. Chiaventone dramatizes Red Cloud's War, which was such a victory for Native Americans that the U.S. government pressured them to sign a peace treaty. Despite the end result, the author takes an even-handed approach. Western Heritage Award.

Coldsmith, Don.

Spanish Bit Series. ★ YA

In the sixteenth century, the Elk-Dog People (an amalgam of Plains Indian tribes) come upon a lost Spanish conquistador named Juan Garcia. The encounter changes their entire way of life. As the Spaniard (renamed "Heads Off") adapts to The People's ways, he introduces them to the horse. This transforms them from a wandering hunter-gatherer society to a race of warriors. Heads Off becomes their chief, and later volumes of this saga detail the lives of his descendants through the late eighteenth century. In these short, character-centered novels, the family stands at the heart of Plains culture, and readers will appreciate the genealogical tables. Common elements include vision quests, encounters with other tribes, trade with French and Spanish traders, and bits of native myth and legend.

Trail of the Spanish Bit. Doubleday, 1980. 180pp.

The Elk-Dog Heritage. Doubleday, 1981. 181pp.

Follow the Wind. Doubleday, 1983. 192pp.

Buffalo Medicine. Doubleday, 1981. 183pp.

Man of the Shadows. Doubleday, 1983. 183pp.

Daughter of the Eagle. Doubleday, 1984. 178pp.

Moon of Thunder. Doubleday, 1985. 179pp.

The Sacred Hills. Doubleday, 1985. 179pp.

Pale Star. Doubleday, 1986. 176pp.

River of Swans. Doubleday, 1986. 176pp.

Return to the River. Doubleday, 1987. 181pp.

Medicine Knife. Doubleday, 1988. 187pp.

The Flower in the Mountains. Doubleday, 1988. 188pp.

Trail from Taos. Doubleday, 1989. 176pp.

Song of the Rock. Doubleday, 1989. 178pp.

Fort de Chastaigne. Doubleday, 1990. 180pp.

Quest of the White Bull. Doubleday, 1990. 180pp.

Return of the Spanish. Doubleday, 1991. 179pp.

Bride of the Morning Star. Doubleday, 1991. 176pp.

Walks in the Sun. Doubleday, 1992. 240pp.

Thunderstick. Doubleday, 1993. 182pp.

Track of the Bear. Doubleday, 1994. 180pp.

Child of the Dead. Doubleday, 1995. 245pp.

Bearer of the Pipe. Doubleday, 1995. 258pp.

Medicine Hat. Univ. of Oklahoma Press, 1997. 266pp.

The Lost Band. Univ. of Oklahoma Press, 2000. 260pp.

Raven Mocker. Univ. of Oklahoma Press, 2001. 253pp.

The Pipestone Quest. Univ. of Oklahoma Press, 2004. 255pp.

Conley, Robert J.

Real People Series. ★

An authentic, continuing series set among the Cherokee (the "Real People"), based on native lore and legend. The timeline begins before European contact (1500s), during a dark period when the Cherokee revolt against their priests. Later volumes cover contact with the Spaniards and the tragedy of the Trail of Tears (1838), when the U.S. government forcibly relocates the Cherokee to Oklahoma. Loosely connected, they can be read in any order. Technically, not all of these books are Westerns, because many take place in the southeastern United States. However, they deal with the history of the Cherokee Nation (of which the author is a member), and most readers consider them Westerns—in style, if not completely in substance. *Dark Island* took home a Spur Award. The novels appear in paperback from the University of Oklahoma Press.

The Way of the Priests. Doubleday, 1992.

The White Path. Doubleday, 1993. 183pp.

The Dark Way. Doubleday, 1993. 179pp.

The Way South. Doubleday, 1994. 176pp.

The Long Way Home. Doubleday, 1994. 182pp.

The War Trail North. Doubleday, 1995. 183pp.

🎗 *The Dark Island.* Doubleday, 1995. 181pp.

War Woman. St. Martin's Press, 1997. 357pp.

The Peace Chief. St. Martin's Press, 1998. 339pp.

Cherokee Dragon. St. Martin's Press, 2000. 289pp. ✍

Spanish Jack. St. Martin's Press, 2001. 210pp.

Sequoyah. St. Martin's Press, 2002. 217pp.

Earling, Debra Magpie.

🎗 *Perma Red.* BlueHen, 2002. 296pp. 📖

On the Flathead Indian Reservation in 1940s Montana, beautiful and tough-minded Louise White Elk yearns to escape. She is held back by her attraction to three very different men, including Baptiste Yellow Knife, who adheres to the Old Ways—and whose attractions are as strong as they are dangerous. Spur Award; Willa Award. **Literary.**

Fergus, Jim.

One Thousand White Women: The Journals of May Dodd. **St. Martin's Press, 1998. 304pp.** 📖

Imagine that in 1875, President Grant signs a peace treaty with Little Wolf of the Cheyenne to send 1,000 white women to the Cheyenne Nation. May Dodd of Chicago, whose parents placed her in a mental institution for having borne two illegitimate children to the wrong man, marries Little Wolf as part of the secret "Brides for Indians" treaty. May records her life among the Cheyenne in her journals. Danger, in the form of liquor and vengeful white men, is never far away.

Garcia y Robertson, R.

American Woman. **Forge, 2001. 349pp.**

"American Woman" was born Sarah Kilory, a blonde Quaker from Pennsylvania who originally headed west to convert the natives to Christianity. Her plans changed when she fell in love with Yellow Legs, a Lakota warrior and medicine man, and became his second wife. As a member of the Lakota tribe, American Woman struggles with her identity as an outsider whose sister-wife takes precedence over her. She also sympathizes with the plight of the Indians at a time when the buffalo are near extinction and the railroad threatens their open lands. Through Sarah's eyes, we see the events leading up to the Little Big Horn from a new viewpoint.

Glancy, Diane.

Pushing the Bear: A Novel of the Trail of Tears. **Harcourt Brace, 1996. 241pp.** 📖

Starting in 1838, thousands of Cherokee—men, women, and children—make the arduous march west from North Carolina to Oklahoma Territory, where the U.S. government has chosen to relocate them. Glancy tells their tale from multiple points of view, the strongest of which belongs to Maritole, a young woman who loses her baby along the way. Her shaky relationship with her husband adds to her anger and pain. **Literary.**

Hill, Ruth Beebe.

🎗 *Hanta Yo.* **Doubleday, 1979. 834pp.**

This mammoth novel, meant to be a fictionalized ethnographic study, describes the life of the Sioux from the 1790s to the 1830s (before the arrival of white settlers) as seen through the eyes of two families. To achieve authenticity, Hill translated her novel from English to Dakotah and then back to early American English. However, this controversial novel was denounced by some Native Americans as inauthentic and disrespectful to their way of life, since (among other things) it focuses on characters' individual strengths, a la Ayn Rand, rather than on their togetherness. Western Heritage Award.

Lambert, Page.

Shifting Stars. **Forge, 1997. 352pp.**

In Wyoming Territory in the 1850s, Skye Macdonald feels torn between her mother's Lakota heritage and the blood of her Scottish father. Having lost her mother as a child, Skye had grown up with her father, but she returns to her mother's people as a young woman. There she learns about her Lakota side from her maternal grandmother and tries to understand her mixed heritage.

McMurtry, Larry, and Diana Ossana.

Zeke and Ned. **Simon & Schuster, 1997. 478pp.** ✍

Ezekiel Proctor and Ned Christie—Zeke and Ned—were Cherokee leaders just after the end of the Civil War who are thought of as folk heroes today. Their personalities shaped by the Cherokees' forced relocation along the Trail of Tears, the heroic pair try to right old wrongs dealt to them by the U.S. government. The women they love stand by them to the end.

Munn, Vella.

Blackfeet Season. **Forge, 1999. 383pp.**

Every winter is a struggle for survival, but for the Blackfeet tribe on the Western plains in the 1860s, it's also a struggle for leadership. Bunch of Lodges, their shaman, wants to use spiritual wisdom to lead his people, but the Blackfoot chief, Sleeps Too Long, chooses the warrior's path. White Calf, a young woman, has visions of a time when white men will steal Blackfoot lands from them, and her marriage to Bunch of Lodges' son sets them on a path to civil war.

Cheyenne Summer. **Forge, 2001. 366pp.**

In the difficult summer of 1800, massive drought causes wildfires to flare up. European settlers are forcing the Cheyenne away from their homeland and onto enemy territory. This causes intense rivalry between the Cheyenne and the Pawnee, who fight not only over their land but also over the limited food supply. Grey Bear and Lone Hawk, two Cheyenne leaders, take different approaches to the matter. While Grey Bear lives for war, Lone Hawk realizes that the Cheyenne and the Pawnee have many things in common.

Soul of the Sacred Earth. **Forge, 2000. 350pp.**

In 1628, in what's now known as Arizona, the Spanish arrive in Oraibi, a Hopi village. Spanish soldiers come seeking riches, while priest Fray Angelico wants to save the Indians' heathen souls. The presence of the Spanish stirs up rivalries between them and the Hopi, who don't want to give up their own beliefs, and also between the Hopi and the Navajo —the former a peaceful people, the latter a warrior race. There's some romance, too, when the Hopi maiden Morning Butterfly falls in love with Cougar, a Navajo who serves as the Hopi interpreter.

Murphy, Garth.
The Indian Lover. **Simon & Schuster, 2002. 439pp.**

In the 1840s, the last years of Spanish rule in California, young seaman Bill Marshall heeds the call of the American frontier and jumps ship in San Diego. When his romance with the major's daughter Lugarda goes awry, Bill heads north with his Indian companion, Pablo Verdi. They take shelter with Pablo's people, and Bill learns their ways, but he never completely forgets Lugarda or his former way of life.

Murray, Earl.
Spirit of the Moon. **Forge, 1996. 304pp.**

In 1841, Spirit of the Moon, a young Nez Perce woman also known by the English name Elizabeth, travels with her adoptive French-Canadian father to the southwestern desert country called the Coyotero. Two fur trappers join them along the way. During the dangerous journey, Elizabeth falls in love with one of the trappers. This threatens to derail her betrothal to the weak-willed man her father wants her to marry.

O'Brien, Dan.
The Contract Surgeon. **Lyons, 1999. 316pp.** ✍

In 1877, the great Sioux chief Crazy Horse died a suspicious death while in the hands of the U.S. Army. Valentine McGillycuddy, a mostly untried physician contracted to the Army as a surgeon during the Great Sioux War, befriends the famed warrior while trying to save his life. Through his experiences, McGillycuddy loses his youthful idealism, including his belief that the government really has the Indians' best interests at heart. Based on a true story. The sequel, *The Indian Agent*, will deal with McGillycuddy's friendship with Red Cloud during the 1880s. Western Heritage Award.

Robson, Lucia St. Clair.
Ghost Warrior. **Forge, 2002. 496pp.** ✍

Lozen of the Apaches was known as the "Apache Joan of Arc" for her role in saving her people. With legendary native warriors Cochise, Geronimo, and her brother Victorio, Lozen fights for Apache freedom when the U.S. Army tries to drive them from their New Mexico homeland. Her gift of second sight lets her see her enemies' plans, but the one white man she makes an exception for is adventurer Rafe Collins. Though their bond never develops into romance, their friendship changes his life forever. Set in the 1850s through the 1880s.

Wilkinson, David Marion.
Oblivion's Altar. **New American Library, 2002. 376pp.** ✍

Part Cherokee and part white, Major Ridge, the Cherokee chieftain known to his people as Kah-nung-da-tla-geh, adapts easily to both worlds. Firmly believing that education will gain the Cherokee freedom and respectability, he brings up his son, John Ridge, in his own image. Major Ridge relies on Andrew Jackson's government to abide by its treaties, but the United States fails to do so, and the Cherokee favor war over peaceful settlement. Although he was betrayed by his people, Ridge is remembered today as a hero for both sides. Set between 1776 and 1839, from Georgia to the Trail of Tears. Spur Award.

Indian Captives

The "Indian captive" theme is a frequent one in Western historical novels, and many involve women captives. Children or adults, forcibly taken by Indians from their white families, fight against their captivity at first. Over time, as they accustom themselves to their new lifestyle, they may marry into the tribe and have children. Although some captives are rescued, they don't always leave willingly. However, the basic plotline isn't as politically correct as that makes it sound. Captives' lives are hardly idyllic, since adjustment is painful, and they don't fit well into either culture. The prototype is the real-life story of Cynthia Ann Parker, fictionalized in Lucia St. Clair Robson's *Ride the Wind*. Captivity stories also appear in novels of America's eastern frontier; see Chapters 2 and 10.

Black, Michelle.

An Uncommon Enemy. Forge, 2001. 398pp.

In November 1868, General Custer penned a letter to his wife in which he mentioned the arrival of a white woman in his camp. In Black's version, the woman is Eden Murdoch, forcibly taken into custody when Custer's frontier army attacks a Cheyenne village. But Eden had found happiness with her Cheyenne family and did not want to be rescued. Although Custer wants to use Eden as an example to justify violence against the Indians, she will do anything to prevent that from happening. Captain Brad Randall, sworn to serve Custer but fascinated by Eden, finds his loyalties torn. Eden's and Brad's adventures continue in Black's <u>Mysteries of the Victorian West</u> (Chapter 7).

Haseloff, Cynthia.

The Chains of Sarai Stone. Five Star, 1995. 218pp.

In 1836, Kiowa and Comanche raiders massacre the family of ten-year-old Sarai Stone and steal her away. Her grandfather, Silas Stone, sends his agents to track her down, but Sarai—having grown up and adjusted to Comanche culture—refuses to come home, at least until she realizes that her way of life is at an end.

<u>Kiowa Series.</u>

Two realistic Western novels set among the Kiowa Indians in the 1860s and 1870s.

Satanta's Woman. Five Star, 1998. 301pp.

Adrianne Chastain is a rancher and relatively young widow captured by Kiowa Indians after a raid in which her daughter and granddaughter were killed. She gradually comes to terms with life among the Kiowas as well as her growing feelings for Satanta, their war chief. Written as a prequel to *The Kiowa Verdict*.

🏵 *The Kiowa Verdict*. Five Star, 1997. 260pp. ✍

Kiowa chieftain Satanta is put on trial in Oklahoma for having murdered white freighters on a raid into Texas. Satanta doesn't deny his involvement and in fact uses the opportunity to boast about his accomplishments. Testimony by his former captive, Adrianne Chastain, may save him. Satanta's trial was real, but Haseloff fictionalized the details. Spur Award.

Horsley, Kate.

Crazy Woman. **La Alameda, 1992. 239pp.**

Growing up with a submissive mother and alcoholic father in Virginia, quiet Sara Franklin always longed to live a life in which her passion could fly free. Sara marries one of her teachers, Reverend Willoughby, a missionary who takes her to New Mexico to help him convert the Indians to Christianity. When Apaches capture her, they name her "Crazy Woman" for her unusual beliefs. Gradually Sara adapts to their way of life and finds love and acceptance at last.

Riefe, Barbara.

Desperate Crossing. **Forge, 1997. 253pp.**

Newlyweds John and Jenny Sanders Pryor are heading back to Kansas from his post in Laramie, Wyoming, when their wagon train is attacked by Sioux Indians. After seeing most of her party massacred, Jenny is taken captive by the Sioux and forced to become the seventh wife of their chief, Ottawa. Meanwhile John, believing that Jenny is still alive, searches tirelessly to get her back. Realistic action scenes, though nearly all Native Americans (except one Christian convert) are presented stereotypically.

Robson, Lucia St. Clair.

Ride the Wind. **Ballantine, 1982. 562pp.** ✍ ★ 📖

In 1836, Cynthia Ann Parker is nine years old. When Comanches raid her family's camp on the Texas frontier, killing most of the men and animals and raping the women, they take Cynthia and several other children back with them. Cynthia grows up with the Comanche, slowly accepting their ways, adopting the name Naduah and becoming the wife of a Comanche warrior named Wanderer. Her son Quanah Parker, loyal to his Comanche heritage, grows up to be the tribe's last free war chief. Robson's novel, replete with descriptions of Comanche culture and religion, is based on a true story.

Texas and Mexico

A whole mythology has grown up around the history of Texas: the bloody conflicts with Indian tribes, the battle for statehood, and perhaps most of all, the 1836 siege of the Alamo, where over 200 Texians lost their lives in a hopeless attempt to wrest territory from Mexican control. Many novelists have attempted to humanize the history of this great state, but in the end, Texas remains larger than life. (The term "Texians" refers to the early Anglo settlers of Texas.)

Harrigan, Stephen M.

The Gates of the Alamo. **Knopf, 2000. 581pp.** ★ 📖

At the 75th anniversary of the siege of the Alamo, Terrell Mott, aged ninety-one in 1911, reminisces about the events leading up to that fateful day. At the center of Harrigan's story are three proud individuals. Edmund McGowan, a naturalist, finally gets up the courage to stand for what he believes in. Mary Mott, Terrell's widowed mother, maintains an inn along the Gulf Coast. Her son, sixteen-year-old Terrell, has a tragic love affair that drives him into the heart of the conflict. Historical personages like David Crockett, James Bowie, Sam Houston, and Mexican General Santa Anna play secondary roles but are well characterized nonetheless. Harrigan strips the mythology from the 1836 siege of the Alamo in this historically based account. Spur Award; Western Heritage Award.

Kelton, Elmer.

Kelton, described as the best living Western writer, is a seven-time winner of the Spur Award. Many of his earlier novels have been republished by Forge in paperback.

Texas Rangers Series.

An ongoing series dealing with the beginning of the Texas Rangers, a group of volunteers who banded together to protect settlers from the Comanche Indians. It also covers Texans' role during the Civil War and Reconstruction. The first three novels were republished as the paperback omnibus *Lone Star Rising* (2003).

The Buckskin Line. Forge, 1999. 287pp.

Davy "Rusty" Shannon, a young red-haired Texas Ranger, was taken in and raised by the man who rescued him from a Comanche raid. When his adoptive father Mike Shannon is killed for his political views, Rusty vows revenge.

Badger Boy. Forge, 2000. 286pp.

Rusty leaves the Rangers to start up his own ranch. When he encounters Badger Boy, a young white boy who was captured by the Comanche as a baby, Rusty gets the chance to reexamine his past.

The Way of the Coyote. Forge, 2001. 283pp.

Ten-year-old Andy Pickard, formerly known as Badger Boy, makes the effort to adapt to white civilization. Rusty tries hard to make a success of his ranch. Comanches kidnap the son of Rusty's former flame. Spur Award.

Ranger's Trail. Forge, 2002. 287pp.

In 1874, Rusty prepares to marry his sweetheart, Josie Monahan, but she is murdered by an outlaw out for revenge on her family. In tracking down her killer, Rusty discovers he may be following the wrong man.

Texas Vendetta. Forge, 2003. 301pp.

With his companion Farley Brackett, Texas Ranger Andy Pickard aims to deliver killer Jayce Landon to the courthouse for trial, but their prisoner escapes.

Michener, James A.

The Eagle and the Raven. State House Press, 1990. 214pp. ✍ ★

Along the San Jacinto River in 1836, Sam Houston (the Raven) takes revenge on the Mexican armies led by General Santa Anna (the Eagle), who had massacred Texians at the Alamo earlier that same year. The Texians' victory led to freedom for Texas and its establishment as a Republic. This short novel was a previously unpublished excerpt from Michener's epic novel *Texas* (Chapter 3).

Shrake, Edwin.

The Borderland. Hyperion, 2000. 416pp. ✍

In 1839, Texas is still a Republic, and war with Mexico rages on. President Mirabeau Lamar angers Sam Houston with his proposal to move the capital inland to a new frontier city, Austin, which sits in the middle of Comanche country. It's the job of Texas Ranger Captain Matthew Caldwell to keep Austin safe from Comanche warriors, who are furious over their territory's invasion. Caldwell and Romulus Swift, a half-Cherokee physician in search of mystical wisdom, battle each other as ferociously as they fight the Mexicans and Comanche. It all takes place on a large scale, with a multitude of characters both real and fictional.

Vaughan, Robert.

Texas Glory. St. Martin's Paperbacks, 1996. 328pp.

Despite the overwhelming odds against them, a determined band of Texians—including famous names like David Crockett and Jim Bowie—defend the Alamo against Mexican armies in 1836.

Wilkinson, David Marion.

Not Between Brothers. Boaz, 1996. 645pp.

Texas in 1816 is an empty, desolate prairie, settled mainly by Indians, Mexicans, and newly arrived Anglos. Remy Fuqua, an orphaned boy of Scots-French heritage, grows up to be an intelligent but hot-tempered man. His Indian counterpart, Kills White Bear of the Comanche, grows up to be the leader of his people. Their lives run in tandem until a debt owed to one by the other turns into a hostile situation. Both possess a strength that propels them through major events in Texas history—the Alamo, the Mexican War, and on until the Civil War. Wilkinson avoids taking sides, and his powerful writing leads smoothly from the personal to the epic.

The Army in the West

Historical novelists re-create real-life battles fought by the U.S. Army on the Western frontier, and the Americans don't always come out looking like heroes. During the Civil

War, the U.S. Army went west to prevent the Confederacy from gaining ground. After the Civil War, American soldiers headed westward to control the rebellious native tribes—who were, of course, only defending their lands against white settlers. Custer's Last Stand, the legendary Battle of the Little Big Horn in Montana, is the most common topic. It was in this battle—fought on June 25, 1876—that General George Armstrong Custer led the officers of the 7th Cavalry in a doomed charge against a much larger army of Cheyenne and Lakota Sioux Indians. Its story has been retold in fiction again and again, each time from a slightly different perspective. Like the 1836 siege of the Alamo, readers seem to never tire of it. (For more novels about the frontier army, see the section on African Americans on the frontier.)

Black, Michelle.
An Uncommon Enemy. Forge, 2001. 398pp.

Annotated under "Indian Captives."

Blake, Michael.
Marching to Valhalla. Villard, 1996. 288pp. ✍

In his journal, written over the last few weeks of his life, George Custer reflects upon his fondest memories—his marriage, the happy years spent with wife Libbie, his stint in the Civil War, the reasons behind his court martial, and the great victory he won over the Washita in 1868. It's a sympathetic portrait that attempts to explore Custer's humanity. His fictional journal ends before the final battle.

Chiaventone, Frederick.
A Road We Do Not Know. Simon & Schuster, 1996. 333pp. ✍

On the morning of July 25, 1876, General Custer comes upon an Indian village. When he makes the fateful decision to attack, he never fully believes that the natives will rise up and retaliate. He's wrong—very wrong. Chiaventone's novel, painstakingly researched from original sources, dispels the myth of the Battle of the Little Big Horn. He brings it alive from many different points of view, including that of Lieutenant Charles Varnum, a recent West Point grad torn between his loyalty to Custer and his friendship with Indian scouts. A gritty, fast-paced tale.

Crawford, Max.
Lords of the Plain. Atheneum, 1985. 307pp.

Captain Philip Chapman, an officer with the U.S. 2nd Cavalry in 1870s Texas, has been given orders to move the Comanche onto the reservation so that the desolate Llano Estacado region can be opened for settlement. Despite his loyalty to the Army, Chapman isn't sure what he's doing is right.

Haycox, Ernest.
Bugles in the Afternoon. Little, Brown, 1944. 306pp. ★

There's dissent within General Custer's famed 7th Cavalry. Private Kern Shafter, a soldier under Custer's command, discovers that his former rival has been appointed his superior. Haycox's classic novel is refreshingly free of sentimentality. Reissued by the University of Oklahoma Press in 2003, with a foreword by the author's son.

Hoyt, Edwin P.

The Last Stand. **Forge, 1995. 316pp.** ✍

Popular with the public but detested by his officers and the Indians, Custer is an enigma to all who know him. Hoyt dwells upon Custer's strengths and foolishness. While his determined charges into battle solidify his reputation as a fearless leader, they also gain him many enemies. Yet Hoyt also shows Custer's romantic side, for he goes out of his way time and again to be near his wife Libbie, even if it means disobeying orders from Washington.

Nagle, P. G.

Far Western Civil War series.

Annotated in Chapter 2.

Shaara, Jeff.

Gone for Soldiers. **Ballantine, 2000. 424pp.**

Annotated in Chapter 2.

Coming of Age

Young men and women grow up in the West in the late nineteenth and early twentieth centuries, losing their innocence and replacing it with knowledge of their place in the world. The protagonists in coming-of-age stories frequently have mentors to show them the way, but in novels set on the rough Western frontier, the young people often have to grow up on their own.

Blakely, Mike.

🏵 *Summer of Pearls.* **Forge, 2000. 224pp.**

In his eighties, Ben Crowell looks back on the magical summer of 1874, his fourteenth year, when he fell in love for the first time. Ben's daring rescue from a riverboat explosion leads to the discovery of pearls in Great Caddo Lake's freshwater mussels. This amazing find leads to prosperity for the sleepy Texas town of Port Caddo, which the railroads had left behind. It also serves as the catalyst for the murder of Judd Kelso, the cruel riverboat owner. His killer remains a mystery for forty years. Spur Award.

Estleman, Loren.

Sudden Country. **Doubleday, 1991. 182pp.** **YA**

It is 1890. Judge Blod, a boarder staying with young David Grayle and his mother in Oklahoma, has an unexpected visitor who changes all their lives. Jotham Flynn, a Confederate soldier newly released from prison, has arrived to tell Blod his life story. He brings along a treasure map of gold hidden in the Black Hills back in 1863. When Flynn is murdered, David and company take the map and search for the treasure, little knowing that their enemy hides among their party.

Gatewood, Robert Payne.
The Sound of the Trees. Holt, 2002. 304pp. YA

> In Depression-era New Mexico, eighteen-year-old Trude Mason and his mother flee from his alcoholic father. After his mother dies en route, Trude is forced to make his way to Colorado alone. Along the way, he comes across a young black woman named Delilah. Likening her abusive past to his, Trude doesn't hesitate to come to her aid when they meet up again in a ruthless border town.

Horsley, Kate.
Careless Love. University of New Mexico Press, 2003. 249pp.

> Bostonian Thomas Hall, disillusioned about lies his mother told him about his birth, heads west in 1889 in search of the adventure he read about in dime novels. Thomas lands in New Mexico, learning over time that life has more to offer than he expected.

Kelton, Elmer.
Cloudy in the West. Forge, 1997. 255pp.

> When twelve-year-old Joey Shipman's father dies in 1885, his greedy stepmother stops at nothing to get rid of him so that she can inherit the farm. To save his life, Joey runs away and takes refuge with Beau Shipman, his drunkard of a cousin.

Pumpkin Rollers. Forge, 1996. 301pp.

> Just after the Civil War, Trey McLean leaves the family cotton farm and heads to Forth Worth to make some money being a cowboy. There he learns about life, love, and why not to trust the first person who comes along.

Turner, Nancy E.
The Water and the Blood. Regan, 2001. 416pp. 📖

> Annotated below, under "Early Twentieth-Century West."

Women of the West

Some of the most popular Western historical novels feature women as main characters, as if Western authors finally are making up for their neglect of the female half of humanity.

Women on the Frontier

When men head westward in search of new lands to settle, their wives and families accompany them. The women bring a touch of civilization to the wild Western frontier, though most find their new way of life to be quite an adjustment. Some independent-minded women make their way westward on their own, but this is usually due to circumstance, not choice. Despite their apparent physical frailty, these frontier women possess an inner strength that helps them survive the harsh conditions both along the trail and at their final destination. The cramped living conditions en route make them reevaluate their relationships with the men in their lives. Many novels appear in the form of letters or diaries written by the women during their journey. This evokes an appropriately old-fashioned atmosphere and makes readers feel as if they are experiencing frontier journeys first-hand. Set between the 1840s and 1880s. Many Christian novels (Chapter 11) fit this same theme.

Ballantine, David.

Chalk's Woman. **Forge, 2000. 288pp.**

Eighteen-year-old Ann, who lost her parents and her arm in the siege of Vicksburg, decides to travel west when she realizes there's nowhere else for her to go. Along the Santa Fe Trail to Oregon, Ann helps out a group of orphaned children stranded with their wagon. She also meets and falls in love with Chalk, a rough cowhand, and together they all forge a new family.

Cather, Willa.

Cather's novels of immigrant pioneer life on the majestic Nebraska prairie in the late nineteenth century, replete with poetic descriptions of the native landscape, have been reprinted many times.

My Ántonia. **Houghton Mifflin, 1918. 418pp.** ★ 📖

Jim Burden, an orphaned ten-year-old boy, comes to live with his grandparents in Black Hawk, Nebraska, at the same time that Ántonia Shimerda, the free-spirited daughter of a Bohemian immigrant family, arrives in town. Obviously smitten with her, Jim describes Ántonia's fascinating life through his own eyes. They remain friends throughout adulthood, despite physical separation and Ántonia's marriage to another, and learn to respect each other's personal and social differences.

O Pioneers! **Houghton Mifflin, 1913. 308pp.** ★ 📖

Alexandra Bergson, a young Swedish woman in the small town of Hanover, Nebraska, inherits her family farm after her father's death—to her younger brothers' consternation. Despite their disapproval, she decides to make a go of it, struggling with the elements and ignoring the pressure to sell the farm and move to the city.

Dallas, Sandra.

The Diary of Mattie Spenser. **St. Martin's Press, 1997. 229pp.** 📖

Mattie Spenser, a new bride in 1865, still can't believe that town heartthrob Luke Spenser asked her to marry him. A week later, she and Luke leave Iowa for the Colorado Territories. Though in love with him, Mattie can't understand Luke's odd reticence or his unwillingness to give her credit when her quick thinking saves their lives. At first, only her journal keeps her company, though Mattie befriends other folks along the way. Through many joys and tragedies, Mattie grows to love her new home.

Elliott, Diane.

The Strength of Stone: The Pioneer Journal of Electa Bryan Plumer, 1862–1864. **Twodot/Globe Pequot, 2002. 375pp.**

During the Civil War, twenty-year-old schoolteacher Electa Bryan comes to Dakota Territory (modern Montana) as a missionary and to help out her married sister. She grows intrigued by the sheriff of the town of Bannack, William Henry Plumer, and soon marries him. In her journals, Electa records her thoughts, feelings, and the real story about her husband's character. Henry Plumer (also called Plummer) is a notorious figure in Montana's history, hanged by vigilantes in 1864 for supposedly abetting organized crime.

Gilchrist, Micaela.

 The Good Journey. **Simon & Schuster, 2001. 396pp.**

After her husband Henry's death in 1842, Mary, his wife of sixteen years, learns how little she really knew him. Her story takes readers back to 1826, when Mary, a young Southern belle from Louisville, decides to marry General Henry Atkinson. A virtual stranger much older than her, Henry takes Mary away from her family to his headquarters in St. Louis. While Henry tries to pacify the nearby Black Hawk Indians, Mary makes a home for herself and tries to get to know the man she married. Based on letters written by the real-life Mary Atkinson. Willa Award.

Holland, Cecelia.

An Ordinary Woman. **Forge, 1999. 223pp.**

Holland's dramatized biography of Nancy Kelsey, the first white woman to reach California, can be read either as a novel or as straight history. An "ordinary woman" with a pioneering spirit, fifteen-year-old Nancy accompanies her husband Ben from Missouri to California in 1838. Over the next three years she braves hunger, thirst, and illness, giving birth to several children along the way (not all of whom survive). The Kelsey family's arrival in California in 1841 is a testament to Nancy's fortitude and the American spirit. Fully documented, with footnotes and a bibliography.

Kelly, Carla.

Here's to the Ladies: Stories of the Frontier Army. **Texas Christian University Press, 2003. 259pp.**

Kelly, a ranger for the National Park Service, sets her collection of eight short stories amid garrison life on Western frontier army posts, but here the army wives have their say. The stories reflect hardship, love, and loss, all told sensitively and with vivid historical detail. Kelly also writes Regency romances.

Lee, Wendi.

The Overland Trail. **Forge, 1996. 317pp.**

In 1846, twenty-one-year-old America Hollis journeys along the Overland Trail from Independence, Missouri, to the Oregon Territories, with her new husband Will by her side and a child (by the lover who abandoned her) on the way. She loses Will and all their belongings during a violent storm, and other pioneers steal her newborn daughter after she gives birth. Two kindly Paiute Indians take her in, and with their help and understanding, America strives to get her child back. Part of Forge's Women of the West series (see this chapter and Index).

Lehrer, Kate.

✦ *Out of Eden*. **Harmony, 1996. 339pp.** 📖

While visiting Paris in the 1880s, Lydia Fulgate, an American widow, meets and befriends Charlotte Duret, a young French socialite. Disillusioned by failed romances and society's restrictions on women, the two decide to settle on the Kansas plains, in twin houses adjacent to one another, and begin a new life as sheep ranchers. Prairie life proves more difficult than they expected. Western Heritage Award.

Levy, JoAnn.

✦ *For California's Gold.* **University Press of Colorado, 2000. 268pp.**

In 1849, Sarah Daniels gives in to her husband Caleb's wishes to leave Illinois for distant California in search of gold. Although they agree to stay in the gold fields for only two years, Sarah doesn't really believe they'll ever come home. Sarah's vivid first-person narration makes Levy's novel seem almost autobiographical. Willa Award. Part of Women's West Series.

Miller, Dawn.

The Journal of Callie Wade. **Pocket, 1996. 330pp.**

Annotated in Chapter 11.

Murray, Earl.

Gabriella. **Forge, 1999. 319pp.**

Beginning on April 5, 1846 in St. Louis, Gabriella Hall, a young Englishwoman, records information about her days in her private journal. Gabriella, a talented artist, accompanies her fiancé, Sir Edward Albert Waterston-Garr III, on a hunting trip along the Oregon Trail. She plans to paint portraits of the native Indians. But Garr has other ideas; he wants to stop Americans from encroaching on the Pacific Northwest, which he believes should belong to Great Britain. As Edward clashes with Quincannon, a trapper and mountain man who wants to open Oregon Territory to trade, Quincannon and Gabriella develop an understanding that turns into love.

Newman, Holly.

A Lady Follows. **Forge, 1999. 382pp.**

In 1846, Carolina Harper, an American widow of Spanish descent, journeys along the Santa Fe Trail from Missouri to New Mexico to care for her orphaned cousins before war with Mexico escalates. Gerald Gaspard, her "mountain man" guide along the route, becomes more than a friend to Carolina. But she can manage well on her own, as shown in her dealings with her uncle, Diego Navarro, who wants to see all Anglos gone from New Mexico. Part of Forge's Women of the West series (see this chapter, and Index).

Osborn, Karen.

Between Earth and Sky. **Morrow, 1996. 306pp.**

Abigail Conklin, her husband, and their children leave Virginia in 1867 on a wagon train bound for New Mexico. Over the next 60 years, Abigail writes to her sister Maggie back home about the hardships forging a life in the Southwestern desert. While Abigail grows to love the landscape of her new home, finding many beautiful scenes worth painting, Maggie remains set in her old-fashioned, occasionally prejudicial ways. An epistolary novel.

Riefe, Barbara.

Against All Odds: The Lucy Scott Mitchum Story. **Forge, 1997. 286pp.**

Lucy Mitchum, her husband Noah, and their daughter Lynette board their prairie schooner in Baltimore in 1849. Noah has caught gold fever, and he means to strike it rich in California. Their six-month journey is fraught with hardship: violent encounters with Indians, illness, and the despair of their fellow travelers. Despite their lack of choice in whether to make the journey, it's the women in Lucy's party who keep up everyone's hope and strength.

Sandifer, Linda.

Raveled Ends of Sky. **Forge, 1998. 349pp.**

Native Bostonian Nancy Maguire, in search of adventure in 1843, yearns to achieve her dream of owning a horse ranch. She goes against her blue-blooded family's wishes by joining Joseph Ballinger Chiles's wagon train to the Mexican province of California. The men in Nancy's party feel threatened by her independence, which comes as a shock to her. Nancy befriends a widowed woman, Lottie England, who shares her adventurous spirit, and falls in love with Hart Daniels, a handsome frontiersman. Part of Forge's Women of the West series (see this chapter and Index).

Smiley, Jane.

The All-True Travels and Adventures of Lidie Newton. **Knopf, 1998. 452pp.**

Around 1855, Lidie Newton and her new husband Thomas make their way from Quincy, Illinois, to K.T. (Kansas Territory) with dreams of settling the verdant prairie and keeping it safe from slavery. The reality is anything but idyllic. Kansas's freezing winters and Kansans' hatred of abolitionists prove dangerous and ultimately tragic. Lidie, once thought to be unmarriageable for her outspokenness and tomboy ways, takes up the challenge and makes the land her own. Spur Award. **Literary.**

Turner, Nancy E.

These Is My Words: The Diary of Sarah Agnes Prine, 1881–1901. **ReganBooks, 1999.** ✍ 📖 **YA**

Sarah Agnes Prine, eighteen years old as she begins her diary in 1881, lives with her family on the frontier settlement near Tucson. Unable to bear the unremitting heat of the Arizona desert, Sarah and her family pack up their wagon and head to Texas. Throughout many deprivations and hardships, the resourceful Sarah embodies the family's strength and spirit, and her writing and poise mature throughout the novel. Initially she resists her attraction to Captain Jack Elliott, the army man assigned to protect the settlers, but their blossoming romance soon takes over her diary and heart. Based on the life of the author's great-grandmother.

Heroines of the West

These courageous Western women take their destinies into their own hands. They take on roles and occupations traditionally held by men: doctor, cattle rancher, businessperson, explorer. Others have a more traditional role, standing fast by their husbands during the times they're needed most. Although their road is paved with difficulty and occasional prejudice, it gains them respect in the long run.

Alter, Judy.

Director of Texas Christian University Press, Judy Alter has written fiction and nonfiction about the American West for both adults and young adults. Her best known works are fictional biographies of Western heroines.

Cherokee Rose. **Bantam, 1996. 308pp.** **YA**

Tommy Jo Burns, a young woman growing up on an Oklahoma ranch, always knew she was destined for greatness. Her skill as a trick roper catches the eye of President Theodore Roosevelt, who calls her America's first cowgirl. Determined to succeed, she joins Zach Miller's 101 Ranch Show, taking the name Cherokee Rose. She performs at Madison Square Garden and other venues, falling in love with several men whose paths cross hers. But despite her successful stage persona, she feels that there is something missing in her life. Based on the life of Lucille Mulhall, a real-life cowgirl.

Jessie. **Bantam, 1995. 436pp.** ✍ **YA**

Jessie Benton, born in 1824, is the daughter of a Missouri senator who grows up knowledgeable about the Washington political scene. She proves to be the perfect wife for John Charles Frémont—mapmaker, explorer, adventurer, and sometime politician—and accompanies him on many of his journeys to California, through the Panama Canal, and to Britain and Europe.

Libbie. **Bantam, 1994. 404pp.** ✍ **YA**

Elizabeth Bacon Custer, determined to protect her husband's name and privacy, left few records of her married life. Alter's imagined version of Libbie's journals records her private thoughts about her husband "Autie," George Armstrong

Custer, the brilliant man who won so many battles against the Indians but lost his life at the Little Bighorn. Despite Libbie's sacrifices on Autie's behalf and his occasional wandering eye, theirs is a true love story.

🎗 *Mattie*. **Doubleday, 1988. 181pp.**

Mattie Armstrong, a poor young woman of illegitimate birth, is taken in by a frontier physician and his family. Strong-willed and intelligent, Mattie becomes the nurse of the physician's wife and caretaker of his daughter, eventually attending college to become a doctor herself. At the age of eighty, Mattie tells her own story, looking back on her long, eventful life. Loosely based on the story of the first female doctor in Nebraska. Spur Award.

Brown, Corinne Joy.

MacGregor's Lantern. **Five Star, 2001. 392pp.**

In the 1870s, when Philadelphia banker's daughter Margaret Dowling weds Scotsman Kerr MacKennon, she looks forward to making a new start out West. When her husband is killed, Maggie shows her true mettle, taking over his partnership in a Colorado cattle ranch.

Burrows, Geraldine.

Chinatown Mission. **Five Star, 2002. 366pp.**

At the turn of the twentieth century, minister's daughter Lorna Davidson travels west to San Francisco to join the staff of the Presbyterian Mission Home, a safe house for young Chinese women victimized by the "yellow slave trade." Together with Donaldina Cameron (whose fictionalized life appears in Lenore Carroll's novel, below), Lorna stands fast in the face of San Francisco's corrupt practices, but doesn't expect to fall in love with the wrong man.

Carroll, Lenore.

One Hundred Girls' Mother. **Forge, 1998. 348pp.** **YA**

A missionary working in 1895 San Francisco, Thomasina McIntyre's ultimate goal is to free Chinese girls from their forced servitude in Chinatown's brothels. Due to her unceasing efforts on their behalf, Thomasina becomes known as Lo Mo, "one hundred girls' mother." Based on the life of real-life Western heroine Donaldina Cameron. Part of Forge's Women of the West series (see this chapter and Index).

Downing, Sybil.

Ladies of the Goldfield Stock Exchange. **Forge, 1997. 319pp.**

In the Gold Rush town of Goldfield, Nevada, in 1906, respectable women were cut off from profiting directly from successful strikes by trading mining stocks. Three enterprising women—college grad Meg Kendall, ex-prostitute Tess Wallace, and spinster Verna Bates—take on the male establishment together, braving scandal to set up their own stock exchange. Fictionalized, but based on historical events. Part of Forge's Women of the West series.

Gear, Kathleen O'Neal.

Thin Moon and Cold Mist. **Forge, 1995. 380pp.**

Robin Heatherton, a half-Cherokee woman spying for the Confederacy in 1864, loses her husband to Yankee gunfire. When Union forces discover her true identity, Robin flees westward to Colorado with her five-year-old son. Thomas Corley, a Union officer determined to see Robin dead for her role in his brother's death, is hot on her trail. After she arrives in Colorado Territory, she stakes a claim in a gold mine, only to find that it has already been claimed by Garrison Parker, a gruff Union army veteran. Part of Forge's Women of the West series.

Levy, JoAnn.

Daughter of Joy. **Forge, 1998. 318pp.** ✍

Ah Toy, a young Chinese woman, arrives in 1840s California as a slave, but protests when merchant Norman As-Sing tries to claim her. As the head of San Francisco's Chinese community, As-Sing is feared by all. Having no other way to survive, Ah Toy becomes a "daughter of joy," a prostitute, but doesn't hesitate to stand up for herself in the face of unfair treatment by As-Sing and others. Based on the life of the first Chinese woman to defend herself in an American court. Willa Award. Part of Forge's Women of the West series.

Robson, Lucia St. Clair.

Fearless. **Ballantine, 1998. 388pp.** ✍

Sarah Bowman, a six-foot, red-haired Amazon of a woman, signs on as a laundress and cook during General Zachary Taylor's campaign to win Texas from Mexico in 1845. Despite the death of her husband before the Mexican War begins, Sarah forges on, making a home for herself on and off the battlefield. Kind, tough, and compassionate, such is the strength of Sarah's personality that Taylor's troops dub her "the Great Western."

Windle, Janice Woods.

True Women Series.

Annotated below, under "Western Sagas."

Women Explorers and Adventurers

Westward exploration wasn't only the province of men. These independent nineteenth-century women, some of whom are historical characters, forge their own way west on scientific and other exploratory missions.

Byrd, Max.

Shooting the Sun. **Bantam, 2004. 306pp.**

In 1840, young astronomer Selena Cott joins an exploration team heading to the Southwest to take the first photograph of a solar eclipse. In charge of the project is Charles Babbage, whose Difference Engine will supposedly predict the correct time and place for best viewing. Yet nothing on this trip is what it seems. Just as an eclipse temporarily conceals the sun, Selena discovers that her fellow travelers are keeping some deadly secrets.

Coleman, Jane Candia.

Lost River. **Five Star, 2003. 213pp.**

In the early twentieth century, photographer Sidra Givens is hired to document an archaeological dig in New Mexico. A fearful atmosphere pervades the town of Lost River, for a powerful landowner kills off anyone who disagrees with him. When the landowner's daughter is murdered in revenge, Sidra courageously hides the main suspect, a ten-year-old boy whose parents were killed by the man's gang.

Murray, Earl.

In the Arms of the Sky. **Forge, 1998. 301pp.**

In 1873, Isabella Lucy Bird, an unmarried Englishwoman and travel writer in her forties, journeys to Estes Park, Colorado to see the great Rocky Mountains for herself. There she encounters danger and adventure, facing it all with aplomb. Isabella falls in love with "Rocky Mountain" Jim Nugent, an outlaw who wants to keep the park as public land. Murray's fictionalized account is based on the real Isabella's own travelogue, *A Lady's Life in the Rocky Mountains.*

Smith, Diane.

Letters from Yellowstone. **Viking, 1999. 226pp.** 📖 **YA**

In the spring of 1898, Dr. Howard Merriam invites A. E. Bartram, a young botanist and medical student from Cornell, to join his field study at Yellowstone National Park in Montana. What he doesn't realize is that the young doctor is really a woman—Alexandria Bartram, whose gender shocks the scientists when she arrives. She recounts her studies and specimen-collecting trips in letters and telegrams home. As the expedition proceeds, Alex accustoms herself to the team members' differing scientific methods, the presence of a Smithsonian researcher who may want to shut them down, and the disapproval of her fiancé back east.

Pictures from an Expedition. **Viking, 2002. 277pp.** 📖

In 1876, just after the Battle of the Little Bighorn, scientific illustrator Eleanor Peterson and her mentor, portrait painter Augustus Starwood, join a paleontological expedition to Montana. Their group is composed of many eccentric scientific-types, of which Starwood is the most flamboyant. As expected, members of the group bicker about proper research techniques and academic politics. A character-centered novel with a detailed backdrop of the stark Montana landscape.

Waldo, Anna Lee.

Sacajawea. Avon, 1984. 1408pp. ✍ ★

A mammoth novel about Sacajawea, the Shoshoni girl who accompanied Lewis and Clark on their journey west to the Pacific. Captured by the Arikara tribe at a young age, Sacajawea is won by trader Toussaint Charbonneau in a game. She travels with him, her son Baptiste on her back, while he works as a translator on Lewis and Clark's expedition. Sacajawea befriends Clark, and he relies on her expertise with native foods and the landscape. Throughout it all, she dreams of being reunited with her family.

Women's Lives and Relationships

These female-centered stories delve into the social issues women faced on the Western frontier: early suffrage, finding friends on the isolated prairie, and raising families. Think of this category as "women's fiction" set in the historical American West.

Brown, Irene Bennett.

<u>Women of Paragon Springs.</u>

Four interconnected novels about the heroism of women's day-to-day lives in Paragon Springs, Kansas, in the late nineteenth and early twentieth centuries.

Long Road Turning. Five Star, 2000. 238pp.

Meg Brennon adopts a new identity to hide from her abusive husband and forms an unlikely family group with Lucy Ann and Laddie, two orphaned children. They settle down on a Kansas farm, attracting other women and children who need help, though Meg always fears that her husband will find her.

Blue Horizons. Five Star, 2001. 311pp.

The little town of Paragon Springs, which Meg Brennon had helped found, continues to thrive. To get a legal divorce, Meg hires a St. Louis attorney, but in doing so, she risks divulging her locale to her cruel husband.

No Other Place. Five Star, 2002. 323pp.

In the 1880s, Aurelia Symington, the newly elected president of the Town Company, does her best to convince Paragon Springs that it needs a railroad to attract more businesses and settlers.

Reap the South Wind. Five Star, 2003. 214pp.

After losing her husband on a trip to claim his land on Oklahoma's Cherokee Strip, Lucy Ann Walsh returns to Paragon Springs and finds the entire town wrapped up in Populist politics. Lucy Ann, surprising herself, takes a stand for women's suffrage and defends the purpose of her neighbor's invention: a new-fangled flying machine.

Callen, Paulette.

Charity. Simon & Schuster, 1997. 310pp.

Schoolteacher Augusta "Gustie" Roemer travels west from Philadelphia with her lover, Clare, at the turn of the twentieth century. In Charity, South Dakota, Gustie mourns Clare, who dies just after their arrival, yet finds love again with the granddaughter of a Sioux matriarch. At the same time, Gustie helps her only friend, Lena Kaiser, solve a family murder. Gustie's search for acceptance is long and difficult, but her kindness and charity eventually win the town over. **Literary.**

Dallas, Sandra.

These character-centered novels, all about women's close-knit lives in the Western United States, tug at the emotions.

Buster Midnight's Café. **Random House, 1990. 277pp.**

Effa Commander, now in her seventies, reminisces about growing up in Butte, Montana, during the Depression. Then, she and her two best friends, Whippy Bird and May Anna, form a camaraderie that remains unbroken throughout their lives. May Anna moves to Hollywood and becomes movie star Marion Street. Rumors of involvement in an unpleasant murder case plague Marion, leaving her two longtime friends to set the record straight.

🎗 *The Chili Queen.* **St. Martin's Press, 2002. 292pp.** 📖

In the 1860s, Emma Roby arrives on a train in Nagitas, New Mexico, to marry a man she's never met. When he fails to show, Addie French, madam at the Chili Queen whorehouse, befriends Emma and takes her in. The pair, along with the whorehouse cook and a local bank robber, concoct a scheme to set them on the road to a better life. Spur Award.

The Persian Pickle Club. **St. Martin's Press, 1995. 196pp.** 📖

In the small farming town of Harleyville, Kansas, in the 1930s, farm wife Queenie Bean lives for the days when her quilting circle meets. Within the Persian Pickle Club, as the group is known, women trade gossip, create quilts, and bond with one another. When a city outsider named Rita infiltrates the group, Queenie befriends her, which causes bad feelings among her friends—especially when Rita drudges up a dark secret from their past.

Wood, Jane Roberts.

Lucy Richards Trilogy. 📖

Although Wood's trilogy may have the classic "prairie novel" plot—a young woman boards a train to take a schoolteacher job in a small West Texas town—Lucy Richards is no mere caricature. In a succession of letters and diary entries, Lucy reveals her hopes, dreams, and adventures in a gently humorous voice. Heartwarming novels brimming with nostalgia.

The Train to Estelline. Ellen C. Temple, 1987. 227pp.

In 1911, seventeen-year-old Lucinda Eliza Richards accepts a teaching position at the White Star School and boards a train to Estelline, Texas. As a single professional woman in an unfamiliar town, she faces numerous challenges.

A Place Called Sweet Shrub. Delacorte, 1990. 307pp.

Just before World War I, Lucy returns home to her family, where she cares for her Aunt Catherine and ponders her fate as an old maid. But her old beau, Josh Arnold, tracks her down. After a brief courtship, they marry and settle in sleepy Sweet Shrub, Arkansas, where Josh gets a job as a school principal.

Dance a Little Longer. Delacorte, 1993. 233pp.

In 1931, Josh and Lucy Arnold pick up and move back to dusty West Texas, where new employment awaits them both. Although they make some friends, the townspeople are hostile to educators. These and other hardships strain their happy marriage.

Romantic Westerns

These are romantic historicals (Chapter 4) set in the American West, mostly during the nineteenth century. The romance and the history play equal roles in the plot, and a happily-ever-after outcome, while rewarding, doesn't always happen. Like novels in the previous section, romantic Westerns are written by women for female readers. Readers should also investigate "Frontier and Western Romances" in Chapter 4; they have similar subjects but focus more on the romance than on history.

Bittner, Rosanne.

Mystic Indian Series.

In this three-book series of romance and adventure set between 1833 and 1876, Bittner illuminates the Lakotas' first encounters with European settlers. The novels are well researched, but readers should expect some role reversal from traditional Westerns: The Native Americans are brave souls with spiritual depth, while most of the whites have few redeeming qualities.

Mystic Dreamers. Forge, 1999. 288pp.

Stalking Wolf, an Oglala warrior, is promised to Star Dancer of the Brule Sioux. Although it's an arranged marriage, the two come to love each other.

Mystic Visions. Forge, 2000. 320pp.

A Lakota couple, holy woman Buffalo Dreamer and her warrior husband Rising Eagle, mourn the loss of their children to smallpox. Rising Eagle vows revenge for their loss.

Mystic Warriors. Forge, 2001. 366pp.

Buffalo Dreamer and her husband Rising Eagle hold the hide (and therefore the power) of the white buffalo, but when white men steal the robe, tragedy befalls the Lakota.

Bonner, Cindy.

McDade Cycle. 📖 **YA**

Four love stories set in Texas, from the 1880s through the 1920s. In Bonner's gritty Western novels, passion and beauty don't last forever, and optimistic endings aren't a given. When Bonner's heroines find true happiness, it is something to be treasured.

Lily. Algonquin Books of Chapel Hill, 1992. 336pp.

On Christmas Day, 1883, Lily DeLony first spots the man destined to become the love of her life—Marion Beatty, the youngest member of an outlaw gang. She runs away from home to be with him, ruining her spotless reputation and angering her father, one of the vigilantes on Beatty's trail.

Looking After Lily. Algonquin Books of Chapel Hill, 1994. 326pp.

When Marion lands in jail, his brother Haywood "Woody" takes charge of looking after Marion's pregnant young wife, Lily. Lily's bravery and resourcefulness make Woody wonder how he ever survived without her.

The Passion of Dellie O'Barr. Algonquin Books of Chapel Hill, 1996. 353pp.

In 1896, Lily's younger sister Dellie has been married for two years to kindly rancher Daniel O'Barr, one of Lily's former suitors. Dellie's overwhelming passion for Andy Ashland, a poor tenant farmer involved in Populist politics, ruins her marriage and leads her to commit a horrible crime.

Right from Wrong. Algonquin Books of Chapel Hill, 1999. 329pp.

Since childhood, Sunny DeLony (Lily and Dellie's niece) has loved her cousin Gil, and he loves her. But their parents disapprove of any romantic relationship between them. To avoid temptation, Gil enlists in the Army and fights during World War I in Europe, while Sunny marries a succession of men she doesn't love.

Brown, Irene Bennett.

Haven. Five Star, 2003. 239pp.

In 1893, Laila Mitchell makes her way to La Grande, Oregon, where she will meet her grandparents and hopefully get a chance to use the medical skills she acquired back home. Along the way she meets a widow, Kate Boston, whose journey to answer a help-wanted ad leads Laila to a new chance at love.

Charbonneau, Eileen.

Rachel LeMoyne. Forge, 1998. 317pp. **YA**

In 1847 Oklahoma, teachers choose Rachel LeMoyne, a half-Choctaw student, to accompany them to Ireland to distribute corn to the country's poor. In Ireland Rachel marries widower Darragh Ronan to rescue him from prison, and she returns with him to America. The couple faces anti-Irish prejudice wherever they go. When Darragh gets in trouble with the law after defending Rachel's name, they are forced to journey from St. Louis all the way to Oregon. Part of Forge's <u>Women of the West</u> series (see this chapter and Index).

Waltzing in Ragtime. **Forge, 1996. 477pp.**

In San Francisco in the early years of the twentieth century, Olana Whittaker is a rich man's daughter assigned to cover the opening of the Sequoia National Park for a local newspaper. Matthew Hart is a gentle park ranger who fears the incursion of lumbermen, such as Olana's father, onto the park's natural lands. The couple's fiery romance is frequently disturbed by Olana's family's influence, secrets from Matt's past, and the 1906 San Francisco earthquake.

Jenner, Gail L.

Across the Sweet Grass Hills. **Creative Arts, 2001. 303pp.**

In the late 1860s, Reverend Ralston brings his spoiled daughter Liza with him to minister to the Pikuni Indians of Montana. When their party is attacked, a half-white, half-Pikuni man named Red Eagle comes to their rescue. Despite the vast cultural differences between them, Liza and Red Eagle come to love each other. Willa Award.

Marvine, Dee.

Sweet Grass. **Five Star, 2003. 282pp.**

Twenty-nine year old Lili Tornquist, worried that she will never find a husband, leaves her Minnesota home to marry Gunnar Jorgeson, a distant cousin who runs a sheep ranch in Montana. When it becomes clear that her new husband isn't interested in marriage, Lili picks up and heads to Butte. There, she takes a job singing in a hurdy-gurdy house and tries to reconcile her need for independence with her affection for two different men.

Munn, Vella.

Seminole Song. **Forge, 1997. 315pp.**

In 1830s Florida, a former slave named Calida—scarred physically and emotionally after a traumatic past—learns to love again with Panther, a war chief of the Seminole.

Spirit of the Eagle. **Forge, 1996. 352pp.**

During the Modoc War of 1872–1873 in what is now southern Oregon, a Modoc woman named Luash finds romance with Jed Britton, an Army officer who survived a Sioux massacre.

Wind Warrior. **Forge, 1998. 350pp.** **YA**

In Alta California in the early 1800s, the invading Spaniards are set on crushing, enslaving, and converting the native Chumash. Lucita, the daughter of a Spanish army colonel, loves the native landscape and is attracted by the beauty of a proud Chumash warrior.

Pendergrass, Tess.

Colorado Trilogy.

A trilogy of three strong-willed Colorado women who find love in the late nineteenth century.

Colorado Shadows. Five Star, 2000. 364pp.

Maggie Parker's parents send her off to Oxtail, Colorado, after she shames them with a love affair. When she arrives, she finds her uncle and his family brutally murdered. Maggie has no choice but to turn to Marsh Jackson, her cousin's drunken brother-in-law.

Colorado Twilight. Five Star, 2001. 355pp.

Jordan Braddock, widowed twice over, heads out West to banish her grief and take up painting once again. When Jordan's train is held up by thieves, the man across the seat reveals himself as reformed gunfighter Elijah Kelly, and proceeds to saves her life.

Colorado Sunrise. Five Star, 2003. 384pp.

Harriet Jackson, distraught after Elijah Kelly's marriage to Jordan, takes up with city slicker Ash Brady even though she doesn't love him. When Elijah's brother Malachi comes to town, Harriet changes her mind.

Williams, Jeanne.

Williams, winner of multiple Spur awards, crafts realistic yet romantic tales of women's survival on the rough Western frontier.

Home Mountain. St. Martin's Press, 1990. 406pp. **YA**

After the deaths of her parents in 1881, sixteen-year-old Katie MacLeod brings her brother and sisters from Texas to Arizona, where they hope to start their own horse ranch. Cowboy Bill Radnor helps them settle in, and he and Katie gradually fall in love, but her dreams are derailed by neighbor Ed Larrimore.

Home Station. St. Martin's Press, 1995. 321pp.

In 1900, Lesley Morland's father Ed takes the job of station master in Bountiful, Kansas. Things go well at first. Bountiful's residents are busy making plans for the arrival of the railroad, and Lesley is thrilled when wagon driver Jim Kelly proposes. After Lesley's father is killed in a robbery, she takes up his duties at the railroad station, but her new responsibilities strain her marriage.

Lady of No-Man's Land. St. Martin's Press, 1998. 382pp. (Alternate title: *Prairie Bouquet*.) **YA**

Swedish immigrant Kirsten Mordal arrives in Texas in 1884 with little more than an instinct for survival. Though she falls in love with Irishman Patrick O'Brien, he is promised to another woman, so Kirsten sets out on the Western frontier armed with her sewing machine. As a "sewing woman" along the No Man's Land strip between Kansas and Texas, Kirsten travels the frontier crafting dresses for the region's pioneer women. She attracts one wealthy admirer who wants to marry her, but her heart remains set on Patrick.

No Roof But Heaven. **St. Martin's Press, 1990. 450pp. (Alternate title:** *Oh, Susanna!***)** **YA**

> Schoolteacher Susanna Alden leaves her Ohio home after the Civil War and settles in Dodge City, Kansas. She falls in love with a young doctor, Matt Rawdon, while struggling to survive in a prairie town where war between the North and the South never really ended.

The Unplowed Sky. **St. Martin's Press, 1994. 307pp.**

> When Hallie Meredith's father dies in 1924, her stepmother kicks her and her half-brother out of her house on the Kansas prairie. To get by, Hallie takes a post as housekeeper for a wealthy couple but is forced to leave when her employer, Quentin Radford, makes a pass at her. She takes a job cooking for the MacLeod brothers' threshing business. Hallie's budding romance with Garth MacLeod takes a back seat to the MacLeods' fight against dirty politics.

Wind Water. **St. Martin's Press, 1997. 309pp.**

> Since childhood, Julie McCloud has traveled the High Plains with her adoptive father, helping him and his crew install windmills. At the end of the nineteenth century, Julie and company settle in Oklahoma's No Man's Land to help three orphaned boys, who need a windmill to bring water to their community. She finds romance with Trace Riordan, who helps them out, but the group makes an enemy of a powerful rancher who wants their land.

Mining Boomtowns and the Gold Rush

After 1848, when miner James Marshall discovered gold at Sutter's Mill in California, people rushed west to California in droves. For fortune seekers around the globe, it was the American dream come to life. In these novels, as men and women head westward with visions of gold and silver, rough frontier communities spring up where they land. Fortunes are won and lost in these bustling mining towns, but the thrill doesn't last forever. When the ore runs out, it leaves behind only disappointment and heartache.

Alef, Daniel.

🏆 *Pale Truth*. **MaxIt, 2000. 588pp.** ✍

> In 1849, gold fever puts San Francisco on the map. Among the railroad magnates and prospectors is Mary Ellen, a pale-skinned slave's daughter from Georgia who sees a chance to make her fortune. In San Francisco, Mary Ellen establishes a large financial empire, guarding her every move in fear that her long-held secret may be revealed. Mary Ellen (Pleasant) and her cohorts are based on historical characters. This was meant to be the first of a trilogy, but subsequent volumes never appeared. *Foreword Magazine's* Book of the Year.

Allende, Isabel.

Daughter of Fortune. **HarperCollins, 1999. 399pp.**

> Annotated in Chapter 10.

Cleary, Rita.

Goldtown. Sunstone, 1996. 269pp.

Goldtown is based on the history of Virginia City, Montana. It's a ghost town today, but in the 1860s its streets were filled with men and women consumed by gold fever. Lee Cameron, a gambler and Confederate veteran, comes to Varina, Montana, with gold in his eyes and lust in his heart for Emma Dubois, his former lover. Unbeknownst to him, Emma gave birth to their child years ago. As the lovers get reacquainted, violence in the streets proves that the Civil War hasn't really ended.

Coleman, Jane Candia.

Matchless. Five Star, 2003. 244pp.

The story of Leadville's Horace Tabor and his second wife Baby Doe is legendary, but what of Horace's first wife, Augusta Pierce? Natives of Maine, Gusta and Horace Tabor make their way west, first to Kansas and then to Colorado, where they settle. When Horace strikes it rich in silver with his Matchless Mine, Gusta wants nothing more out of life, but Horace's greed runs rampant—especially when it involves an enticing young woman named Elizabeth McCourt. Meanwhile, Gusta continues with her successful business ventures, offering to bail Horace out when his fortunes fail.

Holland, Cecelia.

Lily Viner Series.

Two of the best novels from prolific historical novelist Holland, both featuring the intriguing Lily Viner, a young woman from the rough mining town of Virginia City, Nevada, who doesn't always agree with society's definitions of right and wrong.

Railroad Schemes. Forge, 1997. 271pp.

Lily Viner, a motherless fifteen-year-old in 1870s Los Angeles, agrees to help fake a stagecoach robbery provided nobody gets killed. This throws her into the path of "King" Callahan, an Irish outlaw who fights the coming of the railroad.

Lily Nevada. Forge, 1999. 224pp.

Lily starts a new life in San Francisco, where she joins a roving theatrical company and becomes the toast of the stage. But she never gives up her dream of finding the mother she lost long ago.

Jakes, John.

California Gold. Random House, 1989. 658pp.

James Macklin "Mack" Chance arrives in San Francisco in 1887 hoping to make his fortune like so many others have done before him. He's disillusioned quickly by the city's violence and corruption, especially among the railroad bigwigs. With gold mining a thing of the past, Mack strikes it big first with oil and then with the citrus industry—but his career-minded girlfriend refuses to marry him. A classic rags-to-riches story full of historical references. Many of California's great heroes make appearances: Teddy Roosevelt, William Randolph Hearst, and more.

Ledbetter, Suzann.

Megan O'Malley Series. `YA`

Irish immigrant Megan O'Malley doesn't let her gender interfere with her ambition to strike gold. Based on the real-life exploits of Nellie Cashman, subject of the author's Spur-award-winning biography.

Trinity Strike. Signet, 1996. 350pp.

Megan O'Malley, determined to make her way in a man's world, arrives in America from Ireland with her sister Frances. Not discouraged by anti-Irish prejudice, Megan takes a job as the first ever elevator operator. After she and Frances head farther west, Megan prospects for gold, becoming an inspiration to everyone who works for her.

Klondike Fever. Signet, 1997. 350pp.

In 1897, Megan and her teenage son B.D. hop a ship north to Alaska in the hopes of getting B.D. to settle down. In the town of Dawson in the Klondike, Megan strikes gold for real but is surprised by the reappearance of an old flame from her past.

Parker, Ann.

Silver Lies. **Poisoned Pen Press, 2003. 410pp.**

Annotated in Chapter 7.

Vernon, John.

All for Love. **Simon & Schuster, 1995. 235pp.** ✍

The rags-to-riches-to-rags story of "Baby Doe" Tabor is a Western legend. In 1879, Elizabeth McCourt Doe leaves her hometown of Oshkosh, Wisconsin, to make her fortune out west. In Leadville, Colorado, she meets the much-older Horace Tabor, the city's silver magnate, and persuades him to leave his wife Augusta and marry her. But for Baby, as Horace called her, life as a rich man's wife doesn't last long. After Horace dies in 1899, Baby stays on at a shack near their famous Matchless Mine with her two children, and dies impoverished and alone thirty-six years later. Vernon's literary retelling explains the characters' psychological motivations. **Literary.**

Wheeler, Richard S.

Wheeler is at his best when describing the frenetic atmosphere of Western mining boomtowns and the courageous men and women who came in search of wealth and ended up staying. His "Western soap opera" novels are complex psychological portraits of Western towns and their people.

Cashbox. **Forge, 1994. 381pp.**

Silver lures prospectors and adventurers to the small Montana town of Cashbox in the 1880s. Mining magnate Cornelius Daley aims to make his fortune in silver, while Sylvie Duvalier opens a club that caters to men's other needs. Their partnership mirrors the story of Horace and Baby Doe Tabor. Wheeler based the town of Cashbox on historical Castle, Montana.

Goldfield. **Forge, 1995. 379pp.**

Thousands of men and women hungry for wealth pour into Goldfield, Nevada, around the turn of the twentieth century. Among them are Maude Arbuckle, a go-getting woman who does her own prospecting; her lazy husband Harry, who takes credit for her efforts; and Hannibal Dash, a Midwestern professor who protects Maude from Harry's unsavory schemes.

Second Lives. **Forge, 1997. 348pp.**

In the 1880s, people come to Denver with the hope of starting over, but not all of them succeed. Lorenzo "Magnificent" Carthage, a silver mining has-been who has already gone from rags to riches and back to rags, convinces people to invest in his get-rich-quick schemes once again. Rose Edenderry, a saloon woman, tries to put aside her penchant for drink and loose living. Perhaps the most touching story is that of Homer Peabody, an aging attorney who shocks Denver by taking the case of Cornelia Kimbrough, a woman who wants a divorce from her unfeeling husband.

● *Sierra.* **Forge, 1996. 380pp.**

In 1849, Ulysses McQueen leaves his pregnant wife Susannah on their Iowa farm, promising to come back from California a rich man. His journey west is fraught with difficulty. Stephen Jarvis, an Army veteran, finds himself in the right place at the right time—Sutter's Mill, California, right when gold is discovered. Both men can't forget the women they left behind. Spur Award.

Sun Mountain. **Forge, 1999. 304pp.**

In 1900, sixty-year-old journalist Henry Stoddard reminisces about life in the mining boomtown of Virginia City, Nevada, during its heyday—the 1860s, when the Comstock Lode was discovered. Stoddard recounts his acquaintance with Samuel Clemens, the author who used his stories for the *Enterprise* to make his fortune.

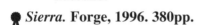

The Mythic West

This is the West as it never was, but perhaps as it should have been. These novels take traditional Western tales and turn them on their heads, which may not be all that much of a stretch given all of the other legends evoked by this period and place. Some of these novels retell old legends using a Western setting, and others create new ones. The characters' wacky and sometimes fantastical adventures are entertaining, humorous, and touching.

Berger, Thomas.

Little Big Man Series.

A fictional autobiography of Jack Crabb, presented as the only white man to survive Custer's Last Stand. Behind his tall-tale adventures and self-deprecating humor lies a serious tone, for this was one of the first novels to look behind the image of the "noble savage" and reveal Native Americans' humanity. Berger presents this theme in an entertaining, non-didactic way.

🎗 *Little Big Man.* Dial, 1964. 440pp. ★

At 111 years old, Jack Crabb has seen and done it all. Born to a white couple but adopted into the Cheyenne, Jack doesn't belong to either group, and he feels guilty whenever he considers the brutality that whites inflict on the American Indians. Between the 1840s and the Battle of the Little Big Horn in 1876, Jack tries a variety of careers: drunkard, hustler, mule-skinner, and more. He meets many famous people along the way and doesn't hesitate to name-drop. Western Heritage Award.

The Return of Little Big Man. Little, Brown, 1999. 432pp.

Crabb, who died at the end of *Little Big Man* at age 112, admits he faked his own death to get out of an unfair publishing contract. He resumes his life story after the Battle of the Little Big Horn and proceeds to meet more famous historical characters like Annie Oakley, Wyatt Earp, and Doc Holliday. Then he joins Buffalo Bill Cody's Wild West show, which already has Sitting Bull as a headliner.

Kimball, Philip.

Liar's Moon. Holt, 2000. 288pp.

A folkloric novel about the so-called winning of the West, told from multiple points of view that alternate and occasionally fade into one another. In one thread, two children—an African-American girl and a white boy—fall off the back of a wagon in 1859. Lost to their people, they are raised by coyotes. In another thread, a young woman captured by Indians from her Texas home helps to track what became of the children. Their paths all cross in the end. Elements of magical realism. **Literary.**

Latham, Aaron.

Code of the West. Simon & Schuster, 2001. 494pp.

Latham takes the classic King Arthur legend and moves it to the Old West. Cowhand Jimmy Goodnight does the impossible when he pulls an axe from an anvil at a local county fair. He creates the Home Ranch, a cattle kingdom, with the prize money. He and handsome horseman Jack Loving are best friends, until Goodnight rescues beautiful Revelie Sanborn from an evil band of outlaws.

Recknor, Ellen.

🎗 *Prophet Annie.* Avon, 1999. 330pp.

Within the body of twice-widowed, twenty-two-year-old Annie Pinkerton Boone Newcastle resides the spirit of her late husband Jonas, who is all too eager to speak his mind through poor Annie's body. She travels with P. T. Barnum throughout the Old West of the 1880s, spouting wisdom and predicting the future. Her exploits make her famous, but not always in a good way. Spur Award; Willa Award.

The Real Wild West

These gritty novels don't pull any punches about life on the Western frontier. They ignore the romantic mythology of the Wild West and focus on the bloody, violent reality. Here there are no good guys or bad guys, just people struggling to stay alive as best they can—even if it means abandoning all morality. With their emphasis on gore, degradation, and physical brutality, these novels aren't for the faint of heart.

Askew, Rilla.

The Mercy Seat. **Viking, 1997. 427pp.**

In 1887, brothers John and Fayette Lodi pick up and move from Kentucky to southeastern Oklahoma so that Fayette can avoid criminal prosecution. Ten-year-old Mattie, John's daughter, observes her family's gradual disintegration. She fights to hold their family together, despite her mother's death, her own youth, and her uncle Fayette's schemes to use John's gunsmithing skills for his own gain. Mattie's gift of foresight, remarked upon by a Choctaw healer, doesn't prevent a violent ending. Western Heritage Award. **Literary.**

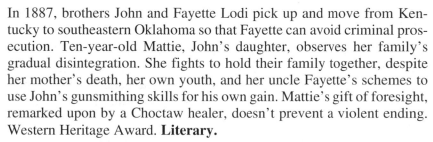

Estleman, Loren.

The Master Executioner. **Forge, 2001. 270pp.**

Over the years, hangman Oscar Stone has honed his skills into an art form. Absorbed by his extraordinary accomplishments, he travels from town to town attending many executions, growing more skillful with each one. When the wife who left him years ago reappears one day with a revelation, he finally comes to terms with his role in life. A haunting psychological Western. Western Heritage Award.

Fackler, Elizabeth.

Texas Lily. **Forge, 1997. 416pp.**

Having lost her father in the infamous Lincoln County War, Lily Cassidy decides to marry her father's old friend, widower Emmett Moss, to provide for her mother and crippled brother. In doing so, she rejects her longtime sweetheart, Jasper Stone. Emmett helps her get revenge on her father's killer, but their plans turn into bloody tragedy.

Houston, James D.

Snow Mountain Passage. **Knopf, 2001. 317pp.**

A novel of the Donner Party's fateful expedition west from Springfield, Illinois, during the winter of 1846–1847. When James Frazier Reed, one of the party's leaders, kills a man in self-defense, he leaves the group and heads on to California alone. Meanwhile, his family gets stranded with the rest of the party in the Sierra Nevadas during a harsh winter. Eight-year-old daughter Patty, from the viewpoint of old age, records their ordeal in her journal—the beauty of the landscape, the frigid weather, and their intense hunger and desperation, which forces some to resort to cannibalism. Despite the gruesome subject matter, Patty tells the story with sensitivity and compassion.

Huebner, Andrew.

American by Blood. **Simon & Schuster, 2000. 245pp.** ✍

Gus Huebner, a scout in the U.S. Army, arrives at the Little Big Horn River one day after the infamous battle and has no choice but to clean up the gruesome mess. He and two other scouts, James Bradley and William Gentle, track down the American Indian tribes that perpetrated the massacre, bent on vengeance for their lost comrades. Written in a literary style, with short sentences and no quotation marks. The author is the protagonist's great-great-grandson. **Literacy.**

Jones, Robert F.

Deadville. **St. Martin's Press, 1998. 244pp.**

In 1833, brothers Dillon and Owen Griffith head into the Wild West in search of wealth, but instead find shocking, bloodthirsty adventure among the Arikara Indians, who still rule the land. Dillon forms a partnership with African-American mountain man/Indian chief James Pierson Beckworth, who hides a murderous past.

McCarthy, Cormac.

Blood Meridian, or, The Evening Redness in the West. **Random House, 1985. 337pp.** ★

The Kid, a fourteen-year old boy from Tennessee, gets a real education in how the West really is when he joins a band of bounty hunters set on obtaining Apache scalps along the Texas–Mexico border in the 1850s. The crimson sunsets, combined with the bloody carnage and the red desert landscape, are nothing less than hell transferred to a Western setting. Lyrically written, but intensely dark and grim; it may be one of the most violent books ever written. **Literary.**

McGiffen, Steve.

Tennant's Rock. **St. Martin's Press, 2001. 257pp.**

Since age thirteen, Sissy has been forced to live with Swann, a violent rapist, on her family's Sacramento Valley farm; she and her mother were powerless to stop him. Now at almost twenty, Sissy has two children by Swann, who has usurped the role of head of the household. When her brother Nate returns from prison, Sissy hopes he can save their family, but she doesn't fully trust him either. An unremittingly grim tale set in 1860s California.

Swarthout, Glendon Fred.

🎗 *The Homesman.* **Weidenfeld & Nicolson, 1988. 239pp.** ★

The realities of the Western frontier—with its harsh winters, lack of comforts, and isolation—prove to be more than some women can handle. Mary Bee Cuddy, a plain-faced schoolmarm, serves as a "homesman," agreeing to escort four young wives from Missouri back home to Iowa after life out West drives them into madness. A ruthless land-grabber, whom Mary saves from a lynching, unwillingly accompanies them all. Spur Award; Western Heritage Award.

The Early Twentieth-Century West

Life on the Western frontier was never easy, but the early twentieth century was particularly tough for individuals and families. These novels deal with social issues out West during the first decades of the last century: racial tension, religious prejudice, organized crime, and the overwhelming poverty of the Great Depression. Readers who don't believe that this occasionally grim setting can work in a romance should investigate Dorothy Garlock's homespun Americana romances (Chapter 4).

Askew, Rilla.

✤ *Fire in Beulah*. Viking, 2001. 376pp.

When Althea Whiteside is thirteen, her brother Japheth is born, setting into motion a chain of events that affect her entire life. She escapes her poverty-stricken family by marrying oil mogul Franklin Dedmeyer and becoming a woman of society. Eventually her uneasy relationship with her young, African-American, live-in maid Graceful Whiteside will reveal her troubled past and culminate in the Tulsa Race Riot of 1921. American Book Award. **Literary.**

Doig, Ivan.

Bucking the Sun. Simon & Schuster, 1996. 412pp.

When the New Deal comes to Montana to put local residents to work constructing the Fort Peck Dam along the Missouri River, it floods the Duff family's farm. Forced out of business, the Duffs—father Hugh, his wife Meg, their sons, and their wives—move to the shanty town that springs up alongside the river. Naturally, they all disagree on how to deal with the changes. **Literary.**

Downing, Sybil.

The Binding Oath. University Press of Colorado, 2001. 200pp.

It's 1922, but for all the respect that Liz O'Brien gets as a reporter for the *Denver Post*, it might as well be Victorian times. When she gets wind of a story about the KKK's involvement in political matters, she immediately suspects that they're also behind a murder in Denver's slums. Nobody believes her, not even her editor.

Fire in the Hole. University Press of Colorado, 1996. 239pp.

Widowed attorney Alex MacFarlane defends the young man who had tried to save her husband in a mining accident. By protecting the interests of immigrant miners, she incites the fury of the coal companies and the

U.S. government. This story about the Ludlow Massacre, in which twenty miners, wives, and children were murdered by Colorado militiamen and other strike-breakers in 1914, was the first volume of the publisher's short-lived <u>Women's West</u> series (which also includes JoAnn Levy's *For California's Gold*).

Turner, Nancy E.

The Water and the Blood. Regan, 2001. 416pp. 📖

Philadelphia "Frosty" Summers, the misfit middle daughter of a devout, bigoted Southern Baptist family in 1940s east Texas, grows up with unclear definitions of sin and righteousness. It's only after Frosty escapes her town and her abusive mother by working for the war effort in California that she realizes she doesn't have to buy into her family's legacy. Frosty's perceptions of racial inequality gradually change, particularly after she finds love with Gordon Benally, a Navajo soldier who works secretly for the war effort. **Literary.**

Williams, Jeanne.

The Longest Road. St. Martin's Press, 1993. 389pp.

During the Great Depression, Laurie Field and her brother Buddy are left with their grandfather when a dust storm kills their mother. Determined to join their father in California, the children walk, ride boxcar trains, and hitch rides throughout the Western states. For Laurie, the gift of a harmonica symbolizes her journey to find a place to belong.

Western Sagas

The harsh life on the Western frontier can bring families together, but it can also force them apart. These family sagas, set between the nineteenth century and the present, are told from a variety of viewpoints: newly arrived immigrants, ranchers, Native Americans, Mexicans, and more. These are somewhat more action-oriented than sagas set in other locales, such as those listed in Chapter 5.

Blakely, Mike.

Holcomb Series.

Saga of the Holcomb family, cattle ranchers who settle in the Pikes Peak region of Colorado just before the Civil War. The theme of country-western music is present throughout, in the form of song lyrics and in the chosen avocation of son Caleb. Blakely is an accomplished western/folk music performer himself.

Shortgrass Song. Forge, 1994. 431pp.

After the Mexican War, Ab Holcomb brings his family—wife Ella, and his three sons Matthew, Pete, and Caleb—to the Colorado ranges in the hope of starting up a cattle ranch. Their fortunes improve, but the stress of frontier life and the threat of Indian raiders weighs them down.

Too Long at the Dance. Forge, 1998. 532pp.

Caleb Holcomb has grown up to be a cowboy musician despite his father's disapproval. Amid his other adventures on the range, his strong moral code prevents him from acting on his attraction to his brother's widow, Amelia.

Bowman, Doug.

The Copelands. **Forge, 1999. 285pp.**

In 1866, having survived the Civil War, Kentuckian Seth Copeland loads up wagons with his parents and six children and heads west to Texas. He achieves his dream of making a fortune in cattle ranching, but the wild ways of his sons threaten to derail all his plans.

Doig, Ivan.

Montana Trilogy. ★ 📖

The continuing saga of two Scottish immigrant families in Montana's rural Two Medicine Country, and the ways they adjust to pioneer life out West. Doig overlays the innate tragedy of Western frontier life with rewarding and human qualities. Set over a hundred-year period in Montana's history, beginning in 1889. **Literary.**

Dancing at the Rascal Fair. Atheneum, 1987. 405pp.

Friends Angus McKaskill and Rob Barclay arrive in Montana from Scotland in 1889 with plans to set up homesteads. They each build up flocks of sheep to raise, but the harsh land and stark winters prove difficult to master. Over the next thirty years, their friendship strains due to both men's stubbornness and Angus's marriage to Rob's sister, whom he only marries after the loss of his first love.

🎗 *English Creek.* Atheneum, 1984. 339pp.

Jick McKaskill, age fourteen in 1939, grows into maturity and wisdom. At his family's ranch in Two Medicine Country, Jick watches his older brother leave to become a cowboy, defying his parents. A dangerous forest fire threatens his community that summer, and as a result, Jick discovers his proper place. Western Heritage Award.

Ride with Me, Mariah Montana. Atheneum, 1990. 324pp.

In 1989, the year of Montana's centennial, Jick McKaskill's daughter Mariah, a news photographer, takes him (and an enterprising reporter) on a whirlwind tour of the state's history.

Jekel, Pamela.

She Who Hears the Sun. **Kensington, 1999. 358pp.**

In 1847, three generations of women—the chief's wife Deezbaa, her daughter Ayoi, and granddaughter Pahe, "she who hears the sun"—discuss how best to hold off European settlers in this time of great change. Jekel takes inspiration from the women of the Navajo people of the

American Southwest, who have survived despite numerous efforts of the U.S. Army to destroy them.

L'Amour, Louis.

Sackett Family Series. ★

At the beginning of this seventeen-book series, Barnabas Sackett travels to the New World after being exiled from Elizabethan England. Over the next ten generations, Sackett descendants settle and conquer the American frontier, from the mountains of Tennessee to the plains of the American West. The first four novels take place between 1600 and 1620, after which the saga jumps to the 1840s and continues straight on to the 1870s. Among this close extended family, readers will find cattle-drivers, sharpshooters, gold-seekers, explorers, and ranchers—all prototypes of the men and women who won the west. L'Amour's *The Sackett Companion* explains his inspiration for the series and serves as a guide to characters, relationships, plots, and commonly used terms. Titles are listed in historical order.

Sackett's Land. Saturday Review, 1974. 198pp.

To the Far Blue Mountains. Saturday Review, 1976. 176pp.

The Warrior's Path. Bantam, 1980. 226pp.

Jubal Sackett. Bantam, 1985. 375pp.

Ride the River. Bantam, 1983. 184pp.

The Daybreakers. Bantam, 1960. 204pp.

Lando. Bantam, 1962. 122pp.

Sackett. Bantam, 1961. 151pp.

Mojave Crossing. Bantam, 1964. 150pp.

The Sackett Brand. Bantam, 1965. 120pp.

The Sky-liners. Bantam, 1967. 151pp.

The Lonely Men. Bantam, 1969. 140pp.

Mustang Man. Bantam, 1966. 137pp.

Galloway. Bantam, 1970. 156pp.

Treasure Mountain. Bantam, 1972. 187pp.

Ride the Dark Trail. Bantam, 1981. 176pp.

Lonely on the Mountain. Bantam, 1980. 194pp.

McMurtry, Larry.

Berrybender Narratives.

When Lord and Lady Berrybender take six of their fourteen children and a large entourage of servants on an exciting hunting expedition on the American frontier, they really have no idea what the West has in store. They encounter a good deal of gruesome violence, but the Berrybenders' selfish attitude won't get them much sympathy from readers. A farcical adventure set in the 1830s.

Sin Killer. Simon & Schuster, 2002. 300pp.

Strong-willed Tamsin Berrybender shocks her parents with her intention to marry Jim Snow, a trapper and mountain man better known as "Sin Killer."

The Wandering Hill. Simon & Schuster, 2003. 302pp.

Along the Yellowstone River, Tamsin, married to Jim Snow and heavily pregnant with his child, watches her father descend into madness.

By Sorrow's River. Simon & Schuster, 2003. 347pp.

As the Berrybenders and company travel south from the Great Plains to Santa Fe, Tamsin tries and fails to bring up her young son Monty as a proper Englishman.

Folly and Glory. Simon & Schuster, 2004. 236pp.

As Americans and Mexicans fight over Texas, officials keep the Berrybenders under house arrest in Santa Fe. Mexican guards release them and escort them on to Vera Cruz, but the journey proves tragic for most of them. The title is ironic, since by the end there's been far more folly than glory on this horrific nightmare of a trip.

Lonesome Dove Saga. ★ **YA**

In this classic saga of Western heroism and tragedy, McMurtry details the adventures, lives, and loves of two former Texas rangers, Augustus "Gus" McCrae and Woodrow F. Call, on the barren Texas landscape. Epic in scope and told in plain language, these character-centered dramas have proven to be hits with thousands of readers. The partnership between Gus, easygoing and sensitive, and Woodrow, a gruff workaholic, is a study in contrasts. Their friendship carries them through many tough times: Indian attacks, periods of drought and hunger, and arguments among their entourage. McMurtry patterned his protagonists on legendary cattle drivers Oliver Loving and Charles Goodnight.

Dead Man's Walk. Simon & Schuster, 1995. 477pp.

Woodrow Call and Gus McCrae, two young and untried Texas Rangers, head to Santa Fe to recapture the city from the Mexicans. Crazed Comanche Indians and deadly forces of nature meet them at every turn, and the treacherous Dead Man's Walk proves to be their greatest challenge. McMurtry portrayed the early lives of the *Lonesome Dove* protagonists in this prequel.

🎗 ***Comanche Moon.*** Simon & Schuster, 1997. 752pp.

Another prequel to *Lonesome Dove*, set in pre-Civil War Texas. Call and McCrae, still relatively young men, get their feet wet wresting control of Texas from the Comanche. Their primary foes are Comanche warrior Buffalo Hump and his son, Blue Duck, who discovers the deadly power of gunfire. Spur Award.

🎗 *Lonesome Dove.* Simon & Schuster, 1985. 843pp.

In the 1870s, former Texas lawmen Gus and Woodrow co-own the Hat Creek Cattle Company in the small town of Lonesome Dove. Though content with their carefree life, another ex-ranger speaks in glowing terms of the Montana grasslands, ideal ranching ground that's still unclaimed. Together, the men pull together a herd of Mexican cattle and proceed to drive them north. The problem is, a bunch of other people insist on coming along for the ride. Pulitzer Prize.

The Streets of Laredo. Simon & Schuster, 1993. 589pp.

The railroad hires Captain Woodrow Call, practically a living legend, to find Joey Garza, a Mexican bandit and train robber. Raised by Apaches, Garza has been impossible to track down. With the help of Pea Eye, Call's former deputy, Call gives it his best shot.

Ryan, Mary.

Hope. St. Martin's Press, 2003. 470pp. ✍

Mary Ryan's great-granduncle, Tom Walsh, emigrates with his sister Maria from Ireland to America in 1869, after their family's estate is seized. They make their way to Ouray, Colorado, where they have heard that gold is available for the taking. Amazingly, Tom strikes it rich, becoming one of the country's richest men over the next thirty years. Having made good, Tom returns to Ireland on a visit, where his attempts to help out the villagers financially are taken as insults and turned down flat. His fortunes turn worse when his daughter Evalyn convinces him to buy the cursed Hope Diamond. Based on a true story.

Sherman, Jory.

Baron Family of Texas.

Saga of a Texas cattle ranching family, the Barons, from the early days of the Texas Republic through the end of the Civil War. Patriarch Martin Baron, a Gulf fisherman from New Orleans, dreams of owning a cattle empire. His Box B Ranch grows to encompass over a million acres on the Texas frontier. Danger comes in the form of Mexicans and Apaches, and Martin's wild son Anson frequently disagrees with him. The first published volume, *Grass Kingdom*, features a later generation of Barons who eke out a living during Prohibition.

The Barons of Texas. Forge, 1997. 319pp.

The Baron Range. Forge, 1998. 320pp.

The Baron Brand. Forge, 2000. 317pp.

The Baron War. Forge, 2002. 318pp.

The Grass Kingdom. Tor, 1994. 412pp.

Stegner, Wallace.

🎗 *Angle of Repose.* Doubleday, 1971. 569pp. ★ 📖

Lyman Ward, a wheelchair-bound historian whose marriage has failed, decides to write a fictional biography about his pioneer grandparents to discover why they grew apart over the years. Through their letters and documents, Lyman pieces together the story of Susan, his grandmother, who moved from the East Coast when she married his grandfather, Oliver Ward, a mining engineer in the late nineteenth century. Pulitzer Prize.

Vanderhaeghe, Guy.

The Last Crossing. **Atlantic Monthly, 2004. 393pp.**

Annotated in Chapter 10.

Williams, Jeanne.

Arizona Saga.

This three-volume saga, set in Arizona from 1847 until the modern day, focuses on the proud women of an Arizona family. It begins with Socorro Quintana, a young Spanish woman whose family is killed by Indians in the mid-nineteenth century. When she rescues Irishman Patrick O'Shea from almost certain death by dehydration in the Arizona desert, he falls in love with her instantly. Over the years, Socorro's original Spanish blood mingles with Irish (via Patrick), English, and even Apache, at the home they call the Rancho del Socorro. There's plenty of romance, plus danger aplenty in the form of Apache raids, starvation, and governmental oppression, yet still the family goes on.

The Valiant Women. Pocket, 1980. 496pp. Spur Award.

Harvest of Fury. Pocket, 1981. 400pp.

A Mating of Hawks. Pocket, 1983. 276pp.

Windle, Janice Woods.

True Women Series.   **YA**

Janice Woods Windle writes imaginatively reconstructed fictional biographies of her own Texas ancestors, who participated in many of the events in the state's long and stormy history and who knew some of Texas's most famous residents, such as Sam Houston and Lyndon Johnson. All are based on thorough primary source research, but the result is anything but dry.

True Women. Putnam, 1993. 451pp.

As a child in the 1830s, Windle's great-great-grandmother, Euphemia Texas Ashby King, flees the wrath of Mexican general Santa Anna with her older sister Sarah. Another ancestor, Georgia Virginia Lawshe Woods, travels with her husband from Georgia to San Marcos, where she and her children fight off Union soldiers on their own. Euphemia's daughter-in-law, Bettie Moss King, survives a frightening encounter with wolves and fights against the rise of the Klan. The TV miniseries *True Women* plays up the friendship between Euphemia and Georgia, though in history they were mere acquaintances.

Hill Country. Longstreet, 1998. 474pp.

In the wild Texas Hill Country in the 1870s, Laura Hoge, the author's maternal grandmother, grows up in a ranch family living alongside the Blanco River. Choosing domestic stability over wild romance, Laura marries Peter Woods, an older man with a love for horses. The life of the Woods family intertwines with that of the Johnsons, their longtime neighbors. Rebekah, later the mother of President Lyndon Johnson, shares Laura's lifelong interest in Hill Country politics.

Will's War. Longstreet, 2002. 366pp.

In 1917, anti-German sentiment runs high, and the German-American families of Seguin, Texas, find themselves the victims of prejudice and persecution. When the federal government accuses Windle's maternal grandfather, union sympathizer Will Bergfeld, of participating in a conspiracy to assassinate President Wilson, his family can't believe it. Unfortunately for his attorney, Will is a kind but exasperatingly hotheaded young man who prefers to handle his own defense. His loving family fights an uphill battle to clear Will's name.

Chapter 7

Historical Mysteries

Historical mysteries present readers with a puzzle to solve—most typically, figuring out who committed a murder or murders. Readers combine their interest in times past with an intellectual challenge, one in which they can try to figure out "whodunit" by delving through clues along with the protagonist. As in Gary Warren Niebuhr's *Make Mine a Mystery* (Libraries Unlimited, 2003), the works covered in this chapter are mystery novels in their most traditional sense. That is, they are works of historical fiction in which detectives try to serve justice by solving crimes.

Today, historical mysteries form one of the most popular subgenres of historical fiction, and the trend shows no signs of slowing down. Most historical mysteries occur in series, which gives readers the chance to get comfortable with the characters, the era, and the physical setting. Readers who enjoy historical mysteries in series find that over time, even unfamiliar settings such as ancient Egypt or feudal Japan can feel like home.

The subgenre is not new, though its current popularity might make readers think otherwise. Agatha Christie's ancient Egyptian mystery *Death Comes at the End* (1944) was an early entry, as were Lillian de la Torre's short story collections starring Dr. Samuel Johnson as detective. Josephine Tey's *Daughter of Time* (1951), about a modern Scotland Yard detective who becomes intrigued by a portrait of England's Richard III, was one of the first modern novels to get readers thinking about historical crimes. Although Tey's novel takes place in the present, it is still beloved by historical mystery fans. In the late 1970s and early 1980s, Ellis Peters started a trend with her popular Brother Cadfael medieval mysteries, which are still widely read. Peters set the bar for the subgenre with her suspenseful plots and historical accuracy.

Many series that first got their start in the 1980s and early 1990s, such as Elizabeth Peters' Amelia Peabody and Steven Saylor's Roma Sub Rosa, are still going strong, with new volumes appearing about every year. Long-running paperback series, such as those by Margaret Frazer and Robin Paige, have grown so popular that their publisher has made the transition to hardcover. New series spring up regularly, as do new stand-alone titles. Many well-known romance writers—Roberta Gellis, Patricia (P. B.) Ryan, Penelope Williamson—have successfully made the transition to historical mystery, to the delight of readers who enjoy novels in both genres. These crossover titles also gain the historical mystery subgenre many new converts.

On the other hand, the sheer number of titles appearing today may make librarians wonder if publishers are choosing quantity over quality. The market may become saturated at some point, but this hasn't happened yet. Only time will tell which new series will survive to become classics. Several major awards in the mystery genre are devoted specifically to historical mysteries, such as the Bruce Alexander Historical Award, the Anthony for best historical mystery (awarded first in 2004), and the Ellis Peters Historical Dagger. This demonstrates both the prevalence and the popularity of this subgenre within the larger mystery field.

In contrast to mysteries set in contemporary times, protagonists in historical mysteries are challenged to solve murder cases without employing modern forensic methods. Instead, they must use whatever tools and clues their era and setting make available. For the protagonists, this means not only being an astute observer of people and personalities, but also being well versed in the era's political and social realities, because these factors are frequently motives for murder. Some historical mystery sleuths have their own investigative specialties as well. For example, Kathy Lynn Emerson's Elizabethan amateur sleuth, Susanna, Lady Appleton, is an expert in herbalism, which means that she's familiar with the effects of plant-based poisons.

Readers have different degrees of tolerance for mysteries featuring historical characters as sleuths, even though traditional biographical novels (covered in Chapter 2) are generally well accepted. The main issue here is plausibility, because the pretext of these novels runs contrary to known historical facts. Did the historical Queen Elizabeth I really disguise herself as a servant and sneak out of her castle at night to solve crimes, as in Karen Harper's novels? Did the real Mark Twain stumble across dead bodies while he was on the lecture circuit, as author Peter Heck imagines? Most likely not. However, if the setting, dialogue, and other factors seem historically authentic, many readers can willingly suspend their disbelief long enough to enjoy the story. Other readers, those who take a more purist view of historical truth, will want to stick with mysteries in which fictional characters do all the sleuthing.

This chapter is organized by historical setting (place and period), as this is of great interest to readers who specifically look for historical mysteries, but there are other factors that will appeal to readers. The mystery genre uses standard terms to define two of these characteristics, as discussed below.

The personal qualities of the main character, as well as some secondary characters, can make or break a mystery for a reader. This is especially true because most historical mysteries occur in series, and the detective must be someone readers are willing to stick with through multiple cases. People may prefer to read about protagonists who are either male or female, of a particular personality type, or with a certain career or role in society. These are noted in the annotations. Readers enjoy solving crimes along with the detective, and the way they go about doing so is determined by the official role the detective has in the investigation, if any. Common terms describing the main character in mysteries are described below. For readers who look for historical mysteries featuring a particular type of detective, these terms will be listed in bold at the end of each title or series annotation.

Public detectives. In the case of historical mysteries, these novels feature members of the local police force, who investigate crimes with the authority of the state behind them. In these novels, which can also be called "police procedurals" (though this term is more often used for modern police detective mysteries), members of a crime-solving team follow official police procedure in solving crimes. These detectives may depend on one another for support or go out on their own. Examples are Lt. Bak (by author Lauren Haney, ancient Egypt) and Sir John Fielding (Bruce Alexander, Georgian England).

Private detectives. These investigators work on their own, for hire. They may have their own investigative agency. Examples are William Monk (Anne Perry, Victorian England) and Marcus Didius Falco (Lindsey Davis, ancient Rome).

Amateur detectives. This is the most common type of protagonist in historical mysteries. Individual members of society get dragged into their first investigation by chance, usually when someone either physically nearby or emotionally close to them is murdered. Over time, word of their success gets around, and people ask them to help solve crimes. Authors must take special care to make these characters' actions believable, because average people tend not to stumble upon murders as often as public or private detectives might. These sleuths also have to be very creative in gathering evidence, because they rarely have an official role in an investigation. Likewise, they may run into opposition from local law enforcement officers, who resent outsiders' interference in police matters. Examples are Sister Frevisse (Margaret Frazer, medieval England), and Catherine Williams (Stephen Lewis, colonial America).

When speaking about historical mysteries, detective type isn't always obvious, because an official "police force" may not have existed at the time the novel is set. However, most eras had judges or other arbiters of law who fulfilled these roles for society. In this book, legal professionals who investigate on behalf of the government and whose word has the force of law are listed as public detectives. Series of this type include Edward Marston's <u>Domesday Books</u> and Peter Tremayne's <u>Sister Fidelma Series</u>. On the other hand, Sharon Kay Penman's <u>Justin de Quincy Series</u>, which involves an untrained young man asked by Eleanor of Aquitaine to look into crimes, is listed as an amateur detective series.

The level of action and violence in historical mysteries serves as another appeal factor for readers. Novels in this chapter are identified with one of the following terms, placed in bold at the end of the title or series annotation, as appropriate.

Hard-boiled. These action-packed mysteries follow lone private detectives who solve brutal murders in the heart of the inner city. They are dark, violent, and suspenseful, with crime scenes graphically described. These aren't common in historical mystery, since hard-boiled novels practically require modern settings. Example are the Nathan Heller series (Max Allan Collins, twentieth century America) and Toby Peters series (Stuart Kaminsky, 1940s Hollywood).

Cozy (also called "soft-boiled") . These lighthearted mysteries use comfortable settings such as English country houses, rural villages, or small towns—places that would normally be pleasant to live in, were it not for the murders that take place nearby. There is no graphic violence, or even much blood; death normally occurs offstage, with the characters discussing it after it happened. Most cozy mysteries use amateur detectives. Examples are <u>Victorian Mysteries</u> (Robin Paige) and <u>Daisy Dalrymple series</u> (Carola Dunn, 1920s England).

Traditional. A term used by Gary Warren Niebuhr in *Make Mine a Mystery* to describe mysteries that fall between "hard-boiled" and "cozy." The level of violence is realistic, but not gratuitously so. Most historical mysteries fit this category.

Other appeal factors in historical mysteries include language (appropriate to the period, or modern), pacing (fast-paced or leisurely), and overall theme. These are delineated in the annotations in this chapter.

Traditional Westerns (in general, as well as historical Westerns in Chapter 5) may appeal to historical mystery readers, especially those involving lawmen of the Wild West who track down outlaws in pursuit of justice. And because many historical thrillers also involve crimes, readers may wish to investigate the novels listed in Chapter 9, which emphasize danger and suspense. One could argue that some of these novels could be described as either thrillers or mysteries. The Mystery FAQ on the ClueLass home page (http://www. cluelass.com), an excellent overview of the mystery genre in general, provides more detail on the mystery/thriller/suspense distinctions as well as a glossary of terms frequently used in the mystery genre.

Ancient Civilizations

Egypt

Mysteries of ancient Egypt blend the unusual with the familiar. Their dry desert setting, colorful character names, and polytheistic religion will seem exotic to readers, but the situations the characters find themselves in—family squabbles and political rivalry—are similar to those found in mysteries with more traditional settings.

Christie, Agatha.

Death Comes As the End. **Dodd, Mead, 1944. 223pp. ★**

Imhotep, a widowed Egyptian landowner and priest, brings his beautiful teenage concubine, Nofret, back to his family home. His sons and daughters immediately object to her acquisitive ways. When Nofret is found dead at the bottom of a cliff, Imhotep's family members become the immediate suspects, but family rivalry may not be the only motive for her murder. Good characterization and Christie's ability to transplant a traditional murder mystery to ancient Egypt make this novel a classic. Widely reprinted. **Amateur detective/Traditional.**

Doherty, P. C.

<u>**Egyptian Mystery Series.**</u> ✍

An action-packed series from the prolific Doherty, set against the background of the accession of Queen Hatusu (Hatshepsut) to the Egyptian throne, circa 1480

BC. As Hatusu attempts to convince the people that a woman is capable of ruling Thebes, her loyal chief judge, Lord Amerotke, solves a series of crimes on her behalf. Most are politically motivated. **Public detective/ Traditional.**

The Mask of Ra. St. Martin's Minotaur, 1999. 244pp.

Pharaoh Tutmosis II has just died in Thebes, leaving the throne open for dispute between his beautiful widow/half-sister, Hatusu, and his illegitimate son. Was the pharaoh's death truly caused by a snake bite, and if so, who planted the snake on the royal barge?

The Horus Killings. St. Martin's Minotaur, 2000. 274pp.

To continue discussion over whether a woman should be allowed to rule, Hatusu invites priests and scholars to Thebes, but a series of murders among the group threatens to upset her reign.

The Anubis Slayings. St. Martin's Minotaur, 2001. 308pp.

Pharaoh Hatusu has finally defeated the Mitanni people, but murders committed by a mysterious individual wearing a mask of the god Anubis cause uneasiness among the Mitanni envoys.

The Slayers of Seth. St. Martin's Minotaur, 2002. 306pp.

Though Lord Amerotke is already busy solving the murder of a young scribe, Hatusu interrupts his efforts and asks him to find out who killed General Balet, a famous Egyptian hero.

Haney, Lauren.

Lieutenant Bak Series.

In the fifteenth century BC, during the reign of the female pharaoh Queen Hatshepsut, Lt. Bak of the Medjay police in the fortress city of Buten (modern Sudan) serves as chief investigator. Though her dialogue is fairly modern, Haney's historical accuracy has been praised by the editors of *KMT*, a scholarly journal of ancient Egypt. **Public detective/Traditional.**

Flesh of the God. Avon, 2003. 338pp.

Exiled to the desolate frontier city of Buhen for offending high-ranking officials in the capital city of Waset, Lt. Bak turns his misfortune into professional advantage when he solves the murder of Nakht, Buhen's commandant. Though published second to last, this novel was written before the others.

The Right Hand of Amon. Avon, 1997. 300pp.

While overseeing the journey of a golden idol of the god Amon up the Nile, where it is being sent to heal a tribal king's son, Lt. Bak discovers the body of a slain soldier.

A Face Turned Backward. Avon, 1999. 286pp.

Someone is smuggling elephant tusks up the river Nile. Besides dealing with this problem, Lt. Bak must solve a farmer's murder.

A Vile Justice. Avon, 1999. 290pp.

In the city of Abu, people—each one more powerful than the last—are being killed off every ten days.

A Curse of Silence. Avon, 2000. 287pp.

Hatshepsut's cousin Amonked arrives in Buhen to decide whether the queen should withdraw her troops from the frontier city. When Lt. Bak uncovers the dead body of a local prince at Amonked's former residence, he suspects someone in Amonked's party is guilty.

A Place of Darkness. Avon, 2001. 285pp.

Lt. Bak heads to Waset, where Hatshepsut's memorial temple is under construction, to look into several mysterious deaths as well as possible sabotage of the temple.

A Cruel Deceit. Avon, 2002. 290pp.

On a visit to Waset for the eleven-day Feast of Opet, Lt. Bak investigates the murder of a Hittite horse trader.

A Path of Shadows. Avon, 2003. 302pp.

Lt. Bak heads north into the desert with his men to find a missing explorer, and a series of deaths follows the Medjay police on their journey.

Robinson, Lynda S.

Lord Meren Series. 📖 YA

At the beginning of King Tutankhamun's reign in the fourteenth century BC, the political environment remains unstable following the death of Akhenaten, Tutankhamun's father. Akhenaten had sought to overthrow worship of the gods and form a monotheistic religion, which made him unpopular with the people. Political intrigue swirls within the royal court as the priests of the ancient Egyptian gods assert their power once again. Lord Meren, the "Eyes and Ears of Pharaoh," investigates a series of mysteries for Tutankhamun, his royal patron and friend, with the help of his adopted son Kysen. Light and entertaining, with good historical detail. Readers who enjoy these may also like Elizabeth Peters's Amelia Peabody series, listed under the Middle East toward the end of this chapter. **Public detective/Traditional.**

Murder in the Place of Anubis. Walker, 1994. 190pp.

The holy Place of Anubis, where the dead are embalmed, has been desecrated by the stabbing death of the scribe Hormin.

Murder at the God's Gate. Walker, 1995. 236pp.

Unas, a priest of Amon, falls to his death from atop a larger-than-life statue of the young King Tutankhamun.

Murder at the Feast of Rejoicing. Walker, 1996. 229pp.

Lord Meren hopes to relax at his country house after working hard at court, but when his cousin's shrewish wife Anhai is murdered, his hopes for a nice vacation go out the window.

Eater of Souls. Walker, 1997. 229pp.

A series of deaths in the royal city of Memphis. In the streets, groups of people are being horrifically murdered, perhaps by a demon goddess.

Drinker of Blood. Mysterious Press, 1998. 229pp.

Meren looks into the death of Queen Nefertiti, Tutankhamun's mother, and tries to prevent the pharaoh from knowing about his suspicions that she was poisoned.

Slayer of Gods. Mysterious Press, 2001. 244pp.

Meren continues his investigations into Nefertiti's death, which endangers the lives of his son and daughter. A mysterious woman named Anath may be Meren's only hope, but is she trustworthy?

Thurston, Carol.

The Eye of Horus. **Morrow, 2000. 308pp.**

Kate McKinnon, a present-day medical illustrator, joins forces with radiologist and Egyptologist Max Cavanaugh to uncover the real story behind the life and death of Tashat, a mummy from 1350 BC who will be part of an exhibit at a Denver museum. Tashat's body had been found with broken ribs and a man's skull between her legs. The journal of Tenre, an ancient Egyptian physician, keeps readers one step ahead of the modern-day investigation and links young Tashat with the beautiful Queen Nefertiti. A multi-period mystery. **Amateur detective/Traditional.**

Greece

A small assortment of mysteries set in ancient Greece, a locale that no mystery novelist has really claimed as his or her own.

Apostolou, Anna.

Mysteries of Alexander the Great. ✍

An action-packed duology set in Greece circa 336–332 BC, and based on historical events. Characterization could be better, as the fictional detectives (the Hebrew brother-sister team of Simeon and Miriam Bartimaeus) are little more than cardboard cutouts, but the strong plotting and colorful descriptions make ancient Greece come alive in all its bloody glory. (Apostolou is one of the many pseudonyms of the prolific Paul Doherty.) **Amateur detective/Traditional.**

A Murder in Macedon. St. Martin's Press, 1997. 243pp.

Because a crowd of people sees Pausanias, captain of the king's guard, kill Philip of Macedon, Alexander's father, the solution to Philip's death seems obvious—until Pausanias himself is killed moments later.

A Murder in Thebes. St. Martin's Press, 1998. 226pp.

Returning from conquests in Thessaly, Alexander discovers that Thebes is in revolt against him, and Memnon, his most trusted captain, has died after falling from his locked tower room.

Doherty, Paul.

Mysteries of Alexander the Great. ✍

This Alexander the Great series is slightly different from the one Doherty wrote as Anna Apostolou, though both feature Alexander's military campaigns against Persia. The fast-paced and occasionally violent plots suit the subject matter, and characterization has improved since the first series. The amateur detectives are Telamon, Alexander's childhood friend and personal physician, and Telamon's Celtic assistant, Cassandra. **Amateur detective/Traditional.**

The House of Death. Carroll & Graf, 2001. 276pp.

In 334 BC, Alexander is eager to conquer Persia. When murders occur among his camp—including some that happen in tents that are under guard—Alexander asks Telamon to alleviate superstition among his followers by solving the crimes.

The Godless Man. Carroll & Graf, 2002. 303pp.

Alexander has conquered Persia's armies at the Battle of the Granicus, but when he enters the city of Ephesus, a Persian assassin known only as the "Centaur" threatens to bring him down.

The Gates of Hell. Carroll & Graf, 2003. 292pp.

Pamenes, a scribe working on cracking the code of the Pythian Manuscript, which holds the secret to defeating the city of Halicarnassus, is found dead in a locked room.

Doody, Margaret.

Aristotle and Stephanos Series. ✍

In *Aristotle, Detective*, set in Athens of 332 BC, a young Greek named Stephanos turns to his former mentor, Aristotle, to disprove a murder charge against his cousin Philemon. But is Philemon really guilty? The pair team up for further investigations in the subsequent novels. Published around the same time as Ellis Peters's first novel, *Aristotle, Detective* became enormously popular in Italy, which led Doody to continue the series twenty-four years later. **Amateur detective/Traditional.**

Aristotle, Detective. Harper & Row, 1978. 278pp. ★

Aristotle and Poetic Justice. London: Century, 2002. 324pp.

Aristotle and the Secrets of Life. London: Century, 2003. 420pp. (Alternate title: *The Secrets of Life.*)

Poison in Athens. London: Century, 2004. 436pp.

Edwards, Michael B.

Murder at the Panionic Games. Academy Chicago, 2002. 260pp.

When an athlete named Tyrestes collapses in a temple during the opening ceremonies of the Panionic Games in 650 BC, a young sub-priest named Bias has the misfortune to catch him as he falls. Now it's up to Bias to remove the taint of Tyrestes's death from his own person by solving the murder himself. Lighthearted and witty. **Amateur detective/Traditional.**

Somoza, José Carlos.

The Athenian Murders. Farrar, Straus, & Giroux, 2002. 272pp.

An ancient Athenian text reveals the death of a handsome adolescent boy, one of the pupils at the prestigious Plato Academy. The boy's teacher believes it to be murder, and he asks Heracles Pontor, Decipherer of Enigmas, to help him prove it. In the present day, the translator of the text finds that the more he reads from the manuscript, the more familiar the case seems to be. Strangely, the text is beginning to reflect the translator's own life, and his fate as a possible victim of violence. This tale wraps around itself, making readers confront what they think they know about time and reality. **Amateur detective/Traditional/Literary.**

The Roman Empire

The Senate, that group of men who dominated the political landscape of ancient Rome, takes center stage in these mysteries. As such, most of the murders are politically motivated. The detectives are well aware of this, though because of the Senate's power, it doesn't make the crimes any easier to solve.

Bell, Albert J.

All Roads Lead to Murder. High Country, 2002. 246pp. ✍

In AD 83, Pliny the Younger, the well-known Roman senator and letter-writer, heads to Rome in a caravan along with the historian Tacitus and some other travelers. When one among their number ends up murdered after spending the night in Smyrna, Pliny takes the case, with Tacitus's help. Things grow complicated after Pliny learns that he himself might have been the intended victim. As a narrator, Pliny is a bit stuffy and priggish, but he freely admits to these faults. **Amateur detective/Traditional.**

Davis, Lindsey.

<u>Marcus Didius Falco Series.</u> ★ **YA**

Davis's detective/narrator is Marcus Didius Falco, a wisecracking, bumbling private investigator in ancient Rome during the reign of Vespasian (circa AD 70). Though originally from the lower classes, Falco somehow manages to capture the heart of a Roman senator's daughter, Helena Justina, an intelligent woman who becomes his ideal mate. With a combination of witty dialogue, idiomatic phrasings, fast pace, and likable characters (imagine the typical cast of 1940s private eye novels, but

dressed in togas), the author brings the period to life without taking it (or herself) too seriously. **Private detective/Traditional.**

The Silver Pigs. Crown, 1989. 258pp.

Falco departs for Britain, where he disguises himself as a slave at a silver mine to discover why veins of silver (pigs) belonging to the emperor are disappearing—and why the niece of Senator Varus was murdered to keep her silent.

Shadows in Bronze. Crown, 1990. 341pp.

Falco knows that Helena Justina, Senator Varus's daughter, is out of his league romantically, but he pursues her nonetheless. In his next adventure, Falco heads to Pompeii to root out more conspiracies against Vespasian.

Venus in Copper. Crown, 1991. 277pp.

A beautiful widow who has buried several rich Roman husbands—and is on the way to obtaining another—arouses Falco's suspicions, especially when her latest fiancé dies.

The Iron Hand of Mars. Crown, 1992. 305pp.

In AD 71, Falco heads to Germania at Vespasian's request to test the loyalty of a rebel chieftain.

Poseidon's Gold. Crown, 1994. 336pp.

Falco still can't obtain authorization to marry his high-born lady love Helena, and he tries to extricate himself and her from a murder charge stemming from his late brother's shady dealings.

Last Act in Palmyra. Mysterious Press, 1996. 476pp.

Falco and Helena head to Syria at Vespasian's request, and they look into the disappearance of a runaway circus musician.

Time to Depart. Mysterious Press, 1995. 400pp.

After Balbinus Pius, the crime underworld boss of ancient Rome, takes the opportunity to flee the Empire, his associates scramble to claim his territory.

A Dying Light in Corduba. Mysterious Press, 1998. 428pp.

Helena has gotten pregnant, which complicates matters for the couple, and Falco journeys to Baetica (Roman Spain) to look into the corrupt behavior of olive oil producers.

Three Hands in the Fountain. Mysterious Press, 1999. 351pp.

Body parts belonging to late citizens of ancient Rome turn up one day in the city's water supply.

Two for the Lions. Mysterious Press, 1998. 390pp.

The lion that had been used to kill high-profile criminals is itself killed. Falco and Helena follow the clues to Tripoli. Ellis Peters Historical Dagger.

One Virgin Too Many. Mysterious Press, 1999. 304pp.

Falco, newly assigned as keeper of the Emperor's sacred geese, gets entangled with an ancient cult, and the young female candidate for a position as Vestal Virgin ends up dead.

Ode to a Banker. Mysterious Press, 2001. 372pp.

Falco looks into the murder of a powerful banker/publisher, a man who belonged to two professions that naturally have a lot of enemies.

A Body in the Bathhouse. Mysterious Press, 2001. 354pp.

Just after discovering a dead body in his father's new bathhouse, Falco reluctantly heads to the cold frontier outpost of Britain to check out possible fraud in a building project.

The Jupiter Myth. Mysterious Press, 2002. 323pp.

In Londinium in AD 75, Falco's called to investigate the murder of Verovolcus, a henchman of one of Rome's Celtic allies.

The Accusers. Mysterious Press, 2004. 368pp.

Back in Rome, Falco attempts to rejuvenate his career as a private investigator by looking into the death of Rubirius Metellus, a senator who may or may not have committed suicide.

Scandal Takes a Holiday. Mysterious Press, 2004. 352pp.

In Ostia investigating the disappearance of a newspaper mogul, Falco also follows up on rumors that pirates are kidnapping Roman citizens.

Finnis, Jane.

Get Out or Die. Poisoned Pen Press, 2003. 350pp.

In AD 91, many Roman citizens choose to make their homes in the frontier province of Britannia, but the native Britons want them gone. Aurelia Marcella, who runs a guesthouse along the road to York, roots out the person (or persons) responsible for a series of murders, including that of Quintus, a Roman traveler who is murdered near her inn. **Amateur detective/ Traditional.**

Larkin, Patrick.

The Tribune. Signet, 2003. 392pp.

Lucius Aurelius Valens used to be a Roman soldier of the 6th Legion, at least until he turned whistleblower. Transferred to patrol duty in distant Galilee during the reign of Tiberius (first century AD), Lucius expects to merely tolerate his job. Things pick up when a detachment of Praetorian Guards is massacred, along with the Roman senator they were protecting. Fast-paced adventure, told in the first person. (Larkin has co-written several technothrillers with Larry Bond, under Bond's name.) **Amateur detective/Traditional.**

Roberts, John Maddox.

SPQR Series.

SPQR, Senatus QuePopulus Romanus, translates as "the Senate and People of Rome." Roberts's series traces the often stormy relationship between the two. His detective, Senator Decius Caecilius Metellus the Younger, doesn't hesitate to plunge into mysteries involving the lower classes if it means that justice will be served. His adventures are amusing: Metellus enjoys a good time as much as anyone, and his playboy attitude usually gets him into trouble. The early paperback versions of books 1–4 are quite rare, but they have recently been reprinted. **Amateur detective/Traditional.**

SPQR I: The King's Gambit. St. Martin's Minotaur, 2001 (c1990). 274pp.

SPQR II: The Catiline Conspiracy. St. Martin's Minotaur, 2001 (c1991). 278pp.

SPQR III: The Sacrilege. Thomas Dunne, 1999 (c1992). 245pp.

SPQR IV: The Temple of the Muses. Thomas Dunne, 1999 (c1992). 231pp.

SPQR V: Saturnalia. St. Martin's Minotaur, 1999. 275pp.

SPQR VI: Nobody Loves a Centurion. St. Martin's Minotaur, 2001. 276pp.

SPQR VII: The Tribune's Curse. St. Martin's Minotaur, 2003. 248pp.

SPQR VIII: The River God's Vengeance. St. Martin's Minotaur, 2004. 290pp.

Saylor, Steven.

Roma Sub Rosa Series. ★ 📖

Both more serious and more suspenseful than Lindsey Davis's novels, Saylor's series begins nearly a hundred years earlier (circa 80 to 48 BC), just before the Roman Republic became the Roman Empire. Gordianus the Finder, a private investigator, is a fairly average Roman citizen—gray-haired and slightly past middle age—but unusual in that high-profile patrons such as Pompey and Cicero request his services. Gordianus's choice of wife—Bethesda, a freed Egyptian-Jewish slave from his household—is also out of the ordinary. Saylor takes on many complicated issues, such as slavery and other traditional Roman values, without moralizing. The novels mix fictional with historical characters, to good effect. **Private detective/Traditional.**

Roman Blood. St. Martin's Press, 1991. 357pp.

Cicero, a young orator, prepares to defend a farmer named Sextus Roscius against the murder of his estranged father, who threatened to disinherit him. To clear his client's name, Cicero hires Gordianus.

The House of the Vestals. St. Martin's Press, 1997. 260pp.

A collection of mystery short stories featuring Gordianus, his adopted son Eco, and his slave-concubine Bethesda, tales that delve further into the background of all three characters. Time-wise, this anthology fits second in the series.

Arms of Nemesis. St. Martin's Press, 1992. 304pp.

Roman law dictates that when slaves kill their master, all of the household's slaves must be murdered. When two runaway slaves are accused of killing the estate manager of Marcus Crassus, Rome's richest citizen, Gordianus and his adopted son Eco travel to the resort city of Baiae to solve the murder and save the doomed slaves. Set against the backdrop of the Spartacan slave revolt.

Catilina's Riddle. St. Martin's Press, 1993. 430pp.

Rivalry between Gordianus's patron Cicero and radical senator Catilina threatens to disrupt the peace found by Gordianus and his family, who have retired to an Etruscan farm. Unsure whether Catilina's rash comments about his rival are really true, Gordianus questions Cicero's motives. Headless corpses found on Gordianus's farm draw him back into the political fray.

The Venus Throw. St. Martin's Press, 1995. 308pp.

Gordianus's old Greek philosophy teacher, Dios, is visiting Rome on behalf of Egypt, and when other envoys are murdered, Dios fears for his own life. When Dios himself is killed, Gordianus is hired to find the killer.

A Murder on the Appian Way. St. Martin's Press, 1996. 304pp.

While traveling along the Appian Way, populist politician Publius Clodius is brutally murdered. Cicero, preparing the defense for Clodius's political rival Titus Milo, asks Gordianus to investigate.

Rubicon. St. Martin's Press, 1999. 276pp.

In 49 BC, Pompey, the leader of the Roman Senate, flees Rome when Julius Caesar and Mark Antony cross the Rubicon River. Before he does, he compels Gordianus to solve the murder of his favorite cousin, who was found dead in Gordianus's own garden. Set during Rome's civil war. Herodotus Award.

Last Seen in Massilia. St. Martin's Minotaur, 2000. 277pp.

While visiting the walled city of Massilia (modern Marseilles, France) to look for his missing son Meto, who had been reported killed, Gordianus watches as a young girl tumbles to her death from a precipice called Sacrifice Rock.

A Mist of Prophecies. St. Martin's Minotaur, 2002. 270pp.

As Rome's civil war rages on, Gordianus—retired from the detective life—becomes romantically involved with Cassandra, a seeress whose visions brought her to the attention of Rome's most powerful women. When Cassandra dies of poison, Gordianus feels compelled to solve the murder.

The Judgment of Caesar. St. Martin's Minotaur, 2004. 290pp. ✍

In Alexandria, Egypt, two claimants to the throne fight for dominance: King Ptolemy and his half-sister Cleopatra. Caesar's choice of who to support will consolidate his own power. Gordianus, in Alexandria to help cure his wife Bethesda's illness, defends his estranged son Meto from a murder charge.

The British Isles

The Middle Ages

Both politics and religion play strong roles in medieval mysteries, and the two are frequently interrelated. Common causes of death include religious differences and feudal disputes.

Beaufort, Simon.

Sir Geoffrey Mappestone Mysteries.

Sir Geoffrey Mappestone survives the First Crusade to Jerusalem in the early twelfth century, but his adventures have only begun. After the Crusaders return to England, he reluctantly takes on crime investigations, both in his homeland on the Welsh border and back in the Holy Land. (Pseudonym of Elizabeth Cruwys, who also writes as Susanna Gregory, and Beau Riffenburgh.) **Amateur detective/ Traditional.**

Murder in the Holy City. St. Martin's Press, 1998. 280pp.

In 1100 Jerusalem, one of Geoffrey's friends and fellow knights meets his end in the bedchamber of a Greek baker, and other deaths soon follow.

A Head for Poisoning. St. Martin's Press, 1999. 378pp.

When he receives word that his father is seriously ill, Geoffrey heads home to his family's Welsh castle only to find that his sister has died and his father is being poisoned.

The Bishop's Brood. Severn House, 2003. 348pp.

Geoffrey and his friend Sir Roger of Durham plan to head back to the Holy Land on Crusade, with Roger carrying a secret message for his father, Bishop Flambard. Then Geoffrey's servant is killed by an arrow meant for Geoffrey.

The King's Spies. Severn House, 2004. 320pp.

In 1102, the illegitimate nephew of the Earl of Shrewsbury is killed, and the trail leads Geoffrey to a murderous plot against Henry I, King of England.

Clare, Alys.

Hawkenlye Mysteries.

At Hawkenlye Abbey in Tonbridge, Kent, during the reign of Richard the Lionheart (late 1100s), Abbess Helewise rules the mixed community of monks and nuns with an iron hand. Yet the Abbey sits on land that has strong pagan roots, and the mysterious residents of nearby Wealden Forest are frequently blamed for strange goings-on. Together with Josse d'Acquin, a French soldier formerly in the king's service, Abbess Helewise sets the record straight. Many additional titles have been published in Britain. (Alys Clare previously wrote time-slip novels under her real name, Elizabeth Harris; see Chapter 12.) **Amateur detective/Traditional.**

Fortune Like the Moon. St. Martin's Minotaur, 2000. 242pp.

The past of a murdered novice, Gunnora, may hold the key to her murder, even though the people of Tonbridge place blame on a group of prisoners recently freed by King Richard.

Ashes of the Elements. St. Martin's Minotaur, 2001. 244pp.

Although the sheriff of Tonbridge thinks a poacher's death was caused by the Forest People, Helewise and Josse don't believe it.

The Tavern in the Morning. St. Martin's Minotaur, 2002. 230pp.

A guest staying at Goody Anne's inn, one of Josse's favorite taverns, dies of wolf's bane poison in his chicken and vegetable pie.

Conway, Sara.

Lord Godwin Novels.

Lord Godwin, bailiff of the town of Hexham in northern England in 1220, is a former Crusader now in the service of the Archbishop of York. He solves murders as a way of atoning for the crimes he committed in the name of God while on Crusade. **Amateur detective/Traditional.**

Murder on Good Friday. Cumberland House, 2001. 311pp.

The body of a young Christian boy, murdered on Good Friday, bears puncture wounds reminiscent of the Crucifixion. An angry mob blames Hexham's Jewish residents for the crime.

Daughters of Summer. Cumberland House, 2003. 204pp.

When Master Gruffydd, a wealthy and abusive merchant, turns up dead, the obvious suspect is his wife Maegden, a noblewoman whose family had forced her to marry him.

Doherty, P. C.

Paul (P. C.) Doherty is the most prolific author of historical mystery series around. Though they are all fairly short, his well-researched, fast-paced stories provide an unsanitized view of life in medieval England. Doherty's many pseudonyms include Anna Apostolou, Ann Dukthas, Michael Clynes, C. L. Grace, and Paul Harding, among others. He also writes under his full name.

Hugh Corbett Mysteries.

Hugh Corbett, Keeper of the King's Secret Seal during the reign of Edward I (late thirteenth to early fourteenth centuries), works as a clerk, courier, and occasional spy for His Royal Majesty. Doherty's novels frequently include supernatural elements, but unlike those in the <u>Canterbury Tale</u> series, here the ghosts and odd happenings are just another mystery for Corbett to solve. **Amateur detective/Traditional.**

Satan in St. Mary's. St. Martin's Press, 1986. 186pp.

The Crown in Darkness. St. Martin's Press, 1988. 187pp.

Spy in Chancery. St. Martin's Press, 1988. 176pp.

The Angel of Death. St. Martin's Press, 1990.

The Prince of Darkness. St. Martin's Press, 1993. 247pp.

Murder Wears a Cowl. St. Martin's Press, 1994. 249pp.

The Assassin in the Greenwood. St. Martin's Press, 1994. 217pp.

The Song of a Dark Angel. St. Martin's Press, 1995. 249pp.

Satan's Fire. St. Martin's Press, 1996. 250pp.

The Devil's Hunt. St. Martin's Press, 1998. 249pp.

The Treason of the Ghosts. London: Headline, 2000. 249pp.

The Demon Archer. St. Martin's Minotaur, 2001. 250pp.

Corpse Candle. St. Martin's Minotaur, 2002. 310pp.

Canterbury Tale Mysteries.

Every night while on the road, the pilgrims from Chaucer's *Canterbury Tales* (fourteenth century) recount eerie stories of murder and mystery. They recount each tale in the third person, but it's clear to their audience that they're speaking about themselves. Supernatural beings—ghosts, demons, vampires—are portrayed as if they're real. Later volumes, published in Britain, are *The Hangman's Hymn* (1999) and *A Haunt of Murder* (2002). **Amateur detective/Traditional.**

An Ancient Evil. St. Martin's Press, 1995. 248pp.

The Knight's Tale. What connects a murderous cult from the time of William the Conqueror and several murders 200 years later in Oxford?

A Tapestry of Murders. St. Martin's Press, 1996. 247pp.

The Man of Law's Tale. Lawyer Nicholas Chirke investigates the strange life and death of Queen Isabella, Edward III's late mother.

A Tournament of Murders. St. Martin's Press, 1997. 249pp.

The Franklin's Tale. In 1356 Poitiers, France, a knight named Gilbert Savage learns the truth about his father's death.

Ghostly Murders. St. Martin's Press, 1998. 250pp.

The Priest's Tale. Father Philip, a new parish priest in Kent, discovers the secrets of the Knights Templar.

Frazer, Margaret.

Sister Frevisse Medieval Mysteries. **YA**

Sister Frevisse, a sharp-witted Benedictine nun at St. Frideswide's in Oxfordshire during the reign of Henry VI (1430s and 1440s), serves as amateur sleuth. Though she chose a religious vocation of her own free will, Frevisse's background as the niece-by-marriage of Thomas Chaucer (Geoffrey's son) gives her entrance into the world beyond the convent. Frevisse's no-nonsense attitude makes her hard to get to know, but her astute knowledge of human behavior stands her in good stead. Like Ellis Peters's novels, the works of Margaret Frazer (pseudonym for Mary Monica Pulver/Kuhfeld and Gail Frazer, and after the sixth novel, Frazer alone) don't dwell on the unpleasant aspects of medieval life. The plots unfold slowly, and they alternate points of view between Frevisse and the title characters. The titles echo verses from Chaucer's *Canterbury Tales.* **Amateur detective/Traditional.**

The Novice's Tale. Berkley Prime Crime, 1992. 229pp.

In 1431, the blasphemous Lady Ermentrude is determined to remove her pious niece, Thomasine, from the convent. Thomasine becomes the obvious suspect when her aunt is brutally murdered.

The Servant's Tale. Jove, 1993. 234pp.

After the nunnery welcomes a troupe of traveling players, three Yuletide murders throw the residents of St. Frideswide's into confusion.

The Outlaw's Tale. Jove, 1994. 217pp.

Sister Frevisse defends her wayward cousin Nicholas, who has fallen in with a band of outlaws, from a murder charge.

The Bishop's Tale. Berkley Prime Crime, 1994. 198pp.

At the funeral feast of Frevisse's uncle, Thomas Chaucer, a cantankerous guest demands that God strike him down if he has told a lie—and he falls down dead.

The Boy's Tale. Berkley Prime Crime, 1995. 233pp.

Someone is trying to kill Henry VI's young half-brothers, Jasper and Edmund Tudor, who take sanctuary with Frevisse at St. Frideswide's.

The Murderer's Tale. Berkley Prime Crime, 1996. 230pp.

Staying one night at Minster Lovell while on pilgrimage, Sister Frevisse tries to clear an epileptic man from a murder charge.

The Prioress' Tale. Berkley Prime Crime, 1997. 246pp.

Domina Alys, St. Frideswide's sharp-tongued new prioress, installs many of her unpleasant relatives on convent grounds, to the nuns' dismay.

The Maiden's Tale. Berkley Prime Crime, 1998. 245pp.

Frevisse stays with her cousin Alice Chaucer in London while on a trip to escort St. Frideswide's new prioress back to Cornwall. While there, she gets caught up in Lancastrian intrigue.

The Reeve's Tale. Berkley Prime Crime, 1999. 274pp.

A controversy over ownership of land in the village of Prior Byfield leads to two murders. The first hardcover.

The Squire's Tale. Berkley Prime Crime, 2000. 277pp.

Landholder Robert Fenner attempts to settle a dispute between his lady wife Blaunche and her former in-laws about her dower property, and Sister Frevisse is asked to arbitrate.

The Clerk's Tale. Berkley Prime Crime, 2002. 312pp.

In the town of Goring, a local official, a man disliked by many, is found dead in the cloister garden of St. Mary's nunnery.

The Bastard's Tale. Berkley Prime Crime, 2003. 309pp.

In 1447, the Bishop of Winchester asks Frevisse to observe a parliamentary session at Bury St. Edmonds on his behalf. There, she becomes the unlikely friend of Arteys, bastard son of the Duke of Gloucester, which affects her relationship with her cousin Alice.

The Hunter's Tale. Berkley Prime Crime, 2004. 336pp.

Nobody seems all that upset at the murder of Sir Ralph Woderove, a brutal landowner who abused his wife and children. After his death, his will continues to control the lives of his family.

Gellis, Roberta.

Magdalene La Bâtarde Mysteries.

An unlikely mystery heroine, Magdalene la Bâtarde runs a high-class whorehouse in London's Southwark district in the mid-twelfth century. Despite her choice of profession (and a past she'd prefer to hide), Magdalene is a woman of integrity. Her women all have physical disabilities that disqualify them from marriage—one is blind, another deaf, another mute—but this doesn't interfere with their work. The Bishop of Winchester, whose guesthouse Magdalene rents, silently accepts their presence on his property. One of the bishop's knights, Sir Bellamy "Bell" of Itchen, grows ever more fascinated by the still-beautiful Magdalene as the series continues. **Amateur detective/Traditional.**

A Mortal Bane. Forge, 1999. 350pp.

Sabina, a blind woman working as one of Magdalene's whores, discovers the body of one of her recent clients, papal messenger Baldassare de Firenze, at the whorehouse gate.

A Personal Devil. Forge, 2001. 316pp.

Sabina has left the whorehouse to become the permanent mistress of a wealthy man. When his jealous wife is killed, Magdalene asks Bell to help her clear her friends' names.

Bone of Contention. Forge, 2002. 431pp.

Magdalene arranges a secret meeting place in Oxford for her patron, the bishop. While there, one of the bishop's men is accused of murdering a man for political reasons.

Grace, C. L.

Kathryn Swinbrooke Mysteries.

Physician and chemist (apothecary) Kathryn Swinbrooke practices her trade in fifteenth-century Canterbury, site of the holy shrine of Thomas Becket. The series begins at the height of the Wars of the Roses in 1471, so it should surprise no one that some of the crimes are politically motivated. Although it may seem anachronistic for female doctors to have existed in medieval England, Grace's research is based on historical evidence. (C. L. Grace is another Paul Doherty pseudonym.) **Amateur detective/Traditional.**

A Shrine of Murders. St. Martin's Press, 1993. 195pp.

The Eye of God. St. Martin's Press, 1994. 198pp.

The Merchant of Death. St. Martin's Press, 1995. 182pp.

The Book of Shadows. St. Martin's Press, 1996. 195pp.

Saintly Murders. St. Martin's Minotaur, 2001. 241pp.

A Maze of Murders. St. Martin's Minotaur, 2003. 239pp.

A Feast of Poisons. St. Martin's Minotaur, 2004. 240pp.

Gregory, Susanna.

Chronicles of Matthew Bartholomew.

Matthew Bartholomew, a physician and university lecturer in Cambridge in the aftermath of the Black Death in mid-fourteenth-century England, uses his knowledge of medicine and human nature to solve murders. The world-renowned university at Cambridge is the centerpiece for these tales, and as in any university locale, town–gown relations are less than perfect. Volumes appear in their correct order below. (Pseudonym of Elizabeth Cruwys.) **Amateur detective/Traditional.**

A Plague on Both Your Houses. St. Martin's Press, 1998. 406pp.

An Unholy Alliance. St. Martin's Press, 1996. 208pp.

A Bone of Contention. St. Martin's Press, 1997. 375pp.

A Deadly Brew. Trafalgar Square (Little Brown UK), 1998. 360pp.

A Wicked Deed. Trafalgar Square (Little Brown UK), 1999. 392pp.

A Masterly Murder. Trafalgar Square (Little Brown UK), 2000. 406pp.

An Order for Death. Trafalgar Square (Little Brown UK), 2001. 470pp.

A Summer of Discontent. Trafalgar Square (Little Brown UK), 2002. 520pp.

A Killer in Winter. Trafalgar Square (Little Brown UK), 2003. 496pp.

The Hand of Justice. Trafalgar Square (Little Brown UK), 2004. 536pp.

Harding, Paul.

The Sorrowful Mysteries of Brother Athelstan.

Harding's joint detectives are Sir John Cranston, Lord Coroner for London in the fourteenth century, and his assistant, Dominican friar Brother Athelstan. Cranston tends to drink too much, so when his judgment is impaired, Athelstan competently takes over. Only two volumes were published in the United States, but many more have appeared in Britain. (A Paul Doherty pseudonym.) **Amateur detective/Traditional.**

The Nightingale Gallery. Morrow, 1991. 252pp.

Red Slayer. Morrow, 1992. 283pp. (Original title: *The House of the Red Slayer.*)

Healey, Judith Koll.

The Canterbury Papers. **Morrow, 2004. 353pp.** ✍

When she was young, Alais Capet, Princess of France, was brought to England to marry Richard Coeur de Lion, but she was discarded due to her affair with his father King Henry. By the year 1200, she is a middle-aged spinster living at her brother's court in Paris. It's then that Eleanor of Aquitaine, Dowager Queen of England, makes Alais an offer she can't refuse. If Alais travels to Canterbury to retrieve some secret papers, Eleanor promises to reveal the whereabouts of Alais's illegitimate child. A nice story, but inaccurate, for the historical Alais was already married at the time. **Amateur detective/Traditional.**

Jecks, Michael.

Medieval West Country Mysteries.

Jecks's series focuses on the peasants of medieval England and their relationship with the land. The detectives are Simon Puttock, Bailiff of Lydford Castle in Devon, and his friend, Sir Baldwin Furnshill, Keeper of the King's Peace. The fourteenth century was a turbulent time for England: The Knights Templar were disbanded, the Hundred Years War began, and the Black Plague hit hard. Even Simon and Baldwin's quiet village sees its share of feudal disputes, religious strife, violence, and murder. **Public detective/Traditional.**

The Last Templar. Trafalgar Square (Headline UK), 1995. 375pp.

The Merchant's Partner. Trafalgar Square (Headline UK), 1995. 377pp.

A Moorland Hanging. Trafalgar Square (Headline UK), 1996. 375pp.

The Crediton Killings. Trafalgar Square (Headline UK), 1997. 378pp.

The Abbot's Gibbet. Trafalgar Square (Headline UK), 1998. 336pp.

The Leper's Return. Trafalgar Square (Headline UK), 1998. 384pp.

Squire Throwleigh's Heir. Trafalgar Square (Headline UK), 1999. 337pp.

Belladonna at Belstone. Trafalgar Square (Headline UK), 1999. 327pp.

The Traitor of St. Giles. Trafalgar Square (Headline UK), 2000. 335pp.

The Boy-Bishop's Glovemaker. Trafalgar Square (Headline UK), 2000. 331pp.

The Tournament of Blood. Trafalgar Square (Headline UK), 2001. 362pp.

The Sticklepath Strangler. Trafalgar Square (Headline UK), 2001. 366pp.

The Devil's Acolyte. Trafalgar Square (Headline UK), 2002. 395pp.

The Mad Monk of Gidleigh. Trafalgar Square (Headline UK), 2002. 460pp.

The Templar's Penance. Trafalgar Square (Headline UK), 2003. 364pp.

The Outlaws of Ennor. Trafalgar Square (Headline UK), 2004. 320pp.

Marston, Edward.

Domesday Books.

The *Domesday Book*, commissioned by William the Conqueror in 1085, was a comprehensive, detailed survey of all lands and other resources held by the king and his people. Because one of its purposes was tax collection, villagers and townspeople rarely welcomed the Domesday commissioners. In Marston's series, veteran soldier Ralph Delchard and his companion, half-Saxon lawyer Gervase Bret, travel throughout the English countryside on the king's business. Along the way, they meet up with numerous people and not a few murders. The novels build on real-life entries from the historical *Domesday Book.* The next volume will be *The Elephants of Norwich.* (Marston is a pseudonym for Keith Miles.) **Public detective/Traditional.**

The Wolves of Savernake. St. Martin's Press, 1993. 242pp.

The Ravens of Blackwater. St. Martin's Press, 1994. 245pp.

The Dragons of Archenfield. St. Martin's Press, 1995. 242pp.

The Lions of the North. St. Martin's Press, 1996. 227pp.

The Serpents of Harbledown. St. Martin's Press, 1998. 277pp.

The Stallions of Woodstock. St. Martin's Press, 1999. 275pp.

The Hawks of Delamere. St. Martin's Minotaur, 2000. 246pp.

The Wildcats of Exeter. St. Martin's Minotaur, 2001. 275pp.

The Foxes of Warwick. St. Martin's Minotaur, 2002. 274pp.

The Owls of Gloucester. St. Martin's Minotaur, 2003. 275pp.

McIntosh, Pat.

The Harper's Quine. Carroll & Graf, 2004. 300pp.

Glasgow, Scotland, circa 1542. Lawyer Gil Cunningham, in training for the priesthood at his family's request, discovers the body of a young woman on the grounds of Glasgow Cathedral. After investigating, he finds that she was a married noblewoman who left her husband to become a harper's mistress (quine).The attractive daughter of the cathedral's French mason helps him out. **Amateur detective/Traditional.**

Morson, Ian.

William Falconer Medieval Mysteries.

William Falconer, Regent Master of Oxford University in 1264, believes his campus to be a peaceful haven from deadly English politics. Nothing could be further from the truth, of course, and Falconer turns amateur detective when murders disturb his town. Fast-paced, with a less romanticized view of medieval England than Ellis Peters's Cadfael novels. **Amateur detective/Traditional.**

Falconer's Crusade. St. Martin's Press, 1995. 190pp.

Falconer's Judgement. St. Martin's Press, 1996. 208pp.

Falconer and the Face of God. St. Martin's Press, 1996. 192pp.

A Psalm for Falconer. St. Martin's Press, 1997. 220pp.

Falconer and the Great Beast. St. Martin's Press, 1999. 220pp.

Penman, Sharon Kay.

Justin de Quincy Series. 📖 YA

During the reign of Richard the Lion Heart in the late twelfth century, young Justin de Quincy , the unacknowledged bastard son of a bishop, becomes the unexpected ally of Eleanor of Aquitaine, the elderly queen dowager, and does her bidding on his travels throughout the British Isles. The crimes he solves are deeply rooted in the politics of medieval Europe. Though lighter and considerably shorter than her epic novels of medieval royalty (Chapter 2), Penman's fun and entertaining mysteries feature many of the same historical characters: the Plantagenets and their political rivals, the native Welsh princes. **Amateur detective/ Traditional.**

The Queen's Man. Holt, 1996. 291pp.

After accidentally discovering the connection between a murdered goldsmith and the fate of King Richard, being held prisoner by the Holy Roman Emperor in Austria, Justin gains Queen Eleanor's attention. She asks him to find the goldsmith's killer.

Cruel as the Grave. Holt, 1998. 242pp.

While King Richard languishes in his Austrian prison, his younger brother John schemes to steal the throne. It becomes Justin's job not only to convince Prince John, holed up in Windsor Castle, to negotiate with him, but also to solve the murder of a Welsh girl.

Dragon's Lair. Putnam, 2003. 322pp.

When Queen Eleanor receives word that part of King Richard's ransom has gone missing in Wales, she sends Justin to recover it. There he discovers suspects aplenty, all powerful men whom it would be unwise to cross. Among them are Welsh prince Davydd ap Owain, Davydd's rebel nephew Llewelyn ab Iowerth, and—of course—Prince John.

Peters, Ellis.

Brother Cadfael Series. ★

During the civil wars that engulf England in the mid-twelfth century, as King Stephen and his cousin the Empress Maud vie for control of the country, not even the Benedictine monastery of St. Peter and St. Paul in the Welsh border town of Shrewsbury remains unaffected. Peters's detective, Brother Cadfael, possesses expertise in both herb lore and human nature that works well with his crime-solving abilities. A former Crusader who joined the monastery late in life, Cadfael has an unusual history that is revealed gradually throughout the series. The author's version of medieval English life is calm, unrushed, and slightly romanticized; while unpleasantries aren't hidden, they're not dwelt upon, either. Her novels proceed at a leisurely pace and are filled with beautiful descriptions of cloister life as well as the English and Welsh countryside. (Peters is a pseudonym for English novelist Edith Pargeter, who died in 1995.) **Amateur detective/Traditional.**

A Rare Benedictine. Mysterious Press, 1988. 118pp.

Three mystery short stories round out the life story of Brother Cadfael, including the early tale of how he came to join the Benedictines.

A Morbid Taste for Bones. Morrow, 1977. 191pp.

In the first full volume, set in 1137, Cadfael heads to the Welsh village of Gwytherin to acquire the remains of St. Winifred for Shrewsbury Abbey. Controversy over the move among the townspeople leads to murder.

One Corpse Too Many. Morrow, 1980. 191pp.

After the hanged bodies of ninety-four supporters of the Empress Maud are recovered from Shrewsbury Castle in 1138, Cadfael discovers the corpse of a ninety-fifth man, who appears to have died quite differently.

Monk's-Hood. Morrow, 1981. 223pp.

Master Gervase Bonel, a guest at the Abbey, is discovered to have been poisoned by a plant, monk's hood, from Cadfael's own herb garden.

St. Peter's Fair. Morrow, 1981. 219pp.

Thomas of Bristol, a rich merchant, dies at St. Peter's Fair in Shrewsbury, and the motive seems not to be robbery.

The Leper of St. Giles. Morrow, 1982. 223pp.

The leper colony of St. Giles, located just on the outskirts of Shrewsbury, may hold the key to a murder.

The Virgin in the Ice. Morrow, 1983. 220pp.

In the harsh winter of 1139, three young people—a teenage boy, his older sister, and a Benedictine nun—mysteriously vanish after fleeing the sacking of Worcester in search of safety at Shrewsbury.

The Sanctuary Sparrow. William Morrow, 1983. 181pp.

Liliwin, a wandering minstrel, takes sanctuary in the abbey after being accused of murder.

The Devil's Novice. Morrow, 1984. 191pp.

Meriet Aspley, the newest novice at the Abbey of St. Peter and St. Paul, has horrible dreams that earn him the nickname the "devil's novice."

Dead Man's Ransom. Morrow, 1984. 189pp.

When Sheriff Gilbert Prestcote is murdered, suspicion falls on the young Welsh prisoner whom his daughter loves, a man who was about to be exchanged as part of Sheriff Prestcote's ransom.

The Pilgrim of Hate. Morrow, 1984. 190pp.

A loyal knight's killer may be hiding among the pilgrims gathering at the celebration of St. Winifred in May 1141.

An Excellent Mystery. Morrow, 1986. 190pp.

Two monks of the Benedictine abbey at Winchester, destroyed by fire, arrive at Shrewsbury in search of shelter. One is a former Crusader at death's door; the other is his mute caretaker. Both have secrets to hide.

The Raven in the Foregate. Morrow, 1986. 201pp.

When harsh Father Ailnoth drowns, suspicion falls on the nephew of a housekeeper who was traveling with him.

The Rose Rent. Morrow, 1986. 190pp.

It is now 1142, and the monks of Shrewsbury must pay rent in the form of a white rose to a widow whose property they are using. When the monk sent to deliver the rent is found murdered in a pile of rose petals, Cadfael investigates.

The Hermit of Eyton Forest. Mysterious Press, 1988. 224pp.

When ten-year-old Richard Ludel comes into a large inheritance, his grandmother Dame Dionysia insists he marry a neighbor's daughter. When he disappears, Dionysia becomes the prime suspect.

The Confession of Brother Haluin. Mysterious Press, 1989. 164pp.

During winter 1142, Brother Haluin, critically injured while repairing the abbey's roof, makes a surprising deathbed confession.

The Heretic's Apprentice. Mysterious Press, 1990. 186pp.

A young clerk named Elave, bringing his master's body back to be buried at St. Peter and St. Paul, holds heretical views that get him into trouble.

The Potter's Field. Mysterious Press, 1990. 230pp.

A young woman whose corpse is found in a newly plowed field turns out to be the wife of a man who once owned the land.

The Summer of the Danes. Mysterious Press, 1991. 251pp.

Cadfael heads to Wales on a diplomatic mission for the Church. There, he gets caught up in a battle among rival Welsh rulers and the Danish fleet that is set on invading the country.

The Holy Thief. Mysterious Press, 1992. 246pp.

During the flood of autumn 1144, someone makes away with the coffin containing the bones of St. Winifred, Shrewsbury Abbey's special protector. Few people besides Brother Cadfael know that the holy relics really lie elsewhere.

Brother Cadfael's Penance. Mysterious Press, 1994. 292pp.

Cadfael's past comes back to haunt him when his illegitimate son Olivier is taken prisoner, and Cadfael decides to rescue him, whatever the cost.

Robb, Candace.

Owen Archer Mysteries.

Owen Archer, an archer of Welsh birth in late fourteenth-century York, works as a spy for John Thoresby, Archbishop of York and Lord Chancellor of England. Like Ellis Peters's Brother Cadfael, Owen formerly served as a soldier, and he lost one eye while fighting in France. But unlike Cadfael, Owen lives very much in the world. Assisting him on occasion is his apothecary wife, Lucie Wilton, introduced in the first book. The novels contain elements of romance and family life, as shown in the growing relationship between Owen and Lucie, but also among the secondary characters. **Amateur detective/Traditional.**

The Apothecary Rose. St. Martin's Press, 1993. 256pp.

John Thoresby sends Owen to York to investigate the death of his ward, a young man who may have died from an herbal remedy. To solve the crime, Owen apprentices himself to Nicholas Wilton, an apothecary, and grows close to Wilton's much younger wife, Lucie.

The Lady Chapel. St. Martin's Press, 1994. 287pp.

In 1365, the Archbishop of York calls upon Owen to solve the murder of wool merchant Will Crounce, slain in York Cathedral, but whose severed hand ends up in a fellow merchant's tavern.

The Nun's Tale. St. Martin's Press, 1995. 355pp.

In 1366, Joanna Calverley, a young nun who died of the plague one year earlier, claims to have risen from the dead. Murders follow her wherever she goes.

The King's Bishop. St. Martin's Press, 1996. 372pp.

King Edward III wants Owen to convince Church leaders to accept his own nominee as Bishop of Winchester, though the Pope doesn't want to see the king's loyal man with ecclesiastical power.

The Riddle of St. Leonard's. St. Martin's Press, 1997. 303pp.

During the summer of 1369, when everyone is wilting from the extreme heat, elderly patients at St. Leonard's Hospital are mysteriously dying.

A Gift of Sanctuary. St. Martin's Press, 1998. 303pp.

Owen accompanies his father-in-law and his friend Geoffrey Chaucer on pilgrimage to Wales, where he is asked to look into the death of a man outside the gates of St. David's.

A Spy for the Redeemer. Mysterious Press, 2002. 305pp.

Still in Wales, Owen prepares to head home, but the death of a stonemason he had hired keeps him there. Back in York, Lucie and their son await his return, though they fear that Welsh rebel Owain Lawgoch has claimed his loyalties.

The Cross Legged Knight. Mysterious Press, 2003. 321pp.

When William Wykeham, Bishop of Winchester, visits York to appease the family of a knight who died in France, attempts are made on Wykeham's life.

Margaret Kerr Mysteries.

Margaret Kerr, a newly married young woman in late thirteenth-century Scotland, discovers that even family members and friends have their own political agendas that take precedence over her life and personal happiness. English-occupied Edinburgh, with all its danger and squalor, comes to life under Robb's pen. Darker and more serious than the Owen Archer series. Volume 2 in the series, *The Fire in the Flint*, is available in Britain. **Amateur detective/Traditional.**

A Trust Betrayed. Mysterious Press, 2001. 255pp.

In 1297, Margaret travels to Edinburgh in search of her missing husband, merchant Roger Sinclair, and to solve her cousin Jack's murder.

Sedley, Kate.

Roger the Chapman Mysteries.

Roger the Chapman, an English peddler living during the Wars of the Roses (1470s), finds that his insatiable curiosity serves him well as a sleuth. After discovering that monastic life doesn't suit his personality, Roger turns to selling miscellaneous household wares door to door throughout the English countryside. He recounts his youthful adventures from the viewpoint of old age. Historically sound, with an engaging protagonist. **Amateur detective/Traditional.**

Death and the Chapman. St. Martin's Press, 1992. 190pp.

The Plymouth Cloak. St. Martin's Press, 1993. 192pp.

The Weaver's Tale. St. Martin's, 1994. 248pp. (Original title: *The Hanged Man.*)

The Holy Innocents. St. Martin's Press, 1995. 280pp.

The Eve of Saint Hyacinth. St. Martin's Press, 1996. 280pp.

The Wicked Winter. St. Martin's Press, 1999. 282pp.

The Brothers of Glastonbury. St. Martin's Minotaur, 2001. 279pp.

The Weaver's Inheritance. St. Martin's Minotaur, 2001. 247pp.

The Saint John's Fern. St. Martin's Minotaur, 2002. 246pp.

The Goldsmith's Daughter. Severn House, 2001. 214pp.

The Lammas Feast. Severn House, 2002. 250pp.

Nine Men Dancing. Severn House, 2003. 252pp.

The Midsummer Rose. Severn House, 2004. 249pp.

Tremayne, Peter.

Sister Fidelma Series.

Sister Fidelma, a young red-haired Irish "religieuse" at St. Brigid's in Kildare, was born the daughter of the King of Cashel in AD 636. Her training in the Brehon law and her role as court advocate make her a perceptive sleuth, especially in matters of politics and law. She's not as adept at matters of the heart, as shown in her affectionate but awkward relationship with Brother Eadulf, a Saxon. As Tremayne (pseudonym for Celtic scholar Peter Beresford Ellis) reveals, early medieval Ireland was the cradle of civilization, and hardly deserving of the term "Dark Ages." In particular, women could serve as judges, political leaders, and lawyers, and nuns and priests were allowed to marry. Tremayne lays the history lesson on a bit thick in places, which can make his novels challenging, yet they can't be beat for a detailed portrait of ancient Ireland. **Public detective/Traditional.**

Hemlock at Vespers. St. Martin's Minotaur, 2000. 398pp.

These fifteen short stories, collected here for the first time, launch the fictional sleuthing career of Sister Fidelma.

Absolution by Murder. St. Martin's Press, 1996. 274pp.

At the Synod of Whitby in 664, at which the Celtic and Roman churches vie for supremacy, Abbess Etain of St. Hilda is murdered—possibly by a Roman. Fidelma reluctantly teams up with Brother Eadulf, a Saxon in the Romans' party, to solve the mystery.

Shroud for the Archbishop. St. Martin's Press, 1996. 340pp.

While in Rome for his investiture as Archbishop, Wighard of Canterbury is found strangled, and Fidelma and Eadulf try to clear an Irish monk of the crime.

Suffer Little Children. St. Martin's Press, 1997. 339pp.

To prevent war between the rival kingdoms of Muman (modern-day Munster) and Laigin (Leinster), Fidelma investigates the death of the Venerable Dacan, a scholar from Laigin.

The Subtle Serpent. St. Martin's Press, 1998. 339pp.

Fidelma connects two odd happenings: the pagan murder of a woman found dead in a well, and the disappearance of a merchant ship.

The Spider's Web. St. Martin's Press, 1999. 325pp.

Fidelma defends Moen, a deaf-mute man, from charges of murdering his chieftain.

Valley of the Shadow. St. Martin's Press, 2000. 269pp.

Sent to a remote, pagan corner of Ireland on behalf of the Church, Fidelma and Eadulf discover what appears to be the ritual murder of thirty-three men.

The Monk Who Vanished. St. Martin's Minotaur, 2001. 272pp.

At the Abbey of Imleach, the relics of St. Ailbe have vanished, as has an elderly monk.

Act of Mercy. St. Martin's Minotaur, 2001. 268pp.

While aboard ship on a pilgrimage to the Holy Shrine of St. James, Fidelma meditates on her complicated relationship with Eadulf, but the murder of another shipboard passenger disturbs her peace.

Our Lady of Darkness. St. Martin's Press, 2002. 270pp.

Learning that Eadulf has been accused of murdering a young girl, Fidelma hastens to the Kingdom of Laigin, and learns that Roman rather than Brehon law will be used to try him.

Smoke in the Wind. St. Martin's Press, 2003. 267pp.

Forced ashore in Wales while en route to Canterbury, Fidelma and Eadulf help King Gwlyddien figure out why the monks of Llanpadern monastery all disappeared without a trace.

The Haunted Abbot. St. Martin's Minotaur, 2004. 298pp.

Fidelma and Eadulf pay a visit to Eadulf's old friend, Brother Botulf, on their way home to Ireland. When they reach Aldred's Abbey, they discover he was murdered.

Unsworth, Barry.
Morality Play. Doubleday, 1995. 206pp.

In fourteenth-century England, a young monk named Nicholas Barber, released from his monastery after failing to observe the vow of chastity, joins a troupe of traveling players. After coming upon a village in which a murder had been committed, the group decides to re-create the deadly event for the stage, only to find that their performance brings them closer to revealing the truth about the murder. Layers of the crime and the possible perpetrators are revealed little by little. The novel poses its own questions on authorship: How much of reality should be used in the stories that we create? **Amateur detective/Traditional/Literary.**

Wolf, Joan.

Hugh Corbaille Series.

In King Stephen's England (1140s), nobleman Hugh Corbaille finds both mystery and love, the latter with a young woman named Cristen. Romance novelist Wolf had moderate success with her mysteries, though not enough for more than two volumes to be published. The action sweeps readers along nicely, but Wolf's hero is a bit stiff, and her love scenes would not be out of place in romance novels. Political intrigue plays a role, but not a major one. **Amateur detective/Traditional.**

No Dark Place. HarperCollins, 1999. 278pp.

When a knight reveals that Hugh Corbaille may be the true heir to the earldom of Wiltshire, Hugh looks into the death of the man who may have been his real father, a nobleman murdered thirteen years earlier.

The Poisoned Serpent. HarperCollins, 2000. 285pp.

While adjusting to his newly-found heritage, which means his beloved Cristen doesn't rank highly enough to marry him, Hugh defends his late foster father's friend, Bernard Radvers, from a charge of killing the hated Earl of Lincoln.

The Tudor Era

Murder and mayhem at the court of the Tudor monarchs: Henry VIII, Mary I, and Elizabeth I. In this unstable political climate, where loyalty to the wrong monarch or religion could cost you your position or even your head, tracking down a killer can be dangerous work.

Buckley, Fiona.

Ursula Blanchard Series.

A solidly researched mystery series set in and around the court of Elizabeth I in the 1560s. Ursula Blanchard, one of the Queen's Ladies of the Presence Chamber, also works as Elizabeth's spy, rooting out possible traitors whenever she finds them. Though Ursula is a well-educated member of the gentry, the death of her husband left her penniless, and she agrees to take on the queen's work to support her young daughter. In Tudor England, beautiful young widows like Ursula don't stay unattached for long, but she doesn't always have the best judgment where men are concerned. (Pseudonym of Valerie Anand.) **Amateur detective/Traditional.**

To Shield the Queen. Scribner, 1997. 278pp. (Original title: *The Robsart Mystery.*)

To squelch any rumors that Queen Elizabeth aims to marry her Master of Horse, Robert Dudley, Ursula travels to the country home of Robert's wife, Amy Robsart. When Amy's body is found at the bottom of a staircase, Ursula feels like a failure. She determines to solve the mystery of Amy's death.

The Doublet Affair. Scribner, 1998. 294pp.

Ursula spies on some of her old friends, the Masons, because Elizabeth suspects them of plotting against her with Mary, Queen of Scots. Ursula also resigns herself to the fact that her new (and Catholic) husband, Matthew de la Roche, remains exiled in France.

Queen's Ransom. Scribner, 2000. 348pp.

In 1562, Ursula travels to France in the company of her former father-in-law, Luke Blanchard, to deliver the queen's letter to France's Queen Mother, Catherine de'Medici. While there, Ursula learns of a deadly plot against her own life.

To Ruin a Queen. Scribner, 2000. 287pp.

Ursula has finally joined her husband Matthew in France, but her daughter Meg goes missing when her passage to France is arranged later on. The trail to recover her daughter leads Ursula to a mysterious Welsh castle.

Queen of Ambition. Scribner, 2002. 286pp.

Sir William Cecil asks Ursula to look into a planned attack on the queen, which may take place when Elizabeth first arrives in Cambridge for a visit. To investigate, Ursula sets her noble bearing aside and disguises herself as a servant in a pie shop.

A Pawn for a Queen. Scribner, 2002. 279pp.

Ursula travels north to Scotland to plead with her cousin Edward, who has been plotting treason against Queen Elizabeth. When Ursula arrives, she finds Edward dead, and the suspects are many.

The Fugitive Queen. Scribner, 2003. 277pp.

Ursula returns to Scotland with her ward, Penelope Mason, to find a husband for Penelope. Ursula also hopes to deliver a secret message from Elizabeth to Mary, Queen of Scots, who is held prisoner at Bolton Castle.

The Siren Queen. Scribner, 2004. 288pp.

In London to meet a suitor for her daughter Meg, Ursula uncovers treasonous behavior involving a Florentine banker, the Duke of Norfolk, and possibly Mary, Queen of Scots.

Chisholm, P. F.

Sir Robert Carey Mysteries. ✍

In the 1590s, Sir Robert Carey, courtier and cousin to Queen Elizabeth, is appointed the new Deputy Warden of the West Marches, assigned to guard the Anglo–Scottish border. As the only arbiter of law and order in this remote land, Robert relies on his innate wit and judgment to keep the peace, similar to what lone sheriffs will have to do 250 years later in the American Wild West. (Chisholm also writes Elizabethan-era thrillers as Patricia Finney; see Chapter 9.) **Public detective/ Traditional.**

A Famine of Horses. Walker, 1995. 271pp.

A local boy's murder distracts Carey from a baffling case: Someone has been stealing horses from all over the border country.

A Season of Knives. Walker, 1996. 231pp.

While Carey leaves his garrison to protect Lady Elizabeth Widdrington, his true love, from a possible kidnapping, murder occurs back at his home.

A Surfeit of Guns. Walker, 1997. 233pp.

One of Carey's men loses his hand in a pistol explosion. The trail to uncover more faulty weapons leads Carey to the court of Scotland's James VI.

A Plague of Angels. Poisoned Pen Press, 2000. 252pp.

Carey's father, Lord Chamberlain Hunsdon, summons him back to London to find his older brother Edmund, who has gone missing.

Clynes, Michael.

Journals of Sir Roger Shallot, A Rogue.

The mysteries in this series (written by British novelist Paul Doherty under a pseudonym) are the fictional recollections of Sir Roger Shallot, a self-proclaimed physician and rogue in Henry VIII's England who makes a living working as a secretary for Cardinal Wolsey's nephew. Shallot's bawdy observations on both life and death, spiced with the author's dry British wit, are humorous and sarcastic. **Amateur detective/ Traditional.**

The White Rose Murders. St. Martin's Press, 1993. 244pp.

Cardinal Wolsey asks his nephew, Benjamin Daunbey, and Roger Shallot to help restore Henry VIII's sister, Margaret Tudor, to the Scottish throne.

The Poisoned Chalice. O. Penzler, 1994. 280pp.

Shallot and his master head to France to look into the murder of a French diplomat who may also be a spy.

The Grail Murders. O. Penzler, 1993. 244pp.

Everyone's in search of Excalibur and the Holy Grail—Henry VIII, Cardinal Wolsey, and the Knights Templar—and someone's out to kill those who want to find it.

A Brood of Vipers. St. Martin's Press, 1996. 247pp.

King Henry asks Roger Shallot to find the murderer of a Florentine diplomat, so he sends him off to Florence—with a secret message for the Medicis.

The Gallows Murders. St. Martin's Press, 1995. 247pp.

Members of the Guild of Hangmen, the royal executioners, are meeting grisly ends themselves.

The Relic Murders. London: Headline, 1997. 247pp.

Shallot discovers a lucrative method of obtaining wealth in the trade of relics, and he proves so apt a dealer that King Henry and Cardinal Wolsey ask him to find the Orb of Charlemagne.

Dukthas, Ann.

Nicholas Segalla Time Travel Mysteries. ✍

Debonair, immortal sleuth Nicholas Segalla, cursed to wander the earth for eternity, tells professional historian Ann Dukthas the real stories behind the deaths of well-known royals. Despite the series title, no time travel is involved, just Segalla recalling events from his vast memory. Other series volumes include *The Time of Murder at Mayerling* (Archduke Rudolf, nineteenth-century Vienna) and *The Prince Lost to Time* (the lost Dauphin, eighteenth-century France). **Amateur detective/Traditional.**

In the Time of the Poisoned Queen. St. Martin's Press, 1998. 273pp.

England, 1558. Is Queen Mary Tudor being poisoned, and if so, by whom? The Catholic Queen Mother of France, Catherine de Medici? Catherine's daughter-in-law, the young Queen of Scots? Or Princess Elizabeth, Mary's own half-sister?

A Time for the Death of a King. St. Martin's Press, 1994. 226pp.

Edinburgh, 1567. Is Mary, Queen of Scots, responsible for the mysterious death of her young husband, Henry Lord Darnley, or is she being framed?

Emerson, Kathy Lynn.

Susanna, Lady Appleton Mysteries. (Also called Face Down Mysteries.) `YA`

Susanna, Lady Appleton, is an Elizabethan noblewoman-by-marriage with a talent for sleuthing. Most of the victims die by poison, so her knowledge of herbs comes in handy. The novels, set in the 1550s and 1560s, present a lively picture of Elizabethan England's numerous residents, from high-ranking courtiers and royalty down to local villagers. The next volume will be *Face Down Below the Banqueting House.* **Amateur detective/Cozy-Traditional.**

Face Down in the Marrow-Bone Pie. St. Martin's Press, 1997. 218pp.

While her husband Robert serves Queen Elizabeth in France, Susanna journeys to his lands in Lancashire to investigate the death of John Bexwith, their steward.

Face Down upon an Herbal. St. Martin's Press, 1998. 295pp.

At Madderly Castle, where Susanna assists in compiling a new herbal, one of the other houseguests is found dead, his face buried in Susanna's book.

Face Down Among the Winchester Geese. St. Martin's Press, 1999. 244pp.

A veiled gentlewoman, someone who may have been one of the many mistresses of Susanna's husband, is found dead in London's brothel district.

Face Down Beneath the Eleanor Cross. St. Martin's Minotaur, 2000. 280pp.

Although her husband had been reported dead, Susanna suspects that he's really alive and in hiding somewhere. Still, Susanna is surprised when she sees Robert tumble to his death, this time for real, from the top of an Eleanor Cross. When it is revealed that poison killed him, Susanna stands accused of his murder.

Face Down Under the Wych Elm. St. Martin's Minotaur, 2000. 250pp.

Constance Crane, Susanna's husband's former mistress, gets jailed for witchcraft in the town of Maidstone.

Face Down Before Rebel Hooves. St. Martin's Minotaur, 2001. 261pp.

Susanna impersonates her friend's late wife, Eleanor Pendennis, to prevent a plot against Queen Elizabeth from succeeding.

Face Down Across the Western Sea. St. Martin's Minotaur, 2002. 227pp.

England and Spain are bitter rivals for land in the New World, so when English scholarship on the subject goes missing, Susanna helps her friend Sir Walter Pendennis find the truth.

Gooden, Philip.

Nick Revill Series.

In the hectic world of Elizabethan theater, Nick Revill belongs to an elite company of actors—Lord Chamberlain's Men, a troupe partially owned by famed playwright William Shakespeare. His witty adventures and investigations in and around the Globe Theatre make for fun reading. **Amateur detective/Traditional.**

Sleep of Death. Carroll & Graf, 2000. 310pp.

Death of Kings. Carroll & Graf, 2001. 310pp.

The Pale Companion. Carroll & Graf, 2002. 280pp.

Alms for Oblivion. Carroll & Graf, 2003. 281pp.

The Mask of Night. Carroll & Graf, 2004. 281pp.

Harper, Karen.

Queen Elizabeth Mystery Series. ✍ YA

In the early years of her reign, when Catholics loyal to the late Queen Mary are devising plots against her life, Elizabeth I forms an impromptu Privy Council among her trustworthy household servants. The novels humanize the young Elizabeth, who sneaks out of her castle in disguise and investigates crimes herself to serve justice. (Harper used to write historical romance and now writes contemporary suspense and historical mysteries.) **Amateur detective/Traditional.**

The Poyson Garden. Delacorte, 1999. 310pp.

While Elizabeth remains in exile at Hatfield House just before Bloody Mary's death, members of the Boleyn family, relatives of Elizabeth's late mother Anne, are being poisoned one by one.

The Tidal Poole. Delacorte, 2000. 290pp.

The murder of a well-born lady during Elizabeth's coronation procession reveals a sinister plot against the new Queen's life.

The Twylight Tower. Delacorte, 2001. 289pp.

Elizabeth's master lutenist falls to his death from a parapet, and he hadn't even been drinking beforehand. The queen abandons her fleeting romance with Sir Robert Dudley to solve the crime.

The Queene's Cure. Delacorte, 2002. 273pp.

In her royal coach, Elizabeth finds a cruel effigy of herself, portrayed as a corpse ravaged by disease. When Elizabeth herself falls ill, her retainers suspect a conspiracy.

The Thorne Maze. Delacorte, 2003. 290pp.

As Elizabeth and her courtiers spend the summer at Hampton Court to escape the plague in London, a lawyer is murdered within the intricate maze in her gardens.

The Queene's Christmas. St. Martin's Minotaur, 2003. 320pp.

Christmas, 1564: Elizabeth would like to forget about the intrigues of Mary, Queen of Scots, but she can't relax after finding her kitchen master dead among his own culinary creations.

Hawke, Simon.

Shakespeare and Smythe Series. ✍

Will Shakespeare, fledgling playwright for the Queen's Men, and his friend, would-be actor and ostler Symington "Tuck" Smythe, would rather focus on their stage careers, but murder keeps following them. As amateur detectives, they sometimes bumble, but always entertain. Fast-paced, with modern dialogue and plenty of puns. **Amateur detective/Cozy-Traditional.**

A Mystery of Errors. Forge, 2000. 240pp.

The Slaying of the Shrew. Forge, 2001. 255pp.

Much Ado about Murder. Forge, 2002. 237pp.

The Merchant of Vengeance. Forge, 2003. 253pp.

Marston, Edward.

Nicholas Bracewell Series.

Nicholas Bracewell, book holder for the acting troupe Lord Westfield's Men, does his best to keep his thespians in line and out of trouble. He's not always successful. Like Hawke's and Gooden's series, Marston's Bracewell novels are set in the world of the Elizabethan stage, circa 1580s–1590s. In comparison, though, Marston's works are both more serious and more politically involved. The Catholic threat to Elizabeth's throne and the Puritan threat to Elizabethan drama are always in the background. (Pseudonym of Keith Miles.) **Amateur detective/Traditional.**

The Queen's Head. St. Martin's Press, 1988. 236pp.

The Merry Devils. St. Martin's Press, 1989. 236pp.

The Trip to Jerusalem. St. Martin's Press, 1990. 222pp.

The Nine Giants. St. Martin's Press, 1991. 235pp.

The Mad Courtesan. St. Martin's Press, 1992. 252pp.

The Silent Woman. St. Martin's Press, 1994. 312pp.

The Roaring Boy. St. Martin's Press, 1995. 260pp.

The Laughing Hangman. St. Martin's Press, 1996. 248pp.

The Fair Maid of Bohemia. St. Martin's Press, 1997. 229pp.

The Wanton Angel. St. Martin's Press, 1999. 279pp .

The Devil's Apprentice. St. Martin's Minotaur, 2001. 273pp.

The Bawdy Basket. St. Martin's Minotaur, 2002. 262pp.

The Counterfeit Crank. St. Martin's Minotaur, 2004. 272pp.

Tobin, Betsy.

🎀 *Bone House.* **Scribner, 2000. 219pp.** 📖

A young, unnamed serving woman, daughter of the local midwife, investigates the life and mysterious death of Dora, a buxom Flemish prostitute living in a rural village in the early seventeenth century. The novel reveals Elizabethans' obsession with the body (the "bone house") and the carnal natures they keep carefully hidden. Herodotus Award. **Amateur detective/Traditional/Literary.**

Tourney, Leonard.

Matthew Stock Novels.

With the help of his loyal wife Joan, Matthew Stock, clothier and county constable, solves crimes on behalf of Good Queen Bess. Matthew and Joan are comfortable, likable characters who act appropriately for their time. An older but still popular Elizabethan series. **Public detective/Traditional.**

The Players' Boy is Dead. Harper & Row, 1980. 192pp.

Low Treason. Dutton, 1982. 233pp.

Familiar Spirits. St. Martin's Press, 1984. 230pp.

The Bartholomew Fair Murders. St. Martin's Press, 1986. 232pp.

Old Saxon Blood. St. Martin's Press, 1988. 250pp.

Knaves Templar. St. Martin's Press, 1991. 282pp.

Witness of Bones. St. Martin's Press, 1992. 262pp.

Frobisher's Savage. St. Martin's Press, 1994. 264pp.

The Stuart Era

Murder mysteries of the Stuart era focus almost exclusively on the Restoration period (late seventeenth century), after Charles II returned to claim the English throne. Their gaudy, bawdy atmosphere reflects the times as well as the character of the Merry Monarch himself.

Brown, Molly.

Invitation to a Funeral. **Thomas Dunne, 1998. 288pp.** ✎

In 1676, playwright Aphra Behn is down on her luck. She owes rent on her London home, critics hated her latest play, and she doesn't have the strength to banish her lover, an alcoholic attorney, from her bed. Aphra hopes to improve her fortune by training the Earl of Rochester's mistress to star in her new play, but the woman can't act to save her life. Even worse, past debts require her to pay for the funeral of her father's old friend. When Aphra suspects he was murdered, she uncovers a plot that threatens to repeat England's Civil War. Bawdy, comic, and colorful; Nell Gwyn and Charles II make appearances. **Amateur detective/Traditional.**

Morgan, Fidelis.

Countess Ashby de la Zouche Mysteries.

Morgan, a British actress and historian, shares her love for Restoration-era comic theater in these murder mysteries. Countess Anastasia Ashby de la Zouche, a former mistress of Charles II, is rescued from debtors' prison by Alpiew, her buxom former maid. Though they can hardly reclaim their extravagant lifestyle, the pair earn some extra income working for a notorious scandal sheet. The series continues with *The Ambitious Stepmother* (2002) and *Fortune's Slave* (2004), published in Britain. **Amateur detective/Traditional.**

Unnatural Fire. Morrow, 2000. 356pp.

It's 1699, and the Countess and Alpiew track Beau Wilson, a merchant, throughout the dirty streets of London on behalf of his wife, who believes that he's in danger. Unfortunately, Mrs. Wilson proves correct, as the pair discover when they find him in Covent Garden with his throat cut.

The Rival Queens. Morrow, 2002. 340pp.

In 1700, Countess Ashby de la Zouche and Alpiew are no better off financially. While on break from assignments for the *London Trumpet*, they witness an actress's murder at the York Building's concert hall.

The Georgian and Regency Eras

Mysteries set during the Georgian period (1714–1837), which includes the Regency era (1811–1820), juxtapose two different sides of English society. They can either re-create the witty dialogue and fashion-conscious world of the upper classes, as Regency romances do, or they can contrast the modes of London's upper crust with the dingy, poverty-stricken side of the city. Some, like Kate Ross's Julian Kestrel series, do both.

Alexander, Bruce.

Sir John Fielding Series. ✍

Sir John Fielding, the half-brother of novelist and magistrate Henry Fielding, took over his sibling's duties as chief of London's first police force, the "Bow Street Runners," from 1754 to 1780. What made his accomplishments all the more remarkable was that he was completely blind. Alexander's mystery series re-creates the efforts of the real-life "Blind Beak" in rooting out criminals in a city overrun with prostitutes, gangs of pickpockets, highwaymen who preyed on travelers, and slum children with no good way to earn a living. Yet Fielding is also a compassionate judge of character, as he proves in the first book when he gives young Jeremy Proctor a break. (Alexander, a pseudonym for Bruce Alexander Cook, died in 2003.) **Public detective/Traditional.**

Blind Justice. Putnam, 1994. 254pp.

In this classic locked-room mystery set in 1768 London, Jeremy Proctor, a penniless thirteen-year-old boy falsely accused of thievery, becomes Magistrate Fielding's protégé and sidekick as he helps the judge investigate the mysterious murder of Lord Richard Goodhope.

Murder in Grub Street. Putnam, 1995. 276pp.

The night before Jeremy Proctor is due to be apprenticed to Ezekiel Grabb, a printer in London's publishing district, Grabb and members of his household are found murdered.

Watery Grave. Putnam, 1996. 265pp.

In the courtroom in 1769 London, ship's lieutenant William Landon stands accused of having pushed his captain overboard two years earlier.

Person or Persons Unknown. Putnam, 1997. 279pp.

In 1770, over a hundred years before Jack the Ripper, someone is brutally murdering prostitutes in Covent Garden.

Jack, Knave and Fool. Putnam, 1998. 279pp.

Jeremy Proctor, now sixteen and unofficially adopted by his mentor, plays a greater role in Fielding's investigations as the two puzzle out two mysteries: the deaths of elderly Lord Laningham and his wife, and the story behind a severed head found in the Thames.

Death of a Colonial. Putnam, 1999. 275pp.

The younger brother of an aristocrat recently executed for murder suddenly reappears after eight years, ready to claim his lost inheritance. Although the young man's mother seems to recognize him, Fielding suspects that there's treachery afoot.

The Color of Death. Putnam, 2000. 279pp.

The perpetrators of a series of robberies and shootings would seem to be black men, but they may really be white men in blackface, disguising themselves to make the crimes seem racially motivated.

Smuggler's Moon. Putnam, 2001. 247pp.

In 1772, citizens in the town of Deal make most of their money from smuggling, and Sir John and Jeremy arrive there to check on the honesty of a local magistrate.

An Experiment in Treason. Putnam, 2002. 247pp.

Treasonous letters have disappeared from the home of a British official responsible for colonial affairs, and they may be connected to Benjamin Franklin and the rebellion of the American colonies.

The Price of Murder. Putnam, 2003. 257pp.

In 1774, the murder of a young girl, a six-year-old sold by her mother into slavery, leads Jeremy to the racetrack.

Barron, Stephanie.

Jane Austen Mysteries. ✍

Jane Austen (1775–1817), whose novels about early nineteenth-century English society and manners were the inspiration for many Regency romance writers, does some investigating of her own. The novels are set in late Georgian England (early nineteenth century), primarily in Bath, where Austen lived. Written in Austen's own style—complete with witty dialogue, formal phrasings, leisurely pacing, and lengthy digressions—Barron's novels let readers experience Austen's keen psychological insight first-hand. Jane narrates each novel, paying attention to even the smallest historical details. Footnotes about the real-life Austen's life and acquaintances are interspersed throughout the text. (The pseudonym "Stephanie Barron" uses the middle and maiden names of mystery novelist Francine Mathews.) **Amateur detective/Cozy.**

Jane and the Unpleasantness at Scargrave Manor. Bantam, 1996. 289pp.

Isobel Payne, the Countess of Scargrave and Jane's good friend, loses her husband after only three months of marriage. A cruel letter accuses her of adultery and murder.

Jane and the Man of the Cloth. Bantam, 1997. 274pp.

On their way to a seaside holiday in Lyme Regis, Dorset, in 1804, Jane and her family take refuge at High Down Grange when their carriage overturns during a storm. Its master, Mr. Geoffrey Sidmouth, intrigues Jane, even after she realizes he may be connected to a laborer's murder.

Jane and the Wandering Eye. Bantam, 1998. 262pp.

At Christmastime in Bath in 1804, Jane accepts an offer from Lord Harold Trowbridge to trail his errant niece, Lady Desdemona. Jane investigates the death of a theater manager when Desdemona's brother is falsely accused of his murder.

Jane and the Genius of the Place. Bantam, 1999. 290pp.

The strangling death of flamboyant French seductress Francoise Grey at the Canterbury Races in summer 1805 may be connected to Napoleon's planned invasion of England.

Jane and the Stillroom Maid. Bantam, 2000. 277pp.

On a vacation in the Derbyshire countryside in 1806, Jane comes upon the body of a young gentleman who had been shot in the head. An autopsy reveals that the deceased was really a woman, a maidservant disguised as her employer.

Jane and the Prisoner of Wool House. Bantam, 2001. 291pp.

Among the French prisoners of war at Wool House, Southampton, in winter 1807, Jane searches for a witness who can clear her brother's Royal Navy friend Captain Tom Seagrave of murder.

Jane and the Ghosts of Netley. Bantam, 2003. 294pp.

In 1808, Lord Harold Trowbridge, an advisor to the British government, asks Jane to spy on suspected French agent Sophia Challoner.

Bebris, Carrie.
Pride and Prescience. Forge, 2003. 287pp.

Elizabeth Bennett and Fitzwilliam Darcy, the happy couple from Jane Austen's *Pride and Prejudice*, have been married in a double ceremony with Elizabeth's sister Jane and her fiancé, Charles Bingley. Though ecstatic over her wedding, Elizabeth is annoyed when Caroline Bingley, Charles's sister, announces her engagement to a rich American on the same day. When Caroline begins sleepwalking through the London streets, and her fiancé's father is murdered, Elizabeth and Darcy put their heads together to solve the mystery. A Regency mystery with gothic elements. **Amateur detective/Cozy.**

Cornwell, Bernard.
Gallows Thief. HarperCollins, 2002. 304pp.

Down on his luck, Captain Rider Sandman, a veteran of Waterloo, takes the case of artist Charles Corday. Corday has been accused of murdering the Countess of Avebury, whose portrait he was painting. Unless Sandman sifts through a political quagmire to prove Corday's innocence, Corday will be hanged within seven days' time. A stand-alone mystery from historical adventure writer Cornwell, with the author's trademark action and suspense. **Amateur detective/ Traditional.**

De la Torre, Lillian.

Dr. Sam Johnson Series. ✍ ★

James Boswell, the real-life biographer of eighteenth-century lexicographer Samuel Johnson, becomes his subject's Dr. Watson in four short story collections. The pair investigate crimes throughout London's dark alleyways and haunts. Some of the earliest examples of the historical mystery subgenre. **Amateur detective/Traditional.**

Dr. Sam Johnson, Detector. Knopf, 1946. 257pp.

The Detections of Dr. Sam Johnson. Doubleday, 1960. 190pp.

The Return of Dr. Sam Johnson, Detector. International Polygonics, 1985. 191pp.

The Exploits of Dr. Sam Johnson, Detector. International Polygonics, 1985. 190pp.

Donachie, David.

The Privateersman Mysteries.

Annotated in Chapter 8.

Gabaldon, Diana.

Lord John Grey Novels.

Lord John Grey began as a minor character from the author's Outlander novels (annotated in Chapter 4). A high-ranking officer in His Majesty's Army in the 1750s, Major Grey, a secret homosexual, solves crimes for the Crown and tries to keep his private life from being discovered. With its darker tone and its vivid depictions of the gay subculture in Georgian England, these well-written mysteries may surprise readers who expect more of Gabaldon's romantic adventure stories. More volumes are expected. **Amateur detective/Traditional.**

Lord John and the Private Matter. Delacorte, 2003. 305pp.

After discovering the true nature of the man about to marry his cousin, Lord John Grey vows to prevent him from destroying his family. At the same time, Grey's investigations into a brutal murder lead him through all the ranks of English society.

Gardner, Ashley.

Captain Gabriel Lacey Series.

A new series starring Captain Gabriel Lacey, a veteran of the Peninsular Campaign against Napoleon. Lacey narrates the tale, which encompasses all classes of people in Regency England. (Pseudonym of Jennifer Ashley, who writes romances under her own name.) **Amateur detective/Traditional.**

The Hanover Square Affair. Berkley Prime Crime, 2003. 262pp.

In 1816, Lacey comes across a mob scene in fashionable Hanover Square. The mob's leader, laid low with a gunshot wound, tells Lacey he was trying to rescue his daughter, who is being held hostage at a house on that same street.

A Regimental Murder. Berkley Prime Crime, 2004. 248pp.

Lacey rescues a widow, Lydia Westin, from an attack on a darkened street, and soon afterwards gets caught up in solving the murder of her late husband.

Lake, Deryn.

John Rawlings Series.

John Rawlings, an apothecary in 1760s London, moves easily from the drawing rooms of upper crust society to the dark alleyways of the city. Lake injects realism into her novels with the presence of Sir John Fielding, Rawlings's blind magistrate friend, who was one of the founders of the Bow Street Runners, London's first official police force. Fielding appears as a main character in Bruce Alexander's series, above. Seven previous volumes in the series have been published overseas. (Deryn Lake is a pseudonym for British historical novelist Dinah Lampitt.) **Amateur detective/Traditional.**

Death at St. James's Palace. Allison & Busby, 2002. 286pp.

At John Fielding's investiture into knighthood at St. James Palace in 1761, a member of the crowd falls down the stairs to his death.

Death in the Valley of Shadows. Allison & Busby, 2003. 288pp.

A stranger dies mysteriously several days after his visit to John Rawlings's apothecary shop, as does the woman who was pursuing him.

Ross, Kate.

Julian Kestrel Series.

Julian Kestrel, an elegantly dressed dandy based on Beau Brummell, is a proper gentleman, except for his tendency to get involved in sordid murder investigations. His Cockney manservant Dipper, a reformed pickpocket, becomes his friend and fellow sleuth. Set in the 1820s. The series ended with Ross's untimely death in 1996. **Amateur detective/Traditional.**

Cut to the Quick. Viking, 1993. 337pp.

While spending a weekend at a friend's country estate, Kestrel discovers the corpse of a beautiful young woman in his bed.

A Broken Vessel. Viking, 1994. 289pp.

Dipper's sister Sally Stokes, a saucy prostitute, takes three men to her bed one evening, and mistakenly steals a note from one of their pockets—a note containing an urgent message from a distraught young woman.

Whom the Gods Love. Viking, 1995. 382pp.

Alexander Falkland, brilliant in any career he sets his mind to, is bludgeoned to death in his study. Giving up on police efforts, Alexander's father asks Julian Kestrel to find the killer.

🎗 *The Devil in Music.* Viking, 1996. 447pp.

While traveling in Italy, Kestrel becomes engrossed in a four-year-old case in which an Italian aristocrat was murdered and his protégé, an English tenor, disappeared. Agatha Award.

Stevens, Rosemary.

Beau Brummell Mysteries. ✍

George Bryan "Beau" Brummell, the real-life Regency dandy, uses his knowledge of early nineteenth-century London society to solve the murders of people within its ranks. Never dressed in less than the height of fashion, Brummell solves mysteries without dirtying either his name or his perfect attire. **Amateur detective/Cozy.**

🎗 *Death on a Silver Tray.* Berkley Prime Crime, 2000. 277pp.

If Brummell doesn't find out who murdered the odious Countess of Wrayburn, it will ruin the good name of the Duchess of York, Brummell's good friend, who hired the Countess's paid companion. Agatha Award.

The Tainted Snuff Box. Berkley Prime Crime, 2001. 292pp.

The Prince of Wales's food-taster, the loathsome Sir Simon, dies after sampling a new brand of snuff supplied by Brummell's friend Petersham.

The Bloodied Cravat. Berkley Prime Crime, 2002. 291pp.

During a birthday celebration for Freddie, the Duchess of York, the badly behaved Lord Kendrick dies—with Freddie's hair ornament lodged in his throat.

Murder in the Pleasure Gardens. Berkley Prime Crime, 2003. 241pp.

Before he can fight a duel over a lost game of chance, government official Theobald Jacombe is found dead in Vauxhall's Pleasure Gardens.

Wynn, Patricia.

Blue Satan Mystery Series.

It is 1715, and George, Elector of Hanover, has become King George I of England. Falsely accused of killing his father, Gideon Fitzsimmons Viscount St. Mars goes into hiding and reemerges as the highwayman Blue Satan. **Amateur detective/Traditional.**

The Birth of Blue Satan. Pemberley Press, 2001. 325pp.

After three years abroad on a Grand Tour, Gideon returns to England and to Isabella Mayfield, the woman he hopes to marry. Gideon soon discovers that his father, the Earl of Hawkhurst, doesn't approve of their marriage, and has been banned from court for his suspected political leanings. Shortly after Gideon argues with him, the earl is murdered, and Gideon looks like the obvious suspect.

Nobody seems to believe him except Mrs. Hester Kean, Isabella's cousin and lady-in-waiting.

The Spider's Touch. Pemberley Press, 2002. 390pp.

"Blue Satan" remains abroad in France, as the English have no tolerance for outlaws. The exiled James Stuart, the Old Pretender, offers Gideon a chance to reclaim his father's estate if he joins the Jacobite cause. Gideon agrees, returning to England on a fact-finding mission for James, but the murder of a Jacobite close to Hester makes him rethink his loyalties.

The Victorian Era

The social lives of men and women of all classes dominate the plots of murder mysteries set in Victorian times (1837–1901). Death strikes both the rich and the poor in equal numbers. If nothing else, these mysteries prove that the wealthier a person is, the more secrets he or she has to hide. In this category, the first pastiches of Conan Doyle's Sherlock Holmes novels begin to appear.

Dickinson, David.

Lord Francis Powerscourt Mysteries.

Murder surrounds the British royal family in the last years of Queen Victoria's reign. Lord Francis Powerscourt, an Irish peer with a talent for espionage, tries to protect their interests. **Amateur detective/Traditional.**

Goodnight, Sweet Prince. Carroll & Graf, 2002. 314pp. ✍

In 1892, Prince Eddy, son of the Prince of Wales and eventual heir to the British throne, has been murdered in his bed at Sandringham, the royals' country house. The Royal family has publicly disclosed that influenza was the cause of death; few except for Powerscourt know that Eddy really died of multiple stab wounds. The secret to Eddy's death probably lies in his dissolute past and his connections to London's homosexual underworld.

Death and the Jubilee. Carroll & Graf, 2003. 344pp.

Thousands of loyal Britons gather to celebrate Queen Victoria's Diamond Jubilee in 1897. When the decapitated body of a German banker is found floating in the Thames, the royal family calls upon Lord Francis Powerscourt to investigate.

Death of an Old Master. Carroll & Graf, 2004. 314pp.

Both Renaissance art and art forgeries are lucrative markets in 1899 Britain. Powerscourt is caught in the fray when his wife's cousin, art critic Christopher Montague, is found garroted in his London flat.

Fawcett, Quinn.

Mycroft Holmes Series.

Mycroft Holmes, renowned detective and international man of mystery, also happens to be Sherlock Holmes's older brother. Sherlock had always acknowledged that Mycroft was the smarter one, but aside from his appearance in several Conan Doyle short stories, readers never really got to see Mycroft in action until now. Paterson Guthrie, Mycroft's secretary, doesn't always comprehend the world of British intelligence in the Victorian era, but he goes along for the ride. Authorized by Dame Jean Conan Doyle. (Pseudonym of Chelsea Quinn Yarbro and Bill Fawcett.) **Private detective/Traditional.**

Against the Brotherhood. Forge, 1997. 319pp.

Embassy Row. Forge, 1998. 384pp.

The Flying Scotsman. Forge, 1999. 320pp.

The Scottish Ploy. Forge, 2000. 352pp.

Gray, John MacLachlan.
The Fiend in Human. St. Martin's Minotaur, 2003. 352pp.

In the gloomy Dickensian atmosphere of 1852 London, tabloid journalist Edmund Whitty derives success from his sensationalist stories of "Chokee Bill," a serial killer who strangles prostitutes with a white silk scarf. After a man named William Ryan is arrested for the crimes, Whitty looks for another story to make his living, but the chokings continue to occur. Unfortunately, nobody but Whitty believes that the killer is still at large. **Amateur detective/Traditional.**

Lovesey, Peter.
Sergeant Cribb Series.

Sergeant Cribb and his sidekick/assistant, Constable Thackery, pursue crime in Victorian England, mainly at local sporting events. Along with puzzling through an enticing mystery, readers get the chance to learn the lingo of the period. **Public detective/Traditional.**

Wobble to Death. Dodd, Mead, 1970. 190pp.

The Detective Wore Silk Drawers. Dodd, Mead, 1971. 188pp.

Abracadaver. Dodd, Mead, 1972. 220pp.

Mad Hatter's Holiday. Dodd, Mead, 1973. 192pp.

The Tick of Death. Dodd, Mead, 1974. 188pp. (Original title: *Invitation to a Dynamite Party.*)

A Case of Spirits. Dodd, Mead, 1975. 160pp.

Swing, Swing Together. Dodd, Mead, 1976. 190pp.

Waxwork. Pantheon, 1978. 239pp.

Bertie Series. ✍

Albert, Prince of Wales—Queen Victoria's son—narrates his intrepid adventures in crime-solving in the 1880s and 1890s. His beautiful, long-suffering wife Alexandra, more intelligent than she's frequently given credit for, gives him a nudge in the right direction now and then. Lovesey seems to enjoy poking fun at typical Victorian stodginess. **Amateur detective/Traditional.**

Bertie and the Tinman. Mysterious Press, 1989. 223pp.

Bertie and the Seven Bodies. Mysterious Press, 1990. 196pp.

Bertie and the Crime of Passion. Mysterious Press, 1995. 245pp.

Paige, Robin.

Victorian Mysteries.

Kathryn (Kate) Ardleigh, an outspoken Irish-American author of penny-dreadfuls (dime novels), hardly fits the image of a proper Victorian gentlewoman. After serving as companion to an aunt she hadn't known she had, Sabrina Ardleigh of Bishop's Keep in Essex, Kate later inherits her estate. There Kate meets Sir Charles Sheridan, a peer of the realm and an amateur scientist, who becomes her sleuthing partner and husband. Cozy mysteries featuring famous people from Victorian times, from literary figures to royalty. ("Robin Paige" is the pseudonym of married authors Susan Wittig Albert and William Albert.) **Amateur detective/Cozy.**

Death at Bishop's Keep. Avon, 1994. 266pp.

Kate's two aunts, women with ties to a secret society, die mysteriously.

Death at Gallows Green. Avon, 1995. 267pp.

Beatrix Potter helps Kate and Sir Charles solve the murder of a local constable.

Death at Daisy's Folly. Berkley Prime Crime, 1997. 274pp.

Murders occur at a weekend party thrown by Daisy, Countess of Warwick—one of the Prince of Wales's mistresses—and His Royal Highness asks for Charles's and Kate's help.

Death at Devil's Bridge. Berkley Prime Crime, 1998. 274pp.

Kate and Charles host an automobile exhibit and race at their estate, and one of the drivers dies in what may not be an accident.

Death at Rottingdean. Berkley Prime Crime, 1999. 290pp.

While on vacation in the seaside town of Rottingdean, Kate and Charles suspect smuggling activities when a coast guard's body washes ashore. Rudyard Kipling helps investigate.

Death at Whitechapel. Berkley Prime Crime, 2000. 276pp.

Kate befriends Jennie Randolph Churchill, who is being blackmailed by someone who claims that Jack the Ripper was the father of Jennie's son Winston.

Death at Epsom Downs. Berkley Prime Crime, 2001. 292pp.

As Kate watches the races at Epsom Downs with Jennie Churchill and Lillie Langtry, a jockey is killed, and Lillie Langtry's jewels are stolen from their vault. The first hardcover volume.

Death at Dartmoor. Berkley Prime Crime, 2002. 324pp.

At filthy Dartmoor prison, Kate researches her latest Gothic novel, and Charles tries to prove a convicted wife-killer's innocence—with the help of Arthur Conan Doyle.

Death at Glamis Castle. Berkley Prime Crime, 2003. 338pp.

Edward VII asks the Sheridans to investigate strange goings-on at Scotland's Glamis Castle, which is rumored to be haunted.

Death in Hyde Park. Berkley Prime Crime, 2004. 304pp.

An anarchist commits suicide at Edward VII's coronation ceremony; author Jack London may or may not be involved.

Perry, Anne.

Thomas & Charlotte Pitt Mysteries. ★ 📖

Perry's vision of Victorian London is a study in contrasts: its elegant houses, drawing rooms, and high society parties exist alongside all the social ills of the day. Police Inspector Thomas Pitt, who grew up as the son of servants, forms an unlikely romantic and professional partnership with Charlotte Ellison, a gently bred young woman. A romantic relationship between a socialite and a policeman is hardly acceptable in Britain's class-conscious society, but Charlotte is never one to follow the rules. Through his marriage to Charlotte, Pitt gains entrance to the world of London's elite. Set in the 1880s and 1890s. **Public detective/Traditional.**

The Cater Street Hangman. St. Martin's Press, 1979. 247pp.

In April 1881, while the Ellison family is out paying calls, someone strangles a maid in their household.

Callander Square. St. Martin's Press, 1980. 221pp.

The bodies of two newborn babies are found buried in a garden in fashionable Callander Square.

Paragon Walk. St. Martin's Press, 1981. 204pp.

In the high-class neighborhood of Paragon Walk, young Fanny Nash is brutally raped and murdered.

Resurrection Row. St. Martin's Press, 1981. 204pp.

The exhumed body of the elderly Lord Augustus Fitzroy-Hammond turns up in an empty hansom cab.

Rutland Place. St. Martin's Press, 1983. 235pp.

Charlotte and her sister Emily try to protect their mother, who loses a locket containing a reminder of an illicit relationship.

Bluegate Fields. St. Martin's Press, 1984. 308pp.

The body of an upper-class boy, a member of the Waybourne family, is discovered in a sewer in the slums of Bluegate Fields.

Death in the Devil's Acre. St. Martin's Press, 1985. 248pp.

A prominent doctor and three other men are found murdered, their bodies sexually mutilated.

Cardington Crescent. St. Martin's Press, 1987. 314pp.

When Charlotte's brother-in-law George is poisoned, her sister Emily becomes the chief suspect, for the family knew of George's infatuation with his cousin's wife.

Silence in Hanover Close. St. Martin's Press, 1988. 341pp.

Pitt reopens a murder case involving a diplomat killed three years earlier in wealthy Hanover Close.

Bethlehem Road. St. Martin's Press, 1990.

Who cut the throat of Sir Lockwood Hammond, a benevolent member of Parliament, and left his body tied to the lamppost of Westminster Bridge?

Highgate Rise. Fawcett Columbine, 1991. 330pp.

Arson caused the fire that killed Clemency Shaw, a doctor's wife, but did her husband set the blaze?

Belgrave Square. Fawcett Columbine, 1992. 361pp.

The motive for moneylender William Weems's death would seem to be blackmail, for he knew secrets that London's wealthiest men would pay to keep hidden.

Farriers' Lane. Fawcett Columbine, 1993. 374pp.

While the Pitts are attending a play, a distinguished judge in the audience dies of opium poisoning.

The Hyde Park Headsman. Fawcett Columbine, 1994. 392pp.

Pitt, newly promoted to police superintendent, feels the pressure to solve a series of beheadings in Hyde Park.

Traitor's Gate. Fawcett Columbine, 1995. 411pp.

The Pitts connect the murders of Thomas's childhood mentor, the death of a society woman near Traitors' Gate, and leaks in Britain's secret policy on colonial Africa.

Pentecost Alley. Fawcett Columbine, 1996. 405pp.

When a club badge belonging to Finlay Fitzjames is found under the dead body of a prostitute in Pentecost Alley, Fitzjames's father suspects a setup.

Ashworth Hall. Fawcett Columbine, 1997. 373pp.

While moderating a meeting on Irish home rule at Ashworth Hall, government official Ainsley Greville is murdered.

Brunswick Gardens. Fawcett Columbine, 1998. 389pp.

The death of Unity Bellwood, assistant to Protestant vicar Ramsay Parmenter, may relate to her feminist and Darwinist beliefs.

Bedford Square. Ballantine, 1999. 330pp.

The body of a man in tattered clothes is found on the doorstep of respectable General Brandon Ballantyne, and the dead man has Ballantyne's snuffbox in his pocket.

Half Moon Street. Ballantine, 2000. 312pp.

The body of portrait photographer Delbert Cathcart, dressed in a green velvet gown with limbs manacled to the edges, is found floating in a boat on the Thames.

The Whitechapel Conspiracy. Ballantine, 2001. 341pp.

Discredited by his enemies, Pitt gets reassigned to cases in London's East End, where Jack the Ripper lurks in the shadows. In trying to restore Pitt's good name, Charlotte and her maid Gracie uncover a political conspiracy.

Southampton Row. Ballantine, 2002. 326pp.

Amid rivalry between the Tories and the Liberals for a critical seat in Parliament, the Liberal candidate's wife, an advocate of spiritualism, attends a séance that leaves the clairvoyant dead.

Seven Dials. Ballantine, 2003. 345pp.

When a diplomat is killed, senior cabinet minister Saville Ryerson swears that the diplomat's tenant, native Egyptian Ayesha Zakhari, must be innocent.

A Christmas Journey. Ballantine, 2003. 180pp.

A Christmas mystery novella featuring a young Lady Vespasia Cumming-Gould, a secondary character from the Pitt novels.

William Monk Novels. ★ 📖

William Monk, a London police detective circa 1856, turns to private investigation after disputing some of the Force's official methods. Affected with amnesia, he occasionally gets glimpses of the man he used to be, and doesn't like what he sees: a hard man, shrewd and intelligent, but disliked by many. Hester Latterly, a no-nonsense nurse who served with Florence Nightingale in the Crimean War, has an uncanny sense of people's true character. As Hester assists in Monk's investigations, she frequently steals the show. Perry's novels all contain excellent depictions of Victorian society—cobblestone streets, gas-lit alleys, and elegant drawing-rooms—that never intrude on the suspense. Most end with dramatic courtroom scenes, with brilliant barrister Oliver Rathbone on the defense. **Private detective/Traditional.**

The Face of a Stranger. Fawcett Columbine, 1990. 328pp.

Following a carriage accident, police detective William Monk loses his memory. Hiding his amnesia, he returns to work, puzzling out the murder of a nobleman named Grey who fought in the Crimean War.

A Dangerous Mourning. Fawcett Columbine, 1991. 330pp.

Octavia Haslett, the widowed daughter of a British aristocrat, is murdered while sleeping in her own bed.

Defend and Betray. Fawcett Columbine, 1992. 385pp.

Alexandra Carlyon readily confesses to murdering her husband in a fit of jealousy, but Hester believes that she's hiding something.

A Sudden, Fearful Death. Fawcett Columbine, 1993. 383pp.

Attending to her administrative duties at the Royal Free Hospital, Lady Cassandra Daviot, Monk's patron, discovers the body of Nurse Prudence Barrymore stuffed in a laundry chute.

The Sins of the Wolf. Fawcett Columbine, 1994. 374pp.

Hired as a nurse, Hester accompanies Mary Farraline, an elderly Scottish woman, to London by train—and gets accused of poisoning her for profit when Mrs. Farraline dies en route.

Cain His Brother. Fawcett Columbine, 1995. 390pp.

Monk investigates the disappearance of businessman Angus Stonefield. His wife Genevieve, who reports him missing, believes that Angus was killed by his violent twin brother, Caleb.

Weighed in the Balance. Fawcett Columbine, 1996. 355pp.

Oliver Rathbone agrees to defend Countess Zorah Restova against charges of slander brought against her by Princess Gisela of Felzburg. Zorah had publicly accused the princess of murdering her husband, and the only way Rathbone can clear Zorah is by proving that her story is true.

The Silent Cry. Fawcett Columbine, 1997. 361pp.

Hester and Monk, independently investigating a brutal assault on a gentleman's son and a series of violent attacks on prostitutes, realize that the two cases might be connected.

A Breach of Promise. Fawcett Columbine, 1998. 374pp. (Original title: *White Sepulchres.*)

Architect Killian Melville broke his promise to marry Zillah Lambert, whose parents sue him because he ruined her chances for marriage. Rathbone, who takes Melville's case, can't get his client to explain his reasons for jilting Zillah.

The Twisted Root. Ballantine, 1999. 346pp.

Monk pursues a missing persons case: Miriam Gardiner, a bride-to-be, apparently fled the scene during a family party. When her coachman turns up dead, suspicion falls on Miriam.

Slaves of Obsession. Ballantine, 2001. 344pp. (Original title: *Slaves and Obsession.*)

Murder explodes at a dinner party hosted by London arms dealer Daniel Alberton, who plays Americans from the Union and the Confederacy against each other. Newlyweds Monk and Hester travel to Washington, D.C., and Virginia in search of a killer.

Funeral in Blue. Ballantine, 2002. 344pp.

Elissa Beck, the beautiful, frigid wife of one of Hester's medical colleagues, is found strangled to death in a London artist's studio.

Death of a Stranger. Ballantine, 2003. 337pp.

Railway magnate Nolan Baltimore meets his end in a London brothel, which distracts Hester from her newly opened clinic—and her patients' odd symptoms of abuse. And Monk, investigating a case for a new client, recovers most of his memory at last.

The Shifting Tide. Ballantine, 2004. 352pp.

Monk skulks around unfamiliar territory, the River Thames, in search of the men who stole precious cargo—ivory tusks—from Clement Louvain's schooner.

Rogow, Roberta.

Charles Dodgson/Arthur Conan Doyle Mysteries. ✍

Arthur Conan Doyle, the future author of the Sherlock Holmes mysteries, plays Dr. Watson to his friend Reverend Charles Dodgson, better known as novelist Lewis Carroll. Set in the 1880s, when Doyle was still an aspiring author. **Private detective/Traditional.**

The Problem of the Missing Miss. St. Martin's Minotaur, 1998. 261pp.

The Problem of the Spiteful Spiritualist. St. Martin's Press, 1999. 281pp.

The Problem of the Evil Editor. St. Martin's Minotaur, 2000. 288pp.

The Problem of the Surly Servant. St. Martin's Minotaur, 2001. 288pp.

Twentieth Century

In Edwardian times (1901–1910) and slightly thereafter, England saw a period of relative prosperity, and the lighthearted atmosphere is reflected in many of these novels. Mysteries set during or after World War I are darker and more suspenseful, not surprisingly, while those set in the 1920s and 1930s, when women were out in the workforce, have a strong social conscience.

Allen, Conrad.

George Porter Dillman/Genevieve Masefield Series.

To escape people's notice, George Porter Dillman, shipboard detective for the Cunard Line in the early twentieth century, blends in among the well-to-do first class passengers. On the maiden voyage of the *Lusitania* in 1907 (detailed in the first book) he meets Genevieve Masefield, a spirited British lady who rejects his overtures of friendship at first. On subsequent voyages she joins him in his sleuthing. A cozy romantic series set aboard luxury liners, as they sail from Britain or New York to ports around the world. (Pseudonym for Keith Miles, who also writes as Edward Marston.) **Amateur detective/Traditional.**

Murder on the Lusitania. St. Martin's Minotaur, 1999. 266pp.

Murder on the Mauretania. St. Martin's Minotaur, 2000. 277pp.

Murder on the Minnesota. St. Martin's Minotaur, 2001. 295pp.

Murder on the Caronia. St. Martin's Minotaur, 2003. 290pp.

Murder on the Marmora. St. Martin's Minotaur, 2004. 295pp.

Dunn, Carola.

Daisy Dalrymple Series.

In this cozy series, Daisy Dalrymple, a Viscount's daughter in 1920s England, takes a job at a magazine after losing nearly everyone she loves in World War I. An emancipated woman with classic flapper style, Daisy hardly blinks an eye over her developing relationship with Scotland Yard inspector Alec Fletcher, though they come from social classes that wouldn't normally mix. While investigating crimes on English country estates or in the big city, Daisy makes a charming amateur sleuth. Dunn also writes Regency romances, and her graceful style spills over into her mysteries. **Amateur detective/Cozy.**

Death at Wentwater Court. St. Martin's Press, 1994. 216pp.

The Winter Garden Mystery. St. Martin's Press, 1995. 226pp.

Requiem for a Mezzo. St. Martin's Press, 1996. 212pp.

Murder on the Flying Scotsman. St. Martin's Press, 1997. 213pp.

Damsel in Distress. St. Martin's Press, 1997. 234pp.

Dead in the Water. St. Martin's Press, 1998. 249pp.

Styx and Stones. St. Martin's Press, 1999. 231pp.

Rattle His Bones. St. Martin's Minotaur, 2000. 243pp.

To Davy Jones Below. St. Martin's Minotaur, 2001. 248pp.

The Case of the Murdered Muckraker. St. Martin's Minotaur, 2002. 262pp.

Mistletoe and Murder. St. Martin's Minotaur, 2002. 260pp.

Die Laughing. St. Martin's Minotaur, 2003. 276pp.

A Mourning Wedding. St. Martin's Minotaur, 2004. 288pp.

King, Laurie R.

Mary Russell Series.

In Mary Russell, King created a feminine equal to Sherlock Holmes, a woman who can match him in both wit and cunning. Mary begins the series as Holmes's bookish and unconventional teenage apprentice, but Mary soon proves that she can hold her own with the distinguished hero. Despite their vast age difference, the obvious chemistry between them proves hard to ignore, and romance soon develops. Later, as his wife and partner-in-crime, Mary proves that she's as good a crime-solver as her famous husband. Set between 1915 and the 1920s, mostly in England. **Amateur detective/Traditional.**

The Beekeeper's Apprentice. St. Martin's Press, 1994. 347pp.

Sherlock Holmes, retired and peacefully keeping bees, comes across Mary Russell while roaming the Sussex Downs one day in 1915. Intrigued by her wit and insight, he makes Mary his apprentice. They examine a series of crimes together: the kidnapping of an American senator's daughter, a landowner's strange illness, and death threats against Holmes and everyone he knows.

A Monstrous Regiment of Women. St. Martin's Press, 1995. 368pp.

Veronica Beaconsfield, one of Mary's old friends, introduces her to an odd religious group/suffrage organization, the New Temple of God, which has been attracting wealthy female supporters. Not long after several of these women change their wills to benefit the group, they turn up dead.

A Letter of Mary. St. Martin's Press, 1996. 276pp.

It's 1923, and amateur archaeologist Dorothy Ruskin approaches Mary and Holmes with an ancient papyrus appearing to be written by Mary Magdalene. When Miss Ruskin dies in a traffic accident the next evening, Mary and Holmes suspect murder.

The Moor. St. Martin's Press, 1998. 307pp.

One of Holmes's closest friends, the Reverend Sabine Baring-Gould, asks Holmes to travel to Dartmoor to look into paranormal events: People have spotted a ghostly coach that leaves death in its wake. Holmes asks Mary, now his wife, to leave her studies temporarily and help him investigate.

O Jerusalem. Bantam, 1999. 384pp.

King shakes things up by taking readers back to the early days of Russell and Holmes. In 1918, they travel to Palestine at the request of his brother Mycroft, and the Arab region is as politically unstable as ever. A series of murders that Holmes investigates must be related, or so he thinks, to rivalry among the religious groups.

Justice Hall. Bantam, 2002. 331pp.

Gabriel Hughenfort, the heir to Justice Hall, died in the trenches in World War I France under mysterious circumstances. While Mary and Holmes search for the next rightful heir to the estate, they discover a mystery that leads from France to the English countryside and the New World.

The Game. Bantam, 2004. 368pp.

With the coming of the New Year 1924, Mary hopes for some quiet time alone with her husband. Instead they wind up traveling to India at Mycroft Holmes's request, in the hopes of tracking down English spy Kimball O'Hara—the model for Rudyard Kipling's novel *Kim.*

Kingsbury, Kate.

Pennyfoot Hotel Mysteries.

In 1906, Cecily Sinclair owns the Pennyfoot Hotel in an English seaside village that the London aristocracy frequently visit. A recent widow, Cecily is left alone to run the hotel with the help of her trusty hotel manager, but it's not easy to explain murder to her guests. (Pseudonym for Doreen Roberts.) **Amateur detective/Cozy.**

Room with a Clue. Jove, 1993. 204pp.

Do Not Disturb. Berkley Prime Crime, 1994. 203pp.

Service for Two. Berkley Prime Crime, 1994. 203pp.

Eat, Drink and Be Buried. Berkley Prime Crime, 1994. 203pp.

Check-Out Time. Berkley Prime Crime, 1995. 217pp.

Grounds for Murder. Berkley Prime Crime, 1995. 236pp.

Pay the Piper. Berkley Prime Crime, 1996. 219pp.

Chivalry Is Dead. Berkley Prime Crime, 1996. 215pp.

Ring for Tomb Service. Berkley Prime Crime, 1997. 236pp.

Death with Reservations. Berkley Prime Crime, 1998. 217pp.

Dying Room Only. Berkley Prime Crime, 1998. 214pp.

Maid to Murder. Berkley Prime Crime, 1999. 214pp.

No Clue at the Inn. Berkley Prime Crime, 2003. 320pp.

Manor House Mysteries.

In the English village of Sitting Marsh during World War II, Lady Elizabeth Hartleigh Compton still plays at being the lady of the manor even though her late husband's gambling debts left her penniless. She lives off the rents paid by the tenants living in cottages on her estate. Times are especially stressful, with bombing raids threatening their lives and American soldiers invading their peaceful existence. Lady Elizabeth turns to amateur sleuthing to keep herself amused and out of necessity, because the villagers depend on her strength and wisdom. **Amateur detective/Cozy.**

A Bicycle Built for Murder. Berkley Prime Crime, 2001. 216pp.

Death Is in the Air. Berkley Prime Crime, 2001. 199pp.

For Whom Death Tolls. Berkley Prime Crime, 2002. 208pp.

Dig Deep for Murder. Berkley Prime Crime, 2002. 199pp.

Paint by Murder. Berkley Prime Crime, 2003. 215pp.

Berried Alive. Berkley Prime Crime, 2004. 202pp.

Linscott, Gillian.

Nell Bray Mysteries. **YA**

Nell Bray, a militant suffragette and amateur sleuth in Edwardian Britain, inherited her radical political beliefs from her father. As a student at Oxford, Nell joins Emmeline Pankhurst's group, the Women's Social and Political Union, after it appears that women may be denied the right to vote. Though she's obviously a feminist, Nell's narrative voice is witty and intelligent rather than anachronistic. The novels jump back and forth in time to reveal bits of Nell's and suffragist history. They can be read in any order. **Amateur detective/Traditional.**

Sister Beneath the Sheet. St. Martin's Press, 1991. 224pp.

The day before her death, courtesan Topaz Brown wills her immense fortune to the Women's Social and Political Union, which is strange since she hardly espoused feminist causes. Nell searches for her killer with the help of Topaz's maid, Tansy. Early twentieth century.

Hanging on the Wire. St. Martin's Press, 1992. 215pp.

Nell helps a friend at a military hospital in Wales, where World War I soldiers are recovering from wounds and shell-shock. One soldier is found shot through the head, hanging over the wire surrounding the hospital, and Nell doesn't believe it is suicide.

Stage Fright. St. Martin's Press, 1993. 188pp.

In 1909, George Bernard Shaw approaches Nell to take a new case: protecting Bella Flanagan, the star of his latest play, from her resentful husband.

An Easy Day for a Lady. St. Martin's Press, 1995. 210pp.

Nell takes a mountain-climbing trip to Chamonix, France, in 1910. Relatives arrive to claim the body of an explorer who died in an avalanche thirty years earlier. Their squabbling reveals murderous intent, both past and present.

Crown Witness. St. Martin's Press, 1995. 218pp.

During George V's pre-coronation parade in 1910, one of Nell's friends gets arrested for murdering a man on a parade float.

Dead Man's Sweetheart. St. Martin's Press, 1996. 246pp.

While visiting her brother Stuart out in the country, Nell grows intrigued with the story of Osbert Newbiggin, a local mill owner who was murdered, especially when the killer's lawyer still proclaims his client's innocence.

Dance on Blood. St. Martin's Minotaur, 1998. 250pp.

In 1912, Nell refuses to participate in a plot to bomb David Lloyd George's house. When Lloyd George hears of it, he strikes a deal with her: He'll drop charges against her friends if she retrieves some indiscreet letters from a barefoot dancer.

Absent Friends. St. Martin's Press, 1999. 282pp.

In 1918, women have won the vote at last, and Nell decides to run for office. One of her Conservative rivals is killed during a fireworks explosion, and his widow asks for Nell's help. Ellis Peters Historical Dagger; Herodotus Award.

The Perfect Daughter. St. Martin's Minotaur, 2000. 308pp.

Verona Bray, a young London art student in 1914 London, dies, apparently a suicide. Verona's father blames the bad influence of her cousin Nell.

Dead Man Riding. St. Martin's Minotaur, 2002. 320pp.

In 1900, Nell and some Oxford friends take a reading holiday in the country, only to find that their host, her friend Alan's uncle, has been accused of murdering a local boy.

Blood on the Wood. St. Martin's Minotaur, 2004. 311pp.

The late Philomena Venn bequeathed a valuable French painting to the Women's Social and Political Union. When Nell discovers that it's a fake, she breaks into the Venns' home to switch it with the original and stumbles onto a corpse.

Monahan, Brent.

The Sceptered Isle Club. St. Martin's Minotaur, 2002. 306pp.

Annotated with the rest of the John Le Brun series, under "United States, Twentieth Century."

Morrissey, J. P.

A Weekend at Blenheim. Thomas Dunne, 2002. 305pp.

Blenheim Palace is the hereditary Oxfordshire seat of the Dukes of Marlborough. In 1905 its duchess, the former Consuelo Vanderbilt, invites American architect John Vanbrugh to renovate her living quarters. While there, John Singer Sargent's sketchbook is stolen, a housemaid is strangled, and Vanbrugh uncovers letters that reveal a past love triangle. **Amateur detective/Traditional.**

Perry, Anne.

World War I Series.

A projected five-book series set against the backdrop of World War I, with new volumes expected annually. Joseph Reavley, the protagonist of the first book, is based on the real-life Captain Joseph Reavley, Perry's grandfather, who served in France during the war. **Amateur detective/Traditional.**

No Graves As Yet. Ballantine, 2003. 339pp.

Joseph Reavley, who teaches biblical languages at Cambridge, learns one day in 1914 that his parents were killed in a car crash—the same day that Archduke Ferdinand was assassinated in Sarajevo. Joseph's brother Matthew reveals that their father possessed a letter supposedly containing information that could destroy Western civilization. But the letter can't be found, and when Joseph learns of the murder of his favorite student, he knows his problems have only begun.

Shoulder the Sky. Ballantine, 2004. 352pp.

It is 1915, and Joseph, Matthew, and Judith Reavley all actively serve in World War I. Though their parents' murder has been solved, sort of, they don't believe that the story's really over. In the midst of the chaos of war, Joseph discovers the dead body of a journalist.

Roberts, David.

Lord Edward Corinth and Verity Browne Series.

A proper British mystery set among the aristocracy in the 1930s. Lord Edward Corinth, the jaded younger brother of the Duke of Mersham, crosses societal lines to investigate crimes with crusading left-wing journalist Verity Browne. **Amateur detective/Traditional.**

Sweet Poison. Carroll & Graf, 2000. 277pp.

At a dinner hosted by the Duke of Mersham, the guests discuss Hitler's sudden rise to power in Germany. General Sir Alistair Craig, who opposes a relationship between England and Hitler, keels over after ingesting a cyanide capsule. Is it suicide or murder?

Bones of the Buried. Carroll & Graf, 2001. 342pp.

Spain is on the verge of civil war in 1936. Verity needs help defending her Communist lover from a murder charge, so Edward travels to Spain at her request—but against his better judgment.

Hollow Crown. Carroll & Graf, 2002. 309pp.

It's no secret that Mrs. Molly Harkness, an old friend of Edward's and a mistress of the Prince of Wales, has stolen some of Wallis Simpson's personal letters. But before Edward can approach her to get them back, Molly is murdered, and the letters disappear.

Dangerous Sea. Carroll & Graf, 2003. 248pp.

In 1937, Edward and Verity cross the ocean aboard the *Queen Mary*, though not together. When the body of a British government official turns up in a refrigeration compartment, they join forces again to find out whodunit and why.

Todd, Charles.

Ian Rutledge Series.

Scotland Yard Inspector Ian Rutledge, shell-shocked after horrific experiences in France during World War I, returns to work to save his sanity. Banishing his personal demons proves just as difficult as solving cases, for the voice of Hamish MacLeod, a young soldier he was forced to execute for cowardice, taunts him constantly inside his head. Elegant prose and beautiful descriptions of English village life combine with haunting, psychologically intense drama. The novels are set a month apart, all in 1919. ("Charles Todd" is a pseudonym for mother-son writing team Carolyn Watjen and David Watjen.) **Amateur detective/Traditional.**

A Test of Wills. St. Martin's Press, 1996. 282pp.

The only witness to the Warwickshire murder of Colonel Harris, a popular military officer, is a shell-shock victim who has lost his grip on reality. Even worse, the top suspect is the Prince of Wales's good friend.

Wings of Fire. St. Martin's Press, 1998. 294pp.

Among three people murdered in a remote Cornwall village is Olivia, a young poet whose written words gave Rutledge hope during the war.

Search the Dark. Thomas Dunne, 1999. 279pp.

Is a mentally disturbed veteran who had lost his wife and children in a bombing raid guilty of murdering a Dorset woman?

Legacy of the Dead. Bantam, 2000. 308pp.

Rutledge travels to Durham to track the last known moments of Eleanor Gray, a young woman whose remains may have been found on a Scottish mountainside.

Watchers of Time. Bantam, 2001. 339pp.

Rutledge discovers connections between a priest murdered in a small Norfolk town and the sinking of the great ship *Titanic*.

A Fearsome Doubt. Bantam, 2002. 295pp.

Nell Shaw, the widow of a man who had been sent to the gallows on Rutledge's evidence, brings Rutledge proof that her husband was innocent.

The Murder Stone. Bantam, 2003. 351pp.

When her grandfather Francis Hatton suffers a stroke in 1916, Francesca Hatton abandons her work with the Red Cross in London and hurries to River's Edge, his rural estate. By that point she's the last of her line, since five of her male cousins have died in World War I. After Francis's death, new revelations come to light about additional property he owned and a murder he may have committed years ago. Todd took a break from the Ian Rutledge series to write this stand-alone novel. **Amateur detective/Traditional.**

Winspear, Jacqueline.

Maisie Dobbs Series. YA

When Maisie Dobbs was fourteen, her mother died, and Maisie went into service to help her father make ends meet. In 1929, thanks to a Cambridge education given to her by her employer's friend, thirty-three-year-old Maisie opens a detective agency in London. **Private detective/Traditional.**

7

Maisie Dobbs. Soho, 2003. 294pp.

Maisie's first case looks like a simple infidelity investigation but soon turns into something more. The trail leads to a convalescent home for war-wounded soldiers in Kent, from which few residents come out alive. Agatha Award.

Birds of a Feather. Soho, 2004. 311pp.

Maisie gets hired to find Charlotte Waite, the missing, difficult daughter of a London grocery magnate, and starts investigating Charlotte's habits and friends. When three of these friends turn up murdered, Maisie gradually connects their deaths to Charlotte's disappearance.

Europe

The Middle Ages

As in mysteries set in medieval England (earlier this chapter), detectives must gather all their knowledge of religion and contemporary politics to solve crimes. These novels also have elements of adventure, as their protagonists often travel back and forth across Europe, either on pilgrimage or on Crusade.

Gordon, Alan.

Fool's Guild Mysteries.

Members of the Fool's Guild, trained as jesters to perform in the courts of Europe and the Middle East in the late twelfth and early thirteenth centuries, work behind the scenes to ensure peace and political stability. Theophilos, aka Feste the Fool, is the primary sleuth, though the mystery content isn't always primary. As fools, Theo and his wife Viola/Claudia/Aglaia can speak freely with their patrons, unlike most courtiers, and this gains them respect. The series juggles dry humor, mystery, history, and fast-paced adventure. The first three should be read in order, but the last two are retrospective tales, and can stand alone. **Amateur detective/ Traditional.**

Thirteenth Night. St. Martin's Minotaur, 1999. 243pp.

In 1200, upon receiving the message "Orsino is dead," Feste returns to the Duchy of Orsino. He suspects the involvement of Saladin's agent, Malvolio, in the Duke's death. A new take on the aftermath of Shakespeare's *Twelfth Night.*

Jester Leaps In. St. Martin's Minotaur, 2001. 276pp.

Feste and Viola venture south from Italy to Constantinople, where other agents of the Fool's Guild have disappeared without trace. The pair, with Viola disguised as Feste's male servant, get caught up in a dispute over the Byzantine throne.

A Death in the Venetian Quarter. St. Martin's Minotaur, 2002. 288pp.

In Constantinople at the time of the Fourth Crusade, circa 1203, Feste and his wife link the death of a silk merchant in the city's Venetian quarter to the trade rivalry between Venice and Byzantium.

The Widow of Jerusalem. St. Martin's Minotaur, 2003. 288pp.

Theophilos relates the story of Scarlet the Dwarf, his superior in the Guild, and their joint adventures in Tyre during the Third Crusade in 1191. Theo befriends the lonely Queen Isabelle of Jerusalem and gets caught up in high-level political intrigue.

An Antic Disposition. St. Martin's Minotaur, 2004. 337pp.

A former Guild member tells of how Terence of York, better known as the fool Yorick, played an integral role in a dispute over the Danish crown in 1157. A retelling of the events behind *Hamlet* from the fools' point of view; very creative, yet more somber than others in the series.

Newman, Sharan.

Catherine LeVendeur Mysteries. **YA**

Catherine LeVendeur begins the series as a novice/scholar at the Convent of the Paraclete in 1139 France, yet her curiosity and outspokenness make her unsuited to a contemplative life. The Jewish ancestry of her father, merchant Hubert LeVendeur, complicates matters for Catherine, as does her attraction to Edgar, a stonemaster's apprentice she encounters in the first book. Newman, a trained medievalist, creates sympathetic characters that belong to their time rather than to ours. Religious piety, romance, and political intrigue combine with lively storytelling. The next volume will be *The Witch in the Well*. **Amateur detective/Traditional.**

Death Comes As Epiphany. TOR, 1993. 319pp.

Catherine's Mother Superior, Abbess Héloïse, asks her to discover the person who is trying to discredit the convent, and why. Catherine journeys to St. Denis to recover a psalter and discover whether it contains heretical passages that could condemn Héloïse's former lover, Peter Abelard.

The Devil's Door. Forge, 1994. 384pp.

One day in 1140, Countess Alys of Tonnerre appears at the Convent of the Paraclete, apparently the victim of abuse. When the Countess deeds some land to the convent after her death, it upsets her husband, Raynald. Catherine and Edgar, who are betrothed, puzzle over the countess's mysterious death and the piece of land that everyone seems to want.

The Wandering Arm. Forge, 1995. 351pp.

Edgar, now Catherine's husband, defends the Jewish community of Paris when a holy relic of St. Aldhelm disappears from Salisbury Cathedral.

Strong as Death. Forge, 1996. 384pp.

Distraught after two miscarriages, Catherine and Edgar go on pilgrimage to the shrine of Santiago de Compostela in Spain to petition St. James for a child. Along the way, several pilgrims traveling in their group are murdered.

🏅 *Cursed in the Blood.* Forge, 1998. 348pp.

Upon hearing news from Scotland that Edgar's two oldest brothers have been ambushed and murdered, Catherine, Edgar, and baby James journey from France to Edgar's home. Separated from her husband while he and his secretive father try to find a killer, Catherine comes upon a plot to wipe out the entire family. Herodotus Award.

7

The Difficult Saint. Forge, 1999. 350pp.

Catherine's sister Agnes, estranged from her family due to religious differences, is accused of murdering her new German husband. Catherine, Edgar, and their children travel to Germany to clear Agnes's name, risking their own safety in the land's anti-Semitic climate.

To Wear the White Cloak. Forge, 2001. 367pp.

When a Knight Templar is found dead in Catherine's Paris home, the long-held secret about Catherine's Jewish heritage threatens to come to light.

Heresy. Forge, 2002. 352pp.

Astrolabe, the son of Abelard and Héloïse, takes refuge with Catherine's family when someone frames him for a young woman's murder.

The Outcast Dove. Forge, 2003. 432pp.

While in Spain, Catherine's cousin Solomon, whose connection to her is kept secret due to his Jewish religion, confronts his estranged father. "Brother James," as he's now known, had abandoned Judaism to become a monk. Having no other choice, James turns to his son Solomon for help when a fellow monk is murdered.

Roe, Caroline.

The Chronicles of Isaac of Girona.

Isaac, a blind, Jewish physician in 1350s Girona, Spain, doesn't need his sight to solve crimes and bring the perpetrators to justice. Medieval Spain is a unique setting in fiction, and Girona's Jewish quarter is richly described. With their numerous plotlines and characters—members of the royal court, religious officials, and Isaac's large family—the books are best read in order. *A Consolation for an Exile* will be the next volume. (Roe is a pseudonym for Medora Sale.) **Amateur detective/Traditional.**

Remedy for Treason. Berkley Prime Crime, 1998. 259pp.

The body of a royal attendant, who went out disguised as a nun, turns up in Girona's public baths. The Bishop of Girona asks Isaac to investigate.

Cure for a Charlatan. Berkley Prime Crime, 1999. 262pp.

What caused the strange illness, delusions, and death of three young men: poison or witchcraft?

An Antidote for Avarice. Berkley Prime Crime, 1999. 274pp.

Isaac accompanies the ailing Bishop Berenguer of Girona to Tarragona for a religious council. Accompanying him is his sharp-tongued wife Judith, who hopes to arrange a marriage for their daughter Raquel. Both en route and elsewhere in Spain, papal messengers turn up dead.

Solace for a Sinner. Berkley Prime Crime, 2000. 277pp.

A respected merchant, found dead in Girona's streets, is killed on his way to buy what he hoped was the Holy Grail.

A Potion for a Widow. Berkley Prime Crime, 2001. 269pp.

Yusuf, Isaac's young Muslim protégé, leaves Girona to deliver a message to King Pedro in Sardinia. Along the way, his party discovers a young woman disguised as a boy.

A Draught for a Dead Man. Berkley Prime Crime, 2002. 322pp.

Isaac travels to Catalonia with a woman and her family for her arranged marriage, but while there, he ends up treating a seriously injured Christian nobleman. The first series hardcover.

A Poultice for a Healer. Berkley Prime Crime, 2003. 320pp.

While Isaac and his assistant Raquel are treating Bishop Berenguer, a herbalist dying of poison comes to warn the bishop of treachery.

The Renaissance and Reformation

In these mysteries, the Italian Renaissance isn't all glitter, romance, and enlightenment; it also conceals lethal intent.

Eyre, Elizabeth.

Sigismondo Series.

In fifteenth-century Venice, the enigmatic knight Sigismondo and his faithful sidekick, Benno, turn up connections between murders of the nobility and political struggles between the Italian city-states. (Eyre is a pseudonym for Jill Staynes and Margaret Storey, who also write as Susannah Stacey.) **Amateur detective/Traditional.**

Death of the Duchess. Harcourt Brace, 1992. 241pp.

Curtains for the Cardinal. Harcourt Brace, 1993. 260pp.

Poison for the Prince. Harcourt Brace, 1993. 309pp.

Bravo for the Bride. St. Martin's Press, 1994. 308pp.

Axe for an Abbot. St. Martin's Press, 1996. 339pp.

Dirge for a Doge. St. Martin's Press, 1997. 344pp.

Gellis, Roberta.

***Lucrezia Borgia and the Mother of Poisons*. Forge, 2003. 336pp.**

Lucrezia Borgia is commonly thought to be a scheming, incestuous tart, but Gellis shows readers a different Lucrezia—an intelligent, beautiful woman who solves crimes. When Lucrezia's husband, the Duke of Ferrara, accuses her of poisoning his mistress, Lucrezia fears that the old, false rumors about her past will come back to haunt her. She takes on the role of lead investigator to clear her own name and reveal a killer. **Amateur detective/Traditional.**

Herman, George.

Leonardo da Vinci Series.

Leonardo da Vinci—inventor, artist, and all-around Renaissance man—joins forces with an educated dwarf, Niccolo da Pavia, to investigate politically motivated crimes throughout 1490s Italy. Leonardo's knowledge of science, medicine, and human nature frequently holds the key to the puzzles. Herman self-published the last volume with IUniverse. **Amateur detective/Traditional.**

A Comedy of Murders. Carroll & Graf, 1994. 355pp.

The Tears of the Madonna. Carroll & Graf, 1996. 279pp.

The Florentine Mourners. IUniverse, 1999. 364pp.

Early Modern Europe

Europe in the eighteenth and nineteenth centuries saw (and foreshadowed) a number of political revolutions. Just like everyone else, the protagonists of these mysteries are forced to take sides, like it or not. Some are adventure stories as well, with the detectives crossing back and forth across country borders in pursuit of justice.

Akunin, Boris.

Erast Fandorin Series.

Erast Fandorin, the newest recruit to the Moscow Police in late nineteenth-century Russia, is a wide-eyed innocent who's eager to please. But Fandorin gets the job done, which is all that matters in the end. His bumbling detective skills are comic, and the bad guys are truly evil, which can make the series seem like a parody at times. First published in Russia, where Akunin's novels are bestsellers. (Pseudonym of Grigory Chkhartishvili.) **Public detective/Traditional.**

The Winter Queen. Random House, 2003. 244pp.

In 1876, a wealthy university student commits suicide in the Alexander Gardens in full view of a large crowd. Fandorin connects this strange death to a murder he himself witnesses, since both dead men had left their fortunes to an orphanage run by the same English lady.

Murder on the Leviathan. Random House, 2004. 224pp.

While on board the S.S. *Leviathan* en route to Japan, Fandorin finds himself a suspect in the murder of a British aristocrat, which is being investigated by a bumbling French police commissioner, the aptly named Gustave Gauche.

Douglas, Carole Nelson.

Irene Adler Series.

Irene Adler, the beautiful opera singer who managed to outwit Sherlock Holmes in the Arthur Conan Doyle short story "A Scandal in Bohemia," takes her place in fiction once more. With her handsome husband, barrister Godfrey Norton, Irene travels throughout Europe in the 1880s on a series of crime-solving adventures. Penelope "Nell" Huxleigh, Irene's prim, younger companion, narrates the tales. Witty and intelligent writing mingle with adventure, murder, and mayhem. **Amateur detective/Traditional.**

Good Night, Mr. Holmes. Tom Doherty Associates, 1990. 408pp.

Nell Huxleigh reveals the real story behind Conan Doyle's "scandal in Bohemia," in which the Crown Prince of Bohemia wrote some indiscreet letters to opera singer Irene Adler and schemed to get them back.

Good Morning, Irene. Tor, 1991. 374pp. (Alternate title: *The Adventuress.*)

The deaths of Irene and Godfrey, reported in the papers, have been greatly exaggerated. Irene, in exile with Godfrey and Nell in Paris, befriends Sarah Bernhardt and solves the mystery of a drowned sailor with a mysterious tattooed chest.

Irene at Large. Tor, 1992. 381pp.

A stranger found poisoned on a Paris street leads the trio to a mystery involving Afghanistan's role in the Great Game.

Irene's Last Waltz. Forge, 1994. 480pp. (Alternate title: *Another Scandal in Bohemia.*)

At Charles Worth's Parisian salon, Irene and Nell meet Queen Clotilde of Bohemia, wife of Irene's former lover, who wants to know why her husband won't consummate their marriage. The trail leads them to Prague, where a mysterious Golem (clay-monster) is supposedly haunting the city.

Chapel Noir. Forge, 2001. 494pp.

The brutal murders of two courtesans in a Paris brothel eerily echo the London killings of Jack the Ripper. Irene closes in on the killer at the 1889 World's Fair in Paris.

Castle Rouge. Forge, 2002. 540pp.

Jack the Ripper, thought to have been captured by Irene in *Chapel Noir*, has escaped—and he's taken Nell Huxleigh with him. Godfrey has also disappeared. Irene heads to Eastern Europe on their trail, accompanied by reporter Nellie Bly, theater manager Bram Stoker (who gets some ideas for *Dracula* along the way), and a British spy.

Femme Fatale. Forge, 2003. 492pp.

Irene, brilliant and enigmatic, has never revealed her past to anyone. American journalist Nellie Bly, who had helped Irene track Jack the Ripper, writes a letter asking Irene to come to New York City. The teaser: Irene's mother is targeted for death.

Dukthas, Ann.

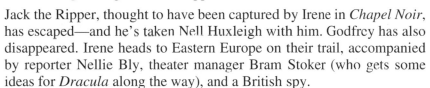

Nicholas Segalla Time Travel Mysteries.

Debonair sleuth Nicholas Segalla, cursed to wander the earth for eternity, tells professional historian Ann Dukthas the real stories behind the deaths of well-known royals. Other series volumes include *A Time for the Death of a King* (Mary Queen of Scots and Henry Lord Darnley) and *In the Time of the Poisoned Queen* (Bloody Mary), listed under Tudor England. **Amateur detective/Traditional.**

The Prince Lost to Time. St. Martin's Press, 1995. 229pp.

Paris, 1793. What really happened to Marie Antoinette's ten-year-old son, the Dauphin, after she was guillotined?

The Time of Murder at Mayerling. St. Martin's Press, 1996. 217pp.

Vienna, 1889. What was the real story behind the suicide-murder of Rudolph, Archduke of Austria, and his mistress Maria Vetsera at Rudolph's private hunting lodge?

O'Brien, Charles.

Anne Cartier Series.

Murder and mystery in pre-Revolutionary Paris, with co-detectives Anne Cartier, a vaudeville actress and teacher of the deaf, and Colonel Paul de Saint-Martin of the French highway patrol. **Amateur detective/Traditional.**

Mute Witness. Poisoned Pen Press, 2001. 325pp.

Official reports state that Anne's stepfather, Antoine Dubois, had first killed his mistress before turning the gun on himself. At the request of another family member, Colonel Paul de Saint-Martin sends for Anne, who is certain that Antoine is not guilty. In Paris, Anne finds a secret witness, a deaf/mute seamstress who's afraid to come forward with what she knows.

Black Gold. Poisoned Pen Press, 2002. 396pp.

In 1787, Paul travels to Bath, England, to visit Anne at her place of employment—tutoring Sir Harry Rogers' deaf son—and to track down Captain Maurice Fitzroy, who raped an aristocrat's daughter in Paris.

Noble Blood. Severn House, 2004. 320pp.

Anne, teacher at the Institute for the Deaf, defends a deaf maid at the French royal court from a murder charge.

Twentieth Century

Mysteries set in the early twentieth-century United States reflect the freewheeling atmosphere of the Roaring Twenties, and this is true for Europe to a small degree. However, the majority of these novels mirror the confusion facing the populace during or after World Wars I and II. Amid the death and destruction of wartime, simple cases of murder can easily be overlooked—or so the perpetrators hope.

Engel, Howard.

Murder in Montparnasse. **Overlook, 1999. 304pp.**

Paris in the 1920s swarms with expatriates, the intellectual and the pseudo-intellectual, the famous and the obscure. When the latest victim of a serial killer turns out to be one of Jason Waddington's friends, Waddington leaves his bar-hopping pursuits and investigates. Readers who enjoy Ernest Hemingway's novels will recognize some of the secondary characters. **Amateur detective/Traditional/ Literary.**

Janes, J. Robert.

St. Cyr & Kohler Mysteries.

The unlikely crime-solving team of Jean Louis St-Cyr, a French inspector with the Sûreté National, and Hermann Kohler, a German agent with the Gestapo, takes to the streets of Occupied Paris. Their partnership and friendship makes the S.S. suspicious. Readers may also enjoy Alan Furst's historical espionage novels (Chapter 9). **Public detective/Traditional-Hard boiled.**

Mirage. D. I. Fine, 1992. 272pp. (Alternate title: *Mayhem.*)

Carousel. D. I. Fine, 1993. 287pp.

Kaleidoscope. Soho, 2001. 293pp. (Originally published 1993.)

Salamander. Soho, 1998. 311pp. (Originally published 1994.)

Mannequin. Soho, 1998. 258pp. (Originally published 1994.)

Dollmaker. Soho, 2002. 258pp. (Originally published 1995.)

Stonekiller. Soho, 1997. 261pp.

Sandman. Soho, 1997. 261pp.

Gypsy. London: Constable, 1997. 256pp.

Beekeeper. London: Orion, 2001. 305pp.

Flykiller. London: Orion, 2002. 408pp.

Pawel, Rebecca.

Carlos Tejada Alonso y León Series.

For those who lived through it, the Spanish Civil War (1936–1939) was more than just a precursor to World War II; it was a social revolution and fervent fight against fascism. Carlos Tejada, a young man moving up the ranks of the Guardia Civil, has always supported the Nationalist cause. In late 1939, when these mysteries take place, the war has ended with a Nationalist victory over the Republican government, but its legacy still remains. The next book will be *The Watcher in the Pine.* **Public detective/Traditional-Hard Boiled.**

Death of a Nationalist. Soho, 2003. 262pp.

Tejada discovers the body of his best friend in the streets of Madrid, and automatically assumes that the Communist woman standing over him is the killer. He shoots her dead, but he may have been wrong. Edgar Award.

7

Law of Return. Soho, 2004. 274pp.

Transferred to Salamanca to keep track of parolees, Tejada follows one of these men to San Sebastian. There he meets up with Elena Fernández, a former romantic interest, who is trying to help one of her father's Jewish friends avoid repatriation to Nazi Germany.

Shields, Jody.

The Fig Eater. Little, Brown, 2000. 311pp. 📖

In 1910 Vienna, a woman named Dora—Freud's famous patient—is found murdered. Her life is reconstructed by an unnamed inspector in the hopes of discovering who and what caused her death. Erzsebet, the inspector's Hungarian wife, does some detecting of her own, though in a more unorthodox fashion. Shields explores Freudian principles in the discussions of early twentieth-century methods of detection, such as newly developed forensic methods, the differing investigative methods of a husband and wife, and the detailed exploration of Dora's famous personality. **Amateur detective/Traditional/Literary.**

United States

Colonial America

In the close-knit settlements in early America, such as those in the Massachusetts Bay and Dutch colonies, tensions can run high, and this frequently leads to murder. The formal tone and dialogue evoke colonial times.

Lewis, Stephen.

Mysteries of Colonial Times.

Midwife Catherine Williams, the intelligent voice of reason in the God-fearing village of Newbury in colonial New England, solves crimes with the help of Massaquoit, a Pequot Indian she takes as a servant after English settlers decimate his tribe. This is a fairly dark series that effectively re-creates the repressive atmosphere of Puritan times. The formal dialogue feels authentic. While lighter moments certainly existed in Puritan society, though, they aren't shown here. The author based Catherine on Anne Hutchinson, a real-life religious reformer. **Amateur detective/Traditional.**

The Dumb Shall Sing. Berkley Prime Crime, 1999. 362pp.

An Irish Catholic girl is accused of murdering a baby she was minding, but Catherine is convinced that the accusations are based on religious intolerance.

The Blind in Darkness. Berkley Prime Crime, 2000. 265pp.

When old man Powell is found murdered in his cabin, the crime disguised as a scalping, the villagers suspect Massaquoit.

The Sea Hath Spoken. Berkley Prime Crime, 2001. 281pp.

Roger and Jane Whitcomb, a Quaker brother and sister, arrive in Newbury seeking religious freedom. The villagers don't welcome them, especially when the body of an English sailor from their ship washes up on shore.

Meyers, Maan.

The Dutchman. **Doubleday, 1992. 306pp.**

The Dutchman's Dilemma. **Bantam, 1995. 254pp.**

Both annotated under "Multi-Period American Series."

Miles, Margaret.

<u>**Bracebridge Mysteries.**</u>

> Charlotte Willett and Richard Longfellow, friends and next-door neighbors in the fictional countryside town of Bracebridge, Massachusetts, in the 1760s, find their peaceful lives repeatedly disturbed by murder. **Amateur detective/Traditional.**

> *A Wicked Way to Burn.* Bantam, 1998. 309pp.

> When a wealthy stranger bursts into flames by the side of the road, is it spontaneous combustion, witchcraft, or something even more sinister?

> *Too Soon for Flowers.* Bantam, 1999. 290pp.

> During a smallpox outbreak in Boston, many Bracebridge residents undergo inoculation, and one of them dies—but from something else.

> *No Rest for the Dove.* Bantam, 2000. 273pp.

> Death follows Richard's European friend Gian Carlo Lahte, an Italian singer nicknamed "the Dove," when he visits Bracebridge in 1765.

> *A Mischief in the Snow.* Bantam, 2001. 322pp.

> Is the death of Alexander Godwin, an unpopular Bracebridge resident, connected to the odd, gothic-like happenings on nearby Boar Island?

The American Revolution

Strangely, the intense political atmosphere of the American Revolution (1775–1783) hasn't inspired many historical mystery novels.

Meyers, Maan.

The Kingsbridge Plot. **Doubleday, 1993. 321pp.**

> Annotated under "Multi-Period American Series."

Swee, Karen.

Life, Liberty, and the Pursuit of Murder. **Bridge Works, 2004. 304pp.**

> In New Brunswick, New Jersey, in winter 1777, widow Abigail Lawrence has her hands full with operating a tavern, raising a teenage daughter, and trying to keep billeted British soldiers from causing a ruckus. When one of her guests dies, pinned to the floor with a sword, the motive probably has something to do with the letters to George Washington he was carrying. **Amateur detective/Traditional.**

Early United States

In mysteries set between the end of the Revolution and the beginning of the Civil War, the emphasis is on America's social history: race relations, women's suffrage, and the growth of cities. These works are entertaining, though serious and occasionally grim.

Hambly, Barbara.

Benjamin January Mystery Series. 📖

Benjamin January, a dark-skinned, mixed-race man in 1830s New Orleans, doesn't fit neatly into any racial category. Returning home after many years abroad in Paris, where he trained as a doctor, Ben decides to teach music because he's not allowed to practice medicine in America. Amid the greed and decadence of the city, where white women tacitly accept their husbands' colored mistresses, Ben risks his life and freedom by voluntarily investigating crimes. **Amateur detective/ Traditional.**

A Free Man of Color. Bantam, 1997. 311pp.

January agrees to preserve the peace by meeting Angelique Crozat, the Creole mistress of an old friend's husband. His honorable act gets him into trouble when Angelique is found strangled to death.

Fever Season. Bantam, 1998. 321pp.

Yellow fever strikes New Orleans in summer 1833. January risks his life by tending the sick and by passing messages between a runaway slave and one of his music students.

Graveyard Dust. Bantam, 1999. 315pp.

When a young man's wife is poisoned, the police accuse January's sister Olympe, a voodoo priestess, of murder.

Sold Down the River. Bantam, 2000. 317pp.

January reluctantly agrees to solve murders happening on the plantation of his former owner, Simon Fourchet. If January doesn't find the real killer, all of Fourchet's slaves will pay the price.

Die Upon A Kiss. Bantam, 2001. 333pp.

Someone is trying to keep impresario Lorenzo Belaggio from presenting the play *Othello*, whose content may be too controversial for New Orleans society to accept.

Wet Grave. Bantam, 2002. 288pp.

Hesione Gros, a corsair's former mistress, had come down in the world since the time January knew her, which is why January can't understand why someone would want to kill her now.

Days of the Dead. Bantam, 2003. 314pp.

In 1835, January and his new wife Rose head to Mexico City to defend his friend Hannibal Sefton from murder accusations.

Dead Water. Bantam, 2004. 320pp.

When a bank president asks January to find Oliver Weems, a bank official who absconded with $100,000 of bank funds, January and Rose follow his trail onto a Louisiana steamboat.

Lawrence, Margaret.

Hannah Trevor Series.

A lyrically written and romantic series with a gritty setting: Rufford, Maine, just after the American Revolution, a town still scarred by memories of war. Hannah Trevor, a midwife and healer, chooses to live alone with her deaf/mute, illegitimate daughter Jennet rather than marry again. The unconventional Hannah has endured much sorrow in her life: the deaths of her husband and her first three children, and the pain of knowing that the man she loves, Jennet's father, is already married. *The Iceweaver* (Chapter 10), a literary historical novel that focuses on Jennet, can be read as a sequel. **Amateur detective/Traditional/Literary.**

Hearts and Bones. Avon, 1996. 307pp.

Anthea Emory dies strangled in her own bed, leaving behind a note implicating one of three men who raped her in the last few days of her life. The townspeople believe that Jennet's father, militia commander Daniel Josselyn, is one of these men.

Blood Red Roses. Avon, 1997. 353pp.

In autumn 1786, when irate farmers roam the Maine countryside in protest over new taxes, Hannah struggles to prevent the courts from taking Jennet away from her. When a man from Hannah's past turns up dead, she fights with all she has to prove her innocence and protect her child.

The Burning Bride. Avon, 1998. 387pp.

Hannah and her lover Daniel Josselyn are finally free to wed, and Hannah is pregnant with his child. But murder comes back to haunt Rufford: Two town leaders are killed in the same fashion.

Linsley, Clyde.

Josiah Beede Mysteries.

Lawyer Josiah Beede gained honor and recognition when serving in the military with Andrew Jackson at New Orleans, but now he's content to live out his life on a New Hampshire farm. Set in the 1830s; Linsley concentrates on social issues of the day. **Amateur detective/Traditional.**

Death of a Mill Girl. Berkley Prime Crime, 2002. 283pp.

When a peddler discovers the body of a beautiful young girl on Josiah's land, Josiah follows the trail to the local fabric mill, which isn't the safest or healthiest place for women to work.

Saving Louisa. Berkley Prime Crime, 2003. 264pp.

Josiah and his servant Randolph return to New Orleans to find and free Randolph's wife Louisa, a slave who was sold away to another plantation.

Meyers, Maan.

The High Constable. Doubleday, 1994. 307pp.

Annotated under "Multi-Period American Series."

Monfredo, Miriam Grace.

Seneca Falls Historical Mysteries (also called Glynis Tryon Mysteries). 📖 YA

Annotated under "Multi-Period American Series."

Schechter, Harold.

Edgar Allan Poe Series. ✍

Edgar Allan Poe, the early nineteenth-century author who wrote creepy gothic tales such as "The Tell-Tale Heart" and "The Murders in the Rue Morgue," stars in two historical mystery series. Silvis's version (next entry) pairs Poe with a much younger sidekick, but Schechter teams him up with historical figures who are his polar opposites, men who are both colorful and larger than life. The narrative switches back and forth between their points of view. If one is to believe Schechter, Poe may have gotten the ideas for his stories from the gruesome murders he investigates. **Amateur detective/Traditional.**

Nevermore. Pocket, 2000. 322pp.

In 1834 Baltimore, frontiersman Davy Crockett tracks down Poe to confront him about a biting review Poe wrote of Crockett's autobiography. This serves as the catalyst for their hunt throughout the city for a serial killer who leaves the word "nevermore" scrawled in blood at the crime scenes.

The Hum Bug. Atria, 2001. 400pp.

In 1844, Poe and his wife Sissy move to New York City, where his suspicions about the provenance of one of P. T. Barnum's exhibits lead to a partnership with the famous showman. The gruesome murder of a young woman imitates the display found in one of Barnum's wax exhibits.

The Mask of Red Death. Ballantine, 2004. 308pp.

Manhattan, 1845: Poe teams up with Kit Carson to unmask a serial killer who scalps his victims. This leads the pair to first suspect a Native American, but the solution isn't that simple.

Silvis, Randall.

Edgar Allan Poe Series. ✍

By 1840, ten-year-old Augie Dubbins, a New York City street urchin, has seen more than his share of pain and tragedy. He forms a kinship with Edgar Allan Poe, an impoverished young journalist who's haunted by demons of his own. The atmosphere is dark, suspenseful, and macabre, not unlike Poe's own stories. Readers may also enjoy Caleb Carr's Kreizler novels (Chapter 9), which also tell of humanity's dark side in nineteenth-century urban America. **Amateur detective/ Traditional.**

On Night's Shore. Thomas Dunne, 2001. 338pp.

When a young woman tosses a baby into the Hudson River, then jumps in herself, Augie decides to profit from the tragedy as best he can. He reveals the story to Poe, and in investigating the woman's motive, the two discover another young woman's body trapped underneath the docks. The trail leads to political corruption at its highest level.

Disquiet Heart. Thomas Dunne, 2002. 322pp.

In 1847, distraught after his young wife's death, Poe accepts the offer of Dr. Alfred Brunrichter, a wealthy philanthropist and admirer, to visit Pittsburgh. The longer Poe stays with Dr. Brunrichter, the more listless Poe seems. Is he being drugged? Meanwhile, Augie tries to establish his own writing career by investigating the mysterious disappearance of several young women.

The Civil War

During the tumult of the Civil War (1861–1865), as thousands of men give their lives for the Union and the Confederacy, political lines are drawn, and tempers run high. Even in this chaotic time, murderers will be caught, and justice served.

Kilian, Michael.

Harrison Raines Civil War Mysteries.

Though he has always abhorred slavery, native Virginian Harrison "Harry" Raines always did his best to avoid politics. But during the Civil War, not even he can remain neutral forever. In most circles Harry's known as a gambler and wastrel, which is why nobody suspects him of being a Union secret agent. Kilian, a Washington journalist, takes readers through the Civil War one key battle at a time. **Amateur detective/Traditional.**

Murder at Manassas. Berkley Prime Crime, 2000. 306pp.

British actress Caitlin Howard asks Harry to escort her to Manassas, where the first Civil War battle will be fought. While there, Harry is the last to see a Federal officer alive, a man who's later murdered and branded as a Union traitor.

A Killing at Ball's Bluff. Berkley Prime Crime, 2001. 374pp.

Harry, now a captain in the Secret Service, gets assigned to guard President Lincoln's friend Colonel Baker. However, Harry's charge wants nothing to do with him. When Baker is killed by a Confederate soldier, Harry tracks down the murderer, trying not to get captured himself.

The Ironclad Alibi. Berkley Prime Crime, 2002.

Traveling deep into Confederate territory to discover the truth about their secret weapon—an ironclad ship—Harry gets distracted by the murder of his former lover.

A Grave at Glorieta. Berkley Prime Crime, 2003. 292pp.

Harry and his partner "Boston" Leahy head to New Mexico to learn about the Confederacy's plans for lands out west, and their local contact gets killed.

The Shiloh Sisters. Berkley Prime Crime, 2004. 384pp.

A Union congressman's wife and her Confederate twin sister are both murdered, and General Grant wants Harry to solve the crime.

McMillan, Ann.

Narcissa Powers/Judah Daniel Series.

Richmond, 1861: Narcissa Powers, a young woman who has just lost her husband and son, strikes up an unlikely friendship with Judah Daniel, a freedwoman and herbalist. The two discover that they have more in common than they think. McMillan's mysteries are socially aware without being politically correct. **Amateur detective/Traditional.**

Dead March. Viking, 1998. 212pp.

After Narcissa's brother Charley dies suddenly, she discovers evidence suggesting that he was murdered. The death of a slave girl whose body was dug up by grave-robbers and sold for science probably isn't accidental, either.

Angel Trumpet. Viking, 1999. 206pp.

In Richmond, the capital of the Confederacy, Col. John Berton returns from service to find his entire family killed. Narcissa and Judah, working as nurses in a local hospital, are asked to discover the murderer and motive.

Civil Blood. Viking, 2001. 196pp.

Smallpox has struck Richmond, and it is being spread throughout the populace by tainted money. The deaths it causes are not accidental but deliberate.

Chickahominy Fever. Viking, 2003. 210pp.

Narcissa continues her work as a war nurse, and her skills are in demand after the Seven Days Battle. Medical supplies keep disappearing, and her patients are dying suspiciously.

Meyers, Maan.

The Lucifer Contract. **Doubleday, 1998. 268pp.**

Annotated under "Multi-Period American Series."

Monfredo, Miriam Grace.

Cain Trilogy. 🕮

Annotated under "Multi-Period American Series."

Parry, Owen.

Abel Jones Series. 🕮

Major Abel Jones, a mild-mannered Union officer working as a clerk in Washington, D.C., in 1861, thought he had left the soldier's life behind. When General George McClellan recruits him to spy for the Union, little does McClellan know that the Welsh immigrant had already seen bloodier battles than he'd likely ever see in America—while fighting with the British Army in India in the 1850s. An elegantly written series that explores the changes the Civil War wrought throughout America. (Pseudonym of Ralph Peters.) **Amateur detective/Traditional.**

Faded Coat of Blue. Morrow, 1999. 338pp.

Anthony Fowler, a fervent abolitionist, dies a martyr's death outside a Union encampment along the Potomac River. General McClellan, determined to win but opposed to war in general, worries that Northern extremists will use Fowler's death as a rallying cry. He asks Abel, a man of known honor and virtue, to investigate. Herodotus Award.

Shadows of Glory. Morrow, 2000. 311pp.

Penn Yann, a small town in the rural Finger Lakes region of New York State, is the site of a potential Irish insurrection against the American government in 1862. In interviewing people about this possible rebellion, Major Jones uncovers an even larger political conspiracy.

Call Each River Jordan. Morrow, 2001. 321pp.

President Lincoln sends Abel to Tennessee, and Abel is the only one to insist upon justice when forty runaway slaves are found hanged at a crossroads. Both Union and Confederate forces are concerned that the event will escalate the war, so Abel crosses enemy lines to solve the murders.

Honor's Kingdom. Morrow, 2002. 328pp.

Abel Jones, still working for Lincoln, heads to London in 1862 to prevent Britain from providing ironclad ships for the Confederacy. All of Britain's political leaders seem to be hiding something. While there, Abel learns of the horrible death of his predecessor—drowned in a tub of eels —and searches throughout London and Glasgow for a killer.

Bold Sons of Erin. Morrow, 2003. 352pp.

Abel returns to his adopted home town—Pottsville, Pennsylvania—to investigate the murder of Carl Stone, a Union general who was recruiting Irish miners for the Northern cause. Did one of the Irishmen take revenge, or has Stone's prewar past caught up with him?

Santangelo, Elena.

Pat Montella Series.

Annotated in Chapter 12.

Reconstruction and the Gilded Age

The expansion of the Western frontier and the high-society atmosphere of America's Eastern cities both hide corruption and social injustice. It's up to the protagonists of these mysteries to make sense of it all.

Black, Michelle.

Mysteries of the Victorian West.

Eden Murdoch and Brad Randall, the engaging protagonists of *An Uncommon Enemy* (Chapter 6), stumble on a series of murders. Black paints colorful portraits of the nineteenth-century American West and its social ills: racial tension, labor unrest, drug addiction, and homosexuality. Her natural dialogue and strong characterization help the plots flow nicely. **Amateur detective/Traditional.**

Solomon Spring. Forge, 2002. 303pp.

Brad leaves his job as Commissioner of Indian Affairs to return to Kansas, both to help the starving Cheyenne and to bring the news to Eden, his former lover, that her firstborn son is still alive. He finds her locked in the county jail for civil disobedience, protesting the development of an exclusive spa at the sacred Solomon Spring. When Eden's cruel first husband reappears in town, and gets killed soon after, Brad finds himself on trial for murder.

The Second Glass of Absinthe. Forge, 2003. 318pp.

In the mining boomtown of Leadville, Colorado, circa 1880, Brad's nephew Kit flees the home of his mistress, mining heiress Lucinda Ridenour, in disgust after recovering absinthe-laced memories of the previous night's debauchery. After Lucinda is found stabbed the next morning, Kit becomes the prime suspect.

Hall, Oakley M.

Ambrose Bierce Mystery Series. ✍

In these mysteries Tom Redmond, fledgling journalist, divulges his crime-solving adventures with Ambrose Bierce, infamous reporter in 1880s San Francisco. No social evil is left unexplored, either in Bierce's cynical journalism or in Hall's novels: prostitution, the plight of the Chinese, the dangers of mining, local politics, greedy railroad barons, and murder. **Amateur detective/Traditional.**

Ambrose Bierce and the Queen of Spades. University of California Press, 1998. 272pp.

Ambrose Bierce and the Death of Kings. Viking, 2001. 288pp.

Ambrose Bierce & the One-Eyed Jacks. Viking, 2003. 216pp.

Ambrose Bierce and the Trey of Pearls. Viking, 2004. 224pp.

Heck, Peter J.

Mark Twain Mysteries. ✍ YA

By the 1890s, author Samuel Clemens (aka Mark Twain) is out of money, so turns to two new pursuits: lecturing and detection. Wentworth Cabot, Clemens's new traveling secretary, has never quite figured out his boss. As Cabot and Clemens wend their way on the lecture circuit throughout the Midwest and Europe, the pair make a droll pair of sleuths, with Cabot playing straight man to the more flamboyant Clemens. The vivid settings provide local color, but most of it comes out of the mouth of the clever, wisecracking author himself. **Amateur detective/Traditional.**

Death on the Mississippi. Berkley Prime Crime, 1995. 290pp.

A Connecticut Yankee in Criminal Court. Berkley Prime Crime, 1996. 311pp.

The Prince and the Prosecutor. Berkley Prime Crime, 1997. 324pp.

Guilty Abroad. Berkley Prime Crime, 1999. 295pp.

The Mysterious Strangler. Berkley Prime Crime, 2000. 290pp.

Tom's Lawyer. Berkley Prime Crime, 2001. 257pp.

Medawar, Mardi Oakley.

Tay-bodal Mysteries. **YA**

Because Tay-bodal, a healer for the Kiowa Nation in 1866, belongs to no individual tribe, he's an outsider among his people. However, his outcast status gives him an advantage when probing suspects. An entertaining, cliché-free look at Native American life in Texas, Oklahoma, and Kansas in the 1860s. (The author is an Eastern Band Cherokee of North Carolina.) **Amateur detective/Traditional.**

Death at Rainy Mountain. St. Martin's Press, 1996. 262pp.

Bands of the Kiowa Nation gather at Rainy Mountain to elect a new leader. When the nephew of one candidate is killed, Cheyenne Robber, a member of a rival band, is accused of his murder.

Witch of the Palo Duro. St. Martin's Press, 1997. 272pp.

In 1864, Kit Carson killed a number of Kiowa who were wintering in Palo Duro Canyon. Now, two years later, the Kiowa blame several murders in the same canyon on ghosts and witchcraft.

Murder at Medicine Lodge. St. Martin's Press, 1999. 272pp.

In 1867, the Kiowa travel to Medicine Lodge, Kansas, to sign peace treaties with the U.S. government. When an army bugler is killed, Tay-bodal sets out to prove the Kiowa representative innocent.

The Ft. Larned Incident. St. Martin's Press, 2000. 288pp.

Tay-bodal has separated from his wife, Crying Wind, which distracts him from investigating the murder of his friend Three Elks, a chief's son. Accused of killing him is a bachelor who may want Crying Wind for himself.

Meyers, Maan.

The House on Mulberry Street. Bantam, 1996. 305pp.

Annotated under "Multi-Period American Series."

Parker, Ann.

🎗 *Silver Lies.* Poisoned Pen Press, 2003. 410pp.

In 1879 Leadville, Colorado, is a silver mining boomtown. Lady Luck doesn't hold out for precious metals assayer Joe Rose, trampled by a horse in the alley behind Inez Stannert's saloon. Inez, no stranger to pain and heartache herself, comforts Joe's grieving widow by settling Joe's accounts. Many things just don't add up, including the presence of the mysterious Reverend J. B. Sands, Leadville's handsome new minister. WILLA Award. **Amateur detective/Traditional.**

Peale, Cynthia.

Beacon Hill Mysteries.

Addington and Caroline Ames, brother and sister, are high-society Brahmins in late nineteenth-century Boston. The enigmatic Addison strives to remain a proper member of society, despite his infatuation for unsuitable actress Serena Vincent, while his spinster sister indulges her desire for good works. Caroline's insatiable curiosity threatens her good reputation, but their boarder, Dr. John MacKenzie, admires her all the more for it. The dialogue is more proper, and the atmosphere less edgy, than Anne Perry's Victorian novels. **Amateur detective/Cozy-Traditional.**

The Death of Colonel Mann. Doubleday, 2000. 342pp.

When Colonel William D'Arcy Mann, publisher of Boston's nastiest gossip newspaper, is shot to death in his hotel room, many Boston Brahmins are relieved.

Murder at Bertram's Bower. Doubleday, 2001. 342pp.

Two residents of Bertram's Bower, a house for fallen women, are found violently murdered. Caroline steps in to defend her friend Agatha, the Bower's proprietress.

The White Crow. Doubleday, 2002. 324pp.

While attending a séance, the elderly gentleman on Caroline Ames's left dies after making contact with his late wife.

Ryan, P. B.

Nell Sweeney Series.

A new series set in Gilded Age Boston, circa 1868. Young Irish immigrant Nell Sweeney—sharper than most Boston Brahmins give her credit for—is comfortable among all social classes, but she conceals an unsavory past. Authentic and suspenseful. (The author writes romances under her full name, Patricia Ryan.) **Amateur detective/Traditional.**

Still Life with Murder. Berkley Prime Crime, 2003. 309pp.

Nell takes a job as a governess with the wealthy Hewitt family. When Viola Hewitt hears that her son William, supposedly killed during the Civil War, is not dead but in prison, she'll do anything to exonerate him—only to find that he doesn't want anyone's help.

Murder in a Mill Town. Berkley Prime Crime, 2004. 272pp.

Bridie Fallon, a mill girl employed by the Hewitts, has disappeared. Nell, searching for Bridie at the request of Viola Hewitt, suspects that Viola's disreputable son Harry may be involved.

Soos, Troy.

Webb-Davies Series.

New York City in the 1890s was a hubbub of activity, quite a lot of it corrupt. Marshall Webb, freelance reporter for *Harper's Weekly* and would-be dime novelist, teams up with social reformer Rebecca Davies. **Amateur detective/Traditional.**

Island of Tears. Kensington, 2001. 280pp.

Christina Van der Waals, a Dutch immigrant girl, arrives at Ellis Island with little more than her dream of becoming a singer. When she disappears, Webb searches tirelessly for her, which leads him to a battered women's shelter run by Rebecca Davies.

The Gilded Cage. Kensington, 2002. 266pp.

Cholera runs rampant in Manhattan in 1893. To keep her shelter open, Rebecca gives her inheritance to a banker to invest for her. When he dies mysteriously, she calls in her boyfriend Marshall Webb for help.

Thompson, Victoria.

Gaslight Mystery Series.

In turn-of-the-twentieth-century New York City, midwife Sarah Brandt teams up with Sergeant Detective Frank Malloy to solve a series of murders taking place amid Manhattan's world of high society and, on the opposite spectrum, its abject poverty. Sarah, a woman born to wealth and privilege, fights her attraction to the gruff Irish policeman, who continues to involve her in his investigations against his better judgment. **Amateur detective/Traditional.**

Murder on Astor Place. Berkley Prime Crime, 1999. 278pp.

Murder on St. Mark's Place. Berkley Prime Crime, 2000. 277pp.

Murder on Gramercy Park. Berkley Prime Crime, 2001. 329pp.

Murder on Washington Square. Berkley Prime Crime, 2002. 326pp.

Murder on Mulberry Bend. Berkley Prime Crime, 2003. 346pp.

Murder on Marble Row. Berkley Prime Crime, 2004. 313pp.

Twentieth Century

Immigrant life, 1920s flappers, the Great Depression, and gangsters are the topics of historical mystery fiction of early twentieth-century America. Though a nostalgic atmosphere prevails overall, these mysteries demonstrate that solving murders back then was anything but simple.

Adams, Harold.

Carl Wilcox Mystery Series.

Carl Wilcox, a former policeman turned itinerant sign painter in Depression-era Minnesota and the Dakotas, takes on odd jobs and occasional amateur sleuthing work. As Wilcox rambles from one small town to another, he stumbles across various murders and gets hired to solve more than a few. The classic bachelor, he gets involved with many attractive women in his travels, at least until marriage to a sharp-witted librarian named Hazel (introduced in the second-to-last book) tames him. These short novels are a charming look at the rural Great Plains during the 1930s, complete with the author's tight writing and witty language. **Private detective/Traditional.**

Murder. Mysterious Press, 1981. 206pp.

Paint the Town Red. Charter, 1982. 214pp.

The Missing Moon. Ace, 1983. 246pp.

The Naked Liar. Mysterious Press, 1985. 265pp.

The Fourth Widow. Mysterious Press, 1986. 195pp.

The Barbed Wire Noose. Mysterious Press, 1987. 184pp.

The Man Who Met the Train. Mysterious Press, 1988. 229pp.

The Man Who Missed the Party. Mysterious Press, 1989. 181pp.

The Man Who Was Taller Than God. Walker, 1992. 156pp.

A Perfectly Proper Murder. Walker, 1993. 150pp.

A Way with Widows. Walker, 1994. 142pp.

Ditched Blonde. Walker, 1995. 157pp.

Hatchet Job. Walker, 1996. 153pp.

The Ice Pick Artist. Walker, 1997. 181pp.

No Badge, No Gun. Walker, 1998. 202pp.

Lead, So I Can Follow. Walker, 1999. 219pp.

Belfer, Lauren.

City of Light. The Dial Press, 1999. 518pp. 📖

At the beginning of the twentieth century, Buffalo, New York, is a showcase for wonders of the scientific world—both at the Pan-American Exposition as well as at Niagara Falls, whose powers are being tapped to bring electricity to the nation. When two suspicious deaths at the power plant occur, Louisa Barrett, the prim headmistress of a girl's school, must use her connections to high-ranking members of society to investigate. **Amateur detective/Traditional/Literary.**

Bowen, Rhys.

Molly Murphy Mysteries.

In this colorful series, Molly Murphy, a young, red-haired Irishwoman, takes another woman's place on a ship to America after killing a landowner's son in self-defense. Molly's first-person narration brings her spunky personality to the forefront and gives readers a prime view of turn-of-the-century New York City through an immigrant's eyes. Handsome police detective Daniel Sullivan, who catches Molly's eye immediately, helps her out (and provides a love interest).

Amateur detective/Traditional, but after the first book it becomes **Private detective/Traditional.**

🎗 *Murphy's Law.* St. Martin's Minotaur, 2001. 226pp.

Aboard a ship heading to Ellis Island, Molly gets into a loud argument with a rude fellow shipmate, but soon regrets it when he turns up dead, his throat slashed. Agatha Award; Herodotus Award.

Death of Riley. St. Martin's Minotaur, 2002. 275pp.

After failing as a lady's maid, Molly tries her hand as a private investigator, and her first case involves solving the murder of her new boss, Paddy Riley.

🎗 *For the Love of Mike.* St. Martin's Minotaur, 2003. 322pp.

Molly decides to take over Paddy Riley's detective agency, and soon she has two cases: industrial espionage in the garment district and looking for the runaway daughter of a Dublin man. Bruce Alexander Historical Award; Anthony Award.

Churchill, Jill.

Grace and Favor Mysteries.

Like all too many Americans, siblings Lily and Robert Brewster lost their family fortune in the 1929 stock market crash. Upon their great-uncle Horatio's death, they move from Manhattan to Westchester County to take up residence in his mansion, the Grace and Favor Cottage. Because they must live there for a decade before it becomes theirs, Lily and Robert take in boarders to make ends meet. Set during the Depression. (Pseudonym for Janice Young Brooks.) **Amateur detective/Cozy.**

Anything Goes. Morrow, 1999. 264pp.

In the Still of the Night. Morrow, 2000. 267pp.

Someone to Watch over Me. Morrow, 2001. 230pp.

Love for Sale. Morrow, 2003. 214pp.

It Had to Be You. Morrow, 2004. 224pp.

Collins, Max Allan.

Nathan Heller Novels.

In this series, private investigator Nate Heller reveals his past involvement in some of the greatest murder/mystery cases of the first half of the twentieth century. Fact and fiction mix as Collins comes up with ingenious solutions. Many historical figures come along for the ride. The novels can be read in any order. **Private detective/Hard-boiled.**

Damned in Paradise. Dutton, 1996. 308pp.

Clarence Darrow and race relations in 1932 Honolulu.

True Detective. St. Martin's Press, 1983. 358pp.

Al Capone and his gangsters in Prohibition-era Chicago.

True Crime. St. Martin's Press, 1984. 357pp.

Death of John Dillinger, 1934 Chicago.

Stolen Away. Bantam, 1991. 514pp.

Kidnapping of the Lindbergh baby, 1935.

Flying Blind. Dutton, 1998. 343pp.

Disappearance of Amelia Earhart, South Pacific, 1935.

Blood and Thunder. Dutton, 1995. 320pp.

Killing of Huey Long, Louisiana, 1935.

The Million Dollar Wound. St. Martin's Press, 1986. 335pp.

Frank Nitti, the ultimate crime boss, Chicago and elsewhere, late 1930s and early 1940s.

Carnal Hours. Dutton, 1994. 324pp.

Murder of Sir Harry Oakes, Nassau, 1943.

Neon Mirage. St. Martin's Press, 1988. 275pp.

Bugsy Siegel and other gamblers in 1946 Chicago and Las Vegas.

Angel in Black. New American Library, 2001. 340pp.

The Black Dahlia murder case, Los Angeles, 1947.

Majic Man. Dutton, 1999. 293pp.

Mysteries surrounding Roswell, New Mexico, 1949.

Chicago Confidential. New American Library, 2003. 292pp.

Organized crime in 1950 Chicago.

The Disasters Series.

Mysteries centered on real-life human tragedies of the early twentieth century; Collins has real-life literary figures investigate. Each novel stands alone. **Amateur detective/Traditional.**

The Titanic Murders. Berkley Prime Crime, 1999. 256pp.

Jacques Futrelle and the sinking of the *Titanic*, 1912.

The Lusitania Murders. Berkley Prime Crime, 2002. 254pp.

Mystery novelist S. S. Van Dine and the sinking of the *Lusitania*, 1915.

The Hindenburg Murders. Berkley Prime Crime, 2000. 272pp.

Leslie Charteris and the *Hindenburg* air disaster, Germany, 1937.

The Pearl Harbor Murders. Berkley Prime Crime, 2001. 272pp.

Edgar Rice Burroughs at the bombing of Pearl Harbor, 1941.

The London Blitz Murders. Berkley Prime Crime, 2004. 224pp.

Agatha Christie and Sir Bernard Spilsbury, pathologist, during the London Blitz, 1942.

Dams, Jeanne M.

Hilda Johansson Mystery Series.

Hilda Johansson, the Swedish maid for the wealthy Studebaker family of South Bend, Indiana, circa 1900, sniffs out clues to murder mysteries right under her employers' noses. While she fights her attraction to Patrick Cavanaugh, a local Irish Catholic policeman, she deals with anti-immigrant prejudice and the realities of servant life. **Amateur detective/ Cozy.**

Death in Lacquer Red. Walker, 1999. 225pp.

Red, White, and Blue Murder. Walker, 2000. 189pp.

Green Grow the Victims. Walker, 2001. 209pp.

Silence Is Golden. Walker, 2002. 226pp.

Day, Dianne.

Fremont Jones Series.

Bored with her humdrum life among the Boston Brahmins and eager to escape an arranged marriage, Caroline Jones relocates to San Francisco in 1905 to begin a career as a "type writer"—that is, a transcriptionist. With an independent mind and an outgoing personality to match, Caroline takes the name of her cousin, frontier adventurer John C. Fremont, and becomes Fremont Jones. Fremont narrates her own tales in charming, humorous style. Through Fremont's observations, the author creates a vivid sense of place. **Amateur detective/Traditional.**

The Strange Files of Fremont Jones. Doubleday, 1995. 229pp.

Fremont suspects that the death of one of one of her clients, Li Wong, relates to the papers she transcribed for him. Another client, Edgar Allan Partridge, writes stories as gothic as those of his namesake.

Fire and Fog. Doubleday, 1996. 241pp.

Having survived the San Francisco earthquake of 1906, Fremont joins the Red Cross, investigates a murder, and tries to puzzle out the mystery of her attractive friend Michael Archer, who she believes may be a spy.

The Bohemian Murders. Doubleday, 1997. 240pp.

Fremont, having relocated to Carmel-by-the-Sea in the aftermath of the 1906 earthquake, temporarily takes over as keeper of the Point Pinos Lighthouse—and finds a dead body floating in the surf.

Emperor Norton's Ghost. Doubleday, 1998. 307pp.

Back in San Francisco in 1908, Fremont starts up a detective agency with friend/lover Michael Archer, befriends Frances McFadden, a young woman with spiritualist leanings, and investigates the deaths of two mediums.

Death Train to Boston. Doubleday, 1999. 258pp.

Fremont and Michael, on a train bound eastward toward Utah, survive a train wreck caused by sabotage. While Michael searches for Fremont, a fanatical Mormon takes her captive, with the intent of making her his sixth wife.

Beacon Street Mourning. Doubleday, 2000. 278pp.

Learning that her father is near death, Fremont heads back to Beacon Street in Boston. When he dies suspiciously in the middle of the night, Fremont suspects that her stepmother is guilty.

Diehl, William.
Eureka. **Ballantine, 2002. 440pp.**

Part mystery, part crime thriller, and part gangster Western, Diehl's novel begins by outlining the background of Thomas Culhane, former World War I hero and now, in 1941, a candidate for governor of California. It's in Culhane's home town of San Pietro, formerly known as Eureka, that rich widow Verna Wilensky meets her demise. Zeke Bannon, police detective, must determine whether or not it's murder, and follow up leads to the mysterious individual who had been sending money to Wilensky over the past twenty years. **Public detective/Traditional.**

Dunning, John.
Two O'Clock Eastern Wartime. **Scribner, 2001. 473pp.**

In the summer of 1942, radio was in its prime. Holly Carnahan's father has gone missing, and she and Jack Dulaney, an aspiring radio star, come to Regina Beach, New Jersey, in hopes of finding him. Old-time radio fans will appreciate the way the author takes them on a tour of the ins and outs of the business, and readers will puzzle at the connections that Jack finds to the radio station's past involvement in nefarious dealings. **Amateur detective/Traditional.**

Hart, Carolyn.
🎗 *Letter from Home.* **Berkley Prime Crime, 2003. 262pp.** 📖

Gretchen "G. G." Gilman, now an aging star journalist, reminisces about the year 1944, when she was thirteen and living in a small town in eastern Oklahoma. Hired as a junior reporter for the *Gazette* in her home town, young Gretchen has a ringside seat to the murder of Faye Tatum, the flamboyant mother of her good friend Barb. Barb's father has disappeared, and the police are convinced that he's the guilty party. A murder mystery combines with a poignant coming-of-age story. Agatha Award. **Amateur detective/Traditional.**

Heffernan, William.
Beulah Hill. **Simon & Schuster, 2001. 301pp.** 📖

In small-town Vermont during the Depression, Constable Samuel Bradley is declared by state law to be officially white. But since he is the product of an interracial relationship that occurred several generations back, society still considers him "bleached." When Bradley is called in to investigate the murder of a white man on property owned by a black family, not only do the hard-won racial victories from years past come into play, but so does his own background. **Amateur detective/Traditional.**

Holden, Craig.

The Jazz Bird. Simon & Schuster, 2001. 314pp.

Charlie Taft, the son of former President William Howard Taft and a prosecutor in 1920s Cincinnati, thinks he has an open-and-shut case when George Remus, a well-known bootlegger, confesses to the murder of his socialite wife, Imogene. All is not what it seems, however, and the more Taft delves into the case, the more facts he manages to uncover. Based on a true story, this tale is reminiscent of F. Scott Fitzgerald's *The Great Gatsby*, with Imogene as the Daisy Buchanan character. For all that she's already dead, Imogene is fascinating and multidimensional. **Public detective/Traditional/Literary.**

Kaminsky, Stuart M.
Toby Peters Series.

When you're a successful detective in 1940s Los Angeles, word gets around. Toby Peters, private investigator, takes on tough cases for a succession of celebrity clients who find themselves in trouble. Classic hard-boiled mysteries, yet they're also humorous, with the author poking gentle fun at the celebrities' odd dilemmas. These mysteries should please readers nostalgic for the Golden Age of Hollywood. **Private detective/ Hard-boiled.**

Murder on the Yellow Brick Road. St. Martin's Press, 1978. 197pp.

Judy Garland, Los Angeles, 1940.

You Bet Your Life. St. Martin's Press, 1979. 215pp.

Marx Brothers, Chicago, 1941.

The Howard Hughes Affair. St. Martin's Press, 1979. 207pp.

Howard Hughes, Los Angeles, 1941.

Bullet for a Star. St. Martin's Press, 1977. 188pp.

Errol Flynn, Los Angeles, 1942.

Never Cross a Vampire. St. Martin's Press, 1980. 182pp.

Bela Lugosi, Los Angeles, 1942.

High Midnight. St. Martin's Press, 1981. 188pp.

Gary Cooper, Los Angeles, 1942.

Catch a Falling Clown. St. Martin's Press, 1982. 182pp.

Emmett Kelly, Los Angeles, 1942.

He Done Her Wrong. St. Martin's Press, 1983. 168pp.

Mae West, Los Angeles, 1942.

The Fala Factor. St. Martin's Press, 1984. 174pp.

Eleanor Roosevelt, Los Angeles, 1942.

Down for the Count. St. Martin's Press, 1985. 178pp.

Joe Louis, Los Angeles, 1942.

The Man Who Shot Lewis Vance. St. Martin's Press, 1986. 194pp.

John Wayne, Los Angeles, 1942.

Smart Moves. St. Martin's Press, 1987. 212pp.

Albert Einstein, New York City, 1942.

Think Fast, Mr. Peters. St. Martin's Press, 1988. 198pp.

Peter Lorre, Los Angeles, 1942.

Buried Caesars. Mysterious Press, 1989. 179pp.

Douglas MacArthur, Los Angeles, 1942.

Poor Butterfly. Mysterious Press, 1990. 179pp.

Leopold Stokowski, San Francisco, 1942.

The Melting Clock. Mysterious Press, 1991. 198pp.

Salvador Dali, Los Angeles, 1942.

The Devil Met a Lady. Mysterious Press, 1993. 194pp.

Bette Davis, Los Angeles, 1943.

Tomorrow Is Another Day. Mysterious Press, 1995. 201pp.

Clark Gable, Los Angeles, 1943.

Dancing in the Dark. Mysterious Press, 1996. 228pp.

Fred Astaire, Los Angeles, 1943.

A Fatal Glass of Beer. Mysterious Press, 1997. 246pp.

W. C. Fields, Los Angeles, 1943.

A Few Minutes Past Midnight. Carroll & Graf, 2001. 234pp.

Charlie Chaplin, Los Angeles, 1943.

To Catch a Spy. Carroll & Graf, 2002. 230pp.

Cary Grant, Los Angeles, 1943.

Mildred Pierced. Carroll & Graf, 2003. 230pp.

Joan Crawford, Los Angeles, 1944.

Lansdale, Joe.

🎗 *The Bottoms.* **Mysterious Press, 2000. 336pp.** 📖

At once a coming-of-age tale, a mystery, and a modern commentary on 1930s race relations, this award winner takes place in Depression-era east Texas. After young Harry Crane finds the mutilated body of a black prostitute in the river bottoms, nobody seems to care about solving the crime except his father, Jacob, the town constable. Harry suspects the killer is the Goat Man, a mysterious figure who lurks around the bridge over the Sabine River. Edgar Award; Herodotus Award. **Amateur detective/Traditional.**

McClendon, Lise.

Dorie Lennox Mysteries.

In this noir mystery series, Dorie Lennox runs a small-time detective agency in 1939 Kansas City along with her partner Amos. The city, barely recovered from the Depression, will soon see more hard times once America enters World War II. The author paints vivid portraits of the Kansas City jazz scene, dance clubs, mob corruption, and murder, seen through the eyes of a tough but kindhearted heroine. **Private detective/Traditional.**

One O'Clock Jump. St. Martin's Minotaur, 2001. 276pp.

Dorie thinks her job is over when the bargirl she was asked to trail jumps off a bridge into the Missouri River, but it's only just beginning.

Sweet and Lowdown. St. Martin's Minotaur, 2002. 278pp.

Eveline Hines, a wealthy woman dying of cancer, is concerned about her wayward daughter Thalia, who keeps getting involved with the wrong men. To protect Thalia's inheritance, Eveline asks Dorie and Amos to look into her daughter's personal life.

Meyers, Annette.

Olivia Brown Series.

Olivia Brown, a free-spirited young poet in 1920s Greenwich Village, lives and loves with gusto. Though hesitant to commit for long to any man, she doesn't give up until crimes are solved. Annette Meyers (half of the Maan Meyers writing team) based Olivia's character on Edna St. Vincent Millay. **Amateur detective/Traditional.**

Free Love. Mysterious Press, 2000. 240pp.

Olivia wants to figure out who has been impersonating her, especially after her mysterious double turns up dead.

Murder Me Now. Mysterious Press, 2001. 290pp.

Two of Olivia's friends host a house party in Croton, but things turn very bad when the body of their nanny is found hanging from a tree.

Monahan, Brent.

John Le Brun Series.

Nothing derails a party more than murder. Murder and mayhem at exclusive social clubs for the wealthy at the turn of the twentieth century: America's Gilded Age and Britain's Edwardian period. **Public detective/Traditional.**

The Jekyl Island Club. St. Martin's Press, 2000. 287pp.

John Le Brun, sheriff of Brunswick, Georgia, is called in to solve a murder at the elite Jekyl Island Club in 1899, right before President McKinley himself pays a visit.

The Sceptered Isle Club. St. Martin's Minotaur, 2002. 306pp.

Geoffrey Moore, a friend Le Brun met at Jekyl Island six years earlier, introduces Le Brun to the London "men's club." While visiting the Sceptred Isle Club with Sir Arthur Conan Doyle, Le Brun hears a series of gunshots go off inside a locked gambling room.

The Manhattan Isle Clubs. St. Martin's Minotaur, 2003. 274pp.

Edmund Pinckney, an unpopular member of the exclusive Metropolitan Club in New York City in 1906, is murdered on club turf, his throat slashed.

Roosevelt, Elliott.

Eleanor Roosevelt Mysteries. ✍

The late Elliott Roosevelt, son of FDR and Eleanor, wrote a series of cozy murder mysteries featuring his mother as amateur sleuth. Eleanor Roosevelt, first lady during the 1930s and 1940s, solves a series of murders from the White House. Most have far-reaching political implications. Well-known politicians, both American and international, make cameo appearances, as do Hollywood actors and notorious mobsters. The author left a number of uncompleted manuscripts at his death in 1990, and the last volume was completed by William Harrington for Roosevelt's estate. They can be read in any order. **Amateur detective/Cozy.**

Murder and the First Lady. St. Martin's Press, 1984. 227pp.

The Hyde Park Murder. St. Martin's Press, 1985. 231pp.

Murder at Hobcaw Barony. St. Martin's Press, 1986. 233pp.

The White House Pantry Murder. St. Martin's Press, 1987. 231pp.

Murder at the Palace. St. Martin's Press, 1987. 232pp.

Murder in the Rose Garden. St. Martin's Press, 1988. 232pp.

Murder in the Oval Office. St. Martin's Press, 1989. 247pp.

Murder in the Blue Room. St. Martin's Press, 1990. 215pp.

A First-Class Murder. St. Martin's Press, 1991. 261pp.

Murder in the Red Room. St. Martin's Press, 1992. 249pp.

Murder in the West Wing. St. Martin's Press, 1992. 247pp.

Murder in the East Room. St. Martin's Press, 1993. 201pp.

A Royal Murder. St. Martin's Press, 1994. 234pp.

Murder in the Executive Mansion. St. Martin's Press, 1995. 197pp.

Murder in the Chateau. St. Martin's Press, 1996. 200pp.

Murder at Midnight. St. Martin's Press, 1997. 216pp.

Murder in the Map Room. St. Martin's Press, 1998. 251pp.

Murder in Georgetown. St. Martin's Minotaur, 1999. 230pp.

Murder in the Lincoln Bedroom. Thomas Dunne Books, 2000. 228pp.

Murder at the President's Door. St. Martin's Minotaur/Thomas Dunne, 2001. 232pp.

Soos, Troy.

Mickey Rawlings Series.

Soos, who wanted to be a baseball player when he grew up, transmits his love of the game into a series of well-researched mysteries set between 1912 and 1922—at baseball stadiums across America, naturally. Mickey Rawlings, a minor leaguer, gets his big break in 1912 when he's bought by the Boston Red Sox. He stumbles onto murders here and there as he follows his teams around the country. **Amateur detective/Traditional.**

Murder at Fenway Park. Kensington, 1994. 252pp.

Murder at Ebbets Field. Kensington, 1995. 280pp.

Murder at Wrigley Field. Kensington, 1996. 296pp.

Hunting a Detroit Tiger. Kensington, 1997. 346pp.

The Cincinnati Red Stalkings. Kensington, 1998. 329pp.

Hanging Curve. Kensington, 1999. 263pp.

Walker, Persia.

Harlem Redux. **Simon & Schuster, 2002. 311pp.**

During the Harlem Renaissance, prominent black lawyer David McKay investigates the death of his sister Lilian, whose behavior had become strangely unstable in the months before her demise. While checking out leads, David rediscovers the strong class barriers among Harlem's elite, and the secret he himself is struggling to keep may be closer to coming out. **Public detective/Traditional/Literary.**

Williamson, Penn (Penelope).

Daman Rourke Series.

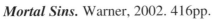

Williamson's romance novels (Chapter 4) are multidimensional portraits of nineteenth-century America, but her police mysteries set in Jazz Age New Orleans are far grittier and darker. The sultry, seductive atmosphere of the Crescent City comes alive. **Public detective/Traditional.**

Mortal Sins. Warner, 2002. 416pp.

Daman Rourke, a brooding homicide detective, tries to prove the innocence of Hollywood movie goddess Remy Lelourie, suspected of brutally stabbing her wealthy husband in a slave shack on his estate. And only Daman, Remy's former lover, knows that she is truly capable of murder.

The Wages of Sin. Warner, 2003. 432pp. (As Penelope Williamson.)

The crucified body of Father Patrick Walsh, a local priest known for his outspoken sermons, turns up in an abandoned New Orleans warehouse. A post mortem reveals the biggest surprise: Walsh was really a woman in disguise.

Woodworth, Deborah.

Sister Rose Callahan Series.

A warmhearted cozy series set in the fictional North Homage Shaker Village of Languor County, Kentucky, in the 1930s. Sister Rose Callahan, the Eldress of the community of believers, takes on the role of sleuth. Interspersed with the mystery plotlines are sensitive portrayals of the Shakers' nonviolent lifestyle. **Amateur detective/Cozy.**

Death of a Winter Shaker. Avon, 1997. 213pp.

The body of a drifter is discovered in the Shakers' herb house, and one of their own members may be a killer.

A Deadly Shaker Spring. Avon, 1998. 289pp.

Someone from the outside is threatening the Shaker community, and Sister Rose discovers a connection between the threats and a twenty-five-year-old scandal.

Sins of a Shaker Summer. Avon, 1999. 261pp.

Two little girls become seriously ill after accidentally ingesting poisonous plants from the Shakers' medicinal herb garden.

A Simple Shaker Murder. Avon, 2000. 246pp.

A member of a group of reformers interested in modernizing the beliefs of North Homage is found hanging from a tree, dead.

Killing Gifts. Avon, 2001. 258pp.

Sister Rose travels to the Hancock Shaker Village in Massachusetts to investigate the death of a fallen woman.

Dancing Dead. Avon, 2002. 320pp.

A successful hostel newly opened by the Shakers may be haunted.

Wright, Edward.

John Ray Horn Series.

Gritty, murderous noir set in post–World War II Los Angeles. **Amateur detective/Traditional-Hard-boiled.**

Clea's Moon. Putnam, 2003. 308pp.

John Ray Horn, a former B-Western movie actor just released from prison, works as a debt collector for an Indian buddy. Scotty, one of Horn's old friends, contacts him about some old photographs he found—photos of Horn's former stepdaughter, Clea. When Scotty gets killed, and Clea disappears, Horn is up to his ears in murder.

While I Disappear. Putnam, 2004. 324pp.

Horn doesn't believe that the strangulation death of Rose Galen, a starlet from his old filmmaker days, was a random act. He teams up with Joseph Mad Crow, his buddy and employer, to look into secrets from Rose's movie past.

Multi-Period American Series

These series follow detectives, who happen to be members of the same family, over multiple time periods in American history.

Meyers, Maan.

Dutchman Mysteries.

A multi-period series featuring members and descendants of the Tonneman family, Dutch settlers in early New York. All volumes can be read independently. (The author is a pseudonym for husband-wife team Martin and Annette Meyers.) **Public detective/Traditional.**

The Dutchman. Doubleday, 1992. 306pp.

In 1664, the Dutch colony of New Amsterdam is threatened from within and without. Pieter Tonneman, Schout (sheriff) of New Amsterdam, tries to keep the peace when the British threaten to invade. Within the city, Pieter accepts the help of beautiful Jewess Racqel Mendoza in investigating a tavern owner's suicide and a fire in Jews Alley.

The Dutchman's Dilemma. Bantam, 1995. 254pp.

It's now 1675, and Pieter Tonneman has made a life and started a family with wife Racqel. When bloody sacrifices appear in public places, rumors of devilry and witchcraft abound, and Racqel's own people—the Jews—are blamed.

The Kingsbridge Plot. Doubleday, 1993. 321pp.

In 1775, John Peter Tonneman, great-great-grandson of Pieter Tonneman from the first books, comes home from abroad and resumes his medical practice. Appointed coroner for the city of New York, Tonneman looks into the decapitation of several red-haired young women. Not surprisingly, the solution is connected to the forthcoming American Revolution.

The High Constable. Doubleday, 1994. 307pp.

John Tonneman from *The Kingsbridge Plot*, sixty years old in 1808, rejoices in his marriage but despairs of his eldest son, Peter, who spends too much time drinking. When both Peter and Peter's boss suddenly vanish, and a corpse appears in the city's water supply, John teams up with his old friend, the high constable of New York, to solve both mysteries.

 7

The Lucifer Contract. Doubleday, 1998. 268pp.

In November 1864, as the Civil War winds down, *New York Evening Post* journalist Pete Tonneman uncovers a plot in which eight Kentucky rebels plan to set fire to Manhattan on election day. He follows a trail strewn with corpses—each with a Lucifer matchstick between its teeth—until he discovers the rebels' true identities.

The House on Mulberry Street. Bantam, 1996. 305pp.

It's 1895, and John "Dutch" Tonneman, son of Peter from *The Lucifer Contract*, follows in the family tradition by working as a police detective. At a violent union rally, John saves the life of Jewish photographer Esther Breslau. When her plates are destroyed, and her boss is killed, John realizes that her camera may have revealed a murderer.

Monfredo, Miriam Grace.

Seneca Falls Historical Mysteries (also called Glynis Tryon Mysteries). 📖 YA

Glynis Tryon, town librarian for Seneca Falls in upstate New York, fights for women's suffrage in the 1840s through the 1860s. Determined to remain unmarried, Glynis concentrates on her career, her role as a proto-feminist (which doesn't always come easy), and her tasks as amateur sleuth. Her on-again, off-again romance with police constable Cullen Stuart complicates her life. Later volumes see more of Glynis's niece, Bronwen Llyr, who serves as the protagonist for Monfredo's Cain Trilogy, below. Excellent depictions of mid-nineteenth-century social history, especially women's rights, slavery, and racism. **Amateur detective/ Traditional.**

Seneca Falls Inheritance. St. Martin's Press, 1992. 259pp.

In 1848, Glynis helps Elizabeth Cady Stanton organize the first Women's Rights Convention. Amid this confusion, the supposed daughter of Mr. and Mrs. Friedrich Steicher, both killed in a boating accident, also turns up dead.

North Star Conspiracy. St. Martin's Press, 1993. 332pp.

In 1854, while helping fugitive slaves escape via the Underground Railroad, Glynis connects several local deaths with the recent escape of Kiri, a former Virginia slave whom Glynis's landlady's son hopes to marry.

Blackwater Spirits. St. Martin's Press, 1995. 328pp.

Jacques Sundown, the Iroquois deputy of Glynis's former beau, Constable Cullen Stuart, is accused of killing several men in town. Only Glynis believes that he's innocent.

Through a Gold Eagle. Berkley Prime Crime, 1996. 386pp.

On a train traveling to Seneca Falls from Illinois in 1859, a male passenger hands Glynis a pouch containing a ring, a bank note, and an eagle coin. Soon after, the man is murdered. Other plot developments include John Brown's raid on Harper's Ferry.

The Stalking-Horse. Berkley Prime Crime, 1998. 340pp.

It's 1861, Lincoln has been elected president, and civil war is on the horizon. Bronwyn Llyr, Glynis's niece, joins the Pinkerton Detective Agency. She travels to Montgomery, Alabama, to investigate Southern railroads and, inadvertently, foil an assassination plot.

Must the Maiden Die. Berkley Prime Crime, 1999. 366pp.

Wealthy Seneca Falls manufacturer Roland Brant is stabbed to death, and his indentured servant girl, conveniently missing, is accused of the crime.

Cain Trilogy.

A continuation of Monfredo's <u>Seneca Falls</u> series, set during the U.S. Civil War. While Bronwen Llyr (niece of Glynis Tryon from the previous books) gets fired from Pinkerton and becomes a spy for the intelligence branch of the Treasury Department, her sister Kathryn nurses wounded Union soldiers in Washington City. **Amateur detective/Traditional.**

Sisters of Cain. Berkley Prime Crime, 2000. 368pp.

The Pinkerton Detective Agency is in trouble in the South after secessionist spies infiltrate its ranks. Though aware of the danger she may face, the treasury chief sends Bronwen into the Confederacy to foil a rebel plot.

🎗 ***Brothers of Cain.*** Berkley Prime Crime, 2001. 323pp.

Seth Llyr, Bronwen's and Kathryn's brother, finds himself a Confederate prisoner of war. The sisters race to rescue him before he's hanged. Herodotus Award.

Children of Cain. Berkley Prime Crime, 2002. 335pp.

Knowing that Lee's troops are preparing for a surprise attack on the Union's supply lines, Bronwen heads north to warn General McClellan before the two armies meet.

Canada

America's northern neighbor doesn't figure in many historical murder mysteries, but Toronto's Maureen Jennings, a native of England, represents her adopted country well.

Jennings, Maureen.

Detective William Murdoch Series.

Toronto in 1895 wasn't the cosmopolitan city it is today. William Murdoch, acting detective with Toronto's Number Four Station, makes his way from the city's darkened alleyways to the parlors of high society in pursuit of justice. These novels are similar in tone and social consciousness to Anne Perry's <u>William Monk Novels</u>, though Murdoch is a more likable protagonist. **Public detective/Traditional.**

Except the Dying. St. Martin's Press, 1997. 255pp.

Therese Laporte, a poor servant girl, is murdered in Toronto's streets. The family that she worked for, the Rhodeses, react strangely to news of her death.

Under the Dragon's Tail. St. Martin's Press, 1998. 243pp.

Few people complain when Dolly Merishaw, midwife and backstreet abortionist, is beaten to death. What puzzles Murdoch is the murder of a young boy in her kitchen not long afterward.

Poor Tom Is Cold. Thomas Dunne, 2001. 278pp.

The death of Constable Oliver Wicken, shot in the temple with his own gun, is ruled to be suicide, but Murdoch uncovers evidence that suggests otherwise.

Let Loose the Dogs. St. Martin's Minotaur, 2003. 320pp.

Harry Murdoch, William's estranged father, is set to be hanged for killing a man he suspects cheated him in a ratting match, a game in which men bet on which dog will kill the most rats. Only William can clear his name.

The Middle East

Detectives, mostly with a Western mindset, confront the mysteries of the ever-fascinating Middle East. (Mysteries of ancient Egypt are annotated earlier in this chapter.)

Gordon, Alan.

Fool's Guild Mysteries.

Annotated under "Europe, Middle Ages."

Holman, Sheri.

A Stolen Tongue. Atlantic Monthly, 1997. 320pp. 📖

In 1483 Father Felix Fabri, a Swabian monk, travels to the Sinai desert to worship the earthly remains of the saint he considers his spiritual wife, Katherine of Alexandria. When he finds that the relics have been desecrated and scattered, he's compelled to go in search of the thief. A woman named Arsinoë, who is known as the "Tongue of St. Katherine" for her ability to channel the saint's words, may know more than she reveals. **Amateur detective/Traditional/Literary.**

Peters, Elizabeth.

Amelia Peabody Series. ★ YA

In the 1880s, Amelia Peabody, a plain Victorian spinster, indulges her outlandish passion for Egyptology by traveling to Egypt and working as an amateur archaeologist. Radcliffe Emerson, an Egyptologist she finds arrogant and stuffy (at least at first), serves as Amelia's guide in both archaeological excavations and crime-solving. Under the bright desert sun, the two fall in love and marry; their son Ramses (real name Walter) solves his own mysteries in later books. Entertaining and smoothly told, with strong character development and vivid historical detail. Amelia's delightful sense of humor appears throughout. Peters is a pseudonym for Barbara Mertz, a Ph.D. in Egyptology who has written a number of nonfiction books on the subject. Peters's *Amelia Peabody's Egypt* (Morrow, 2003, co-written with Kristen Whitbread) is a companion to the series. Those who enjoy Peters's exotic Egyptian settings may also appreciate Lauren Haney's Lord Meren mysteries (under "Ancient Egypt"). **Amateur detective/Traditional.**

Crocodile on the Sandbank. Dodd, Mead, 1975. 273pp.

Having inherited her father's fortune, Amelia journeys to Egypt with her friend, Evelyn Barton-Forbes, who is terrorized by a walking mummy. There she runs into Radcliffe Emerson and, to her amazement, manages to win his heart.

The Curse of the Pharaohs. Dodd, Mead, 1981. 357pp.

Lady Baskerville is convinced that her husband Henry's death was caused by a long-dead pharaoh's curse. Amelia and Emerson, now married, don't believe these tales.

The Mummy Case. Congdon & Weed, 1985. 313pp.

Amelia and Emerson, along with their precocious young son Ramses, investigate the death of an antiquities dealer and the disappearance of a mummy case. The Emersons' archenemy Sethos, the dealer in illegal artifacts whom Amelia calls the "Master Criminal," makes his first appearance in this novel.

Lion in the Valley. Atheneum, 1986. 291pp.

In 1895, Amelia, Emerson, and eight-year-old Ramses return to Egypt, where Amelia will get her chance to excavate the Black Pyramid in Dahshoor. When someone kidnaps Ramses, Amelia knows the Master Criminal is behind it.

The Deeds of the Disturber. Atheneum, 1988. 289pp.

Back in England, a mummy from Egypt's Nineteenth Dynasty is supposedly haunting the British Museum, and his curse is blamed for killing a night watchman on duty. Of course, the real murderer is all too human.

The Last Camel Died at Noon. Warner, 1991. 352pp.

The Emersons journey to the Sudan to find a long-lost British archaeologist, Willoughby Forth, who disappeared in the desert fourteen years ago. Just when the situation looks dire, they come upon a mysterious desert Shangri-La. This book marks the first appearance of the Emersons' beautiful young ward, Nefret.

The Snake, the Crocodile and the Dog. Warner, 1992. 340pp.

When Amelia and Emerson decide to travel from England to a dig in Egypt without their son, they're hoping for a second honeymoon. Little do they know that they're stumbling into a trap; the Master Criminal will stop at nothing to find the secret of the lost oasis.

The Hippopotamus Pool. Warner, 1996. 384pp.

When a masked stranger offers to lead the Emersons to Queen Tetisheri's lost tomb, they can't resist following him. But when the man vanishes without a trace, they're left to find the tomb on their own, hopefully before grave-robbers do.

Seeing a Large Cat. Warner, 1997. 386pp.

It's the 1903 digging season in Cairo, and the Emersons (Amelia, Radcliffe, Ramses, Nefret, and Amelia's nephew David) are warned to stay away from "Site 20–A." Of course, they don't listen, and at the tomb site, Amelia discovers the dead body of a young woman. Meanwhile, her son Ramses is developing into a teenage heartthrob with romantic designs on Nefret.

The Ape Who Guards the Balance. Avon Twilight, 1998. 376pp.

In 1907, Amelia's attendance at a suffragette rally at the home of a Member of Parliament leads to yet another encounter with Sethos, the Master Criminal. The Emersons journey to Luxor on his tail.

The Falcon at the Portal. Avon Twilight, 1999. 366pp.

Just after his wedding, Amelia's nephew David is accused of forging ancient artifacts and sympathizing with Egyptian nationalists. The entire Emerson family pulls together to clear his name.

He Shall Thunder in the Sky. Morrow, 2000. 400pp.

It's 1914, and the coming war complicates the Emersons' annual season in Egypt. Ottoman forces gather for an attack on the Suez Canal, Ramses loudly professes his pacifist beliefs, and David has been imprisoned for political reasons. And Master Criminal Sethos turns up again.

Lord of the Silent. Morrow, 2001. 404pp.

To prevent British intelligence from recruiting Ramses to work for them, Amelia and her entourage leave for another summer of excavation in Egypt. Ramses and his new wife Nefret take center stage. In Luxor, they investigate grave robberies and plunge even deeper into danger.

The Golden One. Morrow, 2002. 429pp.

While World War I rages in 1917, intelligence agents from the British War Office are still trying to recruit Ramses, and looting of the royal tombs at Luxor reveals a dead body.

Children of the Storm. Morrow, 2003. 400pp.

The war is over, and Amelia has become a grandmother, but some things never change: antiquities thefts and mysterious deaths. Ramses' encounter with a strange woman disguised as the Egyptian goddess Hathor deepens the mystery.

Guardian of the Horizon. Morrow, 2004. 399pp.

Amelia's journals from the "lost years" (1907–1908) have recently resurfaced. The Emersons return to the lost oasis they left ten years earlier, during *The Last Camel Died at Noon*, and find danger there once again.

Reed, Mary, and Eric Mayer.

<u>**John the Eunuch Mysteries.**</u>

Sixth-century Byzantium. Though Emperor Justinian follows the new Christian religion, his Lord Chamberlain, John the Eunuch, quietly worships the bull-god Mithras. Wise and respected for his position, John still has trouble dealing with his forced emasculation by barbarian captors years before. A unique protagonist in a singular setting, where paganism rivals Christianity, and survival depends on striking a balance between political factions. **Public detective/Traditional.**

One for Sorrow. Poisoned Pen Press, 1999. 292pp.

One of John's closest friends, royal treasurer Leukos, Keeper of the Plate, gets killed in an alleyway behind a whorehouse.

Two for Joy. Poisoned Pen Press, 2000. 345pp.

The stylites of Constantinople, holy men who live atop tall pillars, are mysteriously bursting into flames.

Three for A Letter. Poisoned Pen Press, 2001. 268pp.

Justinian hopes to use two eight-year-old twins, descendants of the last king of the Ostrogoths, to resurrect the lost Roman Empire. His plans unravel when one of them is murdered.

Four for a Boy. Poisoned Pen Press, 2002. 292pp.

Justinian, heir to Byzantium, plans to marry the actress Theodora regardless of popular opinion. When wealthy philosopher Hypatius is murdered inside a church, Justinian asks a young slave named John to find the killer. This prequel to the series reveals John's early life, something hinted at in previous books.

Five for Silver. Poisoned Pen Press, 2004. 276pp.

In AD 542, plague has overtaken Constantinople. John's elderly servant Peter asks him to discover who killed his old friend Gregory, whose murder Peter had seen in a mysterious vision. John takes to the streets to interview as many witnesses as he can.

Asia

China

China is an uncommon setting for murder mysteries, perhaps because of Robert Van Gulik's outstanding contributions to the genre.

Van Gulik, Robert.

<u>**Judge Dee Murder Mysteries.**</u> ★ ✍

Judge Dee (Di Renjie) was a real-life magistrate during China's T'ang Dynasty, living roughly between AD 630 and 700. Van Gulik, a Dutch novelist, filled in the gaps in Judge Dee's life, imagining scenarios in which Dee solved crimes on his own. However, Van Gulik made the historical background more characteristic of the Ming period (fourteenth to seventeenth centuries). Eleanor Cooney and Daniel Altieri continued the Judge Dee series with their own *Deception* (Morrow, 1993), though they set their novel firmly in seventh-century China. **Public detective/Traditional.**

Celebrated Cases of Judge Dee. Dover, 1976. 237pp. (First published in Japan in 1949.)

The Chinese Bell Murders. Harper & Row, 1959. 262pp.

The Chinese Gold Murders. Harper & Row, 1961. 202pp.

The Chinese Lake Murders. Harper & Row, 1960. 216pp.

The Chinese Nail Murders. Harper & Row, 1961. 231pp.

The Haunted Monastery. Scribner, 1969. 159pp.

The Red Pavilion. Scribner, 1968. 173pp.

The Haunted Monastery and the Chinese Maze Murders. Dover, 1977. 328pp. (Includes previously published novel.)

The Lacquer Screen. Scribner, 1970. 180pp.

The Emperor's Pearl. Scribner, 1964. 184pp.

The Willow Pattern. London: Heinemann, 1965. 183pp.

The Monkey and the Tiger. Scribner, 1966. 143pp.

The Phantom of the Temple. Scribner, 1966. 203pp.

Murder in Canton. Scribner, 1967. 207pp.

Judge Dee at Work. Scribner, 1973. 174pp.

Necklace and Calabash. Scribner, 1971. 143pp.

Poets and Murder. Scribner, 1972. 173pp. (Alternate title: *The Fox-Magic Murders.*)

India

Most historical novels of British rule in India—nineteenth and early twentieth centuries—communicate the harshness with which British soldiers treated the Indian residents. In these mysteries, though, British and Indian detectives work together to catch killers on native soil.

Cleverly, Barbara.

Detective Joe Sandilands Series.

During the last days of the British Raj in the 1920s, Scotland Yard detective Joe Sandilands, ready to return home after a six-month stint with the Bengal Police, gets caught up in political intrigue and murder. Action-packed mysteries in an exotic setting. **Public detective/Traditional.**

The Last Kashmiri Rose. Carroll & Graf, 2002. 287pp.

At the Panikhat post fifty miles north of Calcutta, one military wife has been killed each March for the past five years. On the anniversary of their deaths, red roses appear on their graves. With the end of March approaching again, Joe Sandilands tracks down a serial killer with the help of the Indian police.

Ragtime in Simla. Carroll & Graf, 2003. 288pp.

Sandilands hopes to enjoy a relaxing vacation at a summer mountain resort in Simla but is pulled back into murder investigation when his traveling companion, a Russian opera singer, is killed before his eyes. A year earlier, another man had met the same fate.

🎗 *The Damascened Blade.* Carroll & Graf, 2004. 285pp.

Sandilands finds himself in the mountains of Afghanistan, a hotbed of political activity, while chaperoning a rich American heiress on a tour of the area. When a Pathan prince is killed, one of the prince's relatives takes a hostage, threatening harm if the crime isn't solved within seven days. Ellis Peters Historical Dagger.

Norbu, Jamyang.

Sherlock Holmes: The Missing Years. Bloomsbury, 2001. 279pp. (Alternate title: *The Mandala of Sherlock Holmes.*)

Two years after Sherlock Holmes tumbled to his death from a waterfall, Arthur Conan Doyle brought him back to life, explaining that Holmes had spent the past two years visiting Tibet. In Norbu's version of these missing years, Holmes travels east out of India to avoid Professor Moriarty's henchmen. He and his traveling companion, Hurree Chunder Mookerjee, head to Lhasa, where they meet the Dalai Lama and help him regain his position. Hurree, this novel's Dr. Watson, is a Bengali scholar/spy first mentioned in Rudyard Kipling's adventure novel *Kim*. **Private detective/Traditional.**

Japan

To Westerners, Japanese settings seem exotic and unique, but these mysteries show that some things are always the same: government bureaucracy, class barriers, and quarrelsome family members.

Furutani, Dale.

Samurai Mystery Trilogy.

Matsuyama Kaze is a masterless samurai (*ronin*) in 1603, the year that the Tokugawa Shogunate took over rule of Japan. Kaze values honor above all else, and he continues to roam the Tokaido Road until he finds his late master's lost daughter, who was abducted when her parents were killed. Along the way, Kaze meets with violence, adventure, and not a little mystery. **Amateur detective/Traditional.**

Death at the Crossroads. Morrow, 1998. 210pp.

At a crossroads, Kaze discovers the body of a man who died with an arrow piercing his chest. The authorities immediately accuse the charcoal seller who was with Kaze at the time of discovery.

Jade Palace Vendetta. Morrow, 1999. 222pp.

After saving a merchant along the Tokaido Road from being attacked, Kaze vows to serve as his bodyguard, only to learn later that someone has targeted the merchant for a deadly vendetta.

Kill the Shogun. Morrow, 2000. 230pp.

Kaze traces his lord and lady's young daughter to a house of prostitution in Edo. Once there, Kaze finds himself the subject of a manhunt, since the authorities believe he is plotting to kill the shogun.

Parker, I. J.

Sugarawa Akitada Mysteries.

Lord Sugawara Akitada, a minor government official in the eleventh-century city of Heian Kyo (early Kyoto), jumps at the chance to get out of his boring job by solving crimes. **Amateur detective/Traditional.**

Rashomon Gate. St. Martin's Minotaur, 2002. 336pp.

Professor Hirata, Akitada's old mentor at the Imperial University, asks him to investigate a blackmailer to prevent a scandal. Akitada takes a position as a visiting lecturer and gets caught up in petty academic rivalries. While investigating, he gets sidetracked by other strange happenings, like the disappearance of a student's grandfather.

The Hell Screen. St. Martin's Minotaur, 2003. 338pp.

Akitada, on his way back to Heian Kyo to visit his seriously ill mother, stops at a monastery to rest overnight. His sleep is disturbed by gruesome images of a "hell screen" that was painted by one of the other guests. After being greeted by his squabbling mother and sisters at home, he learns of a horrible murder at the monastery he just left.

Rowland, Laura Joh.

Sano Ichirō Samurai Mysteries.

Due to family obligations, Sano Ichiro reluctantly abandons his career as a history tutor to become a *yoriki*, a senior member of the Edo police force. Despite his samurai status, he's an outsider in the police ranks, and his crime-solving successes make him many enemies. Always inquisitive, Sano looks behind people's masks of politeness to discover the truth behind many murders—and finds political intrigue that could topple the Tokugawa regime. Rowland depicts late seventeenth-century Edo (the city that will eventually become Tokyo) with scenes that contrast its delicate beauty, the excesses of its pleasure quarters, and the ugliness of its prisons and morgues. The first book is **Amateur detective/Traditional,** while the rest are **Public detective/Traditional.**

Shinjū. Random House, 1994. 367pp.

Edo, 1689. The deaths of a beautiful noblewoman and an artist, found drowned together in the Sumida River, are judged to be shinjū, a ritual double suicide committed by forbidden lovers. Sano isn't so sure.

Bundori. Villard, 1996. 339pp.

Sano, now the shogun's Most Honorable Investigator of Events, investigates a serial killer who leaves samurai war trophies, severed heads, in his wake.

The Way of the Traitor. Villard, 1997. 307pp.

In 1690 Nagasaki, where Sano has been exiled, the death of Dutch trader Jan Spaen has immense political implications.

The Concubine's Tattoo. St. Martin's Minotaur, 1998. 326pp.

Lady Harume, the shogun's favorite concubine, dies of a poisoned tattoo. Sano's new fiancée, Lady Reiko, wants to help him find the killer.

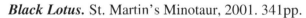

The Samurai's Wife. St. Martin's Minotaur, 2000. 293pp.

In the Imperial city of Miyako, Sano and Lady Reiko expose a killer who can murder men with a single scream.

Black Lotus. St. Martin's Minotaur, 2001. 341pp.

Lady Reiko believes that an orphaned teenage girl, the only survivor of a fire in Edo's Black Lotus Temple, is innocent of the crime.

The Pillow Book of Lady Wisteria. St. Martin's Minotaur, 2002. 292pp.

At a wealthy brothel in the Yoshiwara pleasure quarter, Lord Mitsuyoshi, the shogun's cousin, is found dead in the bed of Lady Wisteria, a famous courtesan.

The Dragon King's Palace. St. Martin's Minotaur, 2003. 340pp.

On their way to Mount Fuki, Lady Reiko and several other powerful women are kidnapped and held hostage.

The Perfumed Sleeve. St. Martin's Minotaur, 2004. 326pp.

The late councilman Makino Narisada, a key advisor to the shogun, left a deathbed message for Sano with his valet: find out who murdered him.

7

Chapter 8

Adventures in History

Historical adventure novels are known for their heroic protagonists, fast pace, and well-realized settings. Daring heroes (and, less occasionally, heroines) travel far and wide in their quest to find treasure, capture pirates, discover new lands, seek justice, fight the enemy on land and sea, or face off against nature. In some novels, the simple thrill of seeking danger in foreign lands becomes a quest in itself.

Physical setting is important to historical adventure novels. The word "adventure" implies a journey of some sort, and the protagonists spend a good part of the story traveling from one place to another. This allows readers to become armchair travelers, learning about new civilizations and different ways of life as they follow the hero on his or her mission. In the case of military novels, the setting incorporates not only the physical location but also the culture of men forced to work closely together in pursuit of victory. Many historical adventure novels feature protagonists from the Western world who are forced to survive in settings far away from home, such as Jerusalem during the Crusades, the icy Arctic in the nineteenth century, or aboard ship during the Napoleonic Wars. In other novels, such as some of those written by Gary Jennings, the exotic narrator belongs to the culture described. This makes the unusual setting even more of a culture shock to readers.

Because the plot involves physical movement, the pace is usually brisk. In this respect, historical adventure novels have much in common with historical thrillers, but in the former, the protagonist's opponent is generally a known commodity. The hero realizes in general who or what the enemy will be—such as a military foe, a warring culture, or simply survival on a lengthy sea voyage—though he may not always know how to combat it. Victory is not always assured, but it is the ultimate aim. There may be romantic subplots, but the romance always remains secondary to the hero's mission.

Characters in historical adventure novels have strong moral codes, which give them mental strength in fighting military rivals and in facing off against the natural dangers found in wild, primitive settings. This moral code may or may not be obvious to readers at the outset. Dorothy Dunnett's Renaissance hero, Francis Crawford of Lymond, has reasons behind his seemingly traitorous acts, though these aren't made clear to readers until the end of the series. Even pirates, normally thought to be the most immoral of rascals, live and die by rules that define their ruthless profession.

The adventure genre as a whole isn't known for strong characterization, though this stereotype doesn't always hold for historical adventure. Some heroes, such as the eunuch slave Taita from Wilbur Smith's Egyptian series, are unbelievably wise and all-powerful, which adds to the exaggerated, larger-than-life setting. Likewise, some villains are one-dimensionally evil. On the other hand, many historical adventure novels emphasize character development. Military novels in series, for example, can also be read as coming-of-age tales. Their protagonists, typically young midshipmen or soldiers as the series begins, grow in courage and stature throughout their long military careers. Also, while characters are forced to choose one side or the other in wartime settings, their choices, just like in real life, aren't always black and white.

Men are the primary characters in historical adventure novels; they are also the primary readers. This shouldn't be surprising, for in history, participation in military action and world exploration has traditionally been a man's role. There are exceptions, of course. Dorothy Dunnett's series of novels, with their swashbuckling action, political intrigue, and romantic heroes, attract more female than male readers. Adventure novels with female protagonists do exist, but they are the minority (see "Women Adventurers," last section).

The themes and types of historical adventure novels, as annotated below, are defined by the nature of the hero's mission and the physical setting—and in most cases, these are related.

Medieval Adventure

Medieval men leave their homes to head out to parts unknown in search of treasure, revenge, or salvation. The Crusades, a series of religious expeditions in medieval times in which men and women from the British Isles and Western Europe headed to the Holy Land to liberate Jerusalem from Muslim "infidels," are an ideal subject for historical adventure. Much of the action and excitement lies not in fighting the enemy, but in the journey itself. See also Pamela Kaufman's Alix of Wanthwaite series at the end of the chapter.

Cornwell, Bernard.

The Grail Quest.

> During the beginning of the Hundred Years War (fourteenth century) in England, Thomas of Hookton joins Edward III's army as an archer after his village is destroyed by French raiders. Determined to recover a holy relic that the rampaging Frenchmen stole from his village church, Thomas heads to France. There he vies with one of his compatriots in the English army for the affections of a beautiful French countess. He also becomes embroiled in a quest to find the Holy Grail, which may be his family's secret inheritance. The author of the Richard Sharpe

series (later this chapter) is in fine form here, with his trademark bloody battle scenes, fast-paced action, and sharp characterization.

The Archer's Tale. HarperCollins, 2001. 374pp. (Original title: *Harlequin.*)

Vagabond. HarperCollins, 2002. 405pp.

Heretic. HarperCollins, 2003. 355pp.

Eisner, Michael Alexander.

The Crusader. Doubleday, 2001. 288pp. `YA`

Brother Lucas, a monk in Spain's Santes Creus monastery in 1275, has agreed to try to exorcise the demons from tormented aristocrat Francisco de Montcada, whose mind has been scattered since his return from the Crusades. Francisco relates horrific tales of atrocities committed in the name of God, which culminated in a siege at the Krak des Chevaliers fortress. What Francisco doesn't know is that Lucas has his own ambitions to contend with in helping him recover his memories.

Lawhead, Stephen R.

Byzantium. HarperPrism, 1996. 645pp. `YA`

In the tenth century, young Aidan is one of a group of Irish monks sent to bring the Book of Kells, a magnificently illuminated manuscript, as a gift to the Byzantine Emperor in the hopes that he will send aid to the beleaguered Irish church. Kidnapped by Viking raiders en route and forced into slavery, Aidan undergoes a series of life-threatening adventures on land and sea that hone his determination and test his faith. Like Lawhead's <u>Celtic Crusades</u> trilogy (below), this novel was marketed as a fantasy, but aside from prophetic dreams, there's little of the supernatural to be found.

The Celtic Crusades. `YA`

Lawhead's trilogy follows several generations of a Scottish family who journey to the Holy Land during the Middle Ages. There they fight Saracens, have otherworldly visions of holy relics, and discover both love and justice. A late Victorian story, in which a Scottish lawyer undergoes initiation into a secret society and sees visions of his ancestors' experiences on Crusade, frames the medieval part of the tale. Lawhead's novels (including *Byzantium*, above) show a strong Christian sensibility, but they should prove accessible for readers of all religious persuasions.

The Iron Lance. HarperPrism/Zondervan, 1998. 498pp.

In late eleventh-century Scotland, Murdo Ranulfson stays home to guard his homeland while his father and brothers head out on the First Crusade to Jerusalem. When a Norseman in collusion with the Church destroys his home, Murdo has no choice but to leave his lady love and head to the Holy Land himself in search of his father. While there, he hears rumors about the holy relic of the title—the iron lance that pierced Christ's flesh at the Crucifixion.

The Black Rood. HarperPrism/Zondervan, 2000. 437pp.

Duncan, Murdo Ranulfson's oldest son, follows in his father's footsteps by heading off on a quest to discover another holy relic, the Black Rood—a piece of the True Cross. Accompanying him is Padraig, a Celtic priest, but their path is blocked at nearly every avenue by bandits, Knights Templar, and Saracens.

The Mystic Rose. HarperPrism/Zondervan, 2001. 512pp.

The Mystic Rose is the Holy Grail, and now that it has once again reappeared in the world, the Knights Templar are determined to possess it. Their one obstacle is a young Scotswoman named Caitriona, the daughter of Duncan Ranulfson, who knows that possessing the Grail is her family's destiny.

Patterson, James, and Andrew Gross.
The Jester. Little, Brown, 2003. 457pp.

In late eleventh-century France, local innkeeper Hugh de Luc heads to Jerusalem on Crusade in the hopes of winning his freedom from his overlord, Lord Baldwin. Returning home two years later, he finds his young son dead and his wife missing, presumably held captive at Lord Baldwin's castle. With the help of a beautiful noblewoman, Hugh decides to infiltrate the castle disguised as a jester, free his wife, and lead a rebellion against Lord Baldwin's tyranny. Despite the excitement and local color, the protagonist is really a twenty-first century man in medieval garb. Patterson is the author of the Alex Cross series of crime thrillers.

Swashbuckling Adventure

These are larger-than-life stories of reckless adventure, swordplay, and derring-do set in Europe between the Renaissance and the eighteenth century. The clever, romantic heroes of swashbuckling adventure fight duels with both weapons and their wits in pursuit of honor or to defend their own good name. The historical novels of French writer Alexandre Dumas, set amid the eighteenth-century royal court, are early examples of the swashbuckling tradition; the most famous of these include *The Three Musketeers* and *The Count of Monte Cristo.* Baroness Orczy's *The Scarlet Pimpernel,* about a dashing rogue who rescues French aristocrats from the guillotine, is another prime example. Pirate novels with dashing heroes, such as Rafael Sabatini's *Captain Blood* (later this chapter), may also be considered works of swashbuckling adventure. Though this is a declining subgenre, the novels mentioned here are classics.

Dunnett, Dorothy.

The novels of the late Scottish novelist Dorothy Dunnett are hard to categorize. Swashbuckling adventures at heart, they are also highly praised in literary circles and beloved by readers in general. Many find Dunnett's novels hard to get into, due to the challenging language and the fact that she drops readers directly into the action without any introduction. Her novels take place on a wide scale, with fictional characters intermingling with historical personalities as they journey through the courts of Europe. Her characters, like the novels themselves, are multifaceted, erudite, and complex. Dunnett's knowledge of Renaissance Europe —politics, art, and personalities included—was encyclopedic, so much so that reading her novels is a true learning experience. Her characters are as apt to speak in Latin or in French (of the sixteenth-century variety) as they are to converse in English. The novels are so full of literary references that two companion volumes (*The Dorothy Dunnett Companion*, vols. 1 and 2, ed. Elspeth Morrison) have been published.

The Chronicles of Lymond. ★

This six-book series is set over a ten-year period, from the 1540s through 1550s, and plays out over a wide stage that includes Europe, Malta, and the Ottoman Empire during the Renaissance. At the beginning of *The Game of Kings*, Francis Crawford of Lymond, the younger son of a sixteenth-century Scottish nobleman, has just returned to Scotland. Edward VI, the child king who was Henry VIII's only legitimate son, is on the English throne. His cousin Mary, Queen of Scots, is still a child. Lymond had betrayed his country to England five years earlier, only to turn around and betray the English in turn. Nobody knows what his next move will be.

Handsome, brilliant, charismatic, and dangerous, Lymond is the ultimate romantic hero. As swift with a sword as he is with his wits, he is an acknowledged rogue who has the uncanny ability to know which way things will tip in the political arena. Yet he is also an anti-hero, for some of his actions seem cruel and inexplicable, and he is only seen through the eyes of other characters. The truth behind the enigma, along with a certain mystery about his birth, is finally revealed at the end. **Literary.**

The Game of Kings. Putnam. 1961. 543pp.

Queens' Play. Putnam, 1964. 432pp.

The Disorderly Knights. Putnam, 1966. 503pp.

Pawn in Frankincense. Putnam, 1969. 486pp.

The Ringed Castle. Putnam, 1972. 521pp.

Checkmate. Putnam, 1975. 581pp.

The House of Niccolò.

Dunnett's second major series is set firmly in the realm of European commerce in the mid-fifteenth century. Claes vander Poele, also called Nicholas and Niccolò, begins the series as an apprentice dyer in the House of Charetty, a trading house in Bruges. Although at first he seems to be a good-natured, unsophisticated lad, behind his buffoonish guise lies one of the sharpest mercantile minds of his era—one he will use to his advantage in taking revenge on the family members who failed him and his mother. As Claes changes before readers' eyes from a simple artisan to courier, master merchant, and engineer in his travels across Europe, the city of Bruges develops into the very center of European trade, with routes open to Scotland, Germany, and Venice, as well as lands as far away as Africa and China. Like the Lymond series, these novels are full of adventure, romance, intrigue, and plenty of mystery, not the least of which is the relationship between Dunnett's two series. **Literary.**

8

Niccolò Rising. Knopf, 1986. 470pp.

The Spring of the Ram. Knopf ,1988. 469pp.

Race of Scorpions. Knopf, 1990. 534pp.

Scales of Gold. Knopf, 1992. 519pp.

The Unicorn Hunt. Knopf, 1994. 656pp.

To Lie with Lions. Knopf, 1996. 626pp.

Caprice and Rondo. Knopf, 1998. 539pp.

Gemini. Knopf, 2000. 672pp.

Sabatini, Rafael.

Scaramouche. **Houghton Mifflin, 1921. 392pp.** ★

Sabatini's masterpiece of a moral adventure tale is set in the years leading up to the French Revolution. To avenge the death of his best friend, killed in an unjust duel against the evil Marquis de La Tour d'Azyr, Andre-Louis Moreau goes underground, feigning to believe in a cause he had previously laughed at. In disguise as "Scaramouche," he hides amid a group of traveling actors and discovers an unexpected talent for rallying crowds against the injustices of the nobility.

Shellabarger, Samuel.

In the 1940s and 1950s, Shellabarger wrote a number of adventurous historical novels set primarily during the Renaissance; these two are the best known.

Captain from Castile. **Little, Brown, 1947. 503pp.**

After the Inquisition destroys his family, nineteen-year-old Pedro de Vargas leaves his home in sixteenth-century Spain to make his fortune in the New World. In Mexico, he and Cortès proceed to conquer Montezuma's Aztec empire for their homeland. Not just a bloody adventure tale, Pedro's heroic journey takes place amid swordfights, political controversy, and romantic intrigue.

Prince of Foxes. **Little, Brown, 1945. 433pp.**

Disguised as an Italian noble, Andrea Orsini joins the entourage of the evil Cesare Borgia in the sixteenth century. Borgia sends Orsini on a mission to persuade the elderly Count of Citadel del Monte to join forces with him, but Orsini's admiration for the Count's honest lifestyle—as well as his lovely wife—makes him rethink his mission.

Military Adventure

These are fast-paced adventure novels that present men's experiences in military encounters throughout history. Here, the hero's goals are twofold: to vanquish the enemy, and, of more immediate concern, simply to stay alive. Among historical adventure fiction, this is the most popular and fastest growing subgenre. Most occur in series. This section does not include general novels of war (found in Chapters 2 and 10), as they concentrate less on the heroes' quest or mission and more on the overall wartime experience, though some readers may enjoy fiction of both types.

Ancient Greece and Rome

These novels re-create ancient battles and portray the military life of long ago. Readers who enjoy them may also want to read Steven Pressfield's novels, starting with *Gates of Fire* (Chapter 2).

Ford, Michael Curtis.

Gods and Legions. **Thomas Dunne, 2002. 384pp.** ✍

Julian the Apostate, a controversial fourth-century Roman emperor, had a renowned military career that is often overshadowed by his later conversion to paganism. After his uncle Constantine proclaims him Caesar of the Western Empire, Julian heads to Gaul, where he triumphs against the native German tribes. Constantine had not expected him to be quite so successful a military leader, however, which sets the stage for their rivalry. Julian's physician, Cacsarius, a fervent Christian who looks down on Julian's pagan beliefs, narrates the tale.

The Last King. **Thomas Dunne, 2004. 384pp.** ✍

Mithridates Eupator VI of Pontus, better known as Mithridates the Great, was one of the greatest threats to the Roman Empire in the first century BC. Strong, stubborn, and well-educated, Mithridates fights for over forty ycars to establish a Greek empire that rivals Rome.

The Ten Thousand. **St. Martin's Press, 2001. 384pp.** ✍

In 400 BC, after Sparta has finally triumphed over Athens, 10,000 Greek and Spartan soldiers—hardened to a life of war—heed the call to arms of Prince Cyrus of Persia. Cyrus is recruiting Greek mercenaries to help him fight his uncle King Artaxcrxes for Persia's throne. Among them is Xenophon, an Athenian soldier-philosopher, who heads south with the Greeks over a thousand miles of treacherous terrain. In Persia, their forces are defeated: Cyrus is killed and other leaders slaughtered. The surviving Greeks want nothing more than to go home, but first they must face Artaxerxes's revenge and their own lack of provisions on the journey back. Ford's novel is based on the historical memoirs of Xenophon, who successfully led the Greek expedition back to the Black Sea.

Iggulden, Conn.

<u>Emperor Series.</u> ✍

A projected four-part series set in ancient Rome. Iggulden is at his best when it comes to plotting, and his action scenes are swift and powerful. He's weaker at characterization, though, and acknowledges playing with history. In reality, his two protagonists Caesar and Brutus were fifteen years apart in age.

Emperor: The Gates of Rome. **Delacorte, 2003. 357pp.**

At the end of the Roman Republic, two boys grow up amid the brutality, violence, and intrigue that pervade the city. They are Gaius, the son of a powerful senator and nephew of one of Rome's greatest leaders, and

Marcus, the bastard son of a prostitute. They train for combat together. Later, Gaius learns the craft of statehood in the Senate, and Marcus becomes a soldier on the battlefields of Greece. Gaius, otherwise known as Gaius Julius Caesar, will grow up to become the most powerful emperor that Rome has ever known; Marcus's identity is hidden until the end. When they meet again as men, their friendship is put to the test.

Emperor: The Death of Kings. Delacorte, 2004. 469pp.

Off the coast of North Africa, pirates kidnap Caesar and hold him captive. After he ransoms himself, he is left to make his own way back to Rome. Meanwhile, back in the heart of the Empire, Brutus rises in political power.

Manfredi, Valerio Massimo.

Alexander Trilogy. ✍

Born to greatness as the heir of Philip of Macedon and his passionate queen, Olympias, young Alexander grows up believing his destiny is to unite the Greek cities of Asia, under himself as their leader. He lives and loves with ambition, as shown by his strength in battle against the Persians and in his romantic pursuit of Barsine, the widow of one of his greatest enemies. Unlike Mary Renault's trilogy (Chapter 2), a serious look at the most significant events in Alexander the Great's life, Italian novelist Manfredi's trilogy recounts Alexander's military and romantic exploits as a grand adventure. Short paragraphs and modern dialogue contribute to this effect.

Alexander: Child of a Dream. Washington Square Press, 2001. 352pp.

Alexander: The Sands of Ammon. Washington Square Press, 2001. 386pp.

Alexander: The Ends of the Earth. Washington Square Press, 2002. 446pp.

Spartan. Atria, 2003. 336pp.

In the ancient Hellenes, two brothers who were separated soon after birth reunite in manhood, but their upbringing influences their destinies. Talos, whose noble Spartan parents abandoned him at birth because of his lameness, is taken in by the Helot people. He is raised hearing about the legend of King Aristodemus, whose valiant deeds he tries to emulate. Talos's healthy brother Bristos grows up to become a Spartan warrior. The two are fated to meet again—as enemies.

Scarrow, Simon.

Cato Series.

This series of novels follow the Roman invasion of Britain in AD 43 from the point of view of the invaders. In Germany, Centurion Lucius Cornelius Macro commands the Second Legion, the most powerful fighting force in the Empire. The soldiers are less than thrilled at being sent to the barbaric British Isles to subdue the native tribes and conquer the lands for Rome. They are also disturbed by the arrival of a new recruit, Quintus Licinus Cato, who is made second in command because of personal connections. As Cato grows from a beardless boy into a hardened soldier, he and Macro fight their way west toward Britain, uncovering not only enemies but also conspiracies against the Emperor Claudius. Scarrow's characters fight and swear like a bunch of Roman soldiers, which, of course, they are.

Under the Eagle. Thomas Dunne, 2001. 246pp.

The Eagle's Conquest. Thomas Dunne, 2002. 310pp.

When the Eagle Hunts. Thomas Dunne, 2004. 272pp.

The Eagle and the Wolves. Thomas Dunne, 2004. 280pp.

The Age of Fighting Sail

These novels take place between 1775 and 1815, a forty-year period that saw Great Britain engage in a number of maritime battles. At its beginning was the American Revolution; at the end was Napoleon's final defeat at Waterloo. The high point for the era—and in many of the novels—was the Battle of Trafalgar in 1805, when Britain's Royal Navy, under Lord Horatio Nelson, succeeded in destroying a combined French–Spanish fleet. Due to its victory at Trafalgar, Britain effectively gained control of the world's oceans for the next 100 years.

Not only do these novels contain pulse-pounding battle scenes aboard ship, but they also provide good doses of character development, scenes of politics and treason, fast-paced action, and enough authentically described nautical detail to make landlubbing readers feel at home on the high seas. The originator of naval fiction set in the Napoleonic era was Captain Frederick Marryat (1792–1848), himself a British naval hero who survived more than fifty shipboard battles. His *Mr. Midshipman Easy* (1808), a humorous yet realistic take on life aboard a British man-of-war, served as a model for works by C. S. Forester, Alexander Kent, and others. The majority of the authors presented here are veteran sailors themselves, which lends a sense of realism to their heroic tales.

Donachie, David.

Nelson and Emma Trilogy. ✍

In 1771, long before he will become England's greatest naval hero, twelve-year-old Horatio Nelson takes up his duties on his first ship, the *Raisonable*. At the same time, in another part of England, young Emma Hamilton settles with her mother into a life of domestic servitude. Nelson's is a brilliant tale of adventure on the high seas, the sort of heroic naval story that Donachie is known for, while the spirited Emma's life is a continual struggle against poverty. The author balances both halves of the tale in a trilogy recounting two of the greatest lovers from history.

On a Making Tide. McBooks, 2003. 448pp.

Tested by Fate. McBooks, 2004. 405pp. (Original title: *Taken at the Flood.*)

Breaking the Line. McBooks, 2004. 268pp.

The Privateersman Mysteries.

In the 1790s, Harry Ludlow, former Royal Navy officer turned privateer, joins forces with his younger brother James to solve a series of crimes aboard ship. Though the books have appeal for mystery fans, readers of naval adventures will appreciate the naval action and intrigue, in which the brothers pursue Britain's interests in the waters of Europe, America, and the West Indies.

The Devil's Own Luck. McBooks, 2001. 318pp.

The Dying Trade. McBooks, 2001. 399pp.

A Hanging Matter. McBooks, 2002. 411pp.

An Element of Chance. McBooks, 2002. 460pp.

The Scent of Betrayal. McBooks, 2003. 448pp.

A Game of Bones. McBooks, 2003. 352pp.

Forester, C. S.

Horatio Hornblower Series. ★

Horatio Hornblower is one of the most engaging and beloved heroes in all of naval literature. With strict technical accuracy, Forester brought to life the Age of Sail with a protagonist based partially on Lord Horatio Nelson, the hero of Trafalgar. In 1793, at the height of the French Revolution, the seventeen-year-old Hornblower joins the British Navy as a midshipman aboard the *Justinian*. He serves British interests in Europe, the Mediterranean, and the West Indies during the Napoleonic Wars, all the while rising in his career until he reaches the rank of Admiral. C. Northcote Parkinson, author of the Richard Delancey series (below), was a devoted Forester fan. His fictional biography of Forester's hero, *The Life and Times of Horatio Hornblower* (Little Brown, 1970), holds up well alongside Forester's own *Hornblower Companion* and does a good job of convincing the reader that Hornblower really lived. They are best enjoyed in historical order, below.

Mr. Midshipman Hornblower. Little, Brown, 1950. 310pp.

Lieutenant Hornblower. Little, Brown, 1952. 306pp.

Hornblower and the Hotspur. Little, Brown, 1962. 344pp.

Hornblower and the Atropos. Little, Brown, 1953. 325pp.

Beat to Quarters. Little, Brown, 1937. 324pp. (Alternate title: *The Happy Return.*)

Ship of the Line. Little, Brown, 1938. 323pp. (Alternate title: *A Ship of the Line.*)

Flying Colours. Little, Brown, 1939. 294pp.

Commodore Hornblower. Little, Brown, 1945. 384pp. (Alternate title: *The Commodore.*)

Lord Hornblower. Little, Brown, 1946. 322pp.

Admiral Hornblower in the West Indies. Little, Brown, 1958. 329pp. (Alternate title: *Hornblower in the West Indies.*)

Hornblower During the Crisis. Little, Brown, 1967. 174pp.

This novel, a compilation of two short stories taking place in 1805 (fourth chronologically), remained unfinished at Forester's death.

Kent, Alexander.

Richard Bolitho Novels.

Kent's lengthy series features conspiracy on the high seas, piracy, honor, loyalty, and treason, all seen through the eyes of Richard Bolitho, a young man who starts out as a midshipman in His Majesty's Navy in 1772. As he matures and gets promoted in rank, he sees action in New York, the Caribbean, India, New South Wales, the Mediterranean, and also back home in Portsmouth, England. The later volumes, beginning with *Second to None*, feature the exploits of Bolitho's nephew, Adam, captain of the frigate *Unrivalled* in the aftermath of Waterloo in 1815. Alexander Kent is the pseudonym for Douglas Reeman, who writes contemporary and historical adventure novels under his own name. The novels, all in print from McBooks, are presented in historical order.

Richard Bolitho, Midshipman. Putnam, 1976. 158pp.

*Midshipman Bolitho and the **Avenger**.* Putnam, 1978. 143pp. (First two novels also published in one volume as *Midshipman Bolitho*.)

Stand into Danger. Putnam, 1981. 296pp.

In Gallant Company. Putnam, 1977. 287pp.

Sloop of War. Putnam, 1972. 319pp.

To Glory We Steer. Putnam, 1968. 328pp.

Command a King's Ship. Putnam, 1974. 320pp.

Passage to Mutiny. Putnam, 1976. 319pp.

With All Despatch. Putnam, 1989. 289pp.

Form Line of Battle! Putnam, 1969. 320pp.

Enemy in Sight! Putnam, 1970. 350pp.

The Flag Captain. Putnam, 1971. 384pp.

Signal—Close Action! Putnam, 1974. 320pp.

The Inshore Squadron. Putnam, 1979. 256pp.

A Tradition of Victory. Putnam, 1982. 296pp.

Success to the Brave. Putnam, 1983. 284pp.

Colours Aloft! McBooks, 2000. 300pp.

Honour This Day. Putnam, 1988. 287pp.

The Only Victor. McBooks, 2000. 384pp.

Beyond the Reef. McBooks, 2000. 349pp.

The Darkening Sea. McBooks, 2000. 351pp.

For My Country's Freedom. McBooks, 2000. 300pp.

Cross of St. George. McBooks, 2001. 320pp.

Sword of Honour. McBooks, 2001. 320pp.

Second to None. McBooks, 2001. 350pp.

Relentless Pursuit. McBooks, 2001. 336pp.

Man of War. McBooks, 2003. 319pp.

Lambdin, Dewey.

Alan Lewrie Naval Adventure Series.

The bastard son of a snobbish London aristocrat, seventeen-year-old Alan Lewrie finds himself banished to the Royal Navy in 1780 by his own father after his latest amorous adventure lands him in hot water. Aboard the *Ariadne*, Lewrie—the bad boy of the high seas—discovers an unexpected liking for seamanship. He acquits himself well in naval battles, though his growth as a sailor does little to tame his scandalous ways on land.

The King's Coat. Fine, 1989. 397pp.

The French Admiral. Fine, 1990. 414pp.

The King's Commission. Fine, 1991. 400pp.

The King's Privateer. Fine, 1992. 360pp.

The Gun Ketch. Fine, 1993. 312pp.

H.M.S. Cockerel. Fine, 1995. 360pp.

A King's Commander. Fine, 1997. 374pp.

Jester's Fortune. Dutton, 1999. 373pp.

King's Captain. St. Martin's Press, 2000. 358pp.

Sea of Grey. Thomas Dunne, 2002. 391pp.

Havoc's Sword. Thomas Dunne, 2003. 384pp.

The Captain's Vengeance. Thomas Dunne, 2004. 352pp.

Mack, William P.

Kilburnie Series.

The rise of Fergus Kilburnie, a Scotsman in Nelson's navy, from lowly sailor to high rank happens more quickly than in most naval fiction. Mack's novels are simply told, but without the extensive nautical detail used by the greats such as O'Brian and Forester.

Captain Kilburnie. Naval Institute Press, 1999. 367pp.

Commodore Kilburnie. Naval Institute Press, 2002. 209pp.

O'Brian, Patrick.

Aubrey/Maturin Series. ★

O'Brian's twenty Aubrey/Maturin novels form the best known, and easily the most admired, historical naval fiction series in existence. Against the backdrop of the Napoleonic Wars, Captain Jack Aubrey of His Majesty's Navy and his friend Stephen Maturin, ship's surgeon and occasional spy, engage the French and

Spanish in a series of fierce sea battles. Though these novels offer as much authentic naval detail as readers can hope for, they provide much more. O'Brian's eloquent dialogue and literary writing style reflect that of the late eighteenth century. He also explores human relationships, using the friendship between Aubrey and Maturin—and the camaraderie that forms among all the men aboard a single vessel—as prime examples. The plots move more slowly than those of most naval adventure novels, but O'Brian's emphasis on thorough research and character development more than compensates. His detailed portraits of these brave men bring the Napoleonic era to life and, at the same time, demonstrate that human nature has not changed over the years. With O'Brian's death in 2000 came the end of the series, or so readers thought. An unfinished final volume, *21*, includes three chapters found on O'Brian's desk after his death.

Master and Commander. Lippincott, 1969. 384pp. 📖

Post Captain. Lippincott, 1972. 413pp.

H.M.S. Surprise. Lippincott, 1973. 318pp.

The Mauritius Command. Stein & Day, 1978. 268pp.

Desolation Island. Stein & Day, 1979. 276pp.

Fortune of War. W.W. Norton, 1991. 329pp.

The Surgeon's Mate. W. W. Norton, 1992. 382pp.

The Ionian Mission. W. W. Norton, 1992. 367pp.

Treason's Harbour. W. W. Norton, 1992. 334pp.

The Far Side of the World. W. W. Norton, 1992. 366pp.

The Reverse of the Medal. W. W. Norton, 1992. 287pp.

The Letter of Marque. W. W. Norton, 1990. 284pp.

The Thirteen Gun Salute. W. W. Norton, 1991. 319pp.

The Nutmeg of Consolation. W. W. Norton, 1991. 315pp.

The Truelove. W. W. Norton, 1992. 256pp. (Original title: *Clarissa Oakes.*)

The Wine-Dark Sea. W. W. Norton, 1993. 261pp.

The Commodore. W. W. Norton, 1995. 281pp.

The Yellow Admiral. W. W. Norton, 1996. 261pp.

The Hundred Days. W. W. Norton, 1998. 280pp.

Blue at the Mizzen. W. W. Norton, 1999. 261pp.

21: The Unfinished Twenty-First Volume in the Aubrey-Maturin Series. W.W. Norton, 2004. 144pp.

The Golden Ocean. J. Day, 1957. 316pp. `YA`

In a sea journey taken around the world in 1740, Peter Palafox, a young Irish midshipman, develops into a competent sailor and an intelligent man. Originally published for a juvenile audience, O'Brian's earliest venture into naval fiction can serve as a prequel to his more successful <u>Aubrey/Maturin series.</u>

***The Unknown Shore.* W. W. Norton, 1995. 313pp. (Originally published in Britain in 1959.)** YA

Like *The Golden Ocean,* O'Brian based this novel on Commodore George Anson's circumnavigation of the globe in the 1740s. Jack Byron, midshipman on the H.M.S. *Wager*, and his best friend, future physician Tobias Barrow, are easily recognized as progenitors for Aubrey and Maturin. Shipwrecked off the southern coast of Chile after becoming separated from Anson's fleet, the *Wager*'s crew struggles to make their way back home.

Parkinson, C. Northcote.

Richard Delancey Novels.

C. Northcote Parkinson is perhaps best known for "Parkinson's Law," a sarcastic treatise on inept managerial style, but he was also a keen military historian. After completing his fictional biography of C. S. Forester's hero Horatio Hornblower (above), Parkinson began his own novels of naval history. His hero Richard Delancey, of Guernsey in England's Channel Islands, joins Britain's Royal Navy in the 1770s as a way of escaping imprisonment after unwittingly becoming involved in a Liverpool labor riot. Between then and 1811, when he returns home from the West Indies as a victorious frigate captain, he sees action aboard ship during America's War for Independence, France's Revolution and Napoleonic Wars, and in Spain during the siege of Gibraltar. All six books, shown in chronological order, have been reprinted by McBooks Press.

The Guernseyman. Houghton Mifflin, 1982.

Devil to Pay. Houghton Mifflin, 1973. 273pp.

The Fireship. Houghton Mifflin, 1975. 185pp.

Touch and Go. Houghton Mifflin, 1977. 230pp.

So Near So Far. Houghton Mifflin, 1981. 268pp.

Dead Reckoning. Houghton Mifflin, 1978. 276pp.

Pope, Dudley.

Lord Ramage Series.

In eighteen books, Dudley Pope follows the career of Lord Nicholas Ramage, son of the tenth Earl of Blazey, as a lieutenant in the Royal Navy during Nelson's time. He and his crew engage in ferocious sea battles not only against France and Spain in Europe and the Mediterranean, but also across the Atlantic in Jamaica. Pope, a naval historian and former member of the British Merchant Navy, writes intelligently and concisely.

Ramage. Lippincott, 1965. 302pp.

Drumbeat. Doubleday, 1968. 269pp. (Alternate title: *Ramage & the Drumbeat.*)

The Triton Brig. Doubleday, 1969. 378pp. (Alternate title: *Ramage & the Freebooters.*)

Governor Ramage R.N. Simon and Schuster, 1973. 340pp.

Ramage's Prize. Simon and Schuster, 1975. 344pp.

Ramage & the Guillotine. Simon & Schuster, 1975. 285pp.

Ramage's Diamond. McBooks, 2001. 332pp. (Originally published in Britain in 1976.)

Ramage's Mutiny. McBooks, 2001. 286pp. (Originally published 1977.)

Ramage & the Rebels. Walker, 1985. 284pp.

The Ramage Touch. Walker, 1984. 226pp.

Ramage's Signal. Walker, 1984. 255pp.

Ramage & the Renegades. McBooks, 2001. 320pp. (Originally published 1981.)

Ramage's Devil. McBooks, 2002. 320pp. (Originally published 1982.)

Ramage's Trial. McBooks, 2002. 347pp. (Originally published 1984.)

Ramage's Challenge. McBooks, 2002. 302pp. (Originally published 1985.)

Ramage at Trafalgar. McBooks, 2002. 254pp. (Originally published 1986.)

Ramage & the Saracens. McBooks, 2002. 304pp. (Originally published 1988.)

Ramage & the Dido. McBooks, 2002. 287pp. (Originally published 1989.)

Stockwin, Julian.

Thomas Paine Kydd Series.

At the end of the eighteenth century, Britain is at war with France, but it lacks sufficient personnel to man its ships. As a result of this shortage, Stockwin's hero Thomas Kydd, a young wig-maker from the landlocked town of Guildford, is pressed into the Royal Navy. The conditions aboard ship are horrible, but Kydd has no choice but to accustom himself to his fate. He befriends fellow novice sailor Thomas Renzi, and the two, to their surprise, find themselves relishing the cutthroat battles and dangerous excitement of the Age of Sail. A relative newcomer to nautical fiction, Julian Stockwin is a retired Lt. Commander in the Royal Navy. His series is expected to last at least eleven volumes.

Kydd. Scribner, 2001. 254pp.

Artemis. Scribner, 2002. 334pp.

Seaflower. Scribner, 2003. 320pp.

Mutiny. Scribner, 2004. 336pp.

Woodman, Richard.

Nathaniel Drinkwater Series.

Woodman's series combines high seas action with political intrigue and espionage. Nathaniel Drinkwater's sea adventures begin at age seventeen, in the year 1779. He joins the crew of the H.M.S. *Cyclops*, whose mission is to prevent American privateers from disrupting British trade. After a departure of twelve years, during which he marries, Drinkwater rejoins the Royal Navy in 1792, just as the French Revolution is engulfing Europe. Later adventures find him defending Britain's interests off the China coast, in the Arctic, off Cape Horn, and back in London, where he works undercover to upset Napoleon's alliance with Russia. The series has been reprinted in its entirety by Sheridan House.

An Eye of the Fleet. Pinnacle, 1983. 213pp.

A King's Cutter. Pinnacle, 1984. 218pp.

A Brig of War. Pinnacle, 1984. 280pp.

The Bomb Vessel. Walker, 1986. 215pp.

Arctic Treachery. Walker, 1987. 232pp. (Original title: *The Corvette.*)

Decision at Trafalgar. Walker, 1987. 209pp. (Original title: *1805.*)

Baltic Mission. Walker, 1988. 211pp.

In Distant Waters. St. Martin's Press, 1989. 246pp.

A Private Revenge. St. Martin's Press, 1989. 247pp.

Under False Colours. Sheridan House, 1999. 247pp.

The Flying Squadron. Sheridan House, 1999. 250pp.

Beneath the Aurora. Sheridan House, 2001. 247pp.

Shadow of the Eagle. Sheridan House, 2002. 260pp.

Ebb Tide. Sheridan House, 2002. 230pp.

American Naval Warfare

Historical naval adventure novels told from the American point of view were rare until relatively recently, but readers now have several growing series to choose from.

Fender, J. E.

Geoffrey Frost Series.

Captain Geoffrey Frost of Portsmouth, New Hampshire, a young but well-trained mariner, becomes a privateer recruited by the American cause during the Revolution against Britain. His friend and aide is Ming Tsun, whom he had rescued, and been rescued by in turn, during their previous naval adventures in China. A ten-volume series is planned. The author is legal counsel for the Portsmouth Naval Shipyard.

The Private Revolution of Geoffrey Frost. University Press of New England, 2002. 297pp.

Audacity, *Privateer out of Portsmouth.* University Press of New England, 2003. 298pp.

Our Lives, Our Fortunes. University Press of New England, 2004. 309pp.

Nelson, James L.

Brethren of the Coast Trilogy.

In 1700, after he kills a man in a duel over a widow's honor, Virginia planter Thomas Marlowe is given command of the Plymouth Prize, a guardship assigned to patrol the Chesapeake Bay against incursion by pirates (the "brethren of the coast") . He must also contend with the vengeful nature of the dead man's family. However, Thomas has a past that comes back to haunt him, for he was once a pirate himself, serving under the maniacal leader of the Brethren. The beautiful widow he protected, Elizabeth Tinling, has her own secrets to keep. Later adventures lead Thomas and his former slave, King James, to Europe during the War of the Spanish Succession, and to Madagascar, a voyage that sorely tempts him to return to piracy.

The Guardship. Post Road, 2000. 372pp.

The Blackbirder. Morrow, 2001. 336pp.

The Pirate Round. Morrow, 2002. 366pp.

Glory in the Name. **Morrow, 2003. 420pp.**

Like Ker Clairborne in David Poyer's *A Country of Our Own*, Samuel Bowater is a reluctant recruit to the Confederate Navy—at least at first. A native of Charleston, South Carolina, on leave from the U.S. Navy, Bowater makes the hard decision to join his state against the Union. Though used to serving on larger vessels, Bowater is pleased enough to receive command of the tug C.S.S. *Cape Fear*, and he and his men use it to defend the Mississippi River against Yankees. More volumes are planned.

Revolution at Sea Saga.

In the American colonies in 1775, Merchant Captain Isaac Biddlecomb is pressed into the British Navy and forced to serve an incompetent leader under horrendous conditions. While there, he develops sympathies for the colonists' revolutionary point of view. Later, as captain of the *Charlemagne*, a naval vessel based in Rhode Island, Biddlecomb is drawn into the events of the American Revolution. He loyally serves General Washington on naval missions to Nassau, England, and France, to which country he delivers diplomat Benjamin Franklin in the newly formed United States' attempt to get military help from the French. The series currently stands at five books, taking the action through 1777.

8

By Force of Arms. Pocket, 1996. 324pp.

The Maddest Idea. Pocket, 1997. 417pp.

The Continental Risque. Pocket, 1998. 372pp.

Lords of the Ocean. Pocket, 1999. 354pp.

All the Brave Fellows. Pocket, 2000. 395pp.

Nicastro, Nicholas.

John Paul Jones Series. ✍

The author dusts off the historical character of John Paul Jones, America's first naval hero, by presenting, in witty style, his adventures on sea, land, and in the bedroom—both in France and in Revolutionary America.

The Eighteenth Captain. McBooks, 1999. 312pp.

Between Two Fires. McBooks, 2002. 384pp.

Poyer, David.

Civil War at Sea Series.

Poyer's novels portray a side of the Civil War rarely seen in fiction: its naval battles.

Fire on the Waters. Simon & Schuster, 2001. 445pp.

In 1861 Eli Eaker, son of a wealthy New York shipping magnate, abandons his father's hopes for him, as well as an arranged marriage to his cousin, by joining the fight for the Union. He signs up as a member of the crew of the U.S.S. *Owanee*, a ship assigned to defend Fort Sumter. There he meets Lt. Ker Clairborne, an Annapolis graduate who must choose between his career in the U.S. Navy and loyalty to his home state of Virginia.

A Country of Our Own. Simon & Schuster, 2003. 429pp.

Ker Clairborne, formerly a lieutenant in the Union Navy, has reluctantly resigned his commission to join his fellow Virginians on the side of the Confederacy. Aboard first the C.S.S. *Montgomery* and later the *Maryland*, he and his compatriots fight, raid, and sink Union vessels in the attempt to block trade goods from reaching their destinations.

Nineteenth-Century Land Warfare

Like novels of the Age of Fighting Sail, these land-based military adventures come in series. They follow a single hero through a series of major army campaigns in Europe, India, and the United States during the nineteenth century.

Cornwell, Bernard.

Richard Sharpe Series.

During the Peninsular Wars, Richard Sharpe, a soldier among the ranks in the British army, saves the life of Sir Arthur Wellesley (later known as the Duke of Wellington) and is rewarded with a field commission. An unusual lieutenant, Sharpe is an outsider; never fully accepted by fellow officers due to his humble background, he nonetheless proves himself time after time on the battle-fields of Europe in the Napoleonic era. Sharpe's earliest adventures, however, began in India. In the first three novels of the series, Private Sharpe fights the evil Tippoo Sultan during the siege of Seringapatam in 1799 and ends up a hero. From India to Spain to Portugal, the series is filled with rip-roaring action, evil villains, fierce battles, and reckless heroism. *Sharpe's Trafalgar*, fourth chronologically, is the only novel to take place aboard ship rather than on land. The novels in this continuing series, most of which are based on real military campaigns, are listed in historical order.

Sharpe's Tiger. HarperCollins, 1997. 385pp.

Sharpe's Triumph. HarperCollins, 1998. 291pp.

Sharpe's Fortress. HarperCollins, 1999. 294pp.

Sharpe's Trafalgar. HarperCollins, 2001. 288pp.

Sharpe's Prey. HarperCollins, 2001. 262pp.

Sharpe's Rifles. Viking, 1988. 304pp.

Sharpe's Havoc. HarperCollins, 2003. 320pp.

Sharpe's Eagle. Viking, 1981. 270pp.

Sharpe's Gold. Viking, 1981. 250pp.

Sharpe's Escape. HarperCollins, 2004. 368pp.

Sharpe's Battle. HarperCollins, 1995. 304pp.

Sharpe's Company. Viking, 1982. 280pp.

Sharpe's Sword. Viking, 1983. 319pp.

Sharpe's Enemy. Viking, 1984. 351pp.

Sharpe's Honour. Viking, 1985. 320pp.

Sharpe's Regiment. Viking, 1986. 301pp.

Sharpe's Siege. Viking, 1987. 319pp.

Sharpe's Revenge. Viking, 1989. 348pp.

Waterloo. Viking, 1990. 378pp. (Alternate title: *Sharpe's Waterloo.*)

Sharpe's Devil. HarperCollins, 1992. 280pp.

Starbuck Chronicles.

These action-adventure novels feature Nathaniel (Nate) Starbuck, son of a Boston abolitionist preacher who becomes an unlikely hero in the Confederate Army during the Civil War. Though never as popular as Cornwell's <u>Richard Sharpe</u> series, perhaps because it's no longer politically acceptable to glorify the Old South, they provide great excitement and overall entertainment.

Rebel. HarperCollins, 1993. 338pp.

Copperhead. HarperCollins, 1994. 375pp.

Battle Flag. HarperCollins, 1995. 356pp.

The Bloody Ground. HarperCollins, 1996. 343pp.

Mallinson, Allan.

Matthew Hervey Series.

Mallinson's novels feature the adventures of Matthew Hervey, a young cavalry officer in the 6th Light Dragoons. In Napoleonic Europe, Matthew Hervey returns from service in Ireland and becomes embroiled in the Battle of Waterloo with the rest of the Duke of Wellington's army. He later makes the sea voyage to India, with the covert mission of forging an alliance with the Raja of Chintalpore. There, he finds that war is a way of life, that battles are fought with money and espionage as often as they are on the field. Fighting the enemy isn't his only problem, though, as he must also navigate his way through the political favoritism, infighting, and petty accusations that characterize his own regiment. Forthcoming volumes, in print in Britain, include *A Call to Arms* and *Rumours of War.*

A Close Run Thing. Bantam, 1999. 306pp.

Honorable Company. Bantam, 2000. 299pp. (Original title: *The Nizam's Daughters.*)

A Regimental Affair. Bantam, 2002. 309pp.

The Sabre's Edge. Overlook, 2004. 319pp.

Rambaud, Patrick.

Napoleonic Trilogy. ✍

In this trilogy, the first two installments of which have been completed, Rambaud recounts the difficulties encountered by Napoleon's army as the French emperor makes a brave but futile attempt to conquer all of Europe in the early nineteenth century. Readers see the action through the eyes of common soldiers as well as those higher in rank. Brilliant characterization combines with ferocious battle scenes that fully convey the carnage and destruction wrought by war.

The Battle. Grove, 2000. 313pp.

Napoleon's first major defeat came at the Battle of Essling, in May 1809, when the French army confronted the armies of the Austro-Hungarian Empire on a wide-open plain outside Vienna. Techniques that had served them well in previous encounters failed here. In a forty-eight hour period, over 40,000 men were killed. Rambaud follows the story from multiple points of view, including that of Henri Beyle, better known as the French novelist Stendhal. Rambaud based this work on research notes left by Honoré de Balzac, who never followed through on his intent to write a novel about the Battle of Essling. Prix Goncourt.

The Retreat. Atlantic Monthly, 2004. 320pp.

The scene turns to Moscow in September 1812. Napoleon, obsessed with power, fully intends to invade Russia with his soldiers—what's left of them, given that three-quarters have already been lost on the long march from Paris. Meanwhile, the cruel Russian winter is approaching, something that the original French title to the novel (*Il Neigeait* = "It snowed") reflects. Napoleon expects the Russian emperor to surrender immediately, but instead his troops discover a hollowed-out shell of a city, for Moscow has already been evacuated. Demoralized and starving in the bitter cold, they quickly realize that defeat is inevitable.

Stuart, V. A.

Alexander Sheridan Adventures.

From the Crimean War in 1854 to India's Sepoy Mutiny of 1857, Colonel Alex Sheridan and his soldiers defend British interests abroad on behalf of the East India Company. Vivian Stuart also wrote the *Phillip Hazard* novels, below.

Victors and Lords. McBooks, 2001. 272pp.

The Sepoy Mutiny. McBooks, 2001. 240pp.

Massacre at Cawnpore. McBooks, 2002. 238pp.

The Cannons of Lucknow. McBooks, 2003. 272pp.

The Heroic Garrison. McBooks, 2003. 256pp.

World Wars I and II

These novels feature fast-paced military maneuvers made by Allied forces against Germany during the two world wars. Classic World War II adventure novels that readers might also enjoy, though not historical fiction by definition, include Nicholas Montsarrat's *The Cruel Sea* (1951) and Alistair MacLean's *The Guns of Navarone* (1957). Readers who enjoy these novels may want to consider reading war thrillers (Chapter 9) set during the same period.

Fullerton, Alexander.

Nicholas Everard Naval Series.

Fullerton, a former submarine officer in the British Navy, brings his background to his series of novels set around naval action during the First and Second World Wars. Nick Everard begins his career as a lowly midshipman on a battleship, but his transfer to the destroyer H.M.S. *Lanyard* means that he'll have a chance to use his abilities first-hand. The action, brutal at times, follows Britain's engagement with the German Navy through the eyes of not only Nick but also his brother and uncle. Soho Press and McBooks Press are in the process of reissuing this lengthy series, of which nine volumes have been published in Britain so far.

The Blooding of the Guns. Soho, 2002. 286pp.

Sixty Minutes for St. George. Soho, 2002. 308pp.

Patrol to the Golden Horn. Soho, 2002. 229pp.

Storm Force to Narvik. McBooks, 2004. 256pp.

Hickam, Homer.

The Keeper's Son. **St. Martin's Press, 2003. 352pp.**

Coast Guard Lt. Josh Thurlow patrols the waters around Killakeet Island, home to a lighthouse off the Outer Banks of North Carolina during

1941–1942. For seventeen years, he and his father, the lighthouse keeper, have been haunted by the disappearance of Josh's baby brother at sea. When German U-boats arrive, the Thurlows find the German commanders to be basically fair men—most of them, anyway—and one of them may even be able to assuage the guilt that torments Josh. First of a planned series; next will be *The Ambassador's Son*.

Reeman, Douglas.

Reeman, who served on destroyers with the British Navy during World War II, is a prolific author of twentieth-century naval adventure fiction. Below is a selection of his World War I and World War II novels. The author also writes as Alexander Kent.

Battlecruiser. **McBooks, 2003. 320pp.**

The captain of the battlecruiser *Reliant*, preparing to invade occupied Europe, knows that a single enemy shell can destroy his vessel, but he heads forth with his mission nonetheless.

H.M.S. Saracen. **Putnam, 1966. 320pp.**

In both World War I and World War II, Royal Navy sailor Richard Chesney and his ship see action in the Mediterranean.

His Majesty's U-Boat. **Putnam, 1973. 320pp.**

Submarine warfare: A British navy commander captures a German U-boat and tries to use it to his advantage before the Germans find out he's taken one of their vessels.

Rendezvous—South Atlantic. **Putnam, 1972. 320pp.**

With the aging battlecruiser the S. S. *Benbencula*, Commander Lindsay fights German U-boats in the North and South Atlantic during World War II.

A Ship Must Die. **Morrow, 1979. 284pp.**

World War II adventure: British ships take on German raiders in the Indian Ocean.

Twelve Seconds to Live. **McBooks, 2003. 368pp.**

During World War II, three men in the Royal Navy press ahead, knowing that any sudden whirr will mean they have hit a mine—and have just twelve seconds left to live.

A Miscellany

A mixture of additional novels featuring military battles in the nineteenth and twentieth centuries.

McCutchan, Philip.

Tom Chatto Series.

These coming-of-age novels star young Irishman Tom Chatto, an apprentice seaman in Britain's late Victorian era. His escapades take him from the southern tip of South America in the 1890s to Patagonia during the early days of World War I. McCutchan is an extremely prolific British author of adventure fiction.

Apprentice to the Sea. St. Martin's Press, 1995. 183pp.

The Second Mate. St. Martin's Press, 1996. 186pp.

The New Lieutenant. St. Martin's Press, 1997. 181pp.

Needle, Jan.

Sea Officer William Bentley Novels.

Aboard the *Welfare* in the early eighteenth century, 14-year-old midshipman William Bentley learns how not to captain a ship by watching the actions of his uncle, Captain Daniel Swift. His decision on whether or not to join a mutiny gives him strength enough to propel him toward his next adventure—catching smugglers on the London River.

A Fine Boy for Killing. McBooks, 2000. 320pp.

The Wicked Trade. McBooks, 2001. 384pp.

The Spithead Nymph. McBooks, 2004. 288pp.

Reeman, Douglas.

Royal Marines Series.

While most works of naval fiction feature officers of the British Royal Navy, Reeman's series have members of the Royal Marines as protagonists. Over ninety years of British history, from the Crimean War in the 1850s through World War II in 1944, four generations of the Blackwood family serve their country with distinction. Their service takes them to the far-flung reaches of the Empire: Africa, China, Gallipoli, and Southeast Asia. All reissued by McBooks. Reeman also writes as Alexander Kent.

Badge of Glory. Morrow, 1984. 357pp.

First to Land. Morrow, 1984. 294pp.

The Horizon. McBooks, 2002. 367pp.

Dust on the Sea. McBooks, 2002. 368pp.

Knife Edge. McBooks, 2005. 304pp.

Stuart, V. A.

The Phillip Hazard Novels.

In 1853, Royal Navy lieutenant Phillip Horatio Hazard heads to Sevastopol aboard ship to support Britain's land forces fighting Russia in the Crimean War. There, he and his men of the steam frigate *Trojan* battle the Russian forces in the Black Sea. The lone woman in an overwhelmingly male subgenre, Stuart had a distinguished military career herself, serving with the British Army in Burma in the mid-twentieth century. McBooks Press is reissuing the Hazard series in trade paperback.

The Valiant Sailors. Pinnacle, 1966. 252pp.

Brave Captains. Pinnacle, 1979. 215pp.

Hazard's Command. Pinnacle, 1972. 251pp.

Hazard of Huntress. Pinnacle, 1972. 217pp.

Hazard in Circassia. London: Hale, 1973. 208pp.

Hazard to the Rescue. Pinnacle, 1974. 206pp.

Guns to the Far East. Pinnacle, 1975. 213pp.

Escape from Hell. McBooks, 2005. 256pp. (Original title: *Sailors on Horseback*; first published in Britain in 1976.)

Suthren, Victor.

Edward Mainwaring Novels.

In the 1740s, Edward Mainwaring, native of the American colonies, serves with distinction in Britain's Royal Navy (hence the title of the first novel), fighting Spanish privateers and the French navy in the Caribbean, Europe, and around Cape Horn.

Royal Yankee. St. Martin's Press, 1987. 189pp.

The Golden Galleon. St. Martin's Press, 1989. 192pp.

Admiral of Fear. St. Martin's Press, 1991. 239pp.

Captain Monsoon. St. Martin's Press, 1992. 220pp.

Voyages of Exploration and Trade

When men (and occasionally women) set out aboard ship to discover new lands or trade in merchandise, they frequently find the journey to be a struggle for survival. In keeping with historical accuracy, the stories don't always end happily. Here the sea, ferocious and all-powerful, becomes almost a character in itself.

Barrett, Andrea.

The Voyage of the Narwhal. W. W. Norton, 1998. 397pp.

Annotated in Chapter 10.

Edge, Arabella.

🎗 *The Company.* Simon & Schuster, 2001. 369pp.

Jeronimus Cornelisz, an apothecary, flees from Amsterdam aboard the *Batavia* in 1629 after discovery of his evil obsession with poisons becomes known. While en route to the Dutch colonies in Asia with members of the Dutch East India Company, Cornelisz incites a mutiny and forces the ship aground off the western coast of Australia. While the ship's leaders head off to seek help, he takes command of the terrified passengers, instigating a reign of murderous terror that lasts for forty days. A combination sea adventure and psychological suspense novel. Herodotus Award.

Edric, Robert.

The Broken Lands. **St. Martin's Press, 2002. 369pp. (Originally published in Britain in 1992.)** ✍

Sir John Franklin's doomed expedition in search of the Northwest Passage across the Arctic is legendary. Setting out from Greenland in 1845 with two ships, the *Erebus* and the *Terror*, all 135 men were never heard from again after August of that year. Edric re-creates what must have been a terrifying journey into the harsh Arctic ice, and the characters' desperation is heightened by readers' foreknowledge that there will be no escape.

Galbraith, Douglas.

The Rising Sun. **Atlantic Monthly, 2001. 520pp.**

At the end of the seventeenth century, a time when European nations were building colonial empires around the globe, Scotland aimed to compete with the English and Dutch by founding its own colony in the New World. To this end, in 1698 five ships left Scotland for Darien (later known as Panama), led by the flagship *Rising Sun.* Roderick Mackenzie, its Superintendent of Cargoes, records the details of this failed attempt in his journal. His detailed account leaves nothing out, from the difficult shipboard voyage to the unpleasant realities of jungle life.

Kneale, Matthew.

English Passengers. **Nan A. Talese/Doubleday, 2000. 446pp.**

Annotated in Chapter 10.

Turteltaub, H. N.

H. N. Turteltaub, the author of *Justinian* (Chapter 2), is the pseudonym for science fiction/alternate history novelist Harry Turtledove. Next will be *Owls to Athens.*

Over the Wine-Dark Sea. Forge, 2001. 381pp.

In the third century BC, two merchants, the scholarly Menedemos and his wilder cousin Sostratos, head out on a trading journey across the Aegean Sea from Rhodes to Pompeii, where they are supposed to be delivering a shipload of exotic cargo. Their escapades are told mostly through dialogue, and they manage to extricate themselves from every scrape, making this an instructive but basically lighthearted adventure.

The Gryphon's Skull. Forge, 2002. 384pp.

Merchants Menedemos and Sostratos, fresh from their adventures in *Over the Wine-Dark Sea*, head across the Aegean to Athens. Along the way they find a mysterious skull in the market of Kaunos, and the intellectual Sostratos believes it may have belonged to a gryphon, a mythological beast. In bringing it to Athens for study, the bickering pair encounter pirates and other warring factions that threaten to bring an end to free trade in the eastern Mediterranean.

The Sacred Land. Forge, 2003. 384pp.

The Rhodian cousins board their trusty vessel *Aphrodite* for Phoenicia, where Sostratos hopes to do some trading with the people of the country of Ioudaia. Little do they know that the Ioudaians have no need for the goods the merchants have brought, and Sostratos also underestimates raiders' uncanny ability to get between him and his destination.

Woodman, Richard.

William Kite Trilogy.

Kite, an apothecary's son in mid-eighteenth-century Cumbria, never intended to make a career at sea, but it proves to be an easy escape route after his affair with a local farmer's daughter is discovered. The *Enterprize* is a slave ship, or Guineaman, en route to Africa, and Kite's sympathies for the slaves' plight leads him into danger. In the second and third volumes, Kite is a successful merchant mariner, and though he doesn't have a military command, he finds himself forced to defend Britain's commercial interests in America during its Revolution as well as in India. For this reason, Woodman's series will also appeal to readers of military fiction.

The Guineaman. Severn House, 2000. 224pp.

The Privateersman. Severn House, 2000. 250pp.

The East Indiaman. Severn House, 2000. 295pp.

Pirate Novels

General

A number of naval adventure novels feature battles against pirates, but novels in this section are told from the pirate's point of view. While older novels, such as those written by Rafael Sabatini, romanticized the pirate's life, those published within the last few years present more realistic scenarios.

Griffin, Nicholas.

🎗 ***The Requiem Shark.*** **Villard, 1999. 319pp.** ✍

William Williams, a fiddler in early eighteenth-century Wales, tells of his unlikely transformation from scholar to pirate after being pressed aboard a slave ship. When it's taken over by a raiding vessel captained by the notorious Bartholomew "Black Bart" Roberts, William finds himself the reluctant scribe for the illiterate pirate king. Soon he awakens to the passion of his captain's bloodthirsty trade, capturing and pillaging ships from Brazil to western Africa, all the while in pursuit of the fabled treasure ship called the *Juliette*. Betty Trask Prize.

Hackman, Gene, and Daniel Lenihan.

Wake of the Perdido Star. Newmarket, 1999. 384pp. **YA**

Actor Hackman and underwater archaeologist Lenihan team up in this rousing adventure of a young man who avenges his parents' deaths by becoming a terror on the high seas. At the turn of the nineteenth century, seventeen-year-old Jack O'Reilly and his parents leave New England aboard the *Perdido Star* for Cuba, his mother's homeland. When his parents are murdered by a wealthy Cuban landowner, he cheats death by escaping aboard the *Perdido Star*, fighting savages and enduring underwater escapades in the South Pacific.

Newcomb, Kerry.

Mad Morgan. St. Martin's Press, 2000. 288pp. ✍

This biographical novel of the real-life pirate Henry Morgan begins with his childhood in the countryside of seventeenth-century Wales, where he was snatched by Spanish raiders and made a slave on their voyage to the Caribbean. He lives to escape captivity, stealing away with a prison ship from Santiago de Cuba. With a fierce company of ex-convicts as his crew, Morgan becomes "El Tigre de Caribe," the most fearsome pirate ever to terrorize the Spanish navy.

Sabatini, Rafael.

Captain Blood Series. ★

In 1680s England, Irish physician Peter Blood does well by saving the life of a man involved in Monmouth's Rebellion, but this noble act is his downfall. Mistakenly declared a traitor by the English government, he is sentenced to ten years of indentured servitude on a Barbados plantation, where he falls in love with the daughter of the man who owns him. He manages to escape on board a stolen Spanish ship and begins a new life as a ruthless pirate on the high seas.

Captain Blood, His Odyssey. Houghton Mifflin, 1922. 356pp. (Alternate title: *Captain Blood.*)

Captain Blood Returns. Houghton Mifflin, 1931. 296pp.

The Fortunes of Captain Blood. Houghton Mifflin, 1936. 240pp.

The Sea-Hawk. Houghton Mifflin, 1923. 366pp. ★

In Elizabethan times, Cornish gentleman Oliver Tressilian is sold into slavery in Arabia by his half-brother, who covets his wealth for himself. Oliver turns the tables by becoming a Barbary pirate and espousing Islam. Though successful in his new life, Oliver—a classic anti-hero—is prepared to give up all he has gained to wreak vengeance on those who have wronged him.

Female Pirates

The historical prototypes for female pirate novels are Anne Bonny and Mary Read, two eighteenth-century women who feature in a number of works themselves.

Garrett, Elizabeth.

The Sweet Trade. **Forge, 2001. 399pp.** ✍

With historical accuracy in mind, Garrett returns to the origins of the Anne Bonny–Mary Read legend. Anne, the spoiled daughter of a rich Irish business-man in the colony of South Carolina in the early eighteenth century, impulsively marries a young sailor named James Bonny and heads away with him to Nassau. There she meets Calico Jack Rackham, a randy pirate who's ready to give it all up until he meets Anne, and they begin a life of piracy on the high seas. Mary Read, an Englishwoman and merchant sailor, has lived most of her life disguised as a boy. When her ship encounters Calico Jack's, Mary befriends the thieving pair and discovers the advantages of the "sweet trade." (Pseudonym of James L. Nelson, who wrote many naval adventure novels under his own name. McBooks Press published Nelson's revised version, with greater emphasis on the naval action, as *The Only Life That Mattered,* in 2004.)

Jensen, Lisa.

The Witch from the Sea. **Beagle Bay, 2001. 321pp.**

In 1823 Boston, sixteen-year-old Tory MacKenzie yearns for the freedom she can't find at the Worthen Academy for Women. Disguising herself as a boy, she stows away aboard a merchant ship, but plans change when pirates board and take over the vessel. Heeding the cliché "if you can't beat them, join them," Tory does just that, learning that pirates, despite being outlaws, have reasons and morals just like everyone else.

Llywelyn, Morgan.

Grania: She-King of the Irish Seas. **Crown, 1986. 437pp.** ✍

Annotated in Chapter 2.

MacLeod, Alison.

The Changeling. **St. Martin's Press, 1996. 324pp.** ✍

This novel of piracy and changing sexual identities begins in eighteenth-century Ireland. Anne Bonny is raised as a boy in Ireland and the Carolinas so that her father can treat her as his heir. Growing up believing that an exciting life awaits her, she leaves her lazy husband for a pirate, Captain Jack Rackham, and begins disguising herself as a man once more. What she doesn't expect is to find another like herself, a cross-dressing woman roaming the high seas.

Simonds, Jacqueline Church.

Captain Mary, Buccaneer. **Beagle Bay, 2000. 301pp.**

Realistic when it comes to describing the brutal life of pirates, Simonds's novel also explores the reasons why women such as Captain Mary may have chosen this unusual way of life. Loyal to her crewmates, beloved by the men and women she takes as lovers, Mary and her brigantine ship *Fury* terrorize the Caribbean during the eighteenth century. She rarely backs down from violent encounters, not hesitating to kill when necessary, yet strives to follow the pirate's unwritten code of honor.

Parody

These humorous novels poke fun at the genre through the picaresque adventures of an incorrigible anti-hero.

Fraser, George MacDonald.

Flashman Papers.

Scotsman George MacDonald Fraser is the so-called editor of the Flashman Papers, a series of bawdy adventure novels that at once belong to and spoof the historical adventure genre. Their hero, British army colonel Sir Harry Flashman, is a completely disreputable and endearing Victorian rogue who somehow manages to turn up at, and participate in, nearly every major event in Victorian-era history. Nothing whatsoever is held sacred. From John Brown's messy raid on Harper's Ferry in 1859, through bumbling Englishmen's squabbles over India, you can be sure that Flashman was there to smooth-talk his way through it all.

Flashman. Knopf, 1969. 256pp.

Royal Flash. Knopf, 1970. 257pp.

Flash for Freedom! Knopf, 1971. 287p.

Flashman at the Charge. Knopf, 1973. 288pp.

Flashman in the Great Game. Knopf, 1975. 340pp.

Flashman's Lady. Knopf, 1978. 330pp.

Flashman and the Redskins. Knopf, 1982. 479pp.

Flashman and the Dragon. Knopf, 1986. 320pp.

Flashman and the Mountain of Light. Knopf, 1990. 365pp.

Flashman and the Angel of the Lord. Knopf, 1994. 394pp.

Flashman and the Tiger. Knopf, 1999. 336pp.

Exotic Adventure

These novels place the protagonist, nearly always male, against the unknown dangers found in exotic lands, such as ancient Egypt, the wilds of Africa, Mexico, and Asia. Because these novels' excitement appeals to men just as romances do to women, they are also called "male romances." Classic novels of exotic adventure, though not historical fiction in the usual definition, include Rudyard Kipling's *Lord Jim*, Joseph Conrad's *Heart of Darkness*, and H. Rider Haggard's *King Solomon's Mines* and *She*. Literary novels of exotic adventure, such as Daniel Mason's *The Piano Tuner* (set in nineteenth-century Burma), are listed in Chapter 10.

Ball, David.

Empires of Sand. **Bantam. 1999. 561pp.**

In the 1870s, at the height of the Franco–Prussian war, two French boys, cousins and best friends, grow up together in a noble household in Paris. But circumstances separate them for a decade. While Paul DeVries trains to be a soldier like his father, his cousin Moussa—the son of a Frenchman and a noblewoman of the nomadic Tuareg tribe—returns to his mother's people. As France proceeds in its foolish attempt to drive a railroad through the heart of the Sahara, a plan bitterly opposed by the Tuareg, the two meet again on opposite sides of the conflict.

Ironfire. **Delacorte, 2004. 667pp.**

Ottoman forces besiege the fortresses on the island of Malta in 1565. Nico Borg, a young Maltese captured by Algerian pirates as a child, hopes the Knights of St. John will eventually rescue him. For now, he adapts to Muslim culture, takes the name Asha, and captains one of the Sultan's warships. His sister Maria, still on Malta, witnessed Nico's abduction. While she plots revenge, she also yearns to escape her surroundings.

Bryan, Francis.

The Curse of Treasure Island. **Viking, 2002. 291pp.** `YA`

Ten years after the events of Robert Louis Stevenson's classic nineteenth-century adventure novel *Treasure Island*, former cabin boy Jim Hawkins and his mother are back home outside Bristol, England, running the Admiral Benbow Inn. He is persuaded by one of the lodgers, the beautiful Grace Richardson, to help her locate Joseph Tate, a pirate last seen on Treasure Island in the South Seas. Thus begins another hair-raising adventure of peril on the high seas, with sufficient continuity for it to appeal to fans of the original.

Bull, Bartle.

Bull's old-fashioned novels of early twentieth-century North Africa combine the exotic noir of the movie *Casablanca* with the evocative African atmosphere of Ernest Hemingway. His latest, *Shanghai Station*, is an unrelated novel.

The White Rhino Hotel. **Viking, 1992. 404pp.**

After the First World War, Europeans flocked to Africa in search of rich new lands to settle and conquer. The chosen outpost of many British adventurers is Lord Penfold's White Rhino Hotel, a lodge in colonial Kenya that is presided over by a British expatriate, his horse-loving wife, and the randy dwarf, Olivio, who serves as its majordomo. Here, would-be pioneers meet, scheme, and fall in love, not realizing that doing business in Kenya is just as complicated and risky as it was back home.

A Café on the Nile. **Carroll & Graf, 1998. 466pp.**

In 1935, Egypt is on the brink of World War II. The capital city of Cairo is the scene for another set of colorful encounters among the *White Rhino Hotel* crowd. Olivio Alavedo, the Goan dwarf from Bull's previous novel, now runs the Cataract Café aboard a barge in the river Nile, a place where many colorful characters gather and engage in intrigue.

The Devil's Oasis. Carroll & Graf, 2001. 336pp.

Back at the Cataract Café in Cairo, it's now 1942, and Rommel and the Afrika Corps are heading in to capture the Suez Canal. The drifters who make up the café's usual entourage find themselves on opposite sides—some with their native Germany, some with the Allies—as friendships and romances are tested.

Shanghai Station. **Carroll & Graf, 2004. 320pp.**

The exotic port city of Shanghai is on the brink of revolution in 1918. Mao Tse-tung incites the peasants to embrace Communism and revolt against their leaders. Alexander Karlov, in Shanghai with his father, plots revenge against the Bolsheviks who killed his mother and kidnapped his sister when they were escaping from Russia.

Clavell, James.

Asian Saga. ★

Epic in scope, the novels in Clavell's Asian Saga, lengthy tales of English adventurers who dare to penetrate exotic foreign markets, are classics of the genre. These sprawling novels incorporate dozens of characters and just as many subplots. In scenes of bloody violence and intense beauty, they portray the experiences of Westerners as strangers in a strange land. The novels are listed in historical order. The saga continues with *King Rat* (c1962, set in World War II Singapore); *Noble House* (c1981, set in 1963 Hong Kong), and *Whirlwind* (c1986, set in 1979 Iran).

Shōgun. Atheneum, 1975. 802pp.

In 1600, Elizabethan adventurer John Blackthorne arrives in Japan after a shipwreck. He seeks to turn this misadventure into an advantage for himself and England, as he envisions a way to wrest control of the Japanese trade from the Portuguese. In Japan he encounters a completely alien culture, one torn by political strife. His captor and mentor is Lord Toranaga, a powerful feudal lord who seeks to use Blackthorne to consolidate power under himself as Shōgun. As Blackthorne learns samurai ways under Toranada's guidance, Lady Mariko, a Catholic woman who dares to fall in love with the barbarian Englishman, is torn between the different ways of life both men represent.

Tai-Pan. Atheneum, 1966. 590pp.

This novel does for China and Hong Kong what *Shōgun* did for Japan. In 1840s Hong Kong, the land has just come under British rule, but its customs and people are still a mystery to most Westerners. Englishman Dirk Struan is Tai-Pan (supreme ruler) of the Noble House Trading Company, whose mission is to supply the hot commodity of tea to hungry English markets. Despite the length and incredible number of characters, it is a fast-moving novel that combines politics, treachery, romance, and adventure to portray the attitudes of the Chinese and English toward each other.

Gai-Jin. Delacorte, 1993. 1038pp.

Clavell returns to Japan with this novel, set in 1862. Noble House, the giant British shipping empire from *Tai-Pan*, has established a base at Yokohama, and Malcolm Struan is its up-and-coming leader. However, the Japanese are less than thrilled at the incursion of yet more greedy foreigners ("gai-jin") into their country, and those who adhere to the old samurai traditions will do anything to see them gone.

Daniel, A. B.

Incas Series.

Bestsellers in France, the novels in this series are meant to do for the Inca Empire of sixteenth-century Peru what Gary Jennings did for the Aztecs. The pace is slower than that of Jennings's novels, but there's still plenty of action, blood, and gore. When Francisco Pizarro arrives in Peru in 1532 with other Spanish explorers, he encounters a culture that reveres their gods through sacrifice. Daniel (a pseudonym for several French authors writing under one name) also includes a romance subplot with the love story of Anamaya, an Incan princess, and Gabriel Montelucar de Flores, a Spanish nobleman.

The Puma's Shadow. Scribner, 2002. 384pp.

The Gold of Cuzco. Scribner, 2002. 384pp.

The Light of Machu Picchu. Scribner, 2003. 335pp.

Highland, Frederick.

Ghost Eater. **Thomas Dunne, 2003. 320pp.**

In 1875, American steamboat captain Ulysses Drake Vanders agrees to navigate through a remote Sumatran jungle to rescue Christian missionaries. In this land of ghosts and exotic superstitions, the members of the Light of the World mission are supposedly being terrorized by bloodthirsty spirits. As the ship maneuvers through these uncharted waters to reach them, a bunch of unlikely stowaways make themselves known to Vanders and then proceed to become part of the crew. When Vanders' group reaches their destination, they come upon a scene more shocking than anything they could have imagined.

Jennings, Gary.

The late Gary Jennings wrote colorful, blood-soaked adventures that emphasize the strange, barbarous customs of cultures largely unknown to Western readers.

Aztec Series.

Mixtli, an Aztec scribe and warrior during the magnificent prime of the Aztec Empire in the sixteenth century, narrates the tale of his rise from commoner to noble. At the same time, he witnesses the arrival of the Spaniards, whose greed for gold and empire-building causes the downfall of Montezuma's people. The shocking descriptions of the Aztecs' religion, sexual habits, and other customs are not for the squeamish, but Jennings also uses them as social commentary. For example, the Spaniards' practice of burning heretics ironically contrasts with the supposed barbarity of the Aztecs' human sacrifices. *Aztec Autumn* and *Aztec*

Blood continue the story with later generations of Aztecs, slaves in the land now called New Spain. The last volume was completed based on detailed notes left by Jennings after his death.

Aztec. Atheneum, 1980. 754pp. ★

Aztec Autumn. Forge, 1997. 380pp.

Aztec Blood. Forge, 2001. 525pp.

The Journeyer. Atheneum, 1984. 782pp. ★ ✍

In the thirteenth century, legendary Venetian explorer Marco Polo made his famous journey across Asia, where he spent many years at the court of Mongol emperor Kublai Khan. Though he kept formal accounts of his journey, few people believed them, yet Marco himself confessed on his deathbed that they didn't reveal the half of his adventures. Jennings fills in the gaps, recounting Marco's travels in his own words. A lover of women, languages, and the thrill of exploration, Marco travels along the Silk Road, encountering all manner of people and exotic customs.

Raptor. Doubleday, 1992. 980pp.

In fifth- and sixth-century Europe, the Roman Empire was in its decline. Thorn, an unconventional Gothic hermaphrodite with strong sexual appetites for both men and women, sojourns across Europe with Wyrd, a former Roman centurion who teaches him the ways of survival in the untamed woodland of the continent. He later becomes a field marshal and spy for Theodoric, King of the Ostrogoths, who manages to take over the remnants of the Roman Empire at a time when paganism clashed with Christianity.

Spangle. Atheneum, 1987. 869pp.

Over a six-year period, from the end of the American Civil War through the Franco–Prussian War, two former Confederate soldiers join the traveling Florilegium Circus in its pageant across Reconstruction Virginia and Europe. Though nineteenth-century Germany, France, and Russia isn't a traditional exotic setting, Jennings treats it as though it were, with plenty of descriptions of circus lore and wild acrobatics, both under the big top and in the bedroom.

Matsuoka, Takashi.
Cloud of Sparrows. Delacorte, 2002. 405pp.

In 1861, Japan has reluctantly reopened its borders to Westerners after two centuries of isolation. In the city of Edo, Lord Genji of the Okamichi clan, the last of his line, has the gift of prophecy, though few believe his gift is real. He foresees the end of the traditional samurai way of life, so he welcomes the presence of several American missionaries who have come to preach the word of God to the Japanese. When henchmen of the Shogunate seek to overthrow Lord Genji and erase his message, he, his missionary guests, and his geisha lover flee over dangerous terrain to

Cloud of Sparrows castle. Here, the hidden motives of everyone in the group are revealed.

Rufin, Jean-Christophe.

Abyssinian Series.

The seventeenth-century adventures of Jean-Baptiste Foncet. Like his hero, French novelist Rufin is a physician and world traveler.

The Abyssinian. W. W. Norton, 1999. 422pp.

In 1699, to establish contact with distant Abyssinia (modern Ethiopia), the French king Louis XIV sought to find an emissary to send to that country's ruler. Rufin takes this historical event and expands upon it. The French consul in Cairo finds the perfect ambassador in Jean-Baptiste Foncet, a man of dubious birth who is secretly practicing medicine without a license. Foncet seizes the opportunity to ingratiate himself with Louis XIV in the hope of winning the hand of the consul's beautiful daughter. As he journeys from Cairo to Abyssinia to Versailles and back, marveling at the exotic countryside, he confronts intrigues at every turn. Prix Goncourt (France).

The Siege of Isfahan. W. W. Norton, 2001. 373pp.

Twenty years after his adventures in *The Abyssinian*, Jean-Baptiste Foncet is an established physician living in Isfahan, Persia's capital. When he receives word that his best friend Juremi is imprisoned in Russia, he heads there to save him but ends up getting captured himself. Their wives fend for themselves in Isfahan during the Afghan siege of the city, just at the same time that Foncet and Juremi end up back there—as Afghan slaves.

Brazil Red. **W. W. Norton, 2004. 448pp.**

During the Renaissance, the French tried to establish a South American empire in Brazil. Two French orphans, Just and Colombe, are sent to the Brazilian jungle as interpreters and begin the colonization process. There they encounter cannibals, a dissolute jungle environment, and an unpleasant expedition leader who may be the devil in disguise.

Smith, Wilbur.

Most exotic adventure novels take a Western man and place him in an alien locale, but the protagonists of Wilbur Smith's fast-paced African and Egyptian novels belong to the unusual culture the author depicts—and are themselves part of the attraction.

Ballantyne Novels.

Smith's Ballantyne family saga follows members of the Ballantyne family of southern Africa from the 1860s until the present day. Their progenitors are a sister and brother, Robyn and Zouga Ballantyne, whose lives are intertwined with the violent history of Rhodesia (now Zimbabwe). The action revolves around the slave trade, piracy, exploration of the African interior, ivory hunts, diamond mining, and clashes with the native tribes.

Flight of the Falcon. Doubleday, 1982 . 545pp. (Original title: *A Falcon Flies.*)

Men of Men. Doubleday, 1983. 518pp.

The Angels Weep. Doubleday, 1983. 468pp.

The Leopard Hunts in Darkness. Doubleday, 1984. 423pp.

The Courtneys.

The extended Courtney series comprises twelve novels, organized into three self-contained series. Like Smith's other African novels, including the Ballantyne saga, they are full of rollicking romance, dangerous elephant hunts, and breathtaking descriptions of the African wilderness.

The first three volumes, beginning with *Birds of Prey*, were written last and continue the saga with earlier generations of Courtneys. Set between the late seventeenth and early eighteenth centuries, at the beginning of South Africa's development as a Dutch colony, they are exotic, swashbuckling adventures complete with piracy and privateering on the high seas.

When the Lion Feeds, *The Sound of Thunder*, and *A Sparrow Falls* form the second Courtney sequence. Between the 1870s and the beginning of World War I, South Africa saw a number of tumultuous events, such as the Zulu Wars, the gold rush, and the Boer War, fought between the British and Dutch over the colony. Two brothers living in the Natal region of South Africa, Sean and Garrick Courtney, become estranged after both a tragic accident and a woman come between them.

The Burning Shore begins the next Courtney sequence with the story of Michael Courtney, Sean's son, and his adventures in World War I. After Michael is killed, his French wife Centaine returns to her late husband's South African homeland. Her two children—one by Michael, one by an Afrikaner—grow up separately, unaware of their blood relationship. Their personal and political rivalry, and that of their descendants, provides considerable action and suspense throughout the series.

Birds of Prey. St. Martin's Press, 1997. 554pp.

Monsoon. St. Martin's Press, 1999. 613pp.

Blue Horizon. St. Martin's Press, 2003. 624pp.

When the Lion Feeds. Viking, 1964. 403pp.

The Sound of Thunder. London: Heinemann, 1966. 437pp.

A Sparrow Falls. Doubleday, 1978. 587pp.

The Burning Shore. Doubleday, 1985. 420pp.

Power of the Sword. Little, Brown, 1986. 618pp.

8

Rage. Little, Brown, 1987. 627pp.

A Time to Die. Random House, 1990. 448pp.

Golden Fox. Random House, 1990. 433pp.

Egyptian Novels.

In his Egyptian adventures, Smith doesn't stint on unpleasantries, such as castrations, bloody murders, and gruesome descriptions of ancient Egyptian surgeries. While there is plenty of local color and action, they require strong stomachs.

River God. St. Martin's Press, 1993. 530pp.

Circa 1780 BC, when the Hyksos tribes were beginning to overrun Egypt, Taita, the eunuch slave of the evil Lord Intef, helps his protégée Lady Lostris—Lord Intef's daughter—carry on a love affair with General Tanus, an army officer. Though Lostris goes ahead with an unwanted marriage to the weak pharaoh, she manages to pass off Tanus's children as the royal heirs. The entire royal court is forced to move to Ethiopia to save themselves from the barbarian invaders. Taita more than makes up for his physical deficiency with extraordinary abilities in art, medicine, and politics, so much so that he seems almost superhuman.

Warlock. Thomas Dunne/St. Martin's Press, 2001. 549pp.

Long after the death of Queen Lostris, the Hyksos still rule in Lower Egypt. Taita, an ancient warlock living in the Egyptian desert, returns to help Lostris's grandson Prince Nefer, the true royal heir, regain his inheritance amid war, treachery, and deceit. With the aid of his undiminished mystical powers, Taita and Nefer take on Lord Naja, the false pharaoh, who will stop at nothing to see Nefer dead.

The Seventh Scroll. St. Martin's Press, 1995. 486pp.

Listed here for the sake of completion, this present-day novel was written as a sequel to *River God.* In ancient Ethiopia, the eunuch slave Taita had carefully hidden the pharaoh's wealth, setting traps so that it would never be found. When modern adventurers find an ancient papyrus written by Taita, it sets off a race against time to find the pharaoh's treasure.

Women Adventurers

While most historical adventure fiction is geared toward men, with limited female involvement, these novels feature strong women who make dangerous journeys through unknown lands. They also incorporate a strong romantic element, which increases their appeal to female readers. Novels of women on the American frontier are presented in Chapter 6; see also the section on female pirates in this chapter.

Bausch, Richard.

Hello to the Cannibals. **HarperCollins, 2002. 661pp.**

Annotated in Chapter 10.

Danze, Philip.

Conjuring Maud. **GreyCore, 2001. 192pp.** 📖

An aging circus magician, David Unger looks back on the African adventures of his youth, which led to a May–December romance with an elusive older woman. At the end of the nineteenth century, David arrives in colonial West Africa, his family torn apart by the lure of the continent's riches. Distraught at British greed, he finds a sympathetic ear in Maud King, a British explorer sixteen years his senior. In Africa, Maud enjoys the freedom she was never able to find in her homeland. As David's life unfolds, bringing him into the British Army during the Zulu Rebellion and into contact with a young Gandhi, his devotion to Maud remains constant. The character of Maud is loosely based on that of Mary Kingsley (a character in *Hello to the Cannibals*, above). **Literary.**

Keywords: West Africa—19th Century

Kaufman, Pamela.

Alix of Wanthwaite Series.

Kaufman also wrote *The Book of Eleanor* (Chapter 2), a novel of Eleanor of Aquitaine.

Shield of Three Lions. Crown, 1983. 474pp. ★

In this bawdy romantic adventure set in the late twelfth century, eleven-year-old Alix of Wanthwaite flees her home on the Scottish border after her family is killed. To regain her lands, she decides to plead her case to King Richard the Lion-Heart, who is in France preparing to go on Crusade. Journeying south disguised as a boy, Alix becomes King Richard's favorite page, and, along with a Scotsman named Enoch who serves as her protector, joins him on the road to Jerusalem. Over time, an unusual love triangle develops among Alix, Enoch, and the homosexual King Richard, who doesn't realize that Alix is really a woman.

Banners of Gold. Crown, 1986. 436pp.

In the sequel to *Shield of Three Lions*, Alix of Wanthwaite, now back in England and married to her friend Enoch, finds that adventure can't leave her behind. Enoch is off at war, and a Jew named Bonel convinces Alix to travel to Germany to help rescue King Richard, who is being held hostage. Richard has never lost his attraction to Alix, despite knowledge of her true identity, and convinces himself that she must have his child.

Keywords: Europe—Middle Ages

Kelley, Douglas.

The Captain's Wife. Dutton, 2001. 304pp. ✍ 📖 **YA**

Kelley re-creates the real-life exploits of Mary Patten, a nine-teen-year-old Bostonian woman who was forced to captain her husband's clipper ship when he became ill. Aboard the *Neptune's Car* as it voyaged around Cape Horn on the way to San Francisco in 1856, the pregnant Mary finds her natural ingenuity stretched to the limit as she nurses her husband day and night, contends with a treacherous first mate, and struggles to earn the respect of her crew.

Keywords: Shipboard Adventure—Early United States

Robson, Lucia St. Clair.
The Tokaido Road. **Ballantine, 1991. 513pp.**

In a fictional retelling of Japan's most well-known revenge story (the "47 Ronin") , Robson describes the journey of young Lady Asano to restore her father's name. After Lord Asano was forced to commit suicide at the hands of the cruel Lord Kira, his daughter, known as Cat, finds herself defenseless and at the mercy of Kira's minions. Trained as a samurai herself, Cat disguises herself as a wandering priest and follows the Tokaido Road to Kyoto, where her father's chief samurai lives. Danger awaits along the road, for a man has been hired to pursue her.

Keywords: Japan—17th Century

Chapter 9

Historical Thrillers

The diverse subgenre of historical thrillers includes novels set in a wide range of locales and eras. What they all share is a common plot pattern and type of protagonist. Historical thrillers are suspenseful stories set in the past that feature intelligent protagonists (typically male) who find themselves in perilous situations. Readers of this subgenre enjoy watching how the heroes manage to use all of their resources, intellectual and emotional as well as physical, to extricate themselves from danger. Because the exact form that the enemy will take is almost always unknown, the protagonists never know what or whom to guard against. This heightens tension considerably. The complex and multifaceted plots of historical thrillers keep readers alert and intent on the story.

When the protagonists are thrust into a dangerous situation, they do not always realize at first how to proceed. One wrong move could mean failure, betrayal, or even death. Throughout these novels, protagonists must make big decisions, often with little warning. As they become more familiar with the situation, they grow more confident. Because of the moral judgments that the heroes are compelled to make, historical thrillers tend to be serious books. Although they may be fast-paced, they are not light, easy reads.

In historical thrillers, the dilemmas in which protagonists find themselves often have political ramifications. On their shoulders may rest the fate of one or more nations. Many historical thrillers are set around pivotal times in political history, such as the French Revolution or the Gunpowder Plot of 1605, when King James I of England was nearly assassinated by an angry Catholic mob. The exception to this rule is psychological suspense novels. In these works, the motives of the protagonists and villains tend to be personal rather than political.

The pacing of historical thrillers depends on the category they fall into, though they all have an engrossing, page-turning quality. Literary thrillers combine an elegant writing style with an abundance of historical detail, and this slows down their pace somewhat. Although there is less physical action in these novels, the numerous plot twists force readers to pay close attention.

On the opposite side of the spectrum, war thrillers are considerably more action-oriented, and readers will cheer and fear for the protagonists as they struggle to stay out of the enemy's clutches. Some novels, like Caleb Carr's literary psychological suspense thrillers, may fall into more than one category.

Historical thrillers share some elements with the mystery and adventure genres. As in historical mysteries, there may be a crime committed and a detective determined to solve it, but this isn't a requirement. David Liss's Edgar Award–winning novel *A Conspiracy of Paper* is an example of this type, and novels of psychological suspense may also fit this description. Readers who enjoy the frenetic pace and twentieth-century settings of war thrillers may also enjoy adventure novels set during World Wars I and II (Chapter 8).

Literary Thrillers

Ever since publication of Umberto Eco's benchmark novel *The Name of the Rose* in 1983, this category has burgeoned. Historical literary thrillers don't necessarily deal with literature and books, although many do. These novels involve intellectual puzzles wrapped inside mysteries and topped off with investigative action, as the protagonists sift through multiple clues to uncover secrets or find a killer. They are set against a detailed, well-researched historical backdrop, one unfamiliar enough for readers to find fascinating. Exciting yet thoughtful books, they allow readers to follow protagonists' internal thought processes as they race to solve a mystery or expose a conspiracy. Most literary thrillers are quite lengthy, and though the pace may not be as fast as others in this subgenre, they are compelling reads nonetheless. The quality of the writing is important, and the language used by the authors is erudite, complex, and appropriate to the period. Literary thrillers have great appeal outside the thriller genre: the labyrinthine, intelligent plots will appeal to readers of literary fiction, and the suspense and detection will please mystery fans as well.

Blissett, Luther.
Q. Harcourt, 2004. 768pp.

After Martin Luther famously nails his ninety-five theses to the door of Wittenberg Cathedral in 1517, papal heretic hunters come out in full force against his supporters. Gustav Metzger, a radical Anabaptist and one of Luther's followers, wanders around Europe rallying people to his cause. Trailing him the whole way is a papal spy known only as "Q." Dense and scholarly in places, but loose and colloquial in others, especially where dialogue is concerned. Blissett is the joint pseudonym for a group of four Italian authors.

Keywords: Germany—Renaissance and Reformation

Eco, Umberto.
The Name of the Rose. Harcourt Brace, 1983. 502pp. 📖 ★

Lengthy, dense, and erudite, filled with Latin and Italian phrases and references to historical figures, Eco's classic work will please readers looking for an intellectual challenge. At its heart is a mystery. In 1327, William of Baskerville, a fifty-year-old monk, becomes involved with investigating a series of bizarre deaths at an Italian monastery. At the same time, the novel also explores philosophical issues, such as complex theological arguments and the nature of art and literature in the Middle Ages. This novel inspired America's fascination with the literary thriller.

> **Keywords:** Italy—Middle Ages

Gleeson, Janet.
The Grenadillo Box. **Simon & Schuster, 2004. 352pp.**

On January 1, 1755, Nathaniel Hopson, apprentice to famed cabinet-maker Thomas Chippendale, installs a library on Lord Montfort's country estate in England. When the nobleman is found dead of a gunshot wound, everyone assumes it must be suicide. Other clues suggest otherwise, such as the trail of blood at the crime scene and the small, carved box found in the victim's dead hand. When a second victim is found brutally killed on the same property, Nathaniel takes action. His investigation leads him through all levels of London society on the trail of a twenty-year-old secret. Someone is ready to kill to prevent the truth from coming out.

> **Keywords:** England—Georgian Era

Jinks, Catherine.
The Inquisitor. **St. Martin's Press, 2002. 400pp.**

First published in the author's native Australia in 1999, Jinks's American debut is set in Lazet, a village in the French Pyrenees, in 1318. Brother Bernard is a friar and Inquisitor of Heretical Depravity—that is, his job is to root out elements of the Cathar heresy and question potential unbelievers. When his superior, the obnoxious ascetic Father Agustin, is murdered in a rather gruesome fashion, Bernard must investigate. In doing so, he grows a little too close to the female members of one Cathar family, to the point of being accused himself of the beliefs he is asked to destroy. This novel's atmosphere is wonderfully realistic, and the fear that the Inquisition inspires in the villagers is palpable.

> **Keywords:** France—Middle Ages

Kerr, Philip.
Dark Matter: The Private Life of Isaac Newton. **Crown, 2002. 347pp.** ✍

In 1696, Isaac Newton, brilliant scientist and Warden of the Royal Mint, teams up with Christopher Ellis, his headstrong assistant (in fiction and in history), to investigate counterfeiting activity that is disrupting the national economy. They discover a conspiracy that reaches much higher and possibly includes a series of murders in the Tower of London.

> **Keywords:** England—Stuart Era

King, Ross.
🔖 *Ex-Libris*. **Walker, 2001. 400pp.** 📖

A mysterious noblewoman asks Isaac Inchbold, a bookseller in Restoration (1660s) London, to locate a dangerous and possibly heretical manuscript that once belonged to her father. In a parallel plot, we are exposed to the philosophical and military battles between Protestants and Catholics during the Thirty Years War in Europe (1618–1648). How this relates to Inchbold's investigation is left for the reader to discover. This novel will appeal to people who enjoy the history of rare books, but King's emphasis on description rather than dialogue slows down the story. Herodotus Award.

Keywords: England—Stuart Era

Liss, David.

Benjamin Weaver Series.

Literary thrillers set amid the world of commerce in eighteenth-century London.

A Conspiracy of Paper. Random House, 2000. 442pp. 📖

London in 1719 is a burgeoning commercial center, and the stock market is the scene for much of the action. Benjamin Weaver, a thief-taker, former boxer, and all-around person-for-hire, turns to investigation once he receives word that his estranged father has been run down in a carriage accident. Suspecting that the death was hardly accidental, Benjamin becomes caught up in the schemes and plots surrounding eighteenth-century London's version of Wall Street, complete with crooks, clandestine meetings, and fortunes to be won and lost. The author evokes the somewhat formal language of two centuries past while keeping with the fast-paced nature of a modern thriller. Edgar Award.

A Spectacle of Corruption. Random House, 2004. 381pp.

Benjamin Weaver returns in this sequel to *A Conspiracy of Paper*, set in mid-eighteenth-century London. Imprisoned for a murder he didn't commit, Benjamin engineers his escape with the help of a mysterious benefactor. To clear his name, he disguises himself as a rich merchant with an interest in politics. His investigations uncover a conspiracy with grave implications for the future of the monarchy.

Keywords: England—Georgian Era

The Coffee Trader. **Random House, 2003. 384pp.** 📖

Miguel Lienzo, a Jewish trader in seventeenth-century Amsterdam, hides a secret: He had escaped from the Inquisition in Portugal years earlier. Using the skills of deception he gained while in hiding for his religion, he forms a partnership with a sexy Dutchwoman in a lucrative scheme to make a fortune in the coffee trade, a commodity that hasn't yet gained popularity. Not only must Miguel gain enough knowledge to succeed in the market, but he must also fend off competition and keep his standing in the Portuguese Jewish community—and there are many who would like to see him fail.

Keywords: Netherlands—Early Modern Era

Mawer, Simon.

The Gospel of Judas. Little, Brown, 2001. 330pp.

Father Leo Newman, a scholar in contemporary Rome, is undergoing a crisis of faith. At a time when his own religious conscience is in doubt, he is summoned to

Jerusalem to devote further study to the origins of some scrolls from the first century AD. These scrolls purport to tell the story of the Gospels from the point of view of Judas. In the version Newman reads, Jesus never did rise from the dead—or so Judas claims. Mawer intertwines several stories, including one set in 1943, when Newman's mother conducts an affair with a Jewish man.

Keywords: Israel—Biblical Era; Italy—World War II

Norfolk, Lawrence.

Lemprière's Dictionary. **Harmony, 1991. 422pp.** ✍ ★ 📖

Ever since his father was killed while watching a nude young woman bathing in a forest, scholar John Lemprière (a historical figure) has seen parallels between his world and that of Greek mythology. He decides to compile a dictionary of classical myth and legend. Soon others begin to die in ways that imitate the Greek stories, and Lemprière gradually unravels a conspiracy that connects his father's death to the beginnings of the East India Company 150 years earlier. A bookish literary thriller in the vein of Ross King's *Ex-Libris*, set in late eighteenth-century London.

Keywords: England—Georgian Era

Palliser, Charles.

The Quincunx. **Ballantine, 1989. 788pp.**

Palliser is at his best when re-creating the brooding, suspenseful atmosphere of nineteenth-century England. The unusual title comes from a family crest of overlapping roses, symbolizing five different families whose heritage and destinies intertwine. John Huffam, a young member of one of these families, moves with his mother to London. There, the two struggle to uncover answers to their family legacy and discover why they are despised by their relations.

Keywords: England—Victorian Era

The Unburied. **Farrar, Straus, & Giroux, 1999. 403pp.**

This literary gothic thriller is set, most appropriately, in an ancient castle in Victorian England. Dr. Edward Courtine is invited for a visit by an old friend from whom he had been estranged for twenty years. Seeing the visit as a chance for reconciliation as well as a way to do research on a medieval document in a nearby cathedral, Courtine makes his journey, but finds his friend strangely tight-lipped. Not only does Courtine discover the cathedral's connection to a murder 250 years prior, but he also becomes witness to a similarly gruesome discovery.

Keywords: England—Victorian Era

Pamuk, Orhan.

My Name Is Red. **Knopf, 2001. 384pp.** 📖

In the sixteenth-century Ottoman Empire, two miniaturists have been murdered, perhaps for their desire to contribute to a masterwork that has been created in the Venetian tradition. Representations from life are considered heretical, so any artist who dares create realistic works of art may find his life in danger. Black, the nephew of one of the slain artists, takes it upon himself to find his uncle's murderer. At the same time, Black becomes infatuated with his beautiful cousin Shekure, who flirts with him by means of notes and mysterious invitations. There are stories nested within stories; the narrators change from chapter to chapter and include inanimate objects and ideas, including the color red (hence the title). A bestseller in the author's native Turkey.

Keywords: Ottoman Empire—16th Century

Pearl, Matthew.
The Dante Club. **Random House, 2003. 372pp.** 📖

The "Dante Club," a group of Boston scholars circa 1865, goes against the Harvard tradition of shunning European literature in favor of classical Greek and Latin texts. Instead, the group—which includes literary geniuses such as Henry Wadsworth Longfellow, James Russell Lowell, and Oliver Wendell Holmes—plans to create the first American translation of Dante's *Divine Comedy*. When a serial killer strikes in a manner taken straight of Dante's *Inferno*, it's clear to these scholars that the murderer cannot be just anyone. The author does his best to re-create the somewhat artificial nature of nineteenth-century academic prose, and his plot leads the characters from the ivy-covered halls of Harvard to the dirty underbelly of downtown Boston.

Keywords: Massachusetts—Reconstruction and Gilded Age

Pears, Iain.
An Instance of the Fingerpost. **Riverhead, 1998. 691pp.** 📖 ★

In 1660s Oxford, England, a fellow of New College is found murdered. Four different people recount the story behind the crime, and each gives a vastly different version of events. Only one of them tells the real truth, but which one? A young woman stands accused of the crime, and though she would seem to have a motive, she may or may not be the killer. Interspersed throughout the text are some wry observations on English life and politics. Full of plot twists, and written with an authentic feel for seventeenth-century language, Pears's novel was hailed as the long-awaited successor to Eco's *The Name of the Rose*.

Keywords: England—Stuart Era

Perez-Reverte, Arturo.
The Fencing Master. **Harcourt, 1999. 256pp.**

In Madrid of 1868, plots are in motion to force Spain's promiscuous and unpopular queen, Isabella II, to abdicate. In this politically unstable climate, a mysterious woman asks Don Jaime Astarloa, an aging fencing master, to teach her a secret move not normally learned by a lady. Soon she wins him over with her skill, but with that one event he is drawn into a dangerous political conspiracy. Spanish novelist Perez-Reverte's other works, such as *The Club Dumas* (1997) and *The*

Nautical Chart (2001), are set wholly in the present but deal with objects or events from the past; historical fiction readers may find them equally intriguing.

Keywords: Spain—Early Modern Era

Ruiz Zafón, Carlos.

The Shadow of the Wind. **The Penguin Press, 2004. 486pp.**

In 1945 Barcelona, ten-year-old Daniel Sempere accompanies his father to a secret rare book library, the Cemetery of Forgotten Books. His father helps him select a volume to take home and read, so that it will never again be forgotten. Daniel selects a copy of *The Shadow of the Wind*, by Julian Carax, and becomes so absorbed in the story that he determines to find other books that Carax wrote. The problem is, someone else has been systematically destroying every copy of Carax's work that he can find. As Daniel comes of age, his life begins to parallel that of the author. A literary gothic thriller, complete with ghostly images, romance, literature, and politics in post–Civil War Spain.

Keywords: Spain—Twentieth Century

Sansom, C.J.

Dissolution. **Viking, 2003. 336pp.**

The dissolution of the title refers to the dismantling of the monasteries in Tudor England. In 1537, Henry VIII reigns, and Anne Boleyn has recently been beheaded. Controversies rage between the Catholics and those loyal to the king and his newly created Church of England. Thomas Cromwell leads the reformers, and when a man loyal to him is murdered at the monastery at Scarnea, Cromwell sends Matthew Shardlake, a lawyer and hunchback, to investigate. Once there, Matthew uncovers more than he bargained for, including sexual scandals, murder, and treason.

Keywords: England—Tudor Era

Taylor, Andrew.

🎗*An Unpardonable Crime.* **Hyperion, 2004. 496pp. (Original title: *The American Boy*.)** ✍

In 1819, ten-year-old Edgar Allan Poe accompanies his foster father to England and enrolls in school at Stoke Newington, outside London. While there he befriends a banker's son, Charlie Frant. After Frant's wealthy father dies a gruesome death, Thomas Shield, the boys' schoolmaster, becomes unwittingly involved in mysterious happenings surrounding the murder. Ellis Peters Historical Dagger.

Keywords: England—Regency Era

Tosches, Nick.

In the Hand of Dante. **Little, Brown, 2002. 377pp.** ✍

The author stars in his own novel about the original, stolen manuscript of Dante's *Divine Comedy.* When a gangster named Louie (from one of the author's previous thrillers) acquires the manuscript, he asks Nick to authenticate it, and the process takes Nick from Arizona to a host of European cities. Dante's own journey to complete the book is detailed in a parallel plot that suffers somewhat in comparison to the whirlwind trip experienced by Nick. However, the historical detail is plentiful, and the author's research is obvious.

Keywords: Italy—Middle Ages

Watkins, Paul.

The Forger. **Picador USA, 2000. 322pp.**

Just before World War II, David Halifax, a young American art student, travels on scholarship to Paris, where he will receive further training in painting. While there, he learns more about his benefactor, Russian painter Alexander Pankratov, as well as his true purpose for being there. Paul is to be trained in a secret mission to forge well-known European paintings and switch the fakes with the originals, so that Hitler's minions will believe they have succeeded in obliterating them. The end is a race against time and the Nazis, as Paul and his compatriots rush to complete the forgeries.

Keywords: France—World War II

Wilson, James.

The Dark Clue. **Atlantic Monthly, 2001. 390pp.**

This thriller is centered on nineteenth-century British landscape painter J. M. W. Turner, and it stars characters taken straight out of Wilkie Collins's literary ghost story *The Woman in White.* The "dark clue" of the title is a hidden element in Turner's paintings that Walter Hartright and Marian Halcombe, two of Collins's literary creations, investigate while writing a biography of the reclusive artist. The story, told in epistolary form, evokes Collins's own writing, but his fans may find the author's evocations of Collins's characters a bit unsettling.

Keywords: England—Victorian Era

Zimler, Richard.

🎗 *The Last Kabbalist of Lisbon.* **Overlook, 1998. 320pp.**

Portugal in the early sixteenth century was a dangerous place for Jews, as demonstrated by the Lisbon massacre of 1506, in which many of the city's Jewish residents were killed by a mob of fanatical Christians. Berekiah Zarco, a manuscript illustrator and secret Jew, witnesses the massacre, which the author describes in all its painful intensity. Even more, Zarco must solve the murder of a well-known kabbalist, his uncle Abraham, whose body was found next to that of a nude young woman. The trail leads him through all of the religious quarters of Lisbon. Herodotus Award.

Keywords: Portugal—Renaissance and Reformation

Psychological Suspense

Psychological suspense is a hard subcategory to define. These novels combine elements of the thriller, horror, mystery, and literary fiction genres to form a category of their own. In a nutshell, they are dark, chilling books whose intense psychological impact causes excitement to build in the reader as the story draws closer to its conclusion. The suspense is usually internal, rather than action-oriented, and mind games are a common plot device. More often than not, the novels conclude with a major plot twist. In historical novels of psychological suspense, the historical background, eerie and atmospheric, plays into the novel's intensity. A typical setting may include the gas-lit streets of Victorian London or a city in nineteenth- or early twentieth-century America. The gloomy, threatening tone enhances the dark atmosphere, and, as in most thrillers, the protagonists find themselves in danger from an unknown source. While there may be a crime committed, as is the case in mystery novels, here the identity of the murderer may or may not be a secret. Instead, this fact may be revealed to the reader early on, so that the novel's suspense lies in the protagonist's desperate hope of unmasking the culprit before he or she strikes again. As in horror novels, ghosts from the past—imagined or real—may be present. Finally, as is the case in literary historicals, the subjects are serious or bleak. The language used by the authors is elegant, but not inaccessibly so, and while pacing may be slower than in most thriller novels, they are compulsive page-turners.

Airth, Rennie.

River of Darkness. Viking, 1999. 386pp.

Just after the end of World War I, Scotland Yard Detective John Madden, a battle-scarred veteran with horrible memories of his wartime experiences, has been called in to help solve a set of murders in the Surrey countryside. A young couple well beloved by their community have been gruesomely stabbed to death in their manor house, along with their servants. After the identity of the killer is revealed, the real mystery becomes a question of whether Madden and his compatriots can stop him in time.

Keywords: England—Twentieth Century

Benson, Ann.

Plague Series.

A series of psychological suspense novels/medical thrillers set in the fourteenth century and in the near future; a third novel is expected.

The Plague Tales. Delacorte, 1997. 474pp.

In England in the year 2005, former surgeon Janie Crowe, in the course of research on virulent disease, unwittingly releases the virus causing the Black Death into the London populace. In a parallel story set in 1348, Spanish physician Alejandro Canches becomes a papal envoy to the court of England's Edward III and finds himself fighting the bubonic plague in the year of its greatest outbreak. There are some gruesome moments, naturally, but also plenty of plot twists as the pair both race to dispel the deadly disease. Suspense rises toward the end, for there is no guarantee that the pair can stop the plague's progress in time.

The Burning Road. Delacorte, 1999. 467pp.

This sequel to *The Plague Tales* picks up with Janie Crowe in 2007, as she continues both her fight against the plague and her discoveries in genetics, helped along by suggestions from Alejandro's journal. Alejandro, back in the fourteenth century, becomes involved with the Hundred Years' War while in France. Both tales portray the triumph against evil and the difficulties of coping in a repressive society.

Keywords: Spain—Middle Ages

Thief of Souls. **Delacorte, 2002. 480pp.**

In fifteenth-century France, Guillemette le Drappiere, assistant to a bishop, knows that the notorious criminal Gilles de Rais is the perpetrator of a string of heinous crimes. Her own son numbers among the victims. Lany Dunbar, an equally strong-willed woman in contemporary Los Angeles, determines to solve the serial murder of a group of young boys. The race is on to catch two serial killers, both of whom are preying on children.

Keywords: France—Middle Ages

Carr, Caleb.

Laszlo Kreizler Series.

Serial killers roam the streets of late nineteenth-century New York. Literary, suspenseful, and occasionally gruesome.

The Alienist. Random House, 1994. 496pp. ★

Before he became president, Theodore Roosevelt was, among other things, the police commissioner for New York. In 1896, a serial killer preying on young male prostitutes stalks the city. Not willing to turn the case over to the corrupt officials who report to him, "T.R." assembles his own group of crime solvers, which include Laszlo Kreizler, a psychologist and the "alienist" of the title. His investigations take him from the crime-ridden underworld of New York to the highest of high society—members of which try to prevent him from continuing, as they fear seeing their names dragged through the mud. All the while, danger is about to strike from another avenue. Anthony Award.

The Angel of Darkness. Random House, 1997. 629pp.

Stevie Taggart, a young urchin saved by Laszlo Kreizler from a life of crime in *The Alienist*, returns to narrate this sequel of sorts. When a young woman appeals to Kreizler and his friends to help her find her kidnapped daughter, they can hardly refuse . . . but the more they find out about the case and the woman's past, they begin to suspect that she may be more involved than she admits. Once again, we are thrust into the shadowy atmosphere of late nineteenth-century New York City in this fast-paced, suspenseful thriller.

Keywords: New York—Reconstruction and Gilded Age

Day, Ava Dianne.

Cut to the Heart. **Doubleday, 2002. 323pp.**

In 1863, Clara Barton, future founder of the Red Cross, is stationed at the Union Army's southern headquarters, Hilton Head Island. There she becomes intrigued by Gullah folk medicine and the freed black slaves who were left to survive after the white men left for war. Evil stalks the town in the form of a doctor who watches Clara's every move.

Keywords: South Carolina—Civil War

Edge, Arabella.

The Company. **Simon & Schuster, 2001. 369pp.**

Annotated in Chapter 8.

Ford, Jeffrey.

The Portrait of Mrs. Charbuque. **Morrow, 2002. 310pp.**

Piero Piambo has built his career on painting portraits of the nouveau riche of 1893 New York City—paintings that improve upon the unattractive reality of his subjects. When a man offers him the lucrative opportunity of painting a portrait of the wealthy Mrs. Charbuque, he naturally accepts. What he doesn't realize is that Mrs. Charbuque will not show her face to him, and that he must divine her likeness only from stories that she tells. As his portrait grows more complete, murders occur throughout the city. When threatened by the woman's husband, Piambo begins to think that his mysterious subject may be connected to the crimes.

Keywords: New York—Reconstruction and Gilded Age

Goddard, Robert.

Painting the Darkness. **Poseidon, 1989. 446pp.** ★

One fine afternoon in 1882, William Trenchard, an Englishman of moderate wealth, sits outside at his country estate when a stranger approaches him. The stranger soon reveals his true identity as Sir James Davenall, a man who had supposedly committed suicide eleven years earlier—and who had previously been engaged to Trenchard's wife. So begins this thriller set among the nineteenth-century British aristocracy. Naturally, Davenall—if it is indeed him—would like to reclaim the estate (and possibly the woman) that had once been his. Goddard, called the literary heir to Daphne du Maurier, is better known in the United Kingdom than he is in the States, and it's hard to understand why.

Keywords: England—Victorian Era

Debt of Dishonour. **Poseidon, 1992. 462pp.**

In England and on the Côte d'Azur in the 1920s, architect Geoffrey Staddon attempts to assuage his guilt over seducing his client's wife years earlier, by trying to extricate her from a murder charge. Consuela Caswell, his former paramour, has been accused of poisoning her niece in an attempt to kill her niece's husband. Geoffrey must return to Clouds

Frome, the magnificent structure he had built, to rescue Consuela and settle old scores. In doing so, he uncovers mysteries from a dozen years ago that he wishes had stayed buried. Most of Goddard's excellent thrillers are either non-historical or only available from his British publishers, but like *Painting the Darkness*, this is an exception.

> **Keywords:** England—Twentieth Century

Gutcheon, Beth.

More Than You Know. **Morrow, 2000. 269pp.**

> Annotated in Chapter 12.

Jakeman, Jane.

In the Kingdom of Mists. **Berkley, 2004. 355pp.** ✑

> This thriller combining art history, crime, and psychological suspense is set in London during the winter of 1900. Artist Claude Monet has rented rooms at the Savoy Hotel to paint images of the light and mists reflecting off the river Thames. On another floor at the Savoy, wounded officers recuperate from injuries received in the Boer War. An Irish policeman believes that mysterious goings-on at the Savoy may be connected to the Ripper-like murders of several young women—and that Monet's paintings may contain some clues.

> **Keywords:** England—Twentieth Century

Monahan, Brett.

The Bell Witch: An American Haunting. **St. Martin's Press, 1997. 199pp.** ✑

> There have been several novelizations of the "true story" behind the Bell Witch incident in Adams, Tennessee, circa 1819, including Melissa Sanders-Self's version (below). Monahan's take on the legend is more tightly constructed, showing the glee taken by the poltergeist in its actions and the horrors suffered by members of the Bell family. Attempts at exorcism by the townspeople do no good, and the action culminates in a horrific event.

> **Keywords:** Tennessee—Early United States

O'Neill, Anthony.

The Lamplighter. **Scribner, 2003. 308pp.**

> As a young girl in the nineteenth century, Evelyn Todd had lived in an Edinburgh orphanage, but she was sent away in disgrace after regaling her fellow orphans with tales of a mysterious lamplighter. Her arrival back in the city years later seems to tie in with the violent murders of some of its most prominent citizens. When Evelyn claims to have dreamed about the murders before they happened, it mystifies police inspectors even in this age of scientific knowledge. It also convinces them to dig deeper into Evelyn's mysterious childhood.

> **Keywords:** Scotland—Victorian Era

Sanders-Self, Melissa.

All That Lives. Warner, 2002. 450pp.

The Bell Witch of Tennessee (see Brent Monahan's novel, above) is an American legend, and this horrific thriller tells the story behind the haunting. When Betsy, daughter of the Bell family, turns thirteen in the early nineteenth century, the poltergeist is stirred up. Its macabre actions begin with pinpricks, mysterious voices, and death threats but soon take on even more appalling forms.

> **Keywords:** Tennessee—Early United States

Smith, Sarah.

<u>Alexander von Reisden Trilogy</u>.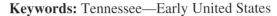

This trilogy of historical suspense novels featuring Swiss nobleman Alexander von Reisden is written in the best gothic tradition, with family secrets, death threats, and a strong dose of the macabre. The novels must be read in order, for the secret of the first book is discussed in the sequels.

The Vanished Child. Ballantine, 1992. 420pp.

In early twentieth-century Switzerland, Baron Alexander von Reisden is recognized by members of a Boston family as the long-lost heir to their family fortune. Thirteen years earlier, an eight-year-old boy named Richard Knight had disappeared from his New England home at the time of his grandfather's murder. Von Reisden, who remembers little of his childhood, abandons his chemistry studies to discover the truth. As he discovers more about the Knight family history, he grows closer to another heir's fiancée, pianist Perdita Halley. He also starts to question his own identity. Is he really Richard Knight? And if he isn't the long-lost heir, is Richard's killer still at large?

> **Keywords:** Switzerland—Twentieth Century; Massachusetts—Reconstruction and Gilded Age

The Knowledge of Water. Ballantine, 1996. 469pp.

Perdita Halley arrives in Paris to be with Alexander von Reisden, the man she loves. However, she will not marry him until she has achieved her dream of becoming a concert pianist, which she cannot do if she weds. Alexander, who directs a mental health institute, continues to be haunted by memories of a lost childhood. Both become involved in a conspiracy after Alexander receives threatening letters. The novel is set against a vibrant, macabre backdrop of art forgeries, the murder of a prostitute, and the flood that overtook Paris in 1910.

> **Keywords:** France—Twentieth Century

A Citizen of the Country. Ballantine, 2000. 420pp.

In 1911, Alexander and Perdita von Reisden are married and have a son. Now that he has come to terms with his own past, Alexander has the chance to help someone else. André du Monde, owner of the Grand

Necropolitan Theatre in Paris, obsesses over his belief that his young wife is destined to kill him. To allay André's fears, Alexander agrees to take part in his first film, but André's horror theater becomes the scene for even more unspeakable happenings.

Keywords: France—Twentieth Century

Vine, Barbara.

Anna's Book. **Harmony, 1993. 394pp. (Original title: *Asta's Book*.)** ★

Anna Westerby, a Danish immigrant in London in early twentieth-century London, meticulously records events from her day-to-day life in her journal. Years later, it is discovered that her diaries, which have gained Anna posthumous fame, may contain the secret to a murder. They may also reveal the true identity of Swanny, Anna's daughter. This is a classic novel of psychological suspense that also gives insight into the lives of immigrants—the struggles they had to adjust to, and the prejudice they faced—in turn-of-the-century London. Vine is a pseudonym for Ruth Rendell.

Keywords: England—Twentieth Century

International Intrigue

In these novels, world history forms a backdrop against which one or more protagonists must race against the clock to solve a puzzle or unmask a killer before danger strikes. The action takes place on one or more continents, typically Europe or Asia, during a time of political unrest. Secrets from the past come back to haunt the protagonists, and the conspiracies they uncover often follow upon one or more political events from the recent past, such as a revolution or war. To investigate, many protagonists enter the hidden arena of the political underworld, going into disguise to uncover a conspiracy, solve a crime, or expose widescale corruption. This is not a large category, but these fast-paced novels are popular with a large variety of readers, including fans of mysteries, traditional historical novels, and modern political thrillers. In these stories, events are set against a grand and global backdrop, often in exotic locales, and the protagonists are sophisticated and cosmopolitan. The stories may include elements of espionage (later this chapter), but this isn't usually the main focus.

Bradby, Tom.

The Master of Rain. **Doubleday, 2002. 448pp.**

The author, a reporter for Britain's ITN television network, sets his first novel in 1920s Shanghai, a city of corruption, intrigue, and international activity. It is here that Richard Field, a Yorkshire policeman, is assigned to solve the grisly murder of a Russian prostitute. His investigations reveal a web of organized crime leading to the highest levels in the business and political arenas of Shanghai.

Keywords: China—Twentieth Century

The White Russian. **Doubleday, 2003. 464pp.**

In 1917 St. Petersburg, the simmering political atmosphere foreshadows revolution. Sandro Ruszky, the city's chief of police, discovers connections between the current political environment and the murder of a couple—a young Russian girl and an American man. As the female victim was formerly a nanny at the Imperial Palace, her killing may be more than it seems.

Keywords: Russia—Twentieth Century

Grant, Tracy.

Fraser Series.

A romantic spy thriller series set in Napoleonic-era London and Scotland.

Daughter of the Game. Morrow, 2002. 483pp.

In 1819 London, Colin, the beloved son of socialite couple Mélanie and Charles Fraser, is kidnapped. The kidnapper's motive is apparently not money, as the Frasers discover when they are asked to come up with the ransom: the Carevalo ring, which, as legend has it, protects its owners from harm. The plot then flashes back seven years, to the time of the Frasers' first meeting in the mountains of Spain. The couple's past connections to the ring and to Spain's war against Napoleon—which are hidden even from each other—cause dissent in their marriage as well as trouble in locating their son, particularly since time is running out. Grant also writes romances, and her thrillers have enough romantic elements to satisfy romance readers.

Beneath a Silent Moon. Morrow, 2003. 427pp.

This prequel of sorts to *Daughter of the Game* reveals the Frasers' early history. Mélanie and Charles Fraser are celebrating the end of the Napoleonic Wars along with the rest of London in 1817. On the night of a house party at the elegant Glenister House, Charles and Mélanie are given papers by a dying man—papers that, once decoded, reveal a connection between the mysterious Elsinore League, the French Revolution, and a beautiful woman whom Charles had been expected to marry. The trail leads them to Perthshire in the Scottish Highlands.

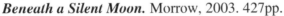

Keywords: England—Regency Era

Neville, Katherine.

The Eight. Ballantine, 1989. 550pp. ★

After the French Revolution, former religious novice Mireille narrowly escapes the guillotine only to find herself caught up in international intrigue. She is charged with scattering pieces of the legendary Montglane Service, a chess set once owned by Charlemagne, around the globe because its power can be dangerous in the wrong hands. Her adventures bring her in contact with some of the greatest political powers of the day, including Robespierre and Talleyrand. In a present-day storyline, computer whiz Catherine Velis teams up with a chess master to reassemble the pieces of the set herself before someone else does. The travels of both women take them across the European continent, from France to Algeria and back again. Chess symbolism, secret codes, numeric patterns, and danger abound.

Keywords: France—Early Modern Era

The Magic Circle. **Ballantine, 1998. 554pp.**

When nuclear scientist Ariel Behn's cousin is murdered, leaving her the heir to ancient scrolls that date from the first century BC, she gets caught up in intrigue that reaches from the United States to Russia. Flashbacks to the scrolls' previous owners reveal the manuscripts' true significance and meaning. A combination historical novel/millennial thriller with elements of New Age philosophy and ancient astronomy.

Keywords: Israel—Ancient/Prehistoric

Redfern, Elizabeth.

Auriel Rising. **Putnam, 2004. 386pp.**

In 1609, Ned Warriner returns from self-imposed exile abroad to reclaim his home and the love of his life, Kate Revill. But Kate is unhappily married to another man, someone sworn to abolish Catholicism in all of England. As Ned had previously helped a Catholic spy escape from prison, he proceeds with caution. He also possesses a secret letter addressed to a mysterious "Auriel," a missive that seems to contain the secret for turning matter into gold. In reality, the letter may include encoded information that could affect the Protestant monarchy.

Keywords: England—Stuart Era

The Music of the Spheres. **Putnam, 2001. 417pp.**

A serial killer stalks young red-haired victims in 1795 London, strangling them with a silken cord. One of these unfortunates was the fifteen-year-old daughter of Jonathan Absey, an agent of the Home Office, who cannot let the matter rest. When Absey convinces himself that the killer may be connected to the Company of Titius, a group of French expatriates who seek to discover a lost planet, he blackmails his estranged brother, a frustrated homosexual, into using his astronomical interests to infiltrate the Company.

Keywords: England—Georgian Era

Stephen, Martin.

The Desperate Remedy. **St. Martin's Press, 2003. 324pp.**

Henry Gresham, a gentleman spy in James I's England, uses a disreputable thief named William Shadwell as his main source of information. When Shadwell is murdered, Gresham is on his own in the underworld of Jacobean (early seventeenth-century) London. Robert Cecil, the King's Chief Secretary, asks Gresham to investigate the sexual depravity of his enemy, Sir Francis Bacon—a task that complicates his life further. The trail of Gresham's investigations leads him to a Catholic conspiracy to eliminate the current monarchy—by blowing up Parliament, killing James I, and setting a Catholic heir on England's throne. First in a projected series.

Keywords: England—Stuart Era

War Thrillers

Nowhere is the battle between good and evil so clearly drawn as in war thrillers. Larger than life heroes battle against dark forces. In wartime, the enemy may be lurking behind every corner, and sometimes it's impossible to tell who the enemy is. A few minutes may mean the difference between success and failure, and in war thrillers, it's a race against time to strike against your enemies before they strike against you. This intensifies the suspense of these fast-paced novels. World War II in particular presents ripe opportunities for authors of historical thrillers, for members of the Nazi party make dastardly villains. Many of these authors also write contemporary war thrillers.

Browne, Marshall.

***The Eye of the Abyss*. Thomas Dunne, 2003. 290pp.**

Franz Schmidt, chief internal auditor at a prominent German bank in 1938, lost one eye defending a Jew from Nazis three years earlier. He claims not to hold a grudge against the Nazis, but finally takes action when the Nazi party deposits large amounts of cash in the bank and demands that Jewish employees be fired. Dietrich, a Nazi henchman, always seems one step ahead of Schmidt, and events spiral out of control as Schmidt tries to keep his family safe.

Carcaterra, Lorenzo.

***Street Boys*. Ballantine, 2002. 400pp.**

In 1943 Naples, a group of orphaned children take it upon themselves to defend their native land against Nazi invaders with the help of an American soldier, who coordinates their assaults. The story of these unlikely heroes, glowing with patriotism, is more than a bit cliché-ridden, but the pace is nonstop and the action is high.

Follett, Ken.

Follett's novels have nonstop thrills and fast-paced action, with larger-than-life heroes and heroines who face danger at every turn. His spy thrillers are listed later in this chapter.

***Hornet Flight*. Dutton, 2002. 420pp.**

By an accident of fate, in June 1941 young Danishman Harald Olufsen stumbles onto a secret German radar installation. He immediately realizes that he needs to get information on the machinery to England. His only way of getting there is by way of an abandoned, rusting Hornet Moth biplane and a dangerous flight of 600 miles across the sea.

***Jackdaws*. Dutton, 2001. 451pp.**

Felicity "Flick" Clairet is a British agent in France during World War II. When her plan to foil the German communication system goes awry, and her husband disappears, she takes it upon herself to form an all-female team—the Jackdaws—whose job it will be to gain access to German

9

lines of communication. However, since the Germans know of their existence, their mission won't be easy.

Night over Water. **Morrow, 1991. 400pp.**

A group of European jet-setters—including a murderer, a thief, an aristocrat, and a scientist—board the Pan American Clipper, a luxurious jumbo jet bound for New York, for one heart-stopping night flight across the Atlantic in 1939.

Gobbell, John J.

Todd Ingram Series.

Gobbell, a former Navy lieutenant, sets his military thrillers in the South Pacific theater of World War II—Japan, the Philippines, and southern China.

The Last Lieutenant. St. Martin's Press, 1995. 360pp.

In 1942, on the island of Corregidor in the Philippines, Lt. Todd Ingram of the U.S. Navy must discover the identity of a Nazi spy—someone hidden among a group of Navy cryptographers deciphering Japanese intelligence about a possible attack on Midway Island.

A Code for Tomorrow. St. Martin's Press, 1999. 320pp.

After escaping from Corregidor, Lt. Ingram hopes to get back to the Philippines to rescue the woman he loves, army nurse Helen Durand. Though Ingram's worst fears come true—he's captured by the Japanese—he underestimates the efficiency of his girlfriend, who works behind enemy lines to rescue him and keep American secrets safe.

When Duty Whispers Low. St. Martin's Press, 2002. 343pp.

Although the Allies celebrate victory at Guadalcanal in 1943, the battle for control of the Pacific continues, for the Japanese want to reclaim control of the island. Ingram, the executive officer of the U.S.S. *Howell*, must defend his vessel and decide whether to obey his commanding officer, whose authority he questions.

The Neptune Strategy. St. Martin's Press, 2004. 344pp.

Rescued by a Japanese submarine after his ship is sunk in the North Pacific, Ingram faces possible torture at the hands of his captors. As the sub heads to France, the American Navy races to save one of their own.

Griffin, W. E. B.

Honor Bound Series.

A trilogy featuring U.S. military officer Clete Frade and his crusade against the evil Nazi empire.

Honor Bound. Putnam, 1993. 474pp.

Because Argentina was a neutral country during World War II, it was prime ground in which both American and German forces could operate covertly. It is the mission of Clete Frade, a lieutenant in the U.S. Marines and a hero of Guadalcanal, to destroy a German-controlled ship that's been supplying enemy submarines. The Allies have more in mind for Frade, such as using the Argentine father he has never met, a famed politician, to throw some support their way.

Griffin's historical accuracy is good, though his secondary characters (especially the women) are little more than cardboard cutouts.

Blood and Honor. Putnam, 1996. 553pp.

Closer to a spy thriller than the first of the series, *Blood and Honor* sees Frade return to Argentina in 1943 with the U.S. ambassador, but he's really there to avenge his father's murder. At the same time, the Argentine military has plans to overthrow the government to bring General Juan Peron to power.

Secret Honor. Putnam, 2000. 497pp.

In 1943 Argentina, Clete Frade, OSS agent, must safeguard the identity of a Nazi pilot who is funneling secrets to him in exchange for protection for him and his family after the war ends.

Higgins, Jack.

Flight of Eagles. **Putnam, 1998. 328pp.**

Max von Halder and Harry Kelso, twins born to a German mother and an American father, spend their lives apart, Max in Germany and Harry in the United States. When World War II strikes, they are both ferocious fighter pilots, but on opposite sides—on a collision course with destiny and with each other.

Lawton, John.

Black Out. **Viking, 1995. 342pp.**

As London suffers through the 1944 Blitz in a maelstrom of fear and destruction, a Scotland Yard detective is asked to look into the possible connection between body parts found a at a bomb site and the disappearance of a scientist studying German atomic rocketry. Conspiracies abound.

Meade, Glenn.

The Sands of Sakkara. **St. Martin's Press, 1999. 436pp.**

The plot of this World War II thriller is familiar at the outset. Two friends, half-German Jack Halder and American Harry Weaver, end up on opposite sides of the conflict. What makes this novel different are the setting and premise. In 1943, four years after their sojourn at Sakkara, an archaeological dig in Cairo, Jack is sent by the Nazis back to Egypt to assassinate Franklin Roosevelt and Winston Churchill, who are meeting there to discuss the Allied war effort. Harry, an American spy, is sent to foil the plot, not knowing who the enemy is. A romantic love triangle develops between them and Rachel Stern, a half-German archaeologist who was also part of the crew at Sakkara in 1939.

Mesce, Bill.

Harry Voss Series.

A series of legal thrillers set in the British Isles and Europe during World War II.

The Advocate. Bantam, 2000. 320pp.

When two U.S. Army pilots stationed in England attack one of their own planes, then attempt to the destroy the farmhouse owned by the civilian spotter and his wife who witnessed the incident, it's up to Judge Advocate General (JAG) Harry Voss to investigate. What he finds makes him think that the American government is less interested in solving the crime than in covering its own tracks. Co-written with Steven Szilagyi.

Officer of the Court. Bantam, 2001. 341pp.

Mesce goes out on his own in the second installation of the Harry Voss series of World War II thrillers. By August 1943, Voss has returned stateside, feeling as if his longed-for trip home was really a bribe in exchange for his silence on his previous case. But when an American officer turns up dead in Scotland's Orkney Islands, Voss can't help but get involved—even though the dead man was hardly one of his favorite people.

The Defender. Bantam, 2003. 277pp.

Lieutenant Dominick Sisto is almost certain to be court-martialed for running from the enemy in the heat of battle in Germany, but when Major Harry Voss takes over as the defense for Sisto's case, he discovers that the official story is far from what really happened. Unfortunately, the one witness to Sisto's heroic conduct may be dead.

Mrazek, Robert J.

🎗 *Stonewall's Gold.* St. Martin's Press, 1999. 240pp. **YA**

This is one of the few war thrillers set in the nineteenth rather than the twentieth century. In the last year of the Civil War in Virginia, fifteen-year-old Jamie Lockhart kills a man who had tried to rape his mother and discovers a secret map in the dead man's pocket. Believing that the map leads to a treasure trove of stolen Confederate gold, Jamie faces considerable danger as he goes behind enemy lines to find it. Michael Shaara Award.

Unholy Fire. St. Martin's Press, 2003. 299pp.

After getting wounded at the 1861 Battle of Ball's Bluff, Lt. John "Kit" McKittridge emerges from a Washington, D.C., area military hospital surprisingly alive but addicted to opium. Assigned to investigate reports of thievery and desertion on behalf of the provost marshal's office, he and a fellow officer turn up a conspiracy that may, if it succeeds, lead to the end of the war and the assassination of the president.

Reich, Christopher.

The Runner. Delacorte, 2000. 440pp.

World War II has ended. Devlin Judge, an American lawyer helping hunt down Nazi war criminals in Europe, is hot on the trail of Erich Seyss, an Olympic runner who was also one of Hitler's elite SS. Judge's mission is also personal, because Seyss, who recently escaped from a POW camp, was responsible for untold wartime atrocities including the murder of Judge's brother. Once Seyss learns that he's being tracked, he aims to catch Judge before he's caught himself.

Robbins, David L.

The End of War. **Bantam, 2000. 398pp.**

In 1945, the war is almost over, but the fight for Berlin has just begun. The three great leaders of World War II—Churchill, Roosevelt, and Stalin —all make plans for triumph during the final months of the war, while secondary characters deal with the realities of war in their day-to-day lives. Character development isn't Robbins's strong point, but fans will keep coming back for the action.

The Last Citadel. **Bantam, 2003. 432pp.**

The Battle of Kursk, in which over two million Russian and German forces clashed in the summer of 1943, was the largest land battle ever fought. Hitler's attempt to conquer Russia culminated at the Soviet city of Kursk, and his plans were given the code name Citadel. German forces gathered their most powerful men, tanks, and other weaponry and headed east. This epic story is told from the point of view of members of a Russian family, a father and his son and daughter, and the formidable Germans who were their enemies.

War of the Rats. **Bantam, 1999. 392pp.**

In this fast-paced blood-and-guts thriller, a Russian and a German sniper battle it out to the end during the Siege of Leningrad in 1942. The story is based on historical events.

Smith, Martin Cruz.

December 6. **Simon & Schuster, 2002. 352pp.**

On December 6, 1941—the day before the Japanese bombed Pearl Harbor —Harry Niles, an American expatriate living in Tokyo, has a feeling about what's coming. He has a chance to catch the last flight out of the country before the attack, though it would mean leaving behind the country and the Japanese woman he loves. The strength of this novel is that it is as much a character and historical study as a thriller.

Spy Thrillers

Spy thrillers take place during or just before wartime, when military intelligence is operating at its highest level. The difference between these and war thrillers is that the protagonists, rather than being men on the front lines of the fighting, are secret agents working undercover for one or both sides. During the Cold War, espionage thrillers were all the rage, for they closely reflected historical reality: spies working covertly amid sinister political intrigue. After the fall of the Soviet

Union in 1991, espionage fiction declined in popularity, but novelists soon found other appealing settings in earlier political conflicts of the twentieth century: World Wars I and II. Common locales include one or more European cities during World War II, such as Paris at the time of the German Occupation. The heroes of espionage thrillers, for they are almost always men, work alone, for in these times of changing political loyalties, there's no one for them to trust. The atmosphere is dark and threatening, with the enemy all around, and they could be betrayed or caught at a moment's notice. The protagonists are as likely to be anti-heroes as heroes, for many are ordinary men forced to become spies due to circumstances beyond their control.

Altman, John.

A Game of Spies. **Putnam, 2002. 259pp.**

Germany's unexpected victory in France and the Low Countries in 1940 is a subject discussed by historians. Eva Bernhardt, a sleeper secret agent for the British, obtains information about Germany's path toward France, but her position is compromised. The question is, by whom: one of the Gestapo officers trailing her, or a British agent secretly working for the Nazis?

Keywords: France—World War II

A Gathering of Spies. **Putnam, 2000. 305pp.**

Harry Winterbotham is a British agent in MI5 who's torn between his duties and wanting to rescue his Jewish wife, a prisoner in Poland. Katarina Heinrich is a Nazi spy married to an American scientist working on the Manhattan Project. When their paths collide in England, blood and mayhem ensue. This first novel by a thirty-year-old writer has its roots in the modern suspense thrillers of Stephen Coonts and Jack Higgins, but Altman takes the espionage activities of World War II as his inspiration.

Keywords: England—World War II

Deaver, Jeffery.

Garden of Beasts. **Simon & Schuster, 2004. 416pp.**

Paul Schumann, a German-American hit man for the New York Mafia, is presented with a choice: either go to prison, or head overseas to assassinate Reinhardt Ernst, the man responsible for helping Hitler rearm Germany. Schumann heads to Berlin and goes undercover as a journalist writing about the 1936 Berlin Olympics. As Schumann stalks Ernst, Hitler's henchmen are out in full force stalking Schumann.

Keywords: Germany—World War II

Deighton, Len.

City of Gold. **HarperCollins, 1992. 375pp.**

As Rommel and his Afrika Corps march toward Cairo (the "City of Gold") in 1942, Bert Cutler, a former police inspector from Glasgow now in the British military, is heading there with prisoner Jimmy Ross, a fellow officer who is about to be tried for murder. When Cutler dies en route to Cairo, Ross takes on his identity.

He also takes on Cutler's other assignment: identifying the spy who has been feeding British secrets to Rommel.

Keywords: Egypt—World War II

Finney, Patricia.

Elizabethan England isn't an unusual setting for historical fiction, but it is for spy thrillers. With their Tudor setting, Finney's thrillers also appeal to mystery and traditional historical novel readers. Though loosely related, the novels can be read in any order. Finney also writes historical mysteries (Chapter 7) as P. F. Chisholm.

Firedrake's Eye. **St. Martin's Press, 1992. 263pp.**

In the year 1583, a conspiracy arises to assassinate the queen, who has been on the throne for twenty-five years. Behind it all may be the mad brother of Tom O'Bedlam, narrator of the tale and would-be foiler of the plot . . . if he can manage to contact the right members of the Elizabethan secret service in time.

Gloriana's Torch. **St. Martin's Press, 2003. 452pp.**

In 1587, the Spanish rely on their secret plan, code-named "Miracle of Beauty," to help them launch the Armada, conquer England, and kill its heretic queen, Elizabeth. David Becket, keeper of the Queen's Ordnance, suspects that a Spanish spy in England is selling gunpowder to the Spaniards, and has terrifying dreams of an alternate reality in which England has come under Spanish control. Meanwhile Becket's friend Simon Ames, an English spy captured by the Inquisition in Lisbon, heads back to England as a galley slave on the Armada. Becket teams up with Ames's wife and a black slave to rescue his friend, but they can only do so if they infiltrate the Armada themselves.

Unicorn's Blood. **Picador USA, 1998. 372pp.**

While Mary Queen of Scots languishes in an English prison at her royal cousin's behest, Queen Elizabeth's diary as a young girl—which names Mary as her heir—may be in the hands of Mary's supporters. It's up to the queen's agents to locate the diary and prove to their mistress that the Catholic monarch deserves to die as a traitor.

Keywords: England—Tudor Era

Fleming, Thomas.
When This Cruel War Is Over. **Forge, 2001. 301pp.**

Annotated in Chapter 5.

Follett, Ken.
Eye of the Needle. **Arbor House, 1978. 313pp.**

When German intelligence discovers that the Allies will be landing in Normandy rather than Calais, British agents must find a way of preventing Die Nadel, a crack German agent, from reaching Hitler before the D-Day invasion can commence.

Keywords: France—World War II

The Key to Rebecca. **Morrow, 1980. 381pp.** ★

Daphne du Maurier's classic novel of romantic suspense holds the key to a code used by one of Rommel's German spies in North Africa during World War II—and it's up to British intelligence to decipher it.

Keywords: Egypt—World War II

Furst, Alan.

Furst's novels are set in Europe prior to or during World War II. His heroes are ordinary people who, in the confusion and political intrigue surrounding the war, become involved in history-changing events—frequently against their better judgment. They can't fully believe in the actions they are forced to take, but they do so because there's no other choice for survival. Furst's scenes call to mind scenes from *Casablanca*: smoke-filled bars, shabby hotels, star-crossed lovers scheduling rendezvous in darkened rooms, and the complexity of military intelligence. While he is a literate writer, his novels are accessible to general readers. All of his novels can stand alone.

Blood of Victory. **Random House, 2002. 237pp.**

Oil is the blood of victory in 1940, as British intelligence makes a second attempt to prevent Romanian oil from reaching its German destination. I. A. Serebin, a Russian journalist living in Paris, gets drawn into the action on the side of the British. The setting here is the Balkans, countries seething with corruption and already destroyed by years of seemingly endless war.

Keywords: Romania, Yugoslavia—World War II

Dark Star. **Houghton Mifflin, 1991. 417pp.**

Polish newspaper correspondent Andre Szara's occasional assignments with the NKVD, a Russian intelligence organization, force him to compromise his journalistic integrity and delve into espionage full-time as war approaches in Europe in 1933.

Keywords: Russia—Twentieth Century

Jean Casson Series. 📖

A duology of novels featuring Jean Casson, a Parisian film producer who becomes a reluctant spy during World War II.

The World at Night. Random House, 1996. 257pp.

Jean Casson starts up his film business again, this time under German auspices. The Germans force him to spy for them against the British, but to save himself, he asks a British agent to bring him into the conflict on the other side. Soon Casson is playing double agent, and though he is determined to avoid political behavior, the more involved he gets, the harder it will be to get out. The complicated intrigue demonstrates how easily a well-intentioned man can get caught up in events beyond his control.

Red Gold. Random House, 1999. 258pp.

Paris, autumn 1941: The real French resistance has begun. Jean Casson, a known enemy to the Gestapo, joins his compatriots in the Parisian underworld. Avoiding Nazi attention is only slightly harder than staying out of the infighting between various factions of the Resistance. Jean's secret romance with a Jewish girl makes his situation even more precarious.

    Keywords: France—World War II

Kingdom of Shadows. **Random House, 2001. 239pp.**

Hungarian expatriate Nicholas Morath, living contentedly in Paris when not making the occasional spy mission to Hungary on behalf of his uncle, is dragged against his will into playing a greater role for the French Resistance during World War II.

    Keywords: France—World War II

Night Soldiers. **Houghton Mifflin, 1988. 437pp.**

In 1934, Khristo Stoianev, a Bulgarian youth, sees his brother murdered by a gang of fascist militia. Vowing to combat fascism, he flees to Russia. There he joins the NKVD, the precursor to the KGB, but the group betrays him during an assignation in Spain during its civil war. Eventually he heads to Paris, where he gathers up enough momentum to fight against his former Communist allies.

    Keywords: Russia—Twentieth Century

The Polish Officer. **Random House, 1995. 325pp.**

Though Poland was partitioned in 1939, a movement against the German invaders continues underground. Captain Alexander de Milja, the Polish officer of the title, changes identities and locales constantly to stay one step ahead of discovery.

    Keywords: Poland—World War II

Griffin, W. E. B.

Men at War Series.

In 1941, President Franklin Roosevelt decides to set up the intelligence organization known as the OSS (Office of Strategic Services), which will be the precursor to the CIA. Between then and 1943, leader "Wild Bill" Donovan and his secret team of agents scatter throughout the world on dangerous missions, such as smuggling uranium ore to be used to develop the atomic bomb.

The Last Heroes. Putnam, 1997. 342pp.

The Secret Warriors. Putnam, 1998. 321pp.

The Soldier Spies. Putnam, 1999. 340pp.

The Fighting Agents. Putnam, 1987. 309pp.

    Keywords: Washington DC; Germany; China; Egypt—World War II

Higgins, Jack.

Eagle Series.

After *The Eagle Has Landed* stood the test of time as a classic World War II thriller, Higgins wrote a sequel—over a decade later.

The Eagle Has Landed. Holt, 1975. 382pp. ★

In 1943, German paratroopers land in the English countryside. Their objective: to kidnap or kill Prime Minister Winston Churchill at his country house in Norfolk. What makes this novel different from most World War II thrillers is that it's told from the Nazi point of view, and a surprisingly human and almost sympathetic one at that. Kurt Steiner, their commander, is on this suicide mission only reluctantly. His efforts are helped on the ground by IRA gunman Liam Devlin, who has been preparing the way for the Germans' arrival. One wrong move, and their cover is blown.

The Eagle Has Flown. Simon & Schuster, 1991. 335pp.

This sequel to *The Eagle Has Landed* picks up at the end of World War II with Liam Devlin, formerly of the IRA. Heinrich Himmler, the head of the German SS, asks Devlin to rescue Kurt Steiner, a POW held by the British in London. What Devlin doesn't know is that Himmler's real plan is to distract them all while he moves in to assassinate Hitler and take over Germany himself.

> **Keywords:** England—World War II

Jakes, John.

On Secret Service. Dutton, 2000. 448pp.

Best known for his <u>North and South</u> trilogy (Chapter 5), Jakes returns to the Civil War period with this novel of espionage, a fast-paced page-turner. Its four protagonists all play a role in the newly formed Secret Service, some unwittingly: Lon Price, an expert in code-cracking; Margaret Miller, Lon's romantic interest and a Rebel spy; Hanna Siegel, an actress who disguises herself as a Union soldier; and Fred Dasher, a U.S. Army major who saves Hanna from possible rape and is demoted as a result. All of the action leads to an inevitable climax: the assassination of President Lincoln at Ford's Theatre in 1865.

> **Keywords:** Washington, DC—Civil War

Kanon, Joseph.

The Good German. Holt, 2001. 496pp. 📖

After *The Prodigal Spy* (1998), set in the 1970s but about the Communist witch hunts of the 1950s, Kanon returned to a slightly earlier period, the postwar era in Berlin. Jake Geismar, a former Berlin news correspondent, returns to Germany to locate his wartime mistress and cover the Potsdam Conference for CBS. When an American soldier is murdered, and nobody will talk about it, Geismar pushes through layers of bureaucratic red tape and Berlin's black market to root out the story.

> **Keywords:** Germany—Twentieth Century

🎗 *Los Alamos*. **Broadway, 1997. 403pp.**

The Manhattan Project, the name given to the secret scientific mission that resulted in the first atomic bomb, took place in Los Alamos, New Mexico, during World War II. Naturally, this is a ripe subject for any writer of spy novels. Michael Connelly, an intelligence officer for the U.S. Army, looks into the death of a security guard in a Santa Fe park. In determining whether the event poses any security risks for the Feds, he turns up evidence of espionage that leads to the highest of the high, J. Robert Oppenheimer himself. Edgar Award.

        Keywords: New Mexico—World War II

King, Benjamin.

The Loki Project. **Pelican, 2000. 352pp.**

This scientific espionage thriller covers the Nazis' failed attempt to develop the atomic bomb, despite its early development by German scientist Otto Hahn in 1938. Dr. Maximilian Lamm, professor of physics, takes up Hahn's lead in the years of World War II, though the Allies and Resistance are on to him.

        Keywords: Germany—World War II

Littell, Robert.

The Company. **Overlook, 2001. 894pp.**

When it comes to official spy organizations, the U.S. Central Intelligence Agency tops the list. This doorstop of a novel is nothing less than the fictionalized epic history of the CIA, or the Company, from Berlin in the postwar years until the present day. From the point of view of three CIA agents and their KGB counterpart, we are taken from the end of World War II through the Cold War and after. An early showdown with Afghanistan gains new meaning in light of events of the early twenty-first century.

        Keywords: Germany—Twentieth Century

Silva, Daniel.

The Unlikely Spy. **Villard, 1996. 481pp.**

At the height of World War II, Professor Alfred Vicary is recruited by MI5, Britain's elite Secret Service, to foil a plot by German intelligence to prevent the Allies' D-Day invasion. Operating undercover in London is German spy Catherine Blake, a ruthless killer who plans to gain information by seducing an American scientist with knowledge of the D-Day project.

        Keywords: Germany—World War II

Skinner, Richard.

The Red Dancer. **Ecco, 2002. 263pp.** ✍

A gorgeous sepia-tinted photo of the most notorious female spy of them all—Mata Hari, born Margaretha Zelle—graces the cover of Skinner's novel. This fictionalized follows her life from her marriage to a Dutch captain, to her sojourn in Europe as an exotic dancer, to her recruitment as a German agent, and finally to her execution by a French firing squad in 1917. Despite the intrigue that continues to surround her, Margaretha (Gerda) is shown primarily from the point of view of people who knew her and from newspaper clips reproduced in the book. Her own narrative is equally mysterious.

Keywords: Germany—World War I

Thayer, James Stewart.

Five Past Midnight. **Simon & Schuster, 1997. 352pp.**

In the declining days of World War II, lone assassin Jack Cray is given the ultimate mission: He is sent by President Roosevelt to find and kill Hitler, who is hiding out in a German bunker. The evil Nazis are clichéd caricatures, and Cray's heroic efforts make the whole thing seem almost too easy. But when the action finally ends at the ruins of Hitler's bunker, as it did in history, readers may find themselves wondering whether it really could have happened this way.

Keywords: Germany—World War II

Topping, Seymour.

The Peking Letter. **Perseus, 1999. 300pp.**

In 1948–1949, as Nationalist China is on the verge of falling to Mao Tse-tung's Communist forces, American Eric Jensen, a scholar of the Taoist religion, decides to remain in the country he has grown to love. However, it's difficult for him to remain apolitical, particularly when the CIA comes recruiting people willing to participate in a secret diplomatic mission between the United States and the Communists. He is also approached by the Communists and agrees to help them out because of his love for Lillian Yang, a student and Communist radical.

Keywords: China—Twentieth Century

Volpi, Jorge.

In Search of Klingsor. **Scribner, 2002. 414pp.**

After World War II, physicist Francis Bacon is assigned to discover the true identity of "Klingsor," the unknown man who advised Hitler on the development of the first atomic bomb. Bacon's search leads him into the dark heart of postwar Germany and a relationship with a beautiful, mysterious woman.

Keywords: Germany—World War II

Wilson, Robert.

The Company of Strangers. **Harcourt, 2001. 480pp.**

One of the few female spies of World War II espionage fiction, Wilson's heroine Andrea Aspinalt is a mathematical genius working for the British in Portugal.

When her cover is blown, she reinvents herself and blends in with the local populace, only to pick up the spy's life years later—but this time her role is more pivotal and more dangerous.

Keywords: Portugal—World War II

Chapter 10

Literary Historical Novels

Literary historical novels use historical settings, eloquent language, and multi-layered plotlines to convey contemporary themes. Librarians and readers may not think of literary fiction as a type of genre fiction, but for readers' advisory purposes, it helps to group them together in this way. Together, these novels form one of the fastest-growing and most popular subgenres of historical fiction. These days, more and more literary novelists are looking back to the past for inspiration, and are doing so with great success.

The use of language is important to readers of literary historicals, and the writing style used in these novels can be described as elegant, poetic, or lyrical. While some literary novelists choose to tell their story in a straightforward fashion, others use a more experimental style, making use of flashbacks, stories-within-stories, and multiple narrative viewpoints. Dialogue can be equally creative. Some authors choose not to enclose their characters' words in quotation marks so that they flow more fully into the story.

These critically acclaimed works are reviewed in major newspapers, and they often win literary prizes. Because they address serious issues, their focus may be darker than most, and they may not have an optimistic ending. Their authors tend to incorporate unique settings, ones not often used by traditional historical novels. The novels themselves are character- rather than plot-driven, and although they tend not to be quick reads, the intriguing, complex characters and multi-layered plots have a way of drawing readers into the story.

In addition to providing a detailed portrait of life during earlier times, authors of literary historical fiction use the past as a vehicle to express a universal or modern theme. Their characters somehow manage to transcend time and speak to us from their own perspective in a way that we, today, can understand. However, despite the assiduous historical research that the authors conduct, their novels are as apt to be labeled "contemporary fiction" as they are "historical fiction." This apparent paradox is due to their emphasis on seemingly timeless subjects. Similarly, with a few notable exceptions like Tracy Chevalier and Beryl Bainbridge, the authors in this chapter are not commonly thought of as historical novelists. Not only are they not tied to a particular historical period, but few of their novels occur in series, and many also write works of fiction set in the present day. Not only will literary historicals appeal to historical fiction fans, but they also have the ability to reach a wide, mainstream audience.

The word "literary" tends to scare off genre fiction readers, but people shouldn't assume that these novels are inaccessible. They can run the gamut from dense, challenging tomes (Umberto Eco) to gentle, uncomplicated reads that are nonetheless beautifully written (Gail Tsukiyama). Most fall somewhere in between. Readers' advisors should also be aware that "literary" refers to a writing style rather than any indication of quality, and that a book's placement in this chapter doesn't necessarily denote a higher quality novel than those found in other chapters. Because literary historicals are thought-provoking works whose ideas can be explored on many levels, they make good choices for reading groups.

Due to the number of literary historical novels currently being published, this is a fairly long chapter. Besides the novels annotated below, readers of literary historicals may appreciate literary thrillers (Chapter 9). Some books found in other chapters, especially Chapter 5 (sagas) and Chapter 7 (Western historical novels), qualify as literary and are tagged with the word **Literary** in bold at the end of the annotation.

Readers who enjoy literary historicals may appreciate some titles from other subgenres that are tagged as appropriate for reading groups ⌺, as they provide thoughtful explorations of historical times. Finally, as described in this book's introduction, many classic or benchmark novels in other chapters, denoted by ★, have cross-genre appeal and may interest readers of literary historical fiction as well.

Biblical

Literary novels with biblical themes tend to be controversial, for they often interpret the lives of characters from the Bible in new and frequently unorthodox ways—especially where their sexuality is concerned. Readers interested in biblical fiction from an evangelical Christian point of view should consult Chapter 11; biblical settings also appear in traditional historical novels (Chapter 2).

Coelho, Paulo.

The Fifth Mountain. HarperFlamingo, 1998. 245pp. ✍

In the ninth century BC, the biblical prophet Elijah confronts and triumphs over challenges to his faith. Having escaped the results of Queen Jezebel's proclamation that non-followers of the pagan god Baal be slaughtered, Elijah finds peace and love in a faraway village. When his contentment is destroyed, he searches within himself for the God-given faith to carry on.

Crace, Jim.

Quarantine. Farrar, Straus & Giroux, 1998. 256pp. ✍

Jesus Christ's forty days of fasting (the "quarantine") in the wilderness becomes an almost hallucinogenic journey. Arriving in the desert with four others, Jesus soon goes off on his own, causing others to confirm their opinions of his eccentricity. Miracles begin to happen as sick people whom he's touched get well. In

the meantime, his body empty of food, Jesus begins to imagine that his companions are spirits sent by the Devil to tempt him.

Diamant, Anita.

The Red Tent. St. Martin's Press, 1997. 321pp. ✍ ★ 📖

The red tent is the haven where women must seclude themselves during menstruation and childbirth. In this novel of Dinah from the Bible, the tent also symbolizes the feminine spirit. The only daughter of Jacob, Dinah grows up with four mothers: Leah, her natural mother, plus Jacob's other wives: Rachel, Zilpah, and Bilhah. Dinah's life story takes a female spin on well-known biblical events, such as Jacob's lengthy courtship of Rachel and the rise to glory of Dinah's half-brother Joseph. Dinah is mentioned in the Bible primarily in the context of her rape and subsequent rescue by her brothers. Here, her relationship with a Canaanite man is a forbidden romance that her brothers destroy with one vengeful act. Other novels of women's lives in biblical times appear in Chapters 2 and 11. Book Sense Book of the Year.

Diski, Jenny.

Only Human. Picador USA, 2001. 215pp. ✍

God in Heaven, realizing that his previous two vessels (Adam and Noah) were both unworthy of him, makes another attempt in Abram. However, Abram's heart is already full, with love of his wife Sarai and their growing family. This oddly comedic love triangle is narrated partly by God (full of grumblings over his creations' refusal to acknowledge his omnipotence) and partly by an outside narrator, who understands Sarai's difficulty in living with a man forced to choose between earthly and divine love.

Fredriksson, Marianne.

According to Mary Magdalene. Hampton Roads, 1999. 235pp. (Original title: *According to Mary*.) ✍

The infamous Mary Magdalene, frustrated because Peter and Paul don't want to hear what really happened between her and Jesus, decides to record her own story for posterity. Orphaned at a young age, the Jewish Mary grows up in a discreet pleasure-house, becoming Jesus's lover and teaching him about the wise ways of women.

Kazantzakis, Nikos.

The Last Temptation of Christ. Simon & Schuster, 1960. 506pp. ✍ ★

Controversial even before Martin Scorsese turned it into a movie, this novel focuses on Christ as a human being: his internal struggles to fulfill the prophecy of his birth, his desire to ignore the voice of God, his sexuality, and his humanity. All combine to make the final acceptance of his death all the more tragic. Though not as irreverent as the media would have people believe, evangelical readers will probably still be offended by it.

Mailer, Norman.

The Gospel According to the Son. **Random House, 1997. 242pp.** ✍

Critical of the Gospels' versions of his life, Jesus Christ decides to set the record straight by narrating his own version. Though this makes the novel sound disrespectful, it wasn't the author's intent. Instead, it serves mainly as a way of making Jesus and his actions more understandable and human. Mailer is less successful at depicting Christ's divinity, but on the whole the novel has a realistic feel, conveyed well by the author's rendering of biblical prose.

Ricci, Nino.

Testament. **Houghton Mifflin, 2003. 464pp.** ✍

Four different views of the historical life of Jesus are shown through the eyes of four characters: Judas, Miryam of Migdal, Jesus's mother Miryam (whose rape by a Roman soldier resulted in his birth), and Simon of Gergesa, a fictional shepherd. There are no miracles here, which is sure to provoke controversy, but Jesus's humility and humanity are sensitively portrayed.

Other Ancient Civilizations

Egypt

The setting for these novels is ancient Egypt, but the tone is decidedly modern. The authors often make wry observations on Egyptian religion, social life, the monarchs' style of ruling, and their habit of marrying close relatives.

Mahfouz, Naguib.

Akhenaten: Dweller in Truth. **American University in Cairo Press, 1999. 180pp.**

It's the fourteenth century BC, and the controversial heretic Pharaoh Akhenaten has just died. Meriamum, a young boy, is given free rein to interview Akhenaten's friends and family, including his alluring wife Nefertiti, to discover why his monarch abandoned the Egyptian gods to follow a monotheistic religion. The more people Meriamum speaks to, the more enigmatic Akhenaten becomes, for each of his subjects has a different impression of what made him tick.

Sprott, Duncan.

The Ptolemies. **Knopf, 2004. 496pp.** ✍

In this retelling, Ptolemy Soter, the first Greek king of Egypt, is the illegitimate son of Philip of Macedon and the half-brother of Alexander the Great. During his reign in the fourth century BC, Ptolemy deals with the constant battles between satraps (governors) of other territories, but he and his descendants manage to hold the Egyptian throne for 300 years. Thoth, scribe and Egyptian god of wisdom, narrates the tale with formality and authority.

West, Paul.

Cheops: A Cupboard for the Sun. **New Directions, 2002. 261pp.** ✍

> The pharaoh Cheops, best known for building the ancient pyramids of Giza circa 2680 BC, meets one of his chief critics, the Greek historian Herodotus, who has been transported back in time to harangue him in person about his notorious wicked deeds. Cheops's final days are narrated by a variety of sarcastic personalities, including the god Osiris, Cheops's daughter, and the pharaoh himself.

Greece

Most literary novels of ancient Greece retell ancient myths with a modern sensibility. This creates obvious parallels between then and now.

Bauchau, Henry.

Oedipus on the Road. **Arcade, 1997. 248pp.**

> After Oedipus has killed his father, married his mother, and put his own eyes out (which summarizes the plot of Sophocles's Greek tragedy), he wanders alone, a blind beggar on his way to Athens. During this contemplative journey, Oedipus learns humility and the power of forgiveness. By the time he reaches the city, he is a changed man with new insight into his past actions.

Cook, Elizabeth.

Achilles. **Picador, 2002. 128pp.**

> Achilles was one of Homer's tragic heroes in the *Iliad*, and poet Cook retells his story in this creative work, told in the form of a tale from long ago. The product of a liaison between a mortal king and a sea nymph, Achilles grows up with great promise and protection, though his famous heel leaves him extremely vulnerable. Only he can win the Trojan War for the Greeks, but he does so at the loss of his own life.

Norfolk, Lawrence.

In the Shape of a Boar. **Grove Press, 2001. 336pp.**

> The first half of this novel takes place in ancient Greece, where warriors hunt the Boar of Kalydon, sent to earth by the goddess Artemis as revenge for a past deed. A romantic triangle develops among Atalanta, the greatest huntress of her era, and two of the other hunters. This portion of the story is laced with lengthy footnotes, which are explained in the second half, when the time period shifts to 1930s Romania and to Greece during World War II. It's only then that the secret behind the boar's existence is revealed.

Unsworth, Barry.

The Songs of the Kings. **Doubleday, 2003. 305pp.** 📖

> Unsworth's novel can be read on two levels. The first is a slightly modernized retelling of the Trojan War, as the Greek fleet—including King

Agamemnon, Achilles, Odysseus, and their crew—are prevented from setting forth to Troy because of unfavorable winds. Zeus's wrath can only be overcome, say the king's advisors, by the sacrifice of his beloved daughter Iphigeneia. The second level has a more contemporary theme: how a group of greedy, power-hungry men can use the excuse of war to achieve their own personal ends.

Vidal, Gore.

Creation. **Random House, 1981. 510pp. Restored edition, Doubleday, 2002. 574pp.**

During the fifth century BC, Cyrus Spitama, a fictional grandson of the great prophet Zoroaster, mingles with great men as he travels far and wide on behalf of his master and great friend, Xerxes of Persia. His encounters with the Buddha, Confucius, Pericles, Socrates, and Lao-Tse teach him about the birth of modern ideas and the path to power. The restored edition includes new material from the original manuscript, such as details on politics of the ancient world and lineages of the Persian kings.

Warner, Marina.

The Leto Bundle. **Farrar, Straus & Giroux, 2002. 416pp.**

A curator at the modern-day Museum of Albion unveils a new acquisition, a female mummy, which comes complete with documents identifying the unknown woman as Leto. The story then switches to Leto herself, a young woman living in the ancient Near East, and her wanderings across Europe with her twin children, a girl and a boy. Leto and her daughter Phoebe turn up in various places across Europe in different eras, always wandering and searching for Leto's son, who was lost in a siege long before.

The Roman Empire

New interpretations of famous figures from Roman times: Ovid, Julius Caesar, the Emperor Hadrian. In other novels, the authors meditate on the reason behind the Roman Empire's decline in the fifth century AD.

Alison, Jane.

The Love-Artist. **Farrar, Straus & Giroux, 2001. 242pp.** ✍

"Two offenses ruined me: a poem and an error," wrote the famed poet Ovid, notorious in ancient Rome for his composition of the erotic *Art of Love*. In history, Ovid was exiled to the Black Sea outpost of Tomis in the first century AD for reasons that have not yet been discovered. Alison's solution to the mystery involves Xenia, a witch and mystic from the far reaches of the empire who becomes Ovid's tragic muse. The atmosphere is dark, eerie, and electrically charged.

De Carvalho, Mario.

A God Strolling in the Cool of the Evening. **Louisiana State University Press, 1997. 265pp.**

Portuguese writer de Carvalho looks at his native land of nearly two millennia ago in this fictional memoir. Lucius Valerius Quincius is ruler of the Roman outpost of Tarcisis, a city on the Iberian Peninsula, but finds its inhabitants more

concerned with day-to-day amusements—such as the persecution of early Christians—than the real possibility of a Moorish invasion. He finds he has to deal with the problem of the Christians sooner rather than later, and his love for Iunia Cantaber, their strong female leader, complicates matters.

Evaristo, Bernardine.
The Emperor's Babe. **Viking, 2002. 272pp.**

Zuleika, a hip, wisecracking Sudanese woman in Londinium of AD 211, is married off at the age of eleven to Lucius Aurelius Felix, a fat Roman senator three times her age. Though happy with her new social status, she's sexually frustrated and bored. When Felix is away on a business trip, she takes up with a new conquest, Septimus Severus, who just happens to be the emperor of Rome, on one of his visits to Britannia. Her story is cleverly told in jaunty free verse.

Haasse, Hella.
Threshold of Fire. **Academy Chicago, 1993. 255pp. (Originally published in 1964 in the Netherlands.)**

In fifth-century Rome, Christianity is the dominant religion, and the pagans —formerly at the forefront of Roman life—are being persecuted. In this clash of cultures and religions during the last years of the empire, the Emperor Hadrian must decide the fate of a man brought to trial for conducting pagan practices. What complicates things is the man's familiarity, for he was once the court poet Claudius Claudianus, who secretly remained in the city after being sentenced to exile years ago.

Panella, Vincent.
Cutter's Island: Caesar in Captivity. **Academy Chicago, 2000. 192pp.** ✍ 📖

At age twenty-five, as is recorded in history, pirates captured Julius Caesar while on his way to study rhetoric on the island of Rhodes. He was held prisoner for nearly forty days. Here, Caesar's encounter with the pirate king Cutter is a character-developing experience, as he finds to his surprise that his forced captivity gives him the needed chance to hone his tactical skills.

Pears, Iain.
The Dream of Scipio. **Riverhead, 2002. 608pp.** 📖

Similar dramas unfold in three different historical periods: the fall of Rome in the fifth century AD, the Black Death in the fourteenth, and World War II in the twentieth. Stories from all three eras intertwine, becoming part of a greater whole. All are set in Provence and have the underlying themes of romantic love, the end of a civilization, and the persecution of one people (the Jews) by another. Connecting the tales together is a neo-Platonic treatise, "The Dream of Scipio," written by

Manlius Hippomanes, the earliest protagonist, and translated and studied by his counterparts in future centuries.

Vidal, Gore.

Julian. **Little, Brown, 1964. 503pp.** ★ ✍

As a youth, Julian Augustus shows incredible military and intellectual ability, promising to become a successful Roman emperor one day. When that day comes, in AD 361, he throws off the yoke of Christianity, which his uncle Constantine the Great had introduced as the official religion, and attempts to restore Rome to worship of its original pagan gods. A fascinating figure, Julian the Apostate—philosopher, scholar, and military genius—was murdered at the age of thirty-two, after reigning for only four years.

Yourcenar, Marguerite.

Memoirs of Hadrian. **Farrar, Straus & Young, 1954. 313pp.** ★ ✍

Hadrian, Emperor of Rome in the second century AD, recounts his life story in the form of letters to his adopted grandson, who later became the Emperor Marcus Aurelius. His eloquent correspondence, as he contemplates the state of the empire during his reign and after he's gone, shows him to be a man of intelligence and strength.

The British Isles

The Middle Ages

These three novels are very different in tone: one heroic and glorious, one bawdy and colorful, and the last grim and realistic. This demonstrates the variety present in literary fiction. All are set in Britain's medieval period, the fifth through fifteenth centuries AD.

Mayse, Susan.

Awen: A Novel of Early Medieval Wales. **Eastern Washington University Press, 1997. 416pp.**

Brys, a disgraced court poet and soldier in eighth-century Powys, sifts his way through political intrigue to unite warring Welsh kingdoms against the Anglian kingdom of Mercia. The ultimate romantic hero, not unlike Dorothy Dunnett's Lymond, Brys survives assassination attempts and numerous battles—and loves women (one in particular) with equal intensity. Somewhat of a sleeper among medieval fiction enthusiasts, *Awen* should appeal to Sharon Kay Penman fans, though its poetic phrasings and densely packed language make it more challenging.

Nye, Robert.

Falstaff. **Arcade, 2001. 464pp. (First published in Britain in 1976.)**

One of Shakespeare's most memorable creations, Sir John Falstaff narrates his memoirs in an irascible, bawdy voice that gives life to both him and his era. The

entire story of the Bard's *Henry IV* is played out to a slightly different tune, as Falstaff gives his own sly interpretations of what really happened during his lengthy life, from the Battle of Agincourt to his own bedroom adventures.

Warner, Sylvia Townsend.

The Corner That Held Them. **Viking, 1948. 367pp.** ★

Between 1349 and 1382, life at the convent of Oby in the Norfolk fenlands proceeds as usual. Though the Benedictine nuns are thought by many to live a quiet life of prayer and contemplation, reality tends to include more worldly concerns, such as jealousy between the women, the struggles to keep vows, and the outbreak of the Black Death. Though this novel is anything but action-oriented, it takes a realistic view of the day-to-day activities among religious communities in the Middle Ages.

The Tudor Era

The Elizabethan period (1558–1603) takes center stage here, and the plots revolve around both the theatrical world and the royal court.

Burgess, Anthony.

A Dead Man in Deptford. **Carroll & Graf, 1995. 272pp.** ✍

Kit Marlowe—brilliant actor, creative playwright, boisterous drunk, atheist, homosexual, and, here, Elizabethan spy—lives dangerously and well, until political intrigues work to bring him down. Stabbed to death in a barroom brawl in Deptford, the true reasons for Marlowe's unfortunate demise are kept hidden. In the last novel written before his death, Burgess re-creates the Tudor underground with aplomb.

Cowell, Stephanie.

Nicholas Cooke: Actor, Soldier, Physician, Priest. **W. W. Norton, 1993. 442pp.**

Fleeing to London after escaping a brutal master in his home city of Cambridge, young Nicholas Cooke begins a journey of self-discovery and professional fulfillment, hobnobbing with the best-known literary figures of the day. *The Physician of London*, its sequel, is annotated in the next section.

The Players. **W. W. Norton, 1997. 252pp.** ✍

Before William Shakespeare was a renowned playwright, he was a glove-maker's son from Stratford. Shakespeare travels to London in search of knowledge and fortune and to escape an unhappy marriage. A sensual young man, his passions lead him to literary immortality as well as into a hopeless love triangle with two unlikely figures: Emilia Bassano, an Italian musician who becomes his "dark lady," and Henry Wriothesley, the Earl of Southampton, the patron for whom he conceives a strong affection.

Garrett, George.

Elizabethan Trilogy. ✎ ★

The poet laureate of Virginia, Garrett's best known works are those comprising his loose trilogy about Elizabethan England, thought by some to be the most imaginative historical re-creations in literature. They are challenging reads to the newcomer, for their plotlines aren't linear, but Garrett's research is impeccable and his prose wonderfully descriptive. The books can be read in any order.

Death of the Fox. Doubleday, 1971. 739pp.

There's political intrigue aplenty as Sir Walter Raleigh, explorer and courtier in Tudor England, meditates on the adventuresome life he led as Queen Elizabeth's captain before his downfall and execution by Elizabeth's successor, King James I.

Entered from the Sun. Doubleday, 1990. 349pp.

The murder of Christopher Marlowe—playwright, actor, and contemporary of Shakespeare—in a tavern brawl in Deptford is presented from the point of view of several witnesses who may also be participants.

The Succession. Doubleday, 1983. 583pp.

In 1603, as Elizabeth I's' reign comes to an end, the succession is still uncertain. Will she choose her distant cousin James VI of Scotland, son of one of her greatest enemies, to follow her? The story of both personalities is told through their own thoughts as well as those of other political leaders of the time, from James's birth in 1566 until Elizabeth's own death in 1603.

Nye, Robert.

Nye's bawdy novels, light and dryly humorous, poke fun at what we think we know about beloved historical figures from Elizabethan times and earlier, yet they're written in language that feels authentic to their time. No stuffy tomes, these.

The Late Mr. Shakespeare. **Arcade, 1998. 398pp.** ✎

In this whimsical fictional biography, a former child actor named Pickleherring recounts his memories of the Bard, making sure to include every possible tidbit of gossip imaginable about his life.

Mrs. Shakespeare: The Complete Works. **Arcade, 1993. 216pp.** ✎

After her husband's death, Anne Shakespeare receives a journal from her daughter Susanna. In it, Anne reveals the truth about her life with the Bard (whose writings she never bothered to read) and the secret about the "second best bed," an intriguing item left to her in his will.

The Voyage of the Destiny. **Putnam, 1982. 387pp.** ✎

Sir Walter Raleigh—courtier, explorer, and supposed lover of Queen Elizabeth—narrates this vicarious tale of his life both in England and at sea via a journal begun in 1616, when he was released from the Tower of London by King James I.

The Stuart Era

These novels deal with the reality of day-to-day life in Stuart England, both at the royal court in London and in outlying areas. Some, specifically those set during the Restoration Period (post-1660) can be fairly ribald. Others set during the English Civil War and Cromwell's Protectorate (1642–1660) can be violent and grim; the same holds true for novels about the bubonic plague and the Great Fire of 1666.

Brooks, Geraldine.
Year of Wonders. **Viking, 2001. 308pp.** 📖

In 1666, the year the bubonic plague revisited England, the small village of Eyam in Derbyshire did the unthinkable—they closed off all access from outside until the disease had run its course. How the townspeople came to this decision is described by Anna Frith, a young widow with a talent for nursing. Despite the improbable ending, Brooks ably re-creates a true historical situation that brought out both the worst and the very best in humanity.

Cowell, Stephanie.
🎗 *The Physician of London.* **W. W. Norton, 1995. 413pp.**

Nicholas Cooke, now a middle-aged man in Stuart England, has achieved his ambition to become a priest and physician. He befriends Thomas Wentworth, a politically astute Yorkshire landowner, and vies with him for the love of Cecelia, a young bluestocking. As in the first part of the trilogy, *Nicholas Cooke* (previous section), Cowell vividly imagines the realities of late sixteenth- and early seventeenth-century England. The third part of the trilogy about Nicholas Cooke has not yet appeared. American Book Award.

George, Sara.
The Journal of Mrs. Pepys. **St. Martin's Press, 1999. 352pp.** 📖 ✍

Elizabeth Pepys begins this account of her life just after her marriage to Samuel, a tally clerk at the Exchequer in London, at age fifteen. Through her eyes, we get a chance to view not only the famed diariest Samuel Pepys but also the events he described in his journal—retold from a woman's point of view.

McCann, Maria.
As Meat Loves Salt. **Harvest, 2003. 584pp.**

Jacob Cullen, a troubled man who can't overcome his tendencies toward violence, is a perfect fit for Cromwell's New Model Army during the English Civil War. A murderer when the novel begins, his other crimes soon include rape and desertion as he follows the compelling (and secretly homosexual) Christopher Ferris home to London. Vividly depicting the colorful background and social problems of late seventeenth-century England, this disturbing tale is not for the faint of heart (or stomach).

Mount, Ferdinand.

Jem (and Sam). **Carroll & Graf, 1999. 425pp.** ✍

As a spoof of Samuel Pepys's famous diaries of Restoration England, this novel is remarkably funny. Jeremiah (Jem) Mount, the author's supposed sixth great-grandfather, has a knack for being at the right place at the right time. That is, until he meets and befriends Samuel Pepys. Jem watches jealously as Sam's career advances and his romantic pursuits succeed, especially after seeing that Sam makes far too little mention of Jem in his journal.

Settle, Mary Lee.

I, Roger Williams. **W. W. Norton, 2001. 312pp.** ✍

Before Roger Williams founded Providence, Rhode Island, he was an active participant in Jacobean politics, when the English Civil War was just on the horizon. Born around 1603, Williams becomes a clerk for jurist Sir Edward Coke and learns his radical political beliefs (separation of church and state) at Coke's knee. Most of the book, which Williams narrates as an elderly man using formal language, takes place in England. In the last few chapters he tells of his flight with his wife to New England, their banishment from the Massachusetts Bay Colony, and his years of hardship and exile with the Narragansett Indians.

Tremain, Rose.

Restoration. **Viking, 1990. 371pp.** 📖

The title refers not only to the restoration of Charles II to England's throne in 1660 but also to that of the title character, Robert Merivel, to his estate after a physical and emotional journey away. Merivel, who narrates, is a flawed and rather foppish character, a physician who leaves his noble profession to take charge of the royal dogs. Merivel garners the king's favor and is granted permission to marry one of Charles II's mistresses, but he loses favor just as easily by falling in love with her.

West, Paul.

A Fifth of November. **New Directions, 2001. 340pp.** ✍

West goes back to the original history behind Guy Fawkes Day—November 5, 1605, the day the English Gunpowder Plot was foiled. A group of Catholics who conspired to blow up Parliament, and with it King James I, confess the plan to Father Henry Garnet, fugitive head of the Jesuits, who wonders to whom his loyalties should belong. Garnet himself is protected by a Catholic noblewoman, Anne Vaux, whose presence serves as both his security and a reminder of his situation.

The Georgian Era

A grim, often shocking undercurrent appears beneath the surface of Georgian society (1714–1837). Some of these authors offer new interpretations of well-known literary figures and stories about the era.

Andahazi, Federico.

The Merciful Women. Grove, 2000. 192pp. ✍

On a dark and stormy night in 1816, Lord Byron, Percy Shelley, Mary Shelley, Mary's stepsister, and Byron's servant John Polidori pass the time in their Swiss villa. They engage in a contest to determine who can write the best Gothic novel. An unexpected contribution comes from Polidori, who (unbeknownst to them) has made a devil's bargain with a mysterious woman.

Bainbridge, Beryl.

According to Queeney. Carroll & Graf, 2001. 242pp. ✍ 📖

Young Hester Thrale, known as Queeney, sharply observes her mother's unusual romantic relationship with literary genius and lexicographer Samuel Johnson in the late eighteenth century. Bainbridge takes us behind closed doors into the dark side of the literary and social atmosphere of Georgian London. In its observations of mental instability and sexual obsession, the novel serves as an ironic counterpoint to the renowned biography of Johnson by James Boswell, his friend and admirer.

Carey, Peter.

Jack Maggs. Knopf, 1997. 306pp.

Carey turns Dickens's *Great Expectations* on its head in this retelling from the point of view of the villainous thief, Magwitch, who was deported to Australia. In London of the 1830s, Jack Maggs, now a gentleman, returns from Down Under incognito and finds himself embroiled in yet more controversy. The novel wryly pokes fun at Dickens's masterpiece while paying homage to the masterful language of the original.

Donoghue, Emma.

Life Mask. Harcourt, 2004. 650pp. ✍

It is the end of the eighteenth century, a time when revolutions and financial disasters grip the world. Eliza Farren, the reigning actress at London's Drury Lane Theatre, forms an unlikely love triangle with two leading figures of the day: the Earl of Derby, an unhappily married member of the House of Lords, and Anne Damer, a wealthy widow, talented sculptor, and supposed lesbian. All three live in the public eye, and none reveals his or her feelings for the world to see.

Slammerkin. Harcourt, 2000. 336pp. ✍ 📖

The title is eighteenth-century British slang for a loose dress or a loose woman, both of which fit Mary Saunders (a historical character), a young woman in 1760s London whose yearnings for beautiful clothing cause her downfall. For a time she rises above her station to become a seamstress, but she eventually turns back to prostitution. In her desire for a better life, Mary is cheeky yet endearing, so much so that one can't help but root for her even when her own poor choices lead her toward a sad end.

Griffin, Nicholas.

The House of Sight and Shadow. **Villard, 2001. 288pp.**

Dr. Joseph Bendix, a former medical student in Paris, arrives in London in the late eighteenth century to continue his studies with Sir Edmund Calcraft, a surgeon who believes in forbidden practices such as the dissection of the dead and other, even more immoral, activities. While the two become more involved in London's criminal underworld, Bendix falls in love with Calcraft's reclusive daughter, Amelia, who suffers from afflictions of her own.

Holman, Sheri.

The Dress Lodger. **Atlantic Monthly, 2000. 291pp.** 📖

In Sunderland, England, during the Industrial Revolution of the 1830s, young Gustine is the "dress lodger" of the title—a prostitute who wears an elegant blue dress to attract wealthy patrons. She allies herself with a doctor of dubious reputation, Henry Chiver, in the hopes that he might help her son, who was born with his heart on the outside of his body. In return, Gustine agrees to help the doctor procure bodies for his gruesome experiments. Dark, atmospheric, and shocking.

Hughes, Glyn.

Brontë. **St. Martin's Press, 1996. 432pp.** ✎

In the early decades of the nineteenth century, the Brontë siblings of Haworth in Yorkshire suffered unbelievable tragedy with the deaths of their mother and two of their older sisters. The author dramatically re-creates the lives of the remaining children, sisters Charlotte, Emily, and Anne and their brother Branwell, with greater insight into their romantic imaginations than their literary works.

Motion, Andrew.

Wainewright the Poisoner. **Knopf, 2001. 276pp.** ✎

Novel or biography? Critics differ on their categorization of this work, the purported confession of Thomas Griffiths Wainewright, a Regency-era literary figure and dandy who also happened to be a thief, forger, and probable murderer. Wainewright's unreliable narrative voice is given credence, and sometimes is contradicted, by footnotes, essays, and other commentary supplied by the author. Using this form, Motion (a noted biographer) manages to portray the charming yet cruel personality of his subject more cannily than he could have done in a straight biography.

Sherwood, Frances.

Vindication. **Farrar, Straus & Giroux, 1993. 435pp.** 📖 ✎

Mary Wollstonecraft, thought of as perhaps the first feminist because of the publication of her *Vindication of the Rights of Women* in 1792, ironically died just as her writing career came to fruition. Her life is re-created in painstaking detail, from her observations of the terror that raged through Paris during the Revolution, to the brutal realities of life for eighteenth-century women, to her intellectual development through friendships with Thomas Paine and William Blake.

Unsworth, Barry.

🏵 *Sacred Hunger.* **Doubleday, 1992. 629pp. ★ 📖**

The "sacred hunger" is imperialist greed, as practiced by a British slaver ship en route from Liverpool in the eighteenth century to the African coast and then to faraway Florida. William Kemp hopes to restore his declining fortunes by overseeing a ship sailing in the slave trade, and his son Erasmus seeks to keep his father's empire afloat. His nephew Matthew Paris, a physician, desires a more ideal world—one in which men don't treat other human beings as chattel—but finds it nowhere. Booker Prize.

White, Edmund.

Fanny. **Ecco, 2003. 384pp.** ✍

Mrs. Frances Trollope, a middle-aged nineteenth-century Englishwoman best known for her harsh critiques of American manners, decides to write a book about her overseas adventures. The story then shifts to the 1820s, when Frances first encountered proto-feminist and abolitionist Fanny Wright. Fanny's energy and determination convince Frances to follow her to America and form a utopian community in Tennessee, which is doomed to failure. Frances's narrative voice is caustic and amusing.

The Victorian Era

These novels of life in Victorian times (1837–1901) recount events and ways of life kept hidden from proper Victorian society: poverty, abuse, homosexuality, and secret love affairs. In this sense they are very modern novels, despite being well researched and written in language appropriate to the time.

Boylan, Clare.

Emma Brown. **Viking, 2004. 435pp.**

At her death in 1855, Charlotte Brontë left behind an incomplete manuscript about a Victorian waif named Matilda, abandoned at a girls' boarding school. Boylan completed her project, recounting a tale of mystery and social conflict in Victorian society. The man who dropped Matilda off fails to pay her tuition, so Isabel Chalfont, a widow, takes her in and cares for her. At first she remembers little of her past, but Matilda soon learns her true identity—Emma Brown—and runs away. Mrs. Chalfont searches for her on London's streets while Emma searches for the mother who sold her.

Byatt, A. S.

🏵 *Possession: A Romance.* **Random House, 1990. 555pp. ★ 📖**

Roland Michell and Maud Bailey are two modern British academics, scholars of Victorian literature. Their interests intersect in the discovery of correspondence found between one of Maud's distant relatives, nineteenth-century feminist poet Christabel LaMotte, and Randolph Henry Ash, a much more famous author of the same era. Were they conducting a secret affair? As Maud and Roland sift through hundred-year-old letters and stumble upon literary clues, they draw continually closer to the truth—and to each other as well. Booker Prize.

Ewing, Barbara.
The Trespass. St. Martin's Press, 2002. 401pp.

Cholera is rampant in 1849 London, so Sir Charles Cooper sends his daughter Harriet to visit cousins in the countryside. Her sister Mary remains with her father. When Harriet returns, her father's abusive actions make it clear that she must escape as soon as possible. Harriet follows her favorite cousin Edward to New Zealand, learning about women's rights and the plight of the poor along the way. Someone is following her, as well.

Faber, Michel.
The Crimson Petal and the White. Harcourt, 2002. 848pp. ★

Sugar, an intellectual prostitute, survives an impoverished childhood to become the mistress of a wealthy nobleman and the confidante of his daughter. It was only after British author Faber found success with a modern psychological novel (*Under the Skin*) and some other shorter efforts that he unveiled his masterpiece, which had languished in a bottom drawer for twenty years. It's an epic, literary page-turner, complete with lush, evocative descriptions of nineteenth-century London. Faber's choice of such a protagonist for his re-creation of a Victorian epic makes it the kind of novel that never would have existed at that time.

Humphreys, Helen.
Afterimage. Metropolitan, 2001. 246pp.

Annie Phelan, a young woman in 1865 England, is hired to work as a maid for the eccentric Dashells on their farm. While Isabelle Dashell, an avid photographer, decides to use Annie as an artist's model, her husband Eldon sees her as a kindred spirit with whom he can discuss his innermost thoughts. Not surprisingly, Annie's multiple roles begin to clash. Canadian author Humphreys took her inspiration from the haunting images of early Victorian photographer Julia Margaret Cameron, who used her maid (shown on the book jacket) as a subject for her creations.

Nattel, Lilian.
The Singing Fire. Scribner, 2004. 321pp.

In 1875, seventeen-year-old Nehama emigrates from Poland to London, where she quickly gets caught up in the unsavory atmosphere of the East End. Trapped briefly into prostitution, she escapes, makes a new life for herself, and marries. In 1886, when she comes across Emilia, a pregnant, unmarried immigrant girl in similar straits, she befriends her and offers her child a home. The child, a daughter named Gittel, links the two women over the years. Some elements of magical realism.

O'Connor, Joseph.

Star of the Sea. Harcourt, 2003. 384pp.

On the twenty-six-day journey from Ireland to America in 1847, during the potato famine, *New York Times* reporter Grantley Dixon chronicles the intrigues that surround the ship's inhabitants. They find that the more they yearn for the promised land of America, the more the past seems to hold them back. Among the passengers are an Irish aristocrat, his wife (and Dixon's lover), the family's maid, her former fiancé, and a thief and murderer. ALA Notable Book.

O'Faolain, Nuala.

My Dream of You. Riverhead, 2001. 500pp.

This sensitive first novel by Dublin memoirist O'Faolain tells about two great loves spaced 150 years apart. In the present, fiftyish Kathleen de Burca abandons her job as a travel writer to research a great love affair between an Irish servant and the wife of his English landlord in the 1850s. In a parallel tale, Marianne Talbot braves class barriers to love William Mullan during the years of the potato famine, but is faced with divorce and the loss of her daughter when her husband finds out. When Irish women finally allow their passion to fly free, are the consequences worth it? Thought-provoking and gently told.

Rogers, Jane.

Mr. Wroe's Virgins. Overlook, 1999. 276pp.

In Lancaster, England, in the 1830s, John Wroe, prophet of the Christian Israelites, asks his congregation for seven virgins "for comfort and succour." Surprisingly, seven families oblige by giving him their daughters. The novel is narrated by four of the girls, all of whom vie for dominance in Wroe's unusual household. All four—beautiful Leah, mute Martha, devoted Joanna, and Hannah, an unbeliever—have distinct voices. As one can imagine, in a household of strong-minded women and one single- minded prophet, there's bound to be trouble. Rogers's novel is based on historical fact.

Roiphe, Katie.

Still She Haunts Me. The Dial Press, 2001. 228pp.

As Lewis Carroll, Oxford mathematician Charles Dodgson wrote two classics of children's literature. His inspiration for *Alice in Wonderland* was a little girl named Alice Liddell, whom he met in 1856 when she was only four. When she turned eleven, Alice's parents abruptly cut off his access to their daughter. In the view of English scholar Roiphe, Dodgson developed an unnatural fondness for the girl, and her novel details his slow descent into madness and obsession.

Tóibín, Colm.

The Master. Scribner, 2004. 338pp. ✍

The author reimagines the inner life of Henry James (1843–1916), a writer sin-gle-mindedly dedicated to his craft. Born an American, James chooses to live and travel overseas during most of his life. Tóibín remains enigmatic about James's sexual identity, which reflects the reality of the time; any hint of homosexuality could have been treacherous for his career. Though his life is essentially a lonely one, James channels significant energy into his masterpieces.

Waters, Sarah.

With her historical novels, British author Waters reclaims Victorian England for a modern lesbian agenda.

Affinity. Riverhead, 1999. 351pp. 📖

When plain Margaret Prior, aged about thirty, goes on a charity visit to the women's ward of Millbank Prison in Victorian London, she finds among the pris-oners Selina Dawes, a beautiful medium whose spirit friend harmed a patron dur-ing a séance. Margaret is drawn to Selina and passionately plans their escape. Signs of the supernatural continue to appear around Selina, which disturbs and amazes Margaret. This is a calm psychological novel with a dark undercurrent —and a surprise twist at the end.

🎗 *Fingersmith*. Riverhead, 2002. 352pp. 📖

Waters takes a third turn at lesbian Victoriana in this novel of Sue Trinder, an or-phan in 1862 London who is raised in a house of pickpockets, or "fingersmiths." When Sue schemes to steal Maud Lilly's inheritance by posing as her maid, plan-ning her marriage to a gentleman, then having her declared insane, she doesn't count on her own unexpected attraction to Maud. The story isn't as straightfor-ward as this appears. Ellis Peters Historical Dagger.

🎗 *Tipping the Velvet*. Riverhead, 1999. 472pp.

Waters's sensual tales of the hidden activities of Victorian England have gar-nered her a devoted following. In 1890s Kent, Nancy Astley is an ordinary work-ing woman shucking oysters for a living when she spies a male impersonator, Miss Kitty Butler, on the cabaret stage. She is lovestruck. Abandoning everything to follow Kitty to London, by turns Nancy becomes her dresser, partner on stage, and lover. So begins Nancy's cultural and sexual awakening, and just as in all coming-of-age tales, her journey is never a smooth one. Betty Trask Award.

Twentieth Century

General

A mélange of literary novels set in twentieth-century Britain and Ireland. The two world wars form part of the background of these novels, but they aren't the focus.

Barker, Pat.

Liza's England. **Picador USA, 2001. 284pp. (Original title:** *The Century's Daughter.*) 📖

Liza Wright, as old as the twentieth century, recalls her life from childhood until the age of eighty-four. Refusing to leave her decrepit house in working-class northern England, she argues with a well-meaning social worker who tries to convince her to go into a nursing home. The wry, cackling voice of the elderly Liza is occasionally grating, occasionally charming as she recounts scenes of heartbreaking poverty and the ever-present hope that things will improve.

Barry, Sebastian.

The Whereabouts of Eneas McNulty. **Viking, 1998. 320pp.**

At the turn of the century, Eneas McNulty grows up in poverty in Sligo, Ireland, and joins the British army during the Great War. Returning home, his connections to the British make him suspect, so he joins the Royal Irish Constabulary. This blacklists him even more. So begins his life of wandering around the globe, a perpetual exile.

Chevalier, Tracy.

Falling Angels. **Dutton, 2001. 324pp.** 📖

On the first day of the Edwardian era in January 1901, two families pay their respects to deceased loved ones in a fashionable London cemetery. Here Maude Coleman, of a well-to-do intellectual upbringing, and Lavinia Waterhouse, whose family is respectably middle-class, meet and become friends. They and their families interact with each other in these changing social times, as women gain more political clout and personal freedom.

Cunningham, Michael.

🎗 *The Hours.* **Farrar, Straus & Giroux, 1998. 229pp.** 📖

Virginia Woolf's novel *Mrs. Dalloway* has an impact on three twentieth-century women of different generations. They are Woolf herself, battling mental illness in 1923 London, and about to start writing her novel; Clarissa Vaughan, a woman in modern New York caring for a friend dying of AIDS; and Laura Brown, a suburban widow living near Los Angeles in 1949. The overall theme: to seize the hours one has to live, and enjoy them before they are gone. Pulitzer Prize; ALA Notable Book.

Dunmore, Helen.

🎗 *A Spell of Winter.* **Atlantic Monthly, 2000. 312pp.**

In this literary gothic, siblings Catherine and Rob Allen are forced to become self-reliant after their mother abandons them for a better life abroad and their father is committed to an asylum. In the house where they're trapped with their grandfather, horrors and madness threaten them at every turn, until Cathy manages to escape from this stifling containment and make a new life for herself at the outbreak of World War I. Orange Prize.

Hansen, Brooks.

Perlman's Ordeal. Farrar, Straus & Giroux, 1999. 400pp.

In Edwardian London, Dr. August Perlman has worked hard to bring respectability to the psychology profession. He listens skeptically to one of his young patients, Sylvie Blum, who unleashes a split personality that may explain her fear of water. Perlman meets up with spiritualist Helena Barrett one night at the symphony, and his rationality clashes with the evidence he discovers.

Knox, Elizabeth.

Billie's Kiss. Ballantine, 2002. 343pp.

Written in the style of a nineteenth-century gothic romance, the novel begins as Billie Paxton, a young passenger on the Swedish *Gustav Edda*, jumps from the ship to shore just before the ship explodes. In doing so, she attracts the attention of Murdo Hesketh, the cousin of the man whom Billie and her family were going to visit at Kiss Castle. Did Billie have forewarning of the tragic event? Vivid imagery and romantic overtones evoke the atmosphere of early twentieth-century Scotland.

Livesey, Margot.

Eva Moves the Furniture. Holt, 2001. 232pp.

After her mother dies in childbirth, Eva McEwan is raised by her father and aunt. Growing up near the Scottish town of Troon in the 1920s, Eva later serves as a nurse in Glasgow during World War II, but her life is interrupted by periodic visions of two ghosts, a woman and a girl whom nobody else can see. Though at first their intentions seem kind and benevolent, later she's not so sure.

Miller, Alex.

Conditions of Faith. Scribner, 2000. 349pp. 📖

In 1923, Australian Emily Stanton is restless, determined to seek out a fulfilling life despite restrictive social barriers. Her marriage to Georges Elder, an older Scots-Frenchman, is hastily arranged. Though Emily moves with him to Paris, her life there is not as exciting as she'd hoped. After an erotic encounter with a priest, she casts off her husband's dream of returning to Sydney and creates a new life for herself.

Stevens, David.

The Waters of Babylon. Simon & Schuster, 2000. 318pp. ✍

T. E. Lawrence ("Lawrence of Arabia") is a legendary figure today, made so in many ways by the well-known film, which was itself based on Lawrence's autobiography. Stevens, the son of one of Lawrence's Royal Air Force compatriots, imagines Lawrence's life after his successful stint aiding the Arabs against the pro-German Turks during World War I. Little is known of Lawrence's later years, but the author fashions a sympathetic portrait of a man frustrated by his unhappy childhood, his homosexuality, and his failure to secure more rights for Arabs after the war.

Tel, Jonathan.

Freud's Alphabet. **Counterpoint, 2003. 192pp.** ✍

> Impressionistic and thought-provoking, this literary novel of Freud's last days in London follows the famed psychoanalyst through the city's streets in 1939. In chapters labeled A to Z, Freud reflects on his own existence and on his environment, the world on the brink of war—but is it reality or just another dream?

Trevor, William.

The Story of Lucy Gault. **Viking, 2002. 228pp.** 📖

> When Ireland is in the midst of civil war in 1921, many Anglo-Irish families decide to leave their homeland for England. The day before her Protestant parents plan to depart, eight-year-old Lucy Gault runs away. When the house's caretakers find her and bring her home, her parents are gone, restlessly wandering around Europe in their grief, for they assume Lucy has drowned. As Lucy grows older, she must assuage the guilt that her long-ago action caused.

The Easter Rising

These works recount the 1916 Easter Rising, that fateful day when Irish citizens tried to throw off oppressive British rule. It was an abysmal failure. Ordinary citizens, even those outside Dublin, get caught up in the conflict.

Davis-Goff, Annabel.

The Fox's Walk. **Harcourt, 2003. 336pp.**

> During the First World War, Alice Moore grows up in a protected environment in her privileged Anglo-Irish family. Her world gradually opens through her conversations with servants, neighbors, and local Catholics. When violence sweeps through the land, she must decide where her loyalties lie.

Doyle, Roddy.

🎗 *A Star Called Henry.* **Viking, 1999. 343pp.** 📖

> Henry Smart, born in 1901 in Dublin, grows up with the century. He spends his childhood on the city streets, becoming an adult early on when he participates in the 1916 Easter Rising for Ireland's independence alongside other patriots. Henry later fights for freedom on the side of Michael Collins and other notables, though he never forgets the woman he loves, Miss O'Shea. ALA Notable Book.

O'Neill, Jamie.

At Swim, Two Boys. **Scribner, 2002. 572pp.** 📖

> In 1915, two Dublin boys agree that by Easter next year, they'll swim the length of Dublin Bay together. They don't realize that it is the planned date for the Republican uprising against British rule, and that by then the two will have fallen in love. It's a tragic and beautiful love story told

against a background of Irish history. The author's prose—filled with lyrical, invented words—has been compared to both Dickens and Joyce.

World War II

Men and women from all walks of life become involved in the Second World War, taking on major responsibilities both on the front and at home. In these somber tales, the atmosphere is overlaid with both tragedy and hope.

Bragg, Melvyn.

Sam Richardson Series.

A thoughtful, character-centered portrait of a family and how war can change their lives. The last volume will be *Crossing the Lines*.

The Soldier's Return. Arcade, 2002. 352pp. 📖

When Sam Richardson returns to his home town of Wigton in 1946, after time spent fighting in Burma, he finds his homecoming bittersweet. His reunion with his wife and son is heartfelt, yet their relationship is strained, as Sam grows frustrated with small-town life. Meanwhile his wife, Ellen, is perfectly content with the life she's always had.

A Son of War. Arcade, 2003. 432pp. 📖

This sequel to *The Soldier's Return* focuses on Ellen Richardson, who knows better than her husband that he's not happy with his newfound factory job. Ellen's and Sam's son, six-year-old Joe, grows up in the post-war years and struggles to get to know the father who had been gone so long.

Corrick, Martin.

The Navigation Log. **Random House, 2003. 292pp.**

In this understated, occasionally humorous tale of the accomplishments of ordinary men, Tom and William Anderson are identical twins born in 1918 England, at the hour when the armistice that ended the Great War was signed. They fulfill their destinies in different ways. Tom grows up fascinated by flight and later serves as a pilot. William, who is more of a poet, becomes an elementary school teacher during the Second World War.

Davis-Goff, Annabel.

This Cold Country. **Harcourt, 2002. 368pp.** 📖

Daisy Creed, formerly a land girl in 1940s England, finds herself in County Waterford, Ireland, after her new husband is called to duty in France. She takes up residence with her eccentric in-laws, taking on more responsibility for the estate. Little by little, Daisy discovers the politics behind Ireland's neutrality in the war.

Frayn, Michael.

Spies. **Metropolitan, 2002. 261pp.** 📖

Stephen Wheatley, now elderly, looks back on his boyhood in England during World War II, when he naively played a dangerous game. The trouble begins

·when his best friend Keith, kidding around, announces that his mother was a German spy. After that, the boys take to rifling through her things and following her everywhere. What they reveal is even more sinister than anything they could imagine.

Humphreys, Helen.

The Lost Garden. W. W. Norton, 2002. 224pp. 📖

In 1941, Londoner Gwen Davis, a young gardener, leaves the city for Devon, where she takes charge of a group of land girls responsible for growing vegetables for the war effort. While there, she and the girls become involved with Canadian soldiers waiting to be called into action. As they form relationships and tend the overgrown gardens of the estate, Gwen begins to find a new purpose in life.

McEwan, Ian.

🎗 *Atonement.* Doubleday, 2002. 351pp. 📖

A girl's childhood mistake has immense repercussions for all around her in this astute psychological novel. When Bryony Tallis, thirteen years old in 1935, thoughtlessly accuses the housemaid's son Robbie of raping her cousin, Robbie is sent to prison and later serves in the Second World War. Only later does Bryony, serving as a nurse in the war, realize that she may have been mistaken. She meditates on how her action may have ruined three lives. National Book Critics' Circle Award; ALA Notable Book.

Europe

The Middle Ages

Novels of medieval Europe show a world on the brink of change. Superstition gives way to reason, clergymen occupy themselves with intellectual pursuits, and adventurers take picaresque journeys throughout the continent.

Aridjis, Homero.

The Lord of the Last Days: Visions of the Year 1000. Morrow, 1995. 259pp.

As the end of the first millennium approaches, monks see portents in the skies, and miracles forecast either civilization's doom or its salvation. In this highly charged arena, twin brothers—one a humble Christian scribe, the other a Muslim military captain—vie for victory over the other. Events in their homelands parallel their actions. As tensions escalate today between the Western world and the Muslim Middle East, this novel serves as both a mirror of, and counterpoint to, our own time.

Audouard, Antoine.

Farewell, My Only One. **Houghton Mifflin, 2004. 336pp.** ✍

William of Oxford, one of medieval philosopher Peter Abelard's most devoted pupils, aids his master's love affair with Héloïse, the beautiful, intelligent niece of Canon Fulbert. But William also loves her, and despite his loyalty to Abelard, his heart breaks at the thought of Héloïse wanting someone else. A lyrical, romantic portrait of early twelfth-century France, a time of great intellectual pursuit.

Cokal, Susann.

Mirabilis. **BlueHen, 2001. 389pp.** 📖

In 1372, the people of Villeneuve, France, are beset by plague and starving to death. Hope arrives in the form of a young woman, Bonne Tardieu, whose mother was either a witch or a saint. Bonne grows up to become a wet-nurse, and her social status in the village changes as the ever-flowing milk from her breasts gives the townspeople succor in their time of need. The author's prose is bawdy and magical, and the atmosphere is overlaid with both sexual and religious connotations.

Cowan, James.

A Mapmaker's Dream. **Shambhala, 1996. 152pp.**

Fra Mauro, an Italian monk living in an island monastery in Venice in the fifteenth century, occupies his time with cartographic pursuits. He muses on the creation of a map of enormous scope, one that encompasses all of the world's people, places, and beliefs. His story is presented in diary form, complete with footnotes by the author, the document's supposed translator.

Eco, Umberto.

Baudolino. **Harcourt, 2002. 528pp.** 📖

In this picaresque fable, Baudolino is an Italian peasant who also happens to be the adopted son of Frederick Barbarossa, Holy Roman Emperor. In 1204, as the Byzantine capital of Constantinople is being sacked by knights on the Fourth Crusade, Baudolino saves the life of a court official. Baudolino tells him the fantastic story of his life, a tale that may or may not be wholly true. It winds from his youth at the University of Paris to his quest to find the kingdom of the legendary Prester John, whose existence Baudolino himself has helped establish.

Haasse, Hella.

In a Dark Wood Wandering. **Academy Chicago, 1989. 574pp. (First published in the Netherlands in 1949.)** ✍ ★

Haasse's first novel to be translated into English is her best known and her most accessible. Her hero is Charles d'Orléans—scholar, poet, courtier, nephew of the mad king Charles VI of France, and prisoner in England for twenty-five years after the Battle of Agincourt during the Hundred Years' War. The real story begins at his birth in 1394, as his mother Valentine Visconti, the Italian-born Duchess of Orléans, lies in childbed. Haasse's vision encompasses all of French and English

society during the fifteenth century: the feuds with each other and with neighboring lands, the coming of Joan of Arc, and the journey of the long-wandering soul to its home, as reflected in Charles's poetry and in the book's title.

Kadare, Ismail.

Elegy for Kosovo. Arcade, 2000. 121pp.

This short novel, written as later events in Kosovo unfolded, takes place in 1389 and evokes an earlier ethnic cleansing of the Kosovars. At the Field of the Blackbirds, an Ottoman army overtakes the Albanian people, which gives them a stronghold in Europe that continues for centuries. Albanian author Kadare has been nominated several times for the Nobel Prize for Literature.

The Three-Arched Bridge. Arcade, 1997. 160pp.

In 1377 Arberia (modern Albania), a Christian monk and translator named Gjon chronicles the building of a bridge over the Ujama e Keqe River. The bridge will end the monopoly of the men who ferry travelers back and forth. It is finally constructed amid controversy on both sides, but the encroaching Ottomans are among the first to cross it. This recounting of troubles in the Balkans in the Middle Ages has obvious implications for today.

Updike, John.

Gertrude and Claudius. Knopf, 2000. 212pp. 📖

In this prequel to Shakespeare's classic play, the focus is on Hamlet's parents: the long-suffering Gertrude (Gerutha), who transforms from unhappy young wife to willing adulterer, and Claudius, brother to the King of Denmark, who has an attraction for her that she can't resist. Hamlet himself is a sullen figure whose odd nature is no doubt due to "too much German philosophy." It's not as compelling as the original, and Updike's love scenes are among the most unappealing in modern literature. However, it is entertaining, as if the author had a good time writing it.

Yehoshua, A. B.

A Journey to the End of the Millennium. Doubleday, 1998. 309pp.

In the year 999, Ben Attar, a Jewish merchant in North Africa, takes a second wife even though his first wife is still living. The German wife of his business partner/nephew disapproves of Attar's behavior. To redeem his character and justify his bigamy, Attar voyages across Europe with his two wives and his Muslim business partner to revisit the issue. Though slow moving in parts, the novel presents an accurate portrait of the cultural influences on early medieval Europe and the religious and legal issues of the time.

The Renaissance and Reformation

New developments in art, science, and religion transform the European world. These novels show how these cultural revolutions affected people's lives. In general, they are set during the years 1450 to 1650, a period especially popular with literary novelists.

Andahazi, Federico.

The Anatomist. Doubleday, 1998. 215pp.

> Christopher Columbus's similarity to Renaissance anatomist Mateo Colombo is made plain here. While Columbus is credited with discovering America, Colombo's own discovery is the clitoris, and with this revelation, he sets forth to claim the land of the female body for himself. His is an erotic journey, as Colombo discovers women's pleasures through experiences with lovely courtesan Mona Sofia.

Bellonci, Maria.

Private Renaissance. Morrow, 1985. 462pp. ★ ✍

> Isabella d'Este, Marchesa of Mantua during the Italian High Renaissance, was the foremost female figure of her era, in a land that was the cultural center of the world at the time. Celebrated for her style, wit, and intelligence, Isabella narrates her own story, from the art and intellect of Leonardo da Vinci to her own Court of Love. Through her eyes, we see the Renaissance as she herself might have seen it.

Bernardi, Adria.

The Day Laid on the Altar. University Press of New England, 2000. 210pp. ✍

> In spare, elegant prose Bernardi juxtaposes two painters during the Italian Renaissance. Bartolomeo de Bartolai, a humble shepherd, cannot read or write, yet he aspires to artistic greatness. The master painter Titian has everything that Bartolomeo does not, including fame and fortune, but he struggles with his family and with the demands that recognition has placed on him. This short novel contemplates the meaning of art and the power it has to transform.

Chevalier, Tracy.

> In her novels, Chevalier explores the relationship between master and servant, and between art and life.

Girl with a Pearl Earring. Dutton, 1999. 233pp. ★ 📖 ✍

> In seventeenth-century Delft, young Griet supports her family by becoming a maidservant in the household of the well-known painter Vermeer. Due to her innate sense of rightness in art, she develops a bond with Vermeer that encourages him to make her the subject of a painting. This not only arouses his wife's jealousy, but it causes scandal among his household and throughout the city. A big hit with female readers and with reading groups.

The Lady and the Unicorn. Dutton, 2004. 250pp. 📖

> In 1490s France, nobleman Jean le Viste commissions Nicolas des Innocents, a skillful and virile painter, to design a set of six tapestries centered on a unicorn.

Nicolas, enraptured by the beauty of Le Viste's daughter Claude, includes her image in his designs. His story intertwines with that of a family of Flemish weavers, who have never created anything of such magnitude before. Little is known of the tapestries' true history, but they can be seen today at the Musée de Cluny in Paris.

The Virgin Blue. **Plume, 2003. 320pp.** 📖

Annotated in Chapter 12.

Dunant, Sarah.
The Birth of Venus. **Random House, 2003. 397pp.** 📖

Fourteen-year-old Alexandra Cecchi, a cloth merchant's daughter, comes of age in fifteenth-century Florence. She dreams of a career as an artist, encouraged by a young painter in her household, but her dreams are dashed when her parents arrange her marriage to a much older man. At the same time, the fanatical monk Savonarola comes to power, loudly preaching that love of art and "pagan" books leads only to damnation. Despite an unhappy married life, Alessandra pursues her attraction to both art and the painter.

Eco, Umberto.
The Island of the Day Before. **Harcourt, 1995. 515pp.**

Erudite but esoteric, Eco's second historical novel (after *The Name of the Rose*, Chapter 9) is set 300 years later, in the mid-seventeenth century. Roberto della Griva, an Italian nobleman, finds himself shipwrecked in the South Pacific not far from the international date line (hence the title). He takes refuge on another ship that he thought was abandoned but that' is occupied by a brilliant Jesuit scientist, Father Caspar, who has mastered the secret of longitude. Roberto tells him the story of his eventful life.

Faunce, John.
Lucrezia Borgia. **Crown, 2003. 277pp.** ✍

Lucrezia Borgia grows up amid a gaggle of corrupt Vatican officials in the fifteenth century, and her father Roderigo (now Pope Alexander) and her cruel brother Cesare are the most rotten of them all. Married off multiple times for political gain, she sees her husbands tossed aside easily when her family no longer finds them useful. She herself is no shrinking violet, never losing her coarse sense of humor and always giving as good as she gets. This Lucrezia is not nearly as evil as her reputation; of the supposed crimes of spousal murder, incest, and poison, she only committed one.

Greenhall, Ken.
Lenoir. **Zoland, 1998. 246pp.**

A young African man named Mbatgha is captured and brought to Amsterdam, a city that thrives on art, literature, and the profits of the Dutch slave trade. To the Dutch, the slave—renamed Lenoir—is an exotic curiosity. He serves as the artist's model for Rembrandt and, in Antwerp, Rubens. But in an ironic role reversal, to Lenoir the Dutch are soulless, godless creatures who have no understanding of humanity.

Haasse, Hella.
The Scarlet City. **Academy Chicago, 1990. 367pp. (First published in the Netherlands in 1952.)** ✍

This somewhat oblique historical novel takes a nonlinear approach to six-teenth-century Italy. At its center is Giovanni Borgia, the *infans Romanus*, or "child of Rome," and his search for his true identity. Trusting no one, his endless quest for the truth is set against a background of the Italian Wars, in which both France and the Holy Roman Empire fought for possession of Italy, with the Italians themselves caught in the middle.

Harris, Joanne.
Holy Fools. **Morrow, 2004. 368pp.**

In Brittany in 1610, a woman known as Soeur Auguste takes refuge in a convent with her daughter Fleur, hoping to hide her past from the world. Previously she had been known as Juliette, an acrobat and rope dancer. When the King of France is murdered, a new abbess comes to power in the convent—Isabelle, a selfish eleven-year-old girl, who brings along her confessor. Juliette immediately recognizes him as Guy LeMerle, the former leader of Juliette's performing troupe, a disreputable seducer she has every reason to hate.

Huddle, David.
La Tour Dreams of the Wolf Girl. **Houghton Mifflin, 2002. 208pp.** ✍

Suzanne Nelson, a contemporary art professor and historian, escapes from thoughts of her philandering husband by meditating on the contrast between French Baroque painter Georges de la Tour's beautiful works of art and his violent way of life. She imagines scenes between the artist and his model, a village girl with an unusual marking on her back, which are recounted in separate chapters. The novel touches on the themes of truth versus lies, and art versus reality.

Lapierre, Alexandra.
Artemisia. **Grove, 1998. 496pp.** ✍

Violently raped by her father's best friend, Artemisia Gentileschi has her name dragged through the Roman courts. However, she grows stronger from the event, and in her art, she portrays women triumphing over tyrannical men. This fictional biography of proto-feminist painter Artemisia does nothing to hide its scholarship; the 150 pages of notes and bibliography at the end give it away. Classification of this title is interesting in itself, because in Europe it was presented as a straight biography rather than a historical novel.

Lovric, Michelle.

The Floating Book. **ReganBooks, 2004. 496pp.**

It is 1468. Wendelin von Speyer has just set up shop in Venice, aiming to make a living from the printing press newly invented by Gutenberg. Sosia Simeon, a Serbian Jew with an immense sexual appetite, forms a love triangle with Bruno Uguccione (Wendelin's editor) and Felice Feliciano, a scribe fascinated by words. All become enraptured with the prose of the Roman poet Catullus. When Wendelin publishes Catullus's poetry for all of literate Venice to read, it brings all of their passions out in the open. Despite these fascinating people, the main character is Venice itself, a "floating book" of sensuality.

Maguire, Gregory.

Confessions of an Ugly Stepsister. **ReganBooks, 1999. 282pp.** 📖

In the 1630s, homely Iris Fisher arrives in the city of Haarlem from England with her dim-witted sister, Ruth, and her ambitious mother, Marguerite. As the trio become involved with both the artistic Van de Meer family and the lucrative tulip trade, the tale turns into an innovative retelling of the familiar Cinderella story. Though Maguire's prose has a light touch, the novel poses some serious questions about the nature of beauty and its power to deceive.

Marlowe, Stephen.

The Death and Life of Miguel de Cervantes. **Arcade, 1996. 495pp.**

This picaresque adventure is written as if Cervantes himself, creator of *Don Quixote*, was the star of one of his own creations. Concentrating on his personal rather than intellectual life, it's a wild romp through Renaissance Spain and all of Europe. Cervantes constantly sidesteps danger, finds romance, and encounters some of the greatest personalities of his day—besides himself, that is.

Matton, Sylvie.

Rembrandt's Whore. **Grove, 2003. 208pp.** ✍

In 1649, twenty-year-old Hendrickje Stoffels travels to Amsterdam to become a model for the painter Rembrandt and ends up staying, becoming first his servant and later his lover. Though his mistress for twenty years, Hendrickje discovers how fickle society can be, labeling her as a whore even as she brings contentment into Rembrandt's life.

Moggach, Deborah.

Tulip Fever. **Delacorte, 2000. 272pp.** 📖

Jan van Loos, an artist in 1630s Amsterdam, is commissioned by Cornelis Sandvoort to paint a portrait of him with his beautiful, bored wife, Sophia. Jan falls in love with her, but before they can run away together, they need money. To get it they make some rash plans involving tulip bulbs, which continue to increase in price and demand.

Murray, Yxta Maya.

The Conquest. Rayo, 2002. 288pp.

Sara Rosario González is a rare book restorer at the Getty Museum in modern Los Angeles. She becomes so involved with her latest project, the translation of a sixteenth-century Spanish manuscript of unknown authorship, that it pushes her longtime boyfriend into the arms of another woman. In a parallel tale, the manuscript itself is narrated by the mysterious Helen, a former member of Montezuma's harem. Disguised as a male juggler, Helen steals away to Rome on Cortés's ship after the burning of Tenochtitlán. This intelligent, romantic, and adventure-filled novel should appeal to bibliophiles.

Norfolk, Lawrence.

The Pope's Rhinoceros. Harmony, 1996. 574pp.

In the early sixteenth century, the Portuguese made an unsuccessful attempt to transport a rhinoceros from Africa to Europe as a bribe for the pleasure-loving Pope Leo X, in the hopes of persuading him to favor Portugal over Spain. This is only the springboard for Norfolk's second novel, a picaresque epic that follows a soldier of fortune and his brutish sidekick from the Baltic coast to Italy and then to the wilds of Africa, where they sign on for the fateful voyage back to Europe. Subplots, intrigue, and odd personalities abound, and if the plotline seems at times to be lost at sea, it's nothing if not entertaining.

Peachment, Christopher.

Caravaggio. Thomas Dunne, 2003. 304pp. ✍

Renaissance artist Caravaggio (1573–1610), unlike his predecessors, painted scenes from the Bible in an all-too-realistic and dramatic way. British author Peachment presumes that his brief life was just as bloody and violent, filled with murder and debauchery of the highest order.

Sherwood, Frances.

The Book of Splendor. W. W. Norton, 2002. 348pp. 📖

This slow-paced but captivating historical novel has an unusual setting: the old city of Prague circa 1601, under the reign of Holy Roman Emperor Rudolph II. Its heroine is Rochel, a young member of Prague's Jewish community, whose future depends on her ability to find a worthwhile husband despite her dubious (possibly illegitimate) birth. Though she settles into marriage, she finds love elsewhere. The emperor experiments with methods both scientific and magical to ensure his immortality.

Stevenson, Jane.

Winter Queen Series.

This is a brilliantly imagined trilogy about the Winter Queen: the beautiful Elizabeth, Queen of Bohemia, the daughter of England's James I, who was forced to flee her adopted homeland with her family after her royal husband was exiled. The trilogy concludes with *The Empress of the Last Days,* about a modern descendant of Elizabeth.

The Winter Queen. Houghton Mifflin, 2002. 307pp. (Original title: *Astraea.*) ✍

It is 1640. Elizabeth Stuart, a widow living in the Netherlands, meets Pelagius van Overmeer, an ex-slave and prince of the Yoruba kingdom of Oyo. The two fall in love and secretly marry. Her pregnancy threatens to expose their precarious relationship.

The Shadow King. Houghton Mifflin, 2003. 304pp. (Original title: *The Pretender.*)

Balthasar Stuart, the secret child of Elizabeth and Pelagius, is the shadow king of the title. He establishes a medical practice in Zeeland, where he encounters Restoration poet Aphra Behn. Never fully at home anywhere, Balthasar travels first to London and then to Barbados in search of his heritage and identity. While he finds happiness with a Barbados woman of gentle birth, ironically he must purchase slaves to survive in her homeland.

Tremain, Rose.

Music and Silence. **Farrar, Straus & Giroux, 2000. 485pp.** 📖

In 1629, British lutenist Peter Claire arrives at the Danish court as the newest member of Christian IV's royal orchestra. The king sees in him a kindred spirit whose playing can distract him from his arrogant queen's adultery and his country's financial troubles. Peter falls in love with Emilia Tilsen, one of the queen's waiting women, who does not have her mistress's permission to return his affection. The musical themes of harmony and dissonance run through the novel, which reaches a near-deafening crescendo of conflict at the end.

Vreeland, Susan.

Girl in Hyacinth Blue. **MacMurray and Beck, 1999. 242pp.** 📖

The ownership of a mysterious painting of a girl garbed in blue, which may be a Vermeer, is traced back in time from its rediscovery in a modern professor's art collection to seventeenth-century Amsterdam. This short novel is as much about the people whose lives it touched and the nature of art as it is about the painting itself.

The Passion of Artemisia. **Viking, 2002. 288pp.** ✍ 📖

In seventeenth-century Rome, Artemisia Gentileschi is publicly humiliated after a rape trial in Rome in which she had accused her painting teacher of assaulting her. To redeem her reputation, she settles for an arranged marriage. However, her new husband is not in favor of her continuing to fulfill her life's passion as a painter, renowned though she is. More accessible than Alexandra Lapierre's documentary novel of Artemisia's life (above), this is nonetheless beautifully told.

Early Modern Europe

Political changes sweep throughout Europe, affecting both royalty and average people. Other novels in this section show changes on a smaller scale, such as how art and music influence people's lives. Set roughly between the late seventeenth century and the early twentieth century.

Bainbridge, Beryl.

🎗 *Master Georgie.* **Carroll & Graf, 1998. 190pp.**

Physician George Hardy heads from Liverpool to the Crimea in 1854, accompanied by Myrtle, his servant and adoring mistress, although he's a secret homosexual who doesn't return her affections. The traumatic and frequently gory experiences of her "Master Georgie" in the Crimean War are told alternately by Myrtle and two others, photographer Pompey Jones (George's sometime lover) and George's brother-in-law Dr. Potter. ALA Notable Book.

Bradbury, Malcolm.

To the Hermitage. **Overlook, 2000. 510pp.** ✍

In the present, a group of scholars travel to St. Petersburg to study Diderot. In an alternate storyline, Diderot himself travels from France to St. Petersburg to present his theories to the Empress Catherine the Great at her palace, the Hermitage. Philosophical ideas flow freely throughout the novel, and its pace drags slightly as a result. This dense, intellectual novel was Bradbury's last. He plays with history, pretending that several historical characters meet when in reality they never did, but slyly admits to such subterfuge in the modern sections.

Chessman, Harriet Scott.

Lydia Cassatt Reading the Morning Paper. **Seven Stories Press and The Permanent Press, 2001. 164pp.** ✍ 📖

Published on the seventy-fifth anniversary of the death of American impressionist painter Mary Cassatt, this short novel sees her from the point of view of her sister and model, Lydia. Each chapter represents a painting of Lydia by her dear "May," an image of which is reproduced in full color within the book. Lydia herself, realizing that she is slowly dying of Bright's disease, is a courageous woman and beloved companion.

Codrescu, Andrei.

Casanova in Bohemia. **Free Press, 2002. 321pp.** ✍

At the end of the eighteenth century, the legendary adventurer and ladies' man Giacomo Casanova was invited to serve as the librarian for Count Waldstein at Dux Castle in Bohemia. Here he reminisces about his youthful romantic conquests. In Bohemia, he writes his memoirs of a life spent gallivanting around Europe, and even starts a new *affaire* of his own with a young Italian maidservant named Laura Brock.

Cowell, Stephanie.

Marrying Mozart. **Viking, 2004. 350pp.**

From the viewpoint of old age, Sophie Weber remembers her carefree youth, when musical prodigy Wolfgang Mozart boarded with her family. In Mannheim in the year 1777, Fridolin and Caecilia Weber have four talented daughters. Beautiful Aloysia captivates Mozart with her looks and talent, Josefa's gorgeous voice amazes him, Constanze's steadfastness intrigues him, and bookish Sophie becomes his good friend. Though he loves them all, he marries only one of them.

Davis, Kathryn.

Versailles. **Houghton Mifflin, 2002. 206pp.**

Marie Antoinette's ghost narrates the tale of her life, first as Archduchess of Austria and later as Dauphine and Queen of France, in a series of witty episodes set mostly in and around the court of Versailles. Constrained by her royal position, Antoinette makes Versailles her home and sanctuary. Antoinette is flirtatious and naïve, and her dialogue breaks into skits at times. She emerges as a more intelligent figure than history has given her credit for being.

De Kretser, Michelle.

The Rose Grower. **Carroll & Graf, 2000. 448pp.**

The Bastille was stormed on July 14, 1789, but repercussions are not yet felt in the French countryside. On this date, American artist Stephen Fletcher crash-lands his hot-air balloon on land belonging to Gascon magistrate Jean-Baptiste de Saint-Pierre. While his married, oldest daughter Claire strikes Stephen's fancy, middle daughter Sophie, a rose grower, pines for him in secret. This leisurely historical starts off slowly but picks up as the Revolution's events touch the family more directly.

de Moor, Margriet.

The Virtuoso. **Overlook, 2000. 201pp.**

In eighteenth-century Naples, twelve-year-old soprano Gasparo Conti undergoes the operation that will allow him to preserve his glorious voice through adulthood—an event that "only one in four fail to survive," as the narrator remarks calmly. The speaker is Carlotta, Duchess of Rocca d'Evandro, a childhood acquaintance who encounters the youthful Gasparo as an adult and swoons with love for the beautiful *castrato*. Nothing is held back in the book's erotic scenes, despite Gasparo's affliction. The novel emphasizes sensuality and supplies lengthy descriptions of the Neapolitan music scene.

Diliberto, Gioia.

I Am Madame X. **Scribner, 2003. 272pp.**

When John Singer Sargent first unveiled his *Portrait of Madame X* in 1884, it was a huge scandal in the Parisian art world. What could the model have been thinking to pose in such an outrageous fashion? His subject—a pale-skinned woman in a sleeveless black gown with deep décolletage, looking away from the artist as if in disdain—was the notorious Virginie Gautreau, a Southern belle from Louisiana who fled to Paris with her family after the Civil War. She narrates her life story.

Ducornet, Rikki.

The Fan-Maker's Inquisition. Holt, 1999. 192pp. 📖 ✍

In 1793 in Paris, the young fan-maker Gabrielle is called before the prudish Comité de Surveillance to testify about her relationship with the notorious sexual libertine, the Marquis de Sade. The novel's first half consists of Gabrielle's inquisition, in which she's asked to respond to questions about pornographic fans she created for de Sade, their joint collaboration on a scandalous book, and her relationship with Olympe de Gouges, a well-known lesbian. In the second half, de Sade—here a sympathetic figure—explains his actions and defends his loyal friend.

Enquist, Per Olov.

The Royal Physician's Visit. Overlook, 2001. 314pp. ✍

In 1760s Denmark, court physician Johann Friedrich Struensee briefly became, in effect, the sole ruler of the country as well as the lover of Queen Caroline Mathilde, the younger sister of England's King George III. Here, the dashing Dr. Struensee forms an alliance with the queen against her husband, the weak-willed and childlike Christian VII, and establishes a good number of political and social reforms. Alas, he isn't politically astute enough to know how to protect himself against his enemies.

Fitzgerald, Penelope.

🎗 *The Blue Flower*. Mariner, 1995. 226pp. ✍

Friedrich "Fritz" von Hardenberg (1772–1801), a philosophy student who later gained fame as the German romantic poet Novalis, outrages his family with his love for a plain twelve-year-old girl, Sophie von Kühn. He is determined to marry her despite all opposition. Through Fritz, the author explores the themes of love, beauty, and philosophy. National Book Critics' Circle Award.

Galloway, Janice.

Clara. Simon & Schuster, 2003. 425pp. ✍ 📖

In her youth, Clara Wieck is a brilliant and renowned pianist, a musical prodigy in her own right. When she marries Robert Schumann against her father's wishes, her own talent fades beside his. They raise a family together, Clara playing the role of dutiful and supportive wife, but his manic depressive periods create difficulties for them both. Though the novel ends before Clara's life is half finished, it's a poignant portrait of a strong woman, a tormented musical genius, and the intersections between creativity and madness.

Hansen, Brooks.

The Monsters of St. Helena. Farrar, Straus & Giroux, 2003. 306pp. ✍

In 1815, Napoleon Bonaparte takes up residence at his final place of exile, the remote Atlantic island of St. Helena. His retinue of 1,500 people worries the island's inhabitants, which include Englishmen in exile, Portuguese settlers and slaves, and the descendants of both. Napoleon befriends and becomes a father figure to young Betsy Balcombe in between time spent writing his memoirs. The novel's most vibrant character is St. Helena itself, given life in the tales told of its ghosts and current residents.

Harrison, Kathryn.

Poison. Random House, 1995. 319pp. ✍ 📖

In seventeenth-century Madrid, Maria Luisa de Borbón, the French-born consort of Spain's King Carlos II, is unable to produce an heir after ten years of marriage. She is being slowly poisoned to death, even though the fault lies with her inbred idiot of a husband. Her life parallels that of Francesca de Luarca, daughter of a Spanish silk grower, whose affair with a Catholic priest attracts the attention of the Inquisition.

Japin, Arthur.

The Two Hearts of Kwasi Boachi. Knopf, 2000. 384pp. ✍

In this novel based on a true story, Ashanti princes Kwasi and Kwame go to Holland in 1837 in a bizarre sort of exchange program that lets European traders use their home country for a fresh supply of slaves. Both attempt to fit into European society, Kwasi more than Kwame, not realizing that they're seen mostly as curiosities rather than as human beings who happen to belong to a different race. They also don't realize that assimilation into white society means leaving their native culture behind forever.

Landis, J. D.

Longing. Harcourt, 2000. 442pp. ✍

In the 1830s, when German Romanticism is at its highest, Robert and Clara Schumann are the ultimate power couple—he, a genius of a composer; she, the finest pianist of her time. Their relationship is passionate yet destructive. As he descends further into madness, she escapes into the arms of Johannes Brahms. Lengthy and erudite, filled with detailed footnotes, the novel is obviously well researched, though the history weighs it down.

Maalouf, Amin.

Balthasar's Odyssey. Arcade, 2002. 391pp.

Balthasar Embriaco, a Genoese merchant, despairs after letting *The Hundredth Name*, a book purporting to reveal the 100th name of God, slip from his grasp. He sets off on a quest across Europe to retrieve it, accompanied by various family members, in the hope that he'll find it before the apocalyptic year of 1666 begins. The author has written a number of historical novels (*Samarkand, Leo Africanus*) on the Middle East and its influence on European culture.

Mariani, Dacia.

The Silent Duchess. **The Feminist Press, 1998. 258pp.** ✍

Due to a childhood trauma, Marianna Ucrìa, the daughter of an aristocratic family in early eighteenth-century Sicily, has been deaf and mute all her life. Silent both literally and metaphorically, she does little to fight against the unnecessary cruel behavior of her parents and her own marriage, at age thirteen, to her uncle Pietro. It's only after her husband's death that she learns how to love and be loved and discovers the reasons for her silence.

Middleton, Haydn.

Grimm's Last Fairytale. **St. Martin's Press, 2001. 256pp.** ✍

Fairy tales mask dark reality in this multi-layered tale of Jacob Grimm, one of the famous Brothers Grimm, set in Germany in 1863. As the elderly Jacob returns to his hometown of Hesse with his niece Auguste so that she may learn more about her family history, he reminisces about life with his late brother Wilhelm and their joint literary creations. His memories take the form of an as-yet-unfinished fairy tale, that of Sleeping Beauty, but this time told by Prince Charming—and with an unsettling ending that has implications for both Grimm and the future political landscape of Germany.

Miller, Andrew.

Casanova in Love. **Harcourt Brace, 1998. 272pp.** ✍

Writing his memoirs in the German castle where he spent his last years, Giacomo Casanova tells a mysterious woman a story from his life. Aged thirty-eight in 1763, Casanova arrives in London to reinvent himself and take a respite from the too-intense feelings that occupy him. But entanglements seem to find him anyway. He befriends both lexicographer Samuel Johnson and the beautiful courtesan Marie Charpillon, with whom he has a tempestuous, doomed love affair.

Nattel, Lilian.

The River Midnight. **Scribner, 1999. 414pp.**

Gabriel García Márquez meets nineteenth-century Poland in this intriguing novel of magical realism in the imaginary shtetl of Blaszka. Misha is the village midwife, a larger than life character beloved by many, and her great secret is the father of her unborn child. The village isn't completely mythical, however, as seen in the author's vivid depictions of Jewish women's lives before the wars.

Petsinis, Tom.

The French Mathematician. **Walker, 1998. 400pp.** ✍

The life story of Evariste Galois, a brilliant mathematician in post-Revolutionary France who was killed in a duel at the young age of twenty, is a tragic one. Galois, who narrates, frequently struggles with his emotions and sexuality. He isn't a likeable character, but the novel succeeds in its portrait of a somewhat self-centered genius who died before his life's ambitions, both intellectually and politically, could be fulfilled.

Reese, James.

The Book of Shadows. Morrow, 2002. 480pp.

In this literary, fantastical gothic, Herculine grows up in a convent in Brittany in the early nineteenth century. She is always uncomfortable with her own identity until she falls in with a group of unusual misfits with whom she feels she belongs. With them, she learns about witchcraft, demonism, and erotic adventure, as well as the true origins of the French Revolution.

Richaud, Frederic.

Gardener to the King. Arcade, 2001. 116pp. ✍

The lush gardens of Versailles symbolize the pomp and splendor of the reigning monarch, the Sun King Louis XIV. In his creations, Jean-Baptiste de Quintinie, royal gardener, has truly managed to triumph over nature. It's fashionable to take well-known events from history and retell them from the point of view of a minor character, a pattern this novel follows to good effect.

Silko, Leslie Marmon.

Gardens in the Dunes. Simon & Schuster, 1999. 479pp. 📖

The reader sees Victorian-era Europe through the eyes of a young Native American woman and finds it wanting. Indigo, a child of the nearly-extinct Sand Lizard tribe of California, is taken in by an English couple during a search for their mother, and the trio voyage through England, Europe, and South America. The female half of the couple, Hattie, is a bluestocking who finds that Indigo can teach her about life as much as she teaches Indigo.

St. Aubin de Terán, Lisa.

The Palace. Ecco, 1999. 263pp.

On a fine May day in 1860, Gabriele del Campo, an apprentice stonemason, languishes in an Italian prison awaiting execution by a firing squad. There he shares experiences with a fellow prisoner and develops a scheme to pass himself off as a wealthy man if he is ever released. He also imagines himself in love with the beauteous Donna Donatella, the wealthy daughter of a landowner whom he had glimpsed but once. When released, Gabriele turns to gambling, garners wealth, becomes a gentleman, and constructs a Taj Mahal-like palace in Donatella's honor.

Thomas, Chantal.

Farewell, My Queen. George Braziller, 2003. 239pp. ✍

Madame Agathe-Sidonie Laborde, whose job it once was to read books to Marie-Antoinette, looks back on the last days of

Versailles—July 14 through 16, 1789. When the palace residents receive word about the fall of the Bastille, their carefully constructed life begins to crumble. Most of them continue their life as always, refusing to believe it. Marie-Antoinette tries to retain some normalcy, though she's not permitted to flee, and most of her friends abandon her.

Welch, James.

The Heartsong of Charging Elk. **Doubleday, 2000. 440pp.**

In this novel based on a true story, Charging Elk, an Oglala Sioux who witnessed the massacre of his people at the Little Big Horn, is recruited by Buffalo Bill's Wild West show. For a time he travels across Europe, performing for crowds. When he falls ill in Marseille in 1892, he finds that the show goes on without him. It's up to Charging Elk to return to where he belongs, if he can only find where that is.

Twentieth Century

General

A selection of novels taking place in Europe during the first half of the twentieth century. Modern wars and revolutions influence the background of these novels to some degree. Those dealing exclusively with World Wars I or II are listed later.

Boetius, Henning.

The Phoenix. **Doubleday, 2001. 320pp.**

Birger Lund, a *Hindenburg* survivor, has never believed the authorities' version of what happened when the airship crashed in flames in Lakehurst, New Jersey, in 1937. Taking the identity of a deceased passenger, he heads overseas to find Edmund Boysen, the ship's pilot, to find out what really happened. Immediacy is granted to this novel through the author's own connections, for Boetius grew up on stories told by his father, the last living survivor of the *Hindenburg* tragedy.

Boyd, William.

🎗 *Any Human Heart*. **Knopf, 2003. 512pp.** 📖

In this fictional autobiography, Logan Montstuart, cultured and intelligent, chronicles his remarkable life and writing career, which spans most of the twentieth century. He begins with his childhood in Uruguay and his youth at a British prep school, and continues through his bohemian existence in Spain and Paris during the wars. In old age, he grows resigned over not having accomplished much, but his own recollections prove otherwise. ALA Notable Book.

Dodd, Susan.

The Silent Woman. **Morrow, 2001. 322pp.** ✍

In 1918 Dresden, painter Oscar Kokoschka emerges from the Great War wounded in body and in spirit. His adored Almi, the widow of composer Gustav Mahler, has married someone else. He seeks to recapture their passion in an affair with Hulda, the housekeeper at the art museum where he works. Though she

yearns to reach him emotionally, he dives head first into madness, remaining obsessed with his former lover.

Ebershoff, David.

The Danish Girl. **Viking, 2000. 270pp.** ✍

The first sex-change operation in history took place in Denmark in 1931. However, this isn't so much the story of artist Einar Wegener as of his marriage, and of his understanding wife Greta. She observes her husband's gradual transformation into a woman and wisely knows when to let him go.

Hegi, Ursula.

Stones from the River. **Poseidon, 1994. 507pp.** 📖

Trudi Montag, a librarian and dwarf living in Germany during the first half of the twentieth century, chronicles the history of the small town of Burgdorf. Through Trudi, a collector of stories, readers are presented with a first-hand look at the effect of Nazism on ordinary Germans. Oprah's Book Club.

Kalfus, Ken.

The Commissariat of Enlightenment. **Ecco, 2003. 304pp.**

In 1910, at the deathbed of Leo Tolstoy, a young cinematographer named Nikolai Gribshin is anxious to capture the moment for the popular press. His path later intersects with Joseph Stalin, and soon Gribshin is honing his skills for the Soviet propaganda machine, the Commissariat of Enlightenment, under the name Comrade Astapov.

Lippi, Rosina.

Homestead. **Delphinium, 1998. 240pp.** 📖

This first novel by Lippi (better known under her pseudonym Sara Donati) is a literary family saga set in Rosenau, a remote Austrian village, beginning in 1909 and ending around 1977. Each chapter tells the story of one of Rosenau's peasant women and her life spent on the dairy farm, with her children, and in discussion with others about the day-to-day events of the Alpine town. The stories all intertwine with one another, leaving a well-rounded impression of how women's lives can change yet stay the same.

Richler, Nancy.

Your Mouth Is Lovely. **Ecco, 2002. 368pp.** 📖

Miriam Lev, writing her memoirs for her young daughter in faraway Canada, sets down the reasons why she got involved with the revolutionary activity that landed her in a dirty Siberian prison camp. Growing up in a Jewish shtetl in Minsk in 1904, Miriam is taught by her haughty stepmother Tsila to look elsewhere for happiness. Her actions lead her nowhere but trouble.

Roberts, Michèle.

The Looking Glass. Holt, 2001. 288pp.

French-English author Roberts's twelfth novel, the second to be published in America, unfolds in a small seacoast village in Normandy in the early twentieth century. Geneviève is a sixteen-year-old maid in the local bar, but she is also a storyteller. As such, she appreciates the undercurrent of sensuality that lies behind traditional French folktales. Fleeing her village, she becomes enraptured by a poet, a storyteller himself, who has captured not only the heart of Geneviève but those of several other young women as well.

Truong, Monique.

The Book of Salt. Houghton Mifflin, 2003. 261pp. ✍

A brief mention of the Indochinese servants of Alice B. Toklas and Gertrude Stein in the *Alice B. Toklas Cook Book* gives rise to the fictional biography of Bình, a Vietnamese man who left his homeland for France and spent five years in the duo's legendary apartment on the Rue de Fleurus. Though lonely and homesick, Bình is a sharp, amusing narrator, interspersing tales of his youth in Vietnam with the pain of exile and glorious descriptions of Parisian food.

World War I

These novels evoke not only the futility and tragedy of the First World War (1914–1918), but also the bustle of activity. They also recount stories of fleeting wartime romances.

Anthony, Patricia.

♟ *Flanders.* Ace, 1998. 384pp.

Travis Lee Stanhope, a young American sharpshooter, joins the British Army during the Great War in hopes of seeing action, but finds it all too close and painful. He writes letters home to his family amid gruesome scenes of fighting on the fields of Flanders, escaping from the horror of trench warfare in dreams. In those dreams he is visited by ghosts of men who can't leave the place where they died. ALA Notable Book.

Bernstein, Michael Andre.

Conspirators. Farrar, Straus & Giroux, 2004. 506pp.

In 1913, Galicia—on the border between modern Poland and Austria—was part of the Austro-Hungarian (Hapsburg) Empire. Conspiracies of rebellion are brewing in one Jewish community, and Count-Governor Wiladowski fears for his life. He hires a Jew, Jakob Tausk, to spy for him as a precaution; the wealthiest man also hires Tausk to keep his son Hans out of trouble. The charismatic new rabbi in town subverts everyone's plans.

Faulks, Sebastian.

Birdsong. Random House, 1993. 412pp. 📖

In 1910, twenty-year-old Englishman Stephen Wraysford meets Isabelle Azaire, the love of his life, on a trip to France, but she is already married. He returns to the

Continent in 1916 to fight in the trenches for France during the Great War. Memories of Isabelle, and the child they conceived, keep hope alive amid the carnage of battle. Decades later, Stephen's granddaughter discovers more about him through his journal.

Gardiner, John Rolfe.

Somewhere in France. **Knopf, 1999. 288pp.**

In 1917, Army physician William Lloyd writes letters to his family in Long Island from a location "somewhere in France." His letters are full of the love and well-meaning advice a man gives to his wife and children in his absence. They also reveal Lloyd's growing closeness to a French-born nurse who uses unorthodox methods of medical treatment.

Makine, Andrei.

Dreams of My Russian Summers. **Arcade, 1997. 320pp.** 📖

In this autobiographical novel, each summer young Andrei and his sister travel to Saranza, a village on the Russian steppe, to visit with their French grandmother Charlotte. Her stories take them back to the mystical world of Paris before and during the Great War, which she remembers with fondness, but her powerful tales may be hiding a truth that's more painful than she cares to reveal directly.

Marcom, Micheline Aharonian.

Three Apples Fell from Heaven. **Riverhead, 2001. 270pp.** 📖

Before the Jewish Holocaust, there was the Armenian genocide, one of the most shameful episodes of World War I. In 1915–1917, the Ottoman government condemned over a million Armenians to death. Their story is related through vignettes narrated by members of this disappearing culture. Anaguil, an Armenian girl, is taken in by a Muslim family but fights to hold on to her heritage, while Dickran, a baby born on the death march, is abandoned under a tree. The novel is based on reminisces of the author's grandmother, a survivor of the Armenian genocide.

Mitchell, Judith Claire.

The Last Day of the War. **Pantheon, 2004. 366pp.**

Yael Weiss, a Jewish girl from St. Louis, disguises herself as a Christian, renames herself "Yale White," and follows the man she loves, Armenian-American Dub Hagopian, across the Atlantic at the end of World War I. In Paris, she works at the YMCA soldiers' canteen and helps Dub in his efforts to avenge the Armenian genocide of 1915. Mitchell occasionally adds excitement and humor to bring to life a very serious subject.

Read, Piers Paul.

Alice in Exile. **Thomas Dunne, 2002. 352pp.** 📖

In 1913, suffragette Alice Fry meets Edward Cobb, a young man with political aspirations, and the two fall in love. When society condemns Alice's father for publishing an erotic sex manual, Edward's family convinces him to break off the match. Edward does not realize she's pregnant with his child. Desperate, Alice accepts the invitation of a Russian baron to return with him to care for his children, but World War I and the Russian Revolution leave Alice to fend for herself. Though the baron falls in love with her, Edward decides he wants her back.

World War II

These novels of World War II in Europe (1939–1945) are serious in tone; some of their scenes can be disturbing, even though few battle scenes are evoked. They emphasize humanity's propensity for survival, love, and hope, even under the harshest of conditions.

Castellani, Christopher.

A Kiss from Maddalena. **Algonquin Books of Chapel Hill, 2003. 338pp.**

In the small Italian village of Santa Cecilia in 1943, most of the men have already left for war. Vito Leone, not quite eighteen, begins courting beautiful Maddalena Piccinelli. She reciprocates his love but is forced to abandon the village when the Germans invade. Vito remains in Santa Cecilia, caring for his sick mother and tending the Piccinelli house. When the war ends, the Piccinellis return, but Maddalena's mother has other marriage plans in mind for her.

De Bernieres, Louis.

Corelli's Mandolin. **Pantheon Books, 1994. 437pp. (Original title:** *Captain Corelli's Mandolin.***)**

On the peaceful Greek island of Cephallonia at the beginning of World War II, soldiers from Italy are beginning their invasion. Pelagia Iannis, the beautiful daughter of the village physician, finds her attentions sought by two rival suitors: Antonio Corelli, captain of the Italian garrison, who'd rather be playing his mandolin and pursuing Pelagia than fighting a war; and Pelagia's fiancé, Mandras, a local fisherman who has gone off to fight for the Greeks.

Doughty, Louise.

Fires in the Dark. **HarperCollins, 2004. 480pp.**

In 1927, Emil is born as the oldest son of Joseph and Anna Ruzicka, who are part of a nomadic Roma (gypsy) tribe living far outside the mainstream of European culture. He grows up with their traditions, always knowing that they are different from the *gadje* (non-Roma) who populate the rest of the continent. When Hitler invades Czechoslovakia and the Ruzickas are sent to a labor camp, only Emil has the strength to survive. A harrowing yet beautifully written tale.

Dunmore, Helen.

The Siege. **Grove Press, 2001. 294pp.** 📖

Leningrad in winter 1941 is the scene of a massive attack by German forces. Members of the Levin family struggle to survive, thrust into sink-or-swim mode by these traumatic events. In this setting of starvation and suffering, love blooms between artist daughter Anna and a young doctor who joins the household. Dunmore's novel captures the tragedy that war held for the civilian population in this lesser-known part of World War II.

Faulks, Sebastian.

Though still more popular in the United Kingdom than in the States, Faulks is fast gaining a reputation here for his atmospheric and unsentimental novels of love in wartime Europe. Like espionage author Alan Furst, he details the ways in which ordinary people get caught up in extraordinary events.

Charlotte Gray. **Random House, 1999. 399pp.** 📖

Charlotte Gray is a young Scotswoman in love with a British RAF officer during the Second World War. Fluent in French, she joins the Secret Service to track down her lover after he goes missing in Occupied France. As she becomes more and more involved with the life of the villagers of Lavaurette, she finds new reasons to go on.

The Girl at the Lion d'Or. **Vintage, 1999. 246pp. (First published in Britain in 1989.)**

In the years leading up to World War II, beautiful Parisian Anne Louvet, hiding from a family disgrace, arrives in the French village of Javilliers with little to lose. While waitressing at the Lion d'Or, a local hotel, she meets Charles Hartmann, a rich, married attorney. The two begin a torrid affair that doesn't remain secret for long, even from his wife.

Giardina, Denise.

Saints and Villains. **Norton, 1998. 487pp.** ✍

Because the humanitarian beliefs of Dietrich Bonhoeffer, a German Protestant theologian and speaker, were contrary to those of the Nazi regime, he spoke out loudly against Hitler's policies. His stance (and failed plot to assassinate Hitler) cost him his life, which ended in a Nazi death camp in 1945. In Giardina's testament to his integrity, Bonhoeffer is a valiant hero.

Harris, Joanne.

Five Quarters of the Orange. **Morrow, 2001. 307pp.** 📖 **YA**

Framboise Dartigen, now a widow, returns to the French village of Les Laveuses to piece together her memories of her life in Occupied France during the years of the Resistance. She hopes to discover why her mother was driven away by her neighbors for collaborating with the Germans. Her mother's journal reveals secrets that explain how the present is still entwined with the past.

Kelby, N. M.

In the Company of Angels. **Hyperion, 2001. 164pp.**

Marie Claire, a young French Jewish girl living on the Belgian border during World War II, loses her entire family during the bombing of her small village. Saved by two Belgian nuns, Marie Claire is removed to their convent, where miracles begin to happen. The miracles always occur simultaneously with the scent of roses, which the girl's grandmother was famous for.

Keneally, Thomas.

🏵 *Schindler's List*. Simon & Schuster, 1982. 400pp. (Original title: *Schindler's Ark*.)
✍

Keneally's version of the inspiring story of German factory owner Oskar Schindler and how he managed to save Jews in his factory from the Holocaust was published well before Steven Spielberg's film version. Here Schindler, a flawed human being who nonetheless managed to perform an incredibly heroic act, is less enigmatic than his film portrayal. Booker Prize.

Knauss, Sibylle.

Eva's Cousin. Ballantine, 2002. 328pp. ✍

Knauss, a German author, has fictionalized the early life story of Gertrude Weisker, who remained with her cousin Eva Braun in the Berghof, Hitler's Bavarian retreat, in 1944 during the last days of the Third Reich. Here Gertrude is renamed Marlene, a twenty-year-old German girl who admires her glamorous older cousin but refuses to be tainted by Fascism.

London, Joan.

Gilgamesh. Grove/Atlantic, 2003. 256pp. 📖

Like the ancient Mesopotamian hero Gilgamesh, who takes a lengthy voyage in search of his beloved friend, a young Australian woman undertakes a dangerous journey across wartime Europe in pursuit of her former lover, the father of her child. Seventeen-year-old Edith, living on a farm in rural Australia in 1937, is seduced by her English cousin's Armenian colleague. Two years later, she and her son Jim make the trip to Soviet Armenia to find him, too engrossed in their task to notice the upcoming war.

Lustig, Arnost.

🏵 *Lovely Green Eyes*. Arcade, 2002. 248pp.

Fifteen-year-old Hanka Kaudersová, a Jew, gets out of Auschwitz by claiming to be an Aryan. The men she services in the German field brothels, over a dozen of them per day, call her "Skinny." Her hatred, and desire to live, keep her alive throughout all of her horrible experiences. ALA Notable Book.

Makine, Andrei.

The Crime of Olga Arbyelina. Arcade, 1999. 256pp.

In 1947, Olga Arbyelina, a beautiful Russian princess and émigrée living in a French village, confesses to the murder of a Russian doctor even though authorities believe it was an accident. The reasons for her self-accusation are gradually revealed through her tormented memories, most of which have to do with her hemophiliac son.

Music of a Life. **Arcade, 2002. 144pp.**

> Alexe Berg, a concert pianist in the 1930s Soviet Union, goes into hiding in the Ukraine after his parents are arrested for supposed anti-governmental activities. He takes on another's identity and fights against Hitler's army, but his musical talent gives him away in the end. Two decades later, he tells his harrowing life story to the novel's narrator, whom he meets at a train station in the Urals.

McBride, James.

Miracle at St. Anna. **Riverhead, 2002. 304pp.** 📖

> St. Anna of Stazzema, a village in Tuscany, is the setting for this novel of four black American soldiers' fight for freedom for themselves as much as their country. One of the group, a giant of a man, protects a mute orphan boy who might know the truth about the person who betrayed the villagers to the Germans.

Ondaatje, Michael.

🎗 *The English Patient.* **Knopf, 1992. 307pp.** ★ 📖

> In an abandoned villa in Italy at the end of World War II, four wounded lives converge. The "English patient," a man burned beyond recognition, gradually reveals a story of romance and adultery that ended tragically. He is cared for by a Canadian nurse who is herself visited by an old family friend. She finds the strength to survive through her growing love for a Sikh man who disarms mines for the British. Difficult for some readers, poetically beautiful for others, this character-driven novel illuminates the human aspect of wartime. Booker Prize; Governor General's Literary Award.

Potok, Chaim.

Old Men at Midnight. **Knopf, 2001. 273pp.**

> The late Rabbi Potok's latest fictional collection is a set of three related novellas about Ilana Davita Dinn, a Jewish woman whose life intersects with three different men over the course of the twentieth century. A survivor of the concentration camps in Poland relates to her the story of the Germans' invasion of his village; a Soviet academic tells her of his experience in the Russian Civil War; and a modern-day professor involves her in the writing of his memoirs. All three novellas are about coming to terms with the painful nature of the past.

Rinaldi, Nicholas.

The Jukebox Queen of Malta. **Simon & Schuster, 1999. 320pp.**

> In 1942, Brooklyn auto mechanic Rocco Raven arrives in Malta to serve as a wireless operator for the American forces. Due to its geographic proximity to Italy, the Mediterranean island is subject to almost daily bombing raids. In this heightened emotional atmosphere, Rocco falls in love with Melita, a woman who repairs jukeboxes that her cousin constructs from leftover metal.

Sanchez, Thomas.

Day of the Bees. **Knopf, 2000. 305pp.**

> Secrets between even the fondest of lovers form the basis for this novel set in German-occupied Vichy, France, during World War II. Frenchwoman Louise Collard and her devoted admirer, the Spanish painter Zermano, are inseparable until he leaves her for Paris. The pair's letters, discovered by an American after Louise's death fifty years later, detail their passion, the reason for Zermano's abandonment of her, and the truths she dared not reveal even to him.

Seiffert, Rachel.

🎗 *The Dark Room*. **Pantheon, 2001. 278pp.** 📖

> The lives of three ordinary Germans during the Third Reich speed by, frame by frame, through the perspective of Seiffert, a film editor. Helmut is a young photographer's assistant who captures 1930s Berlin on camera, though he's unable to understand what he sees. Even when faced with the reality, he continues to espouse the Nazi cause. After the war's end, the teenage Lore takes her younger siblings on a lengthy search for her grandmother while her parents remain Allied captives. Micha, in the present day, is a teacher trying to unearth the reasons why his grandfather was captured by the Russians. Betty Trask Award.

Tapon, Philippe.

The Mistress. **Dutton, 1999. 186pp.**

> Dr. Emile Bastien, a physician in Occupied France in 1942, takes revenge against the Nazi official who propositioned his mistress; he ensures that the stomach operation he performs on the Nazi will have fatal results. In the meantime, Emile's long-suffering wife plots to appropriate for herself the gold bars he has hidden on their country estate.

Thackara, James.

The Book of Kings. **Overlook, 1999. 773pp.**

> First touted as the unpublishable work of an undiscovered genius, this ambitious novel tells of four friends attending the Sorbonne during the 1930s. Their lives are changed with the outbreak of World War II. The author's language is rife with purple prose, and the dialogue is bombastic and unrealistic. Its strength is in character development and the earnestness with which Thackara tells his tale.

Walsh, Jill Paton.

A Desert in Bohemia. **St. Martin's Press, 2000. 288pp.** 🆈🅰

> In Czechoslovakia just after World War II, a young woman fleeing from a massacre rescues an abandoned baby in an empty castle. As she tries to build a new life for them both, the author follows the stories of other residents of this fictional village for the next fifty years, until the fall of the Communist government. All explore philosophical questions, such as the values of capitalism and communism, and the necessity of free will.

Wray, John.
> *The Right Hand of Sleep.* **Knopf, 2000. 325pp.**
>
> After twenty years in the Ukraine, where he fled after deserting his unit in World War I, Oscar Voxlauer returns to Austria to see his mother again. Taking a job as a gamekeeper, Oscar gets caught up in a love triangle with the previous gamekeeper's daughter and her cousin, who happens to be the new S.S. Führer. He is also forced to take sides when a Jewish friend of his loses his livelihood to the Nazis.

The United States

Colonial America

These are tales of survival, as settlers in pre-Revolutionary America make homes for themselves in a new and often harsh land. Their interactions with the land's native inhabitants often turn out differently than expected.

Begiebing, Robert J.
> *Rebecca Wentworth's Distraction.* **University Press of New England, 2003. 264pp.** 📖
>
> London-trained artist Daniel Sanborn arrives in colonial Portsmouth, New Hampshire, and sets up shop as a portrait painter. A wealthy family asks him to paint their twelve-year-old adopted daughter, Rebecca Wentworth. Rebecca proves to be exceptionally talented in art, but she experiences bizarre visions that make her family want to send her away for her own safety. Over the next five years, Sanborn's curiosity about Rebecca's fate causes him to seek out what happened to her. The author's three novels—this one, *Allegra Fullerton* (set in the 1830s), and *The Strange Death of Mistress Coffin* (Chapter 7)—form a loose trilogy of early New England life.

Hebert, Ernest.
> *The Old American.* **University Press of New England, 2000. 287pp.** ✎
>
> Early New Hampshire settler Nathan Blake (a historical figure) was abducted by Algonkian Indians in 1746, during the French and Indian Wars, and held captive in Canada. This novel retells his story, but with one of his captors as the hero. A shrewd and dignified American Indian, Caucus-Meteor (imagined on the cover as the Old Man of the Mountains), brings Blake back to his own settlement rather than sell him to the French. As the bond between them deepens, Blake adapts to Algonkian ways and loses the desire to return to his old life.

Larsen, Deborah.

The White. **Knopf, 2002. 219pp.** ✍ 📖

Sixteen-year-old Mary Jemison, a white woman born at sea on her way to the New World, is captured by a Seneca raiding party in 1758. Her family killed, Mary gradually adapts to Seneca culture. Although by her own choice she never returns to white civilization, an inner voice reminds her of her previous life. Lucia St. Clair Robson's Western historical *Ride the Wind* (Chapter 6) tells a similar tale of Indian captivity, though in a more action-oriented, less literary fashion.

Pye, Michael.

The Drowning Room. **Viking, 1995. 252pp.** ✍

The historical record says little about Gretje Reyniers, the first whore of New York, so the author took it upon himself to flesh out her life and set the record straight. After a rough voyage overseas, life is difficult in seventeenth-century New Amsterdam. Gretje is up to the challenge, living and loving as she wishes and ultimately triumphing over scandal.

The American Revolution

These novels about the founding of the United States (circa 1775–1783) look at the Revolutionary War, and its major participants, in a new light. The portraits are not always flattering.

McGrath, Patrick.

Martha Peake. **Random House, 2000. 367pp.** 📖

Flame-haired Martha Peake escapes the violent rage of her father, a crippled hunchback and perpetual drunk, by fleeing London for the American colonies. Learning that her cousins are ardent Patriots, she soon gets caught up in the Revolution against her homeland. The tale, framed around a Gothic setting, is recounted in a gloomy mansion by a man who once knew both Martha and her father.

Morgan, Robert.

Brave Enemies. **Algonquin Books of Chapel Hill, 2003. 309pp.**

In 1781 in North Carolina, sixteen-year-old Josie Summers disguises herself as a boy after fleeing from the murder of her abusive stepfather. She takes refuge with a Methodist minister, who falls in love with her after discovering that she's a woman. When he is captured by the British, she has no choice but to hide her own identity once again—by joining the militia.

Safire, William.

Scandalmonger. **Simon & Schuster, 2000. 496pp.** ✍

This novel by the well-known language maven and political columnist introduces politics and journalism in the days of America's founding fathers. Readers of Barbara Chase-Riboud's *Sally Hemings* (Chapter 2) will recognize James Callender as the reporter who betrayed his former benefactor, Thomas Jefferson, by revealing his affair with Sally Hemings to the reading public. Callender's ire is directed at other presidential hopefuls as well, including Alexander Hamilton, whose romantic involvement with Maria Reynolds caused a scandal in Washington society.

Vidal, Gore.

Burr. **Random House, 1973. 430pp.** ✎ ★

Vidal, famed man of letters and occasional politician, narrates the story of Aaron Burr (1756–1836), Thomas Jefferson's vice president, making yesterday's political shenanigans seem as fresh and new as today's headlines. An old man, Burr relates his long life to a young journalist, Charlie Schuyler, who was hired to prove that Burr sired presidential candidate Martin Van Buren. In his story, Burr leaves nothing out—his pride in being an American Revolutionary War hero, his 1804 duel with (murder of) Alexander Hamilton, his subsequent feud with Jefferson, and his trial for treason. This classic views America's founding fathers without their usual halos, just as Burr himself might have seen them.

Early United States

Set roughly in the period after the Revolution and before the Civil War (1783–1861), these are novels about a new and growing country, with riches yet to be discovered. Race relations is a common topic, and many novels show the psychological impact of slavery on people both black and white.

Allende, Isabel.

Daughter of Fortune Series.

A two-volume series about Chilean women's coming of age and their experiences with early American culture.

🎖 *Daughter of Fortune.* HarperCollins, 1999. 399pp. 📖

Rich in characterization and the spirit of adventure, this is the story of Eliza Sommers, a young woman of Chilean birth who comes to California in search of her lover Joaquín during the 1849 Gold Rush. Upon arrival, Eliza finds this supposed land of opportunity teeming with prostitutes, ruthless prospectors, and other newly arrived immigrants, including many Chinese, all crazed with gold fever. Willa Award; Oprah's Book Club.

Portrait in Sepia. HarperCollins, 2001. 300pp. 📖

In this sequel to *Daughter of Fortune*, Aurora del Valle, the granddaughter of Eliza Sommers, is brought up in her forebear's homeland of Chile but remains tormented by childhood memories of San Francisco's Chinatown. As she grows up, she decides to uncover her hidden family heritage.

Banks, Russell.

Cloudsplitter. **HarperCollins, 1998. 768pp.** ✎ 📖

Owen Brown, now an elderly man, re-creates the life of his father, abolitionist John Brown, whose murderous action at Harpers Ferry, Virginia, in 1859 contributed to the beginning of the Civil War. John Brown, in his heart an ethical man, honestly believed that God told him to go forth and end slavery. His son's retelling is ambitious, believable, and meticulously researched, if a bit overlong.

Begiebing, Robert.

The Adventures of Allegra Fullerton. **University Press of New England, 1999. 310pp.** 📖

In this lively imagined memoir, Allegra Fullerton is an itinerant portrait painter in 1830s New England who seeks to discover the true nature of art. As she travels from small-town Massachusetts to the drawing rooms of Florence, encountering some of the greatest literary minds of her day, we see her gradual transformation from small-town young woman to learned artist and philosopher.

Blake, Sarah.

Grange House. **Picador USA, 2000. 376pp.**

In this literary homage to Wilkie Collins and Henry James, Blake presents her re-creation of a traditional Victorian novel, complete with family secrets, mysterious handprints, ghosts, and a long-lost diary. In 1816, Maisie Thomas, a cosseted only child, is seventeen years old. She and her parents spend each summer at Grange House on the coast of Maine, but this summer is different. Maisie's imagination re-creates the lives of the house's former residents, the mysterious Grange family, after finding a hidden grave in the woods and from listening to fantastic stories told to her by a Grange daughter.

Brown, John Gregory.

Audubon's Watch. **Houghton Mifflin, 2001. 256pp.** ✎

When John James Audubon is just beginning his renowned career as an ornithologist, in the year 1821, he leaves his wife and family and journeys south to New Orleans to observe and draw birds. Here, he meets physician Emile Gautreaux and his beautiful wife, Myra, with whom Audubon shares a mysterious past. Later, in Audubon's old age, he and Gautreaux reminisce about their shared past, particularly Myra's unexpected death, a mystery that has never yet been solved.

Durban, Pam.

So Far Back. **Picador USA, 2000. 259pp.**

Annotated in Chapter 12.

Durham, David Anthony.

Walk Through Darkness. **Doubleday, 2002. 304pp.** 📖

William, having recently escaped a life of cruel slavery on a Virginia plantation just before the Civil War, heads to Philadelphia to find his pregnant wife Dover and begin a new life of freedom. He's followed at every turn by Andrew Morrison, an immigrant Scot who was hired to track him down. Andrew has had a difficult life himself, one he'd prefer to leave behind him.

Glancy, Diane.

Stone Heart: A Novel of Sacajawea. **Overlook, 2003.** ✍

Sacajawea, the young Shoshoni woman who served as a guide on Lewis and Clark's journey west, is today a legendary figure. Glancy poetically re-creates her voice, juxtaposing Sacajawea's dreamlike thoughts—written in the second person—with excerpts from Lewis and Clark's own diary entries.

Jones, Edward P.

🎗 *The Known World.* **Amistad/HarperCollins, 2003. 400pp.** 📖

Manchester County, Virginia: Henry Townsend, a former slave turned powerful slave owner, dies in 1840. He leaves behind a widow, Caldonia, who doesn't follow Henry's example in keeping a safe distance between her slaves and herself. When Caldonia becomes personally involved with one of her slaves, but fails to free him, it upsets the social order on the plantation—and their known world begins to disintegrate. Jones also details Henry Townsend's history and the social conditions that led him to enslave other African Americans. A powerful, subtle testimonial against slavery. Pulitzer Prize; National Book Critics' Circle Award; ALA Notable Book.

Lawrence, Margaret.

The Iceweaver. **Morrow, 2000. 403pp.**

Not as popular as her early American mysteries but just as beautifully written, this sequel takes up the story of Jennet Trevor, the deaf-mute daughter of detective/midwife Hannah Trevor from the previous books (Chapter 7). Jennet, widely believed to be a madwoman, lives alone in the wilds of upstate New York in 1809. She soon forms an understanding with John Frayne, an adventurer who has come back East to restart his life—and who ends up purchasing her freedom. As the two gradually band together against the icy wilderness, they heal each other's wounds.

Lent, Jeffrey.

Lost Nation. **Atlantic Monthly, 2002. 370pp.**

Appearing in the wilds of northern New Hampshire in 1836 is a man known only as Blood. He brings with him supplies to set up a trading post as well as a sixteen-year-old girl, Sally, whom he won in a card game. When clashes among traders, settlers, and Indians begin to brew, Blood becomes their scapegoat, finding that he can't escape from his secretive past.

Mallon, Thomas.

Henry and Clara. Ticknor and Fields, 1994. 358pp. ✍ 📖

Colonel Henry Rathbone and Clara Harris, his fiancée, were the couple attending Ford's Theatre with the Lincolns on the night the president was assassinated. Mallon reaches farther back in time to illuminate their early history. They were stepsiblings who fought against their family's disapproval of their relationship, and they married after that fateful night. Guilt overshadows their relationship for the next fifty years, for Clara chooses to tend the grief-stricken Mary Lincoln rather than her own wounded fiancé.

Marlowe, Stephen.

The Lighthouse at the End of the World. Penguin, 1995. 324pp. ✍

More than a biographical novel of early thriller/horror writer Edgar Allan Poe, this novel uses Poe's life as a springboard for exploring the themes of passion, madness, and genius. In 1849, Poe disappeared from sight, re-emerging a week later, drunk, in a Baltimore hospital—where he died four days later. This novel is a re-creation (or maybe hallucination) of his entire life, from his youth and early marriage to a thirteen-year-old cousin to his phantom double in Paris. All is seen through the eyes of Poe's own detective, C. Auguste Dupin.

Martin, Valerie.

🏆 *Property*. Doubleday, 2003. 200pp. 📖

This portrait of a female slave holder shows the horrible institution of slavery from a new point of view, and penetrates into the mind of a white woman who honestly believes herself oppressed by the slave she owns. Manon Gaudet, a plantation wife in 1820s Louisiana, never realized her husband's cruelty before she married him. As a result, she is filled with obsessive hatred for her own situation and for her husband's slave mistress, Sarah, who bore him illegitimate children. Orange Prize.

Naslund, Sena Jeter.

Ahab's Wife. Morrow, 1999. 688pp. 📖

"Captain Ahab was neither my first husband nor my last," says Una Spenser at the start of this novel, declaring both her identity and her independence. Herman Melville's *Moby-Dick* was no place for well-developed female characters, a fault Naslund remedies here. Growing up in Kentucky and Massachusetts, Una is a free spirit, running off to sea at sixteen disguised as a boy. Throughout her remarkable, adventurous life, Una searches for intellectual and spiritual grounding, which brings her into the circle of Margaret Fuller, astronomer Maria Mitchell, and abolitionist Frederick Douglass. An epic portrait of nineteenth-century women's social history.

Russell, Josh.

Yellow Jack. W.W. Norton, 1999. 250pp.

"Yellow Jack" is yellow fever, the disease that carried off a number of New Orleans residents in the late 1830s. Into this miasma comes Claude Marchand,

former assistant to photographer Louis Daguerre, who has stolen his mentor's equipment and set up shop in the city. Business is booming, since everyone wants photographic mementos of their deceased loved ones. Marchand's romantic involvement with two local women, one an octoroon, one a shopkeeper's daughter, keeps him occupied. If overly dramatic, the novel is only a product of its locale, the "necropolis of the South."

Sheehan, Jacqueline.

Truth. **Free Press, 2003. 304pp.**

A girl named Isabella is born to the slaves of a Dutch farmer at the beginning of the nineteenth century. She knows the harsh realities of life from childhood. Sold away at age nine, she is owned by a succession of masters, most of whom treat her cruelly. Despite everything, including the loss of her husband and separation from her family, she is convinced that God has a special plan for her. After she is freed and becomes orator Sojourner Truth, she finds her true path hard to follow, but she ultimately triumphs.

The Civil War

These novels show the emotional impact of the Civil War (1861–1865) on all Americans—loyal Union followers, Confederate sympathizers, and those simply caught in the middle. Extended battle scenes aren't necessary to show the immense devastation that war can bring.

Adams, Sheila Kay.

My Old True Love. **Algonquin Books of Chapel Hill, 2004. 289pp.**

Larkin Stanton and his cousin Hackley Norton grow up together in the small mountain town of Sodom, North Carolina, before and during the Civil War years. Both are fascinated by the ballads their grandmother used to sing to them. They develop a friendly rivalry over who is the better singer, but it turns serious when they both fall in love with Mary Chandler. Arty Wallin, sister to the womanizing Hackley and foster mother to Larkin, narrates this tale of war, love, heartbreak, and music. The author is a folklorist and singer.

Adrian, Chris.

Gob's Grief. **Broadway, 2001. 384pp.**

In this honest if surreal historical, Gob and Tomo are the fictional twin sons of early feminist (and presidential candidate) Victoria Woodhull. After the young Tomo runs away and is killed by a bullet in the Civil War, his brother, disgusted by the senseless loss that war brings, stops at nothing to bring him back. For this he enlists Walt Whitman, and the two attempt to construct a machine to bring back all of the Civil War dead.

Bahr, Howard.

The Black Flower. **Nautical & Aviation Club of America, 1997. 267pp.**

Over a forty-eight-hour period in November 1864, during the course of the now-forgotten Battle of Franklin, Tennessee, Confederate soldier Bushrod Carter is wounded and brought to a local residence to recover. He and childhood friends reminisce about past times while trying to distract themselves from the carnage they faced on the battlefield, and the horrors that pass as medical treatment. Anti-war themes figure prominently in this psychologically astute novel. Published first by a small press, this intelligent rendering of the Southern cause has since garnered national attention.

The Year of Jubilo. **Holt, 2000. 376pp.** 📖

This is one of the many post–Civil War novels given life by the success of *Cold Mountain*, yet Bahr moves in a slightly different direction. In 1865, Confederate soldier Gawain Harper returns home to Cumberland, Mississippi. The town, under occupation by Northern soldiers, struggles to find its own identity after the war has left its physical and social fabric tattered. At long last, Harper must confront his fiancée's father, whose goading had pushed him to enlist in the first place.

Baker, Kevin.

Paradise Alley. **HarperCollins, 2002. 688pp.**

During five days in 1863, as a reaction to President Lincoln's instituting the draft, a group of poor, mostly Irish workers in New York City incited a number of riots in the city's streets. The author shows a number of different characters' viewpoints and flashes back on occasion to the lives they left in Ireland during the potato famine years.

Braver, Adam.

Mr. Lincoln's Wars. **Morrow, 2003. 303pp.** ✍

This collection of short stories about Abraham Lincoln shows a human side that will be unfamiliar to most. Lincoln is seen from a variety of perspectives, such as that of his grief-stricken wife after the loss of their son; a Union soldier whom Lincoln indirectly turns into a killer; and John Wilkes Booth, at the fateful assassination. The tone is probing and occasionally modern in its psychological explorations, but it is illuminating to see past events through a present-day conscience.

Frazier, Charles.

🎗 *Cold Mountain*. **Algonquin Books of Chapel Hill, 1997. 356pp.** ★ 📖 **YA**

In 1864, Inman, a wounded Confederate deserter, slowly makes his way home from the Civil War and to the arms of Ada, the woman he loves. In his absence, she ekes out a living on her late father's farm at Cold Mountain in the Blue Ridge Mountains of North Carolina. Ada's life is no less difficult, and she manages to keep the derelict farm going with the help of a drifter named Ruby. Inman's arduous journey, described similarly to *The Odyssey*, is rendered with clarity and lyricism. This novel is the standard to which all Civil War novels, literary and not,

have been compared since its publication. National Book Award; Book Sense Book of the Year; ALA Notable Book.

Gibbons, Kaye.

On the Occasion of My Last Afternoon. **Putnam, 1998. 273pp.** 📖

In this story that celebrates of the strength of Southern women, Emma Garnet Tate Lowell marries a Boston doctor against her father's wishes. The two live in contentment and raise a family in Raleigh, North Carolina. All changes when the Civil War comes to town, for Emma is forced to assist her husband in his surgery. She recalls all these events in the year 1900, when she has made peace with her past and her own family secrets.

Higgins, Joanna.

A Soldier's Book. **The Permanent Press, 1998. 208pp.**

Captured by Confederate forces at the Battle of the Wilderness in 1864, Ira Cahill Stevens is thrown into prison at Andersonville, Georgia, a filthy hell-hole. There, he watches his friends and comrades slowly lose their lives from infection or madness. Ira writes in his journal, hoping to stay alive, knowing his only hope lies in an exchange of prisoners with the Union.

Hummel, Maria.

Wilderness Run. **St. Martin's Press, 2002. 339pp.** 📖

A runaway slave brings cold reality into the lives of two cousins, Isabel ("Bel") and Laurence Lindsey, who lead privileged lives in Vermont in 1859. The pair do their best to save him, but the result leads Laurence to enlist in the Civil War on the side of the Union. Bel remains at home. She begins a romance with her French-Canadian tutor, Louis Pacquette, who later also enlists. Through the men's experiences, the reality of military life is revealed as frequent monotony interrupted occasionally by bloody fighting. After the war, Isabel comes to terms with her true feelings about them both.

Humphreys, Josephine.

Nowhere Else On Earth. **Viking, 2000. 341pp.** 📖

Rhoda Strong, half Scots and half Lumbee Indian, lives in Scuffletown, a poor Indian settlement on North Carolina's Lumbee River. Not only do she and her family have to deal with Union soldiers encroaching on their land, but the men have to avoid being conscripted into labor camps by marauding Confederate gangs. Rhoda falls in love with Henry Berry Lowrie, an outlaw, who helps the townspeople band together.

Jiles, Paulette.

🎗 *Enemy Women.* **Morrow, 2002. 321pp.** 📖

Adair Colley and her two sisters leave their home in southeastern Missouri after Union soldiers set it ablaze. Accused of enemy collaboration,

Adair is captured and forced to live in disgusting conditions in a St. Louis women's prison. Her romance with her Union interrogator sets her free, but then she has to find her way home. Comparisons to *Cold Mountain*, more frequently made than deserved, are fitting in this case. Willa Award.

Lent, Jeffrey.
In the Fall. **Atlantic Monthly, 2000. 542pp.** 📖

In the final years of the Civil War, a runaway slave named Leah nurses Norman Pelham, a wounded Union soldier, back to health. They fall in love, marry, and return to his home in Vermont, where they raise a family and deal with their rural neighbors' racial prejudices. But the past has a way of catching up with people, and so it is with Leah, who returns to her home in the South to wrap up unsolved issues. What she discovers there changes her life and that of her progeny over the next several generations.

O'Nan, Stewart.
A Prayer for the Dying. **Holt, 1999. 195pp.** 📖

Told in the second person through the eyes of Jacob Hansen, a sheriff in post–Civil War Friendship, Wisconsin, this novel is a first-hand view of the horror of diphtheria, a contemporary plague. At first Hansen believes he can fight off the disease and save his family, but reality soon overtakes him, to the point of wondering whether evil in its most virulent form can ever be obliterated.

Randall, Alice.
The Wind Done Gone. **Houghton Mifflin, 2001. 210pp.** 📖

Cindy—also known as Cinnamon or Cynara—is the bastard half-sister of Scarlett O'Hara, the unacknowledged daughter of Scarlett's father and her Mammy. Always an outsider, Cindy goes beyond her class and color to found a new life for herself in the Deep South and in the country's capital. Margaret Mitchell's famous characters move like shadows in the background and are never referred to by name: Scarlett is "Other," Melanie is "Mealy Mouth," and Rhett (their joint romantic interest) is simply "R." Randall's novel was a scandal in the literary world before it was even published, due to claims by Margaret Mitchell's estate that it violated copyright on *Gone with the Wind* (Chapter 4). Eventually it was acknowledged by the courts as a parody, and the whole process lifted it to bestseller status.

Reed, John.
A Still Small Voice. **Delacorte, 2000. 351pp.** 📖

As a young child, Alma Flynt comes to live with her Aunt Bettina in Cotterpin Creek, Kentucky, after her parents' deaths. There she discovers a love for both horses and John Warren, the youngest son of the wealthy Cleveland family. He is called away to war, and she grows to womanhood in his absence, never forgetting her first love and always awaiting his return. Reed's novel of life on the Civil War home front, building on the *Cold Mountain* phenomenon, is reflective and character-driven, and the feminine voice of his narrator rings true.

Vidal, Gore.

Lincoln. **Random House, 1984. 657pp.** ✍ ★

In Washington, D.C., where most of the residents are staunch Confederates, President Lincoln struggles to keep the Union together. He is a canny politician, refusing to be shaped by the powerful men in Washington. Despite the novel's length, this is an illuminating portrait of Lincoln, the man, as seen from the viewpoint of his friends and contemporaries, in particular his secretary John Hay. As with Vidal's other historical novels, the author makes the political background relevant and recognizable to today's readers.

Youmans, Marly.

🎗 *The Wolf Pit.* **Farrar, Straus & Giroux, 2001. 352pp.**

This stylistically strong, poetically written novel relies more on its characterization and beautiful language than on plot. Its two protagonists never meet. Robin, a Confederate soldier, endures the horrors of prison by focusing on family memories and a strange story about green children in a wolf pit. Agate, a mulatto slave, learns to read and write but finds that her accomplishments cause her even more suffering. Michael Shaara Award.

Reconstruction and the Gilded Age

These novels are set between 1865 and 1900. Although the Civil War is over, its legacy remains. Cities reinvigorate themselves in its wake, immigrants flood America's borders, and settlers head west in search of open land. Though slavery has been abolished, racial problems haven't disappeared, not by a long shot.

Boorstin, Jon.

The Newsboys' Lodging House. **Viking, 2003. 342pp.** ✍

This novel re-creates a lost period in the life of one of America's greatest philosophical minds, William James, and is written as his diary. Despondent and nearly suicidal, James—taking inspiration from Horatio Alger's tales of young street urchins who rose to great success—travels incognito to New York City in the 1870s. These were the early days of capitalism in a growing city, where great wealth could be found adjacent to horrible poverty. In the lives of these plucky newsboys, James rediscovers the nature of the American dream.

Bram, Christopher.

The Notorious Dr. August. **Morrow, 2000. 498pp.**

Augustus Fitzwilliam Boyd, better known as Dr. August, is a pianist who claims the ability to communicate with the spirit world through his playing. The action moves from Civil War-era New York to Europe and America in the 1920s. Through a love triangle involving him, the ex-slave Isaac Kemp, and the governess Alice Pangborn, Dr. August investigates the power of love and what it means to be human.

Cambor, Kathleen.

In Sunlight, in a Beautiful Garden. **Farrar, Straus & Giroux, 2000. 258pp.** 📖

Romance and tragedy collide in this fictionalization of the flood that claimed the lives of over 2,200 residents of Johnstown, Pennsylvania, in 1889. Because readers know that many of the people (all vividly depicted) will die before the end, the atmosphere is heavy with foreshadowing. The devastation is made even more heartbreaking by the knowledge that if the town's rich businessmen had not been quite so selfish, the tragedy could have been prevented.

Dew, Robb Forman.

The Evidence Against Her. **Little, Brown, 2001. 327pp.**

Lily Scofield, Robert Butler, and Lily's cousin Warren Scofield are born on the same day in September 1888 in Washburn, Ohio. The three are inseparable until Warren marries an outsider to their circle, sophisticated Agnes Claytor, not long after Lily's marriage to Robert. The emotional dynamics of the trio's relationship, changed by Agnes's presence, reverberates throughout the small town.

Durham, David Anthony.

Gabriel's Story. **Doubleday, 2001. 304pp.**

Annotated in Chapter 6.

Fowler, Karen Joy.

Sister Noon. **Putnam, 2001. 321pp.** 📖

Lizzie Hayes, a fortyish spinster in Gilded Age San Francisco, lives an exemplary life filled with good deeds, such as volunteering at the Ladies' Relief and Protection Society Home. Her rebellious nature emerges when she meets Mary Ellen Pleasant, herself perhaps a former slave, who brings her a young orphan girl to care for.

Mallon, Thomas.

Two Moons. **Pantheon, 2000. 303pp.**

By 1877, Cynthia May, the new human "computer" for the U.S. Naval Observatory in Washington, D.C., has spent nearly half her life in the shadow of the Civil War. Her route to re-joining the civilized world takes two paths, both professional and personal. The "two moons" of the title are not only the newly discovered satellites of Mars, but also two men, consumptive astronomer Hugh Allison and larger-than-life politician Roscoe Conkling. They revolve around Cynthia, affecting her decisions and actions.

Morrison, Toni.

🎗 *Beloved.* **Knopf, 1987. 275pp.** ★ 📖

Sethe, a former slave in post–Civil War rural Ohio, is tormented by memories of her previous life on Sweet Home Farm, from which she had run away. Her most painful memory, revealed gradually in flashbacks, is that she had murdered her infant daughter rather than see her be recaptured. Her daughter later reappears, fully grown, as a ghostly young woman whom Sethe calls Beloved. The ghost's

presence causes difficulties with Sethe's remaining family members, not least of all with Sethe herself. Pulitzer Prize.

Rhodes, Jewell Parker.

Douglass' Women. **Atria, 2002. 358pp.**

Frederick Douglass, African-American abolitionist and orator, loves two women in his life: Anna Murray, the free black woman who later became his long-suffering wife, and Ottilie Assing, a German intellectual and heiress with whom he conducts an illicit affair. When Anna discovers their relationship, she puts up with Ottilie's presence (she even shares their living quarters), but holds fast to her man.

Sontag, Susan.

In America. **Farrar, Straus & Giroux, 2000. 387pp.**

In 1876, Maryna Zalezowska, Poland's leading actress, rejuvenates her life and that of her family by establishing a utopian community in southern California. A consummate actress, she throws herself into this experiment full force and successfully reinvents herself as a strong American woman. When the utopian community fails, Maryna returns to the stage, but with a new sense of purpose. National Book Award.

Vanderhaeghe, Guy.

The Englishman's Boy. **St. Martin's Press, 1997. 333pp.**

Damon Ira Chance, a film mogul in 1920s Hollywood, wants to create a magnificent Western epic in the style of his hero, D. W. Griffith. To this end he finds a film extra named Shorty McAdoo who is rumored to have been a real-life cowboy, and hires Canada native Harry Vincent to seek out his story. In alternating chapters, Vanderhaeghe tells the story of an Englishman's servant who joins a band of wolf-hunters to fight off Indian horse thieves in Montana Territory in the 1870s. His story isn't anywhere near as heroic as Chance expects it to be. The novel explores the power of film to remake history. Governor General's Literary Award.

The Last Crossing. **Atlantic Monthly, 2004. 393pp.**

At their wealthy father's behest, Charles and Addington Gaunt cross the seas from Victorian England to find their brother Simon, who has disappeared somewhere in the American West. They hire a half-Indian, half-Scots guide with his own personal problems to deal with, and the search party steadily accumulates more company along the way. All have their own separate quests, and each is dealt with individually, in between encounters with Indian tribes, mountain men, and other eccentric characters of the wild American West.

Yan, Geling.

The Lost Daughter of Happiness. **Hyperion East, 2001. 288pp.**

Fusang is one of several thousand young Chinese women kidnapped and sold into prostitution in Gold Rush-era San Francisco. In this hotbed of corruption and vice, the life of the silent and enigmatic Fusang is extraordinarily difficult, but it is made more bearable by a Caucasian boy who loves her. Fusang is a historical character about whom little is known, and her character isn't fully fleshed out here, but the author succeeds in conveying the exotic and seedy atmosphere of Chinatown.

Twentieth Century

General

A mélange of fictional portraits set in the United States between 1900 and 1950—a time of nostalgia for many people, but an unfamiliar world to younger readers. This is a large, diverse category showing the wide range of people's experiences in early twentieth-century America. Novels about World War II are listed separately.

Baggott, Juliana.

The Madam. **Atria, 2003. 288pp.**

After a failed get-rich-quick scheme down in Florida, Alma's husband abandons her. She returns home to Marrowtown, West Virginia, a 1920s industrial town with little redeeming value. With the help of two other unconventional women, Alma reclaims her three children and opens a business of her own—a bordello. It's a legitimate way to earn a living, she thinks, until her fifteen-year-old daughter Lettie decides she has had enough. Baggott based this novel on the lives of her great-grandmother and grandmother.

Boyle, T. C.

Riven Rock. **Viking, 1998. 466pp.** ✍

After her marriage to charming Stanley McCormick, wealthy son of inventor Cyrus McCormick, socialite and MIT grad Katherine Dexter must come to terms with his violent behavior toward women. Katherine never gives up hope for his recovery, despite the years he spends incarcerated at Riven Rock, a Santa Barbara sanitarium. He is cared for exclusively by male nurses because of the fear that he would harm anyone female. The early twentieth century goes on without Stanley, while Katherine becomes involved in the suffrage movement.

Braver, Adam.

Divine Sarah. **Morrow, 2004. 224pp.** ✍

The divine stage actress Sarah Bernhardt, aged sixty-one in 1906 in Los Angeles, no longer receives the acclaim she feels she deserves. Not only is she aging less than gracefully, but her shows have been publicly deemed immoral. She decides, with her usual aplomb, to play these theatrical moments for all they're worth. Braver's novel follows a week of Sarah's life, relating her struggles with fame and getting old.

Brown, Carrie.

The Hatbox Baby. **Algonquin Books of Chapel Hill, 2000. 348pp.**

A worried father brings his very premature baby in a hatbox to Dr. Leo Hoffman, world-famous baby doctor, at the Chicago World's Fair in 1933. Here the question of what is and is not normal is moot, for all sorts of human and scientific oddities are on display, from Dr. Hoffman's "infantorium" to dwarves and exotic dancers. Soon many members of the fair's large cast become involved in the baby's future, especially after his father is unexpectedly murdered on the way home.

Chabon, Michael.

🎗 *The Amazing Adventures of Kavalier and Clay.* **Random House, 2000. 639pp.** 📖

In the years just before World War II, the beginning of the Golden Age of comic books, native Brooklynite Sammy Klayman, a Jew, teams up with his cousin Josef Kavalier, newly arrived from Nazi-occupied Prague. Together they create a magnificent comic-book hero, the Escapist, who battles Hitler and his minions on the printed page. At the same time, Joe tries unsuccessfully to rescue his family from Prague. A big-hearted yet serious tale. Pulitzer Prize.

Clarke, Breena.

River, Cross My Heart. **Little, Brown, 1999. 245pp.** 📖 **YA**

After young Clara Bynum drowns in the Potomac River while older sister Johnnie Mae plays nearby, the life of this African-American family in the Georgetown area of Washington, D.C., is never the same. It is 1925, and segregation is in full swing, which is why the siblings were not cooling off in the town pool instead. As she grows, Johnnie Mae and her parents are tormented by Clara's death. Johnnie Mae finds an inner strength in water, becoming a strong swimmer and sneaking into segregated pools at night. Oprah's Book Club.

Day, Cathy.

The Circus in Winter. **Harcourt, 2004. 288pp.**

The Great Porter Circus wintered in the small Midwestern town of Lima, Indiana, between 1884 and 1946. Day weaves the day-to-day lives of circus folk into a collection of related short stories, tying together subjects both comic and tragic. She also includes old photos of circus memorabilia to add to the nostalgic atmosphere.

Doctorow, E. L.

🎗 *Ragtime.* **Random House, 1975. 270pp.** ★

In 1906 in New Rochelle, New York, the lives of some of the most famous people of their time—Emma Goldman, Harry Houdini, Sigmund

Freud—intersect with members of a typical American family. This produces an imaginative and magical romp through the early twentieth century. National Book Critics' Circle Award.

Doig, Ivan.

Prairie Nocturne. **Scribner, 2003. 371pp.** 📖

In Doig's earlier novel about Montana's Two Medicine country, *Dancing at the Rascal Fair* (Chapter 6), Susan Duff was a young girl. Now it is 1924, and she is an unmarried voice teacher in the big city of Helena. Wes Williamson, former gubernatorial candidate and her former lover, asks if she will return to Two Medicine to give voice lessons to his black chauffeur, Monty. He becomes a big success on the New York stage, following in the Harlem Renaissance movement, while Susan and Wes re-evaluate their relationship.

Ebershoff, David.

Pasadena. **Random House, 2002. 485pp.**

When realtor Andrew Blackwood tries to make money by purchasing an old ranch from a farmer in 1944 in Pasadena, California, he gets the chance to hear its complete history, which is the tale of Pasadena itself in miniature. The author's heroine is Linda Stamp, born in 1903, whose affections are torn between the mysterious Bruder, the ranch's later owner, and rich bachelor Willis Poore.

Erdrich, Louise.

The Last Report of the Miracles at Little No-Horse. **HarperCollins, 2001. 361pp.** 📖

Father Damien Modeste, beloved priest of the Ojibwe people on the Little No Horse reservation in rural North Dakota, has kept a secret from his flock for over fifty years: He is, in fact, a woman. Revealed early on, this isn't the greatest mystery of the book. When Father Jude Miller visits to investigate whether the late Sister Leopolda should be made a saint, Father Damien is forced to revisit the past and decide whether he should reveal why her piety may have been false. Erdrich's beautiful prose takes us through decades of reservation history, including that of many families already familiar to readers through her contemporary novels.

The Master Butchers Singing Club. **HarperCollins, 2003. 400pp.** 📖

While Erdrich's novels have traditionally focused on her Native American ancestry, here she looks at her father's forebears, German immigrants who settled on the Great Plains. Fidelis Waldvogel, a master butcher from Germany, arrives in Argus, North Dakota, after World War I with his new wife, Eva. He sets up shop in town. The pair meet and befriend Delphine Watzka, a former circus performer with a heart of gold and generosity to match. Delphine and Fidelis feel some attraction to each other. After Eva's tragic death from cancer, they marry.

Estrin, Marc.

Insect Dreams: The Half-Life of Gregor Samsa. **BlueHen, 2002. 480pp.**

Suppose Gregor Samsa, the man-turned-cockroach of *The Metamorphosis*, survived the untimely end Kafka wrote for him. Here Gregor, rescued by friends, lives to tell the tale of America during the first half of the twentieth century. His path crosses those of Franklin Delano Roosevelt, Einstein, Rilke, and other great political and philosophical minds. The result is a tale at once comical and profound.

Eugenides, Jeffrey.

Middlesex. **Farrar, Straus & Giroux, 2002. 529pp.**

Eugenides tells the story of hermaphrodite Cal (once called Calliope) Stephanides, from her early years growing up as a girl in suburban Michigan to the time she spends discovering her, or his, true nature as a male. But Cal's story truly begins decades earlier with the immigration of his grandparents, brother and sister, from 1920s Greece and Turkey to Detroit during the Prohibition years. Their marriage (and promise to keep their true relationship secret) results in the gender-bending nature of their grandchild. Pulitzer Prize.

Even, Aaron Roy.

Bloodroot. **Thomas Dunne, 2000. 259pp.**

In 1936, near Charlottesville, Virginia, an elderly black caretaker takes the law into his own hands when he shoots and kills a white sheriff sent to force him off his land. This novel, based on historical fact, details the actions that led up to the incident through the eyes of the caretaker, William Wesley, and a young government representative, Elsa Childs.

Feldman, Ellen.

Lucy. **W. W. Norton, 2003. 292pp.**

Feldman celebrates the life of a woman who is little known today but whose role in a presidential marriage caused a scandal in the early twentieth century. Just before the First World War, Franklin Delano Roosevelt, then the Assistant Secretary of the Navy, falls in love with Lucy Mercer, his wife's social secretary. When Eleanor finds their love letters, she demands that they never see each other again. But when the pressures of World War II take their toll on the beleaguered president, he turns once again to Lucy for support.

Fowler, Karen Joy.

The Sweetheart Season. **Holt, 1996. 352pp.**

Irini Doyle's daughter recalls her mother's life as of 1947, when the small town of Magrit, Minnesota, was empty of men because they never came home from the war. Most of Magrit's women work in the local cereal factory. Their employer thinks it's a good idea for them to form a women's baseball team, promoting his product as they tour the circuit.

Gibbons, Kaye.

Divining Women. **Putnam, 2004. 205pp.** 📖

In 1918, in the summer before she begins study at Radcliffe, twenty-two-year-old Mary Oliver pays a visit to her half-uncle Troop and his wife Maureen down in North Carolina. Maureen, heavily pregnant, relies on Mary's presence to shield her from her husband's constant verbal abuse. As Troop's behavior becomes more and more tyrannical, Mary encourages Maureen to fight back.

Gold, Glen David.

Carter Beats the Devil. **Hyperion, 2001. 483pp.**

Charles Carter, aka "Carter the Great," is a magician in vaudeville in San Francisco circa 1923. When President Harding dies unexpectedly several hours after appearing on stage with Carter in an elaborate death-defying stunt, blame is cast on the illusionist. As Carter goes on the run to save his reputation, his antics—like those of the true magician—amaze and fascinate.

Hough, Robert.

The Final Confession of Mabel Stark. **Atlantic Monthly, 2003. 448pp.** ✍

Mabel Stark—tiger tamer extraordinaire in the 1920s—takes center stage in the Barnum and Bailey Circus. Like the dramatic acts she performs, Mabel is herself a larger-than-life personality. In 1968, eighty-year-old Mabel, nursing her latest and worst injuries, speaks about her early escape from a mental institution, her loves and failed marriages, and the job and cats she loves most of all. Based on a true story.

House, Silas.

A Parchment of Leaves. **Algonquin, 2002. 288pp.** 📖

In this tale of tender love and family jealousy, brothers Saul and Aaron Sullivan vie for the love of a beautiful Cherokee woman named Vine in rural Kentucky in 1917. Vine marries Saul, but as she bears his daughter and becomes a real part of the family, the restless Aaron continues to lust after her. When Saul heads out of town to find logging work, Aaron sees the chance to make his move.

Inness-Brown, Elizabeth.

Burning Marguerite. **Knopf, 2002. 237pp.**

One winter morning, on rural Grain Island off the New England coast, James Jack Wright finds the body of his beloved "Tante," ninety-four-year-old Marguerite Deo, lying outside the cabin they shared. As James Jack ponders the mystery of her death, the tale shifts to Marguerite herself, and her life spent raising him after his parents died, in New Orleans during the Depression and World War II.

Johnson, Stephanie.

Belief. **St. Martin's Press, 2002. 485pp.**

In 1899, rural New Zealander William McQuiggin deserts his growing family to go to America after seeing a miraculous vision. He becomes involved with a variety of

religious groups—the Mormons, Jehovah's Witnesses, and utopian believers at Illinois's Zion City. His long-suffering wife Myra and their children eventually catch up and trudge along behind him. Thankfully for readers' patience, Myra grows a tougher skin. Over time William grows mentally unhinged, seeking faith but discovering only emptiness.

Jones, Allen Morris.

Last Year's River. Houghton Mifflin, 2001. 256pp.

After her rich boyfriend rapes her, New York socialite Virginia Price, seventeen years old, is shuttled off to remote Wyoming to have her baby and give it up for adoption. While there she falls in love with Henry Mohr, a war-weary World War I veteran. When the father of her child shows up, Virginia must decide whether to marry her abuser or stay in Big Sky Country with Henry.

Kay, Terry.

Taking Lottie Home. Morrow, 2001. 📖 **YA**

On a train heading north from Augusta, Georgia, in 1904, Ben Phelps meets innocent girl-woman Lottie Barton on his way home from a failed career in professional baseball. Lottie is an angel in disguise destined to change his life, and those of his friends, forever. Full of picturesque descriptions of life in a small Southern town, this is a heartwarming tale of people's unlimited capacity for love.

Kennedy, William.

Roscoe. Viking, 2002. 291pp.

The seventh novel in Kennedy's <u>Albany Cycle</u>, which has become a quasi-epic history of the social and political personalities of Albany, New York, takes on scheming but good-hearted Democrat Roscoe Conway. During the post–World War II years, Conway wants out of politics but can't resist the call to duty when New York's Republican governor threatens the Democrats' power. Previous novels in the Cycle include *Legs*, *Billy Phelan's Greatest Game*, *Ironweed*, *Quinn's Book*, *Very Old Bones*, and *The Flaming Corsage*.

Kilgo, James.

Daughter of My People. University of Georgia Press, 1998. 288pp. 📖

In rural South Carolina in 1918, Jennie Grant, the mixed-race, illegitimate cousin of half-brothers Hart and Tison Bonner, only serves to deepen their rivalry. Hart loves Jennie deeply and takes pains to conceal their longtime affair from the world. When Tison discovers it, he makes insulting overtures to her. This causes Hart to defend her honor and bring her existence out into the open, an action with tragic repercussions.

Laskas, Gretchen Moran.

The Midwife's Tale. **The Dial Press, 2003. 243pp.** 📖

Elizabeth Whiteley, a midwife in the mountains of 1920s West Virginia, is simply following the family tradition with her chosen profession. She has second thoughts when she discovers the meaning behind a red book in which her mother records births. Though Elizabeth falls in love with a man who doesn't reciprocate and discovers that she cannot have children of her own, she finds unexpected rewards in raising her lover's daughter.

Leithauser, Brad.

Darlington's Fall. **Knopf, 2002. 311pp.**

The hero of this novel in verse is naturalist Russel Darlington, who from early childhood in the early twentieth century develops a passion for the natural world, specifically "bugs." He becomes a professor, as expected, but his marriage to a socially conscious woman leaves him frustrated and alone. On a field expedition to the Pacific island of Ponape, he suffers a tragic accident that leaves him crippled. Darlington's second, less literal "fall" is for his much younger housekeeper, Marja, with whom he discovers a new love.

Mallon, Thomas.

Bandbox. **Pantheon, 2004. 306pp.**

Mallon's latest novel, set in the heart of Jazz Age (1920s) New York City, centers on a men's fashion magazine called *Bandbox*. Jimmy Gordon, one of the publication's star editors, has recently defected to a new competitor. This fuels the rivalry between them. As Gordon tries to sink *Bandbox* by stealing away more of its writers, the competition grows fierce and farcical.

Dewey Defeats Truman. **Pantheon, 1997. 355pp.**

In his highly regarded historical novels, Mallon looks beyond the primary players of historical events. Many people have heard about the 1948 presidential election, when newspapers were so certain of Thomas Dewey's victory over Harry Truman that they mistakenly declared him the winner. In Dewey's hometown of Owosso, Michigan, local politics and romance mirror the national contest, as Anne Macmurray chooses between two suitors of opposing political parties.

Martin, Lee.

Quakertown. **Dutton, 2001. 289pp.**

In this novel based on a historical incident, Quakertown is a flourishing African-American neighborhood within the city of Denton, Texas, in the 1920s. When the Klan becomes too strong, gardener Washington Jones is asked by his white employer to do the unthinkable—completely segregate the white and black communities in exchange for access privileges on the white side of town.

Mendlesohn, Jane.

I Was Amelia Earhart. **Knopf, 1996. 145pp.** ✍ **YA**

Imagining what might have happened to the world-famous American pilot Amelia Earhart after her disappearance on her final flight in 1937, Mendelsohn posits that she and her drunken navigator, Fred Noonan, make an emergency landing on a Pacific island. There they grow close over mutual reminiscences.

Millhauser, Steven.

Martin Dressler: The Tale of an American Dreamer. **Crown, 1996. 293pp.**

Dressler, an entrepreneur in turn-of-the-century New York, has dreams of creating beautiful hotels that imitate the natural world and obliterate the need for reality. In this allegory that demonstrates the emptiness of consumerism, his private life is not nearly as pleasant. Pulitzer Prize.

Morgan, Robert.

Gap Creek. **Algonquin Books of Chapel Hill, 1999. 326pp.** 📖 **YA**

For Julie Harmon, a seventeen-year-old newlywed in the mountain country of early twentieth-century North Carolina, life is a struggle to survive. Marriage doesn't make it any easier, yet Julie and her husband hang in there through days of backbreaking labor, starvation, poverty, childbirth, and death. This is an utterly unsentimental look at rural farming life, grim and unpleasant, but accurately conveyed down to the characters' lilting mountain speech. Oprah's Book Club.

This Rock. **Algonquin Books of Chapel Hill, 2001. 323pp.** 📖

Morgan's latest novel about the rewards and troubles of Southern rural Appalachian life in the early twentieth century takes as its protagonists two brothers, Muir and Moody Powell, living in the wilderness of the Carolinas in the 1920s. The seventeen-year-old Muir, his mother's clear favorite, has a Cain-and-Abel-like rivalry with Moody, who turns to bootlegging and prostitution while trying to undermine his brother and his newfound faith.

Murkoff, Bruce.

Waterborne. **Knopf, 2004. 393pp.**

The lives of three strong-minded individuals converge at the building of the Hoover Dam in Boulder City, Nevada, during the Great Depression. Engineer Filius Poe, a workaholic, seeks to forget his tragic past. Lena McCardell wants a new life for herself and her son, and Lew Beck, a bitter man, just wants revenge for all the unfairness he has encountered in life. All of Murkoff's characters, primary and secondary, are fully realized, as is the barren crimson desert setting.

Olafsson, Olaf.

Walking into the Night. **Pantheon, 2003. 272pp.**

Christian Benediktsson, who has worked for years as William Randolph Hearst's reliable butler, pens a series of unsent letters to his wife back in Iceland. In them he reveals why he left her and his children twenty years earlier to run away with a Swedish actress to New York, and what made him settle down to spend his remaining years at remote San Simeon. Set in the 1920s and earlier.

Price, Reynolds.

Roxanna Slade. **Scribner, 1998. 301pp.**

Born in 1900 in rural North Carolina, Roxanna Slade is an "average" woman whose life is actually anything but. Her smooth Southern drawl apparent in her narrative style, the elderly Roxanna takes us through her day-by-day existence over the past century, from the minutiae of chores done to pass the time through her experiences of marriage, childbearing, infidelity, and depression. Her acceptance of all of these things gives her a calm outlook on life.

Rayner, Richard.

The Cloud Sketcher. **HarperCollins, 2000. 435pp.** 📖

Esko Vaananen has survived much in his young life. A fire in his native Finland killed his mother and blinded him in one eye, then came the horrors of the Russian Revolution and the Finnish Civil War. His dream of becoming an architect and his love for a Russian aristocrat's daughter see him through the hard times. By the 1920s, he has come to New York City, gaining fame by designing skyscrapers. His Russian lady-love, also in the city, is married to another. The story begins as Esko is taken away in handcuffs, accused of her husband's murder.

Rossi, Agnes.

The Houseguest. **Dutton, 2000. 294pp.**

In the 1930s, Irishman Edward Devlin, distraught over the death of his wife Agnes, avoids drinking himself into oblivion by escaping overseas to America. He leaves his young daughter Maura in the care of an unloving spinster aunt and feels guilty for leaving his old life behind. Edward ends up as the houseguest of a New Jersey couple; he is welcomed by the jovial husband, and intrigued by his neglected wife. Their relationship affects the lives of all concerned.

Schwarz, Christina.

Drowning Ruth. **Doubleday, 2000. 338pp.** 📖

In 1919, as America's involvement in the First World War is ending, nurse Amanda Starkey returns home to rural Wisconsin after suffering a nervous breakdown. She and her younger sister, the popular and beautiful Mattie, care for Mattie's daughter Ruth after Ruth's father Carl goes off to war. Carl returns home a year later, anxious to begin life again with his beloved wife and child, only to find Mattie drowned under mysterious circumstances and Amanda unwilling to talk about the incident. A novel about family secrets and the repressive nature of small-town life. Oprah's Book Club.

Seymour, Miranda.

The Summer of '39. **Norton, 1999. 230pp. (Original title: *The Telling*.)**

Seymour is a novelist and biographer whose subjects over the years have included Robert Graves, Lord Byron, Medea, and Helen of Troy. Based on her previous biography of Graves, here she re-creates the disastrous summer he spent in

America with the poet Laura Riding and an American couple. The married pair in this novel are Nancy and Chance Brewster, and their story is related by Nancy. She has spent most of her life in a sanitarium, incurably mad, as a result of that fateful summer spent with her European visitors just before World War II.

Shreve, Anita.

All He Ever Wanted. **Little, Brown, 2003. 288pp.** 📖

Man sees woman; man gets woman; man loses woman, only to realize that he never truly had her in the first place. Such is the story of Nicholas Van Tassel, a smarmy academic at a New Hampshire college who spots beautiful Etta Bliss beneath a tree in 1899. He pursues her until she agrees to marry him, but she has a yearning for freedom that won't be denied. When Van Tassel discovers her secret hideaway, his behavior becomes even more paranoid and unreasonable.

Fortune's Rocks. **Little, Brown, 1999. 453pp.** 📖

In New Hampshire in 1899, Olympia Biddeford, the headstrong and precocious fifteen-year-old daughter of a wealthy Boston family, tests the boundaries of her social class by having an affair with a freethinking local physician three times her age. Soon she learns the price of straying. Pregnant and ostracized by society, Olympia must pick up the pieces and invent a new life for herself.

Sea Glass. **Little, Brown, 2002. 384pp.** 📖

This is the third novel of a trilogy, beginning with *The Pilot's Wife* (a contemporary novel) and *Fortune's Rocks* (above), all centered on the inhabitants of a large house on the New Hampshire coast. On a fine June day in 1929, Honora Willard and Sexton Beecher are united in marriage. After the stock market crash, Honora becomes involved with the plight of local mill workers, particularly an Irishman named McDermott. The story is told from the point of view of six characters, whose lives diverge at the beginning but entwine toward the end.

Stonich, Sarah.

These Granite Islands. **Little, Brown, 2001. 310pp.** 📖

Dying in a hospital bed with her son by her side, ninety-nine-year-old Isobel Howard reminisces about the summer of 1936, which she spent in a Minnesota lakefront town with a new friend, the exotic Cathryn Malley. As Cathryn introduces Isobel to her cosmopolitan Chicago ways, she involves her in an illicit affair that she is having with the local forest ranger. When the unspeakable happens, Isobel must herself come to terms with her own definitions of morality.

Strauss, Darin.

The Real McCoy. **Dutton, 2002. 326pp.**

In this recounting of the life of flimflam artist, welterweight champion, and bigamist "Kid McCoy," the legend begins with the theft of the real boxer's identity. Indiana opportunist Virgil Selby takes the dead McCoy's place in the ring, moves to Manhattan, and racks up some championships on his own. All of this mythmaking catches up with him sooner or later, by which point the novel's title takes an even more ironic turn.

Tyler, Anne.
The Amateur Marriage. Knopf, 2004. 306pp. 📖

In Baltimore in 1941, Pauline Barclay and a group of girlfriends stop in the grocery store owned by Michael Anton's Polish Catholic family. Pauline and Michael fall in love and marry as soon as Michael gets out of the Army. The two are polar opposites and really should never have married. Pauline is impulsive and hopeful; Michael is thoughtful and deliberate. Problems start almost immediately, but their marriage survives thirty years and three children, though it seems like one extended argument.

Walker, Alice.
🎗 *The Color Purple*. Harcourt Brace, 1992. 245pp. ★ 📖

From the early twentieth century until the 1940s, an African-American woman, Celie, writes heartfelt letters to her sister Nettie, a missionary in Africa, and to God. In these missives she details her brutal and repressive relationships with both her stepfather and husband. After years of suffering, she eventually finds love and acceptance both from outside and within herself. Pulitzer Prize; National Book Award.

Watson, Brad.
The Heaven of Mercury. Norton, 2002. 288pp.

Mercury, Mississippi, in the first quarter of the twentieth century is the setting for this small-town Southern Gothic novel populated with traditionally quirky characters. Finus Bates falls in love with Birdie Wells instantly after spying her turning cartwheels naked in the woods. Though they are together for a brief time, he doesn't have the courage to pursue her.

Weber, Christin Lore.
Altar Music. Scribner, 2000. 251pp. 📖

The author, a former nun, knows of which she speaks in this thoughtful family saga about women torn between Catholicism and having a life of their own. In rural Minnesota in the first half of the twentieth century, three women—Meghan, her daughter Kate, and Kate's daughter Elise—are devoutly religious. All three discover in different ways that their faith (or, rather, the priests who advise them on it) forces them to give up what they most desire out of worldly life, such as the performance of music or free expression of their sexuality.

Weld, William F.
Stillwater. Simon & Schuster, 2002. 235pp.

In 1938, five towns in western Massachusetts, following a decision made by the state legislature, were flooded to make room for a needed reservoir. The townspeople, knowing that their farms and homes are about to vanish, react in a variety of ways, from denial to panic and madness. This is also a coming-of-age story. Jamieson, a fifteen-year-old boy, discovers love while seeing his world disappear. Weld, a former governor of Massachusetts, proves to be a more than adequate novelist.

Yarbrough, Steve.
Visible Spirits. **Knopf, 2001. 275pp.**

In 1902, racial tension in Loring, Mississippi, runs high. Loda Jackson, America's only African-American postmistress, stands to lose her job to Tandy Payne, a ne'er-do-well white racist who happens to be the mayor's brother. But mayor Leighton Payne sides with Loda, as does Theodore Roosevelt's administration, which uses her case to set an example on civil rights. Based on a historical incident.

Zuber, Isabel.
Salt. **Picador USA, 2002. 352pp.** 📖

Anna Bayley becomes the third wife of a widower in rural North Carolina in the early twentieth century. She never gives up on her dreams of something better, despite the fact that she doesn't really connect with her philandering husband. What she can't have for herself, though, she pursues on her children's behalf.

World War II

These are novels of love and loss set during World War II (1939–1945) on the American home front. The war serves as a catalyst for change for all Americans. Romances blossom and fail as soldiers go off to war. Other soldiers return home and discover that life has altered considerably in their absence. Most shamefully, Asian-American families are torn apart and relocated to internment camps.

Baker, Calvin.
Once Two Heroes. **Viking, 2003. 275pp.**

While fighting in France against the Nazis, Mather Rose (African-American) and Lewis Hampton (Caucasian) know the value of camaraderie and unity, but things take a different turn upon their return stateside. Both come back as war heroes, but racial turmoil in their homeland forces them into a confrontation with each other that changes them both profoundly. Which attitude is truly more difficult to sustain—that of war, or peace?

Canin, Ethan.
Carry Me Across the Water. **Random House, 2001. 206pp.**

August Kleinman, a wealthy Boston Jew aged seventy-eight, looks back on his long life in both Austria and the United States. His story is told in a series of connected vignettes, from his privileged youth in Vienna to his immigration to America in the 1930s and his reminisces of love and war in the Pacific during the 1940s.

Creel, Ann Howard.

The Magic of Ordinary Days. **Viking, 2001. 274pp.** 📖

In this gentle novel, Creel's first book for adults, twenty-four-year-old Olivia Dunne, daughter of a Denver clergyman, is kept sheltered from the world until the realities of war enter her life. A youthful indiscretion forces her into marriage with a kindly farmer she hardly knows. As the two feel their way around their relationship, Olivia strikes up a friendship with two Japanese-American sisters interned at a nearby camp. When the sisters become involved with German POWs, Olivia is drawn into the fray.

O'Nan, Stewart.

A World Away. **Holt, 1998. 338pp.**

World War II brings all family ties into sharp focus, as shown in this sensitive portrait of the Langer family. Son Rennie is missing in action overseas, and his wife Dorothy must give birth without him. In the meanwhile, father James tries to expiate his guilt over an affair he had with one of his high school students, while his wife Anne has a fling of her own with a soldier stationed nearby.

Otsuka, Julie.

When the Emperor Was Divine. **Knopf, 2002. 141pp.** 📖

Otsuka details, with devastating effect, the process by which Japanese-American families were forced to abandon their homes and belongings and were shuttled off to internment camps in the isolated Western desert. This short novel is based on the personal experiences of the author's grandmother.

Singleton, Elyse.

This Side of the Sky. **BlueHen, 2002. 304pp.** 📖

The author takes a unique perspective on the Second World War by showing it from the point of view of two African-American women, Myraleen and Lilian. Best friends, they grow up together in rural Nadir, Mississippi, during the Great Depression. Along the way, they move to Philadelphia and face a new sort of prejudice; later, they become WACs in London during the war and live through the Blitz. There's some romance, also, as darker-skinned Lilian falls for a white German POW while Myraleen sets her heart on an African-American pilot.

Tilghman, Christopher.

Mason's Retreat. **Random House, 1996. 290pp.**

American Edward Mason relocates his family from England to a Chesapeake Bay ranch called The Retreat. His selfless wife Edith restores the dilapidated property with the help of African-American farmhands. Their two sons have different reactions to staying in America. When Edward returns to England to run a factory during World War II, Edith remains behind, falling into the arms of a dashing younger man.

Towler, Katherine.

Snow Island. MacAdam/Cage, 2002. 287pp.

Snow Island is a quiet islet just off the Rhode Island coast where everything happens with slow regularity: the men's annual quahogging activities, the arrival of the summer residents. Alice Daggett, sixteen years old in 1941, finds her life and that of her New England island home transformed by the coming of World War II. A gentle coming-of-age tale.

Trobaugh, Augusta.

Sophie and the Rising Sun. Dutton, 2001. 208pp.

In the years before World War II, the residents of Salty Creek, Georgia, believe that Japanese-American Mr. Oto is the Chinese gardener of Miss Anne, the town's unofficial matriarch. A friendship slowly develops between Mr. Oto and Miss Sophie, an unmarried lady who shares his love of painting. When news of Pearl Harbor hits, Mr. Oto is forced to go into hiding. His and Sophie's growing love for one another forces them to make a big decision. An easy, gentle read.

Walbert, Kate.

The Gardens of Kyoto. Scribner, 2001. 288pp.

In the late twentieth century, a middle-aged woman named Ellen tells her daughter about growing up in the shadow of World War II, when her adored cousin, Randall, was killed at Iwo Jima. The themes of unrequited love and lives ruined by war reappear in her story. Ellen's memory, sweetened on nostalgia and remembered love, may be playing tricks on her, and on the reader as well.

Yarbrough, Steve.

Prisoners of War. Knopf, 2004. 283pp.

In 1943, Dan Timms can think of nothing but leaving his painful past by fighting for his country. Not even Dan's friend Marty Stark, shell-shocked after an overseas tour of duty and assigned to guard German POWs, can change his mind. Both Dan and L. C. Stevens, an African-American man, are employed to drive "rolling stores" of goods through the Mississippi Delta. While Dan yearns to leave Mississippi, L. C. wants nothing more than to escape from the repressive attitudes that surround him. Like Yarbrough's *Visible Spirits*, this novel explores racial prejudice in a rural Mississippi town.

Canada, Greenland, and the Arctic

While Canada and other northern settings don't figure prominently in other subgenres of historical fiction, they proliferate in the literary arena. Many evoke the adventurous spirit of early explorers and the haunting atmosphere of the Canadian Arctic.

Atwood, Margaret.

♠ *Alias Grace*. Doubleday, 1996. 468pp. 📖 ✍

In Canada in 1843, Grace Marks, a young serving girl (and historical figure), has been accused of the brutal double murder of her employer and his mistress—but is she guilty? A jury has judged her so, but the nation isn't entirely convinced. Sixteen years later, Dr. Simon Jordan interviews her at the prison where she now lives, using early psychological methods. Grace's story is one of victimization, both by poverty and by the barbaric prison system of the time, but she is cleverer than she lets on. Giller Prize; ALA Notable Book.

♠ *The Blind Assassin*. Doubleday, 2000. 400pp. 📖

In Toronto in 1945, as the novel begins, twenty-five-year-old Laura Chase drives her car off a bridge. Her story is calmly related by her older sister, Iris, who reports the death as accidental but implies that it was not. Atwood then switches gears, reproducing text from Laura's posthumous novel, a science fiction story featuring a blind assassin. This multi-layered novel is filled with period description and dialogue, not to mention some unexpected twists. It's only at the end that we discover how the pieces finally fit together. Booker Prize; ALA Notable Book.

Barrett, Andrea.

♠ *Ship Fever and Other Stories*. W. W. Norton, 1996. 254pp. 📖

This collection of eight stories emphasizes scientific pursuits, frequently in the face of societal challenges. Most of Barrett's protagonists are scientists themselves, who relate their difficulties reconciling their professional beliefs with their personal lives. Such is the case with the title story, a novella, in which a ship of Irish immigrants fleeing the potato famine arrives in Canada in 1847 only to encounter a typhus epidemic. National Book Award; ALA Notable Book.

♠ *The Voyage of the Narwhal*. W. W. Norton, 1998. 397pp. 📖

In 1855 Erasmus Darwin Wells is a naturalist on board the *Narwhal*, which has a mission to find and recover the lost expedition made by Sir John Franklin over a decade earlier. To his dismay Wells finds himself the victim of foolhardy Zeke Voorhees, the ship's commander and his sister's fiancé, who leads his men into situations that could cost them their lives. When Zeke fails to return on schedule, Wells decides whether to give up on him and seek rescue. ALA Notable Book.

Clark, Joan.

***Latitudes of Melt*. Soho, 2002. 295pp.**

Aurora was found as a baby in 1912, in a basket floating on a piece of ice off the Newfoundland coast. Her unusual origins match her behavior while growing up, for with her white hair and affinity for nature, she seems almost like a fairy child. Aurora marries and raises a family on the island, but it's not until her granddaughter begins investigating that Aurora discovers the truth about her past.

Crummey, Michael.

River Thieves. **Houghton Mifflin, 2002. 335pp.**

Newfoundland in 1810 is a bleak, desolate place inhabited by the native Beothuks (called the "Red Indians"), the Mi'kmaqs, and a handful of trappers and homesteaders originally from Great Britain. Among this latter group are trappers John Peyton Sr. and his son, who are at odds over their vision for the native peoples. John Sr. has hostile intentions toward them, while his son takes the idealistic view of a visiting Navy lieutenant, who believes they can be incorporated into white society. The tragic extinction of the Beothuks is shown from their own point of view in Bernard Assiniwi's *The Beothuk Saga*, annotated in Chapter 3.

Dudman, Clare.

One Day the Ice Will Reveal All Its Dead. **Viking, 2004. 405pp. (Original title:** *Wegener's Jigsaw.***)** ✍

Alfred Wegener is the little-known German meteorologist and Arctic explorer who revolutionized the scientific world with his theory of continental drift. Dudman evokes key episodes in Wegener's life, from his early childhood in Berlin, when he nearly drowned, to his horrific experiences in World War I, to his three expeditions to Greenland and the Arctic, where he formulated his ideas.

Govier, Katherine.

Creation. **Overlook, 2003. 320pp.** ✍

In the summer of 1833, John James Audubon enlisted the help of a group of men to search out new bird species in Newfoundland and Labrador. During this short yet sizzling summer, they see sights no man has ever seen and hear beautiful songs no one else has heard. The paradox is that to depict the birds on paper, they must be silenced forever.

Harrison, Kathryn.

The Seal Wife. **Random House, 2002. 224pp.** 📖

Harrison's latest novel of intimacy and obsession begins in the cold Alaskan winter of 1915, as a young scientist named Bigelow Greene heads to Anchorage to establish a weather station for the U.S. government. Living in this barren and lonely landscape, he falls in love with a mute Aleut woman whose name he doesn't know.

Hay, Elizabeth.

A Student of Weather. **Counterpoint, 2001. 368pp.** 📖

Maurice Dove, a botanist and student of weather, journeys from Ottawa to rural Saskatchewan in the mid-1930s to analyze the climate of the Canadian Great Plains. He stirs up a whirlwind of romantic yearnings in the two Hardy sisters. Though Maurice seems attracted by beautiful Lucinda's many charms, it's eight-year-old Norma-Joyce who stirs his curiosity. Though far from a typical romance, this beautifully written tale explores the staying power of a first love.

Itani, Frances.

Deafening. **Atlantic Monthly, 2003. 378pp.** 📖

Grania O'Neill, a deaf woman living in Canada during World War I, is sent by her family to learn sign language at the Ontario School for the Deaf. After learning how to communicate with the hearing world for the first time, she meets and falls in love with Jim Lloyd. All too soon, he is called away to serve in the war overseas. Through her first novel, Itani explores the power of language to liberate and heal.

Johnston, Wayne.

The Colony of Unrequited Dreams. **Doubleday, 2000. 528pp.** ✍ 📖

This is an epic tale about the early life of Joey Smallwood, who became the first premier of Newfoundland in 1949. Growing up, his background is obscure but his dreams are grand. His goal is to bring respectability and greatness to the poor and downtrodden citizens of the wild province. His sometime foe, sometime lady-love is Sheilagh Fielding, whose life parallels his. ALA Notable Book.

The Navigator of New York. **Doubleday, 2002. 496pp.**

Johnston's latest historical about Newfoundland history evokes the great age of Arctic exploration—the mid-nineteenth to the early twentieth centuries. Devlin Stead is a young orphaned Newfoundland boy who unexpectedly learns more about his family from Dr. Frederick Cook, an explorer who vies with Robert Peary to be the first man to reach the North Pole. Devlin joins Cook in Manhattan and, as the two make plans for an expedition to Greenland, gets caught up in his quest to beat Peary.

Morrissey, Donna.

Downhill Chance. **Mariner, 2003. 429pp.**

Job Gale leaves his isolated Newfoundland fishing village behind when he enlists to serve in World War II. The lives of Job's wife Sare, and daughters Clair and Missy are strongly affected by his absence. Clair watches her homeland change in the aftermath of the war, and external politics and wartime secrets gradually overtake the community.

Smiley, Jane.

The Greenlanders. **Knopf, 1989. 558pp.** ★

Written in the style of the old Norse sagas, Smiley's novel about fourteenth-century Greenland evokes the day-to-day life of the family of landowner Asgeir Gunnarsson. It also describes the intense beauty of the bleak landscape as well as nature's power of destruction. Babies are born, and people die tragically, but neither event causes any more ripples in the community than any other natural occurrence.

Urquhart, Jane.

The Stone Carvers. Viking, 2001. 392pp.

Her mother's early death and her brother's disappearance made Klara Becker's young life sad and difficult. Growing up in a small Ontario town in the years preceding World War I, Klara finds love with an Irish soldier who loses his life in battle. Meanwhile her brother Tilman goes off in search of adventure and loses his leg in the war in France. Their stories remain separate until the 1930s, when they reunite at the site of Walter Allward's monument to the Canadian war dead in Vichy. A bestseller in Canada.

🎗 *The Underpainter*. Viking, 1997. 340pp.

From Rochester, New York, painter Austin Fraser looks back on his life spent creating works of art in the small lakeside town of Davenport, Ontario, and in a small mining village off Lake Superior. His abstract technique of underpainting (painting a scene and then obscuring the details that make it real) is an effect inspired by his relationships with friends and lovers, whose feelings he never reciprocates. Austin's dispassionate nature extends to World War I, for he sits serenely by while his friends' lives are devastated by its effects. Governor General's Literary Award.

Vreeland, Susan.

The Forest Lover. Viking, 2004. 331pp. ✍ 📖

Even as a child, Emily Carr (1871–1945) exhibits the independence and creativity that define her later life. She defies the expectations of Victorian society, becoming an art teacher instead of marrying and having children. Whenever she can, she ventures into the wilderness of British Columbia, fascinated by the native inhabitants' tribal villages, totem poles, and beautifully decorated houses. Like Vreeland's *The Passion of Artemisia*, set in the Italian Renaissance, this is another lyrical portrait of an unconventional painter.

Wright, Richard.

🎗 *Clara Callan*. Holt, 2002. 415pp. 📖

Clara Callan is a thirtyish, single woman in small-town Ontario during the early years of the Depression. Her sister Nora, slightly younger and prettier, follows both sisters' dreams by heading to New York in search of excitement. The more glamorous Nora becomes a radio soap star in the heart of Manhattan, while Clara stays behind, content with her quiet life as an amateur poet and as a schoolteacher in Whitfield. The novel is told through their correspondence, recounting the unemployment and anxieties in the years leading up to World War II. Giller Prize; Governor General's Literary Award.

Latin America and the Caribbean

These novels analyze the turbulent political environments of Latin American and South American countries, primarily in the nineteenth century, and how leaders' policies affected the native populace. Many of the authors relate these historical events to today's political situation.

Allende, Isabel.

Portrait in Sepia. HarperCollins, 2001. 300pp.

Annotated in this chapter, under "Early United States."

Alvarez, Julia.

In the Name of Salomé. Algonquin Books of Chapel Hill, 2000. 357pp. 📖 ✎

Camila Henríquez Ureña, a sixty-five-year-old professor of Spanish at Vassar in 1960, decides to move to Cuba to join Castro's movement. In doing so, she hopes to capture the strength that inspired the mother she never knew, Salomé Ureña, whose poetry inspired the Dominican Revolution. The stories of Camila and Salomé are told in alternating chapters, blurring into one another. Revolution, family, and patriotism are the major themes, in this novel by a well-known author of Hispanic-influenced literary fiction.

Bell, Madison Smartt.

Toussaint L'Ouverture Trilogy. ✎

These novels chronicle the slave rebellion in Haiti (1791–1804), which erupted in terrifying acts of violence and brutality among French plantation owners, their African-American slaves, Spanish settlers, and the British, who wanted the island for themselves. Toussaint L'Ouverture, a slave, is the self-proclaimed leader of the revolt. Later, he takes over the role of governor. Since the novels are told from nearly every point of view but that of Toussaint himself, he remains an enigma. They can be read as one extraordinarily long novel.

All Souls' Rising. Pantheon, 1995. 530pp.

Master of the Crossroads. Pantheon, 2000. 732pp.

The Stone That the Builder Refused. Pantheon, 2004. 768pp.

Braverman, Kate.

The Incantation of Frida K. Seven Stories, 2002. 240pp. ✎

Mexican artist Frida Kahlo, feeble in body but strong in mind, lies on her deathbed at age forty-six, alternately remembering and hallucinating about past episodes in her life. She develops a passion for painter and muralist Diego Rivera, and though the two marry, their relationship is fraught with tension. Rivera's ego tends to get in the way of honest communication, and Frida struggles to prevent her immense physical pain from overtaking her artistic vision.

Carlson, Lori Marie.

The Flamboyant. HarperCollins, 2002. 304pp. 📖

Lenora Demarest, born in 1900, moves with her father from New York to Puerto Rico after her mother's death. An encounter with dashing aviator George Hanson gives her a yearning for flight, though she fears that a permanent relationship with the handsome George may be too confining for her taste.

Conde, Maryse.

Windward Heights. Soho, 1999. 352pp.

Brontë's classic turns Caribbean Gothic in this reworking of *Wuthering Heights*, set on Guadeloupe in the early nineteenth century. Razyé, a hot-tempered African-American man, takes the role of brooding outcast Heathcliff. His Cathy is the wife of a rich white Creole and the daughter of a mulatto landowner. Their story is painful and tragic, but the cold and bitter Razyé has few redeeming qualities. Having been cheated all his life because of his race, he destroys what he loves most.

Danticat, Edwidge.

🎖 *The Farming of Bones*. Soho, 1998. 312pp. 📖

In 1937, Dominican Republic dictator Rafael Leónidas Trujillo institutes a policy of genocide against the Haitian people. Caught in the middle are Haitian maidservant Amabelle Désir, working for a kindly Dominican family, and her lover, cane-cutter Sebastien Onius. Both find themselves in the wrong place at the worst possible time. American Book Award; ALA Notable Book.

Delahunt, Meaghan.

In the Casa Azul. St. Martin's Press, 2002. 308pp. (Alternate title: *In the Blue House*.) 📖 ✎

Leon Trotsky and his wife, voyaging to Mexico City in 1937 in the hopes of avoiding Stalin's deadly plans for him, meet up with Mexican artist Frida Kahlo and her husband Diego Rivera. In vignettes told by friends and other observers, Trotsky and Kahlo have a brief affair. Back in Russia, Stalin betrays one faithful supporter after another. This novel spans nearly seventy years of Mexican and Russian history.

Enright, Anne.

The Pleasure of Eliza Lynch. Atlantic Monthly, 2003. 256pp. ✎

The novel opens with a rather perfunctory sex scene between Francisco Solano Lopez, the future dictator of Paraguay, and the title character, an Irishwoman he met in Paris. Both are rather self-absorbed, which makes them hard to like, but Eliza soon gains our sympathy. Taking high society of 1850s Paraguay by storm despite the disapproval of her lover's family, she rises to become her country's Eva Peron and is for a time the richest woman in the world. But all power has a price, as Eliza discovers when Lopez's ambitions turn violent.

Ephron, Amy.
White Rose: Una Rosa Blanca. **Morrow, 1999. 240pp.** 📖

In 1897, Karl Decker, an American journalist, is sent by William Randolph Hearst to interview Evangelina Cisneros, incarcerated in a Cuban prison for revolutionary activities against the home country of Spain. His secret mission is to rescue her and bring her back to the States, where she has already become famous. Nineteen years old and beautiful, Evangelina and her courageous manner capture Karl's heart, but her mind is set on freedom, not just for herself but for her country.

Esquivel, Laura.
Swift as Desire. **Crown, 2001. 207pp.** 📖 **YA**

Júbilo is a telegraph operator in 1920s Mexico who has the gift of knowing what people mean, rather than simply what they say aloud. But his own once-happy marriage to the beautiful Lucha has turned sour, and it's up to the couple's daughter, Lluvia, to restore the lines of communication between them. A loving memoir to Esquivel's own father.

Ferré, Rosario.
Flight of the Swan. **Farrar, Straus & Giroux, 2001. 262pp.**

The prima ballerina known as "Madame" (based on the dancer Anna Pavlova) brings her dance troupe on tour to Puerto Rico in 1917. They find themselves stranded, and stateless, when revolution overtakes their homeland. Madame and her maid/companion Masha, who narrates, both become involved with Puerto Rico's own revolutionary movement: Madame through her affair with a twenty-year-old rebel who exploits her affections, and Masha through observing the oppression and class distinctions in her newly adopted home.

Fuentes, Carlos.
The Years with Laura Díaz. **Farrar, Straus & Giroux, 2000. 510pp.** 📖

From her birth in 1898 until her death in 1972, Laura Díaz lives through the greatest moments of twentieth-century Mexican history, from the revolutionary activities that are the basis for Mexican politics to the artistic innovations of Frida Kahlo, to whom Laura is a companion and friend. Laura disregards the privileges of her birth to marry a working-class man. Her choice has repercussions for her own children and grandchildren, who themselves get caught up in their country's political struggles.

Hijuelos, Oscar.
A Simple Habana Melody. **HarperCollins, 2002. 342pp.** 📖 **YA**

Back in Habana, Cuba, after many years away, composer Israel Levis attempts to recover from his recent detention by the Nazis, who had mistakenly assumed he was Jewish. His memories take him back to Paris and Habana before the war, when he fell in love with Rita Valladares, a seemingly unattainable singer for whom he wrote his greatest melody.

Mastretta, Angeles.
Lovesick. **Riverhead, 1997. 292pp.**

Emilia Sauri, born in 1893 in Mexico, aspires to study medicine, but the Mexican Revolution of 1911 changes her plans. As she becomes more involved with the unstable political situation, she must also choose between the love of a fellow doctor and her attraction to her childhood love, now a revolutionary.

Montero, Mayra.
The Messenger. **HarperFlamingo, 1999. 218pp.** ✍

During a performance of *Aida* at a Havana opera house, a bomb went off. Tenor Enrico Caruso, in the starring role, disappeared into the street and was not heard from for days. That much is history. Montero imagines that Caruso spends his lost days with Aida Cheng, a Chinese-Cuban mulatto whom he bumps into outside the theater. Through previous conversations Aida had with a Santería priest, she knows that Caruso is doomed but wants to be with him anyway.

Mujica, Bárbara.
Frida. **Overlook, 2001. 366pp.** ✍

Frida Kahlo's sister Cristina, a beautiful woman who grew up in the shadow of her more talented sibling, becomes the surprising rival for the affections of Diego Rivera, Frida's husband. In later life Cristina relates her own version of the pair's tumultuous marriage, and her own involvement in it, to an American psychiatrist.

Poniatowska, Elena.
Here's to You, Jesúsa! **Farrar, Straus & Giroux, 2001. 303pp. (First published in Mexico in 1969.)**

Poniatowska's best known novel, belatedly available in English, fictionalizes the life story of Josefina Bórquez, a fiercely independent woman who fought as a *soldadera* in the Mexican Revolution (1910–1917). Jesúsa, born around the turn of the century in Oaxaca, marries an abusive army officer at age fifteen. Abandoned and widowed after the war, Jesúsa begins again in Mexico City, barely surviving poverty by taking on a varied number of occupations. She lives thereafter on the fringes of society, struggling against authority and becoming increasingly eccentric.

Rhys, Jean.
The Wide Sargasso Sea. **W. W. Norton, 1966. 189pp.** ★

Creole heiress Antoinette Bertha Cosway grows up on a wild, lush island in the West Indies in the 1830s. Her sensual nature mirrors the exotic tropical paradise. Her passion is curtailed after a forced marriage to Edward Rochester, an Englishman who whisks her away from her island home to his English estate. Because of her upbringing, he has misgivings about whether she is a suitable wife. In this repressive atmosphere, her passion for life disguised as madness, Antoinette is kept locked away from the world. Readers will recognize her as the madwoman in the attic of Thornfield Hall, the secret first wife whose presence was discovered by Jane Eyre in Charlotte Brontë's novel.

Runcie, James.

The Discovery of Chocolate. **HarperCollins, 2001. 264pp.**

In this humorous tale, Diego de Godoy, emissary of Emperor Charles V, sets forth from Spain in 1518 on a journey to South America, his lover at home declaring she'll never marry until he returns with "a true and secret treasure." Once he reaches Mexico, his quest is delayed by a beautiful native woman and the drink she gives him—chocolate—which, unbeknownst to him, contains a substance giving him eternal life. Unable to die, our hero travels down through the years, always seeking out the secret of chocolate.

Tuck, Lily.

🎗 *The News from Paraguay*. **HarperCollins, 2004. 248pp.** ✍

In 1854 Paris, Francisco Solano "Franco" Lopez meets Ella Lynch, a beautiful Irishwoman he spies on horseback in the Bois de Boulogne. They become lovers, and he whisks her away to Paraguay, where he becomes the country's dictator after his father's death. They live in opulence, Ella bearing numerous children, while Franco's politics become ever more repressive and tyrannical. Anne Enright's *The Pleasure of Eliza Lynch*, above, has the same subject. National Book Award.

The Middle East

Literary novels with Middle Eastern settings incorporate the themes of religious conflict (among Islam, Judaism, and Christianity, especially during the Crusades), colonialism, and women's personal and sexual liberation.

Ali, Tariq.

The Book of Saladin. **Verso, 1998. 367pp.** ✍

Saladin (Salah-al-Din) was the Kurdish leader who retook Jerusalem for the "infidels" in 1187, nearly a century after the First Crusade. In contrast to Saladin, a reasonable, intelligent leader who becomes his people's savior, the western Crusaders are shown to be violent barbarians, charging in where they don't belong. The action is seen through the eyes of Saladin's Jewish physician, Ibn Maymun, also known as Maimonides.

Connell, Evan S.

Deus Lo Volt!: Chronicle of the Crusades. Counterpoint, 2000. 462pp.

Dense and scholarly, this novel—whose title is translated as the Crusaders' call to arms, "God wills it!"—reads like a real-life chronicle of the Crusades to take back the Holy Land from the Moslems. The story begins in 1095, as Pope Urban appeals to the populace to fight the infidel, and continues for two centuries. Connell, who calls this a "book about the Crusades" rather than a historical novel, has taken great pains to capture the language and spirit of the era, re-creating past conversations that were recounted in medieval documents.

Croutier, Alev Lytle.

The Palace of Tears. Dell, 2000. 192pp.

In Paris in 1868, Casimir de Chateauneuf comes upon a miniature of a beautiful young woman with arresting eyes, one blue and one yellow. Obsessed by her portrait, he follows her trail first to Marseille, then to North Africa and Istanbul, where he finds her residing in the Sultan's Palace of Tears—where men are forbidden to enter. All the while, it turns out that she has been dreaming of him, too.

Eve, Nomi.

The Family Orchard. Knopf, 2000. 316pp. ✍

Annotated in Chapter 5.

Grant, Linda.

✿ *When I Lived in Modern Times*. Dutton, 2000. 260pp. 📖

Evelyn Sert, a twenty-year-old Jewish hairdresser, sails from London to Palestine in 1946, ready to see what the world can offer her. While she doesn't quite fit in with the other Jews, she doesn't really fit anywhere else, either. She leaves the kibbutz, invents a new identity, and moves to Tel Aviv. There she finds love, adventure, and purpose, but none is what she thought it would be. Orange Prize.

Hensher, Philip.

The Mulberry Empire. Knopf, 2002. 476pp.

The anti-colonialist stance of many British historical novels is evident here. This, Hensher's first novel to be published in America, details an earlier war in Afghanistan—this time with the British. In 1839, British forces entered Kabul with the intent of replacing its emir with someone more sympathetic to their trading interests. Three years later, one lone British survivor was left to relate the tale. The story is told from the point of view of Alexander Burnes, an explorer who is the friend of both the British and the emir. Scenes take place not only in Afghanistan but also in London, Calcutta, and St. Petersburg, where many different cultures scheme to take control of the country.

Horch, Daniel.

The Angel with One Hundred Wings. St. Martin's Press, 2002. 260pp.

In this variation of an Arabian Nights tale, ninth-century Baghdad is known as the City of Peace. It is here that Abulhassan, an elderly apothecary, betrays his friend the sultan by helping the Prince of Persia elope with the sultan's favorite concubine. In doing so, he risks his own life, for the path to safety for the lovers is fraught with danger and suspicion. Abulhassan comes to reconsider his own empty marriage and what he once would have done for a love as great as those he aided.

Kazan, Frances.

Halide's Gift. Random House, 2001. 345pp. ✍

Halide Edib (based on a historical figure) is a teenager growing up in Constantinople in the last decade of the nineteenth century. She is torn between the education her father wants for her and the long-held traditions left to her by her late mother. Her mother has bequeathed her another gift as well, the ability to communicate with the dead. In this world where polygamy is the norm and women's intellectual abilities are stifled, Halide decides whether or not to follow her dream.

Makiya, Kanan.

The Rock. Pantheon, 2001. 346pp.

Judaism, Christianity, and Islam all recognize the Rock of Jerusalem, where Abraham offered his son Isaac as a sacrifice to God, as a cornerstone of their faith. Ishaq, a Muslim and Jew, is commissioned to design the Dome of the Rock on this great holy site during the seventh century—a time when the three religions still coexisted in harmony. The last seventy pages comprise notes on historical sources.

Mossanen, Dora Levy.

Harem. Scribner, 2002. 384pp.

Set in fourteenth-century Persia, this novel re-creates its locale's seductive, exotic atmosphere. Rebekah, a young girl in Persia's Jewish quarter, must stand fast against her abusive blacksmith husband to create a safe environment for her daughter. Through Rebekah, her daughter, and granddaughter, who rose to power in the realm, Mossanen depicts the principal path to influence left to women in this era.

Soueif, Ahdaf.

The Map of Love. Anchor, 1999. 529pp. 📖

Two exotic romances spaced a hundred years apart unfold side by side in this tale of Western women in love with Egyptian men, the distances separating the two cultures, and the ties that bring them together. When New Yorker Isabel Parkman uncovers the journals of her ancestor, she turns to Egyptian-American conductor Omar al-Ghamrawi, who takes her to his sister in Cairo for answers. The papers tell the story of Anna Winterbourne, Isabel's great-grandmother, who found romance with an Egyptian in the first decades of the twentieth century. It is not just

a love story, however, but also one involving politics, colonialism, and religion.

Zelitch, Simone.

Louisa. **Putnam, 2000. 377pp.** 📖

In a retelling of the biblical story of Ruth and her gentile daughter-in-law Naomi, Nora, a Hungarian Jew, and her German daughter-in-law Louisa make their way to Israel from Hungary after the war. Both are widows anxious to leave their old life behind, but to Nora, whom Louisa's ingenuity had saved from the Nazis, the younger woman is a bitter reminder of times past. At the same time that Nora revisits memories from the war years, we see how Louisa is never fully accepted by her Jewish brethren in Israel. Still, she remains steadfast at Nora's side.

Asia, Africa, and the Antipodes

Many literary writers choose to set their novels in historical Asia, Africa, Australia, or elsewhere in the Pacific Islands. British, Dutch, and French Imperialism was in full force during the nineteenth century, and common topics include colonialism's effect on distant countries' native peoples. Modernization in general is another theme. When Western visitors pay visits to faraway locales, with the goal of exploration or settlement, change inevitably follows. Readers of exotic adventure (Chapter 8) may enjoy these novels.

Africa

Bausch, Richard.

Hello to the Cannibals. **HarperCollins, 2002. 661pp.** ✑

Lily Austin, a playwright in modern Mississippi, becomes enthralled by a pile of letters addressed by explorer Mary Kingsley to an unknown woman in the future. Back in the 1890s, spinster Mary Henrietta Kingsley, overwhelmed by the responsibility of caring for her family, takes a much-needed opportunity to explore West Africa on her own, the first European to do so. Lily and Mary correspond back and forth, in an odd bit of synchronicity. Though Lily's version occasionally drags, Mary's exotic adventures hold the tale together.

Brink, André.

The Other Side of Silence. **Harcourt, 2003. 320pp.**

In the early twentieth century, Hanna sees a way of escaping years of abuse in her native Germany by traveling to southwest Africa and serving as a "companion" to the predominantly male colonists. The abuse escalates again when she resists the advances of a brutal German officer. As a result Hanna is sent to Frauenstein, a brothel whose horrific conditions would turn anyone's stomach. But she manages to escape, forming a makeshift posse to take on the Germans on their own violent terms.

Foden, Giles.

Ladysmith. **Knopf, 1999. 288pp.**

> For 120 days in 1899, the South African town of Ladysmith is under siege by Boer forces as they wait for British soldiers to arrive. In this time of extreme hardship, Bella Kiernan, a young barmaid, loses some connections to her family but discovers love. Narrated by various people, the novel is a little unfocused in places, and the arresting images of war and gore may make some readers uncomfortable. The maelstrom of activity, though, proves that there was too much going on for anyone to keep track of.

Freed, Lynn.

The Mirror. **Crown, 1997. 224pp.**

> British expatriate Agnes La Grange arrives in Durban, South Africa, in 1920 with a newly made-up last name and a desire to better herself any way she can, regardless of society's constraints on women of the time. Through employment with a Jewish family, an affair with her employer, and marriage to another man, she acquires the wealth she has long desired. It takes longer to acquire her freedom.

Mezlekia, Nega.

The God Who Begat a Jackal. **Picador USA, 2002. 242pp.**

> In seventeenth-century feudal Ethiopia, Aster is the clairvoyant daughter of a fierce tribal chieftain who turns away all suitors for his daughter's hand. When Aster falls in love with Gudu, a court jester and one of the slave men assigned to guard her, their relationship, obviously taboo, can only lead to tragedy.

Australia, New Zealand, and the Pacific Islands

Balint, Christine.

The Salt Letters. **W. W. Norton, 2001. 187pp.**

> On a sea voyage from England to Australia in 1854, young Sarah shares close quarters with other unmarried female immigrants in the belly of the ship, far from daylight. Their living conditions are uncomfortable at best, with disease running rampant and salt water soaking everything in sight. Sarah gradually reveals more of her previous life in Shropshire, with an unwanted suitor and a possible romantic interest. It's easy to believe that this is how early sea voyages must have been, cooped up aboard ship for months on end, but the realism can be claustrophobic.

Ball, Pamela.

The Floating City. **Viking, 2002. 272pp.**

> Hawaii in the 1890s is a nation in turmoil, with different cultural groups vying for supremacy. The natives are loyal to Queen Liliuokalani, while economically conscious politicians from the American mainland want to bring the land to eventual statehood. Eva Hanson, a *haole* (Caucasian) of European origin, is given the responsibility of informing the authorities of a body found on the beach. Though she is accused of his death, she can't bring herself to leave her beloved island, or the Scotsman with whom she's fallen in love.

Carey, Peter.

🎗 *True History of the Kelly Gang*. **Knopf, 2000. 352pp.** ✍ 📖

Ned Kelly is a real-life Australian legend, a nineteenth-century outlaw of Irish descent who was a cold blooded murderer to the English and a hero to the Australian people. In a wry, folksy voice, he narrates his own wild story as if from the grave, so that his baby daughter will grow up knowing who her father was and what he stood for. Booker Prize; ALA Notable Book.

Davenport, Kiana.

Song of the Exile. **Ballantine, 1999. 355pp.** 📖

In the days before Pearl Harbor, Sunny, a Korean-Hawaiian woman, falls in love with Keo, a jazz trumpet player who is a native Hawaiian. Their love is continually tested with the coming of World War II, as Sunny faces unspeakable horror as prisoner of the Japanese. Keo roams the world in search of her.

Flanagan, Richard.

Gould's Book of Fish. **Grove, 2001. 404pp.** 📖

William Gould, an English thief and forger shipped off to a Tasmanian penal colony in the 1830s, lavishly illustrates a scientific book detailing the native fish populations of Sarah Island in order to better his station. His paintings disguise something more: the cruelty of civilization, and his attempts to hang on to his sanity. The chapters themselves are creatively printed in a variety of inks used to convey, frequently humorously, the sense of each.

Gilling, Tom.

The Adventures of Miles and Isabel. **Atlantic Monthly, 2002. 198pp. (Original title: *Miles McGinty*.)**

Miles McGinty and Isabel Dowling are born to two Australian families on the same night in 1856. Their lives begin independently, but they both grow up obsessed by achieving their dreams of flight. The heart of the book is not only the love story between them, but also the picaresque journeys they take, and the quirky characters they meet, along the way.

Johnson, Stephanie.

The Sailmaker's Daughter. **St. Martin's Press, 2003. 255pp. (Original title: *The Heart's Wild Surf*.)**

In Fiji in 1918, twelve-year-old Olive McNab's mother lies dying of the Spanish Flu, quarantined from the rest of her family except Olive's father. He sends Olive and her siblings to the island of Taveuni to stay with her eccentric aunt and uncle. While there, Olive begins to see her island paradise as less than a magical place. When her Aunt Maud assaults a native servant and gets hauled into court, ugly racial tensions, normally ignored, are brought to the forefront.

Keneally, Thomas.

The Office of Innocence. **Doubleday, 2003. 352pp. (Original title:** *An Angel in Australia***.)**

Frank Darragh, a young priest in Australia in World War II, finds his loyalties and faith tested when approached by a parishioner whose husband is a German prisoner in North Africa. After the attractive woman confesses that she's drifting toward infidelity, his thoughts turn more and more to her. When she is found murdered, he is accused of causing her death.

Kneale, Matthew.

🎗 *English Passengers*. **Nan A. Talese, 2000. 446pp.** 📖

This witty, farcical adventure begins in 1857. Captain Kewley, a sea captain from the Isle of Man, takes a group of eccentric passengers on a charter trip to Tasmania to avoid being caught smuggling illegal goods. One passenger, Reverend Wilson, believes Tasmania to be the original Garden of Eden and is dumbfounded when new geological research proves the earth to be younger than the Bible tells. A scientist on the voyage sets out to prove Wilson wrong. And down in Tasmania, a half-breed Aborigine recounts his people's encounters with the invading English, a story that will only get worse once the latest English passengers arrive. ALA Notable Book; Whitbread Award for First Novel.

McConnochie, Mardi.

Coldwater. **Doubleday, 2001. 320pp.**

Charlotte, Anne, and Emily Wolf are sisters living on Coldwater, a penal colony off the Australian coast, in the year 1847. The Wolf sisters, like their literary namesakes the Brontës, are aspiring authors who take up their pens to relieve their dreary, isolated existence. The chains of family break apart when their tyrannical father forbids them their favorite pursuit, and one of the daughters falls in love with an Irish convict on the island.

McDonald, Roger.

Mr. Darwin's Shooter. **Atlantic Monthly, 1999. 384pp.** ✎

Syms Covington is Charles Darwin's shooter on board the *Beagle*, taking a scientific expedition around South America, Australia, and the Pacific Islands. While Covington secures species for Darwin to study, the intrepid scientist devises his own theories of human evolution, ones which—as it turns out—will conflict with the fundamentalist beliefs held by his assistant.

Rogers, Jane.

Promised Lands. **Overlook, 1997. 388pp.**

Arriving in Australia's Botany Bay colony in 1788, Lieutenant William Dawes believes he's reached the Promised Land. It turns out to be no more than a haven for convicts, who are rewarded while the native people are outlawed. In the modern day, Stephen Beech, a school administrator, writes the story of the first British colony in Australia. While Stephen wishes he could change the world, his wife Olla believes that her deformed son will help make the world a better place. As

his own illusions fail, Stephen draws parallels between William Dawes's life and his own.

Tremain, Rose.
The Colour. **Farrar, Straus & Giroux, 2003. 352pp.** 📖

Joseph Blackstone and wife Harriet escape 1860s England with Joseph's mother and head to New Zealand in search of freedom, but what they find is adventure—and greed—in the form of gold specks found in a nearby creek. Joseph is quick to abandon his wife (and mother) in pursuit of "the colour," but conditions in the mining camp are much harsher than expected. Harriet follows him in turn and makes her own, more human, discoveries.

Vanderbes, Jennifer.
Easter Island. **Dial Press, 2003. 320pp.** 📖

Elsa Pendleton discovers her raison d'être while visiting Easter Island with her anthropologist husband in 1913. The island's remoteness keeps her from knowing that World War I has been declared, and that her new homeland is in the direct path of the Germans. In the 1970s, a botanist doing research on the island traces Elsa's path.

Wright, Ronald.
Henderson's Spear. **Holt, 2002. 334pp.**

In the present, Olivia Wyvern travels to Tahiti to locate the father she thought had died in Korea but whom she now believes is living on the island of Taiohae. Jailed on a false murder charge, she has time to fully contemplate the journals of her ancestor, Frank Henderson, a British sailor. In 1879, Henderson had accompanied two of Queen Victoria's grandsons, Edward, Duke of Clarence and his brother George (the future George V), on a South Seas venture gone bad. Olivia also receives a mysterious letter from the daughter she had given up for adoption at sixteen. Henderson's long-ago revelations lead to unexpected connections between the past and present.

China and Hong Kong

Caldwell, Bo.
The Distant Land of My Father. **Chronicle, 2001. 373pp.** 📖

In this memoir-like novel, Anna Schoene, an American girl, grows up in Shanghai in the 1930s. Her father, a millionaire, gives his daughter love, attention, and all of the privileges money can buy. When World War II begins, and the Japanese invade, Anna's father sends his wife and daughter to safety in Los Angeles but remains behind, believing that he will be safe. When he turns up again in California years later, Anna must decide whether she can forgive him. Shanghai is evoked realistically, both to readers and to Joseph Schoene, who unwittingly chooses it over his own family.

Fleischman, Lisa Huang.

Dream of the Walled City. Pocket, 2000. 416pp.

Fleischman fictionalizes the life of her grandmother, an early Chinese feminist and political activist, in her debut novel. Born in 1890, Jade Virtue Liang grows up in a privileged family, only seeing the harsh reality of Changsha, an ancient walled city, after her father dies. Thrust into poverty, she marries into money but discovers her husband is abusive and addicted to opium; she is also forced to deal with the West's incursion into traditional Chinese culture. With the twentieth century come a number of social changes, including freedom for women and the rise of Communism. Jade Virtue deals with both as a path previously unknown to upper-class women.

Harrison, Kathryn.

The Binding Chair, or, A Visit from the Foot Emancipation Society. Random House, 2000. 312pp. 📖

The need of women to escape their bonds, both literal and figurative, is at the heart of this work set in late nineteenth- and early twentieth-century Shanghai. May, a young woman from rural China, spends her days servicing Western men in a Shanghai brothel. She is rescued by well-meaning Arthur Cohen, an Australian member of the Foot Emancipation Society who is determined to put an end to barbaric foot-binding practices (of which May is a victim). He marries her, bringing her back to his estate, where she becomes an unhealthy influence on her impressionable niece-by-marriage.

Heng, Liu.

Green River Daydreams. Grove, 2001. 304pp.

An elderly man known only as Ears recalls his days as a servant in the wealthy Cao family. The younger Cao son, Guanghan, returns from study abroad with a French engineer in tow, hoping to establish a match factory. When Guanghan rejects the marriage his parents arranged for him and becomes embroiled in political revolution, his bride takes comfort in the arms of the Frenchman, though Ears loves her himself.

Ishiguro, Kazuo.

When We Were Orphans. Knopf, 2000. 335pp. 📖

Christopher Banks is a fairly unemotional man. He loses his parents in Shanghai in the early twentieth century, when he is nine. Growing up mostly in England, he returns to Shanghai in the 1930s as a trained detective, convinced that his parents are still alive and determined to find them. Whether this is true, or he is deluding himself into believing they survived, is the novel's great mystery.

Lanchester, John.

Fragrant Harbor. Putnam, 2002. 342pp. 📖

In 1935, Tom Stewart, a young man from Kent, England, sails to Hong Kong (ironically translated as "fragrant harbor") in search of adventure and fortune. Along the way he learns fluent Cantonese from a beautiful nun, Sister Maria, who

becomes a recurring figure in his life. War with the Japanese is soon on the horizon, and Stewart is recruited as a British spy. Over his long life in Hong Kong—which he rarely leaves—the city is presented with sweeping scope, from its colonial origins and millions of immigrants to its grandeur in the realms of banking and finance.

McCunn, Ruthanne Lum.

The Moon Pearl. Beacon, 2000. 316pp. **YA**

Three young Chinese women living in a "girls' house" in the Moon River Delta in the 1830s vow to their gods to become spinsters rather than prepare for marriage. After their families and friends cast them aside, they turn to new pursuits, making their own living in the burgeoning silkworm industry.

Min, Anchee.

Becoming Madame Mao. Houghton Mifflin, 2000. 340pp. ✍ 📖

Jiang Ching, the power-hungry, cruel, and enigmatic wife of Mao Zedong in Communist China, continually reinvents herself throughout her life: from an unhappy child in the 1920s to actress to Communist sympathizer and tyrant. Min, born in China, was fascinated by the beautiful Madame Mao as a child, and it shows in this intense psychological portrait.

Empress Orchid. Houghton Mifflin, 2004. 352pp. ✍

A biographical novel about the Last Empress of China. Tzu Hsi, better known as Orchid, enters China's Forbidden City as a minor concubine to the emperor in 1852. In this insular environment, ritual is everything, and thousands of hopeful women vie for his attention. She sets out to seduce him and succeeds, falling in love and bearing him a much-needed heir. Orchid becomes empress at her husband's death, fighting off calls for her ouster, and holding the troubled country together almost single-handedly. As in her earlier *Becoming Madame Mao*, Min depicts her subject, a much-reviled woman from early twentieth-century Chinese history, sympathetically and convincingly.

Sa, Shan.

The Girl Who Played Go. Knopf, 2003. 312pp. 📖

A teenage girl in remote 1930s Manchuria plays the ancient Chinese game of "go" with a Japanese soldier stationed there with an occupying force. Both narrate in alternating chapters. While the soldier feels homesick and weary of his occupation, the girl grows steadily more comfortable with her own sexuality and how it may be used for political gain. Their growing curiosity about one another, never spoken aloud, takes a back seat to the war raging around them.

Tan, Amy.

Tan explores the complicated relationships between Chinese-born American women and their Americanized daughters.

The Bonesetter's Daughter. **Putnam, 2001. 353pp.** 📖

Ruth Young, a ghostwriter for self-help books in modern San Francisco, is distraught to learn that her mother LuLing is developing Alzheimer's disease. While caring for her, Ruth comes across some writings that LuLing had compiled when she first started noticing her failing memory. Through them, Ruth learns about her mother's previously unknown past in China during the 1920s, as well as that of LuLing's mother, a bonesetter's daughter from the mountainous village of Immortal Heart, Xian Xin. Tan mentions in her author's note that the novel is partly autobiographical.

The Kitchen God's Wife. **Putnam, 1991. 415pp.** 📖

Weili "Winnie" Jiang decides to tell her daughter Pearl about her difficult youth in China, where she survived an arranged marriage that turned abusive, the Japanese invasion, and the Communist takeover. Pearl has never understood her mother's crankiness and difficulty communicating, which is one reason she has never told Winnie about her own multiple sclerosis. Winnie's sharing of her experiences with her daughter brings the two closer together.

Tsukiyama, Gail.

Women of the Silk Series. 📖 **YA**

A gently written two-book series about women's friendships and freedoms in 1920s and 1930s China and Hong Kong.

Women of the Silk. St. Martin's Press, 1991. 278pp. 📖 **YA**

In 1920s rural China, young Pei's poverty-stricken father abandons her at a silk factory, where she is taken in and cared for by the other girls. There she finds contentment and sisterhood, developing independence and deciding against marriage.

The Language of Threads. St. Martin's Press, 1999. 276pp. 📖 **YA**

In this sequel to *Women of the Silk*, Pei, aged twenty-seven in 1938, leaves the silk factory where she grew up, for all intents and purposes, and makes her way to Hong Kong after the Japanese invade Canton. Accompanying her is Ji Shen, an orphaned young woman. Pei obtains a new position with the help of her sisterhood of silk workers, forging a life for herself in a city where appalling poverty and vast wealth exist side by side.

Japan

Baricco, Alexander.

Silk. **HarperCollins, 1997. 96pp.**

In 1861, silk merchant Hervé Joncour travels from France to Japan on business. While in the court of a Japanese baron, he encounters a woman with whom he never speaks, and they manage to conduct an affair with their eyes alone. When he leaves the country, she gives him an erotic note that changes his life forever.

Bock, Dennis.

The Ash Garden. Knopf, 2001. 281pp.

Young Emiko's life and face are both devastated by the bombing of Hiroshima, which kills her younger brother. Anton, a scientist who helped develop the atomic bomb, takes an interest in Emiko's case and follows her life at a distance. Their lives continue to intertwine, never meeting, until Emiko is selected from a group to be brought to the United States for treatment of her scars.

Dalby, Liza.

The Tale of Murasaki. Nan A. Talese, 2000. 426pp. 📖 ✍

Dalby, an anthropologist with an expertise in Japanese culture, was the first Westerner ever to become a geisha herself. Here she presents a fictional autobiography of Lady Murasaki, the eleventh-century author of the classic Japanese novel *The Tale of Genji.* Murasaki Shikibu, a court poet's daughter, is a natural tale-teller who attracts the interest of Japanese society, including that of the empress. Her presence at court leads to romantic and political intrigue.

Golden, Arthur.

Memoirs of a Geisha. Knopf, 1997. 434pp. ★ 📖

In 1929, nine-year-old Chiyo is taken from her home and sold into slavery at a geisha house. Her hair dressed, her make-up perfect, she is given a new name—Sayuri—and trained in the elegant arts of pleasing men. Her virginity is sold to the highest bidder, and her popularity and skill grow steadily, but she never gives up the image of a man who was kind to her as a child. After World War II begins, and industry wins out over tradition, Sayuri must find a new path to forge in the world. What amazed critics and readers alike is how the author, a young American from Boston, could have authentically captured the life of a Japanese woman.

Hazzard, Shirley.

🎗 *The Great Fire.* Farrar, Straus & Giroux, 2003. 288pp. 📖

In 1947, after World War II has ended, several wounded souls meet in Japan, a devastated country still a long way from recovery. Alfred Leith, a war hero, comes to Occupied Japan to survey the damage caused by the atomic bomb on Hiroshima. There he meets Benedict Driscoll, a terminally ill young man, and his precocious sister, seventeen-year-old Helen. Both siblings, children of an Australian army major, are intellectually gifted. Despite the age difference and their unavoidable separation, Leith falls in love with Helen, proving that love serves as a counterpoint to the tumults of war. National Book Award.

Schaeffer, Susan Fromberg.

The Snow Fox. **W. W. Norton, 2004. 438pp.**

In twelfth-century Japan, breathtaking beauty exists alongside intense cruelty, and Schaeffer's novel mirrors both concepts as far as they concern love. Lady Utsu, a poetess at the court of Lord Norimasa, is asked to kill her lover as a test of her loyalty to him. She does so, cementing her dangerous reputation. Despite her unwillingness to cause men more pain, Utsu falls in love with Matsuhito, one of Lord Norimasa's best soldiers. They are torn apart, but their fragile love survives over the years, as each has a pet snow fox that connects them later in life.

Talarigo, Jeff.

The Pearl Diver. **Doubleday, 2004. 240pp.**

In 1948, a Japanese pearl diver is devastated to learn that she has contracted leprosy. Sent away to a leprosarium on the island of Nagashima and told to forget her past, "Miss Fuji" helps care for her fellow patients and adapts to a new civilization. Though treatment contains her illness, her return to normal society is forbidden. A contemplative story of a shameful period of history.

Tsukiyama, Gail.

The Samurai's Garden. **St. Martin's Press, 1995. 211pp.** 📖

Stephen is a young Chinese man sent to his family's residence in Tarumi, Japan, just before World War II, to recover from tuberculosis. He is cared for by four wise local residents who teach him about goodness and beauty, some useful lessons for the time. Though a clear, easy read, Tsukiyama's simplistic style may not appeal to everyone.

South Asia

Literary novels set in Ceylon (modern Sri Lanka), India, Pakistan, and Tibet.

Alai.

🎗 *Red Poppies.* **Houghton Mifflin, 2002. 433pp.**

In the 1930s, before Tibet was occupied by the People's Liberation Army, it was a country run by powerful chieftains who followed traditional feudal customs. The narrator is Second Young Master, the "idiot" son of the high-ranking Maichi family, whose people are the beneficiaries of the government's decision to let them plant opium poppies instead of grain. Because the narrator's advice usually succeeds, nobody seems to know whether he's an idiot or a sage. Either way, he is a reliable observer in this epic tale of tribal maneuverings and political intrigue. Winner of China's top literary award, the Mao Dun Prize.

Baldwin, Shauna Singh.

What the Body Remembers. **Doubleday, 1999. 471pp.** 📖

When Sikh landowner Sardarji takes young Roop to be his second wife, she expects his barren first wife, Satya, to treat her well. But Satya is devoted to her husband and won't relinquish him so easily, especially as Roop's children begin to

arrive. Sardarji himself is preoccupied with the future of India as it moves toward Partition in 1947.

Kakar, Sudhir.

The Ascetic of Desire. **Overlook, 2002. 301pp.** ✍

This first novel by a founder of Indian psychoanalysis takes on the origins of the Kamasutra, the classic treatise on sexual practice written by Vatsyayana in the fourth century AD. A young man, disappointed by his first sexual experience, travels to meet Vatsyayana and write his biography. As he learns from Vatsyayana about his practice of the sexual arts, his research—particularly with the noted author's neglected wife—takes on a more intimate direction than expected.

Kunzru, Hari.

🎗 *The Impressionist.* **Dutton, 2002. 383pp.** 📖

In the 1920s, after living for fifteen years as the privileged child of a high-caste man of India, Pran Nath Razdan's true father is revealed to be a British officer—and he is tossed out on the street. Pran Nath makes his way to England, disguised as an Englishman. There, he is surprised to learn that the man whose identity he has stolen is the heir to a fortune. But even this ideal situation is not to last, and Pran Nath finds he must reinvent himself yet again. Betty Trask Prize.

Meidav, Edie.

The Far Field. **Houghton Mifflin, 2001. 608pp.** 📖

In 1936, idealistic New Yorker Henry Frye Gould leaves his family behind to sail to Ceylon, where hopes to bring a pure Buddhism back to the country's repressed people. He finds obstacles at every turn, from the colonizing British to Ceylon's own warring religious groups. It is hardly the utopia he had imagined, and Gould's arrogant actions don't help the colonists' situation at all.

Moore, Susanna.

One Last Look. **Knopf, 2003. 320pp.**

In 1836, Lady Eleanor accompanies her sister Harriet and brother Henry to Calcutta, where Henry will take up duties as the country's governor-general. All are shocked by the arduous journey and the intense heat and color of their new home. In her journal, Eleanor records her thoughts about the country's native inhabitants, her unusually close relationship with her brother, and her changing feelings about the value of imperialism.

Roberts, Karen.

The Flower Boy. **Random House, 2000. 336pp.**

Chandi is a Ceylonese servant boy on a lush tea plantation in 1930s Ceylon. He vows to protect Lizzie, the white daughter of the house, whom he calls Rose-Lizzie for the flowers he loves. However, the stage is set for disappointment when his mother, a serving woman, develops a relationship with Lizzie's father, Mr. Buckwater. Chandi hopes that their affair will lead him to an education. His friendship with Lizzie parallels their parents' relationship, as both break social taboos.

Wheeler, Kate.
When Mountains Walked. **Houghton Mifflin, 2000. 256pp.** 📖

Maggie Goodwin, in the present day, follows her husband to rural Peru to help him set up a health clinic, but finds herself falling in love with a local revolutionary. In doing so, she follows in the footsteps of her grandmother Althea Baines, who accompanied her geologist husband to the Indian subcontinent in the 1940s. The stories of both women parallel one another, tracing the paths of many women in search of adventure and self-discovery.

Southeast Asia

Includes historical novels set in Burma (modern Myanmar), Cambodia, Indonesia, Laos, Malaysia, the Philippines, Singapore, Thailand, and Vietnam.

Godshalk, C. S.
Kalimantaan. **Holt, 1998. 480pp.**

In 1838 Gideon Barr, a trader with the East India Company, establishes his own private empire on the island of Borneo, in the Malaysian archipelago. In this overheated atmosphere of headhunters and rampant disease, the phrase "survival of the fittest" takes on a new meaning. Barr's eighteen-year-old bride Amelia observes his megalomaniac behavior with strength and compassion. The real-life exploits behind this literary adventure tale are said to have inspired Joseph Conrad's *Lord Jim.*

Holthe, Tess Uriza.
When the Elephants Dance. **Crown, 2002. 368pp.** 📖

At the end of World War II, when the Japanese and Americans fought for control of the Philippines, the Filipino people were caught in the middle. The Karangalan family gathers together in the cellar of their house, recounting stories of Filipino magic and legend to keep their mind off events occurring outside. The author, an American of Filipino heritage, had heard these tales from her parents and grandmother, who survived the Japanese invasion of their homeland.

Lee, Chang-rae.
🎗 *A Gesture Life*. **Riverhead, 1999. 356pp.** 📖

Franklin Hata, a native Korean, tries in vain to make a place for himself in foreign cultures. An officer in Japan's Imperial Army in 1945, Hata is posted to Burma and oversees Korean "comfort girls" sent to service the soldiers. He falls in love with one of them, but the tragedy of that relationship overshadows his life and affects his ability to care for others. After the war, he lives a respectable life as a storekeeper in a New York suburb, never understanding until much later that his isolation did not bring him happiness. ALA Notable Book.

Loh, Vyvyane.

Breaking the Tongue. **W. W. Norton, 2004. 407pp.**

Loh's first novel centers on the fall of Singapore, a British colony, to the Japanese in 1942. Claude Lim's Anglophile father raised him to be a young Englishman and to disdain the family's traditional Chinese culture. His encounters with Jack Winchester, a newly arrived English tourist, and with a beautiful Chinese spy draw him into intrigues and danger that, ultimately, force him to accept his heritage.

Mason, Daniel.

The Piano Tuner. **Knopf, 2002. 336pp.** 📖

In 1886, the British War Office asks piano tuner Edgar Drake to travel to Burma to tune the grand piano owned by a surgeon in the army, Dr. Anthony Carroll, whose music and poetry are keeping the native tribes from war. Drake's journey is difficult, yet magical. The same is true of Carroll, a suave, enigmatic man whose personal beliefs prove strangely persuasive.

Nguyen, Kien.

The Tapestries. **Little, Brown, 2002. 306pp.** ✎

In 1916 Dan Nguyen is married at age seven to Ven, a family servant almost twenty years his senior. Ven manages to hide him when his parents are murdered, but she succumbs to disease and is forced to sell him into slavery for his own protection. Dan's romance with the enemy's granddaughter complicates matters. The author based his novel on the life of his grandfather, an embroiderer in the Vietnamese royal court.

Slouka, Mark.

🎗 *God's Fool.* **Knopf, 2002. 288pp.** ✎

From his home on a North Carolina plantation at the time of the Civil War, Chang Bunker—one of the famous Siamese twins—looks back on his life from his childhood in Siam to his touring stint with P. T. Barnum's circus. Over the years, his rivalry with brother Eng continues, despite their being joined by a fleshy band at the chest. ALA Notable Book.

Strauss, Darin.

Chang and Eng. **Dutton, 2000. 336pp.** 📖 ✎

The first of a pair of novels written about the Bunker twins (see *God's Fool,* above), this version is narrated by the more introspective twin, Eng, who marvels and despairs about their conjoined nature. They are born in Siam in 1811, and their lives are threatened by the superstitious King Rama, who decides to profit from their existence instead. Their life afterwards consists of sideshows and carnival tents until the Civil War years, when they settle in North Carolina and marry a pair of sisters.

Texier, Catherine.

Victorine. **Pantheon, 2004. 323pp.** ✍ 📖

In 1940, Victorine—the author's great-grandmother—looks back on her eventful past. She grows up in Vendée, France, in the late nineteenth century and becomes a schoolteacher. By 1899, she has married and has two children. When she falls in love with a customs officer, Victorine abandons her family and runs off with her lover to Indochina. Hoping to reinvent her life along the Mekong Delta, she discovers that she does not fit in well there, either.

Toer, Pramoedya Ananta.

The Girl from the Coast. **Hyperion, 2002. 280pp.** ✍

The unnamed Girl from the Coast leaves her fishing village at age fourteen to marry an Indonesian aristocrat, the Bendoro, who keeps her a virtual prisoner in his home. While there, she learns she is only a "practice wife," someone who can be put aside on a whim and whose children become the property of her husband. The author, an Indonesian political activist whose books are banned in his native country, based this novel on the courageous life of his grandmother.

Chapter 11

Christian Historical Fiction

Novels in the very popular subgenre of Christian historical fiction, as the name suggests, place historical or fictional characters in conflicts that reflect the Christian worldview of the authors. It's not too tongue-in-cheek to say that these authors preach to the converted, for their main audience is their fellow Christians—and, more often than not, Christian women. The authors share their own deeply held Christian beliefs via thoughtful stories about characters who strive to live a godly life in an imperfect world. As John Mort describes in his thorough analysis, *Christian Fiction: A Guide to the Genre* (Libraries Unlimited, 2002), the major conflict in the novels must deal somehow with Christian principles. The characters struggle to understand God's message for them, since knowing this will guide them in making major life decisions.

Christian historicals have the potential to offer readers one advantage over other historical fiction subgenres: They don't flinch from portraying the religious facets of life in earlier times—eras when, one might suggest, religion played a larger role in the average person's life than it does now. Although biblical novels form the foundation of Christian historical fiction, other authors choose settings in which Christianity was in crisis, such as the Roman Empire right after the Crucifixion. Other authors choose periods of general strife and hardship, such as rural America during the Great Depression, the frontier West in the mid-nineteenth century, or any period of wartime. The struggles the characters face during rough times draw them closer to God, and their faith helps pull them through. While most Christian novels are "gentle reads"—novels with no sexual content, and very little else of shock value—they don't necessarily stint on realism with the historical setting. Of course, this depends on the era and type of novel.

Though Catholic historical novels exist, dealing mostly with saints' lives, this chapter emphasizes the Protestant experience, at least as far as the two branches of the religion diverge. Christian fiction (which may be called inspirational fiction, especially on bookstore shelves) generally does the same. Frequent characters in Christian historicals include members of those cultural/religious groups persecuted throughout history: early Israelites forced to serve as slaves in Egypt, early Christians in ancient Rome, Protestant believers during the European Reformation, slaves and abolitionists during the American Civil War, and finally the Jews, again, during the Holocaust—as well as those Christians sympathetic to their plight. A few Mormon novels are included in this chapter, mainly those that might appeal to general Christian readers.

Christian fiction is considered separately in the publishing world from "secular" trade fiction. Not only does it have its own trade associations in the CBA (Christian Booksellers' Association) and ECPA (Evangelical Christian Publishers Association), but the publishers also differ. While some are book publishers first and foremost (e.g., Bethany House), others are only one part of a larger ministry organization. Some are imprints of a larger publishing firm (HarperCollins' Zondervan, Random House's WaterBrook). For the most part, Christian authors stay within the subgenre, though some started out as secular romance writers (Francine Rivers, Robin Lee Hatcher) before finding their current home in Christian fiction. The personal Christian journeys of many authors mentioned in this chapter are told in Diane Eble's biographical compendium *Behind the Stories* (Bethany House, 2002).

The subgenres of Christian historical fiction form a microcosm of the larger historical fiction genre. Traditional historical novels, sagas, Western historical novels, romances, and even multi-period epics—each given its own chapter in this volume—all appear from a Christian viewpoint. Although no "literary" subgenre is provided here, readers looking for lyrical prose would do well to seek out some of Christian historical fiction's most elegant stylists, such as Lynn Austin, Jane Kirkpatrick, and Liz Curtis Higgs. Because of the Christian fiction label, mainstream readers may give these and other such authors a pass, which would be their loss. As with the rest of this book, only those novels with significant historical content are included.

This chapter equates Christian fiction with evangelical fiction, as this is what most readers mean when they ask for "Christian fiction." However, others define the genre more broadly; for example, John Mort's guide surveys all types of fiction with Christian themes. Readers' advisors must determine the parameters of taste for readers who request Christian historical fiction. Within this book, non-evangelical novels on Christian topics will appear within other chapters, such as the "Biblical Fiction" section of Chapter 2 as well as in Chapter 10. Readers interested in these works can find them using the subject index, under the listings "biblical themes" and "Christian themes."

Christian Historical Novels

Biblical

Both the Old and New Testaments are natural subjects for Christian novelists, as the Bible is the basis for all Christian faith. Through reading these works, readers get the chance to reacquaint themselves with well-known biblical stories and explore the motivations of major figures in depth. The historical background plays a strong role in these novels. This section includes novels set any time from the age of the Patriarchs—Abraham, Jacob, and Joseph—through the time of the Crucifixion. Traditional (Chapter 2) and literary (Chapter 10) historical novelists also set their novels in biblical times.

Austin, Lynn N.

Chronicles of the King. **YA**

Lynn Austin based her Old Testament novels on a character rarely touched upon in fiction. Hezekiah, King of Judah, is a religious reformer who abolishes idol-worship and brings the Jewish people back to God during the eighth and seventh centuries BC. To do so, he survives the schemes of his weak-willed father, King Ahaz, and prevents an Assyrian takeover of the land. *The Lord Is My Salvation* takes readers to the end of Hezekiah's reign, in which his unfruitful wife's deceit threatens to destroy his faith. The last two novels cover the reign of Hezekiah's son, King Manesseh, who nearly ruins everything his father worked for. The author has rewritten this series; it will be republished by Bethany House starting in early 2005. The first volume will be renamed *Gods and Kings*.

The Lord Is My Strength. Beacon Hill, 1995. 206pp.

The Lord Is My Song. Beacon Hill, 1996. 304pp.

The Lord Is My Salvation. Beacon Hill, 1997. 272pp.

My Father's God. Beacon Hill, 1998. 283pp.

Among the Gods. Beacon Hill, 1999. 300pp.

Brouwer, Sigmund.

The Weeping Chamber. Word, 1998. 310pp.

Simeon of Cyrene, a merchant despondent over family tragedies, travels to Jerusalem on business. Over the next week, which will be the last week in the life of Christ, Simeon listens to Christ's final teachings. Christ's suffering and forgiveness of the men who condemned him to death make Simeon believe that redemption is possible.

Card, Orson Scott.

Stone Tables. Deseret, 1998. 432pp.

Little is told about Moses's personal life and political achievements in either *Exodus* or the *Book of Mormon,* so Card fleshes out his character. Moses rejects his Hebrew heritage at first, but grows in God's faith to become the savior of his people. Card, best known for his science fiction, is also a devout Mormon, and some Mormon teachings are reflected in *Stone Tables.* Card based his novel on a stage play of the same name that he wrote in the 1970s.

Women of Genesis Series.

Annotated in Chapter 2.

Cobb, Melvin J.

Vessel of Honor. Moody, 2004. 464pp.

In the eighth chapter of Acts, Luke recorded that the apostle Philip baptized an Ethiopian chamberlain, converting him to Christianity. Answering the question "what happened next," Cobb relates the life story of

Sahlin Malae, royal chamberlain to Queen Amanitore of Ethiopia. A historically based account of the roots of Christianity in first-century Africa.

Douglas, Lloyd C.

The Robe. 1942. Houghton Mifflin, 1942. 695pp. ★ 📖

Marcellus Gallio, a young Roman soldier sent to Judea as punishment, is ordered to carry out the crucifixion of a Jewish upstart. In a dice game, he wins the robe worn by Christ on the cross. Though he's bewildered at first by his new acquisition, it inspires him to find out more about Christ and his teachings. This leads him on adventures throughout the Roman Empire. After learning about Christ and his growing influence in the Roman world, Marcellus finally converts to Christianity. Widely reprinted.

Groot, Tracy.

Brother's Keeper Series.

Two related novels set around the time of the Crucifixion; members of Jesus's family interact with fictional characters.

The Brother's Keeper. Moody, 2003. 396pp. ✍

The slow spiritual awakening of James, brother of Jesus, forms the heart of Groot's debut novel. James doesn't know what to make of his older brother, a charismatic preacher whose teachings have offended nearly everyone in authority. Jesus's followers regularly appear at the carpentry shop James runs with his other brothers after Joseph's death, which confuses them to no end.

Stones of My Accusers. Moody, 2004. 394pp.

Groot's second novel follows up on two characters from *The Brother's Keeper.* A young man named Nathanael has been killed, with his last words directed toward his mother Rivkah, a prostitute. Nathanael's words of forgiveness, which reflect Christ's teachings, eventually affect all concerned: his beloved, Jorah, Jesus's younger sister; Joab, who informs Rivkah of her son's death; and Orion, a Roman official.

Hendricks, Obery M.

Living Water. HarperSanFrancisco, 2003. 367pp. 📖

During the time of Christ, the Samaritans were despised social outcasts; their women were treated like chattel, even by their husbands. After surviving much cruelty in her life, including five unkind spouses, a Samaritan woman finds happiness with her sixth husband. When she meets Jesus at a well and provides him with a drink of water, Jesus inspires them both with God's message of equality.

Hunt, Angela Elwell.

Legacies of the Ancient River. ✍ YA

Hunt based her trilogy on the biblical story of Joseph, the son of Jacob who was sold by his jealous brothers into slavery in Egypt. She embellishes the Old Testament account by adding romantic intrigue and placing the story in a well-researched, recognizable historical setting, Egypt's Eighteenth Dynasty. Less violent than the original accounts.

Dreamers. Bethany House, 1996. 400pp.

Tuya, a beautiful young Egyptian slave, falls in love with Joseph, one of her fellow slaves in the household of Potiphar.

Brothers. Bethany House, 1997. 368pp.

Joseph has established himself as a great vizier of Egypt, and his ten treacherous brothers come to him out of desperation during the famine in Israel. Mandisa, a handmaid in Joseph's household, grows strongly attracted to Simeon, the most arrogant of the brothers.

Journey. Bethany House, 1997. 384pp.

Just before the patriarch Jacob dies, he bestows his blessing on Ephraim, the younger of Joseph's sons. This instigates a lifelong rivalry between Ephraim and Manasseh, his older brother.

Lemmons, Thom.

Daughters of Faith.

Lemmons sensitively renders the lives of three biblical women—Mary Magdalene, Lydia, and the fictional Amanis of Ephesus—who come from three different cultures. He explores how their lives changed after the Crucifixion.

Daughter of Jerusalem. Multnomah, 1999. 325pp. ✍ 📖

Mary Magdalene, distraught at Jesus's horrific death on the Cross, fills with joy at the thought of passing on her beloved teacher's word to others, but she knows she still has to face up to her disreputable past.

Woman of Means. Multnomah, 2000. 320pp. ✍

On her deathbed, Lydia, Paul's first convert to Christianity, reminisces about her long life—from her tomboy days in Greece, where she grew up worshipping the Roman gods, through her marriage, the births of her children, and the running of her uncle's dye shop.

Mother of Faith. Multnomah, 2001. 320pp.

Amanis, an Ethiopian slave, rescues her master's newborn baby daughter from slaughter and brings her to the Jews for safekeeping. After that she flees for her life, takes up with circus performers, and eventually forms a friendship with the apostle John.

Longenecker, Bruce W.

The Lost Letters of Pergamum. **Baker Academic, 2003. 192pp.** ✍

Lost Letters takes the form of an epistolary novel illuminating the role of early Christianity in the Mediterranean world. Luke, the biblical author, corresponds with Antipas, a Roman civic leader, about Christian teachings. As a result, Antipas views the activity of local Christians in a new light.

Lund, Gerald N.

The Kingdom and the Crown.

The basic storyline of this continuing series about the early years of Christ's ministry, and the miracles he performed, will be familiar to many. Where Lund excels is in humanizing the many examples of how Christ and his teachings touched the common people, such as David ben Joseph, a merchant from Capernaum. Lund also brings to life the political and religious background of Israel circa AD 30.

Fishers of Men. Shadow Mountain, 2000. 642pp.

Come Unto Me. Shadow Mountain, 2001. 574pp.

Behold the Man. Shadow Mountain, 2003. 682pp.

Mills, James R.

The Memoirs of Pontius Pilate. Fleming H. Revell, 2000. 222pp. ✍ 📖

Mills creates a sympathetic portrayal of the much-vilified Roman governor, Pontius Pilate, who writes his recollections of Jesus and his followers thirty years after the Crucifixion. In his own mind, Pilate is a benevolent leader. He never accepts the blame for Jesus's death, and never overtly states any belief in any miracles, though Pilate remains open to the possibility that they may have been real.

Morris, Gilbert.

Lions of Judah. ✍

Morris, evangelical fiction's most prolific author, turns to biblical fiction with his trilogy about Christ's Jewish ancestors.

Heart of a Lion. Bethany House, 2002. 352pp.

Noah faces many temptations, such as the lure of a beautiful young woman who worships the pagan god Baal, before God shows him his life's mission.

No Woman So Fair. Bethany House, 2003. 351pp.

Sarai leaves behind a life of riches to follow Abram, the humble shepherd she loves. They wait years before God's promise, that they will one day have a child, is fulfilled.

The Gate of Heaven. Bethany House, 2004. 317pp.

Like the previous two novels, Morris's novel about biblical patriarch Jacob deviates little from Scripture, relating his life from early childhood through his marriages with Leah and Rachel.

Rivers, Francine.

Lineage of Grace Series. ✍ 📖

Five biographical novellas about major biblical women in the lineage of Christ: Tamar, Rahab, Ruth, Bathsheba, and Mary, in that order. They recount how each woman reached God's grace, and each comes complete with scriptural discussion questions at the end. *Unashamed* won the Christy for Best International Historical.

Unveiled. Tyndale House, 2000. 173pp.

🎗 *Unashamed.* Tyndale House, 2001. 165pp.

Unshaken. Tyndale House, 2001. 185pp.

Unspoken. Tyndale House, 2001. 214pp.

Unafraid. Tyndale House, 2001. 212pp.

Sons of Encouragement Series. ✍ 📖

Following upon Lineage of Grace, Francine Rivers began a new series of novellas about biblical men. The first volume deals with Aaron, younger brother of Moses; four more will follow.

The Priest. Tyndale House, 2004. 228pp.

Snyder, James D.

All God's Children. **Pharos, 1999. 658pp.**

This dense, well-documented novel is narrated by Attalos, an ex-slave who dutifully records his impressions of the Roman Empire, the Jewish people, and Christ's loyal followers over the forty years just following the Crucifixion. Snyder's purpose is to show how and why one small segment of the Jewish population decided to break away from their Hebrew beliefs to follow one remarkable man, and why Christ's legacy still remains today.

Tenney, Tommy.

Hadassah: One Night with the King. **Bethany House, 2004. 349pp.** ✍

This fairly standard retelling of the story of the Jewish Queen of Persia who saved her people begins with a modern framing device in which a present-day young woman reads an ancient letter written by Esther, her ancestress. In the first person, Esther speaks about being chosen as Xerxes's queen, the year-long preparation for her marriage, and her transformational night with him (in which the pair do nothing but converse).

Thoene, Bodie, and Brock Thoene.

A.D. Chronicles.

Moshe Sachar, in modern-day Israel, shows his son a collection of ancient scrolls that retell the stories presented in these novels. Many familiar characters from the Thoenes' Zion Legacy series (later in this chapter), which moved from twentieth-century Israel to the first century AD, reappear here. Everyone seems to be searching for the Messiah who can lead them to the light of God. The Thoenes are deservedly popular, but too many characters and subplots interrupt the flow. The next book will be *Third Watch.*

First Light. Tyndale House, 2003. 395pp.

Marcus Longinus, a Roman centurion, hopes to find the prophet Yeshua in time to prevent the slaughter of Jews before Passover. Peniel, a blind young beggar, awaits the coming of the Messiah, and prays that Yeshua is the man he seeks.

Second Touch. Tyndale House, 2004. 354pp.

Twelve-year-old Lily is cast out of her village when she contracts leprosy. She and other lepers, living in exile in the Valley of Sorrows, hear rumors of a Messiah who can heal them all with a miracle.

Wangerin, Walter.

🏵 ***Paul.*** Zondervan, 2000. 512pp. ✍

In accounts told by many different people, Wangerin fleshes out the life of the Apostle Paul, a rabbi who actively persecuted Christians until an encounter with Jesus changed his life. This detailed and frequently scholarly novel does a good job presenting the early years of the Church. Gold Medallion.

The Roman Empire

This section lists novels set after the Crucifixion that deal with Roman citizens other than Christ or his apostles. Christianity was a fledgling religion during the early years of the Roman Empire up until Emperor Constantine's formal conversion, circa AD 312. These novels portray the deeply held faith of early Christians in ancient Rome, forced to practice their religion in secret under threat of death.

Bunn, T. Davis.

To the Ends of the Earth. Thomas Nelson, 1996. 335pp.

It is AD 338; Emperor Constantine, a recent convert to Christianity, has just died. Travis, son of a Carthaginian merchant, sails for Constantinople in the hope of reestablishing the family fortune. There he finds a city torn apart by political and religious factions, but his romance with a young Christian woman, Lydia, turns him toward salvation.

Hagee, John.

Apocalypse Diaries.

Amid the worldly excesses of the Roman Empire in the first century AD, members of one Christian family hold fast to their newfound faith. John of Patmos, prophet from the Book of Revelation, is a major character.

Devil's Island. Thomas Nelson, 2001. 344pp.

Abraham of Ephesus, a wealthy shipping merchant in Domitian's Rome, is forced to decide publicly whether to sacrifice to Caesar or follow the lead of the apostle John, who acknowledges faith in Christ. The consequences for not following Caesar? Either martyrdom to the lions in Rome's Colisseum, or exile to Patmos, called Devil's Island.

Avenger of Blood. Thomas Nelson, 2002. 381pp.

Abraham's children, Jacob and Rebecca, return to Ephesus after Emperor Domitian's death, but their troubles aren't over. Rebecca loses her fiancé after bearing an illegitimate child from rape, and Jacob takes revenge against the perpetrator.

Rivers, Francine.

Mark of the Lion Trilogy. ★ 📖

Political intrigue, adventure, romance, and faith all come together in Rome in AD 70. The violence displayed in the novels evokes these troubled times. These longtime reader favorites have been reprinted often.

A Voice in the Wind. Tyndale, 1993. 442pp.

After the fall of Jerusalem, Hadassah, a virtuous young Christian woman, is sold into slavery in Rome and forced to serve the Valerian family. While they prove to be kind masters, the decadent behavior of their children, Marcus and Julia, worries Hadassah, who longs to share her new faith with them.

🎗 *An Echo in the Darkness.* Tyndale, 1994. 442pp.

Hadassah, believed to be dead, works secretly as a physician's assistant on the outskirts of Rome. The Valerians, humbled by Hadassah's faith, realize how empty their lives are without her. For Marcus, a chance encounter with Hadassah leads to his own conversion. Gold Medallion.

🎗 *As Sure As the Dawn.* Tyndale, 1995. 448pp.

Atretes, an ex-gladiator who appeared briefly in *A Voice in the Wind*, decides to return home to Germany with his infant son. His son's nurse, Rizpah, a widowed Christian woman, accompanies them. Initial animosity between Rizpah and Atretes turns to attraction. Gold Medallion.

Seddon, Andrew.

Imperial Legions. **Broadman & Holman, 2000. 434pp.**

In AD 59, Sergius, a Roman soldier with Christian beliefs, is ordered by Emperor Nero to eradicate all of the Druids living in Britain. This complicates his romance with Ailidh, a young Celtic noblewoman who also happens to be a Christian. Boudicca, the Celtic warrior queen who threatened the power of Rome, also figures strongly in this novel.

The British Isles

The Early and High Middle Ages

In these novels of medieval times, Christianity is the accepted religion, but believers face challenges in making it accessible to the common people.

Cavanaugh, Jack.

Book of Books.

A projected four-book series about the pioneering efforts to make the Holy Bible available in English. Such an idea was considered heresy because religious worship would then circumvent church leaders.

Cavanaugh expertly interweaves historical fact with Christian content. See the section on the Tudor era for the second installment.

Glimpses of Truth. Zondervan, 1999. 320pp.

Thomas Torr, a smarter-than-average peasant in England in 1384, assists John Wycliffe in translating the New Testament into English. Invited to the Vatican to defend his actions, signaling possible tolerance on their part, Thomas meets only with betrayal. He returns home but finds that the woman he wished to marry now loves another.

Moorhouse, Geoffrey.

Sun Dancing: A Vision of Medieval Ireland. Harcourt Brace, 1997. 284pp.

Quiet and contemplative, *Sun Dancing* uses an unusual combination of fiction and history to reconstruct monastic life on the Skellig Islands off Ireland's west coast from the sixth through the twelfth centuries. The first half of the book, "The Tradition," is purely fiction, with the chapters set about a century apart. The remaining chapters, called "The Evidence," are nonfiction, dealing with the influences of different cultures on Celtic Christianity.

Windsor, Linda.

The Fires of Gleannmara.

Three stand-alone titles about strong-willed women in early Christian Ireland; adventure and romance.

Maire. Multnomah, 2000. 355pp.

Maire, Gleannmara's warrior queen in the fifth century AD, finds that her fierce battle prowess is no match for the strong Christian faith of Rowan ap Emrys, one of her hostages.

Riona. Multnomah, 2001. 351pp.

Riona of Dromin, a Celtic noblewoman in the sixth century, had already rejected Lord Kieran of Gleannmara's hand in marriage because of her preference for a religious life. This all changes when she rescues three orphaned children, for she can't formally adopt them without a husband.

Deirdre. Multnomah, 2002. 351pp.

When Alric, bastard son of a Saxon king, captures devout Irish princess Deirdre on a raid along Ireland's coast in the seventh century, he fulfills his mother's prophecy that his earthly kingdom would be won by love.

The Tudor Era

In 1533, King Henry VIII broke with the Catholic Church to divorce Catherine of Aragon and marry Anne Boleyn. With this defiant act, the head of the English church was changed, but religious practice in England was essentially the same as before. These novels clearly take the side of the Protestant cause, still considered heresy by many at that time.

Cavanaugh, Jack.

***Beyond the Sacred Page.* Zondervan, 2003. 336pp.**

> The second novel in Cavanaugh's series begins in 1535. Meg Foxe, a friend of Anne Boleyn, comes upon one of William Tyndale's translations of the New Testament and becomes enraptured with its prose. The problem: Her husband Pernell is an avowed heretic-hunter. Part of the Book of Books series; see the previous volume under "The Early and High Middle Ages," above.

Nuernberg, Leslie.

***Only Glory Awaits: The Story of Anne Askew, Reformation Martyr.* Emerald House, 2003. 255pp.** ✍

> During the 1540s, the Protestant Reformation hasn't yet reached England, and Henry VIII remains staunchly Catholic in practice. Anne Askew, a young gentlewoman forced into an unhappy marriage, never gives in to pressure to recant her strong Protestant faith. First in a projected series called Seasons of Grace.

The Georgian Era

The growth of Britain as a world power: British imperialism vies with individual citizens' religious beliefs.

Bunn, T. Davis, and Isabella Bunn.

Heirs of Acadia.

> These books feature descendants of the characters written about in the Song of Acadia series (listed under Canada), which Bunn co-wrote with Janette Oke.

***The Solitary Envoy.* Bethany House, 2004. 319pp.**

> During the War of 1812 in Washington, D.C., Erica Langston's father is killed, and their family business is destroyed. Afterward, Erica travels alone to England to deal with her father's creditors. There she confronts Gareth Powers, a British major she had first encountered in Washington's streets during the war.

***The Innocent Libertine.* Bethany House, 2004. 320pp.**

> Abigail Aldridge causes a family scandal in London in 1824 by tending to the poor in a dangerous section of Soho. Sent back to America in disgrace, Abbie begins again with the help of her patron, a wealthy countess.

Musser, Joe.

***The Infidel.* Broadman and Holman, 2001. 368pp.** ✍

> Musser's evangelical biographical novel stars John Newton, an eighteenth-century British seaman and slave trader who sins mightily and often. Newton gets sold into white slavery himself and discovers how

inhumane a state it is. He finds redemption later in life, turning to ministry and writing the well-known Christian hymn "Amazing Grace."

The Victorian Era

Christian novels set during the Victorian period (1837–1901) show a mix of social classes—the wealth of the.rich versus the deplorable plight of the poor, especially the Irish.

Blackwell, Lawana.

Tales of London.

Three interconnected gentle reads set in 1870s and 1880s London and surroundings.

The Maiden of Mayfair. Bethany House, 2000. 409pp.

Dorothea Blake, a wealthy widow, brings young Sarah Matthews from a dingy orphanage to her own home at Mayfair, where she raises Sarah as her long-lost granddaughter.

Catherine's Heart. Bethany House, 2002. 414pp.

At eighteen, Catherine Rayborn enjoys the independence of attending college at Cambridge, but mistakenly gives her heart to a man with a disreputable past.

Leading Lady. Bethany House, 2004. 432pp.

Bethia Rayborn works as wardrobe mistress in London's Royal Court Theatre and gets caught up in the vengeful schemes of the production's leading lady.

Thoene, Bodie, and Brock Thoene.

Galway Chronicles.

In the 1830s and 1840s, Irish Catholic tenant farmers suffer mightily under the yoke of their English overlords. For the poor Irish residents of Ballynockanor in Galway, freedom seems to be only a dream. Hope arrives in the form of Joseph Connor, a stranger to the village, whose presence affects everyone in the Donovan family—especially eldest daughter Kate, who lost both her husband and her beauty in a fire several years earlier. Happiness for Kate and Joseph is long in coming, with English treachery at every turn. Though the Thoenes write primarily about ancient and modern troubles in the Holy Land, their portrayal of mid-nineteenth-century Ireland is magnificent. The first novel won a Gold Medallion.

Only the River Runs Free. Thomas Nelson, 1997. 269pp.

Of Men and of Angels. Thomas Nelson, 1998. 320pp.

Ashes of Remembrance. Thomas Nelson, 1999. 320pp.

All Rivers to the Sea. Thomas Nelson, 2000. 320pp.

Europe

The Renaissance and Reformation

Heroes and heroines of the Protestant Reformation, when citizens throughout Europe rejected papal authority in pursuit of individual faith, take center stage here.

Grant, Reg.

Storm. WaterBrook, 2001. 402pp. ✍

After surviving a violent storm, Martin Luther, a young man of the law in early sixteenth-century Germany, swears to St. Anne that he will become a monk. Thus begins this dramatic biographical novel of Luther's life, from his determination to abolish the Catholic Church's granting of indulgences through his romance with former nun Kate von Bora.

Herr, Ethel L.

The Seekers. **YA**

In the mid-sixteenth century, the very Catholic King Philip II of Spain took it upon himself to purge the Netherlands, one of Spain's dominions, of its Protestant heresy. While members of the Inquisition travel the Netherlands to suppress the new faiths that have sprung up in the wake of the Reformation, two young people fall in love. Herr goes to great length to explain the complicated politics and beliefs of the times.

The Dove and the Rose. Bethany House, 1996. 331pp.

In the Dutch city of Breda, bookseller's daughter Aletta Engelshofen and Pieter-Lucas van den Garde, an artist, are kept apart because Pieter-Lucas's parents support the Beggars, a radical Calvinist group.

The Maiden's Sword. Bethany House, 1997. 317pp.

Aletta and Pieter-Lucas, now married, are torn between politics and their faith when Prince Willem van Oranje asks Pieter-Lucas to serve as his messenger.

The Citadel and the Lamb. Bethany House, 1998. 308pp.

Their lives threatened by Spanish soldiers, Pieter-Lucas and Aletta flee to the walled city of Leyden for safety, but danger pursues them even there.

Huggins, James Byron.

Rora. Lion's Head, 2001. 471pp. ✍

The Waldenses were members of a Protestant sect, begun in the Middle Ages, that avowed extreme poverty in protest against the worldliness of the Catholic Church. Declared heretics by the Inquisition, many Waldenses were massacred in the Alpine Valley of Rora in 1655. In Huggins's heroic but little-known novel, Joshua Gianavel, the Waldenses' military leader, takes a brave stand against the army sent to exterminate his people.

Scheib, Asta.

Children of Disobedience. **Crossroad, 2000. 242pp.** ✍

Taking a more serious tone than Grant's *Storm*, above, Scheib focuses her attention on the courtship and marriage of Martin Luther, monk turned reformer, and runaway nun Katharina von Bora. Their passionate relationship, sensitively portrayed, is based on original letters written by Luther to Katharina.

World War II

After the Reformation, the timeline for European Christian fiction jumps right to World War II. It isn't going too far to imply that the Nazis, with their unredeemable policies of evil, represent the devil himself.

Cavanaugh, Jack.

Songs in the Night.

In World War II-era Germany, ordinary Christian citizens take a stand against the evil Nazi regime.

🎗 *While Mortals Sleep.* Bethany House, 2001. 384pp.

Josef Schumacher, a pastor in 1939 Berlin, watches Nazi corruption slowly infiltrate his congregation. When one of his teenage parishioners turns in his own father for listening to BBC radio, Josef actively begins teaching his youthful audience to follow God rather than Hitler. Christy Award.

🎗 *His Watchful Eye.* Bethany House, 2002. 384pp.

It's now 1943, and much to the dismay of Pastor Schumacher, his parishioner Konrad Reichmann joins the Hitler Youth Movement. Faced with the reality of the Third Reich on the Russian front, Konrad vows never to kill again. Christy Award.

Above All Earthly Powers. Bethany House, 2004. 384pp.

The war has ended, but in East Berlin, little has really changed. Mady Schumacher, widow of Josef, picks up where her heroic husband left off, rescuing disabled children from a mental institution.

Goyer, Tricia.

From Dust and Ashes. **Moody, 2003. 463pp.**

In Austria in 1945, Helene, the abandoned wife of a cruel S.S. guard, searches for redemption after American soldiers liberate the concentration camp at Gusen. Determined to make up for her husband's sins, Helene takes refuge with her father and cares for two survivors, a Jewish girl and a Polish Christian woman who helped save Jews during the war. Helene's selfless acts attract the attention of Sgt. Peter Scott, an American GI. Goyer based her novel on interviews with survivors.

Larson, Elyse.

Women of Valor.

Larson dramatizes women's World War II experiences while exploring the faith that sustained them.

For Such a Time. Bethany House, 2000. 352pp.

Jean Thornton, an American Red Cross worker stationed at a Welsh hospital, does her best to rescue her French cousin, Giselle Munier, a member of the Resistance who is captured by the Nazis.

So Shall We Stand. Bethany House, 2001. 352pp.

Nella Killian, a war widow in 1944, returns home to Wales to raise her young daughter alone. When she pursues the true cause of an American serviceman's death, she puts herself in danger. Nella was a minor character in *For Such a Time.*

The Hope Before Us. Bethany House, 2002. 352pp.

Toward the end of the war, nurse Marge Emerson is reassigned to medical duty in France, where she meets a conscientious objector with a faith much stronger than hers.

Thoene, Bodie.

Zion Covenant. ★

Elisa Lindheim, a violinist in Vienna hiding under an Aryan name, joins with her friend Leah Feldstein to rescue their fellow Jews from pre–World War II Austria regardless of the personal cost. John Murphy, a *New York Times* reporter, helps them. Some of the lucky ones escape to the Holy Land or America, but other Jews find that there's nowhere for them to go. Continued by the Thoenes' Zion Chronicles series (listed under Middle East).

Vienna Prelude. Bethany House, 1989. 410pp.

Prague Counterpoint. Bethany House, 1989. 380pp.

Munich Signature. Bethany House, 1990. 396pp.

Jerusalem Interlude. Bethany House, 1990. 400pp.

Danzig Passage. Bethany House, 1991. 413pp.

Warsaw Requiem. Bethany House, 1991. 510pp.

Vaughan, Robert.

Vaughan, a decorated former military officer, paints on a wide canvas in his World War II-era series, focusing not only on military engagements in Britain, Europe, Asia, and North Africa but also on the American home front. His expertise in military aviation is evident.

Touch the Face of God. Thomas Nelson, 2002. 306pp.

In 1943, Lt. Mark White, American pilot of a B-17 bomber, stays in close touch with his sweetheart Emily back home even as he revs up for a fierce fight against Germany. White's best friend, chaplain Lt. Lee Arlington Grant, tries to convert his fellow soldiers in the hope of keeping them strong.

Whose Voice the Waters Heard. Thomas Nelson, 2003. 320pp.

Vaughan's second novel introduces new characters and a different setting. Patrick Hanifin and Diane Slayton rekindle their romantic relationship just as war heats up in the South Pacific.

His Truth Is Marching On. Thomas Nelson, 2004. 320pp.

Dewey Bradley, an American destined for the religious life, joins the infantry to help fight Hitler. Meanwhile, his German counterpart in the novel, Gunter Reinhardt, begins to question Hitler's policies toward Jews.

The United States

Colonial America

As one of America's founding principles was religious freedom, it's not surprising that Christian novelists have been inspired by the colonial period. These novels, particularly those by Ammerman and Schalesky, are comparatively little known, but they're well worth seeking out.

Ammerman, Mark.

Cross and the Tomahawk.

A heavily researched, action-packed fictionalization of the relations between English settlers and the Narragansett Indians, called "praying Indians" for their early conversion to Christianity. The novels begin in early seventeenth-century Rhode Island and continue through the mid-eighteenth century. The author descends from Roger Williams, Rhode Island's founder.

The Rain from God. Horizon, 1997. 320pp.

Katanaquat, known to his tribe as "Rain from God," resents the changes that white people mean to his way of life. He undergoes a spiritual transformation when he meets preacher Roger Williams.

The Ransom. Horizon, 1997. 392pp. ✍

Job Kattenanit, Katanaquat's son (and a historical figure), tells about the growing animosity between his tribe and the English, which leads to King Philip's War.

Longshot. Horizon, 2000. 301pp.

Ammerman moves westward to Pennsylvania, while Anglican minister Christopher Long and Narragansett Indian/witch doctor Caleb Hobomucko, make an adventurous journey to settle the Ohio Country in the 1750s.

Hunt, Angela Elwell.

Keepers of the Ring.

A five-book historical series/family saga about early American colonists and their dependence on, and conflicts with, Native American tribes. Over time, the English families intermarry with the natives, meaning their descendants don't fully belong to either group. The novels interconnect by means of an inscribed wedding ring passed from one generation to the next.

Roanoke: The Lost Colony. Tyndale House, 1996. 512pp.

In this imagined version of what might have happened to the first English colony in America, Jocelyn White (fictional cousin of Eleanor Dare, mother of Virginia) voyages reluctantly to the American colonies. Married to Thomas Colman, a man who doesn't love her, Jocelyn relies on her faith in God to see her through.

Jamestown. Tyndale House, 1996. 432pp.

Only a few children survive the massacre at Roanoke in 1607 and arrive at the Jamestown colony. Pocahontas becomes sister and mentor to young Gilda, just three years old, while Fallon Bailie, a teenager, voyages to England for his education.

Hartford. Tyndale House, 1996. 350pp.

In Connecticut's Hartford colony in the mid-seventeenth century, Fallon's and Gilda's identical twin sons, Daniel and Taregan, compete for nearly everything.

Rehoboth. Tyndale House, 1997. 356pp.

While Daniel's son Mojag ministers to the Indians, Aiyana Bailie, Daniel's daughter, finds love in the colonial village of Rehoboth, Massachusetts, in the 1670s—right about the time when the native inhabitants rise up against English settlers in King Philip's War.

Charles Towne. Tyndale House, 1998. 432pp.

Rachelle Bailie has always believed her father, Mojag, to be dead. When she learns that he is still alive, Rachelle heads for Boston. She has the adventure of her life when her ship is attacked by pirates.

Schalesky, Marlo.

The Winds of Freedom.

It is 1743. English colonists are caught up in the Great Awakening, a religious revival that sweeps through the land and gives people a closer relationship with God. At the same time, they prepare for trouble with the French; by 1755, tensions have exploded into all-out war. Kwelik, a half-breed Indian girl on the Pennsylvania frontier, and Jonathan Grant, an Englishman in search of new beginnings in America, both get caught up in the fray.

Cry Freedom. Crossway, 2000. 379pp.

Freedom's Shadow. Crossway, 2001. 333pp.

The American Revolution

Like traditional historicals, Christian historicals set during the American Revolution (1775–1783) are patriotic tales of freedom and sacrifice.

Carter, Ron.

Prelude to Glory.

Carter has Revolutionary War heroes (Paul Revere, John Paul Jones) interact with members of the fictional Dunson family of Boston, giving his extended saga a sense of realism. Not only does he portray battle scenes with vigor, but he details the philosophical and spiritual underpinnings of the Revolution. However, he crams almost too many historical facts into his series, making it action-packed in places but dry in others. Mormon emphasis.

Our Sacred Honor. Bookcraft, 1998. 605pp.

Times That Try Men's Souls. Bookcraft, 1999. 556pp.

To Decide Our Destiny. Bookcraft, 1999. 499pp.

The Hand of Providence. Bookcraft, 2000. 681pp.

A Cold, Bleak Hill. Bookcraft, 2001. 557pp.

The World Turned Upside Down. Bookcraft, 2002. 517pp.

The Impending Storm. Bookcraft, 2003. 552pp.

A More Perfect Union. Bookcraft, 2004. 560pp.

Morris, Gilbert.
The Spider Catcher. Zondervan, 2003. 352pp.

Heartbroken after his fiancée's death, Welsh physician Rees Kenyon leaves London for America, bringing along his new ward, Callie Summers, a teenage orphan who has led a hard life. During the American Revolution, Rees gets caught up in building fighting ships ("spider catchers") for the American patriots, but continues to deny his growing feelings for Callie.

The Early United States

Between the Revolution and the Civil War, the United States grew into a powerful nation. While some of these novels emphasize emigration and worldwide travel, others look at the social problems within America's borders: the exploitation of mill workers and growing racial tensions in the South.

Gouge, Louise M.

Ahab's Legacy.

A new series of literary Christian fiction.

Ahab's Bride. RiverOak, 2004. 348pp. 📖

Hannah Oldweiler, a gentle girl in early nineteenth-century Nantucket, falls in love with Captain Ahab, a sailor who never lets anything, especially the sea, get the best of him.

Hoff, B. J.

Song of Erin.

Hoff's two-book series, which reads like one long novel, covers both Irish and Irish-American experiences in the 1840s. Jack Kane, an Irish immigrant in New York City, yearns to establish a publishing empire. He falls in love with Samantha Harte, a Christian widow whose past hides a dark secret. Back in Ireland, Terese Sheridan struggles with extreme poverty, and Jack's dissolute younger brother Brady deceives her about his true character.

Cloth of Heaven. Tyndale House, 1997. 400pp.

Ashes and Lace. Tyndale House, 1999. 390pp.

Kraus, Jim, and Terri Kraus.

Circle of Destiny. YA

The adventures of four Harvard classmates in the 1840s—young, energetic, and in charge of their own destinies—will appeal to adult and young adult readers. The action sweeps from small-town Ohio to the California Gold Rush. The historical research and storytelling of this husband-wife team have been compared to those of Bodie Thoene and Brock Thoene, but the Krauses' style is far more preachy.

The Price. Tyndale House, 2000. 300pp.

Joshua Quittner, a preacher's son from rural Ohio, changes his mind about a seminary career after meeting his fellow students, who fire up his spirit for adventure.

The Treasure. Tyndale House, 2000. 300pp.

After graduation, Gage Davis begins running his father's business but discovers that money can't buy happiness.

The Promise. Tyndale House, 2001. 403pp.

Hannah Morgan Collins dreams of becoming a doctor in Massachusetts but has difficulty reconciling her independence with her hopes for a husband and family.

The Quest. Tyndale House, 2002. 300pp.

Jamison Pike, cynical journalist and world traveler, finds Christ and turns his life around. When he returns home, he discovers happiness where he least expects it.

Morris, Gilbert, and Aaron McCarver.

Spirit of Appalachia.

After his wife's death in childbirth, Josh "Hawk" Spencer sets out for a new life in the Appalachian Mountains. The MacNeal family joins his wagon train, and all of these ambitious pioneers rely on God for their survival. The series begins after the Revolutionary War. The last volume, set partly in England, introduces many new characters and seems to be an afterthought.

Over the Misty Mountains. Bethany House, 1997. 334pp.

Beyond the Quiet Hills. Bethany House, 1998. 320pp.

Among the King's Soldiers. Bethany House, 1999. 336pp.

Beneath the Mockingbird's Wings. Bethany House, 2000. 320pp.

Around the River's Bend. Bethany House, 2002. 288pp.

Morris, Gilbert, and Lynn Morris.

The Creoles.

In this projected four-book series, centering on four female friends who met at the Ursuline Convent School, the father-daughter writing team chronicles religious, cultural, and racial differences in early to mid-nineteenth-century Louisiana.

The Exiles. Thomas Nelson, 2003. 267pp.

The search for her baby sister, long thought to be dead, leads red-haired Chantel Fontaine from New Orleans through Louisiana's swampland in search of answers.

The Immortelles. Thomas Nelson, 2004. 255pp.

While Damita De Salvedo's fortunes fall, those of her former slave girl Rissa, now a wealthy independent freedwoman, begin to rise.

Morris, Lynn, and Gilbert Morris.

Cheney Duvall, MD.

Cheney Duvall, a new graduate of the University of Pennsylvania women's medical college in the 1860s, learns that jobs for female doctors are few. She jumps at the chance to serve as shipboard physician on a voyage from New York to Seattle, even though it also means chaperoning 200 frontier brides-to-be. Shiloh Irons, the ship's male nurse, becomes her partner in adventure and, later, her romantic interest. After succeeding in their original mission, detailed in *Stars for a Light*, they travel wherever medical help is needed—Arkansas, cholera-ridden New York City, the Deep South, and San Francisco. The series continues through the Civil War. Another series, Cheney and Shiloh: The Inheritance (see under "Reconstruction and the Gilded Age"), picks up where this one leaves off.

Stars for a Light. Bethany House, 1994. 315pp.

Shadow of the Mountains. Bethany House, 1994. 336pp.

A City Not Forsaken. Bethany House, 1995. 335pp.

Toward the Sunrising. Bethany House, 1996. 338pp.

Secret Place of Thunder. Bethany House, 1996. 335pp.

In the Twilight, In the Evening. Bethany House, 1997. 320pp.

Island of the Innocent. Bethany House, 1998. 320pp.

Driven with the Wind. Bethany House, 2000. 315pp.

Parr, Delia.

Trinity Series.

As midwife in the small town of Trinity, Pennsylvania, in 1833, widowed Martha Cade knows more than her share of the residents' secrets. Martha sees midwifery as her Christian duty, but struggles to balance her career with the needs of her family.

A Place Called Trinity. St. Martin's Press, 2002. 290pp.

One of Martha's great hopes is that her daughter Victoria will follow in her footsteps as a midwife. Heartbroken after Victoria runs away from home, and unable to find her, Martha returns to Trinity only to find that a doctor has set up a practice that rivals hers.

Home to Trinity. St. Martin's Press, 2003. 308pp.

Victoria returns home with her new boss—a female magazine publisher—in tow, and insists that she has found a new career. Meanwhile, Martha remains convinced that the death of a newborn baby in town masks an abusive situation.

Peterson, Tracie, and Judith Miller.

Bells of Lowell.

The mill girls of early nineteenth-century Lowell, Massachusetts, lead difficult lives working in the textile factories that are the town's lifeblood. With the occasionally wooden dialogue, the characters don't seem very realistic, but the setting is well researched, showing the plight of the downtrodden in industrial New England: the young and the Irish. All three novels have romantic elements.

Daughter of the Loom. Bethany House, 2003. 382pp.

With no other means of survival, Lilly Armbruster works in Lowell's textile mills in 1828. Lilly believes it to be God's will that she sabotage the cruel business that killed her father and destroyed her town.

A Fragile Design. Bethany House, 2003. 380pp.

In 1831, Bella Newberry leaves her Shaker community in search of independence in Lowell and discovers that the mill towns are sorely in need of educational and social reform.

These Tangled Threads. Bethany House, 2003. 381pp.

Mill girl Daughtie Winfield fights her attraction to Liam Donohue, an Irish artist who supports her abolitionist beliefs.

Lights of Lowell.

More romantic drama centering on the textile factory town of Lowell, this time in the mid-nineteenth century.

A Tapestry of Hope. Bethany House, 2004. 351pp.

Jasmine Wainwright, a Mississippi planter's daughter, barely tolerates her arranged marriage to an abusive mill owner from Lowell, a man who puts his business before everything.

Rivers, Francine.

🏅 *The Last Sin Eater.* **Tyndale House, 1998. 380pp.** 📖

The residents of one Scottish community in 1850s Appalachia still believe in the practice of human "sin-eaters," individuals who absolve the dead of their sins. Ten-year-old Cadi, spying the sin-eater at her grandmother's gravesite, wants to ask the man to relieve her own guilt over her sister Elen's tragic death. Over time, Cadi hears about Jesus, turns to Christianity, and learns that only Christ can relieve people of sin. Gold Medallion.

Williamson, Denise.

Roots of Faith.

Williamson describes how Christian masters and slaves had to adjust their religious beliefs to reflect the realities of the time. Her research into antebellum Charleston, South Carolina, is evident. Set in the 1830s through 1850s.

The Dark Sun Rises. Bethany House, 1999. 480pp.

Elderly Abram Callcott, a benevolent master, discovers that Joseph Whitsun, one of his field slaves, has learned to read. Rather than punish the young man, as his son Brant tries to do, Abram provides Joseph with an education.

When Stars Begin to Fall. Bethany House, 2000. 480pp.

Manumitted at Abram Callcott's deathbed, Joseph now practices medicine in Pennsylvania, where he helps other slaves escape along the Underground Railroad. He also encounters Mayleda, his former master's daughter, who goes against her in-laws' wishes to help Joseph's cause.

The Civil War

Readers who believe Christian novelists can't write realistic battle scenes or craft compelling social dramas should consider these selections, set between 1861 and 1865.

Austin, Lynn N.

Refiner's Fire.

In this loose trilogy, Austin relates women's Civil War experiences from multiple perspectives. The third novel will be *A Light to My Path*.

🏅 *Candle in the Darkness.* Bethany House, 2002. 431pp.

Caroline Fletcher, daughter of a Virginia plantation family who believe that slave ownership is their God-given right, becomes a fervent abolitionist after a visit to relatives in Pennsylvania. During the early years of the Civil War, she risks all, including loyalty to the South, to put an end to slavery. Christy Award.

🎗 *Fire by Night.* Bethany House, 2003. 429pp.

Austin's second novel of women's coming of age during the Civil War introduces Julia Hoffman, daughter of a well-to-do Northern family, who loses a potential beau's interest due to her self-centered behavior at the Battle of Bull Run. Determined to give her life meaning, Julia becomes a nurse for the Union. In a parallel story, tomboy Phoebe Bigelow disguises herself as a man and follows her brothers into the Union army. Christy Award.

Dwyer, John J.

Heroes in Time. ✍

Long biographical novels about two Confederate heroes.

Stonewall. Broadman & Holman, 1998. 634pp.

Confederate General Thomas J. "Stonewall" Jackson was an intensely devout man, very much anti-war, yet convinced that his actions during the Civil War were guided firmly by God. In occasionally gripping, occasionally long-winded prose, complete with relevant Scripture quotations, Dwyer captures Jackson's life from his youth in Lexington, Virginia, through his death in 1863. The women in Jackson's life also figure prominently.

Robert E. Lee. Broadman & Holman, 2002. 775pp.

This sequel to *Stonewall* picks up where the previous novel left off, at Jackson's funeral, and follows Robert E. Lee, another religious man, through Reconstruction to the end of his life in 1870. The novel is just as much about the people who surrounded Lee as about Lee himself.

Lacy, Al.

Battles of Destiny.

Eight stand-alone novels of love, war, family, and faith, each with a different Civil War battle as a backdrop: Fredericksburg (*Joy from Ashes*), Gettysburg (*Season of Valor*), Chancellorsville (*Turn of Glory*), and more.

A Promise Unbroken. Multnomah, 1993. 307pp.

A Heart Divided. Multnomah, 1993. 320pp.

Beloved Enemy. Multnomah, 1994. 356pp.

Shadowed Memories. Multnomah, 1994. 307pp.

Joy from Ashes. Multnomah, 1995. 285pp.

Season of Valor. Multnomah, 1996. 294pp.

Wings of the Wind. Multnomah, 1997. 300pp.

Turn of Glory. Multnomah, 1998. 300pp.

Morris, Gilbert.

 *Edge of Honor.* **Zondervan, 2000. 373pp.**

At the end of the Civil War, Quentin Larribee, a Union surgeon, accidentally killed a man he was trying to heal. He travels south to give the bad news to the man's widow and see what he can do to help, only to find himself falling in love with her. Quentin finds himself torn between her and his fiancée in New York. Christy Award.

Phillips, Michael.

Shenandoah Sisters.

Reading as one very long novel, Phillips's series follows two young women of Shenandoah County, North Carolina, during and just after the Civil War. Katie Clairborne, orphaned daughter of a white plantation owner, bands together with Mayme Jukes, an escaped African-American slave girl, to keep Katie's family plantation running smoothly. While the white characters and Mayme speak proper English without even a Southern accent, many former slaves use a strong African-American dialect that is incomprehensible at times.

Angels Watching Over Me. Bethany House, 2003. 316pp.

A Day to Pick Your Own Cotton. Bethany House, 2003. 318pp.

The Color of Your Skin Ain't the Color of Your Heart. Bethany House, 2004. 314pp.

Together Is All We Need. Bethany House, 2004. 317pp.

Reconstruction and the Gilded Age

Late nineteenth-century America isn't a common setting; see also the later books of Michael Phillips's <u>Shenandoah Sisters</u>, above.

Hoff, B. J.

American Anthem.

Hoff's latest Christian soap opera takes place primarily in late nineteenth-century New York City. She incorporates multiple plotlines and characters to illustrate a wide range of American immigrant experiences. Susanna Fallon is intrigued by her brother-in-law Michael, a pianist, but worries about the role he may have played in her late sister's death. Andrew Carmichael, a Scottish physician, accepts a female doctor into his practice. Finally, the McGovern family adjusts to a new life in America. A projected trilogy.

Prelude. W Publishing Group, 2002. 281pp.

Cadence. W Publishing Group, 2003. 264pp.

Morris, Gilbert.

Jacob's Way. **Zondervan, 2001. 416pp.**

Just after the Civil War, Reisa Dimitri and her grandfather Jacob emigrate from Russia and find a new home with New York's Jewish community. To earn a living, the Dimitris head south with their new friend Dov and peddle their wares across the Southern states. Jacob's thoughts lead him ever closer to Christianity, and Reisa feels drawn to an ex-con, Ben Driver, who doesn't think he's good enough for her.

Morris, Lynn, and Gilbert Morris.

Cheney and Shiloh: The Inheritance.

Cheney and Shiloh, newly married, return in these sequels to the <u>Cheney Duvall, MD</u>, series (described under "The Early United States"). More adventure and romance await the duo, who take a sailing honeymoon in the Caribbean and begin new lives together in New York City in the late 1860s.

Where Two Seas Met. Bethany House, 2001. 317pp.

The Moon by Night. Bethany House, 2004. 381pp.

The Twentieth Century

With the notable exception of James Scott Bell's legal thrillers, these are thoughtful, family-oriented tales of pain, endurance, and hope during difficult times like the Depression and World Wars.

Austin, Lynn.

🔖 *Hidden Places.* **Bethany House, 2001. 432pp.** 📖

After the deaths of her husband and father-in-law, Eliza Wyatt is left to run Wyatt Orchards and raise three children alone. But it is 1930, money's hard to come by, and the bank threatens foreclosure on her farm. When Eliza discovers a deathly ill stranger on her land, she hopes he might be a guardian angel come to rescue her. The man, Gabe Harper, turns out to be the catalyst for the revelation of long-held family secrets. Christy Award.

Bell, James Scott.

The Trials of Kit Shannon.

James Scott Bell, co-author of the <u>Shannon Saga</u> (later in this section) and a former trial lawyer himself, continues writing about the career and personal trials of Kit Shannon, female lawyer in early twentieth-century Los Angeles. Kit gets tougher, and so do her cases.

A Greater Glory. Bethany House, 2003. 301pp.

To prevent her daughter from discovering a dark secret about her past, society matron Celia Harcourt hires Kit to sue the *Gazette* for a libelous story they threaten to print.

A Higher Justice. Bethany House, 2003. 303pp.

Kit hopes to make the owner of the newly developed Los Angeles Electric Trolley Line take responsibility for the death of Winnie Franklin's son, dead in a streetcar accident, but there is corruption in the company's ranks.

A Certain Truth. Bethany House, 2004. 304pp.

Kit Shannon, finally married to her longtime suitor Ted Fox, returns to California with her new husband on an ocean liner. She decides to defend Wanda Boswell, a fellow passenger whose husband was found dead in her stateroom.

Foster, Sharon Ewell.

✿ *Passing By Samaria.* Alabaster, 2000. 382pp. 📖 **YA**

In Mississippi in 1919, after Alena Waterbridge's best friend is lynched by a mob, her parents send her to live with an aunt in Chicago for her protection. The era's racial tension makes it impossible for Alena to express her opinions freely, and despite her aunt's care, Alena grows bitter and resigned. In Chicago, she meets two men who change her life. One of them proves dangerous to her self-belief, but the other helps restore her faith in God. Christy Award.

Hickman, Patricia.

Millwood Hollow Series. **YA**

A projected four-book series about the three Welby siblings, coming of age in poverty-ridden rural Arkansas during the Depression. The author's humorous situations don't feel contrived, and they make for heartwarming tales of redemption.

Fallen Angels. Warner Faith, 2003. 301pp.

Twelve-year-old Angel Welby cares for her two younger siblings, Willie and Ida May, after their mother runs off. They latch onto Jeb Nubey, an illiterate man hiding from the law, and all are forced into a life of deception when the townspeople of Nazareth, Arkansas, mistake them for a widowed preacher and his three children.

Nazareth's Song. Warner Faith, 2004. 336pp.

The Welbys' deception has been unmasked, but Jeb finds his makeshift talents as preacher are sorely needed when the real Reverend Gracie becomes ill.

Kelly, Leisha.

Wortham Family.

During the Great Depression in rural Illinois, the Wortham family bottoms out financially when father Sam loses his job, but they find the greatest rewards in helping their neighbors. Elderly Emma Graham helps them out in turn when they need it most. Put together, the books read like one long novel.

Julia's Hope. Fleming H. Revell, 2002. 318pp.

Emma's Gift. Fleming H. Revell, 2003. 314pp.

Katie's Dream. Fleming H. Revell, 2004. 330pp.

Lemmons, Thom.

Sunday Clothes. Broadman and Holman, 2004. 404pp.

Against the wishes of her Methodist father, Addie Caswell marries Zeb, a traveling salesman who follows the Church of Christ. Zeb's many infidelities soon have Addie regretting her decision to abandon her home and religion. Set in early twentieth-century eastern Tennessee.

Peterson, Tracie, and James Scott Bell.

The Shannon Saga.

Lynn Morris and Gilbert Morris introduced a nineteenth-century female physician in their <u>Cheney Duvall, MD</u>, series, and Peterson and Bell revisit the same themes with their series about Kathleen "Kit" Shannon. As a female lawyer in early twentieth-century Los Angeles, Kit struggles to make her way in a man's world. Bell wrote the sequel series, <u>The Trials of Kit Shannon</u>, on his own.

City of Angels. Bethany House, 2001. 376pp.

In 1903, Kit moves to Los Angeles to practice law, but encounters prejudice from male attorneys as well as from her Aunt Freddie, who fears she will bring scandal on the family. Her fiancé doesn't approve, either. Kit believes it to be God's will that she defend the innocent, so doesn't hesitate to take the case of a Mexican gardener accused of murder.

Angels Flight. Bethany House, 2001. 381pp.

Kit encounters yet more racism when she defends a Mexican man against a rape charge, and a new suitor comes into Kit's life.

Angel of Mercy. Bethany House, 2002. 379pp.

One of Kit's former foes insists that she's the only lawyer who can defend him. Kit feels conflicted because she's not entirely sure he's innocent.

Tatlock, Ann.

🎗 *All the Way Home.* **Bethany House, 2002. 447pp.** 📖 **YA**

Middle-aged Augie Schuler Callahan remembers her childhood in 1930s Los Angeles, when she befriended a Japanese-American girl, Sunny Yamagata, and found a second home with Sunny's welcoming parents. Their lives diverge when Sunny's family is sent to an internment camp during World War II. When Augie and Sunny meet again in Mississippi twenty-three years later, they ponder the never-ending problem of racism. Christy Award.

I'll Watch the Moon. **Bethany House, 2003. 399pp.** 📖 **YA**

In 1948, nine-year-old Nova Tierney's older brother Dewey is hospitalized with polio, which causes her mother, Catherine, to question God's existence. Josef Karski, a survivor of Auschwitz, rents space in the St. Paul boardinghouse the Tierneys share with their aunt. Josef fills Nova's need for a father figure, while Catherine regains her lost faith after hearing Josef's tale of survival and forgiveness.

Canada

Christian fiction never really took off in Canada, which explains the dearth of entries here. This leaves plenty of fertile ground for American novelists to delve into. See also Janette Oke's other novels, under "Prairie Romances."

Oke, Janette, and T. Davis Bunn.
Song of Acadia. YA

Oke and Bunn's five-part series begins in Acadia in 1753, when tensions between the French and English settlements are simmering. Catherine Price, a gentle English woman, meets Louise Belleveau while out picking wildflowers. Over time, they share thoughts of friendship, faith, and their forthcoming marriages. Through a series of odd circumstances and coincidences, the women end up raising one another's children. Elspeth, Catherine's daughter, travels south to Louisiana with Louise and her husband when they are forced out of Acadia. Meanwhile Louise's daughter Antoinette, renamed Anne, is raised by Catherine and her husband Andrew. A generation later, the young women learn their true identities, traveling back and forth to Louisiana and England to claim their proper birthrights. *The Meeting Place* won a Christy Award.

The Meeting Place. Bethany House, 1999. 282pp.

The Sacred Shore. Bethany House, 2000. 256pp.

The Birthright. Bethany House, 2001. 288pp.

The Distant Beacon. Bethany House, 2002. 288pp.

The Beloved Land. Bethany House, 2002. 288pp.

The Caribbean

One cannot have exotic Caribbean settings without elements of adventure; see also Lynn Morris's and Gilbert Morris's two Cheney Duvall, MD, series.

Kraus, Jim, and Terri Kraus.
Treasures of the Caribbean.

Light but well-researched historical adventure and romance from the Kraus husband–wife team, set in seventeenth-century Devon and Barbados. William Hawkes, seaman and reluctant privateer in the Caribbean, finds romance with Lady Kathryne Spenser, daughter of the governor of Barbados. In the last volume, William's friend, vicar Thomas Mayhew, falls in love with a former prostitute, which threatens to ruin his career.

Pirates of the Heart. Tyndale House, 1996. 501pp.

Passages of Gold. Tyndale House, 1997. 500pp.

Journey of the Crimson Sea. Tyndale House, 1997. 384pp.

The Middle East

The Crusades

Portraying Islam as Christianity's foe, even in historical context, is a political hot potato. This may explain why the Crusades are not a more popular subject, though Chaikin wisely evens things up by making her hero half-Muslim.

Chaikin, Linda.

The Royal Pavilions.

In 1096, Tancred Redwan, an honorable Norman knight, feels torn between following his father's Christianity and his mother's Muslim ancestry. Tancred flees Palermo for Constantinople after being falsely accused of murder, only to get caught up in the turbulence of the First Crusade. He also becomes involved in the family affairs of a young Byzantine noblewoman, Helena Lysander, whose nasty Aunt Irene tries to marry her off to a Muslim.

Swords and Scimitars. Bethany House, 1996. 320pp.

Golden Palaces. Bethany House, 1996. 349pp.

Behind the Veil. Bethany House, 1998. 256pp.

Lawhead, Stephen R.

The Celtic Crusades.

Annotated in Chapter 8.

The Twentieth Century

Bodie Thoene and Brock Thoene dominate this category with their well-researched novels about the birth of modern Israel.

Thoene, Bodie.

Zion Chronicles. ★

Bodie Thoene set her first major series against the backdrop of the formation of the State of Israel in 1947–1948. When Jews who survived the Holocaust head to Jerusalem to found a new nation, they face Arab conspiracies as well as danger from the British forces occupying Palestine. Major characters include Ellie Warne, an American photojournalist, and Rachel Lebowitz, a Holocaust survivor who gets trapped in Jerusalem during the siege. The Thoenes's Zion Covenant series, set in World War II-era Germany, is a prequel to the Zion Chronicles although the Chronicles were written earlier. *Gates of Zion* and *Key to Zion* both won the Gold Medallion.

The Gates of Zion. Bethany House, 1986. 368pp.

A Daughter of Zion. Bethany House, 1987. 330pp.

The Return of Zion. Bethany House, 1987. 343pp.

A Light in Zion. Bethany House, 1988. 352pp.

♟ *The Key to Zion.* Bethany House, 1988. 351pp.

Thoene, Bodie, and Brock Thoene.

♟ ***The Twilight of Courage*. Thomas Nelson, 1994. 614pp.**

In the spring of 1940, more than 300,000 Allied troops were rescued from northern France in what was called the "miracle of Dunkirk." Amid the tumult, an American journalist recently escaped from Warsaw rescues a Jewish baby. This stand-alone novel serves as a bridge between the <u>Zion Covenant</u> and <u>Zion Chronicles</u> series; a sequel was planned but never published. Gold Medallion.

Zion Legacy.

This series, the Thoenes's first attempt to reach a wider audience with a mainstream publisher, follows directly upon their <u>Zion Chronicles.</u> It begins on May 14, 1948, the day the British exit Jerusalem, leaving Jewish and Muslim forces to their own devices. A fictional cast of Jewish characters fights for control of the Old City while the Arabs slowly close in. The plot moves slowly; by the beginning of *Jerusalem Scrolls*, only two weeks have passed. The novels also introduce a subplot that gradually consumes the entire series. A scroll dating from the first century AD, found by one of the Israeli leaders, reveals a romance between a young Jewish widow and a Roman centurion. This earlier plotline begins the <u>A.D. Chronicles</u> series (listed under "Biblical") .

Jerusalem Vigil. Viking, 2000. 322pp.

Thunder from Jerusalem. Viking, 2000. 311pp.

Jerusalem's Heart. Viking, 2001. 328pp.

The Jerusalem Scrolls. Viking, 2001. 272pp.

Stones of Jerusalem. Viking, 2002. 263pp.

Jerusalem's Hope. Viking, 2002. 272pp.

Africa and the Antipodes

These novels, set primarily between the seventeenth and nineteenth centuries, deal with colonization and missionary work in remote places.

Cavanaugh, Jack.

African Covenant.

Perhaps because of the unfamiliar setting, Cavanaugh's two-book series about the settlement of South Africa by Dutch farmers (Boers) wasn't very successful, but readers who enjoy unusual locales are in for a treat.

The Pride and the Passion. Moody, 1996. 331pp.

In 1715, orphaned Margot Campion, a French Huguenot, arrives in Cape Town with little more than her strong will and proto-feminist attitude. There she encounters the country's religious and racial difficulties first-hand.

Quest for the Promised Land. Moody, 1997. 287pp.

A century after *Pride and the Passion*, Margot's descendant Christian van der Kemp lives through conflicts between the British and Xhosa.

Chaikin, Linda Lee.

East of the Sun Trilogy.
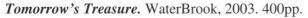

Romantic and suspenseful historical adventure amid the gold and diamond mining industries of 1890s South Africa. Evy Varley leaves her aunt and uncle's English home to return to South Africa, where her parents were killed during the Zulu War of 1878. There she discovers unexpected mysteries about her past. Sir Rogan Chantry, son of a local aristocrat, is right in the thick of it. A projected trilogy.

Tomorrow's Treasure. WaterBrook, 2003. 400pp.

Yesterday's Promise. WaterBrook, 2004. 364pp.

Hickman, Patricia.

Land of the Far Horizon.

Five different accounts of the colonization of Australia, beginning with the 1787 Botany Bay Expedition and continuing through the Australian Gold Rush of 1850. Taken together, these interconnected novels present an epic picture.

Voyage of the Exiles. Bethany House, 1995. 320pp.

Angel of the Outback. Bethany House, 1995. 319pp.

The Emerald Flame. Bethany House, 1996. 288pp.

Beyond the Wild Shores. Bethany House, 1997. 288pp.

The Treasure Seekers. Bethany House, 1998. 320pp.

Leanne, Shelly.

Joshua's Bible. **Warner/Walk Worthy, 2003. 367pp.**

In the 1930s, new seminary graduate Joshua Clay, an African American, travels to South Africa as a missionary to the Xhosa people. Proud to have been selected for this honor by his church, Joshua grows steadily more dismayed as he learns more about the racial tension pervading the country. His love for Nongolesi, a Xhosa woman, compels him to take action against injustice.

Morris, Lynn.

Red and Lowering Sky. **Zondervan, 2004. 303pp.**

In 1811, President Grover Cleveland sends Stockton Livingstone on a diplomatic mission to Samoa. When Stockton arrives in the tropical paradise, with six children in tow, he discovers a land torn among German, US, and British loyalties. Only aptly named Mavis Thoroughgood remembers the downtrodden natives.

Christian Epics

Like the works of Michener and his literary successors (Chapter 3), these epic novels present fictional slices of a given locale's history—a city or country with a long tradition of religious development and conflict. The British Isles and Israel are obvious choices.

Arthur, Kay.

Israel, My Beloved. **Harvest House, 1996. 443pp.**

Arthur tells the story of Israel in a series of short chapters, beginning in 605 BC and continuing through the near future. Through the plight of many strong-willed women, all named Sarah, Arthur portrays the struggles of the Jews and how their belief that they were God's chosen people was challenged by historical events. These include the Crucifixion, anti-Jewish prejudice in the Middle Ages, and the tragedy of the Holocaust. Arthur obviously hopes to introduce Christians to the wide-ranging Jewish experience, and her novel is written from a Jewish viewpoint. Some of her conclusions may annoy evangelical Christians.

Crow, Donna Fletcher.

Crow is a successful writer of inspirational fiction, and in her epics, she traces the history of three parts of the United Kingdom: England, Scotland, and Northern Ireland. Although some of her Christian characters are a little too perfect to be real, her accurate research and smooth storytelling make these novels fascinating reads.

The Banks of the Boyne. **Moody, 1998. 814pp.**

The history of Northern Ireland is given life in the author's fictional story of Mary Hamilton, an American college student relocating to Scotland with her fiancé, a divinity scholar. When he is transferred instead to the violent city of Belfast, Mary's journey to understand the conflict takes her through 400 years of the city's struggles between the Protestants and Catholics.

The Fields of Bannockburn. **Moody, 1996. 707pp.**

Three modern college students and a Scottish storyteller imagine the history of Christian Scotland from St. Columba's time in the sixth century until now. In the author's inspirational retelling of Scottish history, Christianity emerges again and again as the chosen religion of its people.

Glastonbury. **Crossway, 1992. 859pp.**

From its Druid past 1,500 years ago to the dismantling of the monasteries in the Tudor era, Crow retells the history of Glastonbury, England, in a series of stories about its people. Taken together, the tales in this inspirational epic demonstrate how Christianity rose from a minor religion in Joseph of Arimathea's time to become a great religious power during Henry VIII's reign.

Phillips, Michael.

Caledonia Series.

An old Scotsman tells Andrew Trentham, British nobleman and Member of Parliament, about his Scottish heritage in a series of non-sequential historical episodes.

Phillips acknowledges historical novelists James Michener and Nigel Tranter among his influences. He's almost as strong a storyteller as they, but Phillips sometimes slips into mythical fantasy.

Legend of the Celtic Stone. Bethany House, 1999. 538pp.

Andrew Trentham, in present-day London nursing a broken heart, can hardly concentrate on a recent break-in at Westminster Abbey. When the media report that Scottish nationalists may be responsible for the theft of the legendary Stone of Scone, Trentham delves into his Scottish roots. Duncan MacRanald, a shepherd living in a humble stone cottage, regales him with tales of Scotland's past, including the Glencoe massacre of 1692 as well as earlier times: antiquity, 237 BC, AD 105, and AD 563. Phillips gets preachy toward the end, condemning ancient Druid practices as satanic.

An Ancient Strife. Bethany House, 2000. 542pp.

Duncan MacRanald enlightens Andrew Trentham even more about Scotland's lengthy struggle for independence. Episodes include the Battle of Bannockburn, AD 1314; the tragedy of Culloden Moor, AD 1745–1745; the romance between Malcolm Canmore and Anglo-Saxon princess St. Margaret in AD 1068; William the Lion in AD 1172, and legendary king Kenneth MacAlpin, AD 843.

Traylor, Ellen Gunderson.

Jerusalem: The City of God. **Harvest House, 1995. 631pp.**

While Kay Arthur (above) presented the Jewish experience through the voices of fictional characters, Traylor focuses the major part of her epic novel on biblical figures who lived within Jerusalem's walls. These include Melchizidek, Abraham, David, Solomon, King Herod, and Jesus. Then she touches briefly on Judea in AD 66, the Crusades, and finally the Zionist movement in the twentieth century.

Christian Sagas

Sagas celebrate the strength of family over time, so their continued popularity in Christian fiction should be no surprise. In the Christian market, they occur almost exclusively in multi-volume series.

British and European Sagas

These sagas show the strength of family during religious and political crises in British and European history: the Reformation, the Russian Revolution, and more.

De Graaf, Anne.

Hidden Harvest Saga.

Anne de Graaf sets her saga of the Piekarz family against a backdrop of war-torn Krakow in the 1940s—a city first occupied by the Germans and then "liberated" by the Soviets. The trilogy combines thorough historical research with the poignant love story of Hanna Muller, a young German woman, and Tadeusz Piekarz, a Polish prisoner forced to labor for her father's company. The last novel won a Christy Award.

Bread Upon the Waters. Bethany House, 1995. 350pp.

Where the Fire Burns. Bethany House, 1997. 352pp.

🎗 *Out of the Red Shadow.* Bethany House, 1999. 345pp.

Hunt, Angela Elwell.

The Heirs of Cahira O'Connor.

Kathleen O'Connor, a modern-day student writing a research paper, learns about the power wielded by her female ancestors. Every 200 years, a woman with a warrior's spirit is born, and each has the same distinguishing white streak in her bright red hair, the same one Kathleen herself possesses. All descend from Cahira O'Connor, fierce daughter of a medieval Irish king. Through the other women's stories of faith and love, Kathleen learns about her own destiny.

The Silver Sword. WaterBrook, 1998. 403pp.

In fifteenth-century Bohemia, Anika of Prague joins reformer Jan Hus in his holy war against the Roman Catholic Church.

The Golden Cross. WaterBrook, 1998. 412pp.

Aidan O'Connor, a young botanical artist, escapes the slums of the Dutch colony of Batavia in the seventeenth century by disguising herself as a boy and stowing away on board a ship.

The Velvet Shadow. WaterBrook, 1999. 400pp.

After the Civil War flares up, Flanna O'Connor can't leave her Boston medical school to head back home to Charleston, so she joins the Union army as a surgeon.

The Emerald Isle. WaterBrook, 1999. 389pp.

Kathleen O'Connor visits Ireland and finally learns about her greatest ancestress, Cahira O'Connor, a king's daughter from Connacht who fights off Norman invaders in the thirteenth century.

Morris, Gilbert.

The Wakefield Dynasty.

Religious persecution and change, from the licentiousness of Henry VIII's court through the Napoleonic era, is the theme of Morris's dramatic saga. Appropriate given the books' publisher, *Sword of Truth* starts out with the Protestant Reformation, when William Tyndale was executed for heresy after translating the Holy Bible into English. Servant boy Myles Morgan, later recognized as the illegitimate son of Sir Robert Wakefield, interacts with historical figures of the time, such as Tyndale, Henry VIII, and Queen Catherine. The Morgan–Wakefield rivalry carries on through the ages. Subsequent volumes cover Wakefield descendants through the Spanish Armada, the English Civil War, the early Methodist movement in the eighteenth century, and the Napoleonic Wars.

Sword of Truth. Tyndale House, 1994. 409pp.

The Winds of God. Tyndale House, 1994. 380pp.

The Shield of Honor. Tyndale House, 1995. 394pp.

The Fields of Glory. Tyndale House, 1996. 376pp.

The Ramparts of Heaven. Tyndale House, 1997. 361pp.

The Song of Princes. Tyndale House, 1997. 386pp.

A Gathering of Eagles. Tyndale House, 1998. 320pp.

Phillips, Michael.

The Secrets of Heathersleigh Hall.

After Charles Rutherford, Duke of Heathersleigh and Member of Parliament, converts to Christianity, his wife Jocelyn feels lost. So does their daughter Amanda, at first, until her World War I experiences in Europe also bring her to God. As the individual book titles are no doubt meant to do, Phillips's evocation of late nineteenth- and early twentieth-century rural England will appeal particularly to American readers. This rich but occasionally long-winded saga recounts one English family's religious conversion.

Wild Grows the Heather in Devon. Bethany House, 1998. 320pp.

Wayward Winds. Bethany House, 1999. 426pp.

Heathersleigh Homecoming. Bethany House, 1999. 429pp.

A New Dawn Over Devon. Bethany House, 2001. 448pp.

Phillips, Michael R., and Judith Pella.

The Russians.

When Anna Burenin travels from the humble village of Katyk to St. Petersburg and becomes part of the entourage of Princess Katrina, a transformational process of faith begins that keeps them both grounded during the conflict that tears their country apart. Their two families—the aristocratic Fedorcenkos and the peasant Burenins—face a multitude of social changes between the late nineteenth century and the Russian Revolution of 1917. A very popular saga, reprinted by Bethany House in 2001.

By Phillips and Pella:

The Crown and the Crucible. Bethany House, 1991. 410pp.

A House Divided. Bethany House, 1992. 350pp.

Travail and Triumph. Bethany House, 1992. 400pp.

By Pella alone:

Heirs of the Motherland. Bethany House, 1993. 382pp.

The Dawning of Deliverance. Bethany House, 1995. 400pp.

White Nights, Red Mornings. Bethany House, 1996. 400pp.

Passage Into Light. Bethany House, 1998. 400pp.

American Sagas

Christian authors explore the great span of American history, from colonial days through World War II and after.

Austin, Lynn N.

Eve's Daughters. Bethany House, 1999. 428pp.

Spanning four generations of women, from the early nineteenth century through the 1980s, Austin begins by introducing Emma Bauer, a first-generation American who has kept a secret hidden from her family for fifty years. Through the story of her mother Louise, who left Germany for America before World War I, Emma explains to her granddaughter Suzanne how her own past affected subsequent generations.

Cavanaugh, Jack.

American Family Portrait.

Cavanaugh's multigenerational saga of the Morgan family starts out similarly to Gilbert Morris's House of Winslow series, below. A young man, Drew Morgan, infiltrates the Pilgrims in early seventeenth-century England but regrets his decision when he meets a beautiful Puritan woman. Subsequent generations fight in the American Revolution, the Civil War, and World Wars I and II. Up until *The Pioneers*, in which native New Yorker Jesse Morgan heads to Denver in the 1890s, most of the action stays on America's east coast. *The Allies* and *The Victors* take Morgan family members across the Atlantic, and *The Peacemakers* concludes the story amid the social protest of the 1960s.

The Puritans. Chariot Victor, 1994. 426pp.

The Colonists. Chariot Victor, 1995. 482pp.

The Patriots. Chariot Victor, 1996. 530pp.

The Adversaries. Chariot Victor, 1996. 500pp.

The Pioneers. Chariot Victor, 1996. 423pp.

The Allies. Chariot Victor, 1997. 500pp.

The Victors. Chariot Victor, 1998. 500pp.

The Peacemakers. Chariot Victor, 1999. 512pp.

Miller, Evie Yoder.

Eyes at the Window. Good Books, 2003. 518pp.

This detailed and at times slow-moving saga spans over fifty years in an Amish pioneer community in Pennsylvania and Ohio, beginning with the murder of an infant in 1810. Eight men and women narrate alternating chapters. Reuben Hershberger, falsely accused of the baby's murder, is shunned by the community, including those (like his wife) who believe him innocent. Over time, Reuben's refusal to confess tears away at the fabric of the close-knit community.

Morris, Gilbert.

House of Winslow. ★

This very popular saga of the extended Winslow family begins with Gilbert Winslow, who in 1620 becomes a spy for the Church of England against the rabble-rousing Pilgrims. Later Gilbert has a change of heart, remaining with the Pilgrims after their journey to Massachusetts on the *Mayflower*. Subsequent Winslows participate in nearly every major event in American history. Morris jumps 200 years from colonial times to the Civil War over the first eight books, touching briefly on the American Revolution in between. After that, the pace slows considerably, with the last few books set during the 1929 stock market crash and in the 1930s.

The Honorable Imposter. Bethany House, 1987. 331pp.

The Captive Bride. Bethany House, 1987. 238pp.

The Indentured Heart. Bethany House, 1988. 288pp.

The Gentle Rebel. Bethany House, 1988. 285pp.

The Saintly Buccaneer. Bethany House, 1989. 299pp.

The Holy Warrior. Bethany House, 1989. 284pp.

The Reluctant Bridegroom. Bethany House, 1990. 303pp.

The Last Confederate. Bethany House, 1990. 333pp.

The Dixie Widow. Bethany House, 1991. 318pp.

The Wounded Yankee. Bethany House, 1991. 304pp.

The Union Belle. Bethany House, 1992. 334pp.

The Final Adversary. Bethany House, 1992. 301pp.

The Crossed Sabres. Bethany House, 1993. 317pp.

The Valiant Gunmen. Bethany House, 1993. 320pp.

The Gallant Outlaw. Bethany House, 1994. 288pp.

The Jeweled Spur. Bethany House, 1994. 299pp.

The Yukon Queen. Bethany House, 1995. 285pp.

The Rough Rider. Bethany House, 1995. 303pp.

The Iron Lady. Bethany House, 1996. 320pp.

The Silver Star. Bethany House, 1997. 304pp.

The Shadow Portrait. Bethany House, 1998. 304pp.

The White Hunter. Bethany House, 1999. 304pp.

The Flying Cavalier. Bethany House, 1999. 318pp.

The Glorious Prodigal. Bethany House, 2000. 320pp.

The Amazon Quest. Bethany House, 2001. 320pp.

The Golden Angel. Bethany House, 2001. 316pp.

The Heavenly Fugitive. Bethany House, 2002. 320pp.

The Fiery Ring. Bethany House, 2002. 314pp.

The Pilgrim Song. Bethany House, 2003. 316pp.

The Beloved Enemy. Bethany House, 2003. 319pp.

The Shining Badge. Bethany House, 2004. 320pp.

The Royal Handmaid. Bethany House, 2004. 320pp.

Appomattox Saga.

This entertaining saga of the Civil War in Virginia begins in 1840, as Gideon Rocklin and his more reckless cousin Clay both fall in love with the same woman, Melanie Benton. When Melanie decides to marry Gideon, Clay turns to a life of gambling and drink. Over the next twenty years, Clay finds Jesus and turns his life around. Then the Civil War approaches, and it appears that he and Gideon will fight on opposite sides. The remainder of the saga covers other members of the Rocklin clan, their neighbors, and friends, intertwining romance, faith, and ferocious battle scenes. Morris recounts the action from both Union and Confederate viewpoints.

Covenant of Love. Tyndale House, 1992. 361pp.

Gates of His Enemies. Tyndale House, 1992. 337pp.

Where Honor Dwells. Tyndale House, 1993. 355pp.

Land of the Shadow. Tyndale House, 1993. 338pp.

Out of the Whirlwind. Tyndale House, 1994. 316pp.

Shadow of His Wings. Tyndale House, 1994. 270pp.

Wall of Fire. Tyndale House, 1995. 338pp.

Stars in Their Courses. Tyndale House, 1995. 350pp.

Chariots in the Smoke. Tyndale House, 1997. 291pp.

Witness in Heaven. Tyndale House, 1998. 318pp.

Noble, Diane.

California Chronicles.

Spanning the years 1861 to 1923, Noble's saga recounts the lives and loves of three generations of Dearbornes, a ranching family in the San Jacinto, California, area. Family trees included.

When the Far Hills Bloom. WaterBrook, 1999. 373pp.

Aislin Byrne wants two things in life: to save her family home, Rancha de la Paloma, and to spend her life with Jamie Dearborne. Her world falls apart when Jamie is reported killed in the Civil War, but Jamie's brother Spence, a gifted horseman, soon claims her heart. Then Aislin discovers that Jamie may still be alive.

The Blossom and the Nettle. WaterBrook, 2000. 385pp.

Her reputation in ruins, Emmeline Callahan, a Dearborne relation, leaves Washington, D.C., for California to manage her grandparents' ranch. Their rival and neighbor Quaid Dearborne intrigues her, but Quaid has something else to worry about—his rebellious cousin Merci.

At Play in the Promised Land. WaterBrook, 2001. 370pp.

The series concludes with scenes in 1920s California, New York, and Brazil, as Dearborne descendants Juliet and Sully Dearborne, children of Quaid, flex their wings.

Parker, Gary E.

Blue Ridge Legacy.

These three novels recount the century-long life of Abigail Porter, born in the "hollers" of North Carolina's Blue Ridge Mountains in the early twentieth century. Abby tells her life story to her great-granddaughter, Lisa, from birth through her efforts to escape her mountain childhood and forge a new, independent life. The Depression and World War II years are the hardest to endure. Abby ultimately finds her greatest happiness in the mountains from which she came. The lilting mountain dialect adds authenticity, and the religious aspects feel natural for the place and period. Parker's trilogy has been compared to Catherine Marshall's classic novel *Christy*, also about a young girl living in early twentieth-century Appalachia.

Highland Hopes. Bethany House, 2001. 400pp.

Highland Mercies. Bethany House, 2002. 391pp.

Highland Grace. Bethany House, 2003. 396pp.

Pella, Judith.

Daughters of Fortune.

Keagan Hayes, a newspaper mogul in Los Angeles in 1941, has three strong-willed daughters ready to take on the world. Cameron Hayes, the eldest, follows in her father's footsteps as a journalist but wants to distance herself from his legacy. In Moscow, Cameron battles wits with Dr. Alex Rostov, a Russian surgeon, but their squabbling soon turns into something more. Blair Hayes, an aspiring actress, finds herself in the Philippines in search of her estranged husband just as the Japanese attack Pearl Harbor. Back in Los Angeles, Jackie Hayes, a university student, faces racism when her Japanese-American husband lands in an internment camp. The next volume will be *Homeward My Heart.*

Written on the Wind. Bethany House, 2002. 384pp.

Somewhere a Song. Bethany House, 2002. 427pp.

Toward the Sunrise. Bethany House, 2003. 461pp.

Price, Eugenia.

Price's many sagas of the antebellum South are annotated in Chapter 5.

Snelling, Lauraine.

Red River of the North.

In 1880, Roald Bjorklund and his second wife Ingeborg board a ship to the United States from Norway in search of the American dream. Accompanying them are Roald's five-year-old son Thorliff, Roald's brother Carl, Carl's wife Kaaren, and Carl and Kaaren's newborn baby. They struggle through their first years of settlement in the Red River Valley of North Dakota. Though the Bjorklunds persevere in their dream of running a successful farm, the winters are harsh, and the land doesn't cooperate. Snelling spices the dialogue with many authentic Norwegian words and phrases.

An Untamed Land. Bethany House, 1996. 352pp.

A New Day Rising. Bethany House, 1996. 368pp.

A Land to Call Home. Bethany House, 1997. 368pp.

The Reapers' Song. Bethany House, 1998. 368pp.

Tender Mercies. Bethany House, 1999. 304pp.

Blessing in Disguise. Bethany House, 1999. 269pp.

Return to Red River.

This sequel to the Red River of the North series follows an adult Thorliff Bjorklund through his efforts to attend college and become a professional journalist, despite his father's desire that he run the family farm. Thorliff faces another tough decision: reunite with his childhood sweetheart or pursue his dream of writing. Set in 1890s North Dakota.

A Dream to Follow. Bethany House, 2001. 304pp.

Believing the Dream. Bethany House, 2002. 320pp.

More Than a Dream. Bethany House, 2003. 316pp.

Thoene, Bodie.

Shiloh Legacy.

The female half of the Thoene writing team recounts the trials and dreams of several different men—and, later, their children—coming of age from World War I through the Great Depression. As is usual for the Thoenes, not all of the characters are Christians. Birch Tucker, a farm boy from Shiloh, Arkansas, returns from the war and finds it hard to adjust to family life at home. Max Meyer, a Jew, searches for a place for himself on Wall Street. Jefferson Canfield, an African-American sharecropper from Shiloh, arrives home and encounters racism that didn't seem to exist in wartime. *Shiloh Autumn* continues the Tuckers' and Canfields' stories from the 1929 stock market crash through the early 1930s. This last novel was based on the lives of the author's grandparents.

In My Father's House. Bethany House, 1992. 430pp.

A Thousand Shall Fall. Bethany House, 1992. 428pp.

Say to This Mountain. Bethany House, 1993. 447pp.

Shiloh Autumn. Thomas Nelson, 1996. 470pp. (With Brock Thoene.)

Christian Historical Romances

Most of these novels can be described as historical romances rather than romantic historicals (defined in Chapter 4), though all of them end on a hopeful note. It's a given that for the romance to work, both heroine and hero must follow the Christian faith. Romances with non-believers don't lead to marriage unless the non-Christian party discovers God.

The British Isles

With the exceptions of Carol Umberger's and Kathleen Morgan's novels, both set during turbulent periods of Scottish history, British politics remain firmly in the background. This keeps the focus on the developing romance.

Blackwell, Lawana.

The Gresham Chronicles.

A romantic, preachy, well-researched series set in the late Victorian period.

The Widow of Larkspur Inn. Bethany House, 1998. 432pp.

Destitute after her late husband's gambling debts, Julia Hollis and her three children leave London for the quaint village of Gresham, where she transforms an old coaching inn into a lodging house for travelers. Andrew Phelps, the local vicar, sparks her interest.

The Courtship of the Vicar's Daughter. Bethany House, 1998. 400pp.

Julia's and Andrew's wedding day approaches. As Andrew's daughter Elizabeth awaits her own marriage, an old suitor comes back into her life.

The Dowry of Miss Lydia Clark. Bethany House, 1999. 398pp.

Lydia Clark, the spinster schoolteacher of Julia's and Andrew's children, is hired by archaeologist Jacob Pitney to teach him about poetry—so he can impress another woman.

Higgs, Liz Curtis.

Thorn in My Heart Series. 📖

Higgs does a masterful job of transporting the biblical story of Leah, Rachel, Jacob, and Esau to late eighteenth-century Galloway, in the Scottish Lowlands. Since polygamy is hardly legal in 1780s Scotland, Higgs uses an old Scottish custom to get around the problem. She also sprinkles elements of traditional folklore and dialect throughout the story, giving it an authentic feel. Even mainstream romance readers will appreciate the poignant romance, but have some tissues handy. A third novel, *Whence Comes a Prince*, is forthcoming.

Thorn in My Heart. WaterBrook, 2003. 484pp.

Rowena McKie goads her favorite son, Jamie, into claiming his father's birthright over his twin brother. For his protection, she sends Jamie on a journey to visit her own brother, Lachlan McBride, with directions to take one of Lachlan's daughters to wife. Plain Leana falls in love with Jamie, but Jamie is determined to choose her carefree younger sister Rose as his bride.

Fair Is the Rose. WaterBrook, 2004. 464pp.

With Leana's help, Jamie has finally discovered the true meaning of love and marriage. Leana's greedy father Lachlan still refuses to let the couple return to Jamie's home at Glentrool to make a life for themselves, but Lachlan is not their biggest problem. Rose's selfishness, born of a legal loophole, ultimately causes her sister and Jamie more pain than they can bear.

Morgan, Kathleen.
Consuming Fire. Tyndale House, 2003. 389pp.

Maggie Robertson had hoped to lead a religious life, but her father's plans lead her to seek refuge from Adam Campbell, Laird of Castle Achallader. Some of the secondary characters from *Embrace the Down* return in this stand-alone romantic novel set in Scotland in 1694.

Embrace the Dawn. Tyndale House, 2002. 399pp.

After her abusive husband is killed, Killian Campbell ends up in the clutches of Ruarc MacDonald, the Campbell clan's archenemy. Set in the Scottish Highlands in 1691.

Morren, Ruth Axtell.
Winter Is Past. Steeple Hill, 2003. 448pp.

Lady Althea Breton, a practicing Methodist in London in 1817, takes on the noble responsibility of nursing the ailing daughter of Simon Aguilar, a Sephardic Jew and Member of Parliament. To pursue a political career, Simon had converted to the Church of England, but he never felt connected to his faith. Though Althea is discouraged at first by Simon's apathy toward her religion, his caring qualities quietly attract her.

Morris, Gilbert.

God's Handmaiden. **Zondervan, 2004. 337pp.**

After her mother's death, Gervase Howard moves to London and joins her aunt in service to the Wingate family. Her attraction to David, the eldest Wingate son, threatens to break up his engagement. This inspires Gervase to take a position working with Florence Nightingale. When Florence heads to the Crimea, Gervase accompanies her.

Umberger, Carol.

Scottish Crown Series.

A romantic series set during Scotland's Wars for Independence in the early fourteenth century. The next novel will be *The Promise of Peace*.

Circle of Honor. Integrity, 2002. 292pp.

After murdering his chief rival, John Comyn, in 1306, Robert the Bruce became King of Scotland. Gwenyth, Comyn's (fictional) youngest daughter, flees when Bruce destroys her home and family. After being kidnapped and raped by her captor, she escapes into marriage with Adam Mackintosh, who doesn't know that Gwenyth is fomenting a plot against Bruce.

The Price of Freedom. Integrity, 2003. 280pp.

Sir Bryan Mackintosh, one of Scotland's greatest warriors (and the illegitimate son of Robert the Bruce), is forced into marriage with Kathryn de Lindsay, a countess whose father had English loyalties.

The Mark of Salvation. Integrity, 2003. 262pp.

Countess Orelia Radbourne's husband, an English earl, was killed by the Scots in battle. Taken hostage by Robert the Bruce, Orelia is guarded day and night by a soldier named Ceallach whose gruff exterior masks a wounded soul.

Wick, Lori.

The English Garden.

A popular series of four stand-alone romances set in the English countryside village of Collingbourne in the early nineteenth century. Jane Austen's influence is evident in Wick's plotlines, settings, and character names, but the repartee isn't anywhere near as witty. Appropriately for the period, the couples do not call one another by their Christian names.

The Proposal. Harvest House, 2002. 297pp.

In London in 1810, nobody is more surprised than William Jennings when he inherits the guardianship of three children. At his sister's country home, Jennings meets Marianne Walker, a religious woman who he believes will be the perfect mother for his wards. But Marianne won't marry without love.

The Rescue. Harvest House, 2002. 297pp.

In 1811, Anne Gardiner's father, the irascible colonel, forces her into a hasty marriage with a stranger, Robert Weston, when she accidentally stumbles into Mr. Weston's arms.

The Visitor. Harvest House, 2003. 304pp.

Alexander Tate leaves London for Collingbourne in 1812 after a riding accident damages his vision. There he grows intrigued by the voice of Cassie Steele, a plain young woman who reads to him in his convalescence.

The Pursuit. Harvest House, 2003. 304pp.

En route home to Collingbourne from Africa in 1813, Edward Steele plans to keep his word and return by Christmas, but the plight of two strangers draws him into the path of the mysterious Nicola Bettencourt.

Americana Romances

Gentle romantic tales set in America's small towns in the nineteenth and early twentieth centuries.

Crawford, Dianna.
Reardon Brothers.

The romantic tales of three women who journey to Tennessee Territory in the early nineteenth century and marry the three Reardon brothers, frontiersmen determined to establish a Christian community in the wilderness.

Freedom's Promise. Tyndale House, 2000. 312pp.

Finally free from her bonds as an indentured servant, Annie McGregor leaves Carolina by joining Ike Reardon's wagon train to the Tennessee frontier.

Freedom's Hope. Tyndale House, 2000. 300pp.

Brokenhearted after his sweetheart broke their engagement, Noah Reardon is intrigued by feisty Jessica Whitman, against his better judgment.

Freedom's Belle. Tyndale House, 2001. 325pp.

Crystabelle Amherst, a proud Southern belle on the run from an arranged marriage, flees to Tennessee Territory and becomes a schoolteacher. Drew Reardon convinces her of the evils of slavery.

Reardon Valley.

In these frontier romances, three more women find homes and romance in Tennessee's Reardon Valley. Set in the same locale as the Reardon Brothers series.

A Home in the Valley. Tyndale House, 2002. 333pp.

In 1801, Sabina Erhardt flees from the gambler who won her hand in a poker game. Baxter Clay, a widower with four children, takes her in and falls in love with her, despite his desire to marry a wealthy woman.

Lady of the River. Tyndale House, 2003. 332pp.

Belinda Gregg and her family keep to themselves in their home along the river. Their secrets threaten to come to light when the pastor's son, Max, takes an interest in Belinda.

An Echo of Hope. Tyndale House, 2003. 320pp.

Recently widowed and having to deal with unpleasant in-laws, Hope Underwood never expected her childhood beau, Michael Flanagan, to return to town.

Mitchell, Sara.

Sinclair Legacy.

The gentle, old-fashioned love stories of the three Sinclair sisters and of their father, set in the Shenandoah River Valley of Virginia in the early twentieth century. The historical background is sketched lightly. Mitchell was a pioneer in inspirational fiction.

Shenandoah Home. WaterBrook, 2001. 408pp.

Garnet Sinclair, a pen-and-ink artist living at home with her widowed father and younger sister Leah, believes that she'll never marry. This changes when Dr. Sloan MacAllister comes into her life, but before romance can develop, he must face secrets from his past. In another story, Garnet's older sister Meredith, who has moved to the big city to become a success in business, meets her match in J. Preston Clarke.

Virginia Autumn. WaterBrook, 2002. 404pp.

Leah Sinclair, a spinster schoolteacher, hasn't yet found the deep faith that her sisters and father cling to, but naturalist Cade Beringer sees fit to change that. After all his daughters have married, Jacob Sinclair believes himself alone in the world until he meets Fiona Carlton, a concert pianist who teaches him how much he has to offer.

Prairie Romances

In the traditional prairie romance, a young woman heads west as a schoolteacher, housekeeper, or mail-order bride, grows closer to God during difficult times, and discovers romance where she least expects it. The differences between these novels and romantic Christian Westerns (later this chapter) lie in prairie romances' gentle, heartwarming quality and their emphasis on the domesticity of pioneer life. Quiet rather than action-oriented, prairie romances are apt to be set in farming communities on the Midwestern or Canadian plains, rather than on a ranch or in the mountains or the Southwestern desert.

Glover, Ruth.

Saskatchewan Saga.

The quaint fictional pioneer town of Bliss, Saskatchewan, is the locale for Glover's series of prairie romances set in the 1890s. She populates her novels with lively characters. The novels, which can be read in any order, touch on issues common to the place and era: the pain of emigrating from Scotland; the adjustment to a new, harsher way of life in Canada's bush country; and women who become mail-order brides, little knowing what their new life has in store.

A Place Called Bliss. Fleming H. Revell, 2001. 239pp.

With Love from Bliss. Fleming H. Revell, 2001. 240pp.

Journey to Bliss. Fleming H. Revell, 2001. 253pp.

Seasons of Bliss. Fleming H. Revell, 2002. 224pp.

Bittersweet Bliss. Fleming H. Revell, 2003. 271pp.

Back Roads to Bliss. Fleming H. Revell, 2003. 267pp.

Oke, Janette.

This prolific and highly esteemed author, born into a farming family in Alberta during the Depression, writes novels about settlers' experiences throughout North American history. She is best known for her portraits of love, marriage, and family life on the Canadian prairie. In her works, she evokes strong Christian values and presents faith as the cornerstone of romantic love. *Love Comes Softly*, Oke's first novel, became an instant classic and pioneered the inspirational fiction genre.

Beyond the Gathering Storm Series.

Oke continues the story of Henry and Christine Delaney, the adopted children of Elizabeth and Wynn from the <u>Canadian West</u> series (below), who learn some hard lessons just after World War I ends.

Beyond the Gathering Storm. Bethany House, 2000. 256pp.

When Tomorrow Comes. Bethany House, 2001. 288pp.

Canadian West Series.

This four-volume series, set on the Alberta prairie, features a romance between Elizabeth Thatcher, a young schoolteacher from Toronto, and Wynn Delaney, a Royal Canadian Mountie.

When Calls the Heart. Bethany House, 1983. 221pp.

When Comes the Spring. Bethany House, 1985. 255pp.

When Breaks the Dawn. Bethany House, 1986. 223pp.

When Hope Springs New. Bethany House, 1986. 222pp.

Love Comes Softly Series. ★ YA

On the day of her husband's burial, nineteen-year-old Marty Claridge accepts a marriage proposal from Clark Davis, a stranger whose young daughter Missie needs a mother. Thrown together by tragedy, over time Marty and Clark fall in love, form a real marriage, and raise a family. Subsequent volumes deal with their children's and grandchildren's lives. Neither the exact location nor the era is stated, but it is probably somewhere in the Canadian west in the mid-nineteenth century. Little details of pioneer life—making soap, killing chickens, sewing new clothes—add even more character to this gentle, romantic series. Reprinted many times.

Love Comes Softly. Bethany House, 1979. 188pp.

Love's Enduring Promise. Bethany House, 1980. 206pp.

Love's Long Journey. Bethany House, 1982. 200pp.

Love's Abiding Joy. Bethany House, 1983. 217pp.

Love's Unending Legacy. Bethany House, 1984. 224pp.

Love's Unfolding Dream. Bethany House, 1987. 222pp.

Love Takes Wing. Bethany House, 1988. 220pp.

Love Finds a Home. Bethany House, 1989. 221pp.

Prairie Legacy. YA

This sequel to the <u>Love Comes Softly</u> series continues the Davis family saga beginning with Marty's and Clark's confused teenage granddaughter, Virginia Simpson. As in Oke's previous novels, details from the larger world rarely intrude, but the series begins during the Depression years.

The Tender Years. Bethany House, 1997. 384pp.

A Searching Heart. Bethany House, 1999. 256pp.

A Quiet Strength. Bethany House, 1999. 256pp.

Like Gold Refined. Bethany House, 2000. 251pp.

Women of the West. YA

These stand-alone novels all have similar themes: young women surviving on the Western frontier, taking strength from their Christian faith, and finding love in unexpected places. The exact timeframe is vague, but they all seem to be set on the Western frontier in the late nineteenth century.

The Calling of Emily Evans. Bethany House, 1990. 288pp.

Julia's Last Hope. Bethany House, 1990. 204pp.

Roses for Mama. Bethany House, 1991. 222pp.

A Woman Named Damaris. Bethany House, 1991. 288pp.

They Called Her Mrs. Doc. Bethany House, 1992. 222pp.

The Measure of a Heart. Bethany House, 1992. 219pp.

A Bride for Donnigan. Bethany House, 1993. 223pp.

Heart of the Wilderness. Bethany House, 1993. 239pp.

Too Long a Stranger. Bethany House, 1994. 288pp.

A Gown of Spanish Lace. Bethany House, 1995. 251pp.

The Bluebird and the Sparrow. Bethany House, 1995. 251pp.

Drums of Change. Bethany House, 1996. 235pp.

Palmer, Catherine.

A Town Called Hope.

Heartfelt romantic tales set in the small prairie town of Hope, Kansas, just after the Civil War. Palmer writes about difficult topics (illegitimacy, prejudice, physical abuse) with sensitivity.

Prairie Rose. Tyndale House, 1997. 272pp.

Growing up in a Kansas City orphanage, Rosenbloom Cotton "Rosie" Mills always had poor self-esteem because of her illegitimacy. Her life changes when she heads west with Seth Hunter and his young son Chipper, with plans to become their housekeeper.

Prairie Fire. Tyndale House, 1999. 288pp.

Jack Cornwall, who lost custody of his nephew Chipper to Seth, realizes that his life has to change before he can be fully accepted by the people of Hope—especially beautiful Irish immigrant Caitrin Murphy, whose family is prejudiced against people of Cornish heritage.

Prairie Storm. Tyndale House, 1999. 272pp.

Lily Nolan, a widow, wants to open her heart to the possibility of finding love with Hope's local preacher, Elijah Book. First she must come to terms with the abuse she suffered as a child.

Christian Historical Westerns

While Western historical fiction has generally dropped in popularity, it predominates in Christian fiction, which gives Western readers plenty to choose from. The settings are not quite as varied as in traditional Western historicals (Chapter 6). Most of these novels take place during the latter half of the nineteenth century, as men and women make their way westward to settle the land after the Civil War. See also "Prairie Romances."

Traditional Westerns

Readers who believe that Christian-themed westerns don't have enough hard-hitting action to satisfy traditional Western fans may be surprised by these novels. While the heroes occasionally wax philosophical about their relationship with God and their place in the world, the novels are as gritty as those appearing from secular publishers.

Bagdon, Paul.

West Texas Sunrise Series.

Short novels set in Burnt Rock, Texas, in the 1870s; filled with action and romance.

Stallions at Burnt Rock. Fleming H. Revell, 2003. 191pp.

Lee Morgan, strong-willed owner of a horse ranch, sets out to prove that her horses are a match for any man's. Town marshal Ben Flood, a Christian, tries to keep the peace when the rivalry turns deadly.

Long Road to LaRosa. Fleming H. Revell, 2003. 192pp.

When Ben's archenemy Zeb Stone kidnaps Lee, the woman Ben has begun to care for, Ben follows his trail south to LaRosa, Mexico.

The Stranger from Medina. Fleming H. Revell, 2003.

Ben Flood doesn't believe that Burnt Rock's charismatic new preacher is all that he seems to be.

Thunder on the Dos Gatos. Fleming H. Revell, 2003. 189pp.

Lee Morgan's herd of prized mares is nearly destroyed by thugs.

Brouwer, Sigmund.

Sam Keaton: Legends of Laramie.

Sam Keaton, former gunfighter turned sheriff of Laramie, Wyoming, in the 1870s, now lives on the right side of the law. The townspeople still don't trust him, so Sam has to prove himself time and again. There are a lot of unexplained deaths in Laramie, and Sam sets out to solve the mysteries. His struggles with alcoholism set him apart from other Christian heroes, as he's hardly a saintly character.

Evening Star. Bethany House, 2000. 317pp. (Originally published in 1994 as *Morning Star*.)

Silver Moon. Bethany House, 2000. 319pp. (Originally published in 1994 as *Moon Basket*.)

Sun Dance. Bethany House, 2001. 304pp. (Originally published in 1995.)

Thunder Voice. Bethany House, 2001. 304pp. (Originally published in 1995.)

Frontier Novels

Brave nineteenth-century women confront the dangers and opportunities on America's Western frontier. While the discomforts of pioneer life may cause them to question God's existence, they never truly give up hope. Whether written by women or men, Christian frontier novels normally tell the story from a woman's viewpoint. Not surprisingly, women are the principal readers.

Kirkpatrick, Jane.

Dream Catcher Series. ✍ 📖

The tales of these historical nineteenth-century pioneer couples reveal their commitment to the land, one another, and God.

A Sweetness to the Soul. Multnomah, 1995. 425pp.

Ever since she was a young girl in Oregon, Jane Herbert's mother has blamed her for the death of her siblings. Jane finds true love with an older man, Joseph Sherar, who helps her overcome the scars of her early years. Western Heritage Award.

Love to Water My Soul. Multnomah, 1996. 368pp.

Asiam, a six-year-old Caucasian girl, becomes separated from her family as they travel westward to Oregon. Modoc Indians take her in, but they treat her shamefully, trading her to the Paiutes. The Paiutes teach Asiam, now renamed "Shell Flower," to find her own path through life. Based on Kirkpatrick's husband's family history.

A Gathering of Finches. Multnomah, 1997. 300pp.

In the early twentieth century, Cassie Hendrick Stearns Simpson and her husband Louis, a California lumber baron, settle near Coos Bay, Oregon. Though Louis is a man of considerable wealth, Cassie learns that his money can't buy happiness.

Mystic Sweet Communion. Multnomah, 1998. 400pp.

Ivy Cromartie Stranahan, the first English-speaking teacher in Broward County, Florida, in the first decade of the twentieth century, brings the message of God to the Seminole Indians as she teaches their children. Though a frontier novel and part of the <u>Dream Catcher</u> series, technically this isn't a Western.

Kinship and Courage Series. 📖

Kirkpatrick's well-researched series, appropriate for both mainstream and Christian readers, is based on an incident recorded by pioneer Ezra Meeker as he traveled the Oregon Trail in 1852. In his frontier diary, Meeker wrote of encountering a wagon train of eleven women returning east, their husbands all having died on the westward route.

All Together in One Place. WaterBrook, 2000. 406pp.

Madison "Mazy" Bacon is devastated to learn that her husband Jeremy sold their Wisconsin farm and planned to move them both out West. Accompanying them in their wagon train are Ruth Martin, a horsewoman running from an abusive husband; Bryce Cullver and his blind wife Suzanne; the Wilson family, who follow their daughter Tipton westward so that she can be with the man she loves; and four Chinese mail-order brides. The women bond closer together after their men sicken and die, but the road to acceptance of God's will—and of each other's presence—isn't an easy one.

No Eye Can See. WaterBrook, 2001. 388pp.

The wagon train has reached its destination of Shasta City, California. There the women settle into town life, but despite their wish for new beginnings, they haven't left the past behind. Ruth's husband Zane has followed them to California, which frightens her. Sharp-tongued Suzanne adjusts to her disability and learns to accept the help of others.

What Once We Loved. WaterBrook, 2002. 390pp.

As the series wraps up, Tipton adjusts to married life in Shasta City, Suzanne discovers a new way of seeing, and Ruth overcomes great disappointment in her hopes of establishing a horse ranch. All of the women, even Mazy, learn what it takes to effect change in their lives.

Miller, Dawn.

Journals of Callie MacGregor.

As this series begins, eighteen-year-old Callie Wade, traveling with her family from Missouri to California on a wagon train in 1859, records her innermost thoughts in her journal and in letters home. Accompanying them is blacksmith Quinn MacGregor, whom Callie falls in love with and marries. They settle in Montana Territory, raise a family, and survive difficult times with the help of their strong faith. Miller has been called the "Laura Ingalls Wilder of the 21st century" for her heartfelt portrayals of pioneer life on the American frontier. Fans of Janette Oke may enjoy these stories.

The Journal of Callie Wade. Pocket, 1998. 304pp.

Letters to Callie: Jack Wade's Story. Pocket, 2001. 326pp.

Promiseland. Integrity, 2002. 288pp.

The Other Side of Jordan. Integrity, 2003. 243pp.

Finding Grace. Integrity, 2004. 288pp.

Morris, Gilbert.

Lone Star Legacy.

A preachy series about the tumultuous birth of Texas in the 1830s and 1840s as seen through the eyes of a courageous and virtuous woman. Famous figures like David Crockett, Sam Houston, and Jim Bowie make appearances.

Deep in the Heart. Integrity, 2003. 391pp.

Jerusalem Ann Hardin, used to raising her four children alone while her husband Jake is off somewhere, accepts Clay Taliferro's help when the bank threatens to foreclose on her Arkansas farm. Once she's back on her feet with Clay's help, Jerusalem Ann gathers up her family and heads to Austin, Texas, to reunite with Jake.

The Yellow Rose. Integrity, 2004. 400pp.

During Texas's struggle to gain independence from Mexico, Jerusalem Ann's husband dies at the Alamo. Having narrowly escaped death herself, she settles with her family on the Brazos River, and looks forward to a possible romance with Clay. It's still a dangerous time and place, and Comanche raids menace her settlement.

Noble, Diane.

The Veil. WaterBrook, 1998. 379pp.

In 1857, a misguided group of devotees of the Mormon faith massacred a wagon train of settlers moving westward through Utah. Noble tells the grim story of the Mountain Meadows Massacre from the points of view of Hannah McClary, a young Mormon woman who questions the beliefs she's been taught from birth, and the Farrington family, westward-bound pioneers who happen upon the Mormon settlement at just the wrong time.

Peterson, Tracie.

Heirs of Montana.

In the final years of the Civil War, the Chadwick family's journey westward to Montana symbolizes their journey closer to God. Conditions are rough, and not everyone survives. Too many annoying characters populate the series in the beginning, but once they reach Montana, the story comes together. More volumes will follow.

Land of My Heart. Bethany House, 2004. 392pp.

After her father is shot dead in the street in New Madrid, Missouri, feisty sixteen-year-old Dianne Chadwick convinces her mother to move their family west to Idaho Territory. Cole Selby, the second-in-command on their wagon train, can't forgive himself or his father for a devastating incident from his past. Sparks fly between him and Dianne.

The Coming Storm. Bethany House, 2004. 398pp.

At the end of *Land of My Heart*, Dianne had formed an understanding with Cole Selby, but he has failed to return home to Montana after a trip out east. Little does she know that he was captured by Indians. When her Uncle Bram is injured, ranching life proves difficult for Dianne to handle on her own.

Snelling, Lauraine.

Dakotah Treasures Series.

How does one understand and forgive people who seem to deserve it the least? A series set in Snelling's trademark location of North Dakota during the 1880s.

Ruby. Bethany House, 2003. 320pp.

Sisters Ruby and Opal Torvald leave the big city for the Black Hills of Dakotah Territory to claim their inheritance from their dying father. Their dubious legacy turns out to be Dove House, an establishment of ill repute, which comes pre-populated with a collection of soiled doves.

Pearl. Bethany House, 2004. 320pp.

Dove House has become respectable thanks to Ruby's efforts. Chicago native Pearl Hossfuss answers Ruby's ad for a schoolteacher for the town of Little Missouri, but her romance with a local carpenter is derailed by her memories of a scarred childhood.

Whitson, Stephanie Grace.

Pine Ridge Portraits.

A projected trilogy set on a U.S. Army post at Fort Robinson, Nebraska, in the 1870s. Whitson continues sharing her expertise on the Lakota Sioux (see her Dakota Moons trilogy, under "Native Americans"). Gritty and realistic, as authentic Westerns should be.

Secrets on the Wind. Bethany House, 2003. 319pp.

Sergeant Nathan Boone discovers Laina Gray—young, pregnant, and willing to trust no one—hidden in a dugout on an abandoned claim.

Watchers on the Hill. Bethany House, 2004. 320pp.

Charlotte Bishop, a young widow with a son, decides to return to her childhood home at Fort Robinson after her husband's death. Soon she discovers that she hasn't left the past completely behind her.

Native Americans

It is always controversial when non-native authors write about Native Americans, but to their credit, the novelists mentioned here strive to portray their Native American protagonists as realistically as possible. Though not all of the Indians in these novels are Christians, they all share the Christian message that God loves all people.

Kirkpatrick, Jane.

Tender Ties Historical Series. ✍ 📖

This series is based on the true story of Marie Dorion, the Ioway Indian woman who followed in Sacagawea's footsteps, accompanying the first group of white men heading westward over the Rocky Mountains after the Lewis and Clark expedition. Kirkpatrick combines painstaking research with an emotionally involving story about a little-known but courageous woman.

A Name of Her Own. WaterBrook, 2002. 388pp.

When Pierre Dorion agrees to serve as translator for a French fur trading company heading west in 1811, his neglected wife Marie and their two children accompany him. In this way, Marie makes a name for herself in a world that doesn't honor women, especially Indian women. En route, Marie discovers that she's pregnant again, making an otherwise difficult journey even harder. On one of the group's stops, she forms a strong friendship with Sacagawea, who gives Marie the strength to carry on.

Every Fixed Star. WaterBrook, 2003. 422pp.

It is 1814, and Marie, a widow living in the Okanogan settlement (modern-day Washington State) with her children, still searches for her place in the world. With the difficulties she faces in raising her sons and forming friendships in this barren country, Marie doesn't feel that she really deserves God's love.

Hold Tight the Thread. WaterBrook, 2004. 410pp.

In the 1840s, Marie's growing family presents her with difficulties, while the white and native inhabitants of Oregon Territory fight for control of the land. Marie draws on all her strength and faith in God when a long-lost figure from the past comes back into her life.

Schaap, James Calvin.

Touches the Sky. **Fleming H. Revell, 2003. 256pp.**

In the late 1880s, the Ghost Dance craze sweeps through the Lakota Sioux of South Dakota, leading them ultimately toward the massacre at Wounded Knee. Jan Ellerbroek, a Dutch liveryman, doesn't believe that the Sioux were responsible for a Dutch farmhand's death. As Jan searches for the real perpetrator, he wonders how the God of his fellow settlers and the God worshipped by the Lakota could possibly be one and the same.

Schalesky, Marlo M.

Only the Wind Remembers. **Moody, 2003. 376pp.** ✍

In 1911, the last living Yahi Indian leaves his settlement and heads to San Francisco in order to survive. Thomas Morgan, a curator at a Native American museum, rescues him from jail, renames him Ishi, and turns him into a living exhibit. Allison Morgan, Thomas's troubled young wife, learns Ishi's language, and Ishi tells her a fable about the value that God places on all lives.

Whitson, Stephanie Grace.

Dakota Moons Series.

A well-researched trilogy set among the Lakota Sioux in northern Minnesota in the 1860s.

Valley of the Shadow. Thomas Nelson, 2000. 295pp.

Genevieve "Gen" Lacroix, the blue-eyed daughter of a Frenchman and a Sioux woman, arrives at the Renville Mission to help the minister, Simon Dane, and his wife. Tensions between the Sioux and the settlers culminate in the Sioux Uprising of 1862, in which many white men are murdered. Believing that her true love, Daniel Two Stars, is dead, Gen marries Simon after his wife dies in childbirth.

Edge of the Wilderness. Thomas Nelson, 2001. 288pp.

Gen and Simon begin their ministry at the Crow Creek Reservation, where the Indians live in deplorable conditions. As the couple tries to convince the authorities that not all Indians are their enemies, Daniel Two Stars unexpectedly comes back into Gen's life.

Heart of the Sandhills. Thomas Nelson, 2002. 288pp.

Gen and Daniel, together at last, face considerable prejudice as they begin their new life together. Many of their white neighbors believe that all Sioux are murderous savages.

Romantic Westerns

Though more action-oriented and set farther west than prairie romances (previous section), romantic Westerns follow a similar formula: A single woman heads west, learns God's true path for her, and finds a good man. Readers will see some unique Western settings here, like the Yukon, the 1850s California Gold Rush, and the Grand Canyon.

Bittner, Rosanne.

Where Heaven Begins. **Steeple Hill, 2004. 336pp.**

Elizabeth Breckenridge isn't used to the rough company she's forced to keep while sailing to Alaska during the 1890s to find her brother in Dawson. At first she doesn't know what to make of Clint Brady, the bounty hunter who saves her life. Despite their differences, they fall in love, with Elizabeth hoping she can transform Clint into a proper God-fearing man.

Copeland, Lori.

<u>Brides of the West.</u>

These popular, interconnected Western romances have some stereotypical elements (mail-order brides, big misunderstandings between hero and heroine), but Copeland's endearing characters continue to appeal to readers. The first three novels deal with three orphaned sisters—Faith, June, and Hope Kallahan—who travel west in search of husbands in 1872. The last three continue the mail-order bride theme with the title characters.

Faith. Tyndale House, 1998. 350pp.

June. Tyndale House, 1999. 272pp.

Hope. Tyndale House, 1999. 304pp.

Glory. Tyndale House, 2000. 320pp.

Patience. Tyndale House, 2002. 318pp.

Ruth. Tyndale House, 2004. 290pp.

Hatcher, Robin Lee.

Catching Katie. **Tyndale House, 2004. 368pp.**

Suffragette and Vassar grad Katie Jones returns to Homestead, Idaho, in 1916. Her old friend, newspaperman Ben Rafferty, gives her a column to proclaim her feminist views. As Katie and Ben grow closer, she worries that her ideals may compromise a possible marriage. A reworked version of Hatcher's secular romance *Kiss Me, Katie.*

Speak to Me of Love. **Tyndale House, 2003. 273pp.**

Hatcher transformed her previously published romance *Chances Are* into this inspirational novel of Faith Butler, a divorced single mother traveling with a drama troupe through 1880s Wyoming. The sleepy town of Dead Horse welcomes the Butler family when Faith's young daughter falls ill. Faith takes a job as housekeeper to a local ranch owner, Drake Rutledge, who resists her attractions at first.

Heitzmann, Kristen.

Diamond of the Rockies Series.

In the late nineteenth century, Italian heiress Carina Maria DiGratia thinks she's buying a mansion in a quaint little mining town, but her new property in Crystal, Colorado, turns out to be a shack already inhabited by a rough bunch of miners. She thinks she has found a rescuer in darkly handsome Quillan Shephard, but he has a rough past he's unwilling to share with anyone, even the woman he claims he wants to marry.

The Rose Legacy. Bethany House, 2000. 395pp.

Sweet Boundless. Bethany House, 2001. 350pp.

The Tender Vine. Bethany House, 2002. 382pp.

Morgan, Kathleen.

Brides of Culdee Creek.

Four interconnected novels set at Culdee Creek Ranch, just outside Colorado Springs, Colorado, beginning in the 1890s. Kathleen Morgan turned from mainstream historical romance to Christian fiction, beginning her new career with this series.

Daughter of Joy. Fleming H. Revell, 1999. 336pp.

Abigail Stanton comes to Culdee Creek to become the housekeeper for Conor MacKay and teacher to his daughter, Beth. Over time, she teaches them both the meaning of faith and love.

Woman of Grace. Fleming H. Revell, 2000. 304pp.

Former prostitute Hannah Cutler has found God but can't completely forgive herself for leading a sinful life. Devlin MacKay has a troubled past of his own.

Lady of Light. Fleming H. Revell, 2001. 336pp.

Evan MacKay brings his new Scottish bride, Claire Sutherland, back to Culdee Creek. Their married life isn't easy.

Child of Promise. Fleming H. Revell, 2002. 320pp.

Beth MacKay has grown up to become a successful physician, but her heart still yearns for minister Noah Starr, who married someone else.

Orcutt, Jane.

Heart's True Desire.

These well-written Western romances can be read independently.

The Fugitive Heart. WaterBrook, 1998. 339pp.

The Civil War took away everything that Samantha Martin held dear: her Kansas home, her family, and her childhood sweetheart Nathan Hamilton. Samantha relied on her faith in God to survive their separation, but Nathan's wartime experiences have turned him into a haunted, bitter man, with a price on his head.

The Hidden Heart. WaterBrook, 1998. 323pp.

In 1875, Elizabeth Cameron journeys to Belton, Texas, with her young Native American ward, Joseph, to join the Sanctificationists, an all-female religious sect that proclaims independence from men. Former gunfighter Caleb Martin accompanies them to Belton. He and Elizabeth are forced together to keep Joseph's guardianship. Before any romance can develop, both must face up to the past.

Peterson, Tracie.

Desert Roses.

The lives and loves of three Harvey Girls, virtuous young women recruited as waitresses for Fred Harvey's Western restaurants and hotels in the late nineteenth and early twentieth centuries.

Shadows of the Canyon. Bethany House, 2002. 368pp.

Alexandria "Alex" Keegan, a Harvey Girl at the El Tovar Resort at the Grand Canyon in 1923, doesn't trust men after years of watching her philandering father mistreat her mother. Luke Toland, Alex's best friend of four years, loves her, but they both get mixed up with other people.

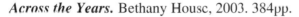

Across the Years. Bethany House, 2003. 384pp.

Ashley Reynolds lost her husband in World War I. Now, in 1929, she supports her ailing grandfather and her young daughter Natalie by working as a Harvey Girl in Winslow, Arizona. An architect on a nearby resort hotel befriends Natalie and tries to heal Ashley's lonely heart.

Beneath a Harvest Sky. Bethany House, 2003. 384pp.

Rainy Gordon, a young woman with a secret past, works as a tour guide for Harvey House Detours in New Mexico in 1931. When she is falsely accused of stealing ancient Hopi artifacts, she's even more shocked to learn that museum curator Duncan Hartford, a man she's grown to admire, has been secretly investigating her role in the thefts.

Yukon Quest.

Three related novels, all romantic adventures set during the Alaskan gold rush of 1897. Characters are painted either wholly good or evil, and their many mishaps wouldn't be out of place in a modern soap opera, but the beautiful northern setting comes alive.

Treasures of the North. Bethany House, 2001. 384pp.

To compensate for a bad business deal, Chicago socialite Grace Hawkins's father arranges her marriage to evil Martin Paxton. She escapes to Alaska with her governess and friend, Karen Pierce, to avoid marrying him. They also hope to locate Karen's missionary father. The young women purchase passage north on a ship owned by handsome Peter Colton, who catches Grace's eye.

Ashes and Ice. Bethany House, 2001. 384pp.

Karen Pierce tries to come to terms with a personal loss, and Grace and Peter's new marriage flounders. Nonetheless, Karen decides to continue their journey north to the gold fields of the Yukon, with her former suitor Adrik Ivankov as their guide.

Rivers of Gold. Bethany House, 2002. 384pp.

Peter Colton's sister Miranda, presumed dead in the second book, is very much alive, and anxious to reunite with her family and friends. English botanist Teddy Davenport abandons his usual workaholic life to care for her.

Rivers, Francine.

Redeeming Love. **Multnomah, 1997. 464pp.** ★ 📖

Angel, a prostitute in Gold Rush-era California, has felt worthless and ill-used ever since she was sold into a life of sin as a child. Her life transforms when Michael Hosea, a devout farmer, marries her. Michael shows her the path to love and salvation, though she'll have none of him at first. This beloved retelling of the classic biblical story of Gomer and Hosea was originally written for the secular market (Bantam, 1991, same title).

Wick, Lori.

The Californians. ★

Wick recounts the romantic trials and tribulations of the Donovan siblings—Kaitlin, Marcail, and Sean Donovan—who leave Hawaii for San Francisco, California, in 1871 to visit their Aunt Maureen. Soon afterward, their mother dies of tuberculosis, and their father heads back to Hawaii to take care of business, leaving the trio on their own. But their real adventure begins when they move to Santa Rosa to help Kaitlin avoid the unwelcome advances of a would-be suitor. There they meet the Taylors, a Christian family. Members of both families feature in all four books.

Whatever Tomorrow Brings. Harvest House, 1992. 323pp.

As Time Goes By. Harvest House, 1992. 279pp.

Sean Donovan. Harvest House, 1993. 269pp.

Donovan's Daughter. Harvest House, 1994. 312pp.

Chapter 12

Time-Slip Novels

A woman spies a painting of an eighteenth-century man hanging on the wall of an English castle and feels as if she might have known him before. A businessman in the present day undergoes hypnosis to help him deal with a psychological issue, and the sessions reveal his past life as a slave in nineteenth-century America. Scientific investigators from the future take a trip back to the fourteenth century to study medieval societies for themselves—but once there, they can't find a way to return home. These three plotlines are all common to the time-slip novel.

Although these novels may not normally be thought of as a subgenre of historical fiction, it can help librarians and readers to consider them as such. Not only do they have many readers in common, but they have a similar appeal. These creatively written novels allow readers to imagine, if only for a time, that slipping from one time period to another is indeed possible. Thus, they appeal to readers' sense of wishful thinking in a way that more straight-forwardly-written historical novels cannot do. Through them, readers will experience the strong pull that the past exerts on characters living in later times.

Time-slip novels appeal to readers of a variety of genres: not only historical fiction, but also fantasy, romance, adventure, and occasionally mystery and even science fiction. They also bridge the gap between them. Because of this, publishers' labels for these books can vary. Works of fiction with a strong emphasis on time travel or the supernatural may be labeled as fantasy, while novels in which people from the future go back into the past are apt to be called science fiction. Time-slips recounting a love that transcends time will appeal strongly to romance readers, as will novels in which a modern-day man or woman returns to an earlier time to find a soul mate. Finally, suspenseful stories of a centuries-old curse carried down through the generations may fall into the category of mystery, thriller, or even horror.

The novels annotated in this chapter include classics of these diverse genres, all of which fit the time-slip definition, as well as recently published titles that explore the same themes. While the subgenre as a whole is not nearly as popular in the United States as it is in Great Britain, time-travel romances continue to be very popular among romance readers. A selected number of these novels are included below, in particular those that provide a significant amount of historical content.

Regardless of the various ways in which they may be categorized, their appeal to historical fiction readers lies in their ability to give additional insight into people who lived, and into events that occurred, at various times in the past. Through them, readers will get the chance to view the past first-hand through a modern character's eyes, and the differences between "now" and "then" are often quite striking. Simultaneously, time-slips often demonstrate that despite these differences, human nature is the same regardless of the era.

Time Travel

In time-travel novels, one or more characters travel back to an earlier time period, either deliberately or by accident. Little by little, they must learn to conduct themselves according to the customs of their new setting, figuring out how best to survive in an era when present-day technology didn't exist. Most of all, they must take care not to appear too modern, for any inappropriate behavior may attract unwanted attention. Characters unlucky enough to be caught in the past without modern conveniences can make for some humorous scenes, though the characters themselves usually see their state of affairs as less than amusing. A common plot device features characters who arrive in the past at a time of particular unrest, such as a time of great war or disease, which makes their continued survival even more precarious. In the end, whether they return to their own era or not, most conclude that life in earlier times wasn't nearly as simple and romantic as they had originally believed.

General

The plotlines of these time-travel novels are fairly straightforward, but there's nothing ordinary about the stories themselves. After the novelty of living in an earlier time wears off, the protagonists must learn how to survive as best they can.

Brock, Darryl.

Sam Fowler Series.

Sam Fowler, a man in present-day Ohio, experiences his greatest passions back in the past—the love of a beautiful woman, and the early days of America's national pastime.

If I Never Get Back. Crown, 1990. 424pp.

In the present day, Sam Fowler steps off a train and finds himself in Ohio in the year 1869. In this earlier time, he becomes a member of the Cincinnati Red Stockings, the first professional baseball team. Viewing the early days of the game is a dream come true for an aspiring sportswriter such as Sam, and that plus a new romance makes him torn about whether to return home.

Two in the Field. Plume, 2002. 382pp.

Back in the present, Sam Fowler is confined to a San Francisco mental hospital after his experiences in nineteenth-century Ohio. His doctor, not buying his story of time travel, lets him go back to Cincinnati to confirm the existence of his nineteenth-century lover, Caitlin O'Neill. An accident sends him right back into the past again.

Butler, Octavia E.

Kindred. **Doubleday, 1979. 264pp.**

Dana, an independent black woman in Los Angeles in 1976, is snatched back in time by her slave-owning ancestor, Rufus, and brought to the antebellum South. She saves Rufus's life more than once, knowing that his continued existence means that he'll survive to capture a free black woman into slavery and rape her—thus ensuring Dana's own birth generations later. While back in the nineteenth century, Dana herself experiences first-hand being enslaved, and realizes how strong her ancestors must have been to endure it.

Finney, Jack.

Time and Again Series.

In a government-sponsored time-travel project, Si Morley is sent back to New York City in 1882.

Time and Again. Simon & Schuster, 1970. 399pp. ★ **YA**

In Si's current mission, he must discover whether the past can coexist with the present. While back in 1880s New York, he falls in love, but then has to make the big decision about whether or not to remain. This classic time-travel novel should appeal to readers interested in learning more about historical Manhattan.

From Time to Time. Simon & Schuster, 1995. 303pp. **YA**

This sequel to *Time and Again* finds Si returning to the future (for him, the twentieth century), where his superiors have a new project for him: learning how to change history to prevent World War I.

Garcia y Robertson, R.

The Spiral Dance. **Morrow, 1991. 227pp.**

Anne Percy, Countess of Northumberland, flees Queen Elizabeth's wrath after the failure of the treasonous Rising of the North (1569–1570). Fulfilling a prophecy by heading north to Scotland's Border Country, she traces her journey back to its beginning, following the ancient pagan ritual known as the Spiral Dance. After traveling back into the past, she meets a madwoman who claims to be an alternate version of herself.

Giardina, Denise.
Fallam's Secret. **W. W. Norton, 2003. 331pp.**

In 2001, Lydde Falcone is a fifty-five-year-old single woman living abroad when she's notified of the death of her Uncle John. Returning home to rural West Virginia to comfort her grieving aunt, she discovers—and follows—some unusual directions that her physicist uncle had left behind. No one could be more surprised than Lydde when she discovers herself in England in the year 1657, the next to last year of Oliver Cromwell's rule. Though the route back home stays open, she finds some compelling reasons to remain, such as her growing attraction to a seventeenth-century Robin Hood who braves the wrath of the town's Puritan leaders to smuggle goods to the poor.

MacAvoy, R. A.
The Book of Kells. **Bantam, 1985. 340pp.**

While taking a rubbing of a Celtic cross, Canadian artist John Thornburn and his Irish colleague are transported back in time to tenth-century Ireland, a land ravaged by Viking invasions. There John falls in love with a lovely young woman named Ailesh. This is one of the rare time-travel novels that doesn't gloss over the difficulty in communicating with people of a completely different era.

Maxim, John R.
Time Out of Mind. **Houghton Mifflin, 1986. 502pp.**

Whenever it snows, Jonathan Corbin finds himself back in New York City of a hundred years earlier, where he sees events and people (including Teddy Roosevelt and J. P. Morgan) through the eyes of his ancestor Tilden Beckworth, who may be a murderer. Back in the present, someone may be out to kill Jonathan for his knowledge of the past. A suspenseful tale.

Tarr, Judith, and Harry Turtledove.
Household Gods. **Tor, 1999. 512pp.**

Nicole Gunther-Perrin, single mother and transplanted Californian, is having the worst week of her life. In desperation, she makes an offering to the two Roman gods on the plaque by her nightstand, asking them to take her back to their time. She awakens the next morning to the overpowering stench of Roman Carnuntum, a frontier town of the Empire, in the year AD 170. Nicole's body is no longer her own; she has become Umma, a widowed tavernkeeper with serious family problems and a steady boyfriend who desperately needs a bath. Umma is also a slave owner, which angers Nicole no end—wasn't life supposed to be more equitable back then?

Romantic

People from the present day travel back in time and end up finding their soul mates. Problems arise when they are forced to decide whether to return to the present, possibly leaving their loved one behind, or remain in the earlier time period with the one they love.

Brown, Rita Mae.

Riding Shotgun. **Bantam, 1996. 341pp.**

Cig Blackwood, a modern Virginia woman, was widowed a year ago—her husband had died while in bed with her sister. Just after she discovers this unpleasant fact, fate steps in and drags her back in time to 1699, where she has two handsome men to choose from.

Deveraux, Jude.

A Knight in Shining Armor. **Pocket, 1989. 341pp. ★**

Abandoned on a trip to England by her callous boyfriend and his annoying teenage daughter, Dougless Montgomery happens upon the tomb of a knight from Elizabethan times. No one is more surprised than she when he appears in the flesh—except perhaps the knight himself, Nicholas Stafford, who is amusingly befuddled by his unexpected appearance. The two grow closer after Dougless hears Nicholas's story, and she travels back in time to 1560s England to help him clear his name. A slightly revised version was reissued by Pocket in 2002.

Legend. **Pocket, 1996. 374pp.**

When Kady Long slips on an antique wedding dress while preparing for her own wedding, she is transported back to Legend, Colorado, in 1873, where she has the chance to stop Cole Jordan from being hanged.

Edghill, Rosemary.

Met by Moonlight. **Pinnacle, 1998. 317pp.**

In this unusual time-travel romance, Diana Crossways, a modern-day practitioner of Wicca, is transported back in time to seventeenth-century England. In this earlier time, Oliver Cromwell is in power and Witchfinder General Matthew Hopkins vigorously pursues his cruel agenda. One of Hopkins's human witch-finding tools is Upright-Before-the-Lord Makepeace, compelled to do his master's will yet strongly attracted to Diana.

Frank, J. Suzanne/Suzanne.

In her later novels, Suzanne Frank dropped the initial "J," and she also dropped the ball somewhat in her final Chloe and Cheftu novel, *Twilight in Babylon*, which she herself admits is short on historical research. This series of romances, humorous and entertaining, is full of modern colloquialisms expressed by her heroine, Chloe, in various historical guises.

Reflections in the Nile. **Warner, 1997. 418pp.**

Chloe Kingsley, an artist in present-day Dallas, is whisked back in time to Egypt in the era of the female Pharaoh Hatshepsut, where she inhabits the body of a priestess. There she falls in love with Cheftu, a court magus, and becomes caught up in a slave revolt led by Moses.

Shadows on the Aegean. Warner, 1998. 481pp.

In ancient Crete, Chloe wakes up in the body of an Oracle of Cybele, and Cheftu shows up as an Egyptian healer.

Sunrise on the Mediterranean. Warner, 1999. 477pp.

This time we're in biblical-era Canaan at the time of King David, and Chloe and Cheftu help their monarch regain Jerusalem.

Twilight in Babylon. Warner, 2002. 480pp.

More fantastical than even her earlier time-travel novels, this final installment picks up in ancient Sumeria. Chloe takes the form of a marsh girl who survives a flood and challenges the patriarchal society of the city of Ur.

Gabaldon, Diana.

Outlander Saga.

Annotated in Chapter 4.

Garcia y Robertson, R.

Knight Errant Series. ✍

While hiking in present-day England, Californian Robyn Stafford encounters Edward, Earl of March, a knight from the fifteenth century. Thus begins their story. This time travel romance never takes itself too seriously, as Robyn somehow manages to bring technological gadgets from the future back with her. The next volume will be *White Rose.*

Knight Errant. Forge, 2001. 479pp. ✍

Acknowledging their mutual attraction, Robyn determines to find Edward, a mysterious knight she spotted in her own time. She arrives in the fifteenth century after participating in a pagan rite, but locating Edward isn't as easy as she thought. Many of the people she meets seem to be reincarnations or alter egos of people she knew in her own time. Plus, it's the height of the Wars of the Roses, Robyn can't remember her history well enough to know what happens next, and she is about to be arrested as a witch.

Lady Robyn. Forge, 2003. 399pp.

Lady Robyn Stafford of Holy Wood, happily betrothed to Edward Plantagenet, realizes that her future father-in-law's bid for England's throne will place her fiancé directly in the line of succession. Given that many royal heirs die young, this isn't something she necessarily wants for herself or her unborn children. While she keeps track of the score between Lancaster and York on her electronic scheduler, her enemies pile up evidence against her, hoping she will make a blunder that will prove she's a witch.

Matheson, Richard.

Bid Time Return. **Viking, 1974. 278pp. (Alternate title:** *Somewhere in Time.***)** ★

Richard Collier, a writer dying of a brain tumor in the 1970s, pays a visit to a turn-of-the-century hotel in San Diego, California. There he spots the portrait of a beautiful actress, Elise McKenna, who performed at the hotel seventy-five years earlier, when the hotel was first built during the 1890s. Having never been in love, Richard grows obsessed by his newfound feelings, and literally wills himself back in time to fall in love with Elise in person. Matheson's novel was made into a well-known film, *Somewhere in Time*, starring Christopher Reeve and Jane Seymour.

McKean, James.
Quattrocento. **Doubleday, 2002. 307pp.**

The Quattrocento is the period of the Italian Renaissance, when fine art flourished. When Matt O'Brien, an art restorer at the Met who's an aficionado of the period, uncovers a painting of a beautiful woman from beneath layers of varnish, he believes he might have uncovered a Da Vinci. Suddenly he's swept back in time, face to face with the woman, whom he had named Anna. Matt finds himself in a love triangle with Anna and another suitor, the dangerous knight Leandro. More leisurely paced than most time-slip novels, this is nevertheless rich in historical detail. **Literary.**

Adventure

Once they are back in the past, protagonists race against time to complete their mission. These are fast-paced, action-oriented time-travel stories.

Crichton, Michael.
Timeline. **Knopf, 1999. 444pp.** `YA`

In this time-travel adventure thriller, a group of historians from 1999 head back in time to France in the year 1357 to rescue their mentor. Little do they realize what dangers await them during the Hundred Years' War, and how close they are to becoming trapped in the past themselves.

Podrug, Junius.
Dark Passage. **Forge, 2002. 464pp.**

Islamic terrorists from the present have found a way to travel through time, so they decide to stop one of the most significant religious events of the Western world: the Crucifixion. Three other characters, sent back to prevent the changing of history, encounter all of the wicked excesses of the first-century Roman Empire, including the brutal exploits of Queen Salome.

Science Fiction

One might think that science fiction and historical fiction are polar opposites that can't be combined, but Kage Baker and Connie Willis prove this idea wrong. They mingle the two genres with their very popular novels about protagonists from the future who make exploratory journeys into the past.

Baker, Kage.

The Company.

Baker's series mixes historical fiction, science fiction, and humor in the adventures of Mendoza, a girl originally born into sixteenth-century Spain. Mendoza is recruited by scientists from the twenty-fourth century to work for Dr. Zeus, Incorporated, a company that makes money preserving cultural artifacts from the past. Trained as a botanist, Mendoza—rendered nearly immortal through drugs and implants—is sent back in time to various eras to safeguard endangered plant species. Her occasionally bumbling colleagues create some very funny scenes. Book 4 of the series, *The Graveyard Game* (2001), goes back from the future to San Francisco in 1996.

In the Garden of Iden. Harcourt, Brace, 1997. 329pp.

Sent back in time to Elizabethan England to collect plants from the garden of Sir Walter Iden, a country squire, Mendoza dons the disguise of a Spanish nobleman's daughter. Her mission is complicated by Nicholas Harpole, Sir Walter's Protestant secretary, with whom she falls passionately in love.

Sky Coyote. Harcourt Brace, 1999. 310pp.

Joseph, the cyborg who had rescued Mendoza from the Spanish Inquisition in her childhood, is sent back with her to pre-Columbian Mexico, where their task is to save a Chumash village before the Europeans come and destroy it with their diseases.

Mendoza in Hollywood. Harcourt Brace, 2000. 326pp.

Sent to Los Angeles during the Civil War, Mendoza spends most of her time mourning for her lover, lost in sixteenth-century England. As she and her colleagues learn how to survive in the Wild West, she meets British spy Edward Alton Bell-Fairfax. A dead ringer for the long-dead Nicholas Harpole, Edward has plans to stop a possible Union victory.

Black Company, White Knights: The Company Dossiers. Golden Gryphon, 2002. 288pp.

This collection of short stories about the adventures of the Company's field agents take them back in time to Santa Barbara in 1844, Los Angeles in 1894, and early twentieth-century Egypt, among other locales.

Willis, Connie.

Doomsday Book. Bantam, 1992. 445pp. ★ 📖

In this classic of both historical fiction and science fiction, Kivrin, a young Oxford scientist in the twenty-first century, is sent back in time to study the Middle Ages first-hand. An accident in calculation places her not in 1320 but in 1348, right before the bubonic plague hit Oxford—and her colleagues can't reach her to bring her back home. Though Kivrin has been inoculated against the plague, she knows true helplessness as she watches the people she's befriended in medieval times succumb to the disease, one by one. Hugo Award; Nebula Award.

Reincarnation

These works presuppose that one or more modern-day characters are the reincarnations of people who had previously lived. Parallel stories, one set now and another in the past, allow readers to explore these characters' connections to an earlier place and time. Within these novels, modern-day individuals are given the opportunity to right wrongs that were set in motion long ago. Many novels about reincarnation center on a love story, in which people are finally given the opportunity to reunite with their soul mates from a previous existence. As the protagonists come to terms with the existence of their past lives, they unlock a psychological healing process.

Baker, Jeanette.

Catriona. **Pocket Books, 1997. 375pp.** ✍

> In this contemporary/historical romance, when modern California lawyer Kate Sutherland travels to the Shetland Islands in search of her roots, she begins seeing visions of an earlier version of herself: Catriona Wells, the first Countess of Bothwell, who in the fifteenth century got caught up in conflicts between Scotland and England.

Bennett, Laura Gilmour.

By All That Is Sacred. **Avon, 1991. 385pp. (Original title:** *A Wheel of Stars***.)**

> In thirteenth-century southern France, a Knight Templar vows to the woman he loves that he will never rest until he finds her again. Seven hundred years later, Louise Carey finds herself irresistibly drawn to a man named Owen Morgan, somehow knowing that they were meant to be together.

Billington, Rachel.

Theo and Matilda. **HarperCollins, 1991. 346pp.**

> Beginning in the eighth century and continuing to an unspecified year in the modern era, lovers Theo and Matilda are reincarnated four times over the centuries. Their unions don't often work out in their favor. Billington is the sister of historical biographer Lady Antonia Fraser.

Costain, Thomas P.

Below the Salt. **Doubleday, 1957. 480pp.** ★

> A U.S. senator tells John Faroday the story of an earlier life of his—beginning 700 years ago, when Faroday was a Saxon freedman present when King John signed the Magna Carta in 1215. Costain has also written a number of classic historical novels.

Danvers, Dennis.

Time and Time Again. Simon & Schuster, 1994. 296pp.

While researching a novel about Susanna Grier, a woman from eighteenth-century Virginia who ran away from her husband with a convict, historian Marion Mead places an ad in the *New York Times Book Review*. She asks for anyone with information on the family to come forward. Marion receives a response from Raymond Lord, a plantation owner who has in his possession a journal written by Susanna's great-granddaughter a hundred years later. While Marion falls immediately in love with Raymond, she's disconcerted by inexplicable coincidences that make her think he knows more about the story than he lets on.

Deford, Frank.

The Other Adonis. Sourcebooks, 2001. 272pp.

When "Bucky" Buckingham, a patient of psychiatrist Nina Winston, claims that he and his lover Constance are the reincarnations of the people who posed for Peter Paul Rubens's painting *Venus and Adonis*, she doesn't know what to believe. After hearing Bucky's recollections of life in seventeenth-century Antwerp while under hypnosis, Nina begins to accept his story. But all isn't as it first seems, for murder and deception that took place long ago may have found their way into the present. A lighthearted, romantic mystery.

Erskine, Barbara.

Erskine, the queen of the British time-slip novel, intertwines her historical works with strong threads of suspense and romance.

Kingdom of Shadows. Dell, 1989. 673pp. ✍

In fourteenth-century Scotland, Isobel of Fife, Countess of Buchan, was a noblewoman of royal blood who had the honor of crowning Robert the Bruce. Isobel was also his distant cousin—and, in Erskine's version, his secret lover. When Clare Royland inherits one of Isobel's family homes, she begins experiencing frightening visions of Isobel's tumultuous and ultimately tragic life.

Lady of Hay. Delacorte Press, 1986. 545pp. ★ ✍

During a session of hypnosis, British journalist Jo Clifford experiences a past life as Matilda de Braose, Lady of Hay, a noblewoman who lived at the time of King John. The beautiful, forthright Matilda was a woman truly ahead of her time, managing her estates as well as a man could. But she made the fatal mistake of taunting King John about the death of his nephew, Prince Arthur, whom John very likely had killed to secure his own succession to the throne. Matilda paid for her mistake most cruelly, and unless Jo can free herself from the memory of her past life, the danger may repeat itself in the present.

Hardwick, Mollie.

I Remember Love. St. Martin's Press, 1983. 335pp.

Joscelyn Conyers and Yolande de Clifford first meet and fall in love during the Wars of the Roses, but the turbulence of war soon tears them apart. Their love calls them back twice more over the centuries, first in Tudor times and next in Victorian London.

Hart, Mallory Dorn.

Fire, Burn! John James, 2002. 397pp.

Lyse, the niece of Charles de Bourbon, is asked by her uncle to help him find the lost treasure of the Knights Templar. To do so, she must regress into the past life of her ancestor, Magdalene, who lived during the time of the Cathar heresy 250 years earlier.

Jones, Liane.

✪ *The Dreamstone.* Signet, 1994. 512pp.

When native North Dakotan Jane Pridden begins an affair with Welsh poet Gwyn Thomas, she discovers their connection to a couple who lived long ago: Ceinwen, a young girl from the twelfth century, and Madoc, a Welsh prince who was one of the first to settle North America. Jones, of Welsh birth herself, tells the stories of both couples in alternating chapters. Betty Trask Prize.

Kearsley, Susanna.

✪ *Mariana.* Bantam, 1998. 339pp.

In this historical gothic romance, Julia Beckett has felt an unexpected connection to Greywethers, a farmhouse in Wiltshire, England, since she was five. Twenty-five years later, she has become the house's new owner, but she can't explain why she finds herself continually drawn into the seventeenth century. While there, she personally experiences the life of a young woman, Mariana, who is hopelessly in love with Richard de Mornay of Crofton Hall—the ancestor of the present-day owner. Catherine Cookson Prize (a short-lived British award).

Long, James.

Long, a British novelist, also writes historical fiction under the pseudonym Will Davenport.

Ferney. Bantam, 1999. 339pp.

When Gally Martin and her husband Mike happen upon a cottage in the English countryside, she feels an immediate connection with the person who lives there, an eighty-three-year-old man named Ferney Miller. In her, Ferney sees a solution to the mystery of his own wife's disappearance half a century earlier. Convincing Gally that she has been his soul mate over many incarnations isn't easy—particularly as she's now married to another man.

Silence and Shadows. Bantam, 2001. 322pp.

Patrick Kane, a former rock star, tries to escape a painful past by heading an archaeological dig in the Welsh village of Wytchlow, where he and others try to recover Roman artifacts. His peace is disturbed by the presence of Bobby Redhead, a woman who reminds him of his late wife, but soon another woman is making her presence felt: a Saxon warrior queen who was buried nearby.

Luke, Mary.

The Nonsuch Lure. **Coward, McCann & Geoghegan, 1976. 319pp.** ★

When wealthy jetsetter Andrew Moffett spies a portrait of a beautiful woman in Tudor garb hanging on the wall of an English mansion, he realizes that he knows her from somewhere. As he explores the history of the house, a royal retreat called Nonsuch, he relives two past lives, one in Elizabethan times, another in the seventeenth century—a time when he loved and lost the woman of his dreams.

Rechy, John.

Our Lady of Babylon. **Arcade, 1996. 353pp.**

In an unnamed European city in the late eighteenth century, the Countess du Muir, accused of her husband's murder, has been having mysterious, erotic dreams about the fallen women of history—Eve, Helen of Troy, Mary Magdalene, Salome, Medea, Cortes's interpreter La Malinche, and others. With the help of a mystic named Madame Bernice, the lady discovers not only that these were her past lives, but also that history has recorded them incorrectly. **Literary.**

Roberts, Nora.

Midnight Bayou. **Putnam, 2001. 352pp.**

When Boston lawyer Declan Fitzgerald returns to New Orleans to purchase the estate known as Manet Hall, he doesn't realize that it comes complete with a tragic history—which Declan can't seem to escape from. A parallel tale relates the story of Abigail Manet, one of its previous residents from the year 1900, and it's her baby that Declan frequently hears crying at night. Only with the help of Lena Simone, owner of a local bar, can Declan come to terms with the past. This is one of the few novels of reincarnation featuring a man with past-life experiences.

Seton, Anya.

Green Darkness. **Houghton Mifflin, 1973. 591pp.** ★

When Celia Marsdon and her husband Richard visit his family's hereditary manor of Medfield Place in Sussex, she begins to relive the experiences of an earlier Celia. In a parallel tale, Celia de Bohun has a love affair with Stephen Marsdon, a priest in England in 1552, that leads to heartbreak and tragedy.

Smouldering Fires. **Doubleday, 1975. 159pp.** **YA**

Seton's short novel features Amy Delatour, a teenager of French Canadian heritage haunted by her past life as Ange-Marie, an Acadian woman from the eighteenth century who yearns to reunite with her lost husband, Paul, after their forced exile from Canada.

Past in the Present

Like novels of reincarnation, novels in this category tell parallel stories: one in the modern day, the other set in the past. Here characters from an earlier period of history manage to communicate with present-day individuals, through dreams and visions or in spirit form. Characters in one era may feel an inexplicable connection to someone living in another time, or ghosts may appear to alert a present-day character to a past event—something that created negative karma that only a living person can put right.

Baker, Jeanette.

Nell. **Sonnet, 1999. 419pp.**

Since childhood, Jillian Fitzgerald has been able to communicate with her ghostly ancestor, Eleanor (Nell) Fitzgerald, an Irish princess whose family was killed by Henry VIII in the sixteenth century. When the Protestant Jillian falls in love with Frankie Maguire, the Catholic son of her family's kennel-keeper, she calls on Nell to help their romance survive. RITA Award for Best Paranormal.

Carey, Lisa.

In the Country of the Young. **Morrow, 2000. 286pp.**

In 1848, the Irish emigrant ship *Tír na nÓg* broke up against the rocky Maine coast, drowning many, including a seven-year-old girl named Aisling. Today, a brooding, fortyish artist named Oisin lives alone on Tiranogue Island, named after the ship that sank long ago on its shores. When Oisin spies young footprints in his house, he assumes, and greatly hopes, that his deceased twin sister's ghost has finally found him. Instead he finds Aisling, no longer a ghost but real, returned to reclaim her lost childhood. **Literary.**

Chevalier, Tracy.

The Virgin Blue. **Plume, 2003. 320pp.**

Ella Turner, a young American woman, moves with her husband to a small French village, begins investigating her ancestry, and inexplicably begins having dreams about the color blue. Four centuries earlier, Isabelle du Moulin, called "La Rousse" for her red hair, marries into a Huguenot family whose members are persecuted because of their Protestant religion. As Ella grows closer to finding out Isabelle's secret, she also becomes closer to Jean-Paul, the dashing librarian who helps her with her research. This was Chevalier's first novel. **Literary.**

Durban, Pam.

So Far Back. **Picador USA, 2000. 259pp.**

For generations, the women of one black Charleston family have served the Hilliards—first as slaves, later as hired servants. When a flood disrupts the contents of Louisa Hilliard Marion's ancestral home, she is forced to sift through old family artifacts. Coming across the 1837 diary of Eliza Hilliard, an early mistress of the house, Louisa learns of the harsh conditions to which the plantation's slaves were subjected—and stirs up an angry ghost. **Literary.**

Erskine, Barbara.

Midnight Is a Lonely Place. **Dutton, 1994. 337pp.**

Author Kate Kennedy decides to rent a cottage on the remote North Essex coast to get away from memories of her recent breakup and to write her latest novel. Her presence irritates the son of her landlord and his teenage daughter Allison, both of whom want her gone. At first Kate blames them when odd things start happening, but in reality Allison's archaeological investigations are to blame: She has called up the ghosts of a Druid prince and his Roman lover, both murdered by the woman's husband in a fit of jealousy and anger. When Kate's boyfriend returns, there's a chance the crime may be re-created.

Gutcheon, Beth.

More Than You Know. **Morrow, 2000. 269pp.** 📖 **YA**

When the elderly Hannah Gray returns to her home town of Dundee, Maine, she has memories of her childhood, when she lived for a time with her unfriendly stepmother and found the love of her life. While growing up, Hannah's family lived in a renovated former schoolhouse that was the scene of a horrible murder a hundred years earlier. In a parallel story, set in the mid-nineteenth century, a young girl named Claris marries a taciturn, solitary man against her parents' wishes and suffers the consequences. The murder of Claris's husband remains a mystery to this day, and the house—Hannah's childhood home—is still haunted by one of its former residents. Worries about whether history will once again repeat itself bring moments of bone-chilling suspense. **Literary.**

Harris, Elizabeth.

During the 1990s, British author Elizabeth Harris wrote a series of time-slip novels, though most were only published in her home country. Harris now writes medieval mysteries as Alys Clare (Chapter 7).

The Herb Gatherers. **Avon, 1993. 298pp.**

While visiting the island of Crete, Rafe awakens the spirit of Alienor, a woman from the Middle Ages who mistakes him for the Crusader lover who abandoned her long ago. Research into Alienor's origins leads him to Kent, England, where he comes upon an herb grower named Nell who looks suspiciously like Alienor.

Jones, Jill.

My Lady Caroline. **St. Martin's Press, 1996. 338pp.** ✍

The ghost of Lady Caroline Lamb, lover of Lord Byron, appears to Boston heiress Alison Cunningham. When Caroline asks Alison to find Byron's secret memoirs to prove that the temperamental poet really did love her, Alison goes to England, where she purchases a manor in which the memoirs may be hidden. She also ends up in the arms of Jeremy Ryder, an antique dealer on the same mission.

The novel takes place mostly in the present, with occasional re-creations of Byron's diaries. Jones has also written *The Scottish Rose*, a time-travel romance, among others.

Joyce, Brenda.

The Third Heiress. **St. Martin's Press, 1999. 408pp.**

As she cradles her dying fiancé in her arms after a car crash, Jillian Gallagher is devastated to hear him call her "Kate." Returning to his London home, Jill discovers a photograph of his grandmother and another woman, Kate Gallagher, an American heiress who disappeared in 1909. With the help of a handsome American tycoon, Jill pieces together Kate's puzzle, wondering if Kate could be her ancestor. Kate's own story is interspersed throughout by means of flashbacks to the early twentieth century.

 12

Lampitt, Dinah.

As Shadows Haunting. **Signet, 1995. 447pp.** ✍

Sidonie Brooks, a concert pianist in twentieth-century England, has been seeing visions of a woman from another time ever since she moved into her new home. Lady Sarah Lennox, whom everyone in eighteenth-century England thinks will be the chosen bride of George III, has been having a similar experience.

Morrison, Toni.

Beloved. **Knopf, 1987. 275pp.** ★

Annotated in Chapter 10.

Perry, Phyllis Alesia.

Stigmata. **Hyperion, 1998. 256pp.** 📖

After coming in contact with a quilt owned by her grandmother, Lizzie DuBose begins to relive her ancestor Ayo's horrific experiences on a slave ship and starts to physically manifest the outward signs of abuse at the hands of a cruel master. Flashbacks return her to earlier time periods. Lizzie doesn't know whether she's going crazy or experiencing past lives, and her parents fear for her sanity. She comes to terms with the past only by creating her own quilt connecting the generations. **Literary.**

Santangelo, Elena.

Pat Montella Series.

A mystery time-slip series set today and during the American Civil War.

By Blood Possessed. **St. Martin's Minotaur, 1999. 326pp.**

After sassy Italian-American Pat Montella learns that she will inherit Bell Run, an estate in Fredericksburg, Virginia, she travels south to meet its present-day owner, Magnolia Shelby, a spry ninety-one-year-old woman. Real estate developers have other plans for the land, of course, but Pat also needs to find out why Miss Maggie thinks she's the estate's rightful owner—and why she's seeing visions of a Civil War battle that happened back in 1863. Even worse, someone in the present day is trying to kill her.

Hang My Head and Cry. St. Martin's Minotaur, 2001. 322pp.

Pat Montella's abilities to see and hear ghosts from the past are back in full force in this sequel to *By Blood Possessed*, in which Miss Maggie and her neighbors turn up a dead body on her estate. This discovery causes Pat to experience the year 1870 through the eyes of a young former slave boy named Emancipation Jackson, who gradually reveals the circumstances behind the long-ago murder.

Ware, Ciji.

A Light on the Veranda. Ivy, 2001. 495pp.

Ware takes readers on a journey back into the past, as classical harpist Daphne Duvallon revisits Natchez, Mississippi, during the antebellum period. A sequel of sorts to *Midnight on Julia Street*, featuring some of the same characters, although both can be read independently.

Midnight on Julia Street. Fawcett, 1999. 470pp.

A modern-day New Orleans TV reporter sees visions of her ancestors and her acquaintances from 150 years earlier, and relives their dreams and passions.

Willis, Connie.

Lincoln's Dreams. Bantam, 1987. 212pp.

Jeff Johnston, researcher for a historical novelist, meets a young woman who has been having vivid dreams of the Civil War—from the perspective of Robert E. Lee. John W. Campbell Memorial Award.

Chapter 13

Alternate History

What if the South won the Civil War? What if the Roman Empire never fell? What if the Spanish Armada succeeded in invading Queen Elizabeth's England? Novels of alternate history (also called "alternative history") examine other possible outcomes for past events. The plots hinge on one particular event—a single military maneuver during a major battle, or the early death of a world leader—and imagine that it turned out differently than in real life. They follow this train of thought in detail, exploring how history might have changed as a result.

Whether alternate history fits as a true subgenre of historical fiction is up for debate. After all, these novels don't just bend the rules of the genre, they break them outright. The plots run counter to accepted historical fact, and they do so deliberately. In addition, historical fiction is set in the past by definition, while some alternate history novels are set in the present—albeit a very different version of it. For these reasons, some historical fiction readers won't touch alternate histories with a ten-foot pole.

On the other hand, the "what if" game is one frequently played by historians as well as historical novelists. Historians often ponder the reasons behind events and the causal relationships between them. To write plausible scenarios of alternate history, novelists not only have to know what really happened, but they also have to know the reasons people acted as they did. They must have a good grasp of the major players and their personalities, enough to be able to speculate how these people might have reacted when faced with alternative situations.

Alternate history novels will appeal to philosophically minded historical novel readers who enjoy pondering the causes and effects of historical events. They give people the opportunity to explore the supposed turning points of history and ponder how inevitable the outcomes really were. Like time-slip novels, alternative histories appeal to people's imaginations and curiosity. It's only human to think about what might have happened if one had the chance to go back and change something in the past. Changing even a seemingly small event could have had enormous repercussions—or it could have made no difference at all.

These works may be fast-paced and action-oriented (those that predict a different outcome to a battle), or they may be leisurely and literary (those based around religious themes). Either way, they are creative and thought-provoking. Readers who like alternate history novels may also appreciate nonfiction works on the same topic. Good places to start are *What If?* (Berkley, 2000) and its sequel *What If? 2* (Berkley, 2001), two essay collections in which prominent historians imagine what might have been. Both are edited by Robert Cowley, the founding editor of *Military History Quarterly.*

In libraries and bookstores, alternate histories tend to be categorized as either general fiction or science fiction. The latter is more typical, but a better catch-all term for them is "speculative fiction." Many appear under science fiction imprints (Baen, DAW, Del Rey) and are written by authors (Harry Turtledove, Harry Harrison) from the science fiction field. A classic example is Philip K. Dick's *The Man in the High Castle*, a Hugo Award winner about an alternative World War II. Short story anthologies are common, though this isn't the case with historical fiction in general.

Following are selected alternate history titles, organized first by historical locale and then by era or theme. Because the focus here is on history and historical plausibility, novels with obvious science fiction plot devices (aliens, modern technology in our historical past, far-future settings, etc.) are excluded. Time-travel alternate histories and "what ifs" for present-day events are also omitted, for the most part, though some anthologies mix these types of stories in with the rest.

World History

The novels in this category show how changing one major event in history might have had repercussions all over the world.

General

Conroy, Robert.
1901. **Lyford, 1995. 374pp.**

> In 1901, Kaiser Wilhelm wants to build an empire. After President McKinley refuses to give up Guam, Puerto Rico, Cuba, and the Philippines to the Germans, the Kaiser retaliates by invading the United States. When the Germans strike first along Long Island, America defends its homeland. An action-packed alternative military history adventure.

Robinson, Kim Stanley.
The Years of Rice and Salt. **Ballantine, 2002. 658pp.** 📖

> In this provocative and thoughtful novel, the divergence from history begins in the fourteenth century. In history, a third of Europe's population died of the Black Death, but what if 99 percent had been killed? With no Europeans to carry on the message of Christianity, the world's population becomes either Buddhist or Muslim. China colonizes the New World, and Asians are the world's greatest philosophers and inventors. Native Americans' roles on earth grow steadily throughout. Over millennia, three characters reincarnate into different historical periods. This

gives readers a grand overview of the place of religion and culture in history, and how individual people can influence historical change.

Stirling, S. M., ed.
Worlds That Weren't. ROC, 2002. 295pp.

A collection of four alternate history novellas. In "The Daimon," Harry Turtledove imagines that ancient Greek philosopher Sokrates accompanied Athenian general Alkibiades to war, with victorious results. S. M. Stirling's "Shikari in Galveston," set in the same universe as his novel *Peshawar Lancers* (not annotated) adds some science fiction elements with his tale of an alternate future Texas—what's left of it, that is, after asteroids destroyed the western United States in the nineteenth century. Walter Jon Williams places Frederick Nietzche in the American Wild West in "The Last Ride of German Freddie." Mary Gentle's "The Logistics of Carthage," a prequel to her science fiction/fantasy/alternate history series  The Book of Ash (Chapter 14), is set in a fifteenth-century, non-Muslim North Africa. The afterwords for each novella provide the "real" historical context without giving away too much.

World Wars I and II

Like adventure novels (Chapter 8) and thrillers (Chapter 9) set during World Wars I and II, these are fast-paced page-turners. How might the world have changed if events during either war had happened differently?

Deighton, Len.
SS-GB. Knopf, 1979. 343pp. ★

Many alternate history novels imagine a German victory in World War II, and this classic was one of the first to do so. It is 1941; Churchill is dead, Germany has won the Battle of Britain, and London is under Nazi occupation. America never comes into the picture at all. A simple murder investigation by Scotland Yard turns into something more sinister as police inspectors uncover a conspiracy involving the S.S. and the British monarchy.

Dick, Philip K.
The Man in the High Castle. Putnam, 1962. 239pp. ★

It is 1962, and America lost World War II in 1947. The country is now divided in two by the Nazis in the East and Japanese in the West. Not only can't they agree with each other on boundaries, but they may be going to war with each other over it. The Americans, living in a bleak, occupied country, feel oppressed and despondent—especially the Jews, who live in hiding. Different parts of the picture are told in overlapping stories. The ending is vague yet thought-provoking. It may seem odd to see Philip K. Dick, a prolific author of speculative and science fiction, in a guide to historical fiction, but this well-known novel is a classic regardless of the genre label. Hugo Award.

Gingrich, Newt, and William Fortschen.
1945. Baen, 1995. 382pp.

The authors' first collaboration (see also *Gettysburg* and *Grant Comes East*, under "The Civil War") imagines a world in which Hitler, injured and comatose after an airplane accident, did not declare war on the United States after Pearl Harbor. This leaves the United States as the only nation left to save the world from the power of the Third Reich. Though panned by critics because of its cartoonish characters and pompous prose, as well as the authors' habits of name-dropping prominent Republican politicians into the action, the novel has military action aplenty. The authors countered that the novel's poor reviews came from leftist-leaning critics from the science fiction world. The truth is left for readers to decide.

Harris, Robert.
Fatherland. Random House, 1992. 338pp. ★

This alternate history thriller begins in 1964, as Hitler is about to celebrate his seventy-fifth birthday. The Third Reich had won World War II twenty years earlier, and a state of cold war exists between the United States and Germany, rather than the United States and the Soviet Union. Just as U.S. President Joseph Kennedy (father of John F.) heads to Germany to meet with Hitler, police investigator Xavier March investigates a drowning in suburban Berlin. The victim is a high-level Nazi, and his death is ruled a suicide. March suspects otherwise, and he and American journalist Charlotte Maguire uncover a conspiracy leading them back to the dark days of the war.

Nagorski, Andrew.
Last Stop Vienna. Simon & Schuster, 2003. 288pp.

Karl Naumann, an average young Berliner in 1920s Germany, grows disillusioned with the country's political climate and joins Hitler's vigilante organization, which later becomes the notorious brownshirts. The Nazi party is divided between Hitler and his rivals, and Karl must decide where his loyalties lie. When he falls in love with Geli Raubal, Hitler's niece, he starts seeing the Führer through her eyes: as a sexual predator who must be stopped. This leads him to take his life, and history, into his own hands.

Niles, Douglas, and Michael Dobson.
Fox Series.

A military history series about World War II, featuring unlikely pairings of allies.

Fox on the Rhine. Forge, 2000. 397pp.

In 1944, Germany is losing the war, at least until Hitler is assassinated by his own generals. When Goering is also killed, Himmler takes over the Third Reich with the help of Rommel, who has survived his wounds in North Africa. Their alliance with the Soviets makes for a very different situation at the Battle of the Bulge and in the European theater as a whole.

Fox at the Front. Forge, 2003. 560pp.

Erwin Rommel has thrown in his lot with the Allies under George Patton, and together they construct a plan to head east and prevent Stalin's Soviet Union from invading Eastern Europe.

Roth, Philip.

The Plot Against America. **Houghton Mifflin, 2004. 391pp.** ✍

What if Charles Lindbergh ran for president against FDR in 1940 and won? This is the premise for Roth's novel, which describes a United States slipping uncontrollably into fascism. Roth tells the story from the viewpoint of himself as a young child, growing up in a Jewish family in Newark, New Jersey. As Lindbergh's influence takes hold, his anti-Semitic policies evoke fear and horror in Jewish communities nationwide, including Roth's. Thoughtful and more leisurely paced than other World War II–era alternate history novels, as it focuses on the home front rather than overseas action. **Literary.**

Stroyar, J. N.

The Children's War. **Pocket Books, 2001. 1157pp.**

More than fifty years after the Nazis won World War II, the Third Reich is as strong as ever. Peter Halifax, a young man captured for having "bad papers" who is tortured by a Nazi who treats him like a slave, becomes an unwitting part of the underground Polish resistance movement. The action parallels that of the real-life resistance during World War II. A very lengthy yet compelling portrait of a society degraded by tyranny.

Thomsen, Brian, and Martin Harry Greenberg, eds.

A Date Which Will Live in Infamy: An Anthology of Pearl Harbor Stories That Might Have Been. **Cumberland House, 2001. 348pp.**

Thirteen original short stories directly relating to December 7, 1941, the day Pearl Harbor was bombed by the Japanese. They fall into three categories: Alternate Architects (the catalysts behind the attack), Alternate Actions, and Alternate Aftermaths. Authors include Jim DeFelice, William Dietz, Brendan DuBois, Tony Geraghty, Ed Gorman, William Hallahan, Simon Hawke, William H. Keith Jr., Allen C. Kupfer, R. J. Pineiro, James Reasoner, and Barrett Tillman.

Turtledove, Harry.

These three series follow one upon the other and are listed in their appropriate reading order.

The Great War Series.

This military history series follows *How Few Remain* (later in this chapter), which imagines that the South won the Civil War. Now it's World War I, and the United States and Germany unite to fight the threat posed by the combined forces of Britain, France, and the Confederacy.

Turtledove's novels are populated by a large cast of characters, showing the action from nearly all angles.

The Great War: American Front. Del Rey, 1998. 503pp.

All the technology of the Great War is the same here as in history, only now the war is fought on American soil. As Britain and France fight Germany in Europe, the Confederacy and the Union, on opposite sides, battle it out in America. Theodore Roosevelt is President of the United States, while Woodrow Wilson leads the Confederacy.

The Great War: Walk in Hell. Del Rey, 1999. 484pp.

In 1915, a Marxist rebellion brews among former slaves of the Confederacy, something that the United States in the north will use to its advantage.

The Great War: Breakthroughs. Del Rey, 2000. 486pp.

The United States, using newly developed weapons technology, finally gets a chance to win against its twice-victorious southern neighbor.

American Empire Series.

Turtledove's next series, set in an alternate post–World War I period, follows immediately upon his three Great War novels. While the focus is mainly North America, the author also covers worldwide political changes. Most of the characters from the previous series show up again. As in the 1920s and 1930s in history, most of the action here is an obvious lead-up to World War II, but a vastly different one.

American Empire: Blood and Iron. Del Rey, 2001. 503pp.

Teddy Roosevelt is President of the United States, and the defeated and bankrupt Confederacy seethes with anger and discontent. Peace is status quo for now, but many people would rather return to war. Farther north, the Canadians try to avoid being colonized by the United States. Paralleling what really happened in 1920s Germany, a land broken down by defeat after World War I, a fanatical Hitler figure named Jake Featherston emerges from the Deep South.

American Empire: The Center Cannot Hold. Del Rey, 2002. 503pp.

Between 1924 and the end of the decade, cities throughout North America and Europe are being rebuilt. Canada has become a U.S.-occupied territory. The Socialists are winning political power in the United States, while in the Confederacy, the fascist Freedom Party gains ground.

American Empire: The Victorious Opposition. Del Rey, 2003. 496pp.

Jake Featherston, elected leader of the Confederacy, has in mind a different sort of Holocaust; in this version of history, the victims are African Americans. Now that the United States is busy trying to quell a bloody rebellion in occupied Canada, Featherston hopes that they will be distracted from the war he hopes to launch against them.

Settling Accounts Trilogy.

Sequel builds upon sequel in this continuation of Turtledove's American Empire series. Two more volumes are forthcoming.

Return Engagement. Ballantine, 2004. 640pp.

The Confederacy, under Jake Featherston, continues its policies of genocide against African Americans and begins launching attacks against Washington, D.C.. U.S. President Al Smith's best hope lies in an untried administrator named Franklin Roosevelt.

The Roman Empire

The power and grandeur of ancient Rome has inspired many historical novelists. But what if Rome never fell, or what if it was conquered before the Roman Empire even began?

Bradshaw, Gillian.

Cleopatra's Heir. Forge, 2002. 447pp.

In history, Caesarion, the son of Julius Caesar and Cleopatra, was assassinated as a teenager by forces loyal to Octavius, his father's successor and grand-nephew. What if Caesarion managed to survive his cousin's death threats by hiding out underground? No longer heir, Caesarion finds a way to deal with his epilepsy—his father's legacy—and discovers a new kind of happiness with lower-class Egyptian people.

Roberts, John Maddox.

Hannibal's Children. Ace, 2002. 359pp.

What if Hannibal succeeded in conquering Rome during the Second Punic War in the third century BC? As conditions of Rome's surrender to Carthage, Romans head into exile up north, where they form their own empire. A century later, descendants of the exiled Romans launch a campaign against the victor's descendants—"Hannibal's children"—to get their country back. For fans of military history.

Silverberg, Robert.

Roma Eterna. EOS, 2003. 396pp.

Imagine that the Eternal City of imperial Rome has endured for two millennia. Silverberg traces the fictional history of this alternate empire in increments by showing what life was like in ten different historical periods. Christianity wasn't this Rome's downfall, because the Jews never escaped Egypt in the first place. Now, in an alternate present-day scenario, Rome has crushed or conquered nearly all of the world's peoples, but a new group called the Hebrews may be both the future and the downfall of the Empire.

Europe and the British Isles

Major events in European history—the Viking invasions of the British Isles, the repulse of the Spanish Armada by England, and others—are given new interpretations.

Harrison, Harry.

Hammer and the Cross Series. ★

A dark and somewhat grim alternate history set in ninth-century England and Europe, a world in which the Vikings never converted to Christianity. The pace is swift, and Harrison's detailed explorations of the conflicts between cultures and religions in these so-called Dark Ages are fascinating. Some fantasy elements: Shef communicates with his gods, and they talk back.

The Hammer and the Cross. Tor, 1993. 414pp.

The Vikings are pillaging England, just as they did in history. When several of England's native kings are killed, the land and its peoples are divided between the greedy Christian church and Norse paganism. Shef Sigvarthsson, a blacksmith and bastard Viking who is a Dark Ages technological genius, discovers a more peaceful way of life and worship.

One King's Way. Tor, 1995. 399pp.

Despite being co-king of the English, Shef would rather go back to being a blacksmith. He takes his large, newly built navy and heads north for exploration and to defend England. Here he meets a group of priests dedicated to the Way, a more civilized form of the pagan Norse religion. Along the way he is pursued by the Knights of the Lance, a fanatical group who want to bring back the Holy Roman Empire.

King and Emperor. Tor, 1996. 384pp.

Shef, now king of the North, watches his religion (the Way) win out over the intolerant religion of Christianity, but the newly resurrected Roman Empire won't let that stand. Together Rome and Byzantium bring in a number of new inventions to help them conquer all of northern Europe.

Kinsolving, William.

Mister Christian. Simon & Schuster, 1996. 380pp. ✍

Fletcher Christian is infamous for his role as the chief mutineer on the H.M.S. *Bounty* on its South Pacific voyage in 1789. In 1810, an inmate in an English insane asylum claims to be Christian, who is apparently not dead at all. He narrates his adventure-filled life from the time he escaped Pitcairn Island. In his story, he returns to England, falls in love with a beautiful duchess, and fights in the Napoleonic Wars.

Leys, Simon.

The Death of Napoleon. Farrar Straus & Giroux, 1992. 129pp. ✍

In this literary alternative history novella, Napoleon manages to escape from his exile at St. Helena in 1815. After sneaking in for an up-close view of the Battle of Waterloo, he returns to France and, in disguise, discovers the joy of the simple life. When he reveals his true identity to the woman who takes him in, of course she doesn't believe him. **Literary.**

Roberts, Keith.
Pavane. **Doubleday, 1968. 279pp.** ★

This classic series of linked stories (six novelettes and a "coda") set in twentieth-century England has the premise that Queen Elizabeth I was assassinated in 1588. The Spanish Armada was successful, meaning that Catholicism triumphed in England. Over time, the Catholic Church hasn't relaxed its anti-scientific stance or its repressive policies, but scientific development happens nonetheless. It is a dark, atmospheric book that imagines how society marches forward through the bleakest of times. The novel's pace takes on characteristics of the title, "pavane," a slow, stately dance of interconnected pieces.

Turtledove, Harry.
Ruled Britannia. **New American Library, 2002. 458pp.**

As in *Pavane*, above, Turtledove's novel presumes the Spanish Armada's victory over Queen Elizabeth's England. Nine years later, in 1597, Roman Catholicism rules the day, and Isabella, daughter of Philip II of Spain, rules the country with her Austrian consort. While Elizabeth I languishes in the Tower of London, her supporters convince young Will Shakespeare to write a play about Boudica, the ancient Queen of the Iceni who rose up against her country's Roman oppressors.

The Americas

These novels recount alternate scenarios for events in North American history, from major events, such as the Civil War and the growth of the Western frontier, to religious and social changes sparked by a single individual.

General

Major events on the American continents turn out vastly different, with political and societal implications for all concerned.

Barnes, Steven.
Lion's Blood Series.

Barnes's novels reverse the roles of master and slave in the Civil War-era South. Not only are they thought-provoking explorations of the history of slavery and the meaning of race, but they also pose questions about Christian–Muslim relations today.

Lion's Blood. Warner, 2002. 461pp.

Imagine a world in which Carthage conquered Rome, and Allah's prophet Bilal convinced the Islamic world to colonize North America. Over a thousand years later, the year is now 1863—at least in Christian terms. The nation of Bilalistan occupies what we know as the American South. To the north is a Viking empire; to the south, the country of the Aztecas. The wealthy plantation owners of Bilalistan are Islamic men of African descent. Their slaves are white men and women captured from Europe by the Vikings and brought to the American South in chains. When slavers destroy an Irish village, a young boy named Aidan arrives in the New World via slave ship, gets sold to a plantation, and befriends Kai, his master's son. Their friendship may not stand the test of time, though, after the whites organize a rebellion.

Zulu Heart. Warner, 2003. 463pp.

Continuing where *Lion's Blood* left off, in an alternate late nineteenth-century America, Kai and Aidan are now grown men. Kai, a wealthy plantation owner, has freed his former slave. Aidan lives out West but doesn't find life easy. Even worse, civil war is about to break out between two ethnic groups of Bilalistan, the Ethiopians and the Egyptians, and Kai and Aidan are caught in the middle.

Blom, Suzanne Alles.

Inca: The Scarlet Fringe. **Forge, 2000. 352pp.** ✍

What if an Incan prince managed to start a rebellion against the Spanish in sixteenth-century Peru? Prince Atahualpa, called Exemplary Fortune in this novel, sees his chance to save his people from conquest and subjugation by Spanish Conquistadors—and takes it. He learns Spanish war tactics from a captured Spaniard and plans to use these new techniques against the invaders, but his enemies will do anything to discredit him. Each chapter begins with a few sentences that explain what really happened in history. The book's cliffhanger ending may disappoint, for it reads as if a sequel had been planned.

The Civil War

The U.S. Civil War (1861–1865) is the most common setting for alternate history novels. This demonstrates how the impact of this long-ago war still resonates with both historians and the American public. What might have happened if a single commander had acted differently, or if the North had lost just one more battle? Might the Confederacy have won?

Gingrich, Newt, and William Fortschen.

Gettysburg Series. ✍

An alternate history of the Civil War, which imagines a Confederate victory at the Battle of Gettysburg.

Gettysburg. St. Martin's Press, 2003. 463pp.

More successful and more widely praised than the authors' previous effort (*1945*, earlier this chapter), *Gettysburg* follows the traditional Civil War history up to July 1863. In this alternative scenario, General Lee succeeds in rebuffing Union forces at the Battle of Gettysburg, which leads to triumph for the South. The military strategies are well-researched, logical, and believable.

Grant Comes East. St. Martin's Press, 2004. 404pp.

After victory at Gettysburg, Lee decides to march on Washington, D.C., and finish off the Union once and for all—even if it means weakening his armies beyond repair. It also means ultimately defeating President Lincoln, who is determined to preserve the Union whatever the cost. Lincoln orders his best general, Ulysses S. Grant, to come east to confront Lee.

Harrison, Harry.

Stars and Stripes series.

An alternative Civil War in which Great Britain gets involved and declares war against the United States. Though it is one of the more creative interpretations of events, Harrison's Americans are a little too perfect, and his British are stereotypically evil and incompetent. This sets up an obvious scenario for war, but Anglophiles will undoubtedly be offended.

Stars and Stripes Forever. Del Rey, 1998. 338pp.

In November 1861, the Civil War is in full swing when a Union ship seizes two Confederate officers bound for Great Britain. They plan to seek outside help for the Southern cause. In history, Britain's Prince Albert prevented his country from taking revenge on the Union Navy, but in Harrison's version, Albert dies before he can defuse the situation. Tensions mount, and when a military accident leads Britain to invade the Confederacy as well, the North and South unite to defeat their common foe.

13

Stars and Stripes in Peril. Del Rey, 2000. 322pp.

It is 1863, and Britain sees its chance to finally triumph against America and possibly win back territory it lost during the Revolution. When Britain decides to attack America's Pacific coast, the United States gets even by attacking Ireland.

Stars and Stripes Triumphant. Del Rey, 2003. 256pp.

The Americans have won the war against Britain, and Britain has turned against Canada and Ireland, both of which are now free nations. After Britain interferes once too often in American trade, then rounds up the Irish populace and transports them to camps, America decides to invade England.

Kantor, MacKinlay.

If the South Had Won the Civil War. Bantam, 1961. 112pp. ★

The title of this slim volume says it all. After Grant's early death, the North is defeated at Gettysburg, President Lincoln is captured by the Confederates, and the South wins the Civil War. With its footnotes and asides, Kantor's version reads like a cross between a novel and a well-researched history text. First published in *Look* magazine in 1960; reprinted by Forge in 2001.

King, Benjamin.

A Bullet for Stonewall. **Pelican, 1990. 267pp.** ✍

On the night of May 2, 1863, the famous Confederate general Jonathan "Stonewall" Jackson was accidentally shot by his own men. King presumes that Stonewall's death was really an assassination planned and carried out by the Union.

McIntire, Dennis P.

Lee at Chattanooga. **Cumberland House, 2002. 276pp.** ✍

The Battle of Chattanooga, in which Braxton Bragg and the Confederate forces were soundly defeated, was a turning point in the Civil War. Would the war have ended differently if Confederate President Jefferson Davis had sent Robert E. Lee to Chattanooga? McIntyre's battle scenes are realistic and plausible, as is his analysis of what might have happened.

Skimin, Robert.

Gray Victory. **St. Martin's Press, 1988. 378pp.**

The South has won the Civil War and established a new country: the Confederate States of America (CSA). Confederate President Jefferson Davis has a military court look into General J. E. B. Stuart's conduct at the Battle of Gettysburg, which resulted in a Northern victory. Stuart's trial coincides with the plans of Southern blacks and Northern abolitionists to assassinate a number of high-ranking Confederate officials.

Thomsen, Brian, and Martin H. Greenberg, eds.

Alternate Gettysburgs. **Berkley, 2002. 342pp.**

The requirements of these twelve original short stories are very specific: What if the Battle of Gettysburg, one of the most famous battles of the Civil War, had turned out differently? Authors include Doug Allyn, Harold Coyle, Jim DeFelice, Brendan DuBois, Jake Foster, Simon Hawke, William R. Forstchen, William H. Keith Jr,, Denise Little, Robert J. Randisi, and Kristine Kathryn Rusch. Four nonfiction essays on Gettysburg (and the text of the Gettysburg Address) conclude the volume.

Turtledove, Harry.

How Few Remain. **Del Rey, 1997. 474pp.**

It is 1881. Sixteen years earlier, the South won the Civil War thanks to General Lee's brilliant military campaigns. Now the United States declares war against the Confederacy once again, this time because of the Confederates' purchase of the states of Chihuahua and Sonora from the Mexican Empire (which still exists). When the North decides to invade the South, England and France join the war on the side of the Confederacy. Several notable historical figures play major roles: Samuel Clemens runs a socialist newspaper in San Francisco, George Custer defends the North/South border in the frontier West, and he and Teddy Roosevelt try to drive the British back into Canada. The pretext of this novel continues in the author's <u>Great War and American Empire</u> series (both above, under "World Wars I and II") , though only a few of the characters from this book are carried over.

Wild West and Native Americans

The U.S. government's poor treatment of Native Americans in the nine-teenth-century West has inspired novelists to imagine alternative scenarios, ones with a more positive outcome.

Page, Jake.

Apacheria. **Del Rey, 1998. 342pp.**

> It is 1884. The United States thinks it can bring the disruptive Apache tribes into line, but it hasn't counted on the military genius of two Apache men, Juh and his son Little Spring. Under their guidance, the Apaches of the Southwestern United States form their own nation, Apacheria, whose members have enough political savvy to challenge the most skilled politicians in Washington.

Sargent, Pamela.

Climb the Wind. **HarperPrism, 1999. 436pp.**

> In this pro-Native American version of an alternate America set just after the Civil War, white men intent on driving Indians off their native lands move steadily westward, but some men assigned to destroy the Cheyenne end up joining the tribes instead. This leads to a strong Indian movement that may yet have enough power to form its own nation—and possibly conquer the existing one.

Skimin, Robert.

Custer's Luck. **Herodias, 2000. 297pp.** ✍

> In 1876, George Armstrong Custer was killed along with all of the 7th Cavalry at the Battle of the Little Big Horn. What might have happened if Custer's luck had held out? Here he not only wins the battle, but he runs for president in 1880 and wins. In the meanwhile, Red Elk, a Sioux Warrior who has never recovered from the humiliation of the battle and the death of his pregnant wife, plots revenge against the man he calls "Long Hair."

An American Miscellany

Additional alternate history novels set in the Americas, ones with narrower scope: they focus on a single person rather than widescale historical changes.

Ackroyd, Peter.

Milton in America. **Nan A. Talese, 1997. 307pp.** ✍

> What if John Milton never wrote *Paradise Lost*? Imagine that the blind poet/philosopher left the licentious court of Restoration (seven-teenth-century) England for America in search of religious freedom. Here, he founds a Puritan settlement and, ironically, preaches against the Catholic beliefs of a nearby colony. Over time, he becomes a tyrant and bigot whose religious intolerance leads to his downfall. **Literary.**

Mann, William J.

The Biograph Girl. **Kensington, 2000. 457pp.** ✎

In 1910, Florence Lawrence was the world's first movie star, attracting larger crowds than even the president. In 1938, depressed over her faltering career, she committed suicide. Mann imagines that the real-life Florence faked her death and lived out her old age in a Buffalo, New York, rest home. It is here, in 1997, that the filmmaking Sheehan brothers find a feisty 106-year-old woman with sharp memories of early Hollywood. Florence, an entertaining narrator, recalls the details of her long life, from her childhood in vaudeville to her years as the celebrated Biograph Girl, the leading lady of numerous silent films.

The Middle East

Turtledove, Harry.

Agent of Byzantium. **Congdon and Weed, 1987. 246pp.** ★

It is an alternate fourteenth century. The prophet Muhammad converted to Christianity centuries earlier, so the Byzantine Empire still stands. In this series of seven connected stories, Basil Argyros, a Byzantine spy, manages to invent or come across a series of new technological developments, from gunpowder to vaccinations.

Chapter 14

Historical Fantasy

This chapter includes historical novels that contain elements of the fantastic: magic, supernatural powers, mythical creatures, and more. Because historical novels depend so much on accurate renderings of past events, it may seem strange to include historical fantasy as a subgenre. Obviously, accuracy isn't an absolute requirement here. Like many examples of genre-blending, these novels bend the rules a little. Historical novelists always combine their research with a good amount of creativity, and in historical fantasy, they explore their imaginations in greater depth.

The historical fiction and fantasy genres have much in common. Both make use of detailed and vividly rendered settings that offer readers the opportunity to slip into another world. Like traditional historical novels, fantasy novels tend to be long books, and they frequently occur in series. Pacing is leisurely, at least in the beginning, but readers quickly become engrossed in the storylines. There is also considerable crossover in terms of both authors and readers, and novels in this chapter bridge the gap. A recent survey of subscribers to *Locus*, a major trade magazine for the fantasy/science fiction field, revealed that 31 percent of its respondents frequently read historical fiction (September 2003, p. 34). A number of popular authors (Judith Tarr, Ann Chamberlin, Morgan Llywelyn, and others) write in both genres.

Novels in this chapter are set firmly in a historical period and reflect the customs of the time. Historical events are included in the story, either as a major part of the plot or as a backdrop. On the fantasy side, both the protagonists and villains make use of magic to achieve their ends. The characters may have the ability to speak with gods and goddesses, or they may be partly divine themselves.

As in most fantasy novels, the plots of historical fantasy revolve around a battle between good and evil—or, put another way, light and dark. As in most heroic tales, the good guys usually win in the end. The roles of light and dark tend to be based on the cultures or religions of the historical period in question, but which one is "good" and which is "evil" can vary. In Stephen R. Lawhead's Pendragon Saga, Christianity is the force of light, but in Marion Zimmer Bradley's classic *The Mists of Avalon*, the protagonists struggle against the encroaching influence of Christianity on a mystical, Goddess-ruled Celtic world.

Much historical fantasy centers on characters from myth and legend, such as heroes from Greek mythology, King Arthur and his entourage, ancient Norse or Irish warriors, and mystical figures from medieval times such as Joan of Arc and the Knights Templar. Other authors use the conventions of myth and legend and build original stories around them. Nearly all historical fantasy novels are set in a pre-industrialized period in the British Isles or Europe. Modern settings exist but aren't common, since they can't always convey the otherworldly atmosphere required by fantasy.

Sometimes the line between historical fiction and fantasy is hard to define. Persia Woolley's Guinevere novels (Chapter 2) contain no magical elements, but readers and librarians often classify them as fantasy because they are based on Arthurian legend and feature characters that may or may not have been historical figures. On the other hand, Rosalind Miles' fantastical Guenevere trilogy (this chapter), which has scenes of enchantment and Celtic rituals, is just as often called historical fiction.

This chapter is organized by subcategories based around cultures (Celtic, Norse) or historical periods (medieval, Renaissance) that have similar characteristics. In general, books that use "alternate" versions of historical settings, such as Orson Scott Card's Alvin Maker series of alternate America, aren't included here. Readers who enjoy these novels, as well as fantasy in general, will want to explore the subject in more depth in Diana Tixier Herald's *Fluent in Fantasy* (Libraries Unlimited, 1999). Time-slip novels (Chapter 12), which include supernatural plot devices, may also be worth investigating.

Fantasy of the Ancient World

Many fantasies set in the ancient world—Greece, Rome, Egypt, and Mesopotamia—take classical myths about powerful heroes from long ago and retell them for a modern audience, with a bit of creative license thrown in. Gods and goddesses get involved in characters' personal lives, affecting history along the way.

Boyd, Donna.
The Alchemist. Ballantine, 2002. 240pp.

Dr. Anne Kramer, a modern-day psychotherapist, is paid a visit by a charismatic man who claims to have committed the greatest crime of his day. He then explains why. As a youth in ancient Egypt, he belonged to the House of Ra. With two other adepts, he unleashed a force of magic so powerful that it changed the course of history.

Bradley, Marion Zimmer.
The Firebrand. Simon & Schuster, 1987. 608pp.

Bradley recounts the story of the Trojan War from the point of view of Kassandra, the tormented Princess of Troy who was cursed with a gift of prophecy. Daughter of Hecuba, a former Amazon tribeswoman, Kassandra grows up believing in the power of matriarchy, but she is forced to live in a world where only men reign. As the Greeks fight with the Trojans for supremacy, the gods on Mount Olympus manipulate everyone to their own ends.

Douglass, Sara.

The Troy Game.

This complex series, of which there will be four volumes in all, traces connections among the Trojan War in ancient times, the founding of Britain by Brutus, the warrior king of Troy, and Britain's role during World War II.

Hades' Daughter. Tor, 2003. 592pp.

Ariadne, Princess of Crete and Mistress of the Labyrinth, takes revenge on her lover Theseus for abandoning her after she gives birth to a daughter. When she undoes the Labyrinth in her grief, it throws the world into chaos. A hundred years later, Brutus, great-grandson of Aeneas, heads to Albion (Britain) to rebuild Troy in all its former glory. When he marries an Eastern princess against her will, one of Ariadne's descendants waits in the wings to take revenge on the Trojan warrior whose ancestor destroyed hers.

Gods' Concubine. Tor, 2004. 557pp.

It is now eleventh-century England, and the Labyrinth constructed by Brutus has turned into London. Brutus has been reincarnated as William, Duke of Normandy, and the rivalry between him and Harold—the two heirs of Edward the Confessor—plays out once again.

Grundy, Stephan.
Gilgamesh. Morrow, 2000. 571pp.

As warrior-king of the Mesopotamian city of Erech circa 2700 BC, Gilgamesh is both revered and feared. When he fails to provide for the good of his people, the priests ask the gods to send him someone who is his equal in all respects—a wild man called Enkidu. He and Gilgamesh become the best of friends as well as lovers, and when Gilgamesh's shortsightedness causes Enkidu's death, he travels to the ends of the earth to bring him back to life. A retelling of the ancient *Epic of Gilgamesh.*

Llywelyn, Morgan, and Michael Scott.
Etruscans. Tor, 2000. 334pp.

It is the sixth century BC. As the city of Rome grows in size and stature, the civilization of the Etruscans, the land's current inhabitants, is declining. Vesi, an Etruscan noblewoman, is raped by a demon and bears him a child. The boy, Horatrim, journeys to Rome, where he discovers that his demon father is out to kill him. Adopted by a Roman who changes his name to Horatius, the boy travels to the ends of the earth to rescue his mother, who has been kidnapped and held hostage in hell.

Tarr, Judith.

Queen of the Amazons. **Tor, 2004. 320pp.**

Hippolyta, Queen of the Amazon clan living in eastern Persia, has given birth to a talented but unusual daughter. Her tribes claim that the girl, named Etta, has no soul. Selene, the niece of the Amazons' seer, becomes her guardian, but not even Selene can stop Etta from running away to see Alexander, the valiant Macedonian conqueror who fights to rule the known world.

Wolfe, Gene.

Latro Series.

Ever since he was injured in battle, Latro, a "barbarian" soldier in Xerxes's army in ancient Greece, has woken up every morning with no memory of his past. He records everything in a daily journal to keep track of what he experiences. His travels and adventures throughout the ancient world make up the plots of both books. To make up for his constant amnesia, Latro is given the ability to speak with gods, and their observations are amusing and astute. Latro's accounts are rambling but also fascinating, particularly in his portrayal of Greece as seen by someone discovering it anew each day. Republished as the single-volume *Latro in the Mist.*

Soldier of the Mist. Tom Doherty Associates, 1986. 335pp.

Soldier of Arete. Tom Doherty Associates, 1989. 354pp.

Arthurian Fantasy

Arthurian fantasies are magical tales set in the mists of Britain's so-called Dark Ages, circa the fifth or sixth centuries AD, after the Romans have abandoned the island and before the Saxons have taken control. In most versions, King Arthur appears as the hero of legend, a great king who manages to unite the warring Celtic tribes for a brief time against Saxon invaders. Included as part of the overall legend are the quest for the Holy Grail, a moral tale marked with Christian symbolism, and the tragic love story of Tristan and Iseult, whose romance began with the drinking of a magical love potion. Authors incorporate fantastical elements in the powers of the great sorcerer Merlin, Arthur's mentor, and the evil necromancy of Morgause and Morgan le Fay, alternately described as Arthur's sisters or aunts. Arthurian fantasies will appeal to readers who enjoy magical, heroic tales of love, honor, and chivalry. Many have romantic elements that appeal to readers, especially women. Because of this, fans may wish to investigate traditional historical novels (Chapter 2) and romantic novels (Chapter 4) set during the early Middle Ages.

Borchardt, Alice.

Tales of Guinevere.

In Borchardt's action-packed Arthurian fantasies, Guinevere is the strong-willed daughter of a pagan warrior queen.

The Dragon Queen. Del Rey, 2001. 473pp.

When her magical powers start to pose a threat to Merlin, the High Druid, young Guinevere is sent into hiding. Growing up in the wild, mysterious world of post-Roman Britain, dragons and wolves are her companions. Her special protector is the shape-shifter Maeniel, a main character from the author's <u>Wolf Series</u> about Dark Ages Gaul (later, this chapter).

The Raven Warrior. Del Rey, 2003. 470pp.

Guinevere, Queen of the Dragon People, leads her people into battle against the invading Saxons, but her sub-commanders refuse to acknowledge a woman as war leader. Her childhood friend, the shape-shifter Black Leg (the future Lancelot), has his own adventures in the South with the Lady of the Lake before reuniting passionately with Guinevere.

Bradley, Marion Zimmer.

The Mists of Avalon. Knopf, 1982. 876pp. ★ YA

Bradley's heroine is Morgaine ("le Fay"), daughter of Igraine of Avalon and her first husband, Gorlois of Cornwall. Trained by her aunt Viviane in the art of being a priestess, Morgaine learns how to lift the mists separating the otherworldly land of Avalon from the Isle of Glastonbury, the site of a Christian monastery. Morgaine's rival throughout her life is Gwynhwyfar, a beautiful Christian woman fostered at Glastonbury as a child. While Morgaine struggles between her love for men and her love for Avalon, Gwynhwyfar's ever-deepening religiosity leads Arthur to abandon his beliefs in the Goddess in favor of his wife's religion, to his and Avalon's downfall. The late Marion Zimmer Bradley's decision to retell Arthurian legend from a feminine viewpoint was ingenious and, at the time, wholly original. Not only did it shed a new light on the religious and gender implications of the traditionally male-dominated story, but her complex, beautifully characterized novel became one of the bestselling fantasy novels of all time.

Bradshaw, Gillian.

<u>Gawain Trilogy.</u> YA

Gwalchmai, the "Hawk of May," throws in his lot with his cousin Arthur rather than follow in his mother Morgawse's footsteps as a master of the Black Arts. Arthur doesn't entirely trust his motives, so Gwalchmai must prove his loyalty time and again, especially when Morgawse, Arthur's stepsister, incites a plot to kill Arthur. Medraut, Arthur's son by Morgawse, becomes the king's nemesis, continually coming between him and his wife Gwynhwyfar. Merlin doesn't play a role here, and the battle between Dark and Light can be seen as the historic conflict between paganism and Christianity.

Hawk of May. Simon & Schuster, 1980. 313pp.

Kingdom of Summer. Simon & Schuster, 1981. 283pp.

In Winter's Shadow. Simon & Schuster, 1982. 379pp.

James, Cary.

King and Raven. Tor, 1995. 384pp.

A revisionist look at the Arthurian legend, set in the thirteenth century. Micah of Greenfarm, a peasant with the nickname "Raven," vows revenge after four of King Arthur's drunken knights rape his sister. His journey takes him to the royal court, where he becomes a witness to Lancelot's affair with Guinevere, and to France, where he travels with the wizard Merlin's help. Everywhere he goes, he can't help but notice the contrasts between the wealth of Camelot and his own lowly station.

Jones, Courtway.

Dragon's Heirs trilogy. YA

In fifth-century England, the remnants of Roman civilization mix uneasily with the land's new-found Christianity and its previous druid practices. Jones gives an anthropological bent to his magical Arthurian trilogy with vivid descriptions of the cultures that made up early Britain.

In the Shadow of the Oak King. Pocket Books, 1991. 290pp.

Arthurian legend from the point of view of Pelleas, King Arthur's bastard half-brother.

Witch of the North. Pocket Books, 1992. 302pp.

Morgan, Arthur's beautiful half-sister, marries the King of the Picts and sets up her own kingdom in the north of Britain.

A Prince in Camelot. Pocket Books, 1995. 367pp.

Mordred, Arthur's bastard son, grows up as "Dylan the Orphan," a boy unaware of his heritage.

Lawhead, Stephen R.

Pendragon Cycle. ★ YA

In Lawhead's hands, Arthurian legend becomes a spiritual tale of magic, adventure, good versus evil, and the triumph of Christian faith. Arthur is a devoted Christian king, and his wife Gwenhwyyvar is faithful to him. At the same time, the novels aren't romanticized or chivalrous in the least; they're set in a grim, realistic sixth-century Britain populated by barbarian chieftains. A sixth and last novel, *Avalon* (Avon, 1999), not historical at all, is set in a future Britain where King Arthur returns to save the modern monarchy from evil. The first three books, first appearing from Christian publisher Crossways, were re-released by Avon in the mid-1990s. Lawhead also writes historical adventures and traditional historicals, as well as epic fantasy.

Taliesin. Crossway Books, 1987. 452pp.

In ancient Atlantis, the druid prince Taliesin falls in love with Charis, princess of that mysterious land, and begets upon her a child named Merlin.

Merlin. Crossway Books, 1988. 445pp.

The aged Myrddin (Merlin), immortal and slightly mad, tells of his journey from warrior to bard to advisor of kings.

Arthur. Crossway Books, 1989. 446pp.

With Myrddin's help, young Arthur rises to greatness.

Pendragon. Morrow, 1994. 436pp.

In a dark and bleak age, Arthur, the Bear of Britain, must stand alone against the Irish and Vandals while Myrddin revisits ghosts from his past.

Grail. Avon, 1997. 452pp.

Gwalchavad (Galahad) narrates a tale in which Morgain, Queen of Air and Darkness, and the disappearance of the Holy Grail both threaten the kingdom.

McKenzie, Nancy.

Arthurian Series.

All four volumes contain a worthwhile mix of chivalry, fantasy, and romance, enlivened by strong and likable characters.

The Child Queen. Del Rey, 1994. 295pp.

Guinevere narrates this and the next volume of this Arthurian tale (republished together as *Queen of Camelot*). Loyal and happily married to her husband Arthur despite loving Lancelot, Guinevere does her best to hold the kingdom and Arthur's family together.

The High Queen. Del Rey, 1995. 439pp.

Acknowledging she will never bear her husband a child, Guinevere brings his bastard son Mordred to court. Mordred betrays Arthur, but Guinevere is herself betrayed by a member of her own family, her jealous cousin Elaine, who seduces and marries Lancelot.

Grail Prince. Del Rey, 2002. 528pp.

The "Grail Prince" is Lancelot's son Galahad, who follows prophetic dreams on a quest for the Holy Grail, only to realize that he searches for something found only within himself.

Prince of Dreams. Del Rey, 2004. 416pp.

Decades after the fall of Camelot, Arthur's enemies move in to destroy his former kingdom. Tristan of Lyonesse is sent by his uncle Markion, King Constantine's heir, to retrieve Markion's bride Essylte. Tristan and Essylte fall in love, risking everything to be together—even Britain's future.

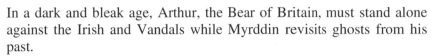

Miles, Rosalind.

Guenevere Trilogy.

Miles's Guenevere, daughter of the Queen of the Summer Country, is the latest in a long line of female rulers who follow the religion of the Goddess. Miles's feminist message comes through in her depiction of the male-dominated Christian church and its hostility to other religions.

Guenevere, Queen of the Summer Country. Crown, 1998. 424pp.

After her mother dies, Guenevere must reclaim her birthright, but can only do so with the help and love of Arthur Pendragon.

The Knight of the Sacred Lake. Crown, 2000. 417pp.

The enchantments of Arthur's half-sisters, Morgause and Morgan, tear away at the strong kingdom that Arthur and Guenevere have built together, as does Guenevere's love for a young French prince named Lancelot.

The Child of the Holy Grail. Crown, 2001. 432pp.

Christianity has become a dominant influence at court, leading to its downfall. Even worse, most of Arthur's knights have abandoned their king to follow Lancelot's son Galahad in search of the Holy Grail. This leaves Arthur's bastard son Mordred to his own evil treachery.

Isolde Trilogy.

In this continuation of Miles's extended series about strong Celtic women, Miles portrays the legendary Isolde as Guenevere's friend and companion. She is also the strong-willed daughter of the Queen of Ireland—a matriarchal land where the Goddess reigns supreme. Miles's smooth storytelling and feminist sensibilities will appeal to women readers.

Isolde, Queen of the Western Isle. Crown, 2002. 432pp.

Princess Isolde's mother, who would rather spend her days in the act of love than in ruling her people, lets her lover Sir Marhaus goad her into invading Cornwall. This leads to Isolde's arranged marriage with the buffoonish King Mark of Cornwall, though her heart belongs to Mark's nephew Tristan of Lyonesse.

The Maid of the White Hands. Crown, 2003. 432pp.

Miles adds originality to the mix with her creative portrayal of Isolde's rival and namesake Isolde of France, called "Blanche Mains" for her white hands. Blanche loves Tristan from afar and will do anything to make him hers, but Isolde won't give him up willingly. Readers expecting the usual tragic ending of the legend have some surprises in store.

The Lady of the Sea. Crown, 2004. 432pp.

Isolde's kingdom of Ireland is beleaguered from within and without. Picts from the north threaten to invade, while some of her treacherous courtiers weaken the traditional mother-right to rule. Without Tristan to rely upon, Isolde turns to the Lady of the Sea for help.

Newman, Sharan.

Guinevere Trilogy. **YA**

Newman's is one of the first modern retellings of the Arthurian legend from Guinevere's point of view. The daughter of a Roman family in Britain, Guinevere grows up in her own fantasy world, adored by all, including a unicorn. Her world is shattered when Saxons kill her older brothers, but she finds peace and contentment in a political marriage to Arthur. Guinevere, a true survivor, lives through the usual intrigues at court, including a fleeting passion for Lancelot plus Modred's betrayal. Unlike many others, she grows wiser through her life experiences.

Guinevere. St. Martin's Press, 1981. 256pp.

The Chessboard Queen. St. Martin's Press, 1983. 296pp.

Guinevere Evermore. St. Martin's Press, 1985. 277pp.

Paxson, Diana L.

The Hallowed Isle Quartet. **YA**

In four slim volumes (later republished as two), Paxson goes back to the original roots of the Arthurian legends. It all begins in the early fifth century, when the Romans have withdrawn from the British Isles. Artoria Argantel, a druid priestess, calls out for a champion worthy of taking up the sword and uniting her warring country. This king is, of course, King Artor (Arthur). What makes Paxson's story unique is her decision to retell the Arthurian legend from the points of view of four tribal cultures that impacted fifth-century Britain: the Romans, the Saxons, the Celtic worshippers of the Old Religion, and the Gauls.

The Book of the Sword. Eos, 1999. 181pp.

The Book of the Spear. Eos, 1999. 200pp.

The Book of the Cauldron. Eos, 1999. 180pp.

The Book of the Stone. Eos, 2000. 192pp.

The White Raven. Morrow, 1988. 409pp. **YA**

Branwen narrates the story of her cousin Esseilte (Iseult), the beautiful daughter of Ireland's High King. Esseilte falls in love with Drustan (Tristan), not realizing that he is the man who killed her beloved uncle Morholt in battle. Though Drustan succeeds in arranging a marriage between Esseilte and his uncle Marc'h, King of Kernow, he and Esseilte fall in love after accidentally drinking a love potion meant for her wedding night with the king. Branwen, queen of the hidden Celtic realm, emerges as the stronger female character when she falls in love with Marc'h herself and proves to be more level-headed than her lovesick cousin. Marion Zimmer Bradley's influence shows in Paxson's interpretation of the Tristan and Iseult legend, set against the conflict between druidic paganism and Christianity of the sixth century.

Radford, Irene.

Guardian of the Balance. DAW, 1999. 529pp.

Arylwren, called Wren, was born of a single night of passion between Myrddin Emrys, the Merlin, and Deirdre, high priestess of the druids. She grows up in her father's shadow, accompanying him on his journeys around Britain as apprentice healer and mage. Their charge is to guard the land and prevent either Christianity or other evil forces from taking hold against the old ways. Although she falls in love with her father's ward Curyll, she has a difficult life, married to a cruel man whom she hates. Radford's characters are hard to care for, but she adds some creative touches to an otherwise worn-out storyline. This is the first volume of the author's Merlin's Descendants series (continued in the medieval and Renaissance sections).

Roberson, Jennifer, ed.

Return to Avalon. DAW, 1996. 398pp.

Roberson, the author of many fantasy and historical novels, compiled this Arthurian short story anthology in honor of Marion Zimmer Bradley. Although most don't hinge on Bradley's *Mists of Avalon* at all, they deal with similar subjects, such as the conflict between Celtic paganism and Christianity. Authors include Diana Paxson, Katharine Kerr, Judith Tarr, Laura Resnick, Melanie Rawn, Dave Wolverton, and Esther Friesner.

Stewart, Mary.

Arthurian Saga. ★ YA

Set in fifth-century Britain, this classic series was based on two medieval sources for Arthurian lore, Geoffrey of Monmouth's *History of the Kings of Britain* and Malory's *Morte d'Arthur*. The novels are tightly written, with multifaceted characters and authentic dialogue that give a realistic feel for the period. The first three volumes are told from the viewpoint of legendary sorcerer Merlin.

The Crystal Cave. Morrow, 1970. 529pp.

The illegitimate son of a Welsh princess, Merlin grows up with the gift of prophecy, which leads him to High King Vortigern and sets him on the path to becoming a royal advisor.

The Hollow Hills. Morrow, 1973. 402pp.

During the reign of Uther Pendragon, prophet Merlin Ambrosius guards the future King Arthur, preparing for the day that Arthur can take up the sword Caliburn and the rule of a kingdom.

The Last Enchantment. Morrow, 1979. 439pp.

Arthur has become king, but foul sorceries—which result in an incestuous liaison with his scheming half-sister Morgause—threaten the future of Camelot. Merlin falls in love with the sorceress Nimue, which leads to his own downfall.

The Wicked Day. Morrow, 1983. 314pp.

Mordred, son of King Arthur and his half-sister, the witch Morgause, never intends to be Arthur's doom, but fate turns against him. A sympathetic portrait of this often maligned character.

Celtic Fantasy

Celtic fantasy novels feature myths and traditions of the Celtic peoples, tribal cultures that lived in the British Isles, all of Western Europe, and lands as far south as Galatia (modern Turkey) from the first millennium BC through the eighth or ninth centuries AD. Frequent topics include the heroic adventures of ancient Celtic warriors, who had the ability to speak with the gods; protagonists' use of magic to prevent invasion by Rome; and the turbulent relationship between earth-based religions and Christianity. Fantasy authors tend to play up the matriarchal aspects of Celtic society, which makes the novels appealing to women. However, the religious rituals frequently owe more to modern paganism than to any ancient tradition. Because some Celtic fantasies are set in post-Roman Britain (fifth or sixth centuries AD), and because many novelists imagine King Arthur as a great Celtic king, there will be some crossover between this and the previous section. In addition, readers will want to investigate traditional historical novels set in prehistoric Europe and Asia (Chapter 2), such as those written by Judith Tarr.

Bradley, Marion Zimmer.

Avalon Series. **YA**

The novels of Bradley's series, completed by novelist Diana Paxson after her death, are mystical works that juxtapose the male-dominated world of ancient Rome against the matriarchal Celts of her imaginary world of Avalon. They can all stand alone, but most readers will want to read *Mists of Avalon* first.

The Forest House. Viking, 1994. 416pp.

Eilan, the clairvoyant daughter of a goddess-worshipping druid in first-century Britain, is chosen to become a priestess of the Forest House. Though she falls in love with half-Celtic, half-Roman soldier Gaius Marcellius, their romance is forbidden. By the time Eilan is selected to be High Priestess, she has another big secret to keep.

Lady of Avalon. Viking, 1997. 460pp.

In Roman Britain, the efforts of three heroic women pave the way for goddess worship in the mystical land of Avalon as well as the coming of King Arthur. The first, Caillean, seals the land of Avalon away from the mortal (Christian) world and fosters the boy-child Gawen, son of Eilan and Gaius from *The Forest House.* Dierna, one of her successors as Lady of Avalon, falls in love with a man she cannot have, and two centuries later, the lady Ana gives birth to five daughters—including Viviane, Igraine, and Morgause—destined to play great roles for Avalon and in *The Mists of Avalon.*

The Mists of Avalon. Knopf, 1982. 876pp.

Annotated under "Arthurian Fantasy."

Priestess of Avalon. Viking, 2001. 394pp. Completed by Diana L. Paxson. ✍

In AD 259, Helena, a ten-year-old British princess, returns to her birthplace of Avalon and reassumes her birth name, Eilan. She becomes a powerful priestess, foreseeing the man she will eventually marry—the Roman Constantius—and the son they will have together, who will be known as Constantine the Great. A fantastical biographical novel of St. Helena, whose own history is largely unknown.

Marion Zimmer Bradley's Ancestors of Avalon. Viking, 2004. 363pp. Written by Diana Paxson.

This prequel to the Avalon series begins in the sea kingdom of Atlantis just before its destruction. Tiriki, high priestess on an Atlantean island, realizes that it's time for her people to begin a new life in the British Isles. She and her lover, Micail, establish separate settlements and try to keep their spiritual beliefs alive, but Damisa, one of Tiriki's acolytes, proves to be a dangerous rival.

Eickhoff, Randy Lee.
Ulster Cycle. `YA`

Eickhoff's works are translations of ancient Irish tales that together are known as the Ulster Cycle. Brought to life for a modern audience, the novels feature heroic men, strong women, brave warriors, and vengeful gods and goddesses, all told with colorful, raw, occasionally bawdy prose. The setting is pre-Christian, Iron Age Ireland, and the author weaves cultural elements of the era into each story. Dr. Eickhoff is a scholar who also writes Western historical novels.

The Raid. Forge, 1997. 283pp.

A translation of the epic *Tain bo Cuailnge*, "Cattle Raid of Cooley," in which the King and Queen of Connacht argue about who is wealthier. This leads to Queen Maeve's attempt to steal a magical bull from the Ulstermen. The warrior hero Cuchulainn defends Ulster against invaders from Connacht.

The Feast. Forge, 1999. 254pp.

Cuchulainn's story continues with this translation of the *Fled Bricrend*, where the trickster Bricriu stages a competition among the warriors of Ulster.

The Sorrows. Forge, 2000. 284pp.

Three stories: "The Fate of the Children of Tuirenn," in which three brothers seek forgiveness for killing their clan's enemy; "The Fate of the Children of Lir," the original "swans" myth in which an evil stepmother turns her four stepsons into swans; and "The Exile of the Sons of Usnech," the tragic story of Deirdre, Naisa, and the end of the Red Branch warriors.

The Destruction of the Inn. Forge, 2001. 238pp.

Conaire Mór, King of Erin, struggles to keep the land safe from his jealous foster-brothers.

He Stands Alone. Forge, 2002. 224pp.

The continued adventures of Cuchulainn, starting from his childhood, including his romance with gentle Emer.

The Red Branch Tales. Forge, 2003. 400pp.

A series of interconnected stories about the Irish warriors of Ulster, including another retelling of Queen Maeve of Connacht's theft of a brown bull (told in *The Raid*).

Guler, Kathleen Cunningham.

Macsen's Treasure series.

Romantic historical fantasy adventure set in the pre-Arthurian period.

Into the Path of Gods. Bardsong, 1998. 413pp.

In the fifth century, a Welsh spy named Marcus ap Iowerth and his clairvoyant lover, Claerwen, join forces to uncover a conspiracy preventing a Celtic high king from claiming the throne of Britain.

In the Shadow of Dragons. Bardsong, 2001. 379pp.

Marcus and Claerwen's latest quest leads them to uncover the treasure of Britain's ancient rulers.

Isidore, Sarah.

Daughters of Bast Trilogy. **YA**

This unusual trilogy mixes Celtic and Egyptian mythologies with quirky yet entertaining results.

The Hidden Land. Avon Eos, 1999. 373pp.

In Gaul at the time of Julius Caesar, a young Celtic woman named Veleda possesses the power of the Egyptian cat goddess Bast. She uses it to unite her people against Roman invaders, who are protected by Bast's dark sister, Sekhmet.

Shrine of Light. Avon Eos, 2000. 352pp.

Damona is the last remaining priestess of Bast in fifth-century Eire (Ireland) at a time when pagan religions are being overcome by Christianity. When the power of Bast deserts her, Damona turns to evil goddess Sekhmet—and lives to regret it.

The World Tree. Avon, 2001. 384pp.

Back in Gaul under the reign of Charlemagne in the ninth century, Bast's last priestess, a healer named Sirona, calls upon all of her powers to prevent the old religion from dying out.

Llywelyn, Morgan.

Morgan Llywelyn has chronicled Irish history from its mythical past through the twentieth century. Here she humanizes the heroes of two of Ireland's greatest myths and places both tales in a historical context.

Finn MacCool. **Forge, 1994. 400pp.** `YA`

In the third century, legendary poet-hero Finn MacCool becomes the leader of Ireland's first army, the Fianna, the fierce fighting force of King Cormac MacAirt.

Red Branch. **Morrow, 1989. 558pp.** `YA`

Iron Age Ireland: This is the life story of the Ulster warrior Cuchulain, of magical birth, and his legendary adventures—which include saving his homeland from destruction by a cattle raid instigated by Queen Maeve of Connaught. A similar tale is recounted in Randy Lee Eickhoff's Ulster Cycle.

Marillier, Juliet.

Sevenwaters Trilogy. `YA`

Marillier's trilogy is set in a mystical ninth-century Ireland, in which the Irish Celts are battling Briton invaders for control of the country. The land's two main religions, a pagan earth magic and early Christianity, meet and mingle. The first volume retells a Celtic legend, but the second and third volumes are original. All have elements of romance.

Daughter of the Forest. Tor, 2000. 400pp.

Sorcha of Sevenwaters and her six elder brothers, children of a wealthy landholder, grow up under the watchful eye of the Lady of the Forest. After their father's new wife Oonagh turns the six young men into swans so that her own future children can inherit, it is left to Sorcha to break the spell by weaving them shirts of nettle. Lovers of Celtic lore will recognize the traditional "Swans" myth in this story, yet Marillier includes a unique twist in the form of Sorcha's love interest.

Son of the Shadows. Tor, 2001. 462pp.

The three children of Sorcha and her British husband, Hugh, continue the tale of the Sevenwaters family. They are Sean, the heir; Liadan, a gifted healer whose destiny lies with one of her family's enemies; and the fey Niamh, who secretly loves a young druid with mysterious connections to her family.

Child of the Prophecy. Tor, 2002. 528pp.

Fainne, daughter of the sorcerer Ciaran and his lost love Niamh, must decide whether to use her powers for good or evil. On one side are the druids of Sevenwaters, her mother's people, who provide her with the family environment she's never known. On the other is her grandmother, the sorceress Oonagh, who uses Fainne as a tool in her attempt to banish the Fair Folk from Ireland forever.

Osborne-McKnight, Juilene.
Bright Sword of Ireland. **Forge, 2004. 304pp.**

Finnabair, plain daughter of the beautiful Queen Medb of Connaught, strikes back when she learns that her mother made her the prize in a game. Medb desires the power of the Brown Cow of Cuailnge for herself. To get it, she promises Finnabair's hand to whoever kills the warrior-boy Cuchulainn in battle. Though crushed by the deaths her mother has wrought, Finnabair survives all to become a peacemaker for her people.

***Daughter of Ireland.* Forge, 2002. 300pp.**

Third-century Ireland is a predominantly pagan land, one not yet conquered by Christianity, but change is on the way. Aislinn ni Sorar, a druid priestess, joins with Eoghan, a poet and Fianna warrior, to protect the reign of Cormac Mac Art and his decision to follow the one true God. Battling against them are druids who hope to keep the Old Ways alive at any cost.

Paxson, Diana L.

***The Serpent's Tooth.* Morrow, 1991. 402pp.**

Paxson sets her retelling of Shakespeare's *King Lear* in Iron Age Britain, around the fifth century BC, and turns the legendary story into a clash of patriarchal and matriarchal tribes. Leir Blatonikos, chieftain of the Quiritani (Celts), has subdued the native tribes by force and by marrying three of their queens. By them he has three beautiful and strong-willed daughters, though only the youngest, Cridilla, is completely loyal to him. Because she only tells him the truth rather than the lies he would prefer to hear, he exiles her out of distrust.

Tolstoy, Nikolai.

***The Coming of the King.* Bantam, 1989. 630pp.**

Merlin is the hero of Tolstoy's massive Celtic fantasy novel set in mid-sixth-century Britain. While it will appeal to readers of Arthurian legend for this reason, in this version Arthur lived two generations before Merlin and isn't even a character. The novel looks back to Britain's mystical past to uncover the original roots of the Celtic legend, and makes no attempt to modernize character or place names. The author, a descendant of Leo Tolstoy, also incorporates elements of the Welsh epic *The Mabinogion* as well as the Anglo-Saxon poem *Beowulf.* Though meant to be the first of a trilogy, subsequent volumes haven't been published.

Norse Fantasy

Norse fantasies, based on the *Nibelungenleid* and other legendary Old Norse sagas, are set in Scandinavia and other Germanic lands in early medieval times. They call to mind a great age of brave Viking warriors and their forebears as well as the brave, beautiful maidens who loved them and occasionally fought alongside them. Many Norse fantasy novels are centered on war, and for this reason, they appeal to readers who like a touch of gritty realism in their fantasy. Magical elements arise as the gods and goddesses in Valhalla get involved in earthly battles.

Anderson, Poul.

***Mother of Kings.* Tor, 2001. 444pp.**

Annotated in Chapter 2.

Godwin, Parke.

The Tower of Beowulf. Morrow, 1995. 246pp. **YA**

In sixth-century Scandinavia, the young warrior named Beowulf has been disowned by his father. Atoning for his sins by attaching himself to King Hrothgar, Beowulf vows to rid him of the monster who has been terrorizing Hrothgar's hall and killing his men. Grendel, in his defense, has his own reasons for his despicable acts, which makes him a surprisingly sympathetic character. A retelling of the Anglo-Saxon poem *Beowulf.*

Grundy, Stephan.

Rhinegold. Bantam, 1994. 719pp.

This retelling of Wagner's Ring Cycle, based itself on the Norse Volsunga Saga, is set firmly in the fifth century. Two warrior clans, the Saxon Walsings and the Burgundian Gebicungs, joined by Wodan's blood, vie with each other over a legendary hoard of gold.

Marillier, Juliet.

Saga of the Light Isles.

A duology of fantasy novels covering the Viking invasion of the Orkney Islands (the "Light Isles") in the eighth century, and the Norsemen's encounters with the native Pictish tribes. Despite the violent clash of cultures that must have occurred, the author's prose is gentle and descriptive, in keeping with her depiction of the Picts' nature-based religion.

Wolfskin. Forge, 2003. 493pp. ✍

Eyvind and Somerled, blood brothers, lead separate lives as adults: while Eyvind becomes the Wolfskin warrior he always wanted to be, Somerled becomes a courtier. Far away, on the Orkney Islands, Nessa of the Folk trains as a priestess. When Eyvind and Somerled are brought back together on a voyage to the Light Isles, it becomes ever clearer what Somerled's plans for the land entail—and Eyvind's previously sworn bond begins to weigh heavily on his soul.

Foxmask. Forge, 2004. 464pp.

Eyvind and Nessa have lived peacefully on the Orkney Isles for the last ten years and more, while Somerled was sent into exile. A young man named Thorvald discovers that he is Somerled's true son and sets out on a quest to learn more about his disgraced father. Creidhe, Eyvind's daughter, loves Thorvald and secretly accompanies him.

Paxson, Diana.

Wodan's Children Trilogy.

Paxson has retold a number of ancient myths and legends in her historical fantasy novels, and this trilogy, set in fifth-century Germania, is based on the classic Norse saga, the *Nibelungenlied,* made famous by Wagner's operas. Worship of the ancient gods rivals the new teachings of Christianity. In Paxson's version, Brunahild is a princess of the Huns and her tragic lover Sigfrid, a shamanic warrior. The novels are less gritty and more fantastic than Stephan Grundy's

Rhinegold (above) and *Attila's Treasure* (Chapter 2), also based on the Norse sagas.

The Wolf and the Raven. Morrow, 1993. 320pp.

The Dragons of the Rhine. Morrow, 1995. 371pp.

The Lord of Horses. Morrow 1996. 373pp.

Medieval Fantasy

These novels are set amid the courts of medieval Europe, but not quite as we know them. Their heroes are men and women with supernatural abilities who manipulate politics from behind the scenes. Settings can vary and may include the British Isles, Europe, and the Middle East (including Byzantium) between the fifth and fifteenth centuries. In keeping with an age in which life was short and difficult, the tone is serious and sometimes dark. Many aspects of medieval times—such as people's belief in miracles, witchcraft, and sorcery—can seem mystical to modern readers. In medieval fantasy novels, these elements truly do become magical.

Borchardt, Alice.

Wolf Series.

Regeane, a young woman living in eighth-century Rome, has the ability to assume wolf shape. Her abilities are both a blessing and a curse, and she struggles to find balance between her female and wolf selves. These are sensual novels told with a touch of the supernatural, as might be expected from an author who is Anne Rice's sister, but they're more romantic and less creepy than those written by Rice herself.

 14

The Silver Wolf. Del Rey, 1998. 451pp.

Regeane's corrupt uncle wants to marry her off appropriately to suit her royal blood. Her destined bridegroom, Maeniel, is a barbarian lord who is keeping his own dark secrets. They become embroiled in the power struggles pervading Charlemagne's empire.

Night of the Wolf. Del Rey, 1999. 454pp.

In this prequel of sorts to *The Silver Wolf*, Maeniel, a gray wolf in Rome during the days of Caesar, discovers how to live with his shape-changing abilities. He becomes a man when he learns the power of love.

The Wolf King. Del Rey, 2001. 375pp.

As Charlemagne's armies cross the Alps in the hopes of adding Lombardy to his holdings, Regeane goes on a mission to rescue her soul-mate Maeniel, who has been captured by Desiderius, King of the Lombards.

Bradshaw, Gillian.

The Wolf Hunt. **Forge, 2001. 380pp.**

Marie Penthièvre, heiress to the Norman lands of Chalandrey in twelfth-century France, falls in love with a noble Breton knight, Tiarnán of Talensac, who rescued her from abduction by outlaws. But Tiarnán falls in love with someone else, a fickle young woman who marries his rival after Tiarnán is reported dead. When a tame wolf with uncanny powers appears in the village, Marie is quick to discover the truth about its true identity. Based on one of the *lais* (poems) of Marie de France.

Chamberlin, Ann.

Joan of Arc Tapestries. ✍

Fifteenth-century France, torn apart by warring Burgundians, Frenchmen, and the English, is the scene for this magical tapestry based on the story of Joan of Arc. The mysterious voices Joan (Jehannette) hears, however, come not from the God of Christianity but from the gods of an ancient pagan religion. Chamberlin's Merlin isn't the famed magician from King Arthur's court, but someone else entirely. *Gloria* will be the next volume.

The Merlin of St. Gilles' Well. Tor, 1999. 320pp.

A young Breton peasant boy named Yann, crippled by an arrow struck by Guy de Rais, begins seeing visions of a young girl who will lead the French to victory. Guy's son Gilles—one day to be known as Bluebeard—is raised alongside Yann in the Old Religion.

The Merlin of the Oak Wood. Tor, 2001. 333pp.

In 1425, France is suffering under years of war and English occupation. Gilles de Rais waits patiently for La Pucelle ("the virgin") to appear, but time is running out. In the novel's second half, Jehannette d'Arc doesn't understand the voices she hears. Yann—now the Merlin—knows that she will emerge as La Pucelle, the savior of her people.

Douglas, L. Warren.

The Sorceress's Tale.

This epic fantasy trilogy, set in Provence between the eighth and tenth centuries AD, includes elements of time travel and alternate history.

The Sacred Pool. Baen, 2001. 402pp.

Pierrette, an apprentice mage, wants to become a great sorceress to avenge her mother's murder. If she doesn't succeed, the Black Time will arrive, or so it is foretold in visions Pierrette sees in a sacred pool.

The Veil of Years. Baen, 2001. 336pp.

Watching history change before her eyes, Pierrette realizes that to put things right, she must travel back in time to when Provence was still a part of Rome.

The Isle Beyond Time. Baen, 2003. 448pp.

The goddess of the sacred pool directs Pierrette to journey to Armorica to kill the sorcerer king, Minho of the Fortunate Isles, whom she had expected to marry.

Gentle, Mary.

The Book of Ash.

In fifteenth-century Burgundy, France, a young woman named Ash grows up in a brutal military camp and becomes a mercenary leader destined to protect and defend her homeland. Like Joan of Arc, she hears voices that give her advice on military strategy. Unlike St. Joan, however, the voices are not divine but something entirely different. The books are full of brutal battlefield scenes and vividly depict the lives of soldiers in medieval armies. Ash's story is framed by words of her manuscript's "translator," Dr. Pierce Ratcliff, who intersperses footnotes and notes of correspondence within Ash's story. Some science fiction elements are present. The series, written as a single novel and published as such in Britain (original title: *Ash: A Secret History*), was divided into four parts in the United States due to its massive length.

A Secret History. Avon/EOS, 1999. 424pp.

Carthage Ascendant. Avon/EOS, 2000. 432pp.

The Wild Machines. Avon/EOS, 2000. 400pp.

Lost Burgundy. Avon/EOS, 2000. 464pp.

Jakober, Marie.

The Black Chalice. **Ace, 2002. 480pp.**

In medieval Germany, a monk named Paul von Arduin is compelled by sorcery to write the truth about his past adventures with nobleman Karelian Brandeis. After returning victorious from the Crusades, Karelian insists on passing through the forest of Helmardin en route to his wedding, despite warnings from his comrades about sorcery. In fact, an enchanted, pagan castle lies within, and its owner, a beautiful half-human, half- eela female named Raven, has deliberately lured Karelian there. Karelian, whose sexual attraction to Raven cannot be denied, must decide between Raven and his vows to his feudal lord. His choice embroils all of Germany in near civil war.

Kurtz, Katherine, and Deborah Turner Harris.

Temple Series.

The mystical Knights Templar become embroiled in Scotland Wars of Independence (late thirteenth to early fourteenth centuries).

The Temple and the Stone. Warner Aspect, 1998. 456pp.

Scotland's Robert Bruce and William Wallace fight for their country's freedom from English dominance. Torquil Lennox and Arnault de Saint Clair belong to the Cercle, a secret organization within the Knights Templar. With the help of magic, they try to restore the powers of the famous Stone of Destiny and vanquish England for good.

The Temple and the Crown. Warner Aspect, 2001. 542pp.

France and England have both turned against the Templars. Arnault de Saint Clair and his Scottish compatriot, Torquil Lennox, band together again to prevent members of the Order of the Black Swan—led by Edward I of England and Philip IV of France—from capturing sacred relics and beating Robert Bruce at the Battle of Bannockburn.

Radford, Irene.

Guardian of the Trust. DAW, 2000. 462pp.

In early thirteenth-century England, rebellion is stirring amongst the nobles, but King John's power is unbreakable so long as he is controlled by the spells of his wicked half-brother. It is up to Resmiranda Griffin, descendant of both King Arthur and Merlin, to banish this evil from the realm. This interesting interpretation of the Magna Carta's origins is volume 2 of the <u>Merlin's Descendants</u> series (also listed under "Arthurian Fantasy" and Tudor and Renaissance Fantasy") .

Shwartz, Susan.

An unnamed series set in medieval Byzantium, written by a well-known fantasist.

Shards of Empire. Tor, 1996.

After the Battle of Manzikert in 1071, at which Byzantium was defeated by the Turks, nobleman Leo Ducas befriends Emperor Romanus, though his family betrays the emperor again and again. When he leaves Constantinople, Leo meets up with a shape-shifter in disguise and a beautiful Jewess, among others, and discovers how to use magic to help fight the Turks.

Cross and Crescent. Tor, 1997.

In this sequel to *Shards of Empire*, the armies of the First Crusade threaten to be as dangerous to Byzantium as the Turks were. Binah, the daughter of Leo Ducas and his magic-wielding wife, befriends and instructs Emperor Alexius's daughter, Anna Comnena, who is a little too ambitious for her own good.

Tarr, Judith.

<u>Alamut Series.</u>

Set in the same world as the <u>Hound and Falcon trilogy</u>, below, this romantic duology sees more clashes between the Christians and Saracens in the Holy Land in the twelfth century.

Alamut. Doubleday, 1989. 470pp.

While in search of his nephew's killer, Prince Aidan, of the elven kingdom of Rhiyana in Wales, falls in love with the Saracen assassin Morgiana.

The Dagger and the Cross. Doubleday, 1991. 474pp.

Lovers Aidan and Morgiana, Christian and Muslim, try to reconcile their religious beliefs, but treachery prevents their marriage.

Hound and Falcon trilogy. ★ YA

A serious yet tenderly romantic trilogy set in Wales and England during the reign of Richard the Lion Heart, and in Byzantium during the Fourth Crusade (early thirteenth century). Later reprinted as the omnibus *Hound and Falcon.*

The Isle of Glass. Bluejay, 1985. 276pp.

Nobody knows for sure that pious Brother Alfred of St. Ruan's Abbey in Ynys Witrin, Wales, is one of the immortal fairy folk, but his youthful appearance has always raised suspicion. Fate steps in when a messenger from the Elvenking asks Alf to intervene in a religious war between England and the Welsh kingdom of Gwynedd. Alf also denies his attraction to Thea, a strong-minded Greek woman with elven blood, for he has taken a vow of chastity.

The Golden Horn. Bluejay, 1985. 262pp.

Alf and Thea arrive in Constantinople, the city on the Golden Horn, only to find it in flames, destroyed by the armies of the Fourth Crusade. Together they try to heal the wounded city. Danger surrounds them; if anyone from the Church discovers their magic, they may be burned as witches, but if the Saracens capture them, they'll be tortured and put to death as traitors.

The Hounds of God. Bluejay, 1986. 344pp.

Now the parents of twins, Alf and Thea return to Rhiyana, the elven kingdom, to raise their children. When a sorcerer captures Thea and the babies and turns them into wild beasts, only Alfred can save them—if he can work his magic while avoiding the wrath of the Church and its hounds of God.

Kingdom of the Grail. **ROC, 2000. 456pp.**

This volume intertwines Arthurian legend with the *Song of Roland.* In the eighth century, centuries after the fall of Camelot, the wizard Merlin remains imprisoned in the forest of Broceliande. Roland, a young warrior with magical abilities, comes upon his ancestor one day and swears to free him. Years later, Roland has become a knight at Charlemagne's court. The consequences of his past oath lead him to romance with a Saracen magician, Sarissa, and a fight with a demon who has beguiled Charlemagne's son.

Richard the Lionheart Series. ✍

A fantastical trilogy set against the Third Crusade to the Holy Land in the late twelfth and early thirteenth centuries. England's King Richard the Lionheart and his Saracen nemesis Saladin both make appearances. Tarr plays with both magic and history; the historical King Richard died in 1199.

Pride of Kings. ROC, 2001. 451pp.

Richard the Lionheart has just been crowned King of England, but he soon heads off on Crusade, leaving his kingdom defenseless against dark magic. Stepping into his shoes is his brother, Prince John, whom history will remember as a traitor who tried to steal Richard's throne. But John's motives are good, and with the help of a magical French youth named Arslan, he fights for the realm against the kingdom's ghostly enemies.

Devil's Bargain. ROC, 2002. 387pp.

It is 1192, and in the Holy Land, Richard the Lionheart is fighting the armies of Saladin during the Third Crusade. Richard's mother, Queen Eleanor, has made a devil's bargain with the sorcerer Sinan: In exchange for Richard's victory, Sinan and the dark lords he serves will be granted Richard's soul. Sioned, Richard's bastard half-sister, arrives to save Richard with her own brand of Celtic magic, but she is torn between helping him and being with the man she loves, Saladin's brother Ahmad.

House of War. ROC, 2003. 376pp.

In the early thirteenth century, Richard has been crowned King of Jerusalem, but his old foe Sinan has returned to torment him. Only Richard's half-sister Sioned, heiress to both Welsh and Angevin magic, can defeat Sinan once again.

Turtledove, Harry.
Thessalonica. **Baen, 1997. 408pp.**

In Thessalonica, Greece, in the seventh century, a humble shoemaker named George finds he needs more than his Christian beliefs to keep the invading Slavs and Avars at bay. For help he turns to the land's native centaurs and satyrs. Byzantine scholar Turtledove also writes alternate histories under his real name and historical sea adventure novels as H. N. Turteltaub.

Tudor and Renaissance Fantasy

Like those set in medieval times, fantasies of the Tudor era (England) and the Renaissance (rest of Europe) feature characters who work their magic around a royal court. Here the tone is lighthearted and whimsical, for the most part, in keeping with this more enlightened age.

Goldstein, Lisa.
The Alchemist's Door. **Forge, 2002. 286pp.** ✍

John Dee, the master of English alchemy during the reign of Elizabeth I, mistakenly unleashes an evil demon on the world. To escape its threats, Dee and his family relocate to Prague. There he meets Rabbi Judah Loew, a mystic who is attempting to create a *golem* (man of clay) to protect the city's Jewish quarter from the soldiers of Rudolf, the Holy Roman Emperor, a master of the black arts. The novel is sketchy on details of the magic but fairly sound historically. Frances Sherwood's *The Book of Splendor* (Chapter 10) is another novel set in this unusual locale.

Hoyt, Sarah A.

Shakespearean Fantasy Trilogy.

In these playful fantasies, young William Shakespeare, not yet the famous playwright, has several encounters with the fairy realm that influence his play *A Midsummer Night's Dream.* Interspersed throughout Hoyt's novels are bits of storyline and dialogue borrowed from the Bard himself.

Ill Met by Moonlight. Ace, 2001. 278pp.

When his wife Nan and baby daughter Susannah are kidnapped by the fairies, Will must enter the elven realm to rescue them. Quicksilver, the rightful elf king, aids him in his quest.

All Night Awake. Ace, 2002. 311pp.

Quicksilver comes to Will's rescue when he is accused by Christopher Marlowe of conspiring against Queen Elizabeth.

Any Man So Daring. Ace, 2003. 336pp.

When his son Hamnet disappears, Will suspects Quicksilver of kidnapping him, but the real culprit is the usurper king of Fairyland.

Maguire, Gregory.

Mirror Mirror. ReganBooks, 2003. 279pp. 📖

Maguire, who retold the Cinderella legend in *Confessions of an Ugly Stepsister* (Chapter 10), sets his version of the Snow White story in fifteenth century Tuscany. While Cesare Borgia sends her father off on a fool's errand, the beauty of the young Bianca de Nevada arouses the jealousy of Cesare's evil sister Lucrezia. Bianca evades Lucrezia's plot to kill her by hiding out in a forest under the protection of seven dwarves.

McIntyre, Vonda N.

The Moon and the Sun. Pocket, 1997. 421pp.

At his court of Versailles in seventeenth-century France, the Sun King, Louis XIV, celebrates fifty years on the throne. Having made France the glory of Europe, the king wants to discover the secret of immortality. When his philosopher, Father Yves de la Croix, returns to the court with a pair of sea creatures, one alive and one dead, the king yearns to test whether the living one is an immortal being. Yves's sister Marie-Josephe sees the creature's humanity and fights to protect it from harm.

Radford, Irene.

Merlin's Descendants.

Other volumes of this ongoing series, *Guardian of the Balance* and *Guardian of the Trust*, are listed under "Arthurian Fantasy" and "Medieval Fantasy." In keeping with the previous volumes, these two novels, with their scenes of bloody violence, are darker than most fantasies of Elizabethan England.

Guardian of the Vision. DAW, 2001. 519pp.

Amid the deadly rivalry between cousins Elizabeth I and Mary, Queen of Scots, twins Donovan and Griffin Kirkwood, heirs to Merlin's power, fight a demon of Chaos.

Guardian of the Promise. DAW, 2003. 544pp.

After Griffin Kirkwood abandons magic to become a Catholic priest, his brother Donovan, in love with Mary, Queen of Scots, tries to avoid Queen Elizabeth's wrath. In the meanwhile, the brothers' children journey to France, where they encounter anti-Protestant sentiment and supernatural animals.

Roessner, Michaela.

Catherine de'Medici trilogy. ✍

Florence, Italy, in the 1530s: Behind the scenes, occult forces are shaping the political destiny of Europe's great houses. Interspersed with the magic, astrology, and political intrigue of the novels are a number of delicious Italian recipes. The last volume has yet to appear.

The Stars Dispose. Tor, 1997. 383pp.

Tommaso Arista, the son of the Medici family's chef, whips up culinary delights for eleven-year-old Caterina. The young heiress, who would rather marry her cousin Ippolito than be married off to the heir of France, confides her fears in her personal maid, Tommaso's sister Ginevra.

The Stars Compel. Tor, 1999. 430pp.

Caterina grows up to become a great sorceress, and with Tommaso's help, she battles against her political fate.

Miscellaneous British and European Fantasy

A miscellany of fantasy novels set in other periods of British or European history, seventeenth through nineteenth centuries.

Brust, Steven, and Emma Bull.
Freedom and Necessity. Tor, 1997. 443pp.

This is a suspenseful historical fantasy/murder mystery/epistolary novel set in England in 1849 , and it's as complex as this brief description suggests. James Cobham, who has been presumed to have drowned, writes to his cousin Richard to announce that he is alive but has lost his memory of the past two months. With the help of another cousin, proto-feminist Susan Voight, he gradually reconstructs his past and investigates who may have tried to murder him. Their trail leads to connections between the Chartists, members of a social revolutionary movement, and a secret occult society that uses magical rituals to gain power.

Clarke, Susanna.

Jonathan Strange and Mr. Norrell. **Bloomsbury, 2004. 782pp.**

Mr. Norrell, a reclusive scholar in England in 1806, has regained the lost art of working magic, becoming the first new magician in hundreds of years. He uses his abilities for England's gain during the Napoleonic Wars. Then out of nowhere comes Jonathan Strange, an arrogant nobleman whose magical abilities rival Norrell's. Mr. Norrell takes Strange as a pupil, but Strange finds Norrell's approach to magic far too restrictive and sedate for his taste. A widely praised, bestselling novel. **Literary.**

Kerr, Peg.

The Wild Swans. **Warner Aspect, 1999. 392pp.** 📖

Like Juliet Marillier's *Daughter of the Forest* (see under "Celtic Fantasy") , this is a retelling of the Celtic "swans" legend, but with a unique twist. Lady Eliza Grey, a young woman banished from her home in England in 1689, goes in search of her eleven brothers, victims of sorcery: They change into wild swans during daylight. She heads to America to find a cure for them, only to be accused of witchcraft. In an alternating tale, Elias Latham is a young gay man living in New York City in the 1980s. Rejected by his family, he finds acceptance and love among the crowd at Fire Island, at least until AIDS strikes his crowd. Though the parallels between the stories aren't always clear, they are powerfully written character studies in well-realized settings.

Lackey, Mercedes.

The Elemental Masters.

Young women in the early twentieth century discover their innate magical powers. A series of re-imagined fairy tales.

Fire Rose. Baen, 2001. 448pp.

This retelling of "Beauty and the Beast" begins in 1905. After her father's death, Rosalind "Rose" Hawkins leaves her Chicago home to become a governess in San Francisco. Her mysterious employer not only has no children, but he is half-wolf, the result of an unsuccessful magic spell.

The Gates of Sleep. DAW, 2002. 389pp. **YA**

In a twist on the "Sleeping Beauty" legend, Marina Roeswood lives with her guardians, friends of her birth parents, in early twentieth-century Cornwall. Here she develops into a well-bred and intelligent young woman with considerable knowledge of magic, but she can't help wondering why her real parents have never seen her or brought her home to Devon. All is revealed after her parents' deaths, when Marina meets her father's sister Arachne, an evil sorceress.

The Serpent's Shadow. DAW, 2001. 343pp. **YA**

Lackey's re-imagined fairy tale is based on "Snow White and the Seven Dwarfs." Dr. Maya Witherspoon, the daughter of a British physician and a Brahmin woman, is a gifted healer in colonial India in 1909. Her mother, a sorceress who could summon the power of native Indian gods, had always warned her daughter to beware the "serpent's shadow." After the mysterious deaths of her parents, Maya flees to London, realizing that the dark magic that killed them both may be stalking her as well.

Phoenix and Ashes. DAW, 2004. 405pp.

A retelling of "Cinderella" set in Warwickshire, England. Eleanor Robinson's father is killed in World War I, and her evil stepmother forces her to do servants' work. Her only hope for freedom lies in Reginald Fenyx, a Master of the Air who is suffering from shell-shock.

Lee, J. Ardian.

Saga of the Ciorram Mathesons.

In Scotland in 1713, the Jacobite rebellion against British tyranny is at its lowest point. To save her homeland, the faerie Sinann calls for a new champion to lead the Scots to victory. He is Dylan Matheson, a modern-day martial arts instructor who is pulled back into the past after picking up an ancient broadsword at a medieval fair. There he finds adventure, danger, and love. The fourth volume continues with Dylan's son Ciaran, who fights in the Battle of Culloden. With its time-travel component and Scottish setting, Lee's four-book series has obvious similarities to Diana Gabaldon's <u>Outlander series</u> (Chapter 4), though Lee's version has more fantasy content, and fewer storylines vie for readers' attention.

Son of the Sword. Ace, 2001. 323pp.

Outlaw Sword. Ace, 2002. 310pp.

Sword of King James. Ace, 2003. 336pp.

Sword of the White Rose. Ace, 2004. 320pp.

Marley, Louise.

The Glass Harmonica. Ace, 2000. 334pp.

Two young women, 250 years apart, experience the healing power of music and an inexplicable connection to one another. When Benjamin Franklin hears Eilish Eam, an Irish orphan, playing water-filled glasses on the streets of London in 1761, he takes her in and teaches her how to play the glass harmonica. In Seattle in 2018, musician Erin Rushton's instrument is the glass harmonica, but she's baffled by strange visions she sees of a girl dressed in old-fashioned clothes. A nice mix of science fiction, fantasy, and historical fiction that should appeal to fans of all three genres, as well as to fans of time-slip novels (Chapter 12).

Saberhagen, Fred.

Dancing Bears. **Tor, 1996. 349pp.**

In 1906, American game hunter John Sherwood heads to Russia to help his friend Gregori hunt man-eating bears on Gregori's estate, only to discover a closely guarded secret about the bears' true nature—they had once been men. However, this may work to their advantage in pre-revolutionary Russia, since it prevents the czar's men from finding them.

Scarborough, Elizabeth Ann.

The Lady in the Loch. **Ace, 1998. 258pp.** ✍

Sir Walter Scott, sheriff of Edinburgh in the late eighteenth century, suspects black magic is afoot when gypsy women on the outskirts of the city begin to go missing . . . and grisly remains are discovered on the banks of the loch. The lilting dialogue evokes the Scottish landscape. Mystery elements.

The Americas

A miscellany of fantasy novels of North America; not a heavily used setting. Most are based on American or Mesoamerican legends.

Bell, Clare.

The Jaguar Princess. **Tor, 1993. 443pp.**

In pre-Columbian Mexico, the Aztecs rule the land amid bloody human sacrifices to their gods. A young girl of the Jaguar People named Mixcatl, sold into slavery with the Aztecs as a young girl, may be the best hope for revolution against Aztec tyranny: she has a talent for shape-changing that links her to the previous Olmec rulers.

Frost, Gregory.

Fitcher's Brides. **Tor, 2002. 398pp.**

In this retelling of the Bluebeard legend, set in the fictional Finger Lakes town of Jekyll's Glen, New York, in 1843, the Reverend Elias Fitcher is the leader of a utopian community that believes that the world will end soon. Three daughters of the Charter family—Vernelia, Amy, and Catherine—each marry Fitcher in turn, only to discover the man's dark side. Not only is this a successful dark fantasy, it is also social commentary on the dangers of religious fervor. Reverend Fitcher is based on William Miller, charismatic leader of the Millerites, a millennial movement in 1840s America.

Hopkinson, Nalo.

The Salt Roads. **Warner, 2003. 304pp.** 📖

In the early nineteenth century, three Caribbean slave women give rise to a new deity in their grief over a stillborn baby. Ezili, the newly created

Afro-Caribbean goddess of sex and love, travels through time and space to discover her own identity. She first inhabits the body of Baudelaire's African mistress, Jeanne Duval, in nineteenth-century France, then that of a Nubian prostitute in the fourth century AD. Finally she returns to where she began, St. Domingue, and becomes embroiled in the Haitian slave revolution. **Literary.**

Irvine, Alexander C.

A Scattering of Jades. **Tor, 2002. 428pp.**

The bloodthirsty gods of the ancient Aztecs roam the streets of 1840s New York City in this horror-tinged fantasy novel. Many of Manhattan's buildings had been destroyed in a huge fire in 1835, and newspaperman Archie Prescott's wife and daughter had perished then as well . . . or so he believed. In reality, his daughter Jane had been kidnapped by worshippers of the Mesoamerican god Tlaloc who are planning to use her as a sacrifice.

Asian Fantasy

This section includes novels set in Japan, China, and India. These cultures can seem exotic and fantastical to Western readers, and in historical Asian fantasy novels, the magic of distant lands becomes part of the story. Rather than retell ancient myths and legends, most of these authors create their own mythologies based on Asian folklore.

Cutter, Leah.

Paper Mage. **ROC, 2003. 343pp.** `YA`

Xiao Yen, a young woman living in China during the Tang Dynasty (circa AD 837), is a paper mage—someone who can create magical creatures and objects out of folded paper. Her gifts are in great demand, but her family doesn't believe that women should work magic. For love of her aunt, Xiao Yen agrees to a dangerous mission: escorting two foreigners through the Middle Kingdom. Here she encounters a goddess who needs her help keeping peace in the land.

Dalkey, Kara.

Blood of the Goddess Series.

Thomas Chinnery, assistant to an English apothecary, arrives in India in the sixteenth century to establish trade for medicinal herbs. His inquiries in this exotic land lead him straight into an enclave of Inquisitors operating in the Portuguese colony of Goa. The Inquisition is busy rooting out heresy in all its forms, as per usual. To this end, they seek a magical substance made from the blood of a goddess, a potion that can supposedly bring the dead back to life. Not only is the potion real, so is the goddess herself.

Goa. Tor, 1996. 252pp.

Bijapur. Tor, 1997. 285pp.

Bhagavati. Tor, 1998. 382pp.

***Genpei.* Tor, 2000. 445pp.**

Japan in the Heian period (twelfth century) is the scene for a series of brutal wars between two rival clans, the Minomoto and the Taira. The conclusion of this thirty-year period of hostility resulted in the death of the last Tairo emperor and the rise of the first shogun. So it is recorded in history, but Dalkey adds some magic to the mix, imagining that gods and demons played a part in the successive rise and fall of each clan.

Hughart, Barry.

Master Li Series. ★ YA

A fantasy trilogy with a mystery bent, set in eighth-century China. The sleuths are Li Kao, aka Master Li, a scholar with "a slight flaw in his character," and his younger companion Number Ten Ox, whose name describes his character well. Their adventures are based partially on ancient Chinese mythology. The narrative uses a formal Chinese style combined with a good dose of black humor, for even the pair's most embarrassing moments are recounted. This makes for some hilarious scenes.

 ***Bridge of Birds.* St. Martin's Press, 1984. 248pp.**

When children from his village fall into a deathly coma, Number Ten Ox recruits Master Li to help him, and they travel together to find the cure: the Great Root of Power. In the course of their adventures, their quest intertwines with the story of the Princess of Birds, a goddess who has been greatly wronged. World Fantasy Award.

***The Story of the Stone.* Doubleday, 1988. 236pp.**

The long-dead Laughing Prince has come back to life, unfortunately so, because he is back to terrorizing his people.

***Eight Skilled Gentlemen.* Doubleday, 1991. 255pp.**

Master Li and Number Ten Ox investigate the deaths of mandarins in the Forbidden City, perhaps by a vampire ghoul.

Johnson, Kij.

Love/War/Death Trilogy.

A projected fantasy trilogy set in Heian (medieval) Japan, a land where animals can assume human form.

***The Fox Woman.* Tor, 2000. 382pp.**

When Kaya no Yoshifuji brings his wife and son to live on his country estate, he doesn't realize that a family of foxes already occupies their property. Kitsune, the young female fox, falls in love with Yoshifuji, to his wife Shijuko's dismay. To steal his heart, Kitsune conjures up a way to turn herself into a beautiful woman. Retelling of a classic Japanese fairy tale.

Fudoki. Tor, 2003. 316pp.

A related novel of animals and humans using the same Heian setting as *The Fox Woman.* The elderly Princess Harueme, half-sister, aunt, and great-great-aunt to emperors, decides to go to a convent to spare her relatives the shame of her death. To fill an empty notebook, she tells the story of a tortoiseshell cat who lost all of her relatives in a fire and wanders until she can find someone to tell her ancestral clan stories to.

Larsen, Jeanne.
Bronze Mirror. Holt, 1991. 357pp.

In twelfth-century Linan, China, young Pomegranate goes into service as a lady's maid to help support her family. Her adventurous tale is part of a storytelling contest held by gods and goddesses above in the heavens, who watch her actions through a bronze mirror. Though they are divine beings, the gods and goddesses have the same personal foibles—jealousies, rivalries, and desires—as the humans down below.

Manchu Palaces. Holt, 1996. 342pp.

Like *Silk Road* and *Bronze Mirror*, this is another of Larsen's thoughtful and adventuresome coming-of-age stories set in Imperial China. In the eighteenth century, China is ruled by the Manchus' Qing Dynasty. Lotus, a young woman living on the outskirts of the palace in Beijing, is chosen to be a bond-servant to the empress. Before she can do so, she is sent on a quest by her late mother and another ghost to find the secret of a mandala.

Silk Road. Holt, 1989. 434pp. ★

In eighth-century China, a general's daughter named Greenpearl is kidnapped by Tibetan raiders and sold into slavery. Her journey back to her family becomes a picaresque adventure, as she encounters fantastical beasts, wondrous lands, and a wide variety of people. In the heavens above, the gods and goddesses try to assist her in her quest. An imaginative fantasy with a strong emphasis on Buddhist and Taoist folktales.

Chapter 15

Resources for Librarians and Readers

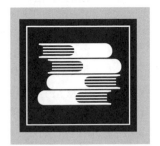

Besides this book, a number of other resources are available to help librarians and readers discover more information on historical fiction. While some are geared toward readers' advisors, others target readers or authors in the genre. Many are fairly general; others are quite specialized or scholarly.

Bibliographies and Biographies

Librarians can consult these sources for lists of novels and/or biographical details on their authors. Only bibliographies generally listing novels for adults are listed, though some cover titles of young adult interest.

> **Adamson, Lynda M.** *American Historical Fiction: An Annotated Guide to Novels for Adults and Young Adults.* Oryx, 1999.
>
> A guide to over 3,300 novels with American settings, mostly published since the 1980s, set in a time "earlier than readers are familiar with." This includes settings up through the 1970s. Arranged by time period, from "North America before 1600" up to "The Late 20th Century." Each entry gives title, citation, number of pages, one-sentence annotation, and genre designation. Extensive indexes by author, title, genre, geography, and subject. Appendixes list award winners and titles of possible young adult interest. Both this and the following volume were written as updates to McGarry's and White's bibliography.
>
> ———. *World Historical Fiction: An Annotated Guide to Novels for Adults and Young Adults.* Oryx, 1999.
>
> Similar in arrangement to *American Historical Fiction,* in this book Adamson annotates more than 6,000 novels set between prehistoric times and the late twentieth century. United States settings are excluded. Primary arrangement is by geographic area, then by time period.

Burt, Daniel S. *What Historical Novel Do I Read Next?* Gale Research, 1997–2003. 3 vol.

Nearly 7,000 titles by 3,000 authors are cited and annotated in volume 1, with historical accuracy evaluation and biographical details. The entries are arranged by author surname. Volume 2 provides eight different indexes to the books mentioned in volume 1. In 2003, volume 3 appeared, covering relevant novels through 2003 plus read-alike titles and review sources. Extensive, but pricey for public libraries.

Gerhardstein, Virginia Brokaw. *Dickinson's American Historical Fiction.* 5th ed. Scarecrow, 1986.

The most recent edition of A. T. Dickinson's classic bibliography *American Historical Fiction*, this volume covers more than 3,000 historical novels set between European colonization and 1984.

Hartman, Donald K., and Gregg Sapp. *Historical Figures in Fiction.* Oryx, 1994.

A bibliographical guide to biographical historical fiction. Includes "4,200 novels in which almost 1,500 historical figures appear as significant characters." The authors include English-language novels that were published since 1940, including some reissues. Young adult and juvenile titles are indicated. There are no annotations, but citations to reviews from major sources (*Booklist, Library Journal,* etc.) are provided. Quite comprehensive, but some of the books are not available in American libraries.

McGarry, Daniel D., and Sarah Harriman White. *World Historical Fiction Guide.* 2nd ed. Scarecrow, 1973.

McGarry and White's work was the first major modern bibliography for historical fiction, and it still has considerable value. Designed for use by both adults and high school students, this selective guide annotates historical novels published since 1900 and judged worthy of inclusion by the authors. Even with these criteria, it's very comprehensive.

Mediavilla, Cindy. *Arthurian Fiction: An Annotated Bibliography.* Scarecrow, 1999.

Mediavilla's bibliography not only lists all of the major (and some minor) Arthurian historical fiction and fantasy novels, but also provides significant critical commentary that will aid librarians, teachers, and readers. More than 200 novels in total, divided into eight categories: Romance of Camelot; Arthur the Roman Leader; Women of Camelot; Merlin, Kingmaker and Mage; Unlikely Heroes of Camelot; the Holy Quest; Return of the King; The Legacy Continues.

Murph, Roxane C. *The English Civil War and the Restoration in Fiction: An Annotated Bibliography, 1625–1999.* Greenwood, 2000.

A comprehensive, scholarly guide to verse, novels, and short stories about the English Civil War in the seventeenth century. The annotations include detailed plot summaries, most of which give away the ending—potential readers beware!

Murph knows her subject, and she always comments on a work's histori-cal accuracy. However, she is contemptuous of romance novels, and her continual harping on their low quality will offend romance readers.

————. *The Wars of the Roses in Fiction: An Annotated Bibliography, 1440–1994.* Scarecrow, 1995.

Murph's first annotated bibliography looks at the Wars of the Roses, the fifteenth-century conflict when rival families Lancaster and York battled for England's crown. Includes novels, short stories, and verse, with com-mentary similar to her later book (above).

Pederson, James P., ed. *St. James Guide to Crime and Mystery Writ-ers.* 4th ed. St. James Press, 1996.

In the same series as *Twentieth Century Western Writers* and *Twentieth Century Romance and Historical Writers*, this volume includes bio-graphical information on 650 crime and mystery writers of the twentieth century. Complete bibliographies (as of 1995) are provided for each.

Simone, Roberta. *The Immigrant Experience in American Fiction: An Annotated Bibliography.* Scarecrow, 1995.

A scholarly guide to novels about forty-one American immigrant groups as well as six "combined groups" (Asian, Hispanic, Jewish, Scandina-vian, Slavic, and West Indian) from the nineteenth century through 1994. Not all are historical novels, but many are.

Sonnichsen, C. L., ed. *Twentieth Century Western Writers.* 2nd ed. Gale, 1992.

In the same series as the two St. James Press titles on crime/mystery and romance writers, this title includes bio-bibliographical information on nearly 500 Western writers.

Van Meter, Vandelia L. *America in Historical Fiction: A Biblio-graphic Guide.* Libraries Unlimited, 1997.

Citations and summaries for over 1,100 historical novels with American settings, from 1492 through the late twentieth century. Additional titles are arranged by state. Geared toward secondary school history classes, and selected with the National Standards for United States History in mind. Many of these titles were originally written for adults.

Vasudevan, Aruna, and Lesley Henderson, eds. *Twentieth-Century Romance and Historical Writers.* 3rd ed. St. James Press, 1997.

A critical, bio-bibliographical guide to significant romantic and histori-cal novelists, emphasizing British writers. The three editions (1990, 1994, 1997) overlap considerably but are not completely cumulative. Unfortunately, no updates are planned. Historical mystery and Western writers are omitted from this volume, since they are covered instead in *St. James Guide to Crime and Mystery Writers* or *Twentieth Century Western Writers.*

History and Criticism

Interested in delving into the history and meaning of historical fiction? Investigate one of these stimulating volumes.

Carnes, Mark C., ed. *Novel History: Historians and Novelists Confront America's Past (and Each Other).* Simon & Schuster, 2001.

An interesting concept: Carnes invited historians to contribute essays on how well historical novels with American settings represented the past. He then invited the authors of the novels to comment on those essays. Novels discussed include Gore Vidal's *Burr*, Larry McMurtry's *Lonesome Dove*, and Charles Frazier's *Cold Mountain*, among others.

Lukacs, Georg. *The Historical Novel.* Beacon Press, 1962; first published in Moscow in 1937. Widely reprinted.

Though decades old, this classical study remains the benchmark work about the genre even though some of its definitions seem dated today. Lukacs describes the rise of the historical novel in the early nineteenth century and tells how practitioners like Walter Scott and Charles Dickens used the literary form to describe and effect social changes in their own time.

Rozett, Martha Tuck. *Constructing a World: Shakespeare's England and the New Historical Fiction.* Albany: State University of New York Press, 2002.

Analyzes the emergence of literary historical fiction in the mid- to late twentieth century, especially as seen through novels set in Shakespearean times.

Solander: The Magazine of the Historical Novel Society. ISSN 1471–7484.

A semiannual literary magazine with critical articles, author interviews, and market reports on historical fiction. $45/year (includes subscription to the *Historical Novels Review*, below under Book Review Sources). To subscribe, visit www.historicalnovelsociety.org

Writing Historical Fiction: A Virtual Conference Session. Albany: Department of History, University at Albany, State University of New York, 1998. Available online at http://www.albany.edu/history/hist_fict/home.htm.

In this online conference, the electronic version of a conference panel presentation, four novelists—Allen Ballard, Steven Leibo, Reed Mitchell, and William Rainbolt—contributed essays on writing historical fiction. Samples of their writing are provided.

Online Resources

Readers' advisory sources for historical fiction proliferate on the Internet, as do discussion groups and Web sites through which authors and fans can share their knowledge of the genre.

Subscription Databases

NoveList

Readers' advisory database from EBSCO Publishing. Includes a searchable interface (author, title, series, keyword) for its database of books, annotations, and full-text reviews. NoveList also offers feature articles, award lists, read-alikes for popular titles, book discussion guides, and staff resources for readers' advisory.

What Do I Read Next?

Thomson Gale's readers' advisory database includes the contents of books in their "What Do I Read Next?" reference book series. Includes the following genres: historical fiction, romance, mystery, Westerns, general fiction, classic fiction, and others. Searchable by title, author, subject, genre, locale, and more.

Discussion Groups

Fiction_L mailing list

http://www.webrary.org/rs/FLbklistmenu.html

Sponsored by Morton Grove Public Library, Illinois, the Fiction_L discussion list serves as a resource for readers' advisory issues. Book lists, many of which are historical fiction-related, are compiled by subscribers and posted to the above Web site. This list is essential for readers' advisors in libraries.

Rec.arts.books.hist-fiction

Low-traffic Usenet group for historical fiction. This group is used most frequently for responses to "stumper" queries rather than discussion.

Yahoo! Groups

http://groups.yahoo.com

Most historical fiction lists on Yahoo! Groups are geared toward writers and readers, but readers' advisors may find them of use. Of particular note are CrimeThruTime (historical mysteries), histfict (historical fiction readers), and HistoricalFictionII (historical fiction writers).

Web Sites

These sites offer a variety of resources: bibliographies, forthcoming books, reviews, short fiction, and more.

Ancient Egypt in Fiction

http://members.aol.com/wenamun/Egyptfiction.html

An online bibliography of novels set in ancient Egypt, arranged by category: young adult, biblical, historical fiction, mysteries, romance, children's, etc.

Bygone Days

http://www.bygonedays.net

A historical fiction e-zine, publishing short stories and book reviews. Hosted by Coachlight Press.

The Copperfield Review

http://www.copperfieldreview.com

Subtitled "a journal for readers and writers of historical fiction," this quarterly online publication offers short stories, author interviews, and book reviews.

CrimeThruTime

http://crimethrutime.tripod.com

A comprehensive historical mystery website, including forthcoming titles, mysteries by time period and locale, and book lists by author.

The Detective and the Toga

http://spotlightongames.com/roman/

A guide to Roman mysteries in many languages; updated frequently.

Fictional Rome

http://www.stockton.edu/~roman/fiction/

A database of historical novels set in Roman times, including book reviews. Housed at Richard Stockton College of New Jersey.

HistFiction.net

http://www.histfiction.net/

This staple in the field, maintained by historical fiction fan Soon-Yong Choi, serves as a meta-index to historical fiction on the Web. It also includes a master list of well-known historical fiction writers, with biographical details. Formerly known as "Soon's Historical Fiction Site."

Historical Mystery Fiction

http://members.tripod.com/~BrerFox/historicalmystery.html

Comprehensive guide to historical mystery novels, arranged by author and time period.

The Historical Novel Society

http://www.historicalnovelsociety.org

Besides describing the Society itself, this site provides lists of forthcoming historical fiction by month, selected articles and interviews from the literary magazine *Solander*, and links to the Web sites of member authors.

History and Lovers

http://www.historyandlovers.com

Maintained by historical novelist Catherine Karp, this site lists romantic historical novels that don't fit the genre romance mold.

The Nautical Fiction List

http://www.boat-links.com/books/nfl/nautfic-01.html

The latest update was in 1999, but despite that flaw, this site offers a searchable database of nautical fiction, much of which is historical.

Of Ages Past

http://www.angelfire.com/il/ofagespast/

Though now defunct, this online magazine for historical fiction has left its archives online for browsing.

Prehistoric Fiction

http://www.trussel.com/f_prehis.htm

Maintained by Steve Trussel, this is a comprehensive guide to prehistoric fiction titles, including definitions and a lengthy bibliography.

Publishers

Following are major publishers (and their imprints) as well as small presses that regularly publish historical novels. Addresses for main company offices, Web sites, and characteristics of the books they publish are listed. These companies publish fiction in a variety of genres, and most also publish nonfiction. The subgenres of historical fiction frequently published by each press are given.

Only American publishers, or British publishers with American offices, are included below. Relevant British publishers with considerable historical fiction output include Hodder Headline, Pan Macmillan, Penguin UK, Random House UK, Robert Hale, Simon & Schuster UK, and Transworld.

Major Publishers

All of the major trade presses publish historical fiction. Only imprints that offer relevant titles for the genre are included.

Farrar, Straus, & Giroux

19 Union Square West
New York, NY 10003
http://www.fsgbooks.com

Part of the Holtzbrinck Publishing Group. Literary historicals.

Five Star Press

295 Kennedy Memorial Drive
Waterville, ME 04901
http://www.galegroup.com/fivestar

Fiction imprint of Thomson Gale, publishing hardcovers for the library market. Beginning in 2003, they also began printing paperbacks for the trade market. Romantic and traditional Westerns, mysteries, historical romances, and women's fiction.

Harlequin Enterprises Ltd.

P.O. Box 5190
Buffalo, NY 14240–5190
http://www.eharlequin.com

Mass-market paperbacks. Non-series imprints include Harlequin Historicals (romance), Mira (women's fiction), and Steeple Hill (Christian). Harlequin also offers many series romance imprints.

HarperCollins Publishers

10 E 53rd Street
New York, NY 10022
http://www.harpercollins.com

Imprints: Amistad (African-American interest), Avon (paperback romance and mystery), Ecco (literary), HarperCollins (traditional and literary), Harper-SanFrancisco (spiritual fiction), Rayo (Hispanic interest), Perennial (paperback).

Henry Holt and Company

115 West 18th Street
New York, NY 10011
http://www.henryholt.com

Part of the Holtzbrinck Publishing Group. Literary historicals. Imprints: Henry Holt, Metropolitan Books.

Houghton Mifflin Company

215 Park Avenue South
New York, NY 10003
http://www.houghtonmifflinbooks.com

Imprints: Houghton Mifflin (literary), Mariner (trade paperback)

Kensington Publishing Corporation

850 Third Avenue
New York, NY 10022
http://www.kensingtonbooks.com

Imprints: Kensington (mystery, romance), Zebra (romance, westerns), Pinnacle (all types of genre fiction)

Penguin Group (USA)

375 Hudson Street
New York, NY 10014

Imprints and trademarks: Ace (fantasy); Berkley and Berkley Signature (romance, western); Berkley Prime Crime (mystery); Dutton (literary and traditional); G.P. Putnam's Sons (literary, mystery); Jove (romance); New American Library (mystery, also historical women's fiction); Penguin (literary and traditional); Plume (trade paperback, literary); Riverhead (literary and traditional); ROC (fantasy); Signet (romance, mystery); Viking (literary and traditional).

Random House

1745 Broadway
New York, NY 10019
http://www.randomhouse.com

Publishers and imprints: Anchor (literary); Ballantine (traditional, romance, mystery); Bantam (traditional, mystery, romance); Broadway (literary), Crown (traditional and literary), Delacorte (literary, traditional, mystery); Dell (romance); Doubleday (literary and traditional); Ivy (romance), Knopf (literary), Pantheon (literary), Random House (literary), Schocken (Jewish influence), Villard (literary).

Severn House Publishers

U.S. Office: Chivers North America
P.O. Box 1450
Hampton, NH 03843-1450
http://www.severnhouse.com

British publisher widely distributed in North America; hardcovers for the library market. Romance, mystery, sagas.

Simon & Schuster

1230 Avenue of the Americas
New York, NY 10020
http://www.simonsays.com

Imprints: Atria (traditional and literary); Free Press (political fiction); Pocket and Pocket Star (mass market paperback, mystery, western); Simon & Schuster (traditional and literary); Scribner (traditional and literary hardcovers and trade paperbacks); Sonnet (romance); Touchstone (trade paperback); Washington Square Press (traditional)

15

St. Martin's Press

175 Fifth Avenue
New York, NY 10010
http://www.stmartins.com

Part of the Holtzbrinck Publishing Group. Imprints: St. Martin's Press (traditional and literary, including sagas; also some romance); Minotaur (mysteries); Picador USA (trade paperbacks).

Time Warner Book Group, Inc.

> 1271 Avenue of the Americas
> New York, NY 10020
> http://www.twbookmark.com

> Part of AOL Time Warner. Imprints: Back Bay (paperbacks); Little Brown (literary); Miramax (traditional and literary); Mysterious Press (mystery); Warner (traditional, mystery, romance).

Tor Books

> 175 Fifth Avenue
> New York, NY 10010
> http://www.tor.com

> Part of the Holtzbrinck Publishing Group. Imprints: Forge (traditional, literary, mystery, occasional romance); Tor (fantasy).

Trafalgar Square Books

> P.O. Box 258, Howe Hill Road
> North Pomfret, VT 05053
> http://www.trafalgarsquarebooks.com

> American distributor of British books. Mysteries, traditional, and literary fiction imported from the United Kingdom.

Small and Independent Presses

Historical fiction thrives in the small and independent press. The following publishers offer at least several new historical novels each year.

Algonquin Books of Chapel Hill

> P.O. Box 2225
> Chapel Hill, NC 27515-2225
> http://www.algonquin.com

> Literary historical fiction.

Arcade Publishing

> 141 Fifth Avenue
> New York, NY 10010
> http://www.arcadepub.com

> Traditional and literary historicals.

Beagle Bay Books

> 3040 June Meadows Road
> Reno, NV 89509
> http://www.beaglebay.com

> Women's historical adventure and romance fiction.

Carroll & Graf Publishers

245 West 17th Street, 11th Floor
New York, NY 10011-5300
http://www.carrollandgraf.com

Imprint of the Avalon Publishing Group. Literary and traditional historicals; also mysteries.

Counterpoint Press

387 Park Ave. South, 12th Floor
New York, NY 10016-8810
http://www.counterpointpress.com

Part of the Perseus Books Group. Literary historical fiction.

Dorchester Publishing

200 Madison Avenue, Suite 2000
New York, NY 10016
http://www.dorchesterpub.com

Mass-market paperbacks. Imprints: LoveSpell (romance), Leisure (romance and Westerns).

Grove/Atlantic

841 Broadway
New York, NY 10003
http://www.groveatlantic.com

Literary historicals. Imprints: Grove Press, Atlantic Monthly Press.

High Country Publishers

197 New Market Center #135
Boone, NC 28607
http://www.highcountrypublishers.com

Traditional historicals and mysteries, often with Appalachian settings.

House of Stratus, Inc.

Thirsk Industrial Park
York Road
Thirsk, North Yorkshire, YO7 3BX
United Kingdom
http://www.houseofstratus.com

Reprints of classic historical novels and sagas. British company whose books are widely distributed in the United States.

MacAdam/Cage Publishing

155 Sansome Street, Suite 550
San Francisco, CA 94104–3615
http://www.macadamcage.com

Traditional and literary historicals.

McBooks Press

ID Booth Building
520 North Meadow Street
Ithaca, NY 14850
http://www.mcbooks.com

Naval historical fiction and other military adventure novels, mainly in series.

Poisoned Pen Press

6962 East First Avenue, Suite 103
Scottsdale, AZ 85251
http://www.poisonedpenpress.com

Historical mystery.

Soho Press

853 Broadway
New York, NY 10003
http://www.sohopress.com

Mystery, traditional historicals, and literary fiction.

The Toby Press, LLC

P.O. Box 8531
New Milford, CT 06776-8531
http://www.tobypress.com

English-language translations of popular European novels, both literary and traditional historicals; some original historical fiction as well.

W. W. Norton & Company

500 Fifth Avenue
New York, NY 10110
http://www.wwnorton.com

Literary and traditional historicals. Norton also distributes books from George Braziller, Inc. (literary) and New Directions (literary).

University Presses

University presses are good choices for regionally based historical fiction. Their works are suitable for both academic and public libraries. These publishers have the greatest output of historical novels.

Texas A&M University Press Consortium

http://www.tamu.edu/upress/

Member publishers with a combined catalog; includes Texas A&M University Press, Texas Tech University Press, and Texas Review Press, among others. Individual publisher addresses listed at Web site. Western-themed historical fiction.

University of Nebraska Press

233 North 8th Street
Lincoln, NE 68588-0255
http://unp.unl.edu

Reprints of classic literature; some literature in translation. No original fiction. Imprints: University of Nebraska Press, Bison Books.

University of New Mexico Press

1720 Lomas Boulevard NE
Albuquerque, NM 87131-1591
http://www.unmpress.com

Literature of New Mexico and the American Southwest.

University of Oklahoma Press

4100 28th Avenue NW
Norman, OK 73069-8218
http://www.oupress.com

Literature of the American West.

University Press of New England

One Court Street
Lebanon, NH 03766
http://www.upne.com

Imprint: Hardscrabble Books (fiction of New England).

Christian Publishers and Imprints

The following Christian publishers and imprints actively publish historical fiction. See also Steeple Hill, the Christian romance imprint of Harlequin.

Bethany House Publishers

11400 Hampshire Avenue South
Minneapolis, MN 55438
http://www.bethanyhouse.com

Part of the Baker Publishing Group.

Broadman and Holman Publishers

127 Ninth Avenue North, MSN 114
Nashville, TN 37234
http://www.broadmanandholman.com

Cook Communications Ministries

4050 Lee Vance View
Colorado Springs, CO 80918-7102
http://www.cookministries.com

Imprint: RiverOak (literary Christian fiction)

Crossway Books

> 1300 Crescent Street
> Wheaton, IL 60187
> http://www.gnpcb.org/home/books/

Fleming H. Revell

> P.O. Box 6287
> Grand Rapids, MI 49516-6287
> http://www.revellbooks.com

> Part of the Baker Publishing Group.

Harvest House Publishers

> 990 Owen Loop North
> Eugene, OR 97402–9173
> http://www.harvesthousepublishers.com

Moody Publishers

> 820 N. LaSalle Boulevard
> Chicago, IL 60610
> http://www.moodypress.com

Thomas Nelson, Inc.

> PO Box 141000
> Nashville, TN 37214
> http://www.thomasnelson.com

Tyndale House Publishers

> 351 Executive Drive
> Carol Stream, IL 60188
> http://www.tyndale.com

WaterBrook Press

> 2375 Telstar Drive, Suite 160
> Colorado Springs, CO 80920
> http://www.randomhouse.com/waterbrook/

> The Christian division of Random House, Inc.

Zondervan

> 5300 Patterson SE
> Grand Rapids, MI 49530
> http://www.zondervan.com

> The Christian imprint of HarperCollins Publishers.

Large Print

Many historical novels are offered in large print format from the following specialized publishers. Some of the major U.S. trade publishers also have large-print divisions or imprints. Historical novels from Britain often make their way into American libraries via large print editions.

Severn House

In "Major Publishers" section above.

Thorndike Press

295 Kennedy Memorial Drive
Waterville, ME 04901
http://www.gale.com/thorndike/index.htm

A Thomson Gale imprint. Significant output, with selections in Christian fiction, historical romance, and Westerns, among others.

Ulverscroft Large Print USA

914 Union Road
West Seneca, NY 14224
http://www.ulverscroft.co.uk

British publisher, with emphasis on romance and family sagas.

Writers' Manuals

All three are written by authors in the genre. Both Martin and Oliver are British, and their works reflect the publishing tastes in the United Kingdom, but many of the concepts are universal.

Martin, Rhona. *Writing Historical Fiction.* St. Martin's Press, 1988.

A short guide to writing in the genre, written by a former winner of the Georgette Heyer Historical Novel Prize.

Oliver, Marina. *Writing Historical Fiction: How to Create Authentic Historical Fiction and Get It Published.* How-To Books, 1998.

Another British handbook written by a former chairman of the Romantic Novelists' Association. Includes assignments that writers can complete while working on their novel.

Woolley, Persia. *How to Write and Sell Historical Fiction.* Writer's Digest Books, 1997.

Beyond creative writing techniques, Woolley describes how to market historical novels to publishers. Woolley has written an Arthurian trilogy about Guinevere.

Book Review Sources

The "big four" book review magazines—*Booklist, Kirkus Reviews, Library Journal,* and *Publishers Weekly*—all review historical fiction regularly. They provide considerable coverage, mainly in their general fiction sections. In addition, the following specialized publications include reviews of many worthwhile titles not mentioned elsewhere. Many relevant Web sites, listed earlier this chapter, also publish book reviews.

All About Romance

Published online at http://www.likesbooks.com

Critical book reviews of novels in the romance genre, with considerable coverage of historical romance. Though the reviews are a highlight, *AAR* also offers reader forums, articles, interviews, and more, all written by enthusiasts who love the romance genre.

Civil War Book Review

ISSN 1528–6592

From the U.S. Civil War Center, *CWBR* reviews nonfiction and historical novels about the Civil War. Fifteen to twenty fiction reviews annually, with blurbs for many more, plus interviews with novelists. Formerly a print publication, *CWBR* is now available free online at http://www.cwbr.com.

The Historical Fiction Review

Published online at http://home.midsouth.rr.com/ochsner/

Maintained by Lynda Ochsner, this free site concentrates on book reviews of historical Christian fiction but occasionally covers other titles. She also includes articles on historical fiction series and related themes.

The Historical Novels Review

ISSN 1471–7492

Published quarterly by the Historical Novel Society since 1997, this magazine reviews new historical fiction from the United States and Great Britain. Reviews are written for readers by readers. 800 reviews annually. $45/year (2005); includes *Solander* subscription (see above, under "History and Criticism"). To subscribe, visit www.historicalnovelsociety.org.

Murder: Past Tense

3 Goucher Woods Court
Towson, MD 21286

A quarterly newsletter dedicated to the historical mystery, published by the Historical Mystery Appreciation Society. Publication was suspended after 2002, though back issues are available. Selected articles are online at http://mywebpages.comcast.net/monkshould/hmas-index.html.

Romantic Times BOOKClub

ISSN 0747–3370

Formerly known as *Romantic Times*, this periodical now boasts the subtitle "the magazine for women who love books." While their coverage of historical romance and Regencies is considerable, they also cover inspirational fiction, mysteries, historical women's fiction, suspense, and traditional historical novels and sagas. $29.95/year (2005).

Roundup Magazine

ISSN 1081–2229

Published bimonthly by Western Writers of America, and presenting information on Western writing and publishing. Several book reviews per issue. $30/year (2005); see http://www.westernwriters.org to subscribe.

Societies and Organizations

No general trade associations exist for historical novelists, as they do for other genres. The Historical Novel Society, an organization welcoming both writers and readers of historical fiction, is the closest match. Historical novelists often join one or more of the following groups to network with their fellow authors and share research and writing tips. The groups also publicize the literature of their genre/subgenre, including those works written by their author members. For specific information on awards granted by these groups, see Appendix A.

Historical Novel Society (HNS)

c/o Debra Tash, U.S. Membership Chair
5239 North Commerce Avenue
Moorpark, CA 93066
http://www.historicalnovelsociety.org

An international organization that actively promotes the genre. Open to all historical fiction enthusiasts: authors, agents, publishers, librarians, and general readers. Based in Britain, with membership offices in Britain, the United States, Canada, and New Zealand. HNS publishes two magazines, the *Historical Novels Review* and *Solander*.

15

Mystery Writers of America

17 East 47th Street, 6th floor
New York, NY 10017
http://www.mysterywriters.org

"The leading association for professional crime writers in the United States" (Web site). Open to anyone interested in mysteries or crime writing. Awards the Edgar Allan Poe Award for excellence in crime fiction.

Novelists, Inc.

P.O. Box 1166
Mission, KS 66222–0166
http://www.ninc.com

An organization for multi-published authors of popular fiction; to qualify for membership, authors must have published at least two print novels generally available to the American public.

Romance Writers of America (RWA)

16000 Stuebner Airline Road, Suite 140
Spring, TX 77379
http://www.rwanational.org

The major American association for published and aspiring romance writers. General membership is open to writers interested in pursuing a career in romance fiction; associate membership is for those in the publishing industry; affiliate memberships are open to librarians and booksellers. RWA's many local chapters offer networking opportunities. Presents the annual RITA Awards at its annual conference.

Romantic Novelists' Association (RNA)

c/o RNA Hon. Membership Secretary
38 Stanhope Road
Reading
Berkshire RG2 7HN
United Kingdom
http://www.rna-uk.org

The British counterpart to Romance Writers of America. Published writers of romantic novels are eligible for membership; associate membership is available to those in the publishing industry. Aspiring writers must enter RNA's New Writers' Scheme to obtain probationary membership. Awards the Parker Romantic Novel of the Year and the Category Romance Award.

Sisters in Crime (SinC)

c/o Beth Wasson, Executive Secretary
P.O. Box 442124
Lawrence, KS 66044-8933

An organization offering networking, advice, and support to mystery authors, and to combat discrimination against women who write mysteries. Open to everyone, including authors, publishers, librarians, booksellers, fans, and more.

Western Writers of America

c/o Secretary-Treasurer James Crutchfield
1012 Fair Street
Franklin, TN 37064
http://www.westernwriters.org

Promotes the literature of the American West, both fiction and nonfiction. Membership is open to published authors writing about the American West. Awards the Spur Awards in many categories.

Women Writing the West

8547 East Arapahoe Road
Greenwood Village, CO 80112-1436
http://www.womenwritingthewest.org

A group dedicated to promoting literature about women's lives in the American West, both fiction and nonfiction. Open to all interested parties. Presents the annual WILLA Literary Awards.

Award-Winning Historical Novels

Although no major award for adult historical fiction currently exists, a number of historical novels have won national and international prizes in recent years. Relevant titles that have been awarded prizes since 1995 are listed below. Since many of these awards are not limited to historical novels, some years may be left blank. Complete lists of winners (and, occasionally, finalists) are often available at the sponsoring organization's Web site. Many lists can also be obtained via the Best Fiction section of NoveList.

Although young adult titles aren't the focus of this book, the Scott O'Dell Award for Historical Fiction is given annually to worthy children's or young adult novels in the genre. To be eligible, novels must be written by American authors and set in the New World, which includes North, South, and Central America. A list of winners is available online at http://www.scottodell.com.

Literary Fiction

ALA Notable Books

The ALA Notable Book distinction is given annually to twenty-five "very good, very readable, and at times very important" works of fiction, nonfiction, and poetry books for adults. The Notable Books Council, which judges this category, fits hierarchically within the Collection Development and Evaluation Section (CODES) of the Reference and User Services Association (RUSA) of ALA. Web site: http://www.ala.org/ala/rusa/rusaprotools/rusanotable/thelists/notablebooks.htm.

2004	*Any Human Heart*, William Boyd
	The Known World, Edward P. Jones
	Star of the Sea, Joseph O'Connor
2003	*Caramelo*, Sandra Cisneros
	Lovely Green Eyes, Arnost Lustig
	Atonement, Ian McEwan
	God's Fool, Mark Slouka
2002	*True History of the Kelly Gang*, Peter Carey
	Bucking the Tiger, Bruce Olds

2001	*The Blind Assassin*, Margaret Atwood
	The Amazing Adventures of Kavalier & Clay, Michael Chabon
	English Passengers, Matthew Kneale
2000	*Master Georgie*, Beryl Bainbridge
	The Hours, Michael Cunningham
	A Star Called Henry, Roddy Doyle
	The Colony of Unrequited Dreams, Wayne Johnston
	A Gesture Life, Chang-rae Lee
1999	*Flanders*, Patricia Anthony
	The Voyage of the Narwhal, Andrea Barrett
	The Farming of Bones, Edwidge Danticat
1998	*Alias Grace*, Margaret Atwood
	Cold Mountain, Charles Frazier
1997	*Ship Fever and Other Stories*, Andrea Barrett

American Book Award

The American Book Award, established by the Before Columbus Foundation, recognizes literary achievement by contemporary American authors. The purpose is to acknowledge the excellence and multicultural diversity in American writing. No Web site.

2002	*Fire in Beulah*, Rilla Askew
1999	*The Farming of Bones*, Edwidge Danticat
1998	*Bitter Grounds*, Sandra Benitez
1996	*The Physician of London*, Stephanie Cowell

Betty Trask Prizes and Awards

These awards were originally funded starting in 1984 by British romance novelist Betty Trask for first novels in English, published or unpublished, written by Commonwealth authors under the age of thirty-five. Novels must be "of a romantic or traditional nature (not experimental)," but this definition has gotten broader over the years. The prize money, divided among all of the winners, is £25,000. The top awardee is granted the Betty Trask Prize; others receive the Betty Trask Award. Presented annually by the Society of Authors at their annual meeting. Web site: http://www.societyofauthors.net/prizes/traskpw.html.

2004	*The Last Song of Dusk*, Siddharth Dhanvant Shangvi (Award)
2003	*Haweswater*, Sarah Hall (Award)
2002	*The Impressionist*, Hari Kunzru (Prize)
2002	*The Dark Room*, Rachel Seiffert (Award)
2000	*The Requiem Shark*, Nicholas Griffin (Award)
1999	*Tipping the Velvet*, Sarah Waters (Award)

Booker Prize

The Man Booker Prize (its official title) is awarded annually by the Booker Prize Foundation for the best English-language novel published in the United Kingdom. Winners must be citizens of the Commonwealth or the Republic of Ireland. Web site: http://www.bookerprize.co.uk.

2001	*True History of the Kelly Gang*, Peter Carey
2000	*The Blind Assassin*, Margaret Atwood
1995	*The Ghost Road*, Pat Barker

Giller Prize: Fiction

Annual literary award for the best Canadian novel published in English; established by Toronto businessman Jack Rabinovitch in honor of his late wife, journalist Doris Giller. Web site: http://www.thegillerprize.ca.

2002	*The Polished Hoe*, Austin Clarke
2001	*Clara Callan*, Richard Wright
1996	*Alias Grace*, Margaret Atwood

Governor General's Literary Award: Fiction (English)

Presented annually by the Canadian Council for the Arts for the best novel in English by a Canadian writer. A separate award is given for French-language works. Web site: http://www.canadacouncil.ca/prizes/ggla/default.asp.

2001	*Clara Callan*, Richard Wright
1997	*The Underpainter*, Jane Urquhart
1996	*The Englishman's Boy*, Guy Vanderhaeghe

National Book Award: Fiction

Sponsored by the National Book Foundation, this literary prize recognizes outstanding achievement in fiction. Web site: http://www.nationalbook.org/nba.html.

2004	*The News from Paraguay*, Lily Tuck
2003	*The Great Fire*, Shirley Hazzard
2000	*In America*, Susan Sontag
1997	*Cold Mountain*, Charles Frazier
1996	*Ship Fever and Other Stories*, Andrea Barrett

National Book Critics' Circle Award: Fiction

Awarded annually by the National Book Critics' Circle, an organization for professional book reviewers and literary critics, for "the finest books published in English." Web site: http://www.bookcritics.org.

2003	*The Known World*, Edward P. Jones
2002	*Atonement*, Ian McEwan
1997	*The Blue Flower*, Penelope Fitzgerald

Orange Prize for Fiction

Awarded to the best full-length English-language novel written by a woman of any nationality, though only works published in the United Kingdom are eligible. Sponsored by the Orange Corporation (British). Web site: http://www.orangeprize.co.uk.

2003	*Property*, Valerie Martin
2000	*When I Lived in Modern Times*, Linda Grant
1996	*A Spell of Winter*, Helen Dunmore

Pulitzer Prize for Literature

Chosen by the Pulitzer Prize Board, housed at Columbia University, for outstanding achievement in fiction. Web site: http://www.pulitzer.org.

2004	*The Known World*, Edward P. Jones
2003	*Middlesex*, Jeffrey Eugenides
2001	*The Amazing Adventures of Kavalier & Clay*, Michael Chabon
1999	*The Hours*, Michael Cunningham
1997	*Martin Dressler, The Tale of an American Dreamer*, Steven Millhauser

General Fiction

Book Sense Book of the Year: Adult Fiction

Prize winners are selected by American Booksellers Association member publishers as the novels they most enjoyed hand-selling to customers. Awarded annually at BookExpo America. Web site: http://www.booksense.com/readup/awards/.

2001	*The Red Tent*, Anita Diamant
1998	*Cold Mountain*, Charles Frazier

Michael Shaara Award

Awarded annually since 1997 by the United States Civil War Center (housed at Louisiana State University) for excellence in Civil War fiction. Web site: http://www.cwc.lsu.edu/cwc/mshaara.htm.

2003	No award given
2002	*Only Call Us Faithful*, Marie Jakober
2001	*The Wolf Pit*, Marly Youmans
2000	*Abe: A Novel of the Young Lincoln*, Richard Slotkin
1999	*Stonewall's Gold*, Robert J. Mrazek
1998	*Jacob's Ladder*, Donald McCaig
1997	*Nashville 1864*, Madison Jones

Oprah's Book Club

Though not an award per se, the novels featured every month as part of Oprah Winfrey's televised Book Club received enormous publicity and became instant bestsellers. Though the program has featured only classic novels since 2003, previous Oprah titles are still very popular. Because of the demand for these books at public libraries, ALA's Web site lists past selections at http://www.ala.org/ala/pio/piopromotions/oprahbookclub.htm.

January 2002	*Fall On Your Knees*, Ann-Marie MacDonald
June 2001	*Cane River*, Lalita Tademy
September 2000	*Drowning Ruth*, Christina Schwarz
February 2000	*Daughter of Fortune*, Isabel Allende
January 2000	*Gap Creek*, Robert Morgan
October 1999	*River, Cross My Heart*, Breena Clarke
February 1997	*Stones from the River*, Ursula Hegi

Mystery Fiction

Agatha Award

The Agatha Award, a fan-generated award named in honor of mystery writer Agatha Christie, is presented annually at the Malice Domestic convention. It is given annually to living authors of traditional mysteries of the type written by Christie (little gratuitous violence, and usually featuring an amateur detective). Web site: http://www.malicedomestic.org/agatha.htm.

2003	*Maisie Dobbs*, Jacqueline Winspear (Best First Novel)
2003	*Letter from Home*, Carolyn Hart (Best Novel)
2001	*Death on a Silver Tray*, Rosemary Stevens (Best First Novel)

2001   *Murphy's Law*, Rhys Bowen (Best Novel)

1997   *The Devil in Music*, Kate Ross (Best Novel)

Anthony Award

The Anthony Award honors the late Anthony Boucher, pseudonym of mystery writer/critic William Anthony Parker White. Presented annually at the Bouchercon world mystery convention.

2004   *For the Love of Mike*, Rhys Bowen (Best Historical Mystery)

1995   *The Alienist*, Caleb Carr (Best First Novel)

Bruce Alexander Historical Award

This award, presented at the Left Coast Crime mystery convention beginning in 2004, honors historical mystery writer Bruce Alexander, who died in 2003.

2004   *For the Love of Mike*, Rhys Bowen

Edgar Award

The Edgars, short for the Edgar Allan Poe Awards, are given annually in several categories by the Mystery Writers of America. Includes mysteries of all types (not just historical). Web site: http://www.mysterywriters.org/awards.html.

2004   *Death of a Nationalist*, Rebecca Pawel (Best First Novel by an
           American Author)

2001   *The Bottoms*, Joe Lansdale (Best Mystery)

2001   *A Conspiracy of Paper*, David Liss (Best First Mystery)

1998   *Los Alamos*, Joseph Kanon (Best First Mystery)

Ellis Peters Historical Dagger

Named in honor of medieval mystery writer Ellis Peters (Edith Pargeter), this award for historical crime fiction has been given since 1999 by the Crime Writers' Association (United Kingdom). It is sponsored by British publishers Headline and Warner/Little Brown as well as the estate of Ellis Peters. Web site: http://www.thecwa.co.uk.

2004   *The Damascened Blade*, Barbara Cleverly

2003   *An American Boy*, Andrew Taylor (US title: *An Unpardonable Crime*)

2002   *Fingersmith*, Sarah Waters

2000   *Absent Friends,* Gillian Linscott

1999   *Two for the Lions*, Lindsey Davis

Herodotus Award

Herodotus Award winners were chosen annually by members of the Historical Mystery Appreciation Society from 1998 to 2001. The U.S. versus International distinction refers to the country of publication, not necessarily the author's nationality. Not all awards were given each year, and the categories changed over the years. Web site: http://mywebpages.comcast.net/monkshould/herodotus.html.

2001	*Brothers of Cain*, Miriam Grace Monfredo (Best Historical Mystery)
2001	*Murphy's Law*, Rhys Bowen (First Historical Mystery)
2000	*The Bottoms*, Joe Lansdale (First U.S. Historical Mystery)
2000	*Bone House*, Betsy Tobin (First International Historical Mystery)
2000	*The Company*, Arabella Edge (International Historical Mystery)
1999	*Faded Coat of Blue*, Owen Parry (First U.S. Historical Mystery)
1999	*Absent Friends*, Gillian Linscott (International Historical Mystery)
1999	*Rubicon*, Steven Saylor (US Historical Mystery)
1998	*The Last Kabbalist of Lisbon*, Richard Zimler (First U.S. Historical Mystery)
1998	*Ex-Libris*, Ross King (International Historical Mystery)
1998	*Cursed in the Blood*, Sharan Newman (U.S. Historical Mystery)

Romantic Fiction

Historical Novel Prize in Memory of Georgette Heyer

This British contest for discovering new talent in historical fiction writing was sponsored by publishers The Bodley Head and Corgi Books from 1978 through 1989. Though the award was named for famed Regency novelist Georgette Heyer, the awardees did not necessarily emulate her style. Because so few prizes are awarded for historical fiction, the winners are listed in full. Most have American editions.

1989	*A Fallen Land*, Janet Broomfield
1988	*Trust and Treason*, Margaret Birkhead
1987	*I Am England*, Patricia Wright
1986	*The Cage*, Michael Weston
1985	*Legacy*, Susan Kay
1984	*The Terioki Crossing*, Alan Fisher (US title: *The Three Passions of Countess Natalya*)
1983	*Queen of the Lightning*, Kathleen Herbert
1982	No award
1981	*Zemindar,* Valerie Fitzgerald
1980	*Children of Hachiman*, Lynn Guest
1979	*The Day of the Butterfly*, Norah Lofts (submitted under a pseudonym; by 1979, Lofts was a well-known novelist!)
1978	*Gallows Wedding*, Rhona Martin

RITA Award

The RITA, the highest commendation in the American romance genre, is awarded annually by the Romance Writers of America in twelve different categories. Relevant winners of the Best Inspirational Romance title are listed below under "Christian Fiction." For a comprehensive guide to winners and finalists, see the Web site: http://www.rwanational.org/rita.cfm.

Best Long Historical

2004   *The Destiny*, Kathleen Givens

2003   *Stealing Heaven*, Madeline Hunter

2002   *The Bridal Season*, Connie Brockway

2001   *Devilish*, Jo Beverley

2000   *Silken Threads*, Patricia Ryan

1999   *My Dearest Enemy*, Connie Brockway

1998   *The Promise of Jenny Jones,* Maggie Osborne

1997   *Conor's Way*, Laura Lee Guhrke

1996   *Something Shady*, Pamela Morsi

1995   *Dancing on the Wind*, Mary Jo Putney

Best Short Historical

2004   *Worth Any Price*, Lisa Kleypas

2003   *The Bride Fair*, Cheryl Reavis

2002   *Tempt Me Twice*, Barbara Dawson Smith

2001   *The Mistress*, Susan Wiggs

2000   *The Proposition*, Judith Ivory

1999   *Merely Married*, Patricia Coughlin

1998   *Heart of a Knight*, Barbara Samuel

1997   *Always to Remember*, Lorraine Heath

1996   *Lord of Scoundrels*, Loretta Chase

1995   *To Tame a Texan's Heart*, Jodi Thomas

Best First Book

2003   *Shades of Honor*, Wendy Lindstrom

2002   *The Border Bride*, Elizabeth English

2000   *The Maiden and the Unicorn*, Isolde Martyn

1999   *My Darling Caroline*, Adele Ashworth

1998   *Brazen Angel*, Elizabeth Boyle

1996   *The Warlord*, Elizabeth Elliot

Best Regency

2004   *Prospero's Daughter*, Nancy Butler

2003   *A Debt to Delia*, Barbara Metzger

2002   *Much Obliged*, Jessica Benson

2001   *A Grand Design*, Emma Jensen

2000   *The Rake's Retreat*, Nancy Butler

1999   *His Grace Endures*, Emma Jensen

1998   *Love's Reward*, Jean Ross Ewing

1997   *The Lady's Companion*, Carla Kelly

1996   *Gwen's Christmas Ghost*, Lynn Kerstan and Alicia Rasley

1995   *Mrs. Drew Plays Her Hand*, Carla Kelly

Paranormal

The Paranormal category occasionally includes time-travel romance, but also covers futuristic and other supernatural titles.

2000   *Nell*, Jeanette Baker

Parker Romantic Novel of the Year Award

Awarded annually by the Romantic Novelists' Association (British organization). Open to both modern and historical novels, with entry limited to citizens of the United Kingdom. These novels may or may not be "historical romances" as defined in this book, but they do have romantic elements. Past winners include Valerie Fitzgerald's *Zemindar* and Reay Tannahill's *Passing Glory*. As of 2005, this award has a new sponsor and has been renamed the FosterGrant Romantic Novel of the Year. Web site: http://www.rna-uk.org.

2002   *The Other Boleyn Girl*, Philippa Gregory

1996   *Coming Home*, Rosamunde Pilcher

Christian Fiction

Christy Award

Named in honor of Catherine Marshall's bestselling inspirational novel *Christy*, the annual Christy Awards recognize excellence in Christian fiction. The award has been organized by representatives from a dozen Christian fiction publishers since 1999; the first awards were given in 2000. The Historical categories include novels set before 1950, while Contemporary is meant to address time periods from 1950 to the present. (Tatlock's *All the Way Home* covers both historical periods.) Before 2004, separate awards were given for International Historical and North American Historical. The Christy has also been awarded in the Western category beginning in 2002, with the exception of 2004, when no award was given. These works are traditional Westerns rather than Western historical novels. Web site: http://www.christyawards.com.

2004	*Fire by Night*, Lynn Austin (Historical)
2003	*All the Way Home*, Ann Tatlock (Contemporary)
2003	*Candle in the Darkness*, Lynn Austin (North American Historical)
2003	*His Watchful Eye,* Jack Cavanaugh (International Historical)
2003	*Toward a New Beginning*, R. William Rogers (Western)
2002	*Hidden Places*, Lynn Austin (North American Historical)
2002	*The Long Trail Home*, Stephen Bly (Western)
2002	*While Mortals Sleep*, Jack Cavanaugh (International Historical)
2001	*Edge of Honor*, Gilbert Morris (North American Historical; tie)
2001	*Passing by Samaria*, Sharon Ewell Foster (First Novel)
2001	*Reaping the Whirlwind*, Rosie Dow (North American Historical; tie)
2001	*Unashamed*, Francine Rivers (International Historical)
2000	*The Meeting Place*, Janette Oke and T. Davis Bunn (North American Historical)
2000	*Out of the Red Shadow*, Anne de Graaf (International Historical)

Gold Medallion Book Award: Fiction

Established in 1978, the Gold Medallion represents the highest quality in evangelical Christian publishing. The Evangelical Christian Publishers Association (ECPA) sponsors the award, and the judges are primarily Christian booksellers. Web site: http://www.ecpa.org/ECPA/Gawards.html.

2001	*Paul, a Novel*, Walter Wangerin
1999	*The Last Sin Eater*, Francine Rivers
1998	*Only the River Runs Free*, Bodie and Brock Thoene
1997	*The Book of God*, Walter Wangerin, Jr.
1995	*The Twilight of Courage*, Bodie and Brock Thoene

RITA Award, Inspirational Category

Awarded annually by the Romance Writers of America for outstanding achievement in inspirational (i.e., Christian) fiction. Contemporary titles have won this award in recent years. Web site: http://www.rwanational.org/rita.cfm.

1997	*The Scarlet Thread*, Francine Rivers
1996	*As Sure As the Dawn*, Francine Rivers
1995	*An Echo in the Darkness*, Francine Rivers

Western Fiction

Spur Award

The Spur Awards are given annually by Western Writers of America for distinguished writing about the American West. In 1997, the award was changed to reflect the year awarded rather than the year published. The distinction between Best Novel of the West and Best Western Novel now depends on length, but in the past, it referred to historical and traditional Westerns. Between 1953 (inception of the Spurs) and 1981, separate awards were given to Novel and Historical Novel. See the Web site for detailed Spur award history: http://www.westernwriters.org/spur_awards.htm.

Best Novel of the West

Western novels over 90,000 words in length are eligible for this award; shorter works are eligible instead for Best Western Novel, below.

2004	*So Wild a Dream*, Win Blevins
2003	*Perma Red*, Debra Magpie Earling
2002	*The Miracle Life of Edgar Mint*, Brady Udall
2001	*The Gates of the Alamo*, Stephen Harrigan
2000	*Prophet Annie*, Ellen Recknor
1999	*The All-True Travels and Adventures of Lidie Newton*, Jane Smiley
1998	*Comanche Moon*, Larry McMurtry
1996	*Sierra*, Richard S. Wheeler
1995	*Stone Song*, Win Blevins

Best Original Paperback Western

Includes Western historical novels as well as traditional Westerns, which are likely to appear in paperback.

2004	*Plain Language*, Barbara Wright
2003	*Oblivion's Altar*, David Marion Wilkinson
2002	*Drum's Ring*, Richard S. Wheeler
2001	*Bound for the Promised Land*, Troy D. Smith
2000	*Mine Work*, Jim Davidson
1999	*Dark Trail*, Hiram King
1998	*Leaving Missouri*, Ellen Recknor
1996	*Potter's Fields*, Frank Roderus
1995	*Thunder in the Valley,* Jim R. Woolard

Best Western Novel

At present, novels under 90,000 words are eligible for this award. This wasn't always the case, however, as Larry McMurtry's epic Western *Lonesome Dove* took home the prize in 1985.

2004   *I Should Be Extremely Happy In Your Company*, Brian Hall

2003   *The Chili Queen*, Sandra Dallas

2002   *The Way of the Coyote*, Elmer Kelton

2001   *Summer of Pearls*, Mike Blakely

2000   *Masterson*, Richard S. Wheeler

1999   *Journey of the Dead*, Loren D. Estleman

1998   *The Kiowa Verdict*, Cynthia Haseloff

1996   *Blood of Texas*, Will Camp

1995   *The Dark Island*, Robert J. Conley

Medicine Pipe Bearers' Award

Awarded for best first Western novel; includes traditional Westerns.

2004   *The Sergeant's Lady*, Miles Hood Swarthout

2003   *Perma Red*, Debra Magpie Earling

2002   *Corps of Discovery*, Jeffrey W. Tenney

2001   *The Chivalry of Crime*, Desmond Barry

2000   *Mine Work*, Jim Davidson

1999   *The Spanish Peaks*, Jon Chandler

1998   *Keepers of the Earth*, LaVerne Harrell Clark

1996   *Death of a Healing Woman*, Allana Martin

1995   *Thunder in the Valley*, Jim R. Woolard

Western Heritage Award: Outstanding Western Novel

Sponsored by the National Cowboy and Western Heritage Museum in Oklahoma City, these awards honor outstanding achievement in Western fiction. Web site: http://www. cowboyhalloffame.org/e_awar.html.

2004   *Spark on the Prairie: The Trial of the Kiowa Chiefs*, Johnny Boggs

2003   *Moon of Bitter Cold*, Frederick Chiaventone

2002   *The Master Executioner*, Loren D. Estleman

2001   *The Gates of the Alamo*, Stephen Harrigan

2000   *The Contract Surgeon*, Dan O'Brien

1999   *Journey of the Dead*, Loren D. Estleman

1998   *The Mercy Seat*, Rilla Askew

1997   *Out of Eden*, Kate Lehrer

1996   *A Sweetness to the Soul*, Jane Kirkpatrick

1995   *Bluefeather Fellini in the Sacred Realm*, Max Evans

WILLA Literary Awards

Awarded annually by Women Writing the West since 1999 for literature featuring women's stories set in the American West. Selectors are librarians unaffiliated with the organization. Separate awards are given for contemporary fiction, historical fiction, and original paperbacks, as well as for children's/young adult fiction and nonfiction. Web site: http://www.womenwritingthewest.org/willamain.html.

Historical Fiction

"Women's stories set in the west before contemporary times."

2004   *Silver Lies*, Ann Parker

2003   *Enemy Women*, Paulette Jiles

2002   *The Good Journey*, Micaela Gilchrist

2001   *For California's Gold*, JoAnn Levy

2000   *Daughter of Fortune*, Isabel Allende

1999   *Daughter of Joy*, JoAnn Levy

Contemporary Fiction

"Women's stories set in the west during contemporary times."

2003   *Perma Red,* Debra Magpie Earling

Original Paperback

2004   *Deliverance Valley*, Gladys Smith

2003   *Small Rocks Rising*, Susan Lang

2002   *Across the Sweet Grass Hills*, Gail Jenner

2000   *Prophet Annie*, Ellen Recknor

1999   *River of Our Return*, Gladys Smith

Reading Lists by
Plot Pattern or Theme

Following are selected lists of recommended titles in popular historical periods and subject areas, and on other commonly requested themes. These lists take a wide-ranging approach, listing authors and titles from a variety of historical fiction subgenres.

Core Authors by Period and Place

The following historical novelists, in the opinion of the author of this book, are consistently reliable in presenting their chosen period of history. Most are quite prolific.

Multi-Period

These exceptional authors have mastered a number of historical periods.

Valerie Anand (also writes as Fiona Buckley)

Barbara Chase-Riboud

Tracy Chevalier

Paul Doherty (many pseudonyms)

Alfred Duggan

Margaret George

Kathryn Harrison

Cecelia Holland

Morgan Llywelyn

Norah Lofts

James Michener

Gilbert Morris

Jean Plaidy (Philippa Carr, Victoria Holt)

Edward Rutherfurd

Anya Seton

Irving Stone

Reay Tannahill

Judith Tarr

Rose Tremain

Bodie Thoene and Brock Thoene

Susan Vreeland

Prehistory

Jean Auel

W. Michael Gear and Kathleen O'Neal Gear

Sue Harrison

Linda Lay Shuler

Judith Tarr

Elizabeth Marshall Thomas

Biblical Times

Orson Scott Card

Angela Elwell Hunt

Francine Rivers

Ancient Egypt

Karen Essex

Pauline Gedge

Lauren Haney

Christian Jacq

Lynda S. Robinson

Judith Tarr

Ancient Greece

Gillian Bradshaw

Steven Pressfield

Mary Renault

The Roman Empire

Gillian Bradshaw

Lindsey Davis

Colleen McCullough

Francine Rivers

Steven Saylor

The British Isles

Early and High Middle Ages

Elizabeth Chadwick

Margaret Frazer

Roberta Gellis

Parke Godwin (Kate Hawks)

Rosemary Hawley Jarman

Edith Pargeter/Ellis Peters

Judith Merkle Riley

Sharon Kay Penman

Rosemary Sutcliff

Nigel Tranter

Peter Tremayne

Jack Whyte

Tudor and Stuart Eras

Pamela Belle

Stephanie Cowell

George Garrett

Karen Harper

Patricia Finney (P. F. Chisholm)

Philippa Gregory

Robin Maxwell

Georgian Era (includes Napoleonic Wars and Regency Era)

Mary Balogh

Jo Beverley

Bernard Cornwell

C. S. Forester

Diana Gabaldon

Georgette Heyer

Carla Kelly

David Liss

Patrick O'Brian

Victorian Era

Catherine Cookson

Michel Faber

Malcolm MacDonald

Anne Perry

Jessica Stirling

Sarah Waters

Twentieth Century

Carola Dunn

Morgan Llywelyn

Charles Todd

Europe

The Middle Ages

Maurice Druon

Sharan Newman

Zoé Oldenbourg

Sigrid Undset

The Renaissance and Reformation

Dorothy Dunnett

Judith Merkle Riley

Samuel Shellabarger

Early Modern Era

Beryl Bainbridge

Sandra Gulland

Rosalind Laker

Twentieth Century

Sebastian Faulks

Alan Furst

Andrei Makine

The United States

Pre–Civil War

Max Byrd

Sara Donati

Howard Fast

Thomas Fleming

Inglis Fletcher

Barbara Hambly

Margaret Lawrence

David Nevin

Mary Lee Settle

Elswyth Thane

James Alexander Thom

Civil War and After

Howard Fast

Dorothy Garlock

John Jakes

MacKinlay Kantor

Thomas Mallon

Eugenia Price

Jeff Shaara

Anita Shreve

Herman Wouk

American West

Judy Alter

Rosanne Bittner

Willa Cather

Don Coldsmith

Robert J. Conley

Loren Estleman

Terry C. Johnston

Elmer Kelton

Jane Kirkpatrick

Louis L'Amour

Larry McMurtry

Maggie Osborne

Lucia St. Clair Robson

Richard S. Wheeler

Jeanne Williams

Canada, Greenland, and the Arctic

Margaret Atwood

Andrea Barrett

Mazo de la Roche

Wayne Johnston

Janette Oke

The Middle East

Ann Chamberlin

Elizabeth Peters

Bodie Thoene and Brock Thoene

Asia, Africa, and the Antipodes

Africa

Wilbur Smith

Australia

Aaron Fletcher

Colleen McCullough

Patricia Shaw

China

Pearl S. Buck

Eleanor Cooney and Daniel Altieri

Amy Tan

Gail Tsukiyama

Robert Van Gulik

India

Valerie Fitzgerald

M. M. Kaye

Rebecca Ryman

Japan

James Clavell

Laura Joh Rowland

Strong Women in History

These novels recount tales of women from history who persevered against overwhelming odds and triumphed in a man's world. They present a strong feminist message without being anachronistic; many of the protagonists are based on historical figures.

Bradley, Marion Zimmer—Avalon Series, especially *The Mists of Avalon*

Chamberlin, Ann—Reign of the Favored Women Series

Cross, Donna Woolfolk—*Pope Joan*

Diamant, Anita—*The Red Tent*

Donnelly, Jennifer—*The Tea Rose*

Edghill, India—*Queenmaker*

Ennis, Michael—*Duchess of Milan*

Essex, Karen—Kleopatra Series

Gillespie, Donna—*The Light Bearer*

Gulland, Sandra—Josephine Bonaparte Trilogy

Holland, Cecelia—*Great Maria*

Kaufman, Pamela—*Shield of Three Lions*

Llywelyn, Morgan—*Grania*

Miles, Rosalind—*I, Elizabeth*; Guenevere Series; Isolde Series

Naslund, Sena Jeter—*Ahab's Wife*

Riley, Judith Merkle—*A Vision of Light*

Robson, Lucia St. Clair—*Fearless*; *Ghost Warrior*

Scott, Manda—Boudica Series

Sundaresan, Indu—*The Feast of Roses*

Tarr, Judith—*Queen of Swords*; *The Eagle's Daughter*

Thom, James Alexander, and Dark Rain Thom—*Warrior Woman*

Vreeland, Susan—*The Passion of Artemisia*, *The Forest Lover*

Windle, Janice Woods—True Women Series

Revisionist Historical Novels

Authors of these novels recount well-known historical episodes from a new viewpoint, putting a different spin on what may have really happened in history. Revered historical figures are seen in a unique and sometimes unflattering light; in other cases, people who have gone down in history as villains are given the opportunity to explain their actions. Because of their subject matter, these works are often controversial.

Alison, Jane—*The Love-Artist*

Bainbridge, Beryl—*According to Queeney*

Brooks, Bill—*The Stone Garden*

Chase-Riboud, Barbara—*Sally Hemings*

Crace, Jim—*Quarantine*

Dunnett, Dorothy—*King Hereafter*

Edghill, India—*Queenmaker*

Ehrlich, Ev—*Grant Speaks*

Gregory, Philippa—*The Other Boleyn Girl*

Hall, Brian—*I Shall Be Extremely Happy in Your Company*

Harr, John Ensor—*Dark Eagle*

Lussier, Paul—*Last Refuge of Scoundrels*

Mailer, Norman—*The Gospel According to the Son*

Mount, Ferdinand—*Jem (and Sam)*

Safire, William—*Scandalmonger*

Vidal, Gore—*Burr*

Vidal, Gore—*Lincoln*

Literary Sequels and Re-Imaginings

Readers have a love–hate relationship with sequels to classic works of literature. While they enjoy getting the opportunity to visit well-loved places and characters once more, it can be disappointing for them when the sequels don't live up to the high literary standards of the originals, or when characters are portrayed in an inconsistent manner. The best literary sequels pay homage to the original works by keeping the style and tone believable. Other authors of sequels retell classic stories based on the point of view of minor characters, either in a straightforward manner or in the form of a parody.

Alleyn, Susanne—*A Far Better Rest* (Charles Dickens' *A Tale of Two Cities*)

Beauman, Sally—*Rebecca's Tale* (Daphne du Maurier's *Rebecca*)

Boylan, Clare—*Emma Brown* (unfinished novel by Charlotte Brontë)

Bryan, Francis—*The Curse of Treasure Island* (Robert Louis Stevenson's *Treasure Island*)

Conde, Maryse—*Windward Heights* (Emily Brontë's *Wuthering Heights*)

Gouge, Louise—*Ahab's Bride* (Herman Melville's *Moby-Dick*)

Naslund, Sena Jeter—*Ahab's Wife* (Herman Melville's *Moby-Dick*)

Randall, Alice—*The Wind Done Gone* (Margaret Mitchell's *Gone with the Wind*)

Reisert, Rebecca—*The Third Witch* (William Shakespeare's *Macbeth*)

Ripley, Alexandra—*Scarlett* (Margaret Mitchell's *Gone with the Wind*)

Rhys, Jean—*The Wide Sargasso Sea* (Charlotte Brontë's *Jane Eyre*)

Tennant, Emma—*Adèle: Jane Eyre's Hidden Story* (Charlotte Brontë's *Jane Eyre*)

Updike, John—*Gertrude and Claudius* (William Shakespeare's *Hamlet*)

African-American Interest

Many historical novels feature African-American characters, but those in the following selected list are told from their own point of view. They show how members of this ethnic group played important roles in history. Additional examples of novels with prominent African-American characters can be found in the subject index.

Barnes, Steven—*Lion's Blood* and *Zulu's Heart*

Butler, Octavia—*Kindred*

Cameron, Christian—*Washington and Caesar*

Chase-Riboud, Barbara—*Sally Hemings*

Clarke, Breena—*River, Cross My Heart*

Durham, David Anthony—*Gabriel's Story*

Foster, Sharon Ewell—*Passing By Samaria*

Haley, Alex—*Roots*

Haley, Alex—*Queen*

Morrison, Toni—*Beloved*

Rhodes, Jewell Parker—*Douglass' Women*

Tademy, Lalita—*Cane River*

Walker, Alice—*The Color Purple*

Walker, Margaret—*Jubilee*

Asian-American Interest

These important novels portray the Asian and Asian-American experience in historical fiction.

Baldwin, Shauna Singh—*What the Body Remembers*

Dalby, Liza—*The Tale of Murasaki*

Golden, Arthur—*Memoirs of a Geisha*

Larsen, Jeanne—*Silk Road*

Lee, Chang-rae—*A Gesture Life*

Levy, JoAnn—*Daughter of Joy*

Liu, Aimee—*Cloud Mountain*

Otsuka, Julie—*When the Emperor Was Divine*

Tan, Amy—*The Bonesetter's Daughter*

Tan, Amy—*The Kitchen God's Wife*

Tatlock, Ann—*All the Way Home*

Trobaugh, Augusta—*Sophie and the Rising Sun*

Tsukiyama, Gail—*Women of the Silk*

Latin American Interest

Similar to the categories above, these novels portray the Latin American historical experience from the point of view of members of this ethnic group.

Allende, Isabel—*Daughter of Fortune*

Alvarez, Julia—*In the Name of Salomé*

Cisneros, Sandra—*Caramelo*

Esquivel, Laura—*Swift as Desire*

Fuentes, Carlos—*The Years with Laura Díaz*

Rosario, Nelly—*Song of the Water Saints*

Native American Interest

In these books, the authors attempt to portray Native American characters sympathetically and/or from their own point of view.

Ammerman, Mark—Cross and the Tomahawk Series

Bittner, Rosanne—Mystic Indian Series and Savage Destiny Series

Black, Michelle—*An Uncommon Enemy*

Blake, Michael—*Dances with Wolves*

Coldsmith, Don—Spanish Bit Series

Conley, Robert J.—Real People Series

Gear, W. Michael and Kathleen O'Neal Gear—The First North Americans Series

Humphreys, Josephine—*Nowhere Else on Earth*

Kirkpatrick, Jane—Tender Ties Historical Series

Robson, Lucia St. Clair—*Ride the Wind* and *Ghost Warrior*

Shuler, Linda Lay—Time Circle Quartet

Silko, Leslie Marmon—*Gardens in the Dunes*

Thom, James Alexander—*The Red Heart*

Thom, James Alexander, and Dark Rain Thom—*Warrior Woman*

Author, Title, and Series Index

Historical Character Index

Place and Time Index

Under each heading, subheadings are listed in order by time period. In general, places are indexed using the terms by which they are most commonly known; for example, novels taking place in Montana Territory before it became a state (1889) are listed under Montana. As with the rest of this book, many novels are grouped by era, with specific years given as follows.

For the British Isles:

Early Middle Ages refers roughly to AD 449–1066

High Middle Ages, 1066–1485

Tudor era, 1485–1603

Stuart era, 1603–1714

Georgian era, 1714–1837, with the exception of the Regency era, 1811–1820

Victorian era, 1837–1901

20th century, 1901–1950, with the exceptions of World War I, 1914–1918, and World War II, 1939–1945

For Europe and some Middle Eastern regions:

Middle Ages, AD 476–1492

Renaissance/Reformation, roughly 1492–1650

early modern era, 1650–1900

20th century, same as above

For the United States:

colonial period, from first European settlement through 1775

American Revolution, 1775–1783

early United States, 1783–1861

Civil War, 1861–1865

Reconstruction/Gilded Age, 1865–1900

20th century, same as above

For other locales, century designations are provided.

Subject Index

About the Author

SARAH L. JOHNSON is Reference Librarian and Assistant Professor at Booth Library, Eastern Illinois University. A longtime reader and collector of historical novels, Johnson is the American book review editor for *Historical Novels Review* (a historical fiction review journal for the United States and Great Britain) and serves as *NoveList's* historical fiction editor.